QUANTITATIVE METHODS, ECONOMICS

CFA® Program Curriculum

2023 • LEVEL 2 • VOLUME 1

WILEY

CONTENTS

◙ indicates an optional segment

◉ indicates an optional segment

Contents

◙ indicates an optional segment

Economics

Ⓞ indicates an optional segment

Contents

◙ indicates an optional segment

indicates an optional segment

How to Use the CFA Program Curriculum

The CFA® Program exams measure your mastery of the core knowledge, skills, and abilities required to succeed as an investment professional. These core competencies are the basis for the Candidate Body of Knowledge (CBOK™). The CBOK consists of four components:

- A broad outline that lists the major CFA Program topic areas (www. cfainstitute.org/programs/cfa/curriculum/cbok)
- Topic area weights that indicate the relative exam weightings of the top-level topic areas (www.cfainstitute.org/programs/cfa/curriculum)
- Learning outcome statements (LOS) that advise candidates about the specific knowledge, skills, and abilities they should acquire from curriculum content covering a topic area: LOS are provided in candidate study sessions and at the beginning of each block of related content and the specific lesson that covers them. We encourage you to review the information about the LOS on our website (www.cfainstitute.org/programs/cfa/curriculum/study-sessions), including the descriptions of LOS "command words" on the candidate resources page at www.cfainstitute.org.
- The CFA Program curriculum that candidates receive upon exam registration

Therefore, the key to your success on the CFA exams is studying and understanding the CBOK. You can learn more about the CBOK on our website: www.cfainstitute.org/programs/cfa/curriculum/cbok.

The entire curriculum, including the practice questions, is the basis for all exam questions and is selected or developed specifically to teach the knowledge, skills, and abilities reflected in the CBOK.

ERRATA

The curriculum development process is rigorous and includes multiple rounds of reviews by content experts. Despite our efforts to produce a curriculum that is free of errors, there are instances where we must make corrections. Curriculum errata are periodically updated and posted by exam level and test date online on the Curriculum Errata webpage (www.cfainstitute.org/en/programs/submit-errata). If you believe you have found an error in the curriculum, you can submit your concerns through our curriculum errata reporting process found at the bottom of the Curriculum Errata webpage.

DESIGNING YOUR PERSONAL STUDY PROGRAM

An orderly, systematic approach to exam preparation is critical. You should dedicate a consistent block of time every week to reading and studying. Review the LOS both before and after you study curriculum content to ensure that you have mastered the applicable content and can demonstrate the knowledge, skills, and abilities described by the LOS and the assigned reading. Use the LOS self-check to track your progress and highlight areas of weakness for later review.

Successful candidates report an average of more than 300 hours preparing for each exam. Your preparation time will vary based on your prior education and experience, and you will likely spend more time on some study sessions than on others.

CFA INSTITUTE LEARNING ECOSYSTEM (LES)

Your exam registration fee includes access to the CFA Program Learning Ecosystem (LES). This digital learning platform provides access, even offline, to all of the curriculum content and practice questions and is organized as a series of short online lessons with associated practice questions. This tool is your one-stop location for all study materials, including practice questions and mock exams, and the primary method by which CFA Institute delivers your curriculum experience. The LES offers candidates additional practice questions to test their knowledge, and some questions in the LES provide a unique interactive experience.

FEEDBACK

Please send any comments or feedback to info@cfainstitute.org, and we will review your suggestions carefully.

Quantitative Methods

Basics of Multiple Regression and Underlying Assumptions

LEARNING OUTCOMES

Mastery	*The candidate should be able to:*
☐	describe the types of investment problems addressed by multiple linear regression and the regression process
☐	formulate a multiple linear regression model, describe the relation between the dependent variable and several independent variables, and interpret estimated regression coefficients
☐	explain the assumptions underlying a multiple linear regression model and interpret residual plots indicating potential violations of these assumptions

INTRODUCTION

1

Multiple linear regression uses two or more independent variables to describe the variation of the dependent variable rather than just one independent variable, as in simple linear regression. It allows the analyst to estimate using more complex models with multiple explanatory variables and, if used correctly, may lead to better predictions, better portfolio construction, or better understanding of the drivers of security returns. If used incorrectly, however, multiple linear regression may yield spurious relationships, lead to poor predictions, and offer a poor understanding of relationships.

The analyst must first specify the model and make several decisions in this process, answering the following, among other questions: What is the dependent variable of interest? What independent variables are important? What form should the model take? What is the goal of the model—prediction or understanding of the relationship?

The analyst specifies the dependent and independent variables and then employs software to estimate the model and produce related statistics. The good news is that the software, such as shown in Exhibit 1, does the estimation, and our primary tasks are to focus on specifying the model and interpreting the output from this software, which are the main subjects of this content.

Exhibit 1: Examples of Regression Software	
Software	**Programs/Functions**
Excel	Data Analysis > Regression
Python	scipy.stats.linregress
	statsmodels.lm
	sklearn.linear_model.LinearRegression
R	lm
SAS	PROC REG
	PROC GLM
STATA	regress

SUMMARY

- Multiple linear regression is used to model the linear relationship between one dependent variable and two or more independent variables.

- In practice, multiple regressions are used to explain relationships between financial variables, to test existing theories, or to make forecasts.

- The regression process covers several decisions the analyst must make, such as identifying the dependent and independent variables, selecting the appropriate regression model, testing if the assumptions behind linear regression are satisfied, examining goodness of fit, and making needed adjustments.

- A multiple regression model is represented by the following equation:

$$Y_i = b_0 + b_1X_{1i} + b_2X_{2i} + b_3X_{3i} + \ldots + b_kX_{ki} + \varepsilon_i, i = 1, 2, 3, \ldots, n,$$

  where Y is the dependent variable, Xs are the independent variables from 1 to k, and the model is estimated using n observations.

- Coefficient b_0 is the model's "intercept," representing the expected value of Y if all independent variables are zero.

- Parameters b_1 to b_k are the slope coefficients (or partial regression coefficients) for independent variables X_1 to X_k. Slope coefficient b_j describes the impact of independent variable X_j on Y, holding all the other independent variables constant.

- There are five main assumptions underlying multiple regression models that must be satisfied, including (1) linearity, (2) homoskedasticity, (3) independence of errors, (4) normality, and (5) independence of independent variables.

- Diagnostic plots can help detect whether these assumptions are satisfied. Scatterplots of dependent versus and independent variables are useful for detecting non-linear relationships, while residual plots are useful for detecting violations of homoskedasticity and independence of errors.

USES OF MULTIPLE LINEAR REGRESSION　　　　　**2**

☐ | describe the types of investment problems addressed by multiple
　 | linear regression and the regression process

There are many investment problems in which the analyst needs to consider the impact of multiple factors on the subject of research rather than a single factor. In the complex world of investments, it is intuitive that explaining or forecasting a financial variable by a single factor may be insufficient. The complexity of financial and economic relations calls for models with multiple explanatory variables, subject to fundamental justification and various statistical tests.

Examples of how multiple regression may be used include the following:

- A portfolio manager wants to understand how returns are influenced by a set of underlying factors; the size effect, the value effect, profitability, and investment aggressiveness. The goal is to estimate a Fama–French five-factor model that will provide an understanding of the factors that are important for driving a particular stock's excess returns.

- A financial adviser wants to identify whether certain variables, such as financial leverage, profitability, revenue growth, and changes in market share, can predict whether a company will face financial distress.

- An analyst wants to examine the effect of different dimensions of country risk, such as political stability, economic conditions, and environmental, social, and governance (ESG) considerations, on equity returns in that country.

Multiple regression can be used to identify relationships between variables, to test existing theories, or to forecast. We outline the general process of regression analysis in Exhibit 2. As you can see, there are many decisions that the analyst must make in this process.

For example, if the dependent variable is continuous, such as returns, the traditional regression model is typically the first step. If, however, the dependent variable is discrete—for example, an indicator variable such as whether a company is a takeover target or not a takeover target—then, as we shall see, the model may be estimated as a logistic regression.

In either case, the process of determining the best model follows a similar path. The model must first be specified, including independent variables that may be continuous, such as company financial features, or discrete (i.e., dummy variables), indicating membership in a class, such as an industry sector. Next, the regression model is estimated and analyzed to ensure it satisfies key underlying assumptions and meets the analyst's goodness-of-fit criteria. Once the model is tested and its out-of-sample performance is deemed acceptable, then it can be used for further identifying relationships between variables, for testing existing theories, or for forecasting.

Exhibit 2: The Regression Process

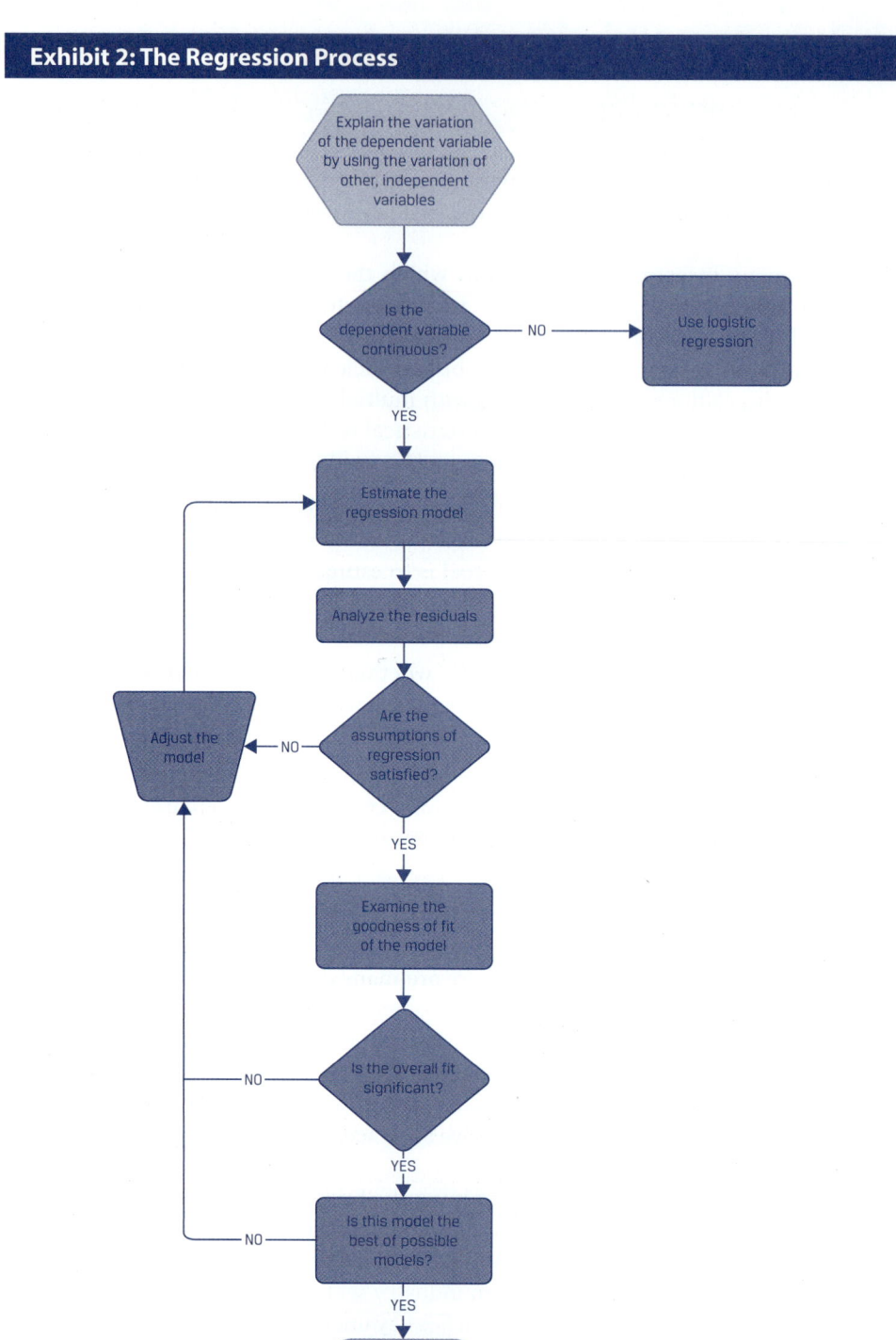

KNOWLEDGE CHECK

Assessment: Multiple Regression—Types of Investment Problems and Process

1. You are a junior analyst assisting in the development of various multiple regression models for your industry sector. Identify the action you should take to resolve each of the following issues:

Issue	Action
The dependent variable takes on a value of 1 if the company is a merger target and 0 otherwise.	
The analyst estimates a model with five independent variables, and none of these variables are significant explanatory variables.	
The residuals do not appear to be homoskedastic, thus violating a regression assumption.	
The regression assumptions are satisfied, the overall fit is significant, and the model is the best model of the possible models.	

Solution

Issue	Action
The dependent variable takes on a value of 1 if the company is a merger target and 0 otherwise.	Use logistic regression.
The analyst estimates a model with five independent variables, and none of these variables are significant explanatory variables.	Adjust the model and re-estimate.
The residuals do not appear to be homoskedastic, thus violating a regression assumption.	Adjust the model and re-estimate.
The regression assumptions are satisfied, the overall fit is significant, and the model is the best model of the possible models.	Use the model for analysis and prediction.

THE BASICS OF MULTIPLE REGRESSION   3

☐ formulate a multiple linear regression model, describe the relation between the dependent variable and several independent variables, and interpret estimated regression coefficients

The goal of simple regression is to explain the variation of the dependent variable, Y, using the variation of an independent variable, X. The goal of multiple regression is the same, to explain the variation of the dependent variable, Y, but using the variations in a set of independent variables, $X_1, X_2, \ldots, X_k$. Recall the variation of Y is

$$\text{Variation of } Y = \sum_{i=1}^{n}(Y_i - \overline{Y})^2,$$

which we also refer to as the sum of squares total. The simple regression equation is

$$Y_i = b_0 + b_1 X_i + \varepsilon_i, \ i{=}1, 2, 3, \ldots, n.$$

When we introduce additional independent variables to help explain the variation of the dependent variable, we have the multiple regression equation:

$$Y_i = b_0 + b_1 X_{1i} + b_2 X_{2i} + b_3 X_{3i} + \ldots + b_k X_{ki} + \varepsilon_i, \ i = 1, 2, 3, \ldots, n. \qquad (1)$$

In this equation, the terms involving the k independent variables are the deterministic part of the model, whereas the error term, ε_i, is the stochastic or random part of the model. The model is estimated over n observations, where n must be larger than k.

It is important to note that a slope coefficient in a multiple regression, known as a **partial regression coefficient** or a *partial slope coefficient*, must be interpreted with care. A partial regression coefficient, b_j, describes the impact of that independent variable on the dependent variable, holding all the other independent variables constant. For example, in the multiple regression equation,

$$Y_i = b_0 + b_1 X_{1i} + b_2 X_{2i} + b_3 X_{3i} + \varepsilon_i,$$

the coefficient b_2 measures the change in Y for a one-unit change in X_2 assuming X_1 and X_3 are held constant. The estimated regression equation is

$$Y_i = \hat{b}_0 + \hat{b}_1 X_{1i} + \hat{b}_2 X_{2i} + \hat{b}_3 X_{3i},$$

with ^ indicating estimated coefficients.

Consider an estimated regression equation in which the monthly excess returns of a bond index (RET) are regressed against the change in monthly government bond yields (BY) and the change in the investment-grade credit spreads (CS). The estimated regression, using 60 monthly observations, is

$$\text{RET} = 0.0023 - 5.0585 \text{BY} - 2.1901 \text{CS}.$$

We learn the following from this regression:

1. The bond index RET yields, on average, 0.0023% per month, or approximately 0.028% per year, if the changes in the government bond yields and investment-grade credit spreads are zero.

2. The change in the bond index return for a given one-unit change in the monthly government bond yield, BY, is −5.0585%, holding CS constant. This means that the bond index has an empirical duration of 5.0585.

3. If the investment-grade credit spreads, CS, increase by one unit, the bond index returns change by −2.1901%, holding BY constant.

4. For a month in which the change in the credit spreads is 0.001 and the change in the government bond yields is 0.005, the expected excess return on the bond index is

$$\text{RET} = 0.0023 - 5.0585(0.005) - 2.1901(0.001) = -0.0252, \text{ or } -2.52\%.$$

KNOWLEDGE CHECK

An institutional salesperson has just read the research report in which you estimated a regression of monthly excess returns on a portfolio, RETRF, against the Fama–French three factors:

- MKTRF, the market excess return;

- SMB, the difference in returns between small- and large-capitalization stocks; and
- HML, the difference in returns between value and growth stocks.

All returns are stated in whole percentages (that is, 1 for 1%), and the estimated regression equation is

$$\text{RETRF} = 1.5324 + 0.5892\text{MKTRF} + -0.8719\text{SMB} + -0.0560\text{HML}.$$

Before this salesperson meets with her client firm, she asks you to do the following regarding your estimated regression model:

1. Interpret the intercept.

Solution

If the market excess return, SMB, and HML are each zero, then we expect a return on the portfolio of 1.534%.

2. Interpret each slope coefficient.

Solution

Each slope coefficient is interpreted assuming the other variables are held constant.
- For MKTRF, if the market return increases by 1%, we expect the portfolio's return to increase by 0.5892%.
- For SMB, if the size effect returns increase by 1%, we expect the portfolio's return to decrease by 0.8719%.
- For HML, if the value effect returns increase by 1%, we expect the portfolio's return to decrease by 0.056%.

3. Calculate the predicted value of the portfolio's return if

$$\text{MKTRF} = 1, \text{SMB} = 4, \text{ and } \text{HML} = -2.$$

Solution

Given the expected values of the independent variables, the expected return on the portfolio is

$$R = 1.534 + 0.5892(1) - 0.8719(4) - 0.0560(-2) = -1.2524.$$

ASSUMPTIONS UNDERLYING MULTIPLE LINEAR REGRESSION   4

☐ | explain the assumptions underlying a multiple linear regression model and interpret residual plots indicating potential violations of these assumptions

Before we can conduct correct statistical inference on a multiple linear regression model estimated using ordinary least squares (OLS), we need to know whether the assumptions underlying that model are met. Suppose we have n observations on the dependent variable, Y, and the independent variables, $X_1, X_2, \ldots, X_k$, and we want to estimate the model

$$Y_i = b_0 + b_1 X_{1i} + b_2 X_{2i} + b_3 X_{3i} + \ldots + b_k X_{ki} + \varepsilon_i, \ i = 1, 2, 3, \ldots, n.$$

In simple regression, we had four assumptions that needed to be satisfied so that we could make valid conclusions regarding the regression results. In multiple regression, we modify these slightly to reflect the additional independent variables:

1. Linearity: The relationship between the dependent variable and the independent variables is linear.

2. Homoskedasticity: The variance of the regression residuals is the same for all observations.

3. Independence of errors: The observations are independent of one another. This implies the regression residuals are uncorrelated across observations.

4. Normality: The regression residuals are normally distributed.

5. Independence of independent variables:

    5a. Independent variables are not random.

    5b. There is no exact linear relation between two or more of the independent variables or combinations of the independent variables.

The independence assumption is needed to enable the estimation of the coefficients. If there is an exact linear relationship between independent variables, the model cannot be estimated. In the more common case of approximate linear relationships, which may be indicated by significant pairwise correlations between the independent variables, the model can be estimated but its interpretation is problematic. In empirical work, the assumptions underlying multiple linear regression do not always hold. The statistical tools to detect violations and methods to mitigate their effects will be addressed later.

Regression software produces diagnostic plots, which are a useful tool for detecting potential violations of the assumptions underlying multiple linear regression. To illustrate the use of such plots, we first estimate a regression to analyze 10 years of monthly total excess returns of ABC stock using the Fama–French three-factor model. As noted previously, this model uses market excess return (MKTRF), size (SMB) and value (HML) as explanatory variables.

$$\text{ABC\_RETRF}_t = b_0 + b_1 \text{MKTRF}_t + b_2 \text{SMB}_t + b_3 \text{HML}_t + \varepsilon_t$$

We start our analysis by generating a **scatterplot matrix** using software. This matrix is also referred to as a *pairs plot*.

CODE: SCATTERPLOT MATRIX

Using Python

```python
import pandas as pd

import matplotlib.pyplot as plt

import seaborn as sns

df = pd.read_csv("ABC_FF.csv",parse_dates=True,index_col=0)

sns.pairplot(df)

plt.show()
```

Using R

```
df <- read.csv("data.csv")

pairs(df[c("ABC_RETRF","MKTRF","SMB","HML")])
```

The pairwise scatterplots for all variables are shown in Exhibit 3. For example, the bottom row shows the relationships for the following three pairs: ABC_RETRF and MKTRF, ABC_RETRF and SMB, and ABC_RETRF and HML. The simple regression line and corresponding 95% confidence interval for the variables in each pair are also shown, along with the histogram of each variable along the diagonal.

Exhibit 3: Scatterplot Matrix of ABC Returns and Fama–French Factors

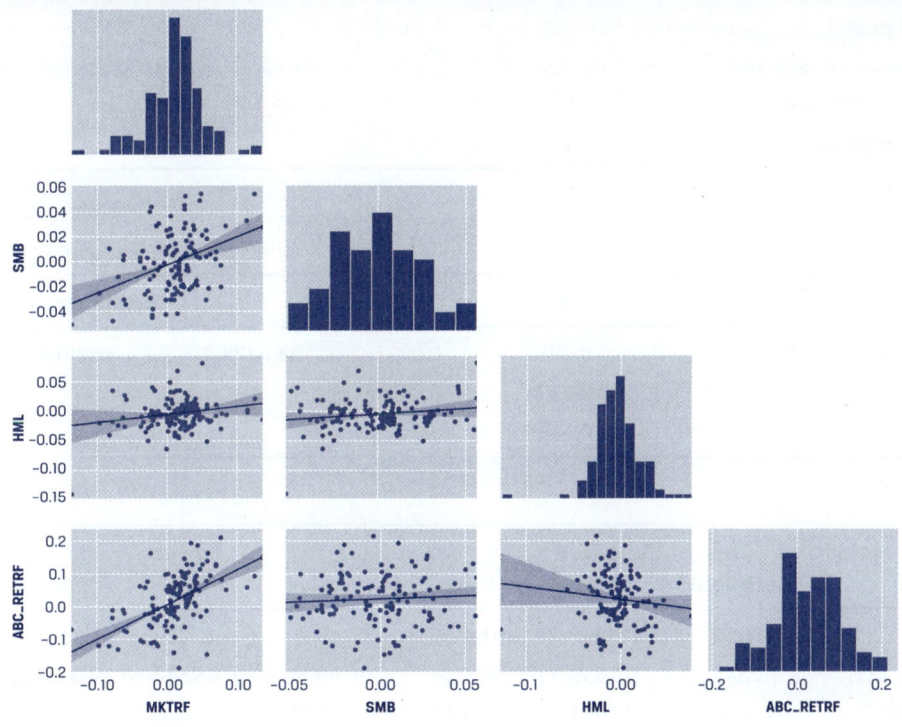

You can see the following from the lower set of scatterplots between ABC_RET and the three independent variables:

- There is a positive relationship between ABC_RETF and the market factor, MKTRF.
- There seems to be no apparent relation between ABC_RETRF and the size factor, SMB. The reason is the scatterplot compares the two variables in isolation and does not show the "partial" correlation picked up by the regression, which explains why SMB is significant in the regression (see Exhibit 4) but not in the scatterplot.
- There is a negative relationship between ABC_RETF and the value factor, HML.

Looking at the scatterplots between the independent variables, SMB and HML have little or no correlation, as indicated by the relatively flat line for the SMB–HML pair. This is a desirable characteristic between explanatory variables.

An additional benefit of the scatterplot matrix is that all data points are displayed, so it can also be used to identify extreme values and outliers.

We now estimate the model of ABC's excess returns using software such as Microsoft Excel, Python, or R; results are shown in Exhibit 5. Focusing on the regression residuals, we look for clues to potential violations of the assumptions of multiple linear regression.

Exhibit 4: ABC Returns Explained Using Fama–French Three-Factor Model

Regression Statistics

Multiple R	0.6238
R-Squared	0.3891
Adjusted R-Squared	0.3733
Standard Error	0.0628
Observations	120

ANOVA

	Df	SS	MS	F	Significance F
Regression	3	0.2914	0.0971	24.6278	0.0000
Residual	116	0.4575	0.0039		
Total	119	0.7489			

	Coefficient	Standard error	t-Stat.	P-value	Lower 95%	Upper 95%
Intercept	0.0052	0.0061	0.8435	0.4007	−0.0070	0.0173
MKTRF	1.2889	0.1538	8.3791	0.0000	0.9842	1.5935
SMB	−0.5841	0.2664	−2.1922	0.0304	−1.1118	−0.0564
HML	−−0.6810	0.2231	−3.0523	0.0028	−1.1229	−0.2391

Exhibit 5: ABC Returns Explained Using Fama–French Three-Factor Model

Regression Statistics

Multiple R	0.6238
R-Squared	0.3891
Adjusted R-Squared	0.3733
Standard Error	0.0628
Observations	120

ANOVA

	Df	SS	MS	F	Significance F
Regression	3	0.2914	0.0971	24.6278	0.0000
Residual	116	0.4575	0.0039		
Total	119	0.7489			

	Coefficient	Standard error	t-Stat.	P-value	Lower 95%	Upper 95%
Intercept	0.0052	0.0061	0.8435	0.4007	−0.0070	0.0173
MKTRF	1.2889	0.1538	8.3791	0.0000	0.9842	1.5935
SMB	−0.5841	0.2664	−2.1922	0.0304	−1.1118	−0.0564
HML	−−0.6810	0.2231	−3.0523	0.0028	−1.1229	−0.2391

CODE: REGRESSION

Using Python

```
import pandas as pd

from statsmodels.formula.api import ols

df = pd.read_csv("data.csv")

model = ols('ABC_RETRF ~ MKTRF+SMB+HML',data=df).fit()

print(model.summary())
```

Using R

```
df <- read.csv("data.csv")

model <- lm('ABC_RETRF~ MKTRF+SMB+HML',data=df)

print(summary(model))
```

We start by looking at a scatterplot of residuals against the dependent variable, as shown in Exhibit 6. We can use this scatterplot to uncover potential assumption violations and to help identify outliers in our data.

Exhibit 6: Residuals vs. Predicted Value of Dependent Variable

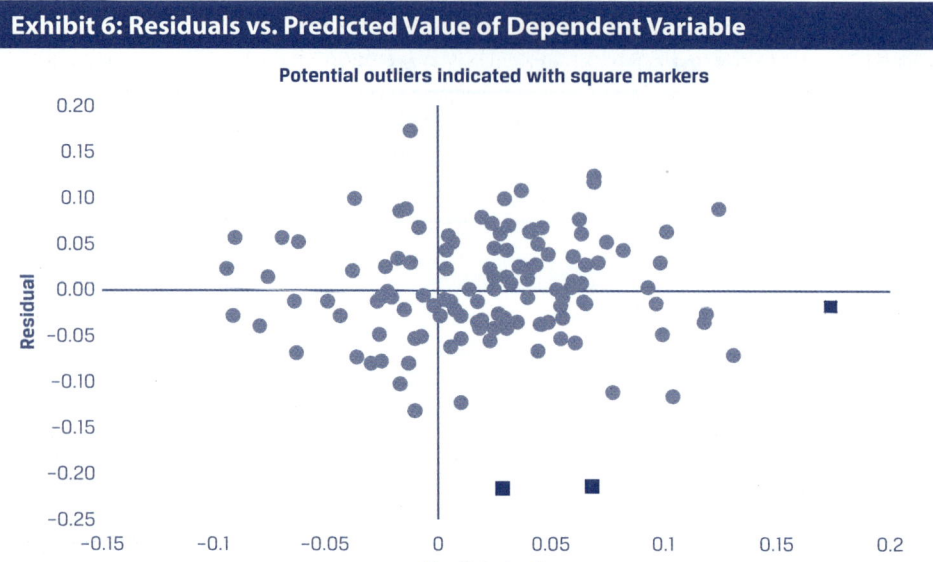

Potential outliers indicated with square markers

As indicated by the line centered near residual value 0.00, a visual inspection of Exhibit 6 does not reveal any directional relationship between the residuals and the predicted values from the regression model. This outcome is good, because we want residuals to behave in an independent manner compared to what the model predicts, and suggests the regression's errors have a constant variance and are uncorrelated with each other, thereby satisfying several of the underlying assumptions of multiple linear regression. Notably, we detect three residuals (square markers) that may be outliers, Months 7, 25, and 95. This information can be used to check for shocks from factors not considered in the model that may have occurred at these points in time.

Exhibit 7 presents plots of the regression residuals versus each of the three factors in Panels A, B, and C. A visual inspection does not indicate any directional relationship between the residuals and the explanatory variables, suggesting there is no violation of a multiple linear regression assumption. Importantly, the three potential outliers detected in the residual versus predicted value plot are also apparent in Exhibit 7, as indicated by the square markers.

Exhibit 7: Regression Residuals vs. Factors (Independent Variables)

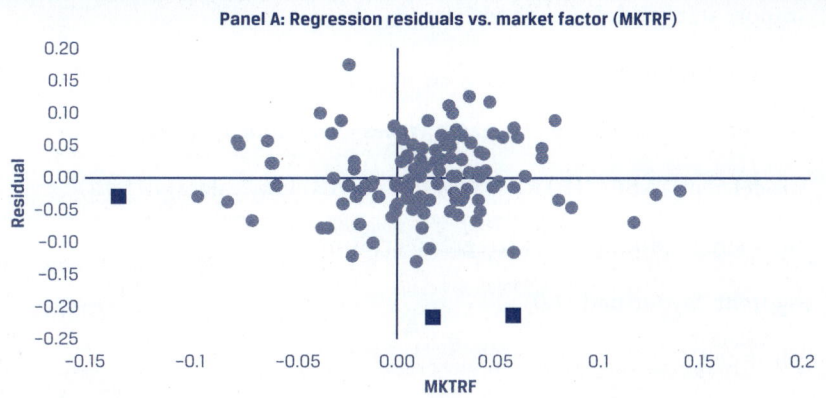

Panel A: Regression residuals vs. market factor (MKTRF)

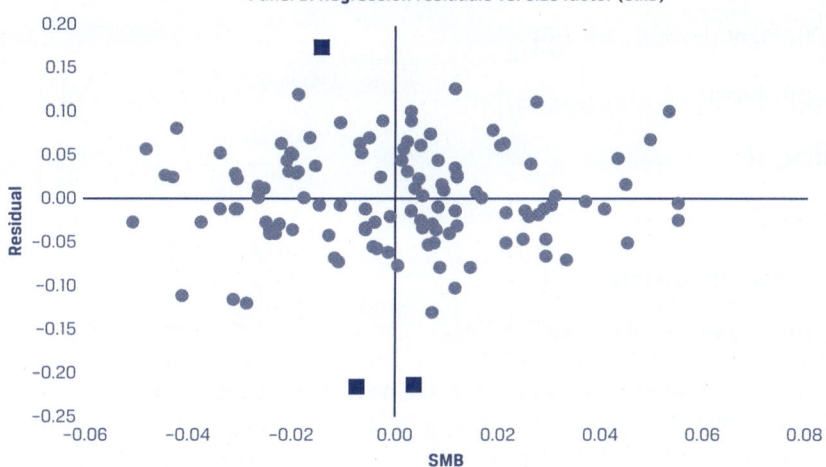

Panel B: Regression residuals vs. size factor (SMB)

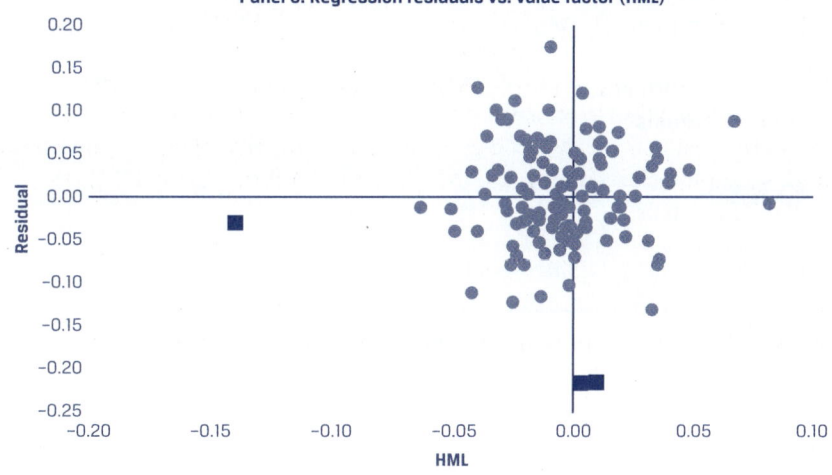

Panel C: Regression residuals vs. value factor (HML)

CODE: RESIDUAL ANALYSIS

Using Python

```
import pandas as pd
```

```
import matplotlib.pyplot as plt

import statsmodels.api as sm

import numpy as np

df = pd.read_csv("data.csv",parse_dates=True,index_col=0)

model = ols('ABC_RETRF ~ MKTRF+SMB+HML',data=df).fit()

fig = sm.graphics.plot_partregress_grid(model)

fig.tight_layout(pad=1.0)

plt.show()

fig = sm.graphics.plot_ccpr_grid(model)

fig.tight_layout(pad=1.0)

plt.show()
```

Using R

```
library(ggplot2)

library(gridExtra)

df <- read.csv("data.csv")

model <- lm('ABC_RETRF~ MKTRF+SMB+HML',data=df)

df$res <- model$residuals

g1 <- ggplot(df,aes(y=res, x=MKTRF))+geom_point()+
xlab("MKTRF")+ylab("Residuals")

g2 <- ggplot(df,aes(y=res, x=SMB))+geom_point()+ xlab("SMB")+
ylab("Residuals")

g3 <- ggplot(df,aes(y=res, x=HML))+geom_point()+ xlab("HML")+
ylab("Residuals")

grid.arrange(g1,g2,g3,nrow=3)
```

Finally, in Exhibit 8 we present a **normal Q-Q plot**. A normal Q-Q plot, or simply a Q-Q plot, is used to visualize the distribution of a variable by comparing it to a normal distribution. In the case of regression, we can use a Q-Q plot to compare the model's standardized residuals to a theoretical standard normal distribution. If the residuals are normally distributed, they should align along the diagonal. Recall that 5% of observations that are normally distributed should fall below -1.65 standard deviations, so the 5th percentile residual observation should appear at -1.65 standard deviations.

Exhibit 8: Normal Q-Q Plot of Regression Residuals

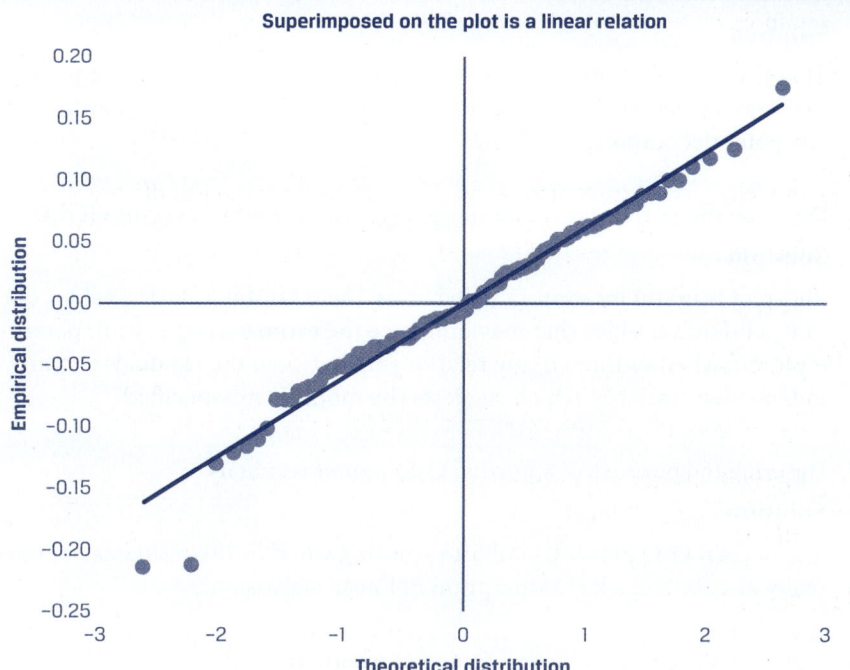

Superimposed on the plot is a linear relation

However, after −2 standard deviations, observations 25 and 95 fall well below the theoretical standard normal distribution range, while Observation 7, lying above the diagonal line around +2.5 standard deviations, is somewhat above the theoretical range. This evidence again suggests these three residual observations are potential outliers. However, setting them aside, the normal Q-Q plot does provide ample evidence that the regression residuals overall are distributed consistently with the normal distribution. Thus, we can conclude that the regression model error term is close to being normally distributed.

KNOWLEDGE CHECK

You are analyzing price changes of a cryptocurrency (CRYPTO) using the price changes for gold (GOLD) and a technology stock index (TECH), based on five years of monthly observations. You also run several diagnostic charts of your regression results. In a meeting with your research director, she asks you to do the following:

1. Identify any assumptions that may be violated if we examine the correlation between GOLD and TECH and find a significant pairwise correlation.

   Solution

   This result may indicate an approximate linear relation between GOLD and TECH, which would be a violation of the independence of independent variables, and should be explored further.

2. Describe the purpose of a plot of the regression residuals versus the predicted value of CRYPTO.

   Solution

   This plot is useful for examining whether there is any clustering or pattern that may suggest the residuals are not homoskedastic and whether there are any potential outliers.

3. Describe the purpose of a plot of the regression residuals versus GOLD.

   Solution

   This plot is useful for examining whether there are any extreme values of the independent variables that may influence the estimated regression parameters and whether there is any relationship between the residuals and an independent variable, which suggests the model is misspecified.

4. Describe the purpose of a normal Q-Q plot of residuals.

   Solution

   The normal Q-Q plot is useful for exploring whether the residuals are normally distributed, a key assumption of linear regression.

5. A pairwise scatterplot is used to detect whether:

   A. there is a linear relationship between the dependent and independent variables.

   B. the residual terms exhibit heteroskedasticity.

   C. the residual terms are normally distributed.

   Solution

   A is correct. The pairwise scatterplot is useful for visualizing the relationships between the dependent and explanatory variables.

6. Interpret this scatterplot showing price changes for the cryptocurrency (CRYPTO) and the tech index (TECH):

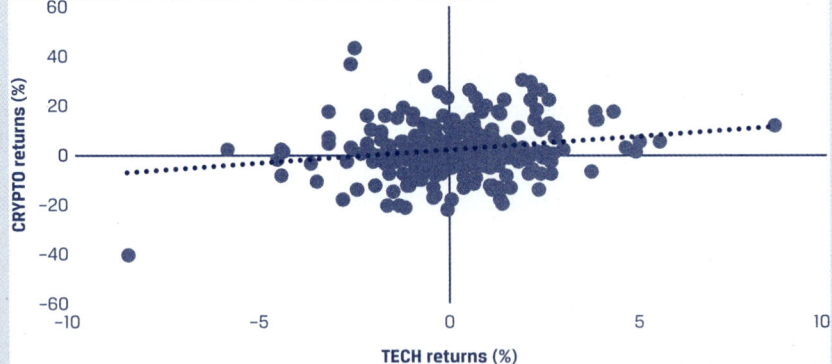

   Solution

   Based on the plot, there appears to be a positive relationship between CRYPTO and TECH, which may be significant. Several potential outliers are also apparent.

7. A normal Q-Q plot is used to detect whether:

   A. there is a linear relationship between the dependent and independent variables.

   B. the regression residual terms exhibit heteroskedasticity.

   C. the regression residual terms are normally distributed.

Solution

C is correct. The normal Q-Q plot is useful for exploring whether the residuals are normally distributed.

8. Interpret this normal Q-Q plot from our regression of CRYPTO price changes:

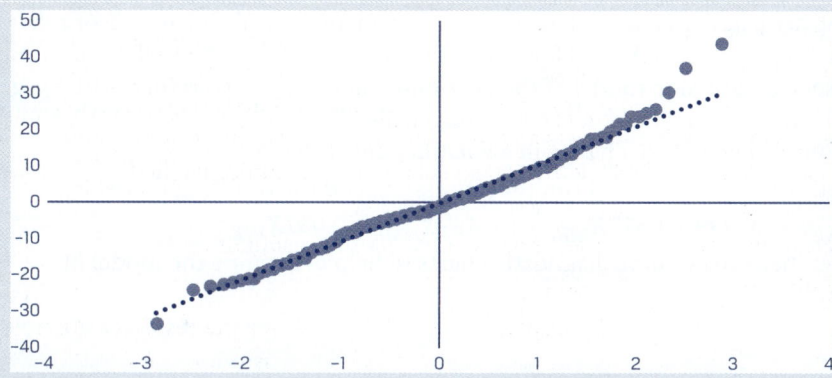

Solution

Based on the plot, the residuals are not normally distributed, as indicated by the deviation of residuals from the diagonal evident past ±2 standard deviations, and several potential outliers are also apparent. This normal Q-Q plot suggests the distribution of residuals is "fat-tailed." Note that fat-tailed distributions of residuals are a commonly observed feature of financial data time series.

PRACTICE PROBLEMS

The following information relates to questions 1-5

You are a junior analyst at an asset management firm. Your supervisor asks you to analyze the return drivers for one of the firm's portfolios. She asks you to construct a regression model of the portfolio's monthly excess returns (RET) against three factors: the market excess return (MRKT), a value factor (HML), and the monthly percentage change in a volatility index (VIX).

You collect the data and run the regression, and the resulting model is

$Y_{RET} = -0.999 + 1.817X_{MRKT} + 0.489X_{HML} + 0.037X_{VIX}$.

You then create some diagnostic charts to help determine the model fit.

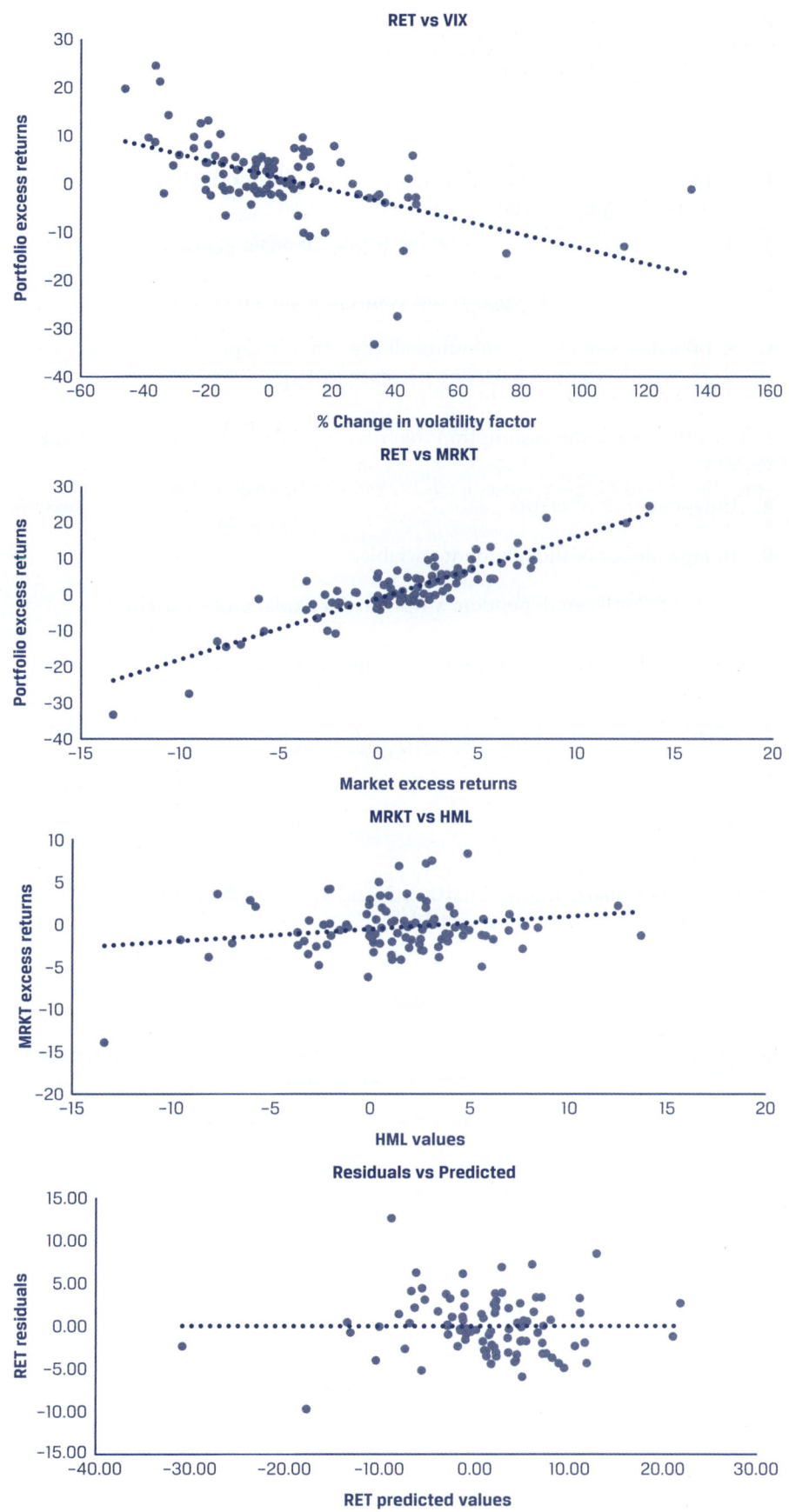

1. Determine the type of regression model you should use.

   A. Logistic regression

   B. Simple linear regression

   C. Multiple linear regression

2. Determine which one of the following statements about the coefficient of the volatility factor (VIX) is true.

   A. A 1.0% increase in X_{VIX} would result in a -0.962% decrease in Y_{RET}.

   B. A 0.037% increase in X_{VIX} would result in a 1.0% increase in Y_{RET}.

   C. A 1.0% increase in X_{VIX}, holding all the other independent variables constant, would result in a 0.037% increase in Y_{RET}.

3. Identify the regression assumption that may be violated based on Chart 1, RET vs. VIX.

   A. Independence of errors

   B. Independence of independent variables

   C. Linearity between dependent variable and explanatory variables

4. Identify which chart, among Charts 2, 3, and 4, is *most likely* to be used to assess homoskedasticity.

   A. Chart 2

   B. Chart 3

   C. Chart 4

5. Identify which chart, among Charts 2, 3, and 4, is *most likely* to be used to assess independence of independent variables.

   A. Chart 2

   B. Chart 3

   C. Chart 4

SOLUTIONS

1. C is correct. You should use a multiple linear regression model since the dependent variable is continuous (not discrete) and there is more than one explanatory variable. If the dependent variable were discrete, then the model should be estimated as a logistic regression.

2. C is correct. The coefficient of the volatility factor (X_{VIX}) is 0.037. It should be interpreted to mean that holding all the other independent variables constant, a 1% increase (decrease) would result in a 0.037% increase (decrease) in the monthly portfolio excess return (Y_{RET}).

3. C is correct. Chart 1 is a scatterplot of RET versus VIX. Linearity between the dependent variable and the independent variables is an assumption underlying multiple linear regression. As shown in the following Revised Chart 1, the relationship appears to be more curved (i.e., quadratic) than linear.

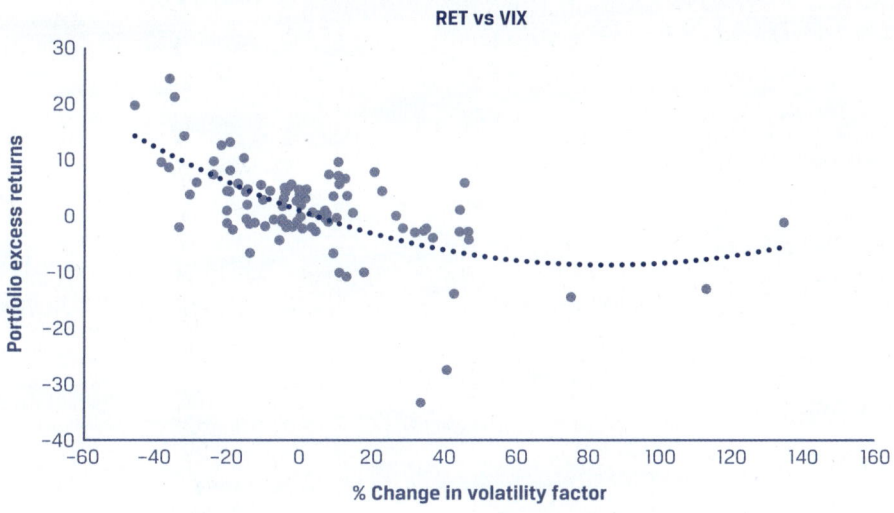

4. C is correct. To assess homoskedasticity, we must evaluate whether the variance of the regression residuals is constant for all observations. Chart 4 is a scatterplot of the regression residuals versus the predicted values, so it is very useful for visually assessing the consistency of the variance of the residuals across the observations. Any clusters of high and/or low values of the residuals may indicate a violation of the homoskedasticity assumption.

5. B is correct. Chart 3 is a scatterplot comparing the values of two of the independent variables, MRKT and HML. This chart would most likely be used to assess the independence of these explanatory variables.

Evaluating Regression Model Fit and Interpreting Model Results

SUMMARY

- In multiple regression, adjusted R^2 is used as a measure of model goodness of fit since it does not automatically increase as independent variables are added to the model. Rather, it adjusts for the degrees of freedom by incorporating the number of independent variables.

- Adjusted R^2 will increase (decrease) if a variable is added to the model that has a coefficient with an absolute value of its t-statistic greater (less) than 1.0.

- Akaike's information criterion (AIC) and Schwarz's Bayesian information criteria (BIC) are also used to evaluate model fit and select the "best" model among a group with the same dependent variable. AIC is preferred if the purpose is prediction, BIC is preferred if goodness of fit is the goal, and lower values of both measures are better.

- Hypothesis tests of a single coefficient in a multiple regression, using t-tests, are identical to those in simple regression.

- The joint F-test is used to jointly test a subset of variables in a multiple regression, where the "restricted" model is based on a narrower set of independent variables nested in the broader "unrestricted" model. The null hypothesis is that the slope coefficients of all independent variables outside the restricted model are zero.

- The general linear F-test is an extension of the joint F-test, where the null hypothesis is that the slope coefficients on all independent variables in the unrestricted model are equal to zero.

- Predicting the value of the dependent variable using an estimated multiple regression model is similar to that in simple regression. First, sum, for each independent variable, the estimated slope coefficient multiplied by the assumed value of that variable, and then add the estimated intercept coefficient.

- In multiple regression, the confidence interval around the forecasted value of the dependent variable reflects both model error and sampling error (from forecasting the independent variables); the larger the sampling error, the larger is the standard error of the forecast of Y and the wider is the confidence interval.

1   GOODNESS OF FIT

☐ | evaluate how well a multiple regression model explains the dependent variable by analyzing ANOVA table results and measures of goodness of fit

In the simple regression model, the **coefficient of determination**, also known as R-squared or R^2, is a measure of the goodness of fit of an estimated regression to the data. R^2 can also be defined in multiple regression as the ratio of the variation of the dependent variable explained by the independent variables (sum of squares regression) to the total variation of the dependent variable (sum of squares total).

$$R^2 = \frac{\text{Sum of squares regression}}{\text{Sum of squares total}} = \frac{\sum_{i=1}^{n}\left(\hat{Y}_i - \overline{Y}\right)^2}{\sum_{i=1}^{n}(Y_i - \overline{Y})^2},$$

where n is the number of observations in the regression, Y_i is an observation on the dependent variable, $\hat{Y}_i$ is the predicted value of the dependent variable based on the independent variables, and $\overline{Y}$ is the mean of the dependent variable.

In multiple linear regression, however, R^2 is less appropriate as a measure of a model's goodness of fit. This is because as independent variables are added to the model, R^2 will increase or will stay the same, but it will not decrease. Problems with using R^2 in multiple regression include the following:

- The R^2 cannot provide information on whether the coefficients are statistically significant.

- The R^2 cannot provide information on whether there are biases in the estimated coefficients and predictions.

- The R^2 cannot tell whether the model fit is good. A good model may have a low R^2, as in many asset-pricing models, and a bad model may have a high R^2 due to overfitting and biases in the model.

Overfitting of a regression model is a situation in which the model is too complex, meaning there may be too many independent variables relative to the number of observations in the sample. A result of overfitting is that the coefficients on the independent variables may not represent true relationships with the dependent variable.

An alternative measure of goodness of fit is the **adjusted R^2 ($\overline{R}^2$)**, which is typically part of the multiple regression output produced by most statistical software packages. A benefit of using the adjusted R^2 is that it does not automatically increase when another independent variable is added to a regression. This is because it adjusts for the degrees of freedom as follows, where k is the number of independent variables:

$$\overline{R}^2 = 1 - \left(\frac{\text{Sum of squares error}/(n - k - 1)}{\text{Sum of squares total}/(n - 1)} \right). \tag{1}$$

Mathematically, the relation between R^2 and $\overline{R}^2$ is

$$\overline{R}^2 = 1 - \left[\left(\frac{n - 1}{n - k - 1} \right)(1 - R^2) \right]. \tag{2}$$

Note that if $k \geq 1$, then R^2 is strictly greater than adjusted R^2. Further, the adjusted R^2 may be negative, whereas the R^2 has a minimum of zero.

The following are two key observations about $\overline{R}^2$ when adding a new variable to a regression:

- If the coefficient's t-statistic $> |1.0|$, then $\overline{R}^2$ increases.
- If the coefficient's t-statistic $< |1.0|$, then $\overline{R}^2$ decreases.

Note that a t-statistic with an absolute value of 1.0 does not indicate the independent variable is different from zero at typical levels of significance, 5% and 1%. So, adjusted R^2 does not set a very high bar for the statistic to increase.

Consider the regression output provided in Exhibit 1, which shows the results from the regression of portfolio returns on the returns for five hypothetical fundamental factors, which we shall call Factors 1 through 5. The goal of this regression is to identify the factors that best explain the returns on the portfolio.

Exhibit 1: Regression of Portfolio Excess Returns on Five Factors

Multiple R	0.7845
R-Squared	0.6155
Adjusted R-Squared	0.5718
Standard Error	0.0113
Log-Likelihood	-74.054
Observations	50

ANOVA Table

Source	Degrees of freedom	Sum of squares	Mean squares	F-statistic	Significance of F-statistic
Regression	5	90.6234	18.1247	14.0853	< 0.0000
Residual	44	56.6182	1.2868		
Total	49	147.2416			

	Coefficient	Standard error	*t*-Statistic	*P*-value	95% confidence interval	
					Lower bound	Upper bound
Intercept	2.1876	0.1767	−12.3787	0.0000	−2.5437	−1.8314
Factor 1	1.5992	0.2168	7.3756	0.0000	1.1622	2.0361
Factor 2	0.1923	0.7406	0.2596	0.7964	−1.3002	1.6847
Factor 3	−0.7126	0.5854	−1.2172	0.2300	−1.8925	0.4673
Factor 4	3.3376	1.3493	2.4736	0.0173	0.6182	6.0570
Factor 5	−2.6832	8.3919	−0.3197	0.7507	−19.5959	14.2295

CODE: REGRESSION STATISTICS

Using Microsoft Excel

Let depvar be the range of cells for the dependent variable, and let indvar be the range of cells for the independent variables.

```
=LINEST(depvar,indvar,TRUE,TRUE) or Data Analysis > Regression
```

Using Python

Let df be the data frame containing the data.

```
import statsmodels.api as sm

from statsmodels.stats.anova import anova_lm

from statsmodels.formula.api import ols

formula='Portfolio ~ Factor1+Factor2+Factor3+Factor4+Factor5'

results=ols(formula,df).fit()

print(results.summary())
```

Using R

Let df be the data frame containing the data.

```
model11 <- lm(df$Portfolio ~

df$Factor1+df$Factor2+df$Factor3+df$Factor4+df$Factor5)

anova(model11)

summary(model11)
```

We see in Exhibit 1 that R^2 is 0.6155, or 61.55%, and can we visualize this relationship using the graph in Exhibit 2.

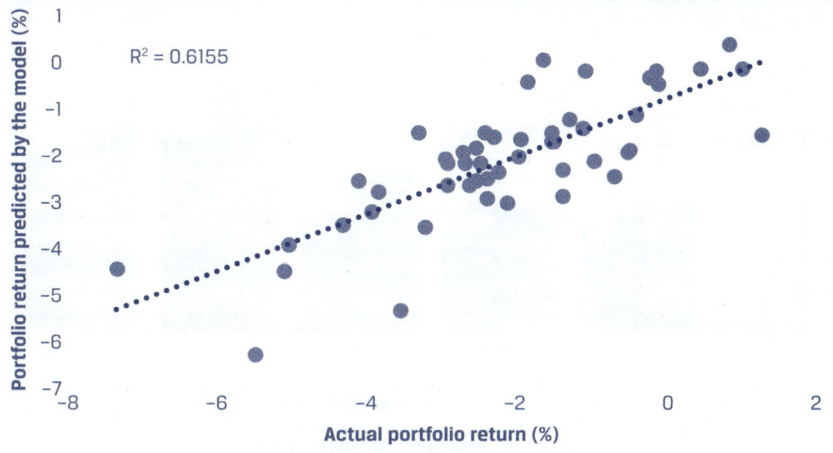

Exhibit 2: Predicted vs. Actual Portfolio Excess Returns Based on Regression of Returns on a Model with Five Factors

We can use the **analysis of variance (ANOVA)** table in Exhibit 1 to describe the model fit. We know from simple regression that the R^2 is the ratio of the sum of squares regression to the sum of squares total. We confirm this as

$$R^2 = \frac{\text{SSR}}{\text{SST}} = \frac{90.6234}{147.2416} = 0.6155$$

and the adjusted R^2 (using Equation 3) as

$$\overline{R}^2 = 1 - \left[\left(\frac{50 - 1}{50 - 5 - 1} \right) \left(1 - \frac{90.6234}{147.2416} \right) \right] = 0.5718.$$

The effect of successively adding each factor to the model is shown in Exhibit 3. The regression of the portfolio returns starts with the returns of Factor 1, then in the next model adds Factor 2, and so on, until all five are included in the full model. Note that with each added variable, the R^2 either stays the same or increases. However, while the adjusted R^2 increases when Factors 3 and 4 are added, it declines when Factors 2 and 5 are added to those models, respectively. This illustrates the relationship between the $|t\text{-statistic}|$ of the added variable and adjusted R^2.

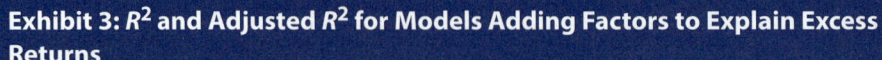

Exhibit 3: R^2 and Adjusted R^2 for Models Adding Factors to Explain Excess Returns

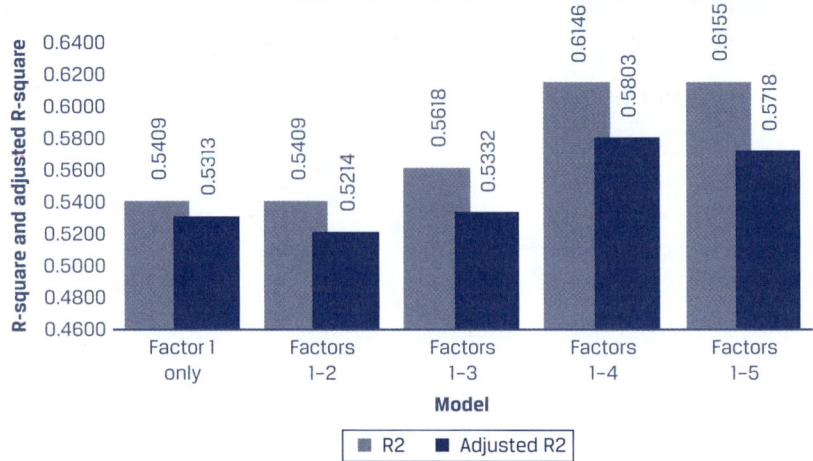

Importantly, the following should be noted:

- Unlike in simple regression, there is no neat interpretation of the adjusted R^2 in a multiple regression setting in terms of percentage of the dependent variable's variation explained.

- The adjusted R^2 does not address whether the regression coefficients are significant or the predictions are biased; this requires examining residual plots and other statistics.

- R^2 and adjusted R^2 are not generally suitable for testing the significance of the model's fit; for this, we explore the ANOVA further, calculating the F-statistic and other goodness-of-fit metrics.

KNOWLEDGE CHECK

You are a junior portfolio manager (PM) reviewing your firm's research on diversified manufacturers. You are considering Model 1, a cross-sectional regression of return on assets (ROA) for a sample of 26 diversified manufacturing companies on capital expenditures scaled by beginning year PPE (CAPEX):

Model 1: $\text{ROA}_i = b_0 + b_{CAPEX}\text{CAPEX}_i + \varepsilon_i.$

Multiple R	0.9380
R-Squared	0.8799
Adjusted R-Squared	0.8749
Standard Error	1.5274
Log-Likelihood	−46.842
Observations	26

Partial ANOVA Results

	Coefficient	Standard error	t-Statistic	P-value	95% confidence interval Lower bound	95% confidence interval Upper bound
Intercept	4.7856	0.6468	7.3988	0.0000	3.4507	6.1206
CAPEX	1.2495	0.0942	13.2623	0.0000	1.0551	1.4440

Adding a second feature, the prior year's ratio of advertising expenditures to revenues (ADV), results in Model 2:

Model 2: $\text{ROA}_i = b_0 + b_{CAPEX}\text{CAPEX}_i + b_{ADV}\text{ADV}_i + \varepsilon_i.$

Multiple R	0.9384
R-Squared	0.8805
Adjusted R-Squared	0.8701
Standard Error	1.55666
Log-Likelihood	−46.795
Observations	26

Partial ANOVA Results

	Coefficient	Standard Error	t-Statistic	P-value	95% confidence interval Lower 95%	95% confidence interval Upper 95%
Intercept	4.9961	0.9144	5.4638	0.0000	3.1045	6.8876
CAPEX	1.2415	0.0990	12.5410	0.0000	1.0367	1.4463
ADV	−0.0345	0.1039	−0.3320	0.7429	−0.2495	0.1805

1. Interpret and contrast R^2 and adjusted R^2 for Models 1 and 2 using the regression output provided.

   Solution

   The R^2 for Model 1 (CAPEX only) indicates that 87.99% of the variation of ROA is explained by CAPEX. For Model 2 (CAPEX and ADV), the R^2 increases to 88.05%. However, the adjusted R^2 for Model 2 declines to 0.8701 (87.01%) from 0.8749 for Model 1. The lower adjusted R^2 is consistent with the |t-statistic| for ADV's coefficient < 1.0 (i.e., 0.3302) and the coefficient not being different from zero at typical significance levels (P-value = 0.7429). To conclude, adding the ADV variable does not improve the overall statistical performance and explanatory power of the model.

As both the R^2 and adjusted R^2 may increase when we add independent variables, we risk model overfitting. Fortunately, there are several statistics to help compare model quality and identify the most parsimonious model, including two statistics more commonly known by their acronyms, AIC and BIC.

We can use **Akaike's information criterion (AIC)** to evaluate a collection of models that explain the same dependent variable. It is often provided in the output for regression software, but AIC can be calculated using information in the regression output:

$$\text{AIC} = n \ln\left(\frac{\text{Sum of squares error}}{n}\right) + 2(k + 1). \tag{3}$$

As the formula indicates, the AIC statistic depends on the sample size (n), the number of independent variables in the model (k), and the sum of squares error (SSE) of the model. One goal in multiple regression is to derive the best fitting model without adding extraneous independent variables. AIC is a measure of model parsimony, so a lower AIC indicates a better-fitting model. The term $2(k + 1)$ is the penalty assessed for adding independent variables to the model.

In a similar manner, **Schwarz's Bayesian information criterion (BIC or SBC)** allows comparison of models with the same dependent variable, as follows:

$$\text{BIC} = n \ln\left(\frac{\text{Sum of squares error}}{n}\right) + \ln(n)(k + 1). \tag{4}$$

Compared to AIC, BIC assesses a greater penalty for having more parameters in a model, so it will tend to prefer small, more parsimonious models. This is because $\ln(n)$ is greater than 2, even for very small sample sizes. Because we also use BIC to choose the best model among a set of models (i.e., the one with the lowest BIC), when do we prefer one measure over the other?

Practically speaking, AIC is preferred if the model is used for prediction purposes, but BIC is preferred when the best goodness of fit is desired. Importantly, the value of these measures considered alone is meaningless; the relative values of AIC or BIC among a set of models is what really matters.

For the regression of portfolio returns on five factors, we present several goodness-of-fit measures in Exhibit 4 generated for five models out of the 31 possible combinations ($_5C_r$, $r = 1{-}5$) of models using these five variables.

Exhibit 4: Goodness-of-Fit Measures for Portfolio Excess Returns Regressed on Different Sets of Factors

	R^2	Adjusted R^2	AIC	BIC
Factor 1 only	0.541	0.531	19.079	*22.903*
Factors 1 and 2	0.541	0.521	21.078	26.814
Factors 1, 2, and 3	0.562	0.533	20.743	28.393
Factors 1, 2, 3, and 4	0.615	0.580	*16.331*	25.891
Factors 1, 2, 3, 4, and 5	0.615	0.572	18.215	29.687

The following are important observations that can be made from Exhibit 4:

- The R^2 increases or remains the same as we add variables to the model.
- The adjusted R^2 increases with the addition of some variables (Factors 3 and 4) but decreases with the addition of other variables (Factors 2 and 5).
- The AIC is minimized with the model using Factors 1, 2, 3, and 4.
- The BIC is minimized with the model using Factor 1 only.

If we are developing a model for prediction purposes, then we would likely select the four-factor model that AIC indicates, whereas if we are seeking the most parsimonious, best-fitting model, we would choose the one-factor model. We now have a framework for selecting the best model from a given set of models.

KNOWLEDGE CHECK

1. The research report you are reviewing presents goodness-of-fit statistics for the two models explaining the variation in return on assets (ROA) for the sample of diversified manufacturers, as follows:

	Model 1: CAPEX Only	Model 2: CAPEX and ADV
R^2	0.880	0.881
Adjusted R^2	0.875	0.870
AIC	23.899	25.804
BIC	26.523	28.792

The senior PM as asks you to interpret the given goodness-of-fit statistics and justify which is the better model.

Solution

The goodness-of-fit results for this sample regression indicate the following:

- 88% of the variation in ROA is explained by CAPEX, and 88.1% of this variation is explained by CAPEX and ADV together.
- Adjusted R^2 declines when ADV is added, indicating its coefficient is not significant and has a $|t\text{-statistic}| < 1.0$ (note that for ADV, the P-value = 0.7429 and the t-statistic is −0.3320).
- AIC and BIC both indicate that Model 1 is a better model as these metrics are lower for Model 1 than for Model 2.

To conclude, adding ADV does not improve the explanatory or predicting power of the original model using just CAPEX.

TESTING JOINT HYPOTHESES FOR COEFFICIENTS

2

☐ | formulate hypotheses on the significance of two or more coefficients in a multiple regression model and interpret the results of the joint hypothesis tests

In multiple regression, the interpretation of the intercept and slope coefficients is similar to that in simple regression, but with a subtle difference. In simple regression, the intercept is the expected value of the dependent variable if the independent variable is zero. In multiple regression, the intercept is the expected value of the dependent variable if *all* independent variables are zero.

Regarding interpretation of slope coefficients, as noted earlier, in multiple regression, the slope coefficient for a given independent variable is the expected change in the dependent variable for a one-unit change in that independent variable *with all other independent variables remaining constant.*

Tests of a single coefficient in a multiple regression are identical to those in a simple regression. The hypothesis structure is the same, and the t-test is the same. For a two-sided alternative hypothesis that the true coefficient, b_j, is equal to a hypothesized value, B_j, the null and alternative hypotheses are

H_0: $b_j = B_j$ and H_a: $b_j \neq B_j$,

where b_j is the coefficient on the jth independent variable and B_j is the hypothesized slope (0, 1, or something else). A one-sided test for a single coefficient is also the same in multiple regression as in simple regression:

One-sided coefficient test, left side	One-sided coefficient test, right side
H_0: $b_j \geq B_j$, H_a: $b_j < B_j$	H_0: $b_j \geq B_j$, H_a: $b_j > B_j$

If we are testing simply whether a variable is significant in explaining the dependent variable's variation, the hypotheses are H_0: $b_j = 0$ and H_a: $b_j \neq 0$.

By default, statistical software produces the t-statistics and the P-values for a test of the slope coefficient against zero for each independent variable in the model. If we want to test the slope against a hypothesized value other than zero, we need to

- perform the test by adjusting the hypothesized parameter value, B_j, in the test statistic or

- compare the hypothesized parameter value, B_j, with the confidence interval bounds for the coefficient generated in the regression output.

There are times when we want to test a subset of variables in a multiple regression jointly. Just to motivate the preliminary discussion and frame the problem, suppose we want to compare regression results for a portfolio's excess returns using Fama and French's three-factor model (MKTRF, SMB, HML) with those using their five-factor model (MKTRF, SMB, HML, RMW, CMA). Because the two models share three factors (MKTRF, SMB, HML), a comparison involves examining whether the two other variables—the return difference between the most profitable and the least profitable firms (RMW) and the return difference between firms that invest most conservatively and those that invest most aggressively (CMA)—are needed. A key objective in determining the better model is parsimony, achieved by identifying groups of independent variables that are most useful in explaining variation in the dependent variable.

Now consider a more general model:

$Y_i = b_0 + b_1 X_{1i} + b_2 X_{2i} + b_3 X_{3i} + b_4 X_{4i} + b_5 X_{5i} + \varepsilon_i.$

We refer to this full model, with all five independent variables, as the **unrestricted model**. Suppose we want to test whether X_4 and X_5 together do not provide a significant contribution to explaining the dependent variable—that is, to test whether $b_4 = b_5 = 0$. We compare the full model with five independent variables to

$Y_i = b_0 + b_1 X_{1i} + b_2 X_{2i} + b_3 X_{3i} + \varepsilon_i.$

This model is referred to as the **restricted model** because by excluding them from the model, we have restricted the slope coefficients on X_4 and X_5 to be equal to zero. These models are also described as **nested models**, because the restricted model is "nested" within the unrestricted model. This comparison of models implies a null hypothesis that involves a joint restriction on two coefficients—that is, H_0: $b_4 = b_5 = 0$ against H_A: b_4 and/or $b_5 \neq 0$.

We can use a statistic to compare nested models, where the unrestricted model is compared to a restricted model in which one or more of the slope coefficients is set equal to zero. This statistic focuses on the impact of the joint restriction on the ability of the restricted model to explain the dependent variable relative to the unrestricted model. We test the role of the jointly omitted variables using the following F-distributed test statistic:

$$F = \frac{(\text{Sum of squares error restricted model} - \text{Sum of squares error unrestricted})/q}{\text{Sum of squares error unrestricted model}/(n-k-1)}, \quad (5)$$

where q is the number of restrictions, meaning the number of variables omitted in the restricted model compared to the unrestricted model.

Suppose we want to compare a model with five independent variables to a restricted model having only three of these variables (X_1, X_2, and X_3).

Unrestricted model: $Y_i = b_0 + b_1 X_{1i} + b_2 X_{2i} + b_3 X_{3i} + b_4 X_{4i} + b_5 X_{5i} + \varepsilon_i$.

Restricted model: $Y_i = b_0 + b_1 X_{1i} + b_2 X_{2i} + b_3 X_{3i} + \varepsilon_i$.

Here, $q = 2$ since we are testing the null hypothesis of $b_4 = b_5 = 0$. Also, note the F-statistic for this test has q and $n - k - 1$ degrees of freedom.

To summarize, the unrestricted model has the larger set of explanatory variables, while the restricted model has q fewer independent variables because the slope coefficients on the excluded variables are constrained to equal zero.

The general form for hypotheses for testing a nested (restricted) model is

$H_0: b_m = b_{m+1} = \ldots = b_{m+q-1} = 0; H_a:$ At least one slope of the q slopes $\neq 0$,

where m is the first restricted slope, $m + 1$ is the second restricted slope, and so on, up to the qth restricted slope.

Why not simply perform hypothesis tests on the individual variables and then draw conclusions about the set from that information? Often in multiple regression involving financial variables, there is some degree of correlation between the variables, so there may be some sharing of explanatory power that is not considered with the tests of individual slopes.

We now apply this test to the model of portfolio returns with the five hypothetical factors (Factors 1–5), introduced in Exhibit 1, as independent variables. Partial ANOVA results for the restricted model with just Factors 1, 2, and 3 and for the unrestricted model with all five factors are shown in Exhibit 5, Panel A. The **joint test of hypotheses** for the slopes of Factors 4 and 5 using the F-test are in Panel B, using a 1% significance level. As demonstrated, we fail to reject the null hypothesis that the slopes of Factors 4 and 5 are both zero.

Exhibit 5: Comparison of Regression Models of Portfolio Excess Returns Using Three Factors and Five Factors (from Exhibit 1)

Panel A Partial ANOVA Results for Models Using Three Factors and Five Factors

Source	Factors	Degrees of freedom	Residual sum of squares	Mean square error
Restricted model	1, 2, 3	46	64.5176	1.4026
Unrestricted model	1, 2, 3, 4, 5	44	56.6182	1.2868

Panel B Test of Hypotheses for Factors 4 and 5 at 1% Level of Significance

Step 1	State the hypotheses.	$H_0: b_{Factor4} = b_{Factor5} = 0$ vs. $H_a:$ At least one $b_j \neq 0$

Step 2	Identify the appropriate test statistic.	$F = \dfrac{(\text{Sum of squares error restricted model} - \text{Sum of squares error unrestricted})/q}{\text{Sum of squares error unrestricted model}/(n - k - 1)}$ with $q = 2$ and $n - k - 1 = 44$ degrees of freedom.
Step 3	Specify the level of significance.	$\alpha = 1\%$ (one-tail, right side).
Step 4	State the decision rule.	Critical F-value = 5.120. Reject the null if the calculated F-statistic exceeds 5.120.
Step 5	Calculate the test statistic.	$F = \dfrac{(64.5176 - 56.6182)/2}{56.6182/44} = \dfrac{3.9497}{1.2868} = 3.0694$
Step 6	Make a decision.	Fail to reject the null hypothesis because the calculated F-statistic does not exceed the critical F-value. There is not sufficient evidence to indicate that at least one slope coefficient among b_4 and b_5 is different from zero.

This joint hypothesis test indicates Factors 4 and 5 do not provide sufficient explanatory power (i.e., SSE declines by just $7.8994 = 64.5176 - 56.6182$) to compensate for the loss of two degrees of freedom by their inclusion in the unrestricted model. Thus, we conclude the restricted, more parsimonious model fits the data better than the unrestricted model.

CODE: COMPARING NESTED REGRESSION MODELS USING THE FIVE FACTORS (FROM EXHIBIT 1)

Python

Let df be the data frame containing the data.

```
from statsmodels.stats.anova import anova_lm

from statsmodels.formula.api import ols

formula='Portfolio ~ Factor1+Factor2+Factor3+Factor4+Factor5'

results=ols(formula,df).fit()

hypotheses='(Factor4=Factor5=0)'

f_test = results.f_test(hypotheses)

print(f_test)
```

R

Let df be the data frame containing the data.

```
model5 <- lm(df$Portfolio ~ df$Factor1+df$Factor2+df$Factor3+df$Factor4+df$Factor5)

model3 <- lm(df$Portfolio ~ df$Factor1+df$Factor2+df$Factor3)
```

```
anova(model5,model3)
```

We can extend the F-distributed joint test of hypotheses for coefficients to test the significance of the whole regression equation, which is often referred to as a goodness-of-fit test. For the multiple linear regression,

$$Y_i = b_0 + b_1X_{1i} + b_2X_{2i} + b_3X_{3i} + \ldots + b_kX_{ki} + \varepsilon_i,$$

where k is the number of independent variables, we can use the **general linear F-test** to test the null hypothesis that slope coefficients on all variables are equal to zero:

$$H_0: b_1 = b_2 = b_3 = \ldots = b_k = 0$$

against the alternative that at least one slope coefficient is different from zero:

$$H_a: \text{At least one } b_j \neq 0.$$

This F-statistic is calculated in the same way as in simple regression—the ratio of the mean square regression (MSR) to the mean square error (MSE)—but the degrees of freedom are now k in the numerator and $n - k - 1$ in the denominator:

$$F = \frac{\text{MSR}}{\text{MSE}}.$$

Using the ANOVA table in Exhibit 1 for the five-factor model of portfolio returns,

$$F = \frac{18.1247}{1.2868} = 14.0853.$$

We present partial ANOVA results in Exhibit 6, Panel A, and show in Panel B the steps for the hypothesis test for model goodness of fit using the F-statistic at the 5% significance level.

Exhibit 6: Test of Hypothesis for Goodness of Fit Using *F*-Statistic for Model of Portfolio Returns Regressed against Five Factors

Panel A Partial ANOVA Results (repeated from Exhibit 1)

Analysis of Variance

Source	Degrees of freedom	Sum of squares	Mean squares
Regression	5	90.6234	18.1247
Residual	44	56.6182	1.2868
Total	49	147.2416	

Panel B Hypothesis Testing

Step 1	State the hypotheses.	$H_0: b_1 = b_2 = b_3 = b_4 = b_5 = 0.$
		$H_a:$ At least one $b_j \neq 0.$
Step 2	Identify the appropriate test statistic.	$F = \frac{\text{MSR}}{\text{MSE}}$, with 5 and 44 degrees of freedom.
Step 3	Specify the level of significance.	$\alpha = 5\%$ (one-tail, right side).
Step 4	State the decision rule.	Critical F-value = 2.427. Reject the null if the calculated F-statistic is greater than 2.427.
Step 5	Calculate the test statistic.	$F = \frac{18.1247}{1.2868} = 14.0853.$

Step 6	Make a decision.	Reject the null hypothesis because the calculated F-statistic exceeds the critical F-value. There is sufficient evidence to indicate that at least one slope coefficient is different from zero.

Exhibit 7 summarizes the statistics we have introduced for judging the goodness of fit of multiple regression models. Importantly, finding the "best" model is not a straight-line process but is, rather, iterative, because it depends on reviewing the regression results and adjusting the model accordingly.

Exhibit 7: Assessing Model Fit Using Multiple Regression Statistics

Statistic	Criterion to use in assessment
Adjusted R^2	The higher the better
Akaike's information criterion (AIC)	The lower the better
Schwarz's Bayesian information criterion (BIC)	The lower the better
t-Statistic on a slope coefficient	Outside bounds of critical t-value(s) for the selected significance level
F-test for joint test of slope coefficients	Exceeds the critical F-value for the selected significance level

Exhibit 8 shows model fit statistics visually for all 31 possible models from our example of regressing portfolio returns on the five factors. Here the models are ranked by BIC, from lowest (best model) to highest (worst model). Note that AIC and BIC may differ because BIC imposes a greater penalty on more complex models.

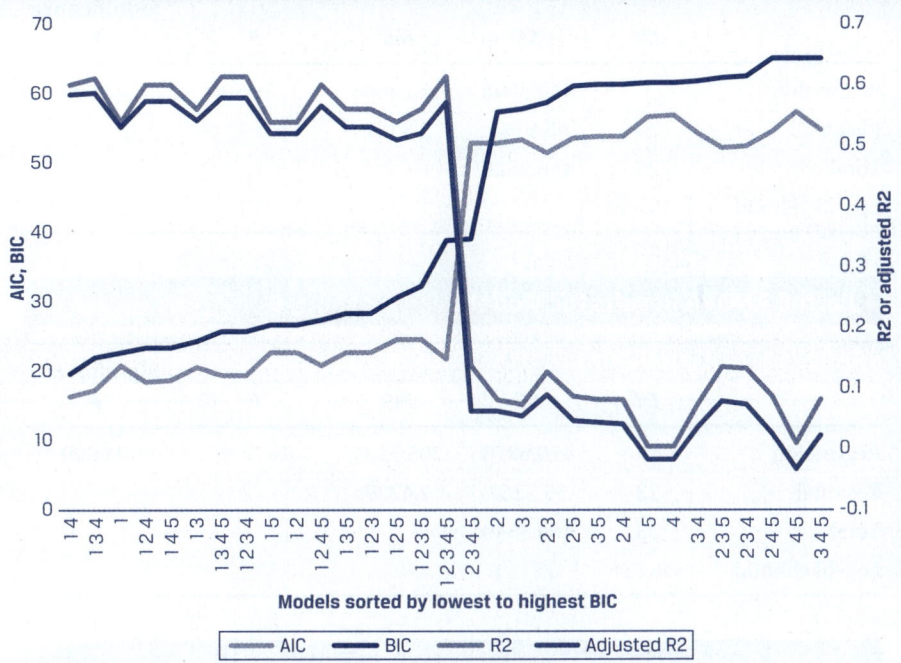

Exhibit 8: All 31 Models of Excess Portfolio Returns Regressed on Up to Five Factors

Note: Each model is designated by its factors. For example, "1 2 4" is the model incorporating Factors 1, 2, and 4 only.

The best model of all 31 models is the model with just Factors 1 and 4. This model has the lowest BIC and AIC and the highest adjusted R^2. Note the model with the highest R^2 has all five factors and ranks relatively poorly on all the other metrics. This visual demonstrates the consistency between AIC and BIC when comparing models and how these statistics differ from the R^2 and adjusted R^2 in selecting the best model.

KNOWLEDGE CHECK

You are a junior analyst tasked with determining important signals of higher ROA for companies. At today's investment meeting, the PM suggested three possible reasons: higher capital investment, higher advertising costs, and higher R&D spending. You cover the manufacturing sector, and you want to determine which factors, if any, signal improved ROA. You estimate the following three models for ROA for a sample of 26 diversified manufacturers:

Model 1: $\text{ROA}_i = b_0 + b_{CAPEX}\text{CAPEX}_i + \varepsilon_i$;

Model 2: $\text{ROA}_i = b_0 + b_{CAPEX}\text{CAPEX}_i + b_{ADV}\text{ADV}_i + \varepsilon_i$;

Model 3: $\text{ROA}_i = b_0 + b_{CAPEX}\text{CAPEX}_i + b_{ADV}\text{ADV}_i + b_{R\&D}\text{R\&D}_i + \varepsilon_i$

Where:

- CAPEX is capital expenditures scaled by beginning-year PPE;
- ADV is the prior year's ratio of advertising expenditures to revenues; and
- R&D is the prior period's R&D expenditures divided by revenues.

Partial ANOVA Results for Model 1

	Df	SS	MS	F	Significance F
Regression	1	410.3606	410.3606	175.8896	0.0000
Residual	24	55.9934	2.3331		
Total	25	466.3540			
Log-likelihood	−46.842				

Partial ANOVA Results for Model 2

	Df	SS	MS	F	Significance F
Regression	2	410.6278	205.3139	84.7396	0.0000
Residual	23	55.7263	2.4229		
Total	25	466.3540			
Log-likelihood	−46.795				

ANOVA Results for Model 3

Source	Degrees of freedom	Sum of squares	Mean squares	F-statistic	Significance of F-statistic
Regression	3	410.9591	136.9864	54.4039	0.0000
Residual	22	55.3949	2.5180		
Total	25	466.3540			
Log-likelihood	−46.716				

	Coefficient	Standard error	t-Statistic	P-value	95% confidence interval Lower bound	Upper bound
Intercept	4.7022	1.2349	3.8078	0.0010	2.1412	7.2633
CAPEX	1.2302	0.1056	11.6490	0.0000	1.0112	1.4492
ADV	−0.0371	0.1062	−0.3490	0.7304	−0.2572	0.1831
R&D	0.1029	0.2837	0.3628	0.7203	−0.4854	0.6913

Before the next investment meeting, the PM asks you to do the following:

1. Demonstrate the relationship between R^2 and adjusted R^2 for Model 3.

   Solution

   For Model 3, the R^2 is 0.8812 and the adjusted R^2 is 0.8650, as follows:

   $$R^2 = \frac{410.9591}{466.3540} = 0.8812.$$

Adjusted $R^2 = 1 - \left[\frac{25}{22}(1 - 0.8812)\right] = 0.8650$.

2. Determine whether Model 3 explains ROA using a 1% significance level.

   Solution

   The test of the full (unrestricted) Model 3 is as follows:

Step 1	State the hypotheses.	$H_0: b_{CAPEX} = b_{ADV} = b_{R\&D} = 0$. H_a: At least one $b_j \neq 0$.
Step 2	Identify the appropriate test statistic.	$F = \frac{MSR}{MSE}$, with 3 and 22 degrees of freedom.
Step 3	Specify the level of significance.	$\alpha = 1\%$ (one-tail, right side).
Step 4	State the decision rule.	Critical F-value = 4.8166. Reject the null hypothesis if the calculated F-statistic exceeds 4.8166.
Step 5	Calculate the test statistic.	$F = 54.4039$, as given in the regression output. (*Note small difference vs. MSR/MSE from rounding.*)
Step 6	Make a decision.	Reject the null hypothesis because the calculated F-statistic exceeds the critical F-value. There is sufficient evidence that at least one slope coefficient is different from zero.

3. Determine whether each slope coefficient in Model 3 is different from zero at the 1% significance level.

   Solution

   The test of whether each slope coefficient in Model 3 is different from zero is as follows:

Step 1	State the hypotheses.	$H_0: b_j = 0$ vs. $H_a: b_j \neq 0$.
Step 2	Identify the appropriate test statistic.	$t = \frac{\hat{b}_j - B_j}{s_{\hat{b}_j}}$, with $26 - 3 - 1 = 22$ degrees of freedom.
Step 3	Specify the level of significance.	$\alpha = 1\%$ (two-tail).
Step 4	State the decision rule.	Critical t-values = ± 2.8188. Reject the null hypothesis if the calculated t-statistic is greater than 2.8188 or less than −2.8188.
Step 5	Calculate the test statistic.	CAPEX: $t = \frac{1.2302 - 0}{0.1056} = 11.649$. ADV: $t = \frac{-0.0371 - 0}{0.1062} = 0.3493$. R&D: $t = \frac{0.1029 - 0}{0.2837} = 0.3627$. *Note calculated t-statistics may differ from output due to rounding.*

Step 6	Make a decision.	Reject the null hypothesis for CAPEX because the calculated t-statistic exceeds the critical t-value. There is sufficient evidence to indicate the slope coefficient for CAPEX is different from zero.
		Fail to reject the null hypothesis for both the ADV and R&D variables because the calculated t-statistics are within the bounds of the critical values. There is not sufficient evidence to indicate that the slope coefficients of ADV or R&D are different from zero.

4. Determine whether ADV and R&D together contribute to the explanation of ROA in Model 3 at a 1% significance level using the joint F-test.

Solution

The joint test of whether ADV and R&D together contribute to the explanation of ROA in Model 3 is as follows:

Step 1	State the hypotheses.	H_0: $b_{ADV} = b_{R\&D} = 0$ vs. H_a: At least one $b_j \neq 0$.
Step 2	Identify the appropriate test statistic.	$F = \dfrac{(\text{Sum of squares error restricted model} - \text{Sum of squares error unrestricted model})/q}{\text{Sum of squares error unrestricted model}/(n - k - 1)}$, with 2 and 22 degrees of freedom
Step 3	Specify the level of significance.	$\alpha = 1\%$ (one-tail, right side).
Step 4	State the decision rule.	Critical F-value = 5.7190. Reject the null hypothesis if the calculated F-statistic exceeds 5.7190.
Step 5	Calculate the test statistic.	$F = \dfrac{(55.9934 - 55.3949)/2}{55.3949/22} = 0.1188$.
Step 6	Make a decision.	Fail to reject the null hypothesis because the calculated F-statistic does not exceed the critical F-value. There is not sufficient evidence to indicate that at least one of the two slope coefficients is different from zero. This evidence suggests that Model 1, using only CAPEX, is the better model compared to Model 3.

5. State and justify your conclusion based on these tests of hypotheses.

Solution

The conclusion is the variation of ROA in this sample is explained by CAPEX. The variables of ADV and R&D by themselves or together do not explain the variation in ROA. The justification for this conclusion is as follows:

- Adjusted R^2 is higher for Model 1 (CAPEX) versus Model 3 (all three variables).
- ADV and R&D are each insignificant based on t-tests of Model 3.
- ADV and R&D together are insignificant based on the joint F-test using Model 1 (restricted) and Model 3 (unrestricted).

6. Consider the following statistics on all possible ROA models:

Variable(s) in Model	R^2	Adjusted R^2	AIC	BIC
CAPEX	0.8803	0.8753	23.8988	26.5226

Variable(s) in Model	R^2	Adjusted R^2	AIC	BIC
R&D	0.0866	0.0486	76.7297	73.9100
ADV	0.0619	0.0228	77.4233	74.5737
CAPEX, R&D	0.8809	0.8706	25.7594	28.7575
CAPEX, ADV	0.8807	0.8703	25.8044	28.7917
ADV, R&D	0.1473	0.0731	76.9431	72.5325
CAPEX, ADV, R&D	0.8814	0.8653	27.6481	31.0365

Recommend the best model from the set and justify your choice.

Solution

The simple regression model with CAPEX alone is the best model among those presented. This model has the highest adjusted R^2 and the lowest AIC and BIC. These model-fit statistics confirm that the model with CAPEX alone, which is the most parsimonious, is the best-fitting model.

FORECASTING USING MULTIPLE REGRESSION

3

☐ | calculate and interpret a predicted value for the dependent variable, given the estimated regression model and assumed values for the independent variable

The process for predicting the value of the dependent variable using an estimated multiple regression model is similar to that in simple regression, but with more items to sum, as shown in the following formula:

$$\hat{Y}_f = \hat{b}_0 + \hat{b}_1 X_{1f} + \hat{b}_2 X_{2f} + \dots + \hat{b}_k X_{kf} = \hat{b}_0 + \sum_{j=1}^{k} \hat{b}_j X_{jf}. \qquad (6)$$

As the formula indicates, to determine the predicted (forecasted) value of the dependent variable $\left(\hat{Y}_f\right)$, the analyst must sum, for each independent variable, the estimated slope coefficient multiplied by the assumed value for that variable $\left(\hat{b}_j X_f\right)$ and then add the estimated intercept coefficient $\left(\hat{b}_0\right)$ times the assumed value for the intercept of 1.

We can use the regression results from Exhibit 1 of portfolio returns on the five factors to predict the portfolio return using the following model:

$$Y_i = b_0 + b_1 \text{Factor}_{1i} + b_2 \text{Factor}_{2i} + b_3 \text{Factor}_{3i} + b_4 \text{Factor}_{4i} + b_5 \text{Factor}_{5i} + \varepsilon_i,$$

which now uses assumed values of the factors. This model becomes

$$\hat{Y}_f = -2.1876 + 1.5992 \text{ Factor}_1 + 0.1923 \text{ Factor}_2 - 0.7126 \text{ Factor}_3 + 3.3376 \text{ Factor}_4 - 2.6832 \text{ Factor}_5,$$

and the assumed values of the five factors are as follows:

Factor	1	2	3	4	5
Assumed Value	0.110	0.040	0.080	−0.010	0.001

Exhibit 9 shows the calculation of the predicted value of the portfolio return, −2.0971%.

Exhibit 9: Predicting Portfolio Returns Using the Five-Factor Model			
	(1)	**(2)**	**(1) × (2)**
	Assumed value	*Estimated coefficient*	*Product*
Intercept	1.000	−2.1876	−2.1876
Factor 1	0.110	1.5992	0.1759
Factor 2	0.040	0.1923	0.0077
Factor 3	0.080	−0.7126	−0.0570
Factor 4	−0.010	3.3376	−0.0334
Factor 5	0.001	−2.6832	−0.0027
			−2.0971

There are cautions regarding predicting with a multiple regression model:

- If a regression model is estimated using all five independent variables, for example, any prediction of the dependent variable must also include all five variables—even the ones that are not statistically significant. This is because correlations between these variables were used in estimating the slope coefficients.

- For any prediction of the dependent variable, we must also include the intercept term.

As with simple linear regression forecasts, we are often interested in the level of uncertainty around the forecast of the dependent variable in terms of the standard error of the forecast. In any regression estimation, there are residuals because not all observations lie on the estimated line. This is basic uncertainty in the model—the *model error*—which is the stochastic part of the model that involves the regression residual, ε_i.

When the independent variables themselves are forecasts and thus out-of-sample predictions, there is an added source of error arising from errors associated with forecasting the independent variables. In such cases, the forecast error for the dependent variable is dependent on how well the independent variables (X_{1f}, X_{2f} ..., X_{kf}) were forecasted, hence introducing *sampling error*. The combined effect of the model error and the sampling error results in a standard error of the forecast for $\hat{Y}_f$ that is larger than the standard error of the regression. This larger forecast error results in a prediction interval for the dependent variable that is wider than the within-sample error.

Although the calculation of the forecast interval for multiple regression is overly detailed for our purposes, we can use software to produce this interval and the corresponding standard error of the forecast. For the five-factor portfolio return model, the standard error of the forecast is 1.1466, the upper 95% confidence bound is 0.2119, and the lower 95% confidence bound is −4.4098, compared with the point estimate, noted above, of −2.0971.

KNOWLEDGE CHECK

1. Your research report includes the following regression equation:

ROA = 4.7022 + 1.2302CAPEX − 0.0371ADV + 0.1029R&D.

An institutional salesperson at your firm asks you to determine the predicted ROA for a company with assumed values for the three independent variables of CAPEX = 5%, ADV = 4%, and R&D = 3%.

Solution

The predicted ROA is 11.0135%, calculated as follows:

$$\widehat{ROA}_f = 4.7022 + 1.2302(5) - 0.0371(4) + 0.1029(3) = 11.0135.$$

PRACTICE PROBLEMS

The following information relates to questions 1-5

You are a junior analyst at an asset management firm. Your supervisor asks you to analyze the return drivers for one of the firm's portfolios. She asks you to construct a regression model of the portfolio's monthly excess returns (RET) against three factors: the market excess return (MRKT), a value factor (HML), and the monthly percentage change in a volatility index (VIX). You collect the data and run the regression. After completing the first regression (Model 1), you review the ANOVA results with your supervisor.

Then, she asks you to create two more models by adding two more explanatory variables: a size factor (SMB) and a momentum factor (MOM). Your three models are as follows:

Model 1: $RET_i = b_0 + b_{MRKT}MRKT_i + b_{HML}HML_i + b_{VIX}VIX_i + \varepsilon_i$.

Model 2: $RET_i = b_0 + b_{MRKT}MRKT_i + b_{HML}HML_i + b_{VIX}VIX_i + b_{SMB}SMB_i + \varepsilon_i$.

Model 3: $RET_i = b_0 + b_{MRKT}MRKT_i + b_{HML}HML_i + b_{VIX}VIX_i + b_{SMB}SMB_i + b_{MOM}MOM_i + \varepsilon_i$.

The regression statistics and ANOVA results for the three models are shown in Exhibit 1, Exhibit 2, and Exhibit 3.

Exhibit 1: ANOVA Table for Model 1

$RET_i = b_0 + b_{MRKT}MRKT_i + b_{HML}HML_i + b_{VIX}VIX_i + \varepsilon_i$

Regression Statistics			Coefficient	Std. Error	t-Stat.	P-Value
Multiple R	0.907	Intercept	−0.999	0.414	−2.411	0.018
R-Squared	0.823	MRKT	1.817	0.124	14.683	0.000
Adjusted R-Sq.	0.817	HML	0.489	0.118	4.133	0.000
Standard Error	3.438	VIX	0.037	0.018	2.122	0.037
Observations	96.000					

ANOVA

	Df	SS	MS	F	Significance F
Regression	3	5058.430	1686.143	142.628	0.000
Residual	92	1087.618	11.822		

ANOVA

	Df	SS	MS	F	Significance F
Total	95	6146.048			

Exhibit 2: ANOVA Table for Model 2

$RET_i = b_0 + b_{MRKT}MRKT_i + b_{HML}HML_i + b_{VIX}VIX_i + b_{SMB}SMB_i + \varepsilon_i$

Regression Statistics			Coefficient	Std. Error	t-Stat.	P-Value
Multiple R	0.923	Intercept	−0.820	0.383	−2.139	0.035
R-Squared	0.852	MRKT	1.649	0.121	13.683	0.000
Adjusted R-Sq.	0.846	HML	0.434	0.109	3.970	0.000
Standard Error	3.161	VIX	0.025	0.016	1.516	0.133
Observations	96.000	SMB	0.563	0.133	4.223	0.000

ANOVA

	Df	SS	MS	F	Significance F
Regression	4	5236.635	1309.159	131.000	0.000
Residual	91	909.413	9.994		
Total	95	6146.048			

Exhibit 3: ANOVA Table for Model 3

$RET_i = b_0 + b_{MRKT}MRKT_i + b_{HML}HML_i + b_{VIX}VIX_i + b_{SMB}SMB_i + b_{MOM}MOM_i + \varepsilon_i$

Regression Statistics			Coefficient	Std. Error	t-Stat.	P-Value
Multiple R	0.923	Intercept	−0.823	0.385	−2.136	0.035
R-Squared	0.852	MRKT	1.719	0.280	6.130	0.000
Adjusted R-Sq.	0.844	HML	0.412	0.138	2.989	0.004
Standard Error	3.177	VIX	0.026	0.017	1.532	0.129
Observations	96.000	SMB	0.553	0.139	3.987	0.000
		MOM	−0.067	0.242	−0.276	0.783

ANOVA

	Df	SS	MS	F	Significance F
Regression	5	5237.402	1047.480	103.751	0.000
Residual	90	908.647	10.096		
Total	95	6146.048			

Your supervisor asks for your assessment of the model that provides the best fit as well as the model that is best for predicting values of the monthly portfolio return. So, you calculate Akaike's information criterion (AIC) and Schwarz's Bayesian information criterion (BIC) for all three models, as shown in Exhibit 13.

Exhibit 4: Goodness-of-Fit Measures		
	AIC	BIC
Model 1	241.03	251.29
Model 2	225.85	238.67
Model 3	227.77	243.16

1. Determine which one of the following reasons for the change in adjusted R^2 from Model 2 to Model 3 is *most likely* to be correct.

   A. Adjusted R^2 decreases since adding MOM does not improve the overall explanatory power of Model 3.

   B. Adjusted R^2 increases since adding SMB improves the overall explanatory power of Model 2.

   C. Adjusted R^2 decreases since adding MOM improves the overall explanatory power of Model 3.

2. Identify the model that provides the best fit.

   A. Model 1

   B. Model 2

   C. Model 3

3. Identify the model that should be used for prediction purposes.

   A. Model 1

   B. Model 2

   C. Model 3

4. Calculate the predicted RET for Model 3 given the assumed factor values: MRKT = 3, HML = −2, VIX = −5, SMB = 1, MOM = 3.

   A. 3.732

   B. 3.992

   C. 4.555

5. Calculate the joint *F*-statistic and determine whether SMB and MOM together contribute to explaining RET in Model 3 at a 1% significance level (use a critical value of 4.849).

   A. 2.216, so SMB and MOM together do not contribute to explaining RET

   B. 8.863, so SMB and MOM together do contribute to explaining RET

   C. 9.454, so SMB and MOM together do contribute to explaining RET

SOLUTIONS

1. A is correct. Adjusted R^2 in Model 3 decreases to 0.844 from 0.846 in Model 2. Model 3 includes all independent variables from Model 2, while adding MOM. Adding variables to a regression model always either increases R^2 or causes it to stay the same. But adjusted R^2 only increases if the new variable meets a threshold of significance, $|t\text{-statistic}| > 1$. MOM does not meet this threshold, indicating it does not improve the overall explanatory power of Model 3.

2. B is correct. BIC is the preferred measure for determining which model provides the best fit, and a lower BIC is better. Since Model 2 has the lowest BIC value, it provides the best fit among the three models.

3. B is correct. AIC is the preferred measure for determining the model that is best used for prediction purposes. As with BIC, a lower AIC is better. Model 2 also has the lowest AIC value among the three models; thus, it should be used for prediction purposes.

4. A is correct. The regression equation for Model 3 is

   RET = −0.823 + 1.719MRKT + 0.412HML + 0.026VIX + 0.553SMB − 0.067MOM.

   Using the assumed values for the independent variables, we have

   RET = −0.823 + (1.719)(3) + (0.412)(−2) + (0.026)(−5) + (0.553)(1) − (0.067)(3)
   = 3.732.

5. B is correct. To determine whether SMB and MOM together contribute to the explanation of RET, at least one of the coefficients must be non-zero. So, H_0: $b_{SMB} = b_{MOM} = 0$ and H_a: $b_{SMB} \neq 0$ and/or $b_{MOM} \neq 0$.
   We use the F-statistic, where

   $$F = \frac{(\text{SSE of restricted model} - \text{SSE of unrestricted model})/q}{\text{SSE of unrestricted model}/(n-k-1)},$$

   with $q = 2$ and $n - k - 1 = 90$ degrees of freedom. The test is one-tailed, right side, with $\alpha = 1\%$, so the critical F-value is 4.849.

   Model 1 does not include SMB and MOM, so it is the restricted model. Model 3 includes all of the variables of Model 1 as well as SMB and MOM, so it is the unrestricted model.

   Using data in Exhibit 1 and Exhibit 3, the joint F-statistic is calculated as

   $$F = \frac{(1087.618 - 908.647)/2}{908.647/90} = \frac{89.485}{10.096} = 8.863.$$

   Since 8.863 > 4.849, we reject H_0. Thus, SMB and MOM together do contribute to the explanation of RET in Model 3 at a 1% significance level.

3

Model Misspecification

LEARNING OUTCOMES

Mastery	The candidate should be able to:
☐	describe how model misspecification affects the results of a regression analysis and how to avoid common forms of misspecification
☐	explain the types of heteroskedasticity and how it affects statistical inference
☐	explain serial correlation and how it affects statistical inference
☐	explain multicollinearity and how it affects regression analysis

SUMMARY

- Principles for proper regression model specification include economic reasoning behind variable choices, parsimony, good out-of-sample performance, appropriate model functional form, and no violations of regression assumptions.

- Failures in regression functional form are typically due to omitted variables, inappropriate form of variables, inappropriate variable scaling, and inappropriate data pooling; these may lead to the violations of regression assumptions.

- Heteroskedasticity occurs when the variance of regression errors differs across observations. Unconditional heteroskedasticity is when the error variance is not correlated with the independent variables, whereas conditional heteroskedasticity exists when the error variance is correlated with the values of the independent variables.

- Unconditional heteroskedasticity creates no major problems for statistical inference, but conditional heteroskedasticity is problematic because it results in underestimation of the regression coefficients' standard errors, so t-statistics are inflated and Type I errors are more likely.

- Conditional heteroskedasticity can be detected using the Breusch–Pagan (BP) test, and the bias it creates in the regression model can be corrected by computing robust standard errors.

- Serial correlation (or autocorrelation) occurs when regression errors are correlated across observations and may be a serious problem in time-series regressions. Serial correlation can lead to inconsistent coefficient estimates, and it underestimates standard errors, so t-statistics are inflated (as with conditional heteroskedasticity).

- The Breusch–Godfrey (BG) test is a robust method for detecting serial correlation. The BG test uses residuals from the original regression as the dependent variable run against initial regressors plus lagged residuals, and H_0 is the coefficients of the lagged residuals are zero.

- The biased estimates of standard errors caused by serial correlation can be corrected using robust standard errors, which also correct for conditional heteroskedasticity.

- Multicollinearity occurs with high pairwise correlations between independent variables or if three or more independent variables form approximate linear combinations that are highly correlated. Multicollinearity results in inflated standard errors and reduced t-statistics.

- The variance inflation factor (VIF) is a measure for quantifying multicollinearity. If VIF_j is 1 for X_j, then there is no correlation between X_j and the other regressors. $VIF_j > 5$ warrants further investigation, and $VIF_j > 10$ indicates serious multicollinearity requiring correction.

- Solutions to multicollinearity include dropping one or more of the regression variables, using a different proxy for one of the variables, or increasing the sample size.

1   MODEL SPECIFICATION ERRORS

☐ | describe how model misspecification affects the results of a regression analysis and how to avoid common forms of misspecification

Model specification refers to the set of variables included in the regression and the regression equation's functional form. Here we provide broad guidelines for correctly specifying a regression and then describe common types of model misspecification.

The principles for good regression model specification are presented concisely in Exhibit 1.

Exhibit 1: Principles for Proper Regression Model Specification

Principle	Explanation
Model should be grounded in economic reasoning.	Provide economic reasoning behind choice of variables.
Model should be parsimonious.	Each variable included in regression should play an essential role.
Model should perform well out of sample.	Model may explain only the specific dataset on which it was trained, meaning it is overfit.

Principle	Explanation
Model functional form should be appropriate.	If a nonlinear relationship between regressors is expected, model should incorporate the appropriate nonlinear terms.
Model should satisfy regression assumptions.	If heteroskedasticity, serial correlation, or multicollinearity are detected, revise regression variables and/or functional form.

We now cover model specification errors. Understanding them will lead to better model development and more informed use of investment research.

MISSPECIFIED FUNCTIONAL FORM   2

When estimating a regression, we assume it has the correct functional form, an assumption that can fail in different ways, as shown in Exhibit 2.

Exhibit 2: Failures in Regression Functional Form

Failures in Regression Functional Form	Explanation	Consequence
Omitted variables	One or more important variables are omitted from the regression.	May lead to heteroskedasticity or serial correlation
Inappropriate form of variables	Ignoring a nonlinear relationship between the dependent and independent variable	May lead to heteroskedasticity
Inappropriate variable scaling	One or more regression variables may need to be transformed before estimating the regression.	May lead to heteroskedasticity or multicollinearity
Inappropriate data pooling	Regression model pools data from different samples that should not be pooled.	May lead to heteroskedasticity or serial correlation

Omitted Variables

First, consider **omitted variable bias**, the bias resulting from the omission of an important independent variable from a regression. If the true regression model is

$$Y_i = b_0 + b_1 X_{1i} + b_2 X_{2i} + \varepsilon_i$$

but we estimate the model as

$$Y_i = b_0 + b_1 X_{1i} + \varepsilon_i,$$

the latter model is misspecified because X_2 is omitted.

If the omitted variable is uncorrelated with X_1, the residual will be $b_2 X_{2i} + \varepsilon_i$. Therefore, the residual in the misspecified regression will not have an expected value of zero nor will it be independent and identically distributed, depending on the behavior of X_2. This means that the estimate of the intercept will be biased, although in this instance, the coefficient for X_1 will still be estimated correctly.

If instead the omitted variable (X_2) is correlated with the remaining variable (X_1), the error term in the model will be correlated with X_1 and the estimated values of the regression coefficients in the latter model will be biased and inconsistent. The estimated coefficient on X_1, the intercept, and the residuals will be incorrect. The estimates of the coefficients' standard errors will also be inconsistent, so these cannot be used for conducting statistical tests.

Inappropriate Form of Variables

Another misspecification error in regression models is using the wrong form of the data when a transformed version is appropriate. For example, an analyst may fail to account for nonlinearity in the relationship between the dependent variable and one or more independent variables by specifying a linear relation. When specifying a regression model, we should consider whether economic theory suggests a nonlinear relation. We can often confirm nonlinearity by plotting the data. For example, if the relation between variables becomes linear when one or more of the variables is represented as a proportional change in the variable, then we can correct the misspecification by taking the natural logarithm of the variable we want to represent as a proportional change.

Inappropriate Scaling of Variables

The use of unscaled data in regressions when scaled data are more appropriate may cause model misspecification. Often, analysts must decide whether to scale variables before they compare data across companies. For example, analysts often compare companies using common-size financial statements. Common-size statements make comparability across companies much easier, allowing the analyst to quickly compare trends in profitability, leverage, efficiency, and so on, for a group of companies.

Inappropriate Pooling of Data

Finally, another common misspecification error is pooling data from samples that should not be pooled. Inappropriate pooling data may occur when the sample spans structural breaks in the behavior of the data. This might arise from a change in government regulation or a regime change from a low-volatility period to a high-volatility period. In a scatterplot, such data would appear in discrete, widely separated clusters with little or no correlation, because the means of the data for each cluster would be very different. When available data results from discernible subsamples, the analyst should estimate the model using the subsample most representative of conditions during the forecasting period.

KNOWLEDGE CHECK

You are a junior analyst at a firm specializing in precious metals funds. The firm's outlook is for increasing stock market volatility over the next six months, so the research director tasks you with modeling the relation between gold returns and changes in stock market volatility. You collect 32 months of returns to gold (GOLD) and changes in the CBOE VIX Index (VIX), estimate a model with GOLD as the dependent variable and VIX as the independent variable, and create the following two scatterplots.

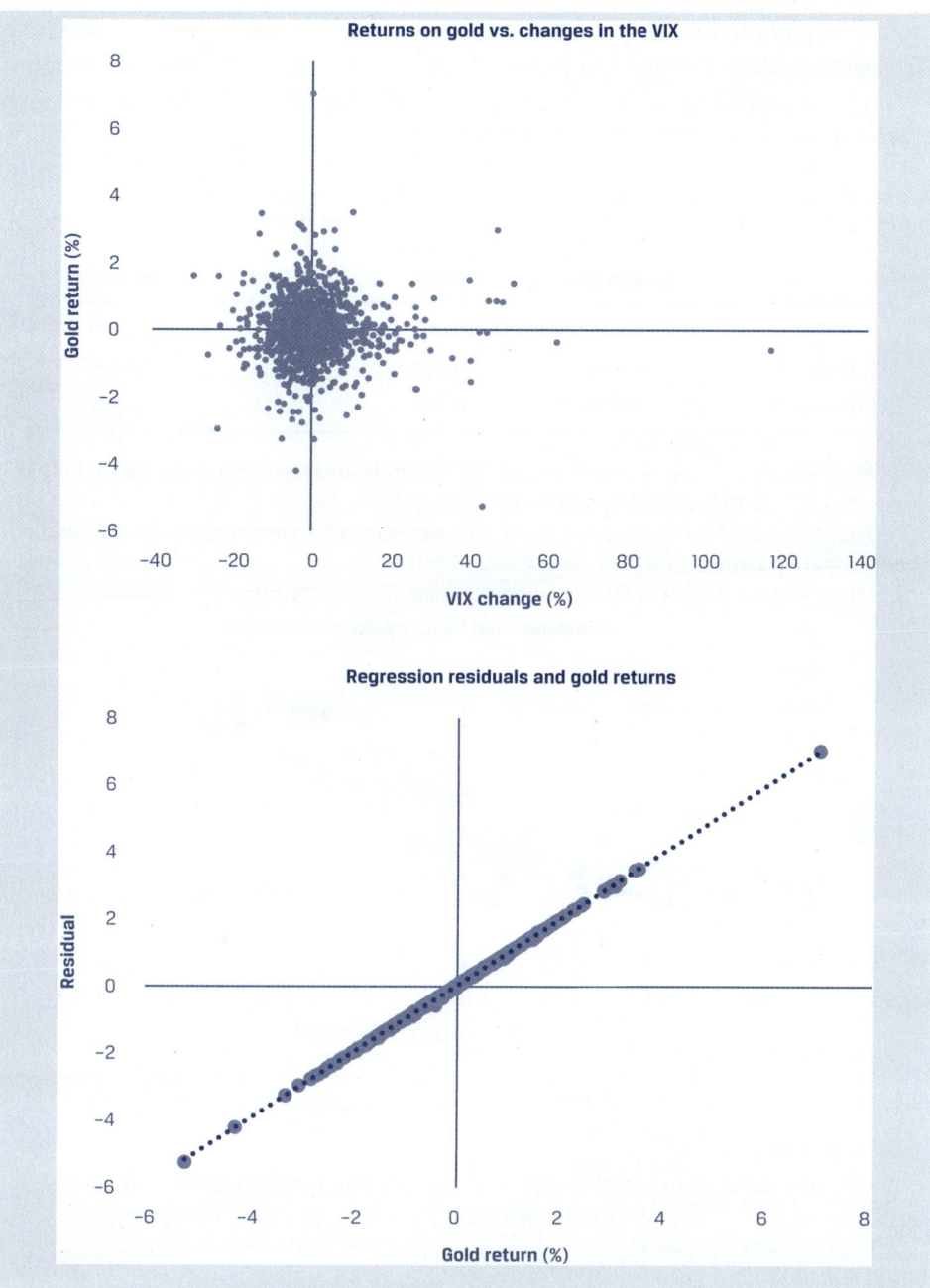

1. Discuss whether these scatterplots provide evidence of any violations of regression assumptions.

Solution

The residuals display a strong positive relationship (not noise) versus GOLD, which is a concern. This suggests the residuals are not normally distributed, are correlated, have a non-zero expected value, and are heteroskedastic. The conclusion, apparent in the lack of linear relation between gold returns and changes in the VIX, is that VIX does not capture the entire explanation of the variation in GOLD.

2. Describe how to address any violations that may be indicated.

Solution

The model should be modified to include additional features—such as market returns, economic drivers such as expected inflation, and even an indicator variable to classify periods of high versus low geopolitical risk—that may better explain the variation in gold returns.

Next, you are assigned to study a factor model for explaining the excess returns to precious metals Portfolio A (PORTA), estimated as

$PORTA_i = b_0 + b_1 X_{1i} + b_2 X_{2i} + \varepsilon_i,$

with the following results:

	Coefficient	Standard Error	t-Stat.	P-Value
Intercept	0.013	0.005	2.671	0.009
X_1, Factor 1	1.896	0.208	9.111	0.000
X_2, Factor 2	0.170	0.186	0.916	0.361

Also, adjusted R^2 is 43%, and the general F-test indicates rejection of the null hypothesis that the coefficients on X_1 and X_2 are equal to zero.

You are asked if it is appropriate to include excess stock market return (MKTRF) as an additional explanatory variable, so you examine the residuals from the estimated model and their relationship with MKTRF using the following scatterplot:

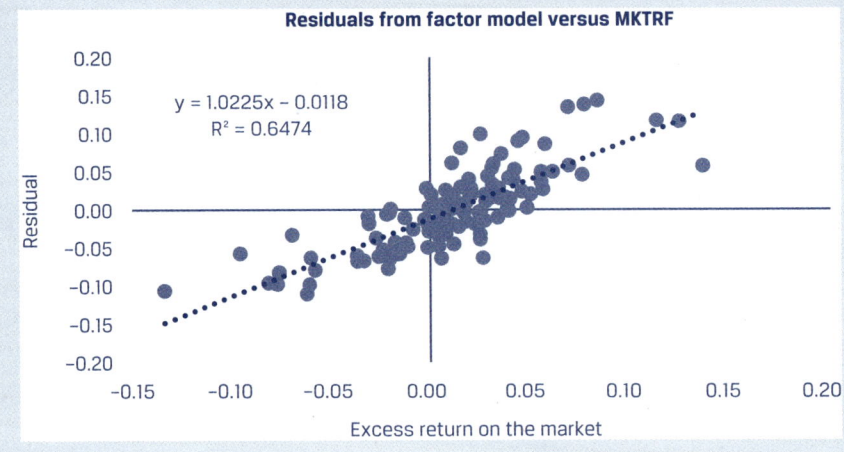

Residuals from factor model versus MKTRF

$y = 1.0225x - 0.0118$
$R^2 = 0.6474$

1. Identify the type of model misspecification suggested by the scatterplot.

   Solution

   The model has two variables (X_1 and X_2), but the residuals from this model have a clear relationship with MKTRF. Therefore, the type of misspecification error is the omitted variable bias.

2. Describe how the misspecification affects the estimated model.

   Solution

   The estimated coefficients for X_1 and X_2 are biased and inconsistent, as are their standard errors, so the model cannot be relied on for making statistical inferences.

3. Recommend a correction for the misspecification.

   Solution

   The recommended correction for this misspecification error is to include the omitted variable, MKTRF, and re-estimate the revised model.

VIOLATIONS OF REGRESSION ASSUMPTIONS: HETEROSKEDASTICITY

3

☐ | explain the types of heteroskedasticity and how it affects statistical inference

An important assumption underlying linear regression is that the variance of errors is constant across observations (errors are homoskedastic). Residuals in financial model estimations, however, are often **heteroskedastic**, meaning the variance of the residuals differs across observations. Heteroskedasticity may arise from model misspecification, including omitted variables, incorrect functional form, and incorrect data transformations, as well as from extreme values of independent variables.

The difference between homoskedastic and heteroskedastic errors can be seen in Exhibit 3. Panel A shows the values of the dependent and independent variables and a fitted regression line for a model with homoskedastic errors; there is no apparent relationship between the regression residuals and the value of the independent variable. Panel B shows the relationship when there are heteroskedastic errors. There is a systematic relationship between the value of the independent variable and the regression residuals: The residuals, which are the distance from the line, are larger for larger values of the independent variable.

Exhibit 3: Homoskedastic and Heteroskedastic Residuals

Panel A: Homoskedastic residuals

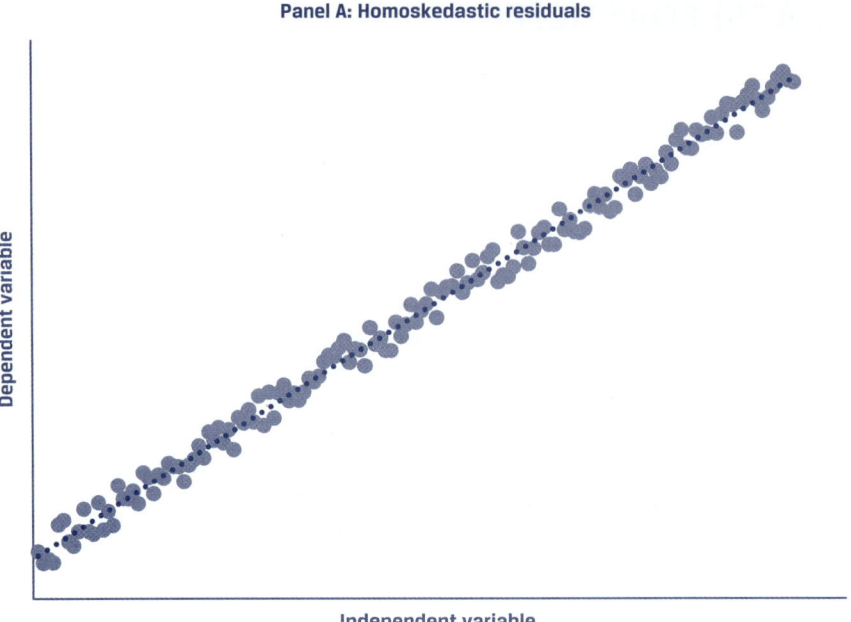

Panel B: Heteroskedastic residuals

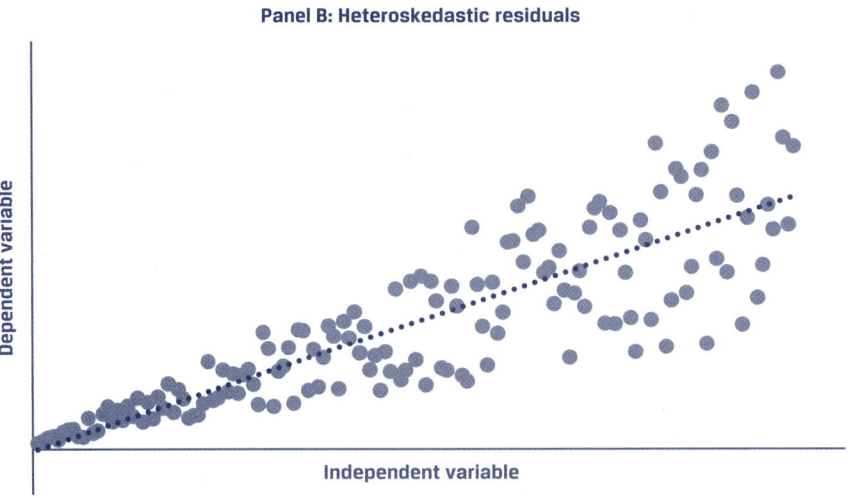

The Consequences of Heteroskedasticity

There are two broad types of heteroskedasticity: unconditional and conditional. **Unconditional heteroskedasticity** occurs when the error variance is not correlated with the regression's independent variables. Although it violates a linear regression assumption, this form of heteroskedasticity creates no major problems for statistical inference.

  Conditional heteroskedasticity is more problematic for statistical inference—when the error variance is correlated with (conditional on) the values of the independent variables. This type of heteroskedasticity may lead to mistakes in statistical inference. When errors are conditional heteroskedastic, the *F*-test for the overall regression significance is unreliable because the MSE becomes a biased estimator of the true population variance. Moreover, t-tests of individual regression coefficients are unreliable because heteroskedasticity introduces bias into estimators of the standard error of regression coefficients. Thus, in regressions with financial data, the most likely impacts of conditional heteroskedasticity are that standard errors will be underestimated, so t-statistics will be inflated. If there is conditional heteroskedasticity in the estimated model, we tend to find significant relationships where none actually exist and commit more Type I errors (rejecting the null hypothesis when it is actually true).

Testing for Conditional Heteroskedasticity

The **Breusch–Pagan (BP) test** is widely used in financial analysis to diagnose potential conditional heteroskedasticity and is best understood via the three-step process shown in Exhibit 4. Fortunately, many statistical software packages easily test for and correct conditional heteroskedasticity.

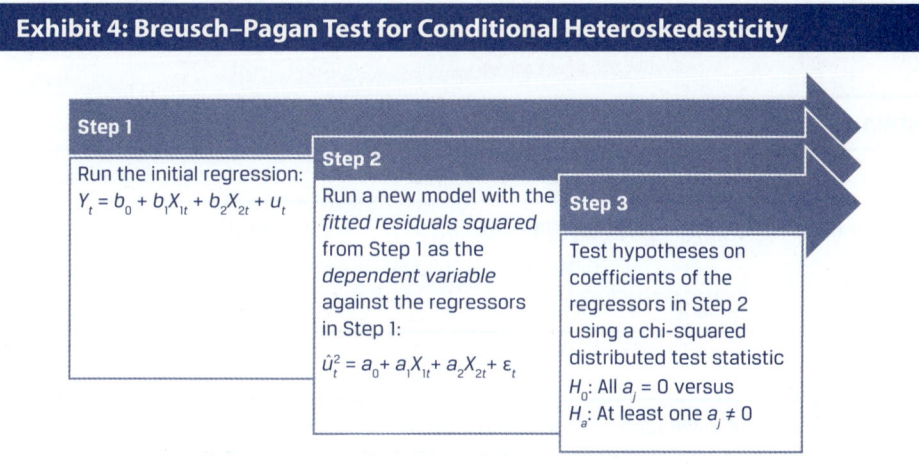

Exhibit 4: Breusch–Pagan Test for Conditional Heteroskedasticity

Step 1

Run the initial regression:
$Y_t = b_0 + b_1 X_{1t} + b_2 X_{2t} + u_t$

Step 2

Run a new model with the *fitted residuals squared* from Step 1 as the *dependent variable* against the regressors in Step 1:

$\hat{u}_t^2 = a_0 + a_1 X_{1t} + a_2 X_{2t} + \varepsilon_t$

Step 3

Test hypotheses on coefficients of the regressors in Step 2 using a chi-squared distributed test statistic

H_0: All $a_j = 0$ versus
H_a: At least one $a_j \neq 0$

If conditional heteroskedasticity is present in the initial regression, the independent variables will explain a significant portion of the variation in the squared residuals in Step 2. This is because each observation's squared residual is correlated with the independent variables if the independent variables affect the variance of the errors.

The BP test statistic is approximately chi-square distributed with k degrees of freedom, where k is the number of independent variables in Step 1:

$$X^2_{BP,k} = nR^2, \tag{1}$$

and here R^2 is from Step 2. The null hypothesis is that there is no conditional heteroskedasticity; the regression's squared residuals are uncorrelated with the independent variables. The alternative is that there is correlation with at least one independent variable. This is a one-tail, right-side test.

The BP test is illustrated in Exhibit 5. Here, an analyst uses 10 years of monthly data to assess exposures of Stock XYZ's excess returns (STOCK_RETRF) using the Fama–French three-factor model; the regressors are excess market return (MKTRF), the size factor (SMB), and the value factor (HML). The regression output is in Panel A.

The regression yields significant estimated MKTRF (1.2414) and SMB (1.0953) exposures. To validate the results, the analyst can conduct a residual analysis by plotting regression residuals against each of the three factors to look for clues to violations of linear regression assumptions, including conditional heteroskedasticity. However, the BP test (results shown in Panel B) is more rigorous. In this case, the null hypothesis is rejected at the 1% level of significance, indicating conditional heteroskedastic residuals.

Exhibit 5: Testing for Conditional Heteroskedasticity in Fama–French Three-Factor Model

Panel A Explaining XYZ Returns Using Fama–French Three-Factor Model

Regression Statistics

Multiple R	0.9375
R-Squared	0.8788
Adjusted R-Squared	0.8757
Standard Error	0.0246
Observations	120

ANOVA

	df	SS	MS	F	Significance F
Regression	3	0.5074	0.1691	280.4951	0.0000
Residual	116	0.0699	0.0006		
Total	119	0.5773			

	Coefficient	Standard Error	t-Stat.	P-Value
Intercept	−0.0026	0.0024	−1.0735	0.2853
MKTRF	1.2414	0.0601	20.6419	0.0000
SMB	1.0953	0.1042	10.5147	0.0000
HML	−0.1065	0.0872	−1.2205	0.2248

Panel B Breusch–Pagan Test for Heteroskedasticity

BP test statistic	13.40264
P-value	0.00038

CODE: BREUSCH–PAGAN TEST FOR HETEROSKEDASTICITY

Using Python

```
from statsmodels.formula.api import ols

import statsmodels.api as sm

model = ols('XYZ_RETRF ~ MKTRF+SMB+HML',data=df).fit()
```

```
print(model.summary())

test = sm.stats.diagnostic.het_breuschpagan(model.resid, model.model.
exog)

print(test)
```

Using R

```
library(lmtest)

model <- lm('XYZ_RETRF~ MKTRF+SMB+HML',data=df)

print(summary(model))

bptest(model)
```

Correcting for Heteroskedasticity

It is important to note that market efficiency implies that in efficient markets, heteroskedasticity should generally not be observed in financial data. However, if heteroskedasticity is detected, for example, in the form of volatility clustering—where large (small) changes tend to be followed by large (small) changes—then it presents an opportunity to forecast asset returns that should be exploited to generate alpha. So, analysts should not only correct problems in their models due to heteroskedasticity but also understand the underlying processes in their data and capitalize on them.

The easiest method to correct for the effects of conditional heteroskedasticity in linear regression is to compute **robust standard errors**, which adjust the standard errors of the regression's estimated coefficients to account for the heteroskedasticity. Many software packages easily compute robust standard errors, and we recommend using them. Note that robust standard errors are also known as *heteroskedasticity-consistent standard errors* or *White-corrected standard errors*.

Returning to the prior example, where the model's error variance is heteroskedastic, Exhibit 6 shows the results when the regression coefficients' standard errors are corrected for conditional heteroskedasticity. Comparing these standard errors to those in the initial regression (in Exhibit 5), the standard errors for the MKTRF and SMB increase from 0.060 to 0.091 and from 0.104 to 0.111, respectively. Note the regression coefficients did not change; rather, the problematic standard errors are corrected.

Exhibit 6: Explaining XYZ Returns Using Fama–French Three-Factor Model with Standard Errors Corrected for Conditional Heteroskedasticity

	Coefficient	Standard Error	t-Stat.	P-Value
(Intercept)	−0.0026	0.0021	−1.2347	0.2194
MKTRF	1.2414	0.0910	13.6483	0.0000
SMB	1.0953	0.1111	9.8605	0.0000
HML	−0.1065	−0.1015	−1.0488	0.2965

KNOWLEDGE CHECK

The summer intern presents to the investment team three multiple regression models, A, B and C, that use various ESG factors to explain stock returns. The research director then asks you, a junior analyst, to examine them for potential heteroskedasticity. You run scatterplots of the regression residuals against factors X_1, X_2, and X_3, respectively, and Breusch–Pagan tests for each of the models.

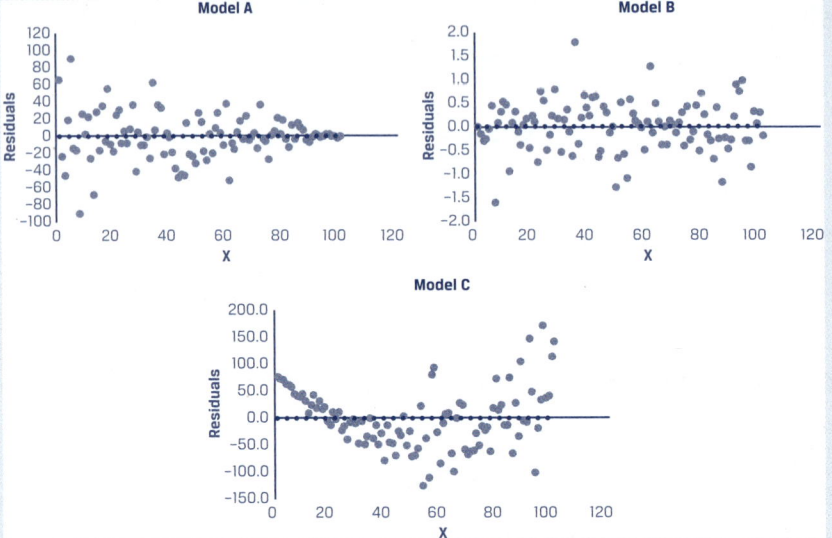

In a follow-up meeting with the research director, she asks you to do the following:

1. Interpret the scatterplot for each regression model, and determine if it suggests heteroskedasticity is a potential problem.

Solution

The Model A scatterplot shows the spread of residuals narrowing dramatically as the value of X_1 increases, suggesting heteroskedasticity is an issue. The Model B scatterplot shows no discernible pattern, just noise, for residuals versus X_2 and thus suggests no heteroskedasticity issue. The Model C scatterplot shows the spread of residuals widening dramatically in a non-linear pattern as the value of X_3 increases, suggesting the presence of both heteroskedasticity and non-linearities.

2. Identify the correct conclusion in the following table for BP tests of the three models using a 5% level of significance.

Model	BP test statistic	P-value	Conclusion: Homoskedastic or heteroskedastic residuals
A	7.183	0.0072	
B	0.035	0.8523	
C	29.586	0.0001	

Solution

If the BP test statistic's P-value is less than 0.05, then conclude the residuals are heteroskedastic.

	BP test statistic	P-value	Conclusion: Homoskedastic or heteroskedastic residuals
A	7.183	0.0072	Heteroskedastic residuals

	BP test statistic	P-value	Conclusion: Homoskedastic or heteroskedastic residuals
B	0.035	0.8523	Homoskedastic residuals
C	29.586	0.0001	Heteroskedastic residuals

3. Given heteroskedastic residuals, describe the expected effect of applying White's correction on coefficient standard errors, calculated t-statistics, and corresponding P-values for the independent variables.

Solution

By applying White's correction for heteroskedasticity, the coefficient standard errors will increase, thereby decreasing estimated t-statistics and increasing corresponding P-values for the independent variables.

VIOLATIONS OF REGRESSION ASSUMPTIONS: SERIAL CORRELATION

4

☐ | explain serial correlation and how it affects statistical inference

A common and serious problem in multiple linear regression is violation of the assumption that regression errors are uncorrelated across observations. When regression errors are correlated across observations, they are serially correlated. **Serial correlation** (or *autocorrelation*) typically arises in time-series regressions. If we have panel data, which is cross-sectional time-series data, serial correlation may also arise. We discuss three aspects of serial correlation: its effect on statistical inference, tests for it, and methods to correct for it.

The Consequences of Serial Correlation

The main problem caused by serial correlation in linear regression is an incorrect estimate of the regression coefficients' standard errors. If none of the regressors is a previous value—a lagged value—of the dependent variable, then the estimated parameters themselves will be consistent and need not be adjusted for the effects of serial correlation. But if one of the independent variables is a lagged value of the dependent variable, serial correlation in the error term causes all parameter estimates to be inconsistent—that is, invalid estimates of the true parameters. These key points are summarized in Exhibit 7.

Exhibit 7: Impact of Serial Correlation on Multiple Regression Model

Independent Variable Is Lagged Value of Dependent Variable	Invalid Coefficient Estimates	Invalid Standard Error Estimates
No	No	Yes
Yes	Yes	Yes

Positive serial correlation is present when a positive residual for one observation increases the chance of a positive residual in a subsequent observation, resulting in a stable pattern of residuals over time. Positive serial correlation also means a negative residual for one observation increases the chance of a negative residual for another observation. Conversely, **negative serial correlation** has the opposite effect, so a positive residual for one observation increases the chance of a negative residual for another observation, and so on. We examine positive serial correlation because it is the most common type and assume **first-order serial correlation**, or correlation between adjacent observations. In a time series, this means the sign of the residual tends to persist from one period to the next.

Positive serial correlation does not affect the consistency of regression coefficients, but it does affect statistical tests. First, the F-statistic may be inflated because the MSE will tend to underestimate the population error variance. Second, positive serial correlation typically causes standard errors to be underestimated, so t-statistics are inflated, which (as with heteroskedasticity) leads to more Type I errors.

Importantly, if a time series exhibits serial correlation, this means that there is some degree of predictability to it. In the case of asset prices, if these prices were to exhibit a pattern, investors would likely discern this pattern and exploit it to capture alpha, thereby eliminating such a pattern. This idea follows directly from the efficient market hypothesis. Consequently, assuming market efficiency (even weak form), we should not observe serial correlation in financial market data.

Testing for Serial Correlation

There are a variety of tests for serial correlation, but the most common are the **Durbin–Watson (DW) test** and the **Breusch–Godfrey (BG) test**. The DW test is a measure of autocorrelation and compares the squared differences of successive residuals with the sum of the squared residuals. However, the DW test is limiting because it applies only to testing for first-order serial correlation. The BG test is more robust because it can detect autocorrelation up to a pre-designated order p, where the error in period t is correlated with the error in period $t - p$. The steps and logic of the procedure are outlined in Exhibit 8.

Exhibit 8: Breusch–Godfrey Test for Serial Correlation

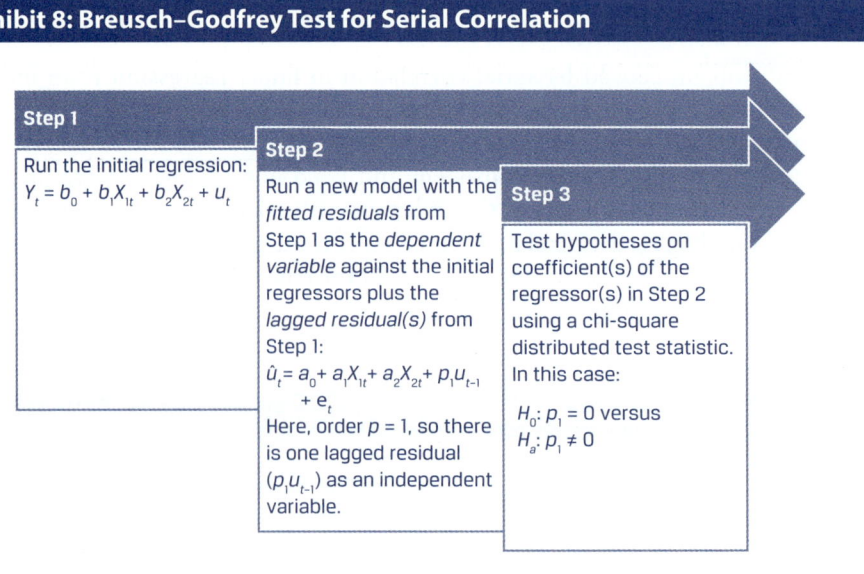

Step 1

Run the initial regression:
$Y_t = b_0 + b_1 X_{1t} + b_2 X_{2t} + u_t$

Step 2

Run a new model with the *fitted residuals* from Step 1 as the *dependent variable* against the initial regressors plus the *lagged residual(s)* from Step 1:
$\hat{u}_t = a_0 + a_1 X_{1t} + a_2 X_{2t} + p_1 u_{t-1} + e_t$
Here, order $p = 1$, so there is one lagged residual $(p_1 u_{t-1})$ as an independent variable.

Step 3

Test hypotheses on coefficient(s) of the regressor(s) in Step 2 using a chi-square distributed test statistic. In this case:

$H_0: p_1 = 0$ versus
$H_a: p_1 \neq 0$

The null hypothesis of the BG test is that there is no serial correlation in the model's residuals up to lag p. As noted in Exhibit 8, to keep things simple for illustrative purposes, the order p in Step 2 is 1, so there is one lagged residual, u_{t-1}, as an independent variable. The alternative hypothesis is that the correlation of residuals for at least one of the lags is different from zero and serial correlation exists up to that order. The test statistic is approximately F-distributed with $n - p - k - 1$ and p degrees of freedom, where p is the number of lags. This F-statistic is provided in most statistical software, so to evaluate the hypotheses, the resulting P-value can be compared with the desired level of significance.

Suppose you want to assess the sensitivity of quarterly changes in GDP to changes in personal consumption expenditures (CONS). You use 30 years of quarterly data and estimate a model with the results shown in Exhibit 9, Panel A.

The coefficient of CONS is different from zero at the 1% significance level, as indicated by the t-statistic and the corresponding P-value. But because this is a time-series model, the analyst must also assess the presence of serial correlation in the regression residuals, especially given the significant F-statistic for the BG test in Panel B.

Exhibit 9: Regression of GDP on Consumer Expenditures

Panel A Regression Results

Regression Statistics

Multiple R	0.946
R Squared	0.896
Adjusted R Squared	0.895
F-statistic	1023.0
Prob. of F-statistic	0.000
Observations	121

	Coefficients	Standard Error	t Stat	P-value	Lower 95%	Upper 95%
Intercept	0.0991	0.050	1.974	0.051	0.000	0.198
CONS	0.8696	0.027	31.990	0.000	0.816	0.923

Panel B Breusch–Godfrey Test for Serial Correlation

	Test Statistic	P-value
F-test	23.6113	0.0230

CODE: BREUSCH–GODFREY TEST

Using Python

```
import statsmodels.api as sm

from statsmodels.formula.api import ols
```

```
from statsmodels.graphics.tsaplots import plot_acf

df = pd.read_csv("data.csv")

model = ols('RETRF ~ MKTRF',data=df).fit()

print(model.summary())

r = model.resid

results = sm.stats.diagnostic.acorr_breusch_godfrey(model,nlags=10)

print(results)
```

Using R

```
library(lmtest)

df <- read.csv("data.csv")

model <- lm(df$RETRF~df$MKTRF)

summary(model)

bgtest(model,order=10,type=c("Chisq","F"))

r <- model$res
```

Correcting for Serial Correlation

The most common "fix" for a regression with significant serial correlation is to adjust the coefficient standard errors to account for the serial correlation. Methods for adjusting standard errors are standard in many software packages. The corrections are known by various names, including **serial-correlation consistent standard errors**, *serial correlation and heteroskedasticity adjusted standard errors*, *Newey–West standard errors*, and *robust standard errors*. An advantage of these methods is that they also correct for conditional heteroskedasticity. The robust standard errors, for example, use heteroskedasticity- and autocorrelation-consistent (HAC) estimators of the variance–covariance matrix in the regression estimation.

Exhibit 10 shows the results of correcting standard errors from the regression of GDP on CONS. The coefficients for both the intercept and slope are unchanged. However, the robust standard errors are larger than the original OLS standard errors, so the t-statistics are now smaller and the P-values are larger. The key point is serial correlation in the regression error caused OLS to underestimate the uncertainty about the estimated parameters. Also, serial correlation is not eliminated, but the standard errors now account for it.

Exhibit 10: Regression of GDP on Consumption Expenditures with Robust Standard Errors (Correction for Serial Correlation)

Regression Statistics	
Multiple R	0.946
R Squared	0.896
Adjusted R Squared	0.895

Regression Statistics	
F-statistic	591.0
Prob. of *F*-statistic	0.000
Observations	121

	Coefficients	Standard Error	t Stat	P-value	Lower 95%	Upper 95%
Intercept	0.0991	0.058	1.701	0.091	−0.016	0.214
CONS	0.8696	0.036	24.310	0.000	0.799	0.940

As a reminder, correcting for serial correlation and heteroskedasticity is important for performing meaningful statistical tests. However, market efficiency implies these conditions should not arise in financial market data. If serial correlation and/or heteroskedasticity are observed, then discernible patterns in the fitted residuals contain information that has the potential to be exploited before they are eliminated by the trading activities of other market participants.

KNOWLEDGE CHECK

The senior analyst provides you, the junior analyst, with the following table for various multiple regression models he has estimated and then asks you to do the following:

1. Determine the critical *F*-value and correct conclusion for BG tests using a 5% significance level.

Model	Breusch–Godfrey F-statistic	Degrees of freedom	Critical F-value	Conclusion: Is there evidence of serial correlation of residuals?
A	5.1634	4, 13		
B	22.0560	6, 15		
C	2.3400	4, 15		
D	1.9800	3, 35		

Solution

Conclusions for each model based on the comparison of the BG statistic and the correct critical *F*-value are as follows:

	Breusch–Godfrey F-statistic	Degrees of freedom	Critical F-value	Conclusion: Is there evidence of serial correlation of residuals?
A	5.1634	4, 13	3.1791	Yes
B	22.0560	6, 15	2.7905	Yes
C	2.3400	4, 15	3.0556	No
D	1.9800	3, 35	2.8742	No

2. Describe robust standard errors and why they are useful.

   Solution

   Robust standard errors are regression coefficient standard errors that are corrected for possible bias arising from autocorrelation and heteroskedasticity. They are larger than OLS standard errors and allow the regression model results to be used for statistical inference.

5   VIOLATIONS OF REGRESSION ASSUMPTIONS: MULTICOLLINEARITY

☐ | explain multicollinearity and how it affects regression analysis

An assumption of multiple linear regression is that there is no exact linear relationship between two or more independent variables. When this assumption is violated, it becomes impossible to estimate the regression. However, **multicollinearity** may occur when two or more independent variables are highly correlated or when there is an approximate linear relationship among independent variables. With multicollinearity, the regression can be estimated, but interpretation of the role and significance of the independent variables is problematic. Multicollinearity is a serious concern because approximate linear relationships among economic and financial variables are common.

Consequences of Multicollinearity

Multicollinearity does not affect the consistency of regression coefficient estimates, but it makes these estimates imprecise and unreliable. Moreover, it becomes impossible to distinguish the individual impacts of the independent variables on the dependent variable. These consequences are reflected in inflated standard errors and diminished t-statistics, so t-tests of coefficients have little power (ability to reject the null hypothesis).

Detecting Multicollinearity

Except in the case of exactly two independent variables, using the magnitude of pairwise correlations among the independent variables to assess multicollinearity is generally inadequate. With more than two independent variables, high pairwise correlations are not a necessary condition for multicollinearity. For example, despite low pairwise correlations, there may be approximate linear combinations among several independent variables (which are unobservable) and that themselves are highly correlated.

The classic symptom of multicollinearity is a high R^2 and significant F-statistic but t-statistics for the individual estimated slope coefficients that are not significant due to inflated standard errors. While the coefficient estimates may be very imprecise, the independent variables as a group may do a good job of explaining the dependent variable.

Fortunately, we can use the **variance inflation factor (VIF)** to quantify multicollinearity issues. In a multiple regression, a VIF exists for each independent variable. Suppose we have k independent variables $X_1, \ldots, X_k$. By regressing one independent variable (X_j) on the remaining $k - 1$ independent variables, we obtain R_j^2 for the regression—the variation in X_j explained by the other $k - 1$ independent variables—from which the VIF for X_j is

$$VIF_j = \frac{1}{1 - R_j^2}.$$ (2)

For a given independent variable, X_j, the minimum VIF_j is 1, which occurs when R_j^2 is 0, so when there is no correlation between X_j and the remaining independent variables. VIF increases as the correlation increases; the higher the VIF, the more likely a given independent variable can be accurately predicted from the remaining independent variables, making it increasingly redundant. The following are useful rules of thumb:

- $VIF_j > 5$ warrants further investigation of the given independent variable.
- $VIF_j > 10$ indicates serious multicollinearity requiring correction.

IDENTIFYING MULTICOLLINEARITY AS A PROBLEM

Consider an analyst who is researching Fidelity Select Technology Portfolio (FSPTX), a mutual fund specializing in technology stocks. She wants to know if the fund behaves more like a large-cap growth fund or a large-cap value fund, so she estimates the following regression using 60 months of data:

$$FSPTX_t = b_0 + b_1 SGX_t + b_2 SVX_t + \varepsilon_t,$$

Where

FSPTX$_t$ is the monthly return to the Fidelity Select Technology Portfolio

SGX$_t$ is the monthly return to the S&P 500 Growth Index

SVX$_t$ is the monthly return to the S&P 500 Value Index

The regression results in Exhibit 11 indicate that the coefficients of SGX and SVX are different from zero at the 1% and 5% levels, respectively, implying the returns to the FSPTX fund are associated with returns to the growth index and returns to the value index.

Exhibit 11: Results of Regressing FSPTX Returns on Returns of the S&P 500 Growth and Value Indexes

Regression Statistics

Multiple R	0.884
R-Squared	0.782
Adjusted R-Squared	0.774
Standard Error	0.027
Observations	60

ANOVA

	df	SS	MS	F	Significance F
Regression	2	0.1486	0.0743	102.2425	0.0000
Residual	57	0.0414	0.0007		
Total	59	0.1900			

	Coefficients	Standard Error	t-Stat.	P-Value	Lower 95%	Upper 95%
Intercept	−0.0069	0.004	−1.896	0.063	−0.014	0.000
SGX	1.7765	0.196	9.064	0.000	1.384	2.169
SVX	−0.4488	0.196	−2.292	0.026	−0.841	−0.057

Suppose the analyst runs another regression, adding returns to the S&P 500 Index (SPX) to the model with SGX and SVX. Importantly, the S&P 500 Index includes the component stocks of these two style indexes (large-cap growth and value), so the analyst is inadvertently introducing severe multicollinearity and is over-specifying the model.

The results of the new regression are shown in Panel A of Exhibit 12. While the adjusted R^2 is little changed, now standard errors of the coefficients are higher: 6.166 for SGX and 5.503 for SVX versus 0.196 for both regressors in the prior model. Adding SPX returns does not explain any more of the variance in FSPTX fund returns, but now the coefficients for SGX and SVX are no longer statistically significant. This situation represents classic multicollinearity. We can visualize this in Panel B, with the correlogram representing the pairwise correlations between the variables.

Exhibit 12: Results of Regressing FSPTX Returns on Returns to the S&P 500 Growth and Value Indexes and the S&P 500 Index

Panel A Regression Results with SGX, SVX, and SPX

Regression Statistics

Multiple R	0.884
R-Squared	0.782
Adjusted R-Squared	0.770
Standard Error	0.027
Observations	60

ANOVA

	df	SS	MS	F	Significance F
Regression	3	0.1486	0.0495	66.9683	0.0000
Residual	56	0.0414	0.0007		
Total	59	0.1900			

	Coefficients	Standard Error	t-Stat.	P-Value	Lower 95%	Upper 95%
Intercept	−0.0070	0.004	−1.877	0.066	−0.014	0.000
SGX	1.5302	6.166	0.248	0.805	−10.822	13.883
SVX	−0.6686	5.503	−0.121	0.904	−11.693	10.356
SPX	0.4658	11.657	0.040	0.968	−22.887	23.818

Panel B Correlogram of variables

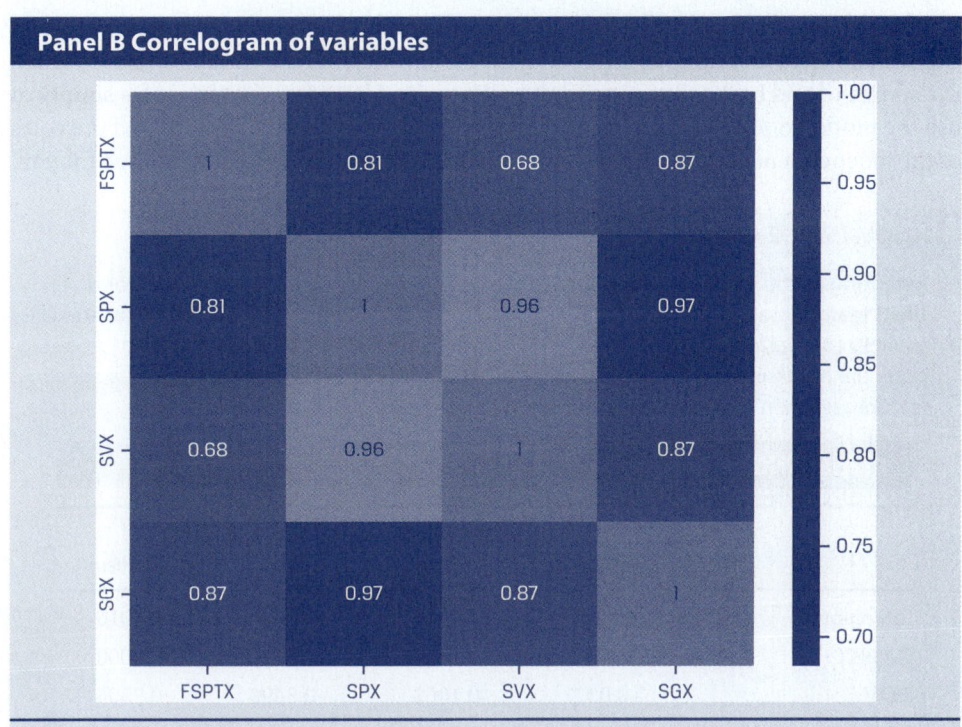

To understand the size of the multicollinearity problem, the analyst may compute VIFs for each independent variable in both regressions, as shown in Exhibit 13. Clearly, all three variables in the regression with SPX have large VIFs, indicating the error variances of their estimated coefficients are highly inflated and these variables are highly correlated. In contrast, VIFs for the coefficients of the two independent variables in the regression without SPX are both less than 5, suggesting multicollinearity is likely not a concern.

Exhibit 13: Variance Inflation Factors and Multicollinearity Problem

Model Explaining FSPTX Returns

With S&P 500		Without S&P 500	
Independent Variable	**VIF**	**Independent Variable**	**VIF**
SGX	3,863.85	SGX	3.97
SVX	3,083.22	SVX	3.97
SPX	12,904.81	–	

Correcting for Multicollinearity

Possible solutions to multicollinearity include

- excluding one or more of the regression variables,
- using a different proxy for one of the variables, and
- increasing the sample size.

Often, however, there is no easy solution for handling multicollinearity. So, you must experiment with including or excluding different independent variables to determine the source of and best solution to multicollinearity. However, if your goal is simply to use the model to predict the dependent variable—rather than to understand the roles of the independent variables—then multicollinearity may not be a major issue for you.

KNOWLEDGE CHECK

Returning to the example of the three-feature (CAPEX, ADV, R&D) ROA model for diversified manufacturers, for which the adjusted R^2 is 86.50% and the overall F-statistic is 54.4039 (partial ANOVA results shown below), the senior analyst is concerned about potential multicollinearity. So, she asks you, the junior analyst, to estimate VIF for each feature and then do the following:

Partial ANOVA Results				
	Coefficient	**Standard Error**	**t-Stat.**	**P-Value**
Intercept	4.7022	1.2349	3.8078	0.0010
CAPEX	1.2302	0.1056	11.6490	0.0000
ADV	−0.0371	0.1062	−0.3490	0.7304
R&D	0.1029	0.2837	0.3628	0.7203

Variable	**VIF**
CAPEX	1.164
ADV	1.068
RD	1.095

1. Determine whether multicollinearity is a concern using the regression results alone.

   Solution

   The overall F-statistic is significant, indicating at least one slope coefficient is non-zero. This is consistent with CAPEX's highly significant t-statistic, so multicollinearity should not be a concern.

2. Determine whether multicollinearity is a concern using the VIF results.

   Solution

   VIF for all features is well below 5 (closer to 1), indicating variances are not inflated, t-statistics are reliable, and multicollinearity is not an issue.

Exhibit 14 provides a summary of the violations of the assumptions of multiple linear regression that we have covered, the issues that result, and how to detect and mitigate them.

Exhibit 14: Summary of Violations of Assumptions from Model Misspecification

Assumption	Violation	Issue	Detection	Correction
Homoskedastic error terms	Heteroskedastic error terms	Biased estimates of coefficients' standard errors	Visual inspection of residuals; Breusch–Pagan test	Revise model; use robust standard errors
Independence of observations	Serial correlation	Inconsistent estimates of coefficients and biased standard errors	Breusch–Godfrey test	Revise model; use serial- correlation consistent standard errors
Independence of independent variables	Multicollinearity	Inflated standard errors	Variance inflation factor	Revise model; increase sample size

PRACTICE PROBLEMS

The following information relates to questions 1-4

You are a junior analyst at an asset management firm. Your supervisor asks you to analyze the return drivers for one of the firm's portfolios. She asks you to construct three regression models of the portfolio's monthly excess returns (RET), starting with the following factors: the market excess return (MRKT), a value factor (HML), and the monthly percentage change in a volatility index (VIX). Next you add a size factor (SMB), and finally you add a momentum factor (MOM). Your three models are as follows:

Model 1: $RET_i = b_0 + b_{MRKT}MRKT_i + b_{HML}HML_i + b_{VIX}VIX_i + \varepsilon_i$.

Model 2: $RET_i = b_0 + b_{MRKT}MRKT_i + b_{HML}HML_i + b_{VIX}VIX_i + b_{SMB}SMB_i + \varepsilon_i$.

Model 3: $RET_i = b_0 + b_{MRKT}MRKT_i + b_{HML}HML_i + b_{VIX}VIX_i + b_{SMB}SMB_i + b_{MOM}MOM_i + \varepsilon_i$.

Your supervisor is concerned about conditional heteroskedasticity in Model 3 and asks you to perform the Breusch–Pagan (BP) test. At a 5% confidence level, the BP critical value is 11.07. You run the regression for the BP test; the results are shown in Exhibit 15.

Exhibit 1: Testing for Conditional Heteroskedasticity

Regression Statistics	
Multiple R	0.25517
R-Squared	0.06511
Adjusted R-Squared	0.01317
Standard Error	18.22568
Observations	96

Now the chief investment officer (CIO) joins the meeting and asks you to analyze two regression models (A and B) for the portfolio he manages. He gives you the test results for each of the models, shown in Exhibit 16.

Exhibit 2: Breusch–Godfrey and Durbin-Watson Test Results

	Test Type	Test Statistic	Critical Value	Independent Variable Is Lagged Value of Dependent Variable
Model A	Breusch–Godfrey	12.124	3.927	Yes
Model B	Durbin–Watson	5.088	4.387	No

The CIO also asks you to test a factor model for multicollinearity among its four explanatory variables. You calculate the variance inflation factor (VIF) for each of the four factors; the results are shown in Exhibit 17.

Exhibit 3: Multicollinearity Test Results		
Variable	R^2	**VIF**
X_1	0.748	3.968
X_2	0.451	1.820
X_3	0.942	17.257
X_4	0.926	13.434

1. Calculate the BP test statistic using the data in Exhibit 15 and determine whether there is evidence of heteroskedasticity.

    A. 1.264, so there is no evidence of heteroskedasticity

    B. 6.251, so there is no evidence of heteroskedasticity

    C. 81.792, so there is evidence of heteroskedasticity

2. Identify the type of error and its impacts on regression Model A indicated by the data in Exhibit 16.

    A. Serial correlation, invalid coefficient estimates, and deflated standard errors.

    B. Heteroskedasticity, valid coefficient estimates, and deflated standard errors.

    C. Serial correlation, valid coefficient estimates, and inflated standard errors.

3. Determine using Exhibit 17 which one of the following statements is *most likely* to be correct. Multicollinearity issues exist for variables:

    A. X1 and X2.

    B. X2 and X3.

    C. X3 and X4.

4. Identify the correct answer related to the following statement.

    Possible solutions for addressing the multicollinearity issues identified in Exhibit 17 include:

    1. excluding one or more of the regression variables.
    2. using a different proxy for one of the variables.
    3. increasing the sample size.

    A. Only Solution 1 is correct.

    B. Only Solution 2 is correct.

    C. Solutions 1, 2, and 3 are each correct.

SOLUTIONS

1. B is correct. The BP test statistic is calculated as nR^2, where n is the number of observations and R^2 is from the regression for the BP test. So, the BP test statistic $= 96 \times 0.06511 = 6.251$. This is less than the critical value of 11.07, so we cannot reject the null hypothesis of no heteroskedasticity. Thus, there is no evidence of heteroskedasticity.

2. A is correct. The Breusch–Godfrey (BG) test is for serial correlation, and for Model A, the BG test statistic exceeds the critical value. In the presence of serial correlation, if the independent variable is a lagged value of the dependent variable, then regression coefficient estimates are invalid and coefficients' standard errors are deflated, so t-statistics are inflated.

3. C is correct. A VIF above 10 indicates serious multicollinearity issues requiring correction, while a VIF above 5 warrants further investigation of the given variable. Since X3 and X4 each have VIFs above 10, serious multicollinearity exists for these two variables. VIFs for X1 and X2 are both well below 5, so multicollinearity does not appear to be an issue with these variables.

4. C is correct. Possible solutions for addressing multicollinearity issues include all of the solutions mentioned: excluding one or more of the regression variables, using a different proxy for one of the variables, and increasing the sample size.

Extensions of Multiple Regression

LEARNING OUTCOMES

Mastery	The candidate should be able to:
☐	describe influence analysis and methods of detecting influential data points
☐	formulate and interpret a multiple regression model that includes qualitative independent variables
☐	formulate and interpret a logistic regression model

SUMMARY

- Two kinds of observations may potentially influence regression results: (1) a high-leverage point, an observation with an extreme value of an independent variable, and (2) an outlier, an observation with an extreme value of the dependent variable.

- A measure for identifying a high-leverage point is leverage. If leverage is greater than $3\left(\frac{k+1}{n}\right)$, where k is the number of independent variables, then the observation is potentially influential. A measure for identifying an outlier is studentized residuals. If the studentized residual is greater than the critical value of the t-statistic with $n - k - 2$ degrees of freedom, then the observation is potentially influential.

- Cook's distance, or Cook's D (D_i), is a metric for identifying influential data points. It measures how much the estimated values of the regression change if observation i is deleted. If $D_i > \sqrt[2]{k/n}$, then it is highly likely to be influential. An influence plot visually presents leverage, studentized residuals, and Cook's D for each observation.

- Dummy, or indicator, variables represent qualitative independent variables and take a value of 1 (for true) or 0 (for false) to indicate whether a specific condition applies, such as whether a company belongs to a certain industry sector. To capture n possible categories, the model must include $n - 1$ dummy variables.

- An intercept dummy adds to or reduces the original intercept if a specific condition is met. When the intercept dummy is 1, the regression line shifts up or down parallel to the base regression line.

- A slope dummy allows for a changing slope if a specific condition is met. When the slope dummy is 1, the slope changes to $(d_j + b_j) \times X_j$, where d_j is the coefficient on the dummy variable and b_j is the slope of X_j in the original regression line.

- A logistic regression model is one with a qualitative (i.e., categorical) dependent variable, so logistic regression is often used in binary classification problems, which are common in machine learning and neural networks.

- To estimate a logistic regression, the logistic transformation of the event probability (P) into the log odds, $\ln[P/(1 - P)]$, is applied, which linearizes the relation between the transformed dependent variable and the independent variables.

- Logistic regression coefficients are typically estimated using the maximum likelihood estimation (MLE) method, and slope coefficients are interpreted as the change in the log odds that the event happens per unit change in the independent variable, holding all other independent variables constant.

1   INFLUENCE ANALYSIS

☐   describe influence analysis and methods of detecting influential data points

Besides violations of regression assumptions, there is the issue that a small number of observations in a sample could potentially influence and bias regression results. An **influential observation** is an observation whose inclusion may significantly alter regression results. We discuss how to detect them and how to determine whether they do influence regression results.

Influential Data Points

Two kinds of observations may potentially influence regression results:

- A **high-leverage point**, a data point having an extreme value of an independent variable

- An **outlier**, a data point having an extreme value of the dependent variable

Both are substantially different from the majority of sample observations, but each presents itself in different ways.

Exhibit 1 shows a high-leverage point (triangle) in a sample of observations. Its X value does not follow the trend of the other observations; rather, it has an unusually high, possibly extreme, X value relative to the other observations. This observation should be investigated to determine whether it is an influential high-leverage point. Also, note the two estimated regression lines: The dashed line includes the high-leverage point in the regression sample; the solid line deletes it from the sample.

Exhibit 1: Illustration of High-Leverage Point

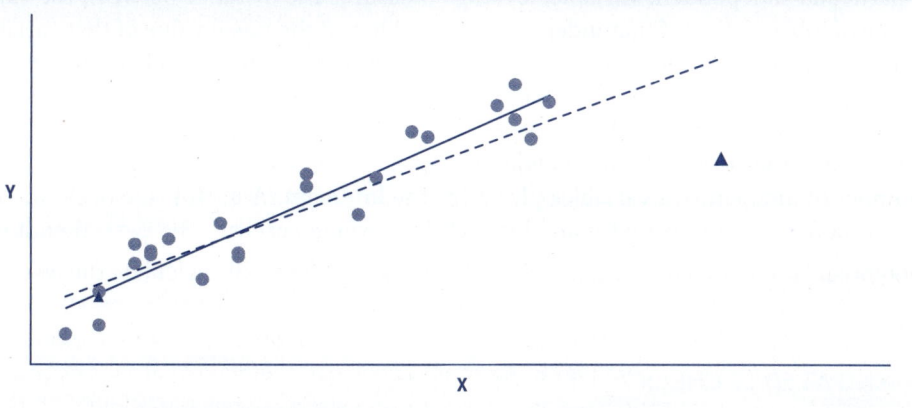

Exhibit 2 shows an outlier data point (triangle) in a sample of observations. Its *Y* value does not follow the trend of the other observations; rather, it has an unusual, possibly extreme, *Y* value relative to its predicted value, $\hat{Y}$, resulting in a large residual, $Y - \hat{Y}$. This observation should be investigated to determine whether it is an influential outlier. Also, note the two estimated regression lines: The dashed line includes the outlier in the regression sample; the solid line deletes it from the sample.

Exhibit 2: Illustration of Potentially Influential Outlier

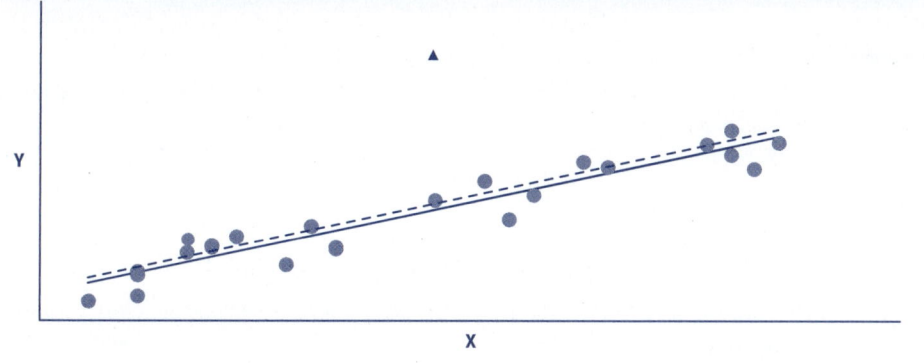

Outliers and high-leverage points are unusual but not necessarily a problem. For instance, a high-leverage point may deviate substantially from the other observations (in terms of values of the independent variable), but it may still lay close to the (solid) regression line. Problems arise if the high-leverage point or the outlier point are distant from the regression line. In these cases, the effect of the extreme value is to "tilt" the estimated regression line toward it, affecting slope coefficients and goodness-of-fit statistics.

Detecting Influential Points

A scatterplot is a straightforward way to identify outliers and high-leverage points in simple linear regression. However, multiple linear regression requires a quantitative way to measure the extreme values to reliably identify influential observations.

A high-leverage point can be identified using a measure called **leverage** (h_{ii}). For a particular independent variable, leverage measures the distance between the value of the ith observation of that independent variable and the mean value of that variable across all n observations. Leverage is a value between 0 and 1, and the higher the leverage, the more distant the observation's value is from the variable's mean and, hence, the more influence the ith observation can potentially exert on the estimated regression. The sum of the individual leverages for all observations equals $k + 1$, the number of independent variables plus 1 for the intercept. A useful rule of thumb for the leverage measure is that if an observation's leverage exceeds $3\left(\frac{k+1}{n}\right)$, then it is a potentially influential observation. Software packages can easily calculate the leverage measure.

KNOWLEDGE CHECK

Exhibit 3: Regression of Operating Profit Margin and Statistical Leverage Measure

Panel A OPM Regression Results with Full Sample

	Coefficient	Standard Error	t-Statistic	P-Value
Intercept	7.03	13.60	0.52	0.61
PROD	0.77	0.28	2.70	0.02
ONLINE	−0.29	0.28	−1.02	0.33

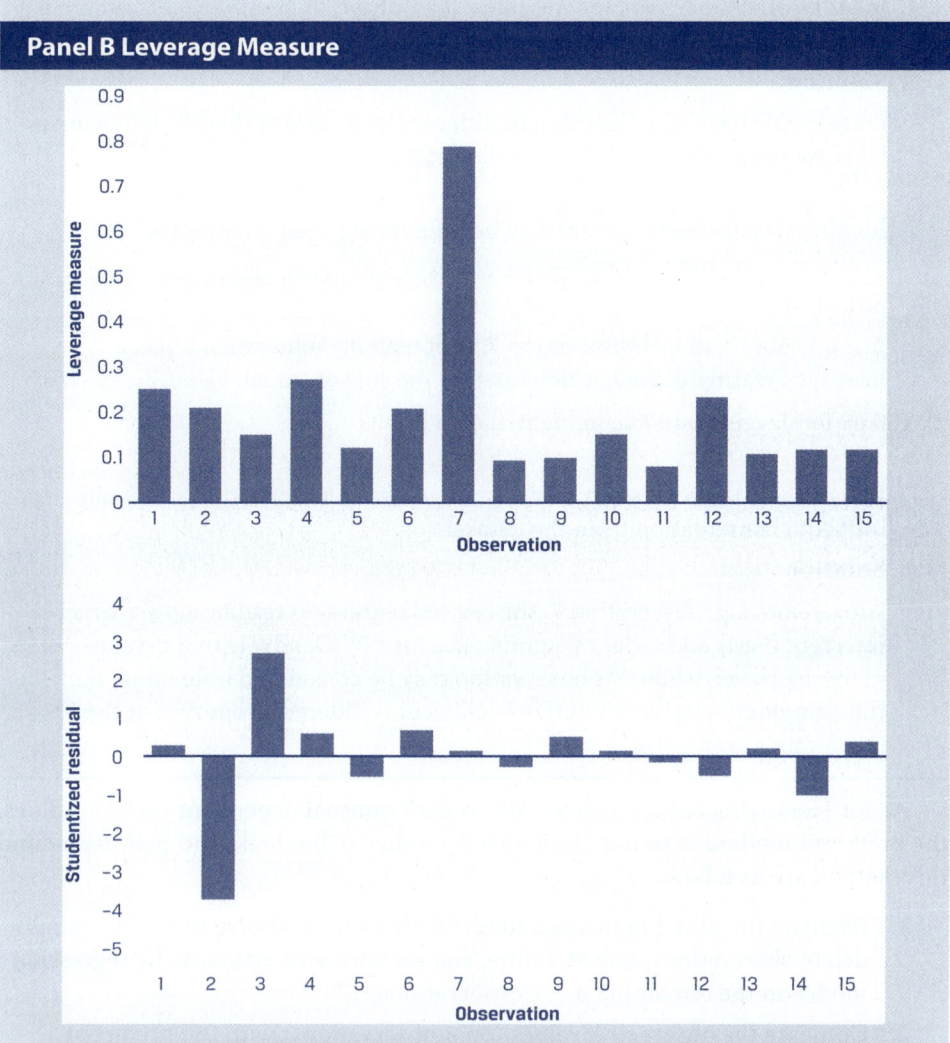

Panel B Leverage Measure

Panel C OPM Regression Results after Removing One Sample Observation

	Coefficient	Standard Error	*t*-Statistic	*P*-Value
Intercept	9.81	24.80	0.40	0.70
PROD	0.74	0.33	2.25	0.05
ONLINE	−0.36	0.61	−0.59	0.57

Given the broad themes of "health consciousness" and "aging population," the senior specialty retail analyst tasks you, the junior analyst, with initiating coverage of nutritional supplement retailers. You begin by analyzing a cross-sectional dataset of 15 such specialty retailers to determine the impact of the number of their unique products (PROD)—such as vitamins, probiotics, antioxidants, and joint supplements—and the percentage of their online sales (ONLINE) on operating profit margins (OPM).

Your partial regression results are shown in Exhibit 3, Panel A, the leverage measure for each observation (i.e., company) is presented in Panel B, and your revised regression results after removing an observation from the sample are shown in Panel C.

1. Identify which independent variables, if any, have slope coefficients different from zero at the 5% significance level.

   Solution

   Only PROD has a slope coefficient different from zero at the 5% significance level; more specifically, it has a P-value of 0.02, or 2%.

2. Identify which observation(s) may be influential based on leverage, and justify your answer.

   Solution

   Just one observation, Observation 7, is potentially influential. It has a leverage measure of 0.80, which exceeds the rule of thumb value, $3\left(\frac{k+1}{n}\right)$, of 0.60 for flagging possible influential data points.

3. Discuss how the regression results change after removing the potentially influential observation from the dataset.

   Solution

   After removing Observation 7, the revised regression results show a larger intercept (9.81) and reduced significance for PROD, now with a P-value of 5%. However, while this observation may be considered influential, the full-sample conclusion—PROD's coefficient is different from zero at the 5% significance level—still holds.

As for identifying outliers, observations with unusual dependent variable values, the preferred method is to use studentized residuals. The logic and process behind this method are as follows:

1. Estimate the initial regression model with n observations, then sequentially delete observations, one at a time, and each time re-estimate the regression model on the remaining $n - 1$ observations.

2. Compare the observed Y values (on n observations) with the predicted Y values resulting from the models with the ith observation deleted (on $n - 1$ observations). For a given observation i, the difference (or residual) between the observed Y (Y_i) and the predicted Y with the ith observation deleted ($\hat{Y}_{i*}$) is $e_i^* = Y_i - \hat{Y}_{i*}$.

3. Divide this residual by the estimated standard deviation, s_{e*}, which produces the **studentized residual**, t_{i*}:

$$t_{i*} = \frac{e_i^*}{s_{e*}} = e_i \sqrt{\frac{n-k-1}{SSE(1-h_{ii})-e_i^2}}. \tag{1}$$

Also, note the equivalent formula (on the right) for t_{i*}, whose terms are all based on the initial estimated regression with n observations, where

e_i^* is the residual with the ith observation deleted

s_{e*} is the standard deviation of the residuals

is the number of independent variables

SSE is the sum of squares error of the initial regression model

h_{ii} is the leverage value for the ith observation.

Studentized residuals are effective for detecting influential outlying Y observations. Exhibit 4 presents a rule of thumb for using them to flag outliers and the test to determine whether the outlier is influential. Note the studentized residual value must be compared to the critical value of the t- distributed statistic with $n - k - 2$ degrees of freedom at the selected significance level to conclude whether the observation is potentially influential.

Exhibit 4: Using Studentized Residuals to Identify Influential Outliers

If . . .	Then . . .
$|t_{i*}| > 3$	Flag observation as being an outlier
$|t_{i*}| >$ critical value of t-statistic with $n - k - 2$ degrees of freedom at selected significance level	Flag outlier observation as being potentially influential

---

Consider the junior analyst testing the OPM regression model with two regressors (PROD and ONLINE) based on the sample of 15 nutritional supplement retailers. The analyst wants to detect outliers and, if any, determine whether they are influential. A visual of the studentized residuals for the regression model is provided in Exhibit 5. Note that the absolute value of the studentized residuals for Observations 2 and 3 exceeds the critical t-value of 2.2010 for 11 (=15 − 2 − 2) degrees of freedom, indicating they may be influential. Consequently, these observations should be flagged for further examination.

Exhibit 5: Detecting Influential Outliers Using Studentized Residuals

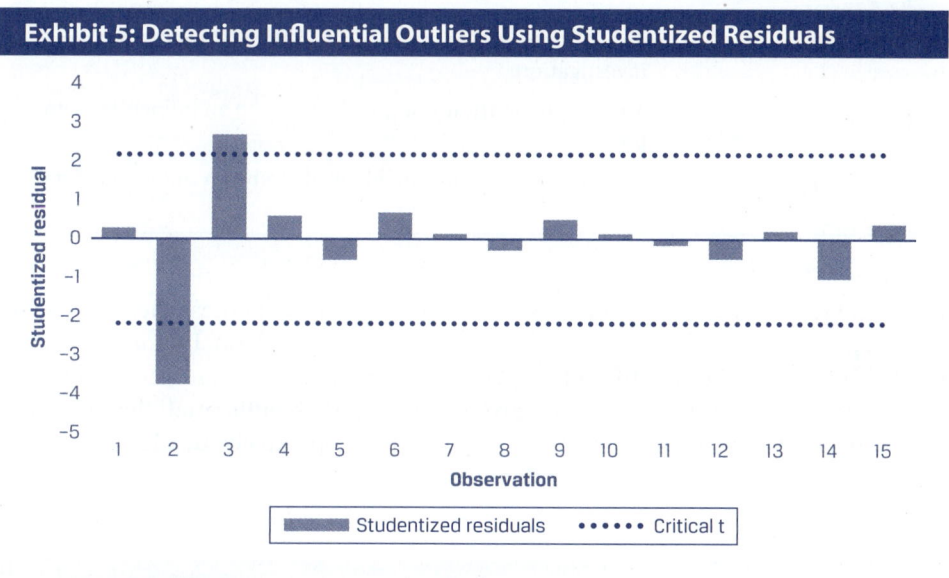

Outliers and high-leverage points are not necessarily influential. An observation is considered influential if its exclusion from the sample causes substantial changes in the estimated regression function. **Cook's distance**, or Cook's D (D_i), is a metric for identifying influential data points. It measures how much the estimated values of the regression change if observation i is *deleted* from the sample and is expressed as

$$D_i = \frac{e_i^2}{k \times \text{MSE}} \left[\frac{h_{ii}}{(1 - h_{ii})^2} \right], \tag{2}$$

where

e_i is the residual for observation i

is the number of independent variables

MSE is the mean square error of the estimated regression model

h_{ii} is leverage value for observation i

The following are some key points to note about Cook's D:

- It depends on both residuals and leverages (dependent and independent variable information plays a role), so it is a composite measure for detecting extreme values of both types of variables.

- In one measure, it summarizes how much all of the regression's estimated values change when the ith observation is deleted from the sample.

- A large D_i indicates that the ith observation strongly influences the regression's estimated values.

Practical guidelines for using Cook's D are shown in Exhibit 6. The challenge is that there are alternative rules of thumb for using Cook's D. Besides these guidelines, the analyst should examine any observation with an unusual Cook's D, which should be further investigated as being potentially influential.

Exhibit 6: Using Cook's D to Identify Influential Observations: Common Guidelines

If D_i is greater than:	Conclusion
0.5	The ith observation may be influential and merits further investigation.
1.0	The ith observation is highly likely to be an influential data point.
$\sqrt[2]{k/n}$	The ith observation is highly likely to be an influential data point.

The roles of leverage, studentized residuals, and Cook's D in detecting influential data points are summarized in Exhibit 7. Although the calculation of these measures seems daunting, most statistical software packages readily provide them. Importantly, while Cook's D by itself can identify influential data points, the leverage and studentized residuals measures can reveal why a given observation is influential, that is, due to it having an extreme X value or an extreme Y value, respectively. In addition, we can use data visualization for clues of influence.

Exhibit 7: Summary of Measures of Influential Observations

Measure	Influence of . . .		Process	Is observation influential?
	Dependent variable	Independent variable		
Leverage		x	h_{ii} ranges from 0 to 1	If $h_{ii} > 3\left(\frac{k+1}{n}\right)$, then potentially influential

	Influence of . . .			
Measure	**Dependent variable**	**Independent variable**	**Process**	**Is observation influential?**
Studentized residual	x		Compare calculated $|t\text{-statistic}|$ with critical t-value	If calculated $|t\text{-statistic}|$ > critical t-value, then potentially influential
Cook's distance	x	x	Compare calculated Cook's D against $\sqrt[2]{k/n}$	If calculated Cook's D > $\sqrt[2]{k/n}$, then highly likely influential

Exhibit 8 presents an **influence plot** for the OPM regression model of the 15 nutritional supplement retailers, which shows leverages on the x-axis, studentized residuals on the y-axis, and values of Cook's D as proportional to the sizes of the circles for each observation.

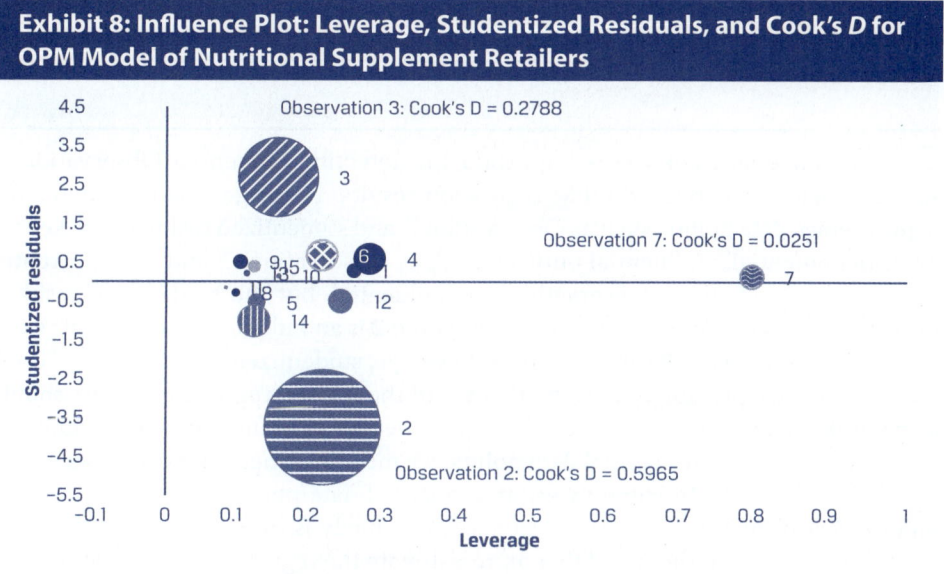

Exhibit 8: Influence Plot: Leverage, Studentized Residuals, and Cook's D for OPM Model of Nutritional Supplement Retailers

Using the Cook's D guideline of $\sqrt[2]{k/n}$, which for this sample is 0.7303 (= $\sqrt[2]{2/15}$, we see that Observations 7 and 3 are not influential, despite being a high-leverage point and an outlier, respectively. Observation 2, as indicated by its large circle, has a relatively large Cook's D, 0.5965, which exceeds the 0.5 guideline for "potential influence," but this value still falls below the threshold of 0.7303 for "highly likely to be influential."

Re-estimating the OPM model for the sample of nutritional supplement retailers after removing the high Cook's D Observation 2 reveals that this data point is indeed influential. In Exhibit 9, the full-sample regression results are repeated in Panel A and the revised results are shown in Panel B. It is clear that after removing Observation 2, the regression function changes substantially. Now, the slope coefficient for PROD increases (to 0.93) and its significance increases to the 1% level (P-value = 0.00), while the coefficient for ONLINE decreases substantially (to −0.47) and becomes significant at the 5% level (P-value = 0.04).

> **Exhibit 9: Comparison of OPM Regression Results with and without High Cook's *D* Observation 2**
>
> ### Panel A OPM Regression Results with Full Sample (repeated from Exhibit 3)
>
> | | Coefficient | Standard Error | *t*-Statistic | *P*-Value |
> |-----------|-------------|----------------|---------------|-----------|
> | Intercept | 7.03 | 13.60 | 0.52 | 0.61 |
> | PROD | 0.77 | 0.28 | 2.70 | 0.02 |
> | ONLINE | −0.29 | 0.28 | −1.02 | 0.33 |
>
> ### Panel B OPM Regression Results after Removing High Cook's *D* Observation 2
>
> | | Coefficient | Standard Error | *t*-Statistic | *P*-Value |
> |-----------|-------------|----------------|---------------|-----------|
> | Intercept | 10.81 | 9.48 | 1.14 | 0.28 |
> | PROD | 0.93 | 0.20 | 4.64 | 0.00 |
> | ONLINE | −0.47 | 0.20 | −2.35 | 0.04 |

To summarize, Cook's D is important for detecting influential Observation 2, as confirmed by the revised OPM regression results. Leverage is key for detecting high-leverage data points, such as Observation 7, and studentized residuals are key for revealing potentially influential outliers, such as Observations 3 and 2. Importantly, Cook's D by itself shows Observation 2 is influential, but the studentized residual measure reveals why it is influential: Observation 2 is an influential *outlier*. This exercise demonstrates why all three measures (leverage, studentized residuals, and Cook's D), the influence plot for visualizing them, and the revised regression results should all be evaluated when the analyst's objective is detection of influential data points.

Besides detecting influential data points, we must investigate why they occur and determine a remedy. In some cases, an influential data point is simply due to data input errors or inaccurate measurements. The remedy is to either correct the erroneous data or discard them and then to re-estimate the regression using the cleansed sample. In other cases, the influential data points are valid, which may indicate that important explanatory variables are omitted from the model or regression assumptions are being violated. We must resolve these issues by identifying and including potentially useful explanatory variables and/or checking that our model satisfies all regression assumptions.

KNOWLEDGE CHECK

You are analyzing a regression model of companies' ROA estimated with 26 observations and three independent variables and are concerned about outliers and influential observations. Using software, you calculate the studentized residual *t*-statistic and Cook's *D* for each observation, as shown below.

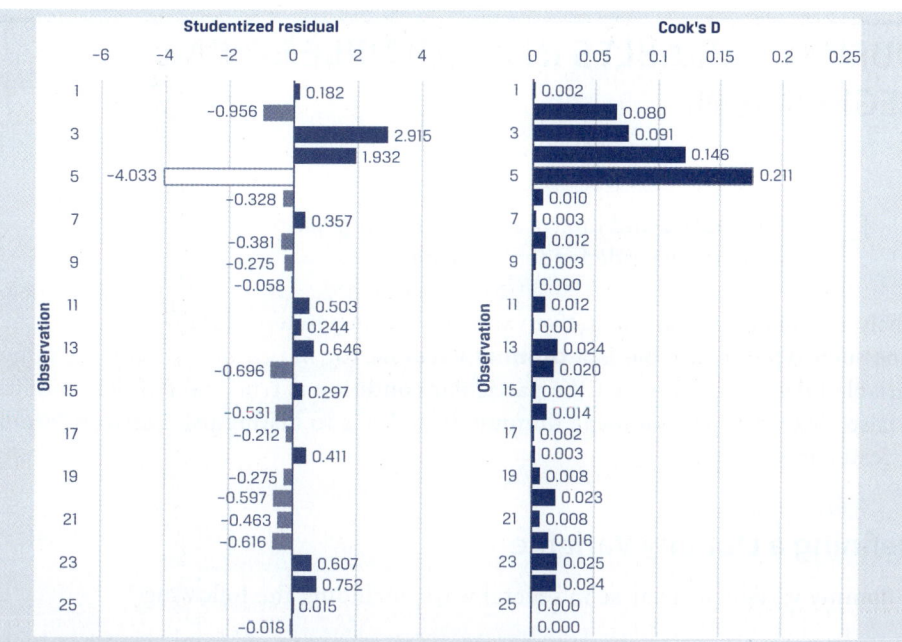

While meeting with the research director to discuss your results, she asks you to do the following:

1. Identify which observations, if any, are considered outliers using studentized residuals at a 5% significance level.

   Solution

   There are 21 (= 26 − 3 − 2) degrees of freedom, so the critical t-statistics are ±2.080. Therefore, Observations 3 and 5 are considered outliers based on the studentized residuals.

2. Identify which observations, if any, are considered influential observations based on Cook's D.

   Solution

   Using the 0.5 and 1.0 guidelines for Cook's D, there are no influential observations. Using the alternative approach, $\sqrt[2]{k/n} = \sqrt[2]{3/26} = 0.679$, there are no influential observations. However, on visual inspection, Observation 5 has a Cook's D much different from those of the other observations.

3. Recommend what actions, if any, you should take to deal with any influential observations.

   Solution

   From the results of studentized residuals and Cook's D, the analyst should investigate outlier Observation 5 to ensure there are no data entry or quality issues.

2   DUMMY VARIABLES IN A MULTIPLE LINEAR REGRESSION

☐ | formulate and interpret a multiple regression model that includes qualitative independent variables

Analysts often must use qualitative variables as independent variables in a regression. One such type of variable is a **dummy variable** (or *indicator variable*). A dummy variable takes on a value of 1 if a particular condition is true and 0 if that condition is false. A key purpose of using dummy variables is to distinguish between "groups" or "categories" of data.

Defining a Dummy Variable

A dummy variable may arise in several ways, including the following:

- It may reflect an inherent property of the data (i.e., industry membership).
- It may be a characteristic of the data represented by a condition that is either true or false (i.e., a date before or after a key market event).
- It may be constructed from some characteristic of the data where the dummy variable reflects a condition that is either true or false (i.e., firm sales less than or greater than some value).

We must be careful when choosing the number of dummy variables in a regression to represent a specific condition. If we want to distinguish among n categories, we need $n - 1$ dummy variables. So, if we use dummy variables to denote companies belonging to one of five industry sectors, we use four dummies, as shown in in Exhibit 10. The analysis still applies to five categories, but the category not assigned becomes the "base" or "control" group and the slope of each dummy variable is interpreted relative to the base. In this case, the base group is Food & Beverage.

Exhibit 10: Using Dummies to Represent Membership in Industry Sector

	Dummy Variables			
Industry Sector	Technology	Financial Services	Health Care	Energy
Technology	1	0	0	0
Financial Services	0	1	0	0
Health Care	0	0	1	0
Energy	0	0	0	1
Food & Beverage*	0	0	0	0

Food & Beverage is the base (i.e., control) group.

The reason for using $n - 1$ dummy variables is to avoid violating the assumption that no exact linear relationship exists between two or more independent variables. If we included dummy variables for all n categories, rather than $n - 1$, the regression would fail because the dummies would sum to the variable used to estimate the intercept in the regression.

Visualizing and Interpreting Dummy Variables

A common type of dummy variable is the **intercept dummy**. Consider a regression model for the dependent variable Y that involves one continuous independent variable, X, and one intercept dummy variable, D.

$$Yi = b_0 + d_0 D_i + b_1 X_i + \varepsilon_i. \tag{3}$$

This single regression model estimates two lines of best fit corresponding to the value of the dummy variable:

- If $D = 0$, then the equation becomes $Y = b_0 + b_1 X + \varepsilon$ (*base category*).
- If $D = 1$, then the equation becomes $Y = (b_0 + d_0) + b_1 X + \varepsilon$ (*category to which the changed intercept applies*).

Exhibit 11, Panel A, shows the effect of the intercept shift from a dummy variable; it is the vertical distance d_0. The shift can be positive or negative (here it is positive). The solid line where the dummy takes the value of zero ($D = 0$) relates to the base category; the parallel dashed line where the dummy variable takes the value of 1 ($D = 1$) relates to the category to which the dummy variable applies.

Exhibit 11: Visualizing Intercept and Slope Dummies

Panel A: Model with intercept dummy variable

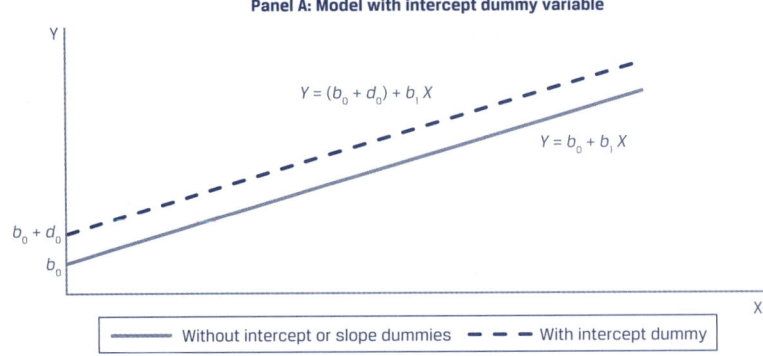

Panel B: Model with slope dummy variable

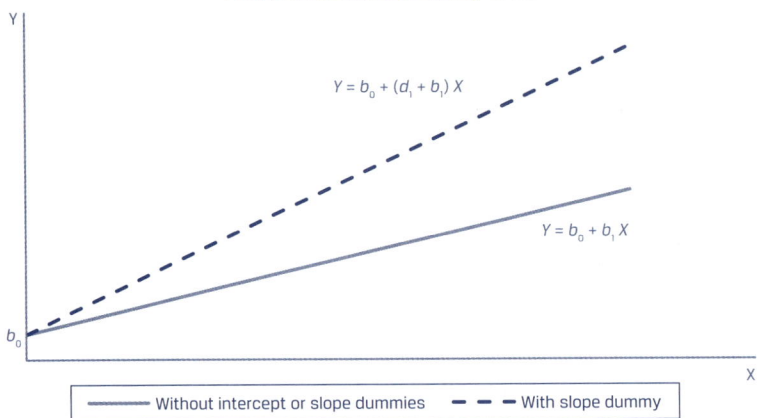

Panel C: Model with intercept and slope dummy variable

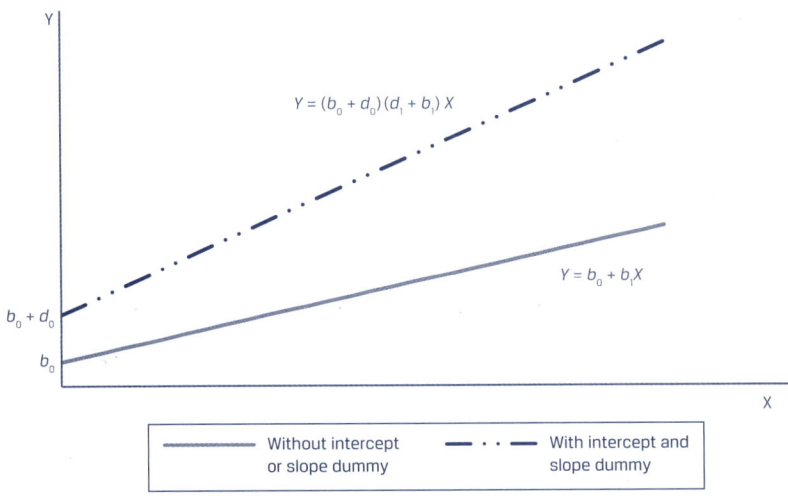

A different scenario uses a dummy that allows for slope differences, a **slope dummy**, and can be explained using a simple model with one continuous variable (X) and one slope dummy variable (D).

$$Y_i = b_0 + b_1 X_i + d_1 D_i X_i + \varepsilon_i. \qquad (4)$$

The slope dummy variable creates an **interaction term** between the X variable and the condition represented by $D = 1$. The slope dummy is interpreted as a change in the slope between the categories captured by the dummy variable:

- If $D = 0$, then $Y = b_0 + b_1X + \varepsilon$ (*base category*).
- If $D = 1$, then $Y = b_0 + (b_1 + d_1)X + \varepsilon$ (*category to which changed slope applies*).

As before, the case of $D = 0$ is the base category. The dummy variable allows for slopes to differ between the two categories. In Exhibit 11, Panel B, the base category is the same as before (shown by the solid line). For the other category, the relationship between Y and X is shown by the steeper-sloping dashed line for $Y = b_0 + (b_1 + d_1)X$. The difference between slopes may be positive or negative, depending on the scenario (here it is positive).

It is also possible for a regression to use dummies in both slope and intercept. To do so, we combine the two previous models.

$$Y_i = b_0 + d_0D_i + b_1X_i + d_1D_iX_i + \varepsilon_i. \tag{5}$$

- If $D = 0$, then $Y = b_0 + b_1X + \varepsilon$ (*base category*).
- If $D = 1$, then $Y = (b_0 + d_0) + (b_1 + d_1)X + \varepsilon$ (*category to which both changed intercept and changed slope apply*).

This model allows for a change in both intercept and slope across the two groups, shown in Panel C of Exhibit 11 by the line above the solid line. In this more complex treatment, the difference between the two categories depends on both an intercept effect (d_0) and a slope effect (d_1X) that varies with the size of the independent variable. Note in this scenario $d_1 > 0$. Finally, these scenarios are based on only two categories. We may have more categories with more dummies and more independent variables; in this case, the graphs would show more fitted lines, one relating to each category.

Testing for Statistical Significance of Dummy Variables

As explained, dummy variables are useful for distinguishing between categories of data. Tests of whether a regression function is different for one group versus another is straightforward with dummy variables. Individual t-tests on the dummy variable coefficients indicate whether they are significantly different from zero.

Exhibit 12 illustrates dummy variables in a regression using a cross-section of mutual fund data. An analyst has been tasked with analyzing how mutual fund characteristics affect fund returns. She uses a large database of mutual funds that includes several styles: blend, growth, and value.

The dependent variable is fund five-year average annual return. The independent variables are

- fund expense ratio (EXP),
- fund portfolio cash ratio (CASH),
- fund age (AGE), and
- the natural logarithm of fund size (SIZE).

Given three possible style categories, she uses $n - 1 = 2$ dummy variables:

- BLEND, which takes a value of 1 if the fund is a blend fund and 0 otherwise;
- GROWTH, which takes a value of 1 if the fund is a growth fund and 0 otherwise; and
- VALUE, the base category without a dummy.

The classification for the dummy variables is shown in Panel A of Exhibit 12. The regression model is

$$\text{Returns}_i = b_0 + b_1\text{EXP}_i + b_2\text{CASH}_i + b_3\text{AGE}_i + b_4\text{SIZE}_i + d_1\text{BLEND}_i + d_2\text{GROWTH}_i + \varepsilon_i.$$

The regression output in Panel B shows all slope coefficients and the intercept are significantly different from zero. The dummy coefficients—0.66 for BLEND and 2.50 for GROWTH—suggest blend funds deliver average annual returns exceeding those of the value category by 0.66% while growth funds deliver 2.50% more than the base value category. Moreover, the intercept coefficient suggests that an average annual return of −2.91% is unexplained by the model's independent variables.

Exhibit 12: Analysis of Mutual Funds in Different Categories

Panel A Classification of Mutual Funds

Mutual Fund Style	Dummy Variable	
	Blend	Growth
Blend	1	0
Growth	0	1
Value*	0	0

*Value is base (i.e., control) group.

Panel B Explaining Mutual Fund Returns with Fund Type Dummies

Regression Statistics

R^2	0.1230
Adjusted R^2	0.1228
Standard Error	4.224
Observations	23,025

ANOVA	Df	SS	MS	F	Significance F
Regression	6	57,636.46	9,606	538	0
Residual	23,018	410,816.9	17.85		
Total	23,024	468,453.3			

	Coefficient	Standard Error	t-Statistic	P-Value
Intercept	−2.909	0.2990	−9.738	0.00
EXP	−0.586	0.0495	−11.824	0.00
CASH	−0.032	0.0029	−11.168	0.00
AGE	0.074	0.0033	22.605	0.00
SIZE	0.267	0.0141	18.924	0.00
BLEND	0.661	0.0678	9.749	0.00
GROWTH	2.498	0.0748	33.394	0.00

The analyst extends the study by adding slope dummies. Initial results suggested a small impact of fund age on returns, 0.07% per year of age. She wonders whether this relationship between age and performance differs by fund type. For example, does the age factor affect growth or blend funds differently from how it affects value funds? To explore this idea, she introduces two interaction variables, AGE_BLEND and AGE_GROWTH, and estimates the following model:

$$\text{Returns}_i = b_0 + b_1\text{EXP}_i + b_2\text{CASH}_i + b_3\text{AGE}_i + b_4\text{SIZE}_i + d_1\text{BLEND}_i + d_2\text{GROWTH}_i + d_3\text{AGE\_BLEND}_i + d_4\text{AGE\_GROWTH}_i + \varepsilon_i.$$

When BLEND = 1, the interaction term AGE_BLEND takes the value of AGE. Similarly, when GROWTH = 1, the interaction term AGE_GROWTH takes the value of AGE. Exhibit 13 presents the revised regression results.

Exhibit 13: Explaining Mutual Fund Returns with Intercept and Slope Dummies

Regression Statistics

R^2	0.123
Adjusted R^2	0.123
Standard Error	4.224
Observations	23,025

ANOVA	Df	SS	MS	F	Significance F
Regression	8	57,760.46	7,220	404.6	0.000
Residual	23,016	410,692.9	17.84		
Total	23,024	468,453.3			

	Coefficient	Standard Error	t-Statistic	P-Value
Intercept	−2.810	0.3060	−9.183	0.00
EXP	−0.587	0.0496	−11.839	0.00
CASH	−0.032	0.0029	−11.211	0.00
AGE	0.065	0.0059	11.012	0.00
SIZE	0.267	0.0141	18.906	0.00
BLEND	0.603	0.1088	5.546	0.00
GROWTH	2.262	0.1204	18.779	0.00
AGE_BLEND	0.005	0.0077	0.627	0.53
AGE_GROWTH	0.020	0.0081	2.478	0.01

These results show that the values and significance of the slope coefficients are little changed. But the revised model provides more information on AGE. For the base group (value funds), the AGE coefficient suggests those funds earn an extra return of 0.065 as time passes. This is when BLEND = GROWTH = 0.

The interaction term AGE_GROWTH is statistically significant, implying for growth funds an extra annual return with each year of age equal to the sum of the AGE and AGE_GROWTH coefficients, or 0.085% (= 0.065% + 0.020%). So, the "slope" coefficient for GROWTH (with respect to AGE) is the sum of those two coefficients. Finally, we can interpret the overall result as suggesting that growth funds' returns exceed those of value funds by 2.347%, or 2.262% (GROWTH) plus 0.085% (AGE + AGE_GROWTH), for each year of a fund's age.

KNOWLEDGE CHECK

You are interviewing for the position of junior analyst at a global macro hedge fund. The managing director (MD) interviewing you outlines the following scenario: You are tasked with studying the relation between stock market returns and GDP growth for multiple countries and must use a binary variable in your regression model to categorize countries by stock market type, emerging (1) or developed (0) markets. He provides three choices, saying the following:

1. Identify the new variable and its function.

    A. Slope dummy: It allows for a change in slope to classify countries into weak stock performance countries and strong stock performance countries.

    B. Intercept dummy: It allows for a change in intercept to classify countries by their stock market development status.

    C. Interaction term: It allows for a change in intercept to classify countries into low-GDP growth and high-GDP growth countries.

    Solution

    B is correct. The new variable, an intercept dummy, allows for a change in intercept to classify countries by emerging versus developed stock market status.

2. The MD continues, indicating that you must refine the model to capture the effect on stock returns of the interaction of each country's GDP growth and its stock market development status. He then asks you to do the following:

    Identify the model you should use (noting these definitions).

    GDPG: Country GDP growth

    EM: Indicates emerging stock market country

    DM: Indicates developed stock market country

    A. Stock return $= b_0 + b_1\text{GDPG} + d_1\text{EM} + d_2\text{DM} + d_3(\text{EM} \times \text{GDPG}) + \varepsilon$.

    B. Stock return $= b_0 + b_1\text{GDPG} + d_1\text{EM} + d_2\text{DM} + \varepsilon$.

    C. Stock return $= b_0 + b_1\text{GDPG} + d_1\text{EM} + d_2(\text{EM} \times \text{GDPG}) + \varepsilon$.

    Solution

    C is correct. This model includes a variable for country GDP growth, (GDPG); one dummy for emerging stock market status (EM = 1, 0 otherwise), with developed market status as the base case; and a term (EM × GDPG) for the interaction of EM status with GDP growth.

3. Another MD joins the interview and mentions that an analyst on her team estimated a regression to explain a cross-section of returns on assets of companies using a regulation dummy variable (REG = 1 if regulated, 0 otherwise), market share (MKTSH), and an interaction term, REG_MKTSH, the product of REG and MKTSH. She notes the resulting model is

$$RET = 0.50 - 0.5REG + 0.4MKTSH - 0.2REG\_MKTSH$$

and asks you to do the following:

Identify which of the following statements is *correct* regarding interpretation of the regression results (indicate all that apply).

A. The average return for a regulated firm is 0.5% lower than for a non-regulated firm, holding the market share constant.

B. Non-regulated companies with larger market shares have lower ROAs than regulated companies.

C. For each increase in market share, a regulated firm has a 0.3 lower return on assets than a non-regulated firm.

Solution

A and C are correct.

A is correct because the coefficient on REG is –0.5.

C is correct because the sum of coefficients is –0.3 = –0.5REG + (0.4MKTSH + –0.2REG_MKTSH).

B is not correct because the coefficient on MKTSH is positive and the coefficient on REG is negative.

MULTIPLE LINEAR REGRESSION WITH QUALITATIVE DEPENDENT VARIABLES

3

☐ | formulate and interpret a logistic regression model

Qualitative dependent variables (categorical dependent variables) are outcome variables describing data that fit into categories. For example, to predict whether a company will go bankrupt or not, we need a qualitative dependent variable (bankrupt or not bankrupt) and company financial performance data (e.g., return on equity, debt-to-equity ratio, or debt rating) as independent variables. This qualitative dependent variable is binary, but a dependent variable that falls into more than two categories is also possible.

In contrast to a linear regression, the dependent variable here is not continuous but discrete (binary). Estimating such a model using linear regression is not appropriate. If we were to try to estimate this using the qualitative dependent variable, such as Y = 1 if bankrupt and 0 if not, in a linear model with three independent variables, then we would be estimating a linear probability model:

$$Y_i = b_0 + b_1X_{1i} + b_2X_{2i} + b_3X_{3i} + \varepsilon_i.$$

The problem with this form is that the predicted value of the dependent variable could be greater than 1 or less than 0, depending on the estimated coefficients b_i and the value of observed independent variables. Generating predicted values above 1.0 or below 0 would be invalid, because the probability of bankruptcy (or of anything) cannot be greater than 1.0 or less than 0. Moreover, linear regression assumes the relationship between the probability of bankruptcy and each financial variable is linear over the range of the financial variable, which might be unrealistic. For example, one can reasonably expect that the probability of bankruptcy and the debt-to-equity ratio are not linearly related for very low or high levels of that variable.

To address these issues, we apply a nonlinear transformation to the probability of bankruptcy and relate the transformed probabilities linearly to the independent variables. The most commonly used transformation is the **logistic transformation**. Let P be the probability of bankruptcy or, generally, that a condition is fulfilled or an event happens. The logistic transformation is

$$\ln[P/(1 - P)]. \tag{6}$$

The ratio $P/(1 - P)$ is a ratio of probabilities—the probability that the event of interest happens, P, divided by the probability that it does not happen $(1 - P)$, with the ratio representing the odds of an event happening.

For example, if the probability of a company going bankrupt is 0.75, $P/(1 - P)$ is $0.75/(1 - 0.75) = 3$. So, the odds of bankruptcy are 3 to 1, implying the probability of bankruptcy is three times as large as the probability of the company not going bankrupt. The natural logarithm (ln) of the odds of an event happening is the **log odds**, which is also known as the *logit function*.

The logistic transformation tends to linearize the relation between the dependent and independent variables. So, instead of a linear regression to estimate the probability of bankruptcy (or the probability of any categorical dependent variable), we use logistic regression for this kind of estimation.

Logistic regression (logit) uses the logistic transformation of the event probability (P) into the log odds, $\ln[P/(1 - P)]$, as the dependent variable:

$$\ln\left(\frac{P}{1-P}\right) = b_0 + b_1 X_1 + b_2 X_2 + b_3 X_3 + \varepsilon. \tag{7}$$

Once the log odds is estimated, the event probability can be derived as

$$P = \frac{1}{1 + \exp\left[-(b_o + b_1 X_1 + b_2 X_2 + b_3 X_3)\right]}. \tag{8}$$

Exhibit 14 shows the linear probability model (Panel A) and logistic regression model (Panel B). The logit model's nonlinear function takes on a sigmoidal shape and is approximately linear except when probability estimates are close to 0 or 1. Moreover, logistic regression assumes a logistic distribution for the error term; the distribution's shape is similar to the normal distribution but with fatter tails.

Exhibit 14: Linear Probability Model vs. Logistic Regression Model

A. Linear Probability Model

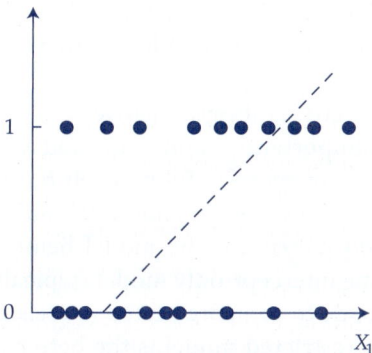

B. Logit Model

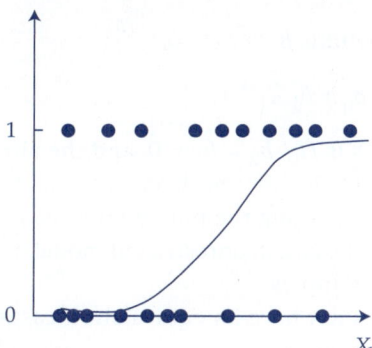

Logistic regression coefficients are typically estimated using the **maximum likelihood estimation (MLE)** method rather than by least squares. The MLE method estimates logistic regression coefficients that make it most likely that the choices in the sample would occur by maximizing the likelihood function for the data. The probability distribution used to construct the likelihood function for the data is the binomial distribution because each outcome is binary. MLE in a logistic model is implemented as an iterative process where the goal is to maximize the log likelihood. Each iteration results in a higher log likelihood, and the iterating process stops when the difference in the log likelihood of two successive iterations is quite small. Therefore, software is required to perform the computations necessary in estimating a logistic regression model using MLE.

Because the logistic transformation of event probability is the dependent variable in logistic regression, the interpretation of regression coefficients is not as intuitive as in regression with a continuous dependent variable. In a logit model, the slope coefficient is the change in the log odds that the event happens per unit change in the independent variable, holding all other independent variables constant.

Applying the exponential function (*exp* or *e*)—the inverse of the natural log function (ln)—to the slope coefficient, e^{b_i}, yields the odds ratio, which is the ratio of the odds the event happens with a unit increase in the independent variable to the odds the event happens without an increase in the independent variable. A hypothesis test that a logit regression coefficient is significantly different from zero follows the same six-step process as the test in ordinary least squares regression.

The **likelihood ratio (LR) test** is a method to assess the fit of logistic regression models and is based on the log-likelihood metric that describes the fit to the data. The LR test statistic is

$LR = -2$ (*Log likelihood restricted model − Log likelihood unrestricted model*).

The test is similar to the joint F-test of hypotheses used in least squares multiple regression (seen in an earlier learning module) in that it compares the fit of the restricted and unrestricted models; however, it uses the log likelihoods of each model. The LR test is distributed as chi-squared with q degrees of freedom (i.e., number of restrictions).

Note the log-likelihood metric is always negative, so higher values (closer to 0) indicate a better fitting model. Importantly, unlike adjusted R^2 (or $\overline{R}^2$), the log-likelihood metric for a given model is not meaningful by itself but is useful when comparing regression models that have the same dependent variable. Most statistical software produces the log-likelihood metric for the model being estimated, as well as the log-likelihood metric for the intercept-only model (typically designated as LL-Null).

As with the joint F-statistic to compare nested models, the null hypothesis for the LR test is that the smaller, restricted model is the better model. For example, if we compare the unrestricted Model A

Model A: $\ln\left(\frac{P}{1-P}\right) = b_0 + b_1 X_1 + b_2 X_2 + b_3 X_3 + \varepsilon$

to Model B, with restrictions $b_2 = b_3 = 0$,

Model B: $\ln\left(\frac{P}{1-P}\right) = b_0 + b_1 X_1 + \varepsilon$,

then the null hypothesis is H_0: $b_2 = b_3 = 0$, and the alternative hypothesis is that at least one of the coefficients is different from zero. So, the LR test is a joint test of the restricted coefficients. Rejecting the null hypothesis is a rejection of the smaller, restricted model in favor of the larger, unrestricted model. Finally, the LR test performs best when applied to large samples.

Logistic regression does not have an equivalent measure to R^2 because it cannot be fitted using least squares. Pseudo-R^2 has been proposed to capture the explained variation in a logistic regression and is generated in standard software output. The pseudo-R^2 must be interpreted with care because it can be used only to compare different specifications of the same model (not models based on different datasets).

Logistic regression plays a key role in binary classification problems in machine learning and neural networks. For example, to enhance fundamental investment analysis, logistic regression can be applied with natural language processing techniques to classify the sentiment of financial texts, such as press releases. The dependent variable is sentiment class: positive sentiment (1) and negative sentiment (0), which signal "good" or "bad" corporate news, respectively. The independent variables are tokens (key words or phrases) from financial text, such as company annual reports, earnings releases, and corporate announcements. The logistic regression model is trained to recognize and classify these tokens into good or bad news and is then tested and deployed to enhance investment valuation models.

KNOWLEDGE CHECK

You are assigned to examine the propensity of companies to repurchase their shares, so for a sample of 500 companies, you have identified those that repurchased shares (Repurchase = 1) and those that did not (Repurchase = 0). You also collected company data for the year prior to the repurchase, including cash-to-total-assets ratio (CASH), debt-to-equity ratio (DE), and net profit margin (NPM), and estimated the following logistic regression:

$\text{Repurchase}_i = b_0 + b_1 \text{CASH}_i + b_2 \text{DE}_i + b_3 \text{NPM}_i + \varepsilon_i.$

Your regression results are shown in Exhibit 15.

Exhibit 15: Logistic Regression Results

Dep. Variable	Repurchase	No. Observations	500
Model:	Logit	Df Residuals	496
Method:	MLE	Df Model	3
		Pseudo-R^2	0.0271
		Log-Likelihood	−304.20
Converged:	TRUE	LL-Null	−312.68
Covariance Type:	Non-Robust	LLR-P-value	0.0007

					95% CI	
	Coefficient	**Std. Error**	**z-Stat.**	**P-Value**	**Lower**	**Upper**
Intercept	−0.4738	0.196	−2.415	0.016	−0.858	−0.089
CASH	−0.9118	1.154	−0.790	0.430	−3.174	1.351
DE	−0.3186	0.133	−2.396	0.017	−0.579	−0.058
NPM	0.9407	0.417	2.255	0.024	0.123	1.758

In the weekly research team meeting, the research director asks you to explain your logistic regression model and assess how the model fits the data, as follows:

1. Interpret the logit regression intercept.

   Solution:

   The intercept of −0.4738 is the log odds of the probability of being a share repurchaser if CASH, DE, and NPM are all zero. The odds are $e^{-0.4738}$ = 0.6226, and the probability (P) = 0.6226/(1 + 0.6226) = 0.3837, or 38.37%.

2. Interpret the role of each independent variable in explaining companies' probability to repurchase shares.

   Solution:

   A coefficient is interpreted as the expected change in the log odds for a one-unit change in the variable. Converting each coefficient from log odds into odds and then into probability results in the following:

Independent variable	Coefficient (log odds)	Odds ($e^{log\ odds}$)	Probability [Odds/(1 + Odds)]
CASH	−0.9118	0.4018	0.2866
DE	−0.3186	0.7272	0.4210
NPM	0.9407	2.5618	0.7192

   - The interpretation of the CASH coefficient is that a one-unit change in the cash-to-total assets ratio results in a 28.7% increase in the probability of repurchasing shares, all other variables held constant.
   - The interpretation of the DE coefficient is that a one-unit change in the debt-to-equity ratio results in a 42.1% increase in the probability of repurchasing shares, all other variables held constant.

- The interpretation of the NPM coefficient is that a one-unit change in the net profit margin results in a 71.9% increase in the probability of repurchasing shares, all other variables held constant.

3. Evaluate how your logistic regression model fits the data using the LR test and an intercept-only model as the restricted model.

   Solution:

   The log likelihood statistics from the logistic regression results are

Model	Log-likelihood
Restricted: Intercept only	−312.68
Unrestricted: Intercept, CASH, DE, NPM	−304.20

   The LR test is a test of the hypothesis for the restrictions, using the standard six-step hypothesis test process, as follows:

Step 1	State the hypotheses.	H_0: $b_{1(CASH)} = b_{2(DE)} = b_{3(NPM)} = 0$, H_a: at least one $b_j \neq 0$
Step 2	Identify the appropriate test statistic.	Likelihood Ratio (LR) = −2 (Log likelihood restricted model − Log likelihood unrestricted model), and degrees of freedom = 3
Step 3	Specify the level of significance.	$\alpha = 5\%$
Step 4	State the decision rule.	Critical chi-square-value = 7.8150, reject the null hypothesis if the calculated LR is greater than 7.8150
Step 5	Calculate the test statistic.	$LR = -2(-312.68 - -304.20) = 16.960$
Step 6	Make a decision.	Reject the null hypothesis because the calculated chi-square-statistic is greater than the critical chi-square-value. We conclude that the unrestricted model fits the data better than the restricted model.

   Based on the LR test, your conclusion is that the unrestricted model fits the data better than the intercept-only model, indicating that the three explanatory variables are jointly significant. Note the regression results show the LR test statistic's *P*-value is 0.0007. Moreover, individual (z-statistic) tests of the coefficients show that DE and NPM are each significant at the 5 percent level.

CODE: LOGISTIC REGRESSION

In Python:

```
import pandas as pd

from statsmodels.formula.api import logit

df = pd.read_csv("data.csv")

formula = ('Repurchase ~ CASH + DE + NPM')
```

```
model=logit(formula=formula,data=df).fit(method='newton')

print(model.summary())
```

In R:

```
df <- read.csv('data.csv')

logit <- glm(Repurchase ~ CASH+DE+NPM,
family=binomial(link="logit"),data=df)

summary(logit)
```

PRACTICE PROBLEMS

The following information relates to questions 1-5

The CIO asks you to analyze one of the firm's portfolios to identify influential outliers that might be skewing regression results of its return drivers. For each observation, you calculate leverage, the studentized residual, and Cook's D. There are 96 observations and two independent variables ($k = 2$), and the critical t-statistic is 2.63 at a 1% significance level. Partial results of your calculations are shown in Exhibit 1.

Exhibit 1: Regression Data for Detecting Influential Observations

	h_{ii}	Studentized Residual	Cook's D
Observation 1	0.043	2.784	0.161
Observation 2	0.022	−0.103	0.000
Observation 3	0.036	−0.731	0.010
Observation 4	0.059	−0.122	0.000
Observation 5	0.011	−0.660	0.002
Observation 6	0.101	−2.906	0.347
...	...	...	...
Observation 45	0.042	2.117	0.094
Observation 46	0.013	0.172	0.000
Observation 47	0.015	−0.672	0.003
Observation 48	0.012	−0.734	0.003
Observation 49	0.064	0.475	0.008
Observation 50	0.141	−2.788	0.594
Observation 51	0.011	1.679	0.016
Observation 52	0.023	−1.218	0.017
...	...	...	...
Observation 91	0.035	−1.260	0.029
Observation 92	0.025	3.001	0.106
Observation 93	0.017	1.483	0.019
Observation 94	0.097	−0.172	0.001
Observation 95	0.017	0.046	0.000
Observation 96	0.011	1.819	0.019

Finally, you are tasked with investigating whether there is any monthly seasonality in the excess portfolio returns. You construct a regression model using dummy variables for the months; your regression statistics and ANOVA results are shown in Exhibit 2.

Exhibit 2: Analysis of Monthly Seasonality of Excess Portfolio Returns

Regression Statistics

Multiple R	0.321
R-Squared	0.103
Adjusted R-Squared	−0.014
Standard Error	8.100
Observations	96.000

ANOVA

	df	SS	MS	F	Signif. F
Regression	11	634.679	57.698	0.879	0.563
Residual	84	5511.369	65.612		
Total	95	6146.048			

	Coeff.	Std. Error	t-Stat.	P-Value
Intercept	1.263	2.864	0.441	0.660
Jan	1.311	4.050	0.324	0.747
Feb	−3.756	4.050	−0.927	0.356
Mar	3.495	4.050	0.863	0.391
Apr	0.174	4.050	0.043	0.966
May	0.714	4.050	0.176	0.861
Jun	0.944	4.050	0.233	0.816
Jul	−0.571	4.050	−0.141	0.888
Aug	−0.445	4.050	−0.110	0.913
Sep	−1.744	4.050	−0.431	0.668
Oct	4.261	4.050	1.052	0.296
Nov	−5.311	4.050	−1.311	0.193

1. Determine and justify the potentially influential observation(s) in Exhibit 1 using the leverage measure.

   A. Observation 50, because it has the highest leverage, at 0.141

   B. Observations 6 and 50, because their leverage exceeds 0.100

   C. Observations 6, 50, and 94, because their leverage exceeds $3\left(\frac{k+1}{n}\right)$

2. Determine and justify the potentially influential observations in Exhibit 1 using the studentized residuals measure.

   A. Observations 1 and 92, because the values of their studentized residuals exceed 2.63

   B. Observations 1, 6, 50, and 92, because the absolute values of their studentized residuals exceed 2.63

C. All the observations shown except observation 95, because the absolute value of its studentized residual is less than 0.094

3. Determine and justify the potentially influential observations in Exhibit 1 using the criteria for Cook's D involving k and n.

   A. Observations 6 and 50, because their Cook's D values exceed 0.144

   B. Observations 6 and 50, because their Cook's D values exceed 0.289

   C. Observations 1, 6, 50, and 92, because their Cook's D values exceed 0.100

4. Identify both the base month and the coefficient that represents its returns in Exhibit 2.

   A. December is the base month, and the intercept coefficient represents its returns.

   B. November is the base month, and the intercept coefficient represents its returns.

   C. December is the base month, and the average of the coefficients for the other 11 months represents its returns.

5. Determine using Exhibit 2 which one of the following statements is *most likely* to be correct. Monthly seasonality in the firm's portfolio is_____.

   A. highly likely

   B. highly unlikely

   C. not able to be determined from the given data

The following information relates to questions 6-12

Your second-round interview for the Junior Quantitative Analyst position went well, and the next day, you receive an email from the investment firm congratulating you for making it this far. You are one of four remaining candidates from more than 100 who applied for the position.

Because the position involves quantitative analysis, you are given an assignment to complete within 72 hours. You are provided a dataset and tasked with creating two logistic regression models to predict whether an ETF will be a "winning" fund, that is, whether the ETF's monthly return will be one standard deviation or more above the mean monthly return across all ETFs in the dataset, or whether the ETF will be an "average" fund.

The variables in the dataset are as follows:

	Variable	Description
1	net_assets	Net assets of ETF in USD
2	small_fund	Dummy Variable = 1 if a small-size fund, and 0 otherwise, with large size fund as the base

	Variable	Description
3	medium_fund	Dummy Variable =1 if a medium-size fund, and 0 otherwise, with large-size fund as the base
4	portfolio_stocks	Percentage of portfolio invested in stocks (1–100)
5	portfolio_bonds	Percentage of portfolio invested in bonds (1–100)
6	price_earnings	Ratio of price per share to earnings per share
7	price_book	Ratio of price per share to book value per share
8	price_sales	Ratio of price per share to sales per share
9	price_cashflow	Ratio of price per share to cash flow per share
10	label (dependent variable)	1 = winning fund, an ETF whose monthly return is one standard deviation or more above the mean monthly return across all ETFs in the dataset, and 0 = average fund, otherwise

For the first logistic regression, you are asked to use all the independent variables, except for the fund size dummy variables (small_fund and medium_fund). For the second logistic regression, you are asked to use all the independent variables except the fund size continuous variable (net assets).

You use a standard software package (in Python or R) to develop the logistic regression models. Your results are as follows:

Logistic Regression 1

Logistic Regression Results

Model: Logit			Pseudo-R^2:	0.057			
Dependent Variable:		label					
No. Observations:		1594	Log-Likelihood:	−451.66			
Df Model:		7	LL-Null:	−478.86			
Df Residuals:		1586	LLR	P-Value:	1.97E−9		
No. Iterations:		10					
	Coefficient	Std.Err.	z-Statistic	P-Value > $|z|$	[0.025	0.975]
Intercept	−2.0350	0.5221	−3.8979	0.0001	−3.0583	−1.0118
net_assets	−0.7667	1.3571	−0.5649	0.5721	−3.4265	1.8932
portfolio_stocks	−0.0089	0.0051	−1.7550	0.0793	−0.0188	0.0010
portfolio_bonds	−0.1113	0.0729	−1.5263	0.1269	−0.2543	0.0316
price_earnings	0.0292	0.0200	1.4647	0.1430	−0.0099	0.0683
price_book	−0.0390	0.1029	−0.3791	0.7046	−0.2407	0.1627
price_sales	0.3432	0.0777	4.4160	0.0000	0.1909	0.4956
price_cashflow	−0.0502	0.0363	−1.3805	0.1674	−0.1214	0.0211

Logistic Regression 2

Logistic Regression Results

	Coefficient	Std.Err.	z-Statistic	P-Value > |z|	[0.025	0.975]
Model: Logit			Pseudo-R^2:	0.059		
Dependent Variable:		label				
No. Observations:		1594	Log-Likelihood:	-450.4		
Df Model:		8	LL-Null:	-478.86		
Df Residuals:		1585	LLR	P-Value:	1.87E–09	
No. Iterations:		10				
Intercept	−1.9589	0.5254	−3.7283	0.0002	−2.9886	−0.9291
small_fund	−0.4794	0.3719	−1.2888	0.1975	−1.2083	0.2496
medium_fund	−0.3509	0.2348	−1.4948	0.1350	−0.8111	0.1092
portfolio_stocks	−0.0092	0.0051	−1.8099	0.0703	−0.0191	0.0008
portfolio_bonds	−0.1121	0.0727	−1.5433	0.1228	−0.2546	0.0303
price_earnings	0.0389	0.0211	1.8467	0.0648	−0.0024	0.0802
price_book	−0.0803	0.1068	−0.7519	0.4521	−0.2897	0.1291
price_sales	0.3453	0.0796	4.3362	0.0000	0.1892	0.5014
price_cashflow	−0.0510	0.0376	−1.3573	0.1747	−0.1247	0.0227

6. Identify which one of the following choices is *most likely* to be correct: "Logistic regression is the appropriate regression method for your assignment because the _____."

   A. independent variables include dummy variables for small- and medium-size funds

   B. dependent variable is binary rather than continuous

   C. dependent variable is not continuous, and the independent variables include dummy variables for small- and medium-size funds

7. Identify which one of the following statements *best describes* the interpretation of an independent variable's slope coefficient in a logistic regression model: "The slope coefficient is the change in the ___."

   A. log odds that the event happens per unit change in the independent variable, while all other independent variables increase by one unit

   B. odds that the event happens per unit change in the independent variable, holding all other independent variables constant

   C. log odds that the event happens per unit change in the independent variable, holding all other independent variables constant

8. Determine which one of the following statements is *true*. "The intercept in these logistic regressions is interpreted as the ___."

    A. probability of the ETF being a winning fund if all independent variables are one

    B. log odds of the ETF being a winning fund if all independent variables are zero

    C. log odds of the ETF being an average fund if all independent variables are zero

9. Determine for Logistic Regression 1 which of the following is *closest to* the change in the probability that an ETF will be a winning fund if net_assets increase by one unit, and all else stays constant.

    A. 31.7%

    B. 76.7%

    C. 100.0%

10. Determine for Logistic Regression 2 which of the following is *closest to* the change in probability that an ETF will be a winning fund if the size of the ETF changes from small to medium, and all else stays constant.

    A. 3.1%

    B. 12.9%

    C. 41.3%

11. Identify which one of the following statements about the logistic regression model fit is *most likely* to be correct. "Based on the log-likelihood criteria, ___."

    A. Model 2 has a better fit because it has a higher log-likelihood value

    B. Model 2 has a better fit because it has a lower log-likelihood value

    C. Model 1 has a better fit because it has a higher log-likelihood value

12. Determine, using the significant variable(s) in Logistic Regression 2 and the information provided, which of the following is *closest to* the probability of the Alpha ETF being a winning fund and whether it would be classified as a winning fund.

    Alpha ETF variable values: small_fund = 0, medium_fund = 0, portfolio_stocks = 99.3%, portfolio_bonds = 0.7%, price_earnings = 25.0, price_book =1.1, price_sales = 4.0, and price_cashflow = 5.7.

    Use significance level of 5% and probability threshold for being a winner of 65%.

    A. 27.4%, and the Alpha ETF is not classified as a winning fund

    B. 36.0%, and the Alpha ETF is not classified as a winning fund

    C. 82.2%, and the Alpha ETF is classified as a winning fund

SOLUTIONS

1. C is correct. The rule of thumb for the leverage measure is that if it exceeds 3 $\left(\frac{k+1}{n}\right)$, where k is the number of independent variables, then it is a potentially influential observation. Since $n = 96$ and $k = 2$, then $3\left(\frac{2+1}{96}\right) = 0.09375$. Three observations exceed this value: 6, 50, and 94. So, they are potentially influential observations.

2. B is correct. For the studentized residuals measure, the critical t-value is 2.63. So, any observation with a studentized residual whose absolute value exceeds 2.63 is a potentially influential observation. The studentized residuals for observations 1, 6, 50, and 92 have absolute values exceeding 2.63; therefore, they are potentially influential observations.

3. B is correct. The required criteria for using Cook's D to identify influential observations is

$$D_i > \sqrt[2]{\frac{k}{n}}$$

which implies the ith observation is highly likely to be an influential data point. Since $n = 96$ and $k = 2$, then $\sqrt[2]{\frac{k}{n}} = \sqrt[2]{\frac{2}{96}} = 0.289$. Only two observations, 6 and 50, have a Cook's D that exceeds 0.289, so they are highly likely to be influential observations.

4. A is correct. December is the base month, and the intercept coefficient represents its returns. We use 11 dummy variables to represent the returns for each month from January through November. December results are measured when each of these dummy variables equals zero, leaving the intercept coefficient to represent December returns.

5. B is correct. Monthly seasonality in the firm's portfolio is highly unlikely. The variance explained by the model (R-squared) is only 10.3%, and after adjusting for the number of independent variables (adjusted R-squared), it becomes negative. Also, the insignificant F-statistic indicates a 56.3% chance that all variable coefficients are zero. Finally, t-statistics and associated p-values indicate that all the variable coefficients are insignificant (i.e., not significantly different from zero). Consequently, monthly seasonality is highly unlikely to exist in this portfolio.

6. B is correct. Logistic regression is the appropriate regression method because the dependent variable is binary rather than continuous.

7. C is correct. An independent variable's slope coefficient in a logistic regression model is the change in the log odds that the event happens per unit change in the independent variable, holding all other independent variables constant.

8. B is correct. The intercept in these logistic regressions is interpreted as the log odds of the ETF being a winning fund if all independent variables are *zero*.

9. A is correct. In Logistic Regression 1, the slope coefficient (i.e., log odds) for net_assets is −0.7667. Therefore, the odds are $e^{-0.7667} = 0.46454$, and the probability (P) is $0.46454/(1.46454) = 0.31719$, or 31.72%. So, a one-unit increase in net_assets results in a 31.72% increase in the probability that the EFT is a winning fund, all other variables held constant.

10. A is correct. The net impact on the probability that an ETF will be a winning fund as it grows from a small-size into a medium-size fund is shown in three steps:

    1. The probability of a medium-size fund is: odds are $e^{-0.3509} = 0.70405$, and probability (P) = 0.70405/(1.70405) = 0.41316, or 41.32%.

    2. The probability of a small-size fund is: odds are $e^{-0.4794} = 0.61915$, and probability (P) = 0.61915/(1.61915) = 0.38239, or 38.24%.

    3. The net impact on the probability that an ETF will be a winning fund by growing from a small fund into a medium fund is: 41.32% − 38.24% = 3.08%.

11. A is correct. Model 2 has a better fit because it has a higher (less negative) log-likelihood value, −450.40 versus −451.66, compared to Model 1.

12. B is correct. Besides the significant intercept, the only significant (at 5% level) variable in Logistic Regression 2 is price_sales. Using these factors, the probability of this ETF being a winning fund is calculated to be 35.95%, as follows:

    Probability of being a winning fund = $0.3595 = \dfrac{1}{1 + \exp[-(-1.9589) + (0.3453)(4.0)]}$

    Because this probability is well below the 65% threshold for being a winner, the Alpha EFT would not be classified as a winning fund.

5

Time-Series Analysis

by Richard A. DeFusco, PhD, CFA, Dennis W. McLeavey, DBA, CFA, Jerald E. Pinto, PhD, CFA, and David E. Runkle, PhD, CFA.

Richard A. DeFusco, PhD, CFA, is at the University of Nebraska-Lincoln (USA). Dennis W. McLeavey, DBA, CFA, is at the University of Rhode Island (USA). Jerald E. Pinto, PhD, CFA, is at CFA Institute (USA). David E. Runkle, PhD, CFA, is at Jacobs Levy Equity Management (USA).

LEARNING OUTCOMES

Mastery	The candidate should be able to:
☐	calculate and evaluate the predicted trend value for a time series, modeled as either a linear trend or a log-linear trend, given the estimated trend coefficients
☐	describe factors that determine whether a linear or a log-linear trend should be used with a particular time series and evaluate limitations of trend models
☐	explain the requirement for a time series to be covariance stationary and describe the significance of a series that is not stationary
☐	describe the structure of an autoregressive (AR) model of order p and calculate one- and two-period-ahead forecasts given the estimated coefficients
☐	explain how autocorrelations of the residuals can be used to test whether the autoregressive model fits the time series
☐	explain mean reversion and calculate a mean-reverting level
☐	contrast in-sample and out-of-sample forecasts and compare the forecasting accuracy of different time-series models based on the root mean squared error criterion
☐	explain the instability of coefficients of time-series models
☐	describe characteristics of random walk processes and contrast them to covariance stationary processes
☐	describe implications of unit roots for time-series analysis, explain when unit roots are likely to occur and how to test for them, and demonstrate how a time series with a unit root can be transformed so it can be analyzed with an AR model
☐	describe the steps of the unit root test for nonstationarity and explain the relation of the test to autoregressive time-series models

LEARNING OUTCOMES

Mastery	The candidate should be able to:
☐	explain how to test and correct for seasonality in a time-series model and calculate and interpret a forecasted value using an AR model with a seasonal lag
☐	explain autoregressive conditional heteroskedasticity (ARCH) and describe how ARCH models can be applied to predict the variance of a time series
☐	explain how time-series variables should be analyzed for nonstationarity and/or cointegration before use in a linear regression; and
☐	determine an appropriate time-series model to analyze a given investment problem and justify that choice

1 INTRODUCTION

As financial analysts, we often use time-series data to make investment decisions. A **time series** is a set of observations on a variable's outcomes in different time periods: the quarterly sales for a particular company during the past five years, for example, or the daily returns on a traded security. In this reading, we explore the two chief uses of time-series models: to explain the past and to predict the future of a time series. We also discuss how to estimate time-series models, and we examine how a model describing a particular time series can change over time. The following two examples illustrate the kinds of questions we might want to ask about time series.

Suppose it is the beginning of 2020 and we are managing a US-based investment portfolio that includes Swiss stocks. Because the value of this portfolio would decrease if the Swiss franc depreciates with respect to the dollar, and vice versa, holding all else constant, we are considering whether to hedge the portfolio's exposure to changes in the value of the franc. To help us in making this decision, we decide to model the time series of the franc/dollar exchange rate. Exhibit 1 shows monthly data on the franc/dollar exchange rate. The data are monthly averages of daily exchange rates. Has the exchange rate been more stable since 1987 than it was in previous years? Has the exchange rate shown a long-term trend? How can we best use past exchange rates to predict future exchange rates?

Exhibit 1: Swiss Franc/US Dollar Exchange Rate, Monthly Average of Daily Data

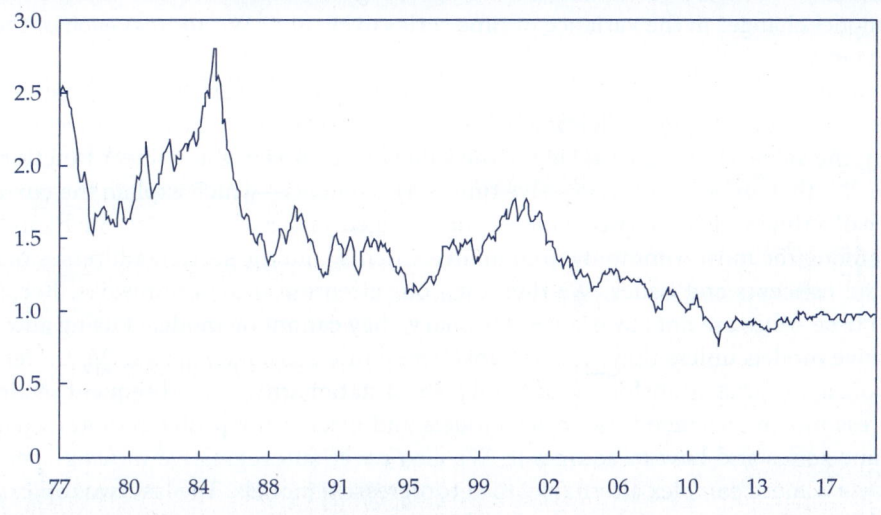

Source: Board of Governors of the Federal Reserve System.

As another example, suppose it is the beginning of 2020. We cover retail stores for a sell-side firm and want to predict retail sales for the coming year. Exhibit 2 shows monthly data on US retail sales. The data are not seasonally adjusted, hence the spikes around the holiday season at the turn of each year. Because the reported sales in the stores' financial statements are not seasonally adjusted, we model seasonally unadjusted retail sales. How can we model the trend in retail sales? How can we adjust for the extreme seasonality reflected in the peaks and troughs occurring at regular intervals? How can we best use past retail sales to predict future retail sales?

Exhibit 2: Monthly US Retail Sales

US Dollars (millions)

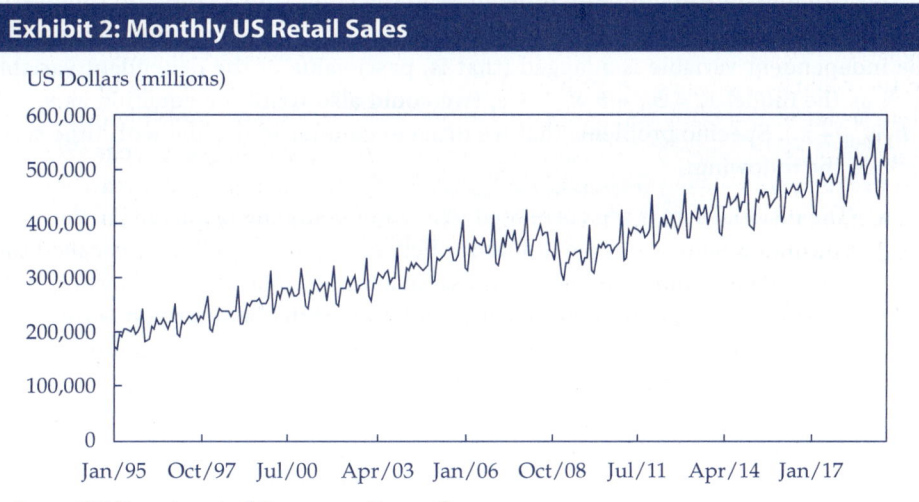

Source: US Department of Commerce, Census Bureau.

Some fundamental questions arise in time-series analysis: How do we model trends? How do we predict the future value of a time series based on its past values? How do we model seasonality? How do we choose among time-series models? And how do we model changes in the variance of time series over time? We address each of these issues in this reading.

We first describe typical challenges in applying the linear regression model to time-series data. We present linear and log-linear trend models, which describe, respectively, the value and the natural log of the value of a time series as a linear function of time. We then present autoregressive time-series models—which explain the current value of a time series in terms of one or more lagged values of the series. Such models are among the most commonly used in investments, and the section addresses many related concepts and issues. We then turn our attention to random walks. Because such time series are not covariance stationary, they cannot be modeled using autoregressive models unless they can be transformed into stationary series. We therefore explore appropriate transformations and tests of stationarity. The subsequent sections address moving-average time-series models and discuss the problem of seasonality in time series and how to address it. We also cover autoregressive moving-average models, a more complex alternative to autoregressive models. The last two topics are modeling changing variance of the error term in a time series and the consequences of regression of one time series on another when one or both time series may not be covariance stationary.

Challenges of Working with Time Series

Throughout the reading, our objective will be to apply linear regression to a given time series. Unfortunately, in working with time series, we often find that the assumptions of the linear regression model are not satisfied. To apply time-series analysis, we need to assure ourselves that the linear regression model assumptions are met. When those assumptions are not satisfied, in many cases we can transform the time series or specify the regression model differently, so that the assumptions of the linear regression model are met.

We can illustrate assumption difficulties in the context of a common time-series model, an autoregressive model. Informally, an autoregressive model is one in which the independent variable is a lagged (that is, past) value of the dependent variable, such as the model $x_t = b_0 + b_1 x_{t-1} + \varepsilon_t$ (we could also write the equation as $y_t = b_0 + b_1 y_{t-1} + \varepsilon_t$). Specific problems that we often encounter in dealing with time series include the following:

- The residual errors are correlated instead of being uncorrelated. In the calculated regression, the difference between x_t and $b_0 + b_1 x_{t-1}$ is called the residual error (ε_t). The linear regression assumes that this error term is not correlated across observations. The violation of that assumption is frequently more critical in terms of its consequences in the case of time-series models involving past values of the time series as independent variables than for other models (such as cross-sectional models) in which the dependent and independent variables are distinct. As we discussed in the reading on multiple regression, in a regression in which the dependent and independent variables are distinct, serial correlation of the errors in this model does not affect the consistency of our estimates of intercept or slope coefficients. By contrast, in an autoregressive time-series regression, such as $x_t = b_0 + b_1 x_{t-1} + \varepsilon_t$, serial correlation in the error term causes estimates of the intercept (b_0) and slope coefficient (b_1) to be inconsistent.

- The mean or variance of the time series changes over time. Regression results are invalid if we estimate an autoregressive model for a time series with mean or variance that changes over time.

Before we try to use time series for forecasting, we may need to transform the time-series model so that it is well specified for linear regression. With this objective in mind, you will observe that time-series analysis is relatively straightforward and logical.

LINEAR TREND MODELS

2

☐ | calculate and evaluate the predicted trend value for a time series, modeled as either a linear trend or a log-linear trend, given the estimated trend coefficients

Estimating a trend in a time series and using that trend to predict future values of the time series is the simplest method of forecasting. For example, we saw in Exhibit 2 that monthly US retail sales show a long-term pattern of upward movement—that is, a **trend**. In this section, we examine two types of trends—linear trends and log-linear trends—and discuss how to choose between them.

Linear Trend Models

The simplest type of trend is a **linear trend**, one in which the dependent variable changes at a constant rate with time. If a time series, y_t, has a linear trend, then we can model the series using the following regression equation:

$$y_t = b_0 + b_1 t + \varepsilon_t, t = 1, 2, \ldots, T, \tag{1}$$

where

y_t = the value of the time series at time t (value of the dependent variable)

b_0 = the y-intercept term

b_1 = the slope coefficient

t = time, the independent or explanatory variable

ε_t = a random error term

In Equation 1, the trend line, $b_0 + b_1 t$, predicts the value of the time series at time t (where t takes on a value of 1 in the first period of the sample and increases by 1 in each subsequent period). Because the coefficient b_1 is the slope of the trend line, we refer to b_1 as the trend coefficient. We can estimate the two coefficients, b_0 and b_1, using ordinary least squares, denoting the estimated coefficients as $\hat{b}_0$ and $\hat{b}_1$. Recall that ordinary least squares is an estimation method based on the criterion of minimizing the sum of a regression's squared residuals.

Now we demonstrate how to use these estimates to predict the value of the time series in a particular period. Recall that t takes on a value of 1 in Period 1. Therefore, the predicted or fitted value of y_t in Period 1 is $\hat{y}_1 = \hat{b}_0 + \hat{b}_1(1)$. Similarly, in a subsequent period—say, the sixth period—the fitted value is $\hat{y}_6 = \hat{b}_0 + \hat{b}_1(6)$. Now suppose that we want to predict the value of the time series for a period outside the sample—say, period $T + 1$. The predicted value of y_t for period $T + 1$ is

$\hat{y}_{T+1} = \hat{b}_0 + \hat{b}_1(T+1)$. For example, if $\hat{b}_0$ is 5.1 and $\hat{b}_1$ is 2, then at $t = 5$ the predicted value of y_5 is 15.1 and at $t = 6$ the predicted value of y_6 is 17.1. Note that each consecutive observation in this time series increases by $\hat{b}_1 = 2$, irrespective of the level of the series in the previous period.

EXAMPLE 1

The Trend in the US Consumer Price Index

It is January 2020. As a fixed-income analyst in the trust department of a bank, Lisette Miller is concerned about the future level of inflation and how it might affect portfolio value. Therefore, she wants to predict future inflation rates. For this purpose, she first needs to estimate the linear trend in inflation. To do so, she uses the monthly US Consumer Price Index (CPI) inflation data, expressed as an annual percentage rate, (1% is represented as 1.0) shown in Exhibit 3. The data include 228 months from January 1995 through June 2019, and the model to be estimated is $y_t = b_0 + b_1 t + \varepsilon_t$, $t = 1, 2, \ldots, 294$. The table in Exhibit 4 shows the results of estimating this equation. With 294 observations and two parameters, this model has 292 degrees of freedom. At the 0.05 significance level, the critical value for a t-statistic is 1.97. The intercept $\left(\hat{b}_0 = 2.7845\right)$ is statistically significant because the value of the t-statistic for the coefficient is well above the critical value. The trend coefficient is negative $\left(\hat{b}_1 = -0.0037\right)$, suggesting a slightly declining trend in inflation during the sample time period. However, the trend is not statistically significant because the absolute value of the t-statistic for the coefficient is below the critical value. The estimated regression equation can be written as

$y_t = 2.7845 - 0.0037t.$

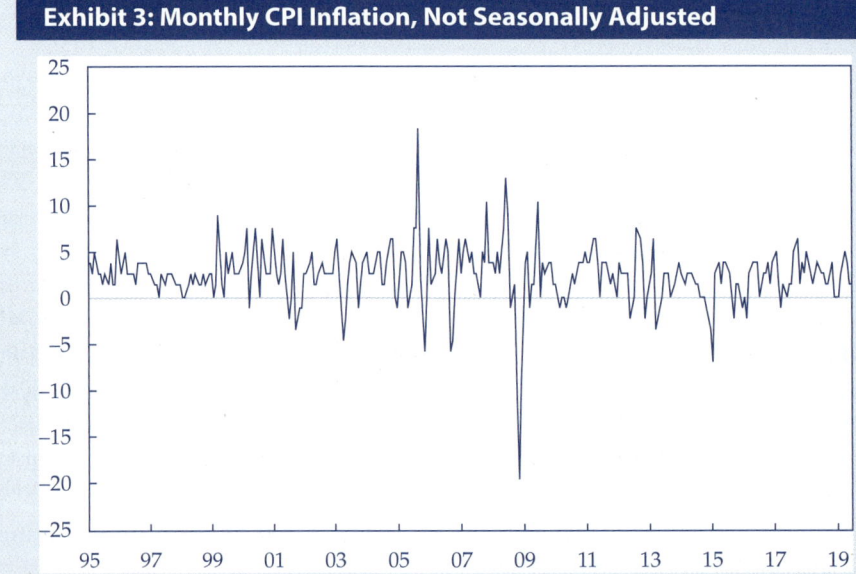

Exhibit 3: Monthly CPI Inflation, Not Seasonally Adjusted

Source: Bureau of Labor Statistics.

Exhibit 4: Estimating a Linear Trend in Inflation: Monthly Observations, January 1995–June 2019

Regression Statistics	
R^2	0.0099

Regression Statistics	
Standard error	3.1912
Observations	294
Durbin–Watson	1.2145

	Coefficient	Standard Error	t-Statistic
Intercept	2.7845	0.3732	7.4611
t (Trend)	−0.0037	0.0022	−1.68

Source: US Bureau of Labor Statistics.

Because the trend line slope is estimated to be −0.0037, Miller concludes that the linear trend model's best estimate is that the annualized rate of inflation declined at a rate of about 37 bps per month during the sample time period. The decline is not statistically significantly different from zero.

In January 1995, the first month of the sample, the predicted value of inflation is $\hat{y}_1$ = 2.7845 − 0.0037(1) = 2.7808%. In June 2019, the 294th, or last, month of the sample, the predicted value of inflation is $\hat{y}_{228}$ = 2.7845 − 0.0037(294) = 1.697%. Note, though, that these predicted values are for in-sample periods. A comparison of these values with the actual values indicates how well Miller's model fits the data; however, a main purpose of the estimated model is to predict the level of inflation for out-of-sample periods. For example, for June 2020 (12 months after the end of the sample), t = 294 + 12 = 306, and the predicted level of inflation is $\hat{y}_{306}$ = 2.7845 − 0.0037(306) = 1.6523%.

Exhibit 5 shows the inflation data along with the fitted trend. Consistent with the negative but small and statistically insignificant trend coefficient, the fitted trend line is slightly downward sloping. Note that inflation does not appear to be above or below the trend line for a long period of time. No persistent differences exist between the trend and actual inflation. The residuals (actual minus trend values) appear to be unpredictable and uncorrelated in time. Therefore, using a linear trend line to model inflation rates from 1995 through 2019 does not appear to violate the assumptions of the linear regression model. Note also that the R^2 in this model is quite low, indicating great uncertainty in the inflation forecasts from this model. In fact, the estimated model explains only 0.99% of the variation in monthly inflation. Although linear trend models have their uses, they are often inappropriate for economic data. Most economic time series reflect trends with changing slopes and/or intercepts over time. The linear trend model identifies the slope and intercept that provides the best linear fit for all past data. The model's deviation from the actual data can be greatest near the end of a data series, which can compromise forecasting accuracy. Later in this reading, we will examine whether we can build a better model of inflation than a model that uses only a trend line.

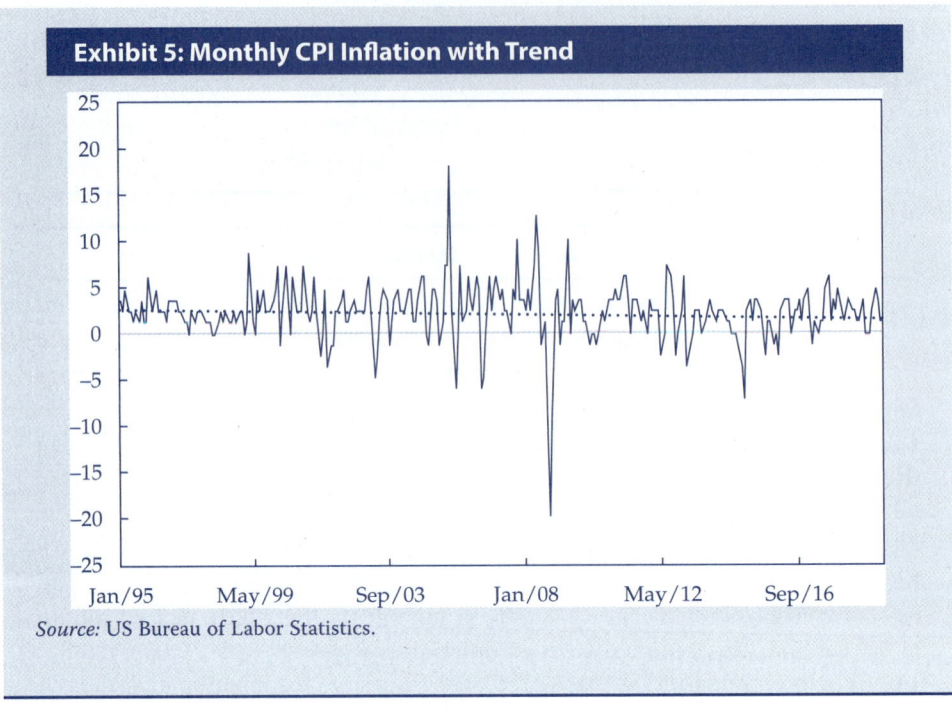

Exhibit 5: Monthly CPI Inflation with Trend

Source: US Bureau of Labor Statistics.

3

LOG-LINEAR TREND MODELS

☐ calculate and evaluate the predicted trend value for a time series, modeled as either a linear trend or a log-linear trend, given the estimated trend coefficients

☐ describe factors that determine whether a linear or a log-linear trend should be used with a particular time series and evaluate limitations of trend models

Sometimes a linear trend does not correctly model the growth of a time series. In those cases, we often find that fitting a linear trend to a time series leads to persistent rather than uncorrelated errors. If the residuals from a linear trend model are persistent, then we need to employ an alternative model satisfying the conditions of linear regression. For financial time series, an important alternative to a linear trend is a log-linear trend. Log-linear trends work well in fitting time series that have exponential growth.

Exponential growth means constant growth at a particular rate. For example, annual growth at a constant rate of 5% is exponential growth. How does exponential growth work? Suppose we describe a time series by the following equation:

$$y_t = e^{b_0 + b_1 t}, \quad t = 1, \quad 2, \quad \ldots, \quad T. \tag{2}$$

Exponential growth is growth at a constant rate $\left(e^{b_1} - 1\right)$ with continuous compounding. For instance, consider values of the time series in two consecutive periods. In Period 1, the time series has the value $y_1 = e^{b_0 + b_1 (1)}$, and in Period 2, it has the value $y_2 = e^{b_0 + b_1 (2)}$. The resulting ratio of the values of the time series in the first two periods is $y_2 / y_1 = \left(e^{b_0 + b_1 (2)}\right) / \left(e^{b_0 + b_1 (1)}\right) = e^{b_1 (1)}$. Generally, in any period t, the time series has the value $y_t = e^{b_0 + b_1 (t)}$. In period $t + 1$, the time series has the value $y_{t+1} = e^{b_0 + b_1 (t+1)}$. The ratio of the values in the periods $(t + 1)$ and t is $y_{t+1}/y_t =$

$e^{b_0+b_1(t+1)}/e^{b_0+b_1(t)} = e^{b_1(1)}$. Thus, the proportional rate of growth in the time series over two consecutive periods is always the same: $(y_{t+1} - y_t)/y_t = y_{t+1}/y_t - 1 = e^{b_1} - 1$. For example, if we use annual periods and $e^{b_1} = 1.04$ for a particular series, then that series grows by $1.04 - 1 = 0.04$, or 4% a year. Therefore, exponential growth is growth at a constant rate. Continuous compounding is a mathematical convenience that allows us to restate the equation in a form that is easy to estimate.

If we take the natural log of both sides of Equation 2, the result is the following equation:

$$\ln y_t = b_0 + b_1 t, \ t = 1, 2, \ldots, T.$$

Therefore, if a time series grows at an exponential rate, we can model the natural log of that series using a linear trend (an exponential growth rate is a compound growth rate with continuous compounding). Of course, no time series grows exactly at a constant rate. Consequently, if we want to use a **log-linear model**, we must estimate the following equation:

$$\ln y_t = b_0 + b_1 t + \varepsilon_t, \ t = 1, 2, \ldots, T. \tag{3}$$

Note that this equation is linear in the coefficients b_0 and b_1. In contrast to a linear trend model, in which the predicted trend value of y_t is $\hat{b}_0 + \hat{b}_1 t$, the predicted trend value of y_t in a log-linear trend model is $e^{\hat{b}_0 + \hat{b}_1 t}$ because $e^{\ln y_t} = y_t$.

Examining Equation 3, we see that a log-linear model predicts that $\ln y_t$ will increase by b_1 from one time period to the next. The model predicts a constant growth rate in y_t of $e^{b_1} - 1$. For example, if $b_1 = 0.05$, then the predicted growth rate of y_t in each period is $e^{0.05} - 1 = 0.051271$, or 5.13%. In contrast, the linear trend model (Equation 1) predicts that y_t grows by a constant amount from one period to the next.

Example 2 illustrates the problem of nonrandom residuals in a linear trend model, and Example 3 shows a log-linear regression fit to the same data.

EXAMPLE 2

A Linear Trend Regression for Quarterly Sales at Starbucks

In September 2019, technology analyst Ray Benedict wants to use Equation 1 to fit the data on quarterly sales for Starbucks Corporation shown in Exhibit 6. Starbucks' fiscal year ends in June. Benedict uses 74 observations on Starbucks' sales from the second quarter of fiscal year 2001 (starting in April 2001) to the third quarter of fiscal year 2019 (ending in June 2019) to estimate the linear trend regression model $y_t = b_0 + b_1 t + \varepsilon_t$, $t = 1, 2, \ldots, 74$. Exhibit 7 shows the results of estimating this equation.

Exhibit 6: Starbucks Quarterly Sales by Fiscal Year

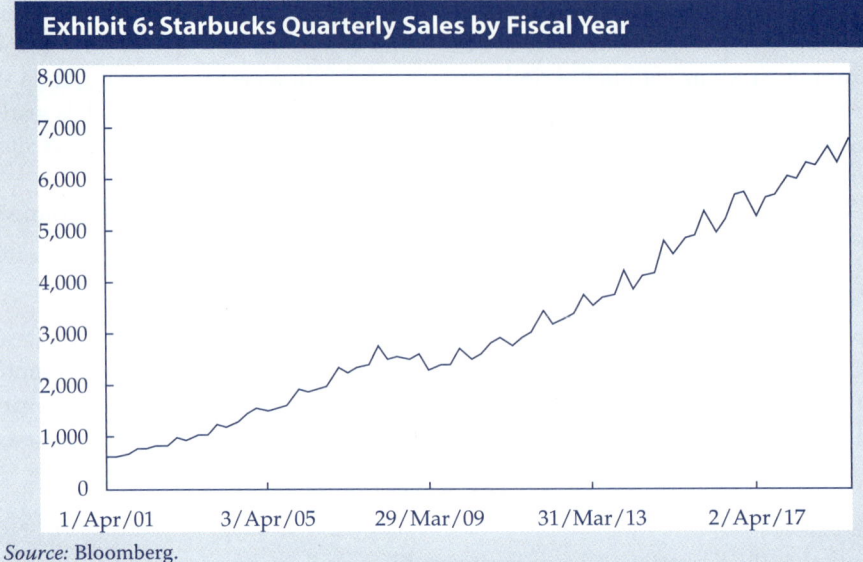

Source: Bloomberg.

Exhibit 7: Estimating a Linear Trend in Starbucks Sales

Regression Statistics

R^2	0.9603
Standard error	353.36
Observations	74
Durbin–Watson	0.40

	Coefficient	Standard Error	*t*-Statistic
Intercept	137.4213	82.99	1.6559
t (Trend)	80.2060	1.9231	41.7066

Source: Bloomberg.

At first glance, the results shown in Exhibit 7 seem quite reasonable: The trend coefficient is highly statistically significant. When Benedict plots the data on Starbucks' sales and the trend line, however, he sees a different picture. As Exhibit 8 shows, before 2008 the trend line is persistently below sales. Subsequently, until 2015, the trend line is persistently above sales and then varies somewhat thereafter.

Exhibit 8: Starbucks Quarterly Sales with Trend

Source: Bloomberg.

Recall a key assumption underlying the regression model: that the regression errors are not correlated across observations. If a trend is persistently above or below the value of the time series, however, the residuals (the difference between the time series and the trend) are serially correlated. Exhibit 9 shows the residuals (the difference between sales and the trend) from estimating a linear trend model with the raw sales data. The figure shows that the residuals are persistent: They are consistently negative from 2008 to 2015 and consistently positive from 2001 to 2008 and from 2017 to 2019.

Because of this persistent serial correlation in the errors of the trend model, using a linear trend to fit sales at Starbucks would be inappropriate, even though the R^2 of the equation is high (0.96). The assumption of uncorrelated residual errors has been violated. Because the dependent and independent variables are not distinct, as in cross-sectional regressions, this assumption violation is serious and causes us to search for a better model.

Exhibit 9: Residual from Predicting Starbucks Sales with a Trend

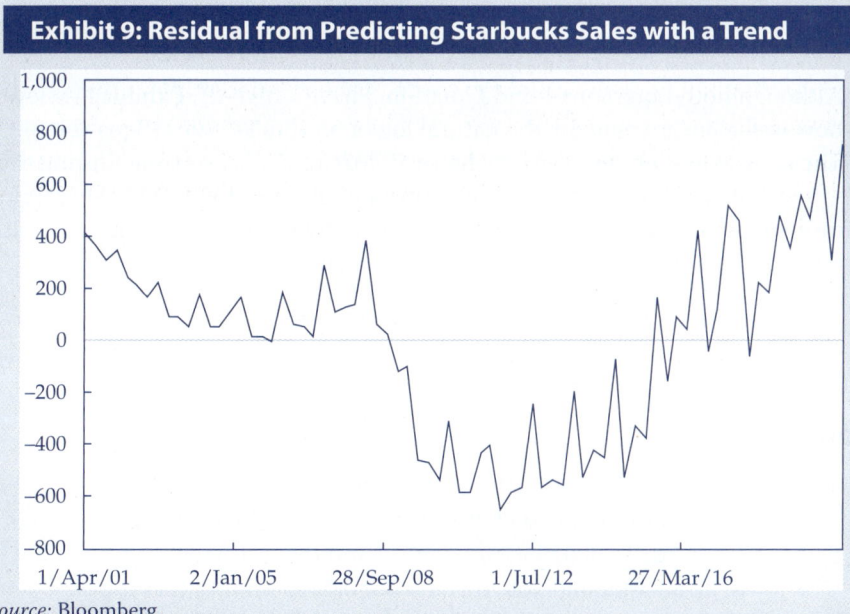

Source: Bloomberg.

EXAMPLE 3

A Log-Linear Regression for Quarterly Sales at Starbucks

1. Having rejected a linear trend model in Example 2, technology analyst Benedict now tries a different model for the quarterly sales for Starbucks Corporation from the second quarter of 2001 to the third quarter of 2019. The curvature in the data plot shown in Exhibit 6 provides a hint that an exponential curve may fit the data. Consequently, he estimates the following linear equation:

$$\ln y_t = b_0 + b_1 t + \varepsilon_t, \ t = 1, 2, \ldots, 74.$$

This equation seems to fit the sales data well. As Exhibit 10 shows, the R^2 for this equation is 0.95. An R^2 of 0.95 means that 95% of the variation in the natural log of Starbucks' sales is explained solely by a linear trend.

Exhibit 10: Estimating a Linear Trend in Lognormal Starbucks Sales

Regression Statistics	
R^2	0.9771
Standard error	0.1393
Observations	74
Durbin–Watson	0.26

	Coefficient	Standard Error	t-Statistic
Intercept	6.7617	0.0327	206.80
t (Trend)	0.0295	0.0008	36.875

Source: Compustat.

Although both Equations 1 and Equation 3 have a high R^2, Exhibit 11 shows how well a linear trend fits the natural log of Starbucks' sales (Equation 3). The natural logs of the sales data lie very close to the linear trend during the sample period, and log sales are not substantially above or below the trend for long periods of time. Thus, a log-linear trend model seems better suited for modeling Starbucks' sales than a linear trend model is.

1. Benedict wants to use the results of estimating Equation 3 to predict Starbucks' sales in the future. What is the predicted value of Starbucks' sales for the fourth quarter of 2019?

Solution

The estimated value $\hat{b}_0$ is 6.7617, and the estimated value $\hat{b}_1$ is 0.0295.

Therefore, for fourth quarter of 2019 ($t = 75$), the estimated model predicts that $\ln \hat{y}_{75} = 6.7617 + 0.0295(75) = 8.9742$ and that sales will be $\hat{y} = e^{\ln \hat{y}_{75}} = e^{8.9742} = \$7,896.7$ million. Note that a $\hat{b}_1$ of 0.0295 implies that the exponential growth rate per quarter in Starbucks' sales will be 2.99475% ($e^{0.0295} - 1 = 0.0299475$).

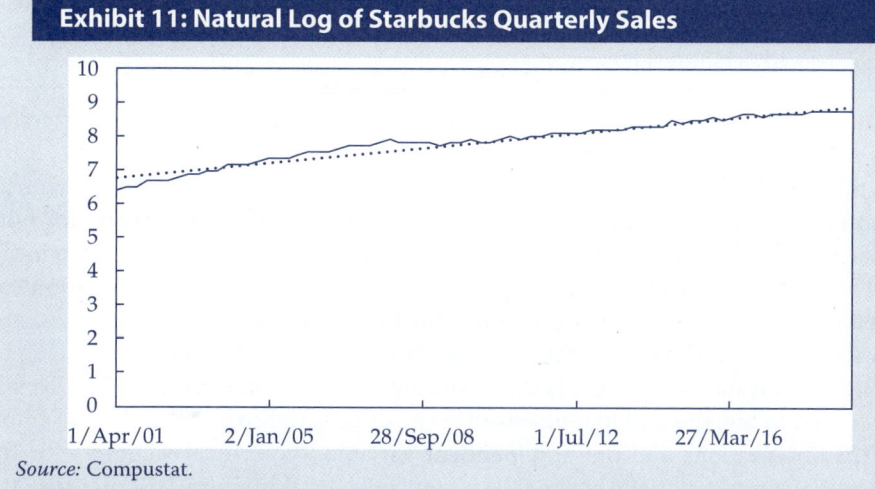

Exhibit 11: Natural Log of Starbucks Quarterly Sales

Source: Compustat.

2. How much different is the previous forecast from the prediction of the linear trend model?

Solution

Exhibit 7 showed that for the linear trend model, the estimated value of $\hat{b}_0$ is 137.4213 and the estimated value of $\hat{b}_1$ is 80.2060. Thus, if we predict Starbucks' sales for the fourth quarter of 2019 ($t = 75$) using the linear trend model, the forecast is $\hat{y}_{75} = 137.4213 + 80.2060(75) = \$6{,}152.87$ million. This forecast is far below the prediction made by the log-linear regression model. Later we will examine whether we can build a better model of Starbucks' quarterly sales than a model that uses only a log-linear trend.

TREND MODELS AND TESTING FOR CORRELATED ERRORS

4

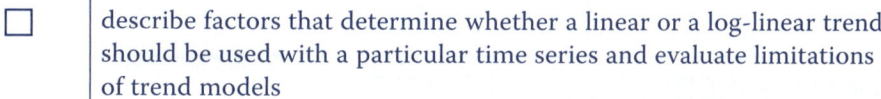

☐ describe factors that determine whether a linear or a log-linear trend should be used with a particular time series and evaluate limitations of trend models

Both the linear trend model and the log-linear trend model are single-variable regression models. If they are to be correctly specified, the regression model assumptions must be satisfied. In particular, the regression error for one period must be uncorrelated with the regression error for all other periods. In Example 2 in the previous section, we could infer an obvious violation of that assumption from a visual inspection of a plot of residuals (Exhibit 9). The log-linear trend model of Example 3 appeared to fit the data much better, but we still need to confirm that the uncorrelated errors assumption is satisfied. To address that question formally, we must carry out a Durbin–Watson test on the residuals.

LOGICAL ORDERING OF TIME-SERIES OBSERVATIONS

In contrast to cross-sectional observations, time-series observations have a logical ordering. They must be processed in chronological order of the time periods involved. For example, we should not make a prediction of the inflation rate using a CPI series in

> which the order of the observations had been scrambled, because time patterns such as growth in the independent variables can negatively affect the statistical properties of the estimated regression coefficients.

In the reading on regression analysis, we showed how to test whether regression errors are serially correlated using the Durbin–Watson statistic. For example, if the trend models shown in Examples 1 and 3 really capture the time-series behavior of inflation and the log of Starbucks' sales, then the Durbin–Watson statistic for both of those models should not differ significantly from 2.0. Otherwise, the errors in the model are either positively or negatively serially correlated, and that correlation can be used to build a better forecasting model for those time series.

In Example 1, estimating a linear trend in the monthly CPI inflation yielded a Durbin–Watson statistic of 1.09. Is this result significantly different from 2.0? To find out, we need to test the null hypothesis of no positive serial correlation. For a sample with 228 observations and one independent variable, the critical value, d_l, for the Durbin–Watson test statistic at the 0.05 significance level is above 1.77. Because the value of the Durbin–Watson statistic (1.09) is below this critical value, we can reject the hypothesis of no positive serial correlation in the errors. (Remember that significantly small values of the Durbin–Watson statistic indicate positive serial correlation; significantly large values point to negative serial correlation; here the Durbin–Watson statistic of 1.09 indicates positive serial correlation.) We can conclude that a regression equation that uses a linear trend to model inflation has positive serial correlation in the errors. We will need a different kind of regression model because this one violates the least squares assumption of no serial correlation in the errors.

In Example 3, estimating a linear trend with the natural logarithm of sales for the Starbucks example yielded a Durbin–Watson statistic of 0.12. Suppose we wish to test the null hypothesis of no positive serial correlation. The critical value, d_l, is above 1.60 at the 0.05 significance level. The value of the Durbin–Watson statistic (0.12) is below this critical value, so we can reject the null hypothesis of no positive serial correlation in the errors. We can conclude that a regression equation that uses a trend to model the log of Starbucks' quarterly sales has positive serial correlation in the errors. So, for this series as well, we need to build a different kind of model.

Overall, we conclude that the trend models sometimes have the limitation that errors are serially correlated. Existence of serial correlation suggests that we can build better forecasting models for such time series than trend models.

5   AR TIME-SERIES MODELS AND COVARIANCE-STATIONARY SERIES

☐ | explain the requirement for a time series to be covariance stationary and describe the significance of a series that is not stationary

A key feature of the log-linear model's depiction of time series, and a key feature of time series in general, is that current-period values are related to previous-period values. For example, Starbucks' sales for the current period are related to its sales in the previous period. An **autoregressive model (AR)**, a time series regressed on its own past values, represents this relationship effectively. When we use this model, we can drop the normal notation of y as the dependent variable and x as the independent variable because we no longer have that distinction to make. Here we simply use x_t. For example, Equation 4 shows a first-order autoregression, AR(1), for the variable x_t:

$$x_t = b_0 + b_1 x_{t-1} + \varepsilon_t. \tag{4}$$

Thus, in an AR(1) model, we use only the most recent past value of x_t to predict the current value of x_t. In general, a pth-order autoregression, AR(p), for the variable x_t is shown by

$$x_t = b_0 + b_1 x_{t-1} + b_2 x_{t-2} + \ldots + b_p x_{t-p} + \varepsilon_t. \tag{5}$$

In this equation, p past values of x_t are used to predict the current value of x_t. In the next section, we discuss a key assumption of time-series models that include lagged values of the dependent variable as independent variables.

Covariance-Stationary Series

Note that the independent variable (x_{t-1}) in Equation 4 is a random variable. This fact may seem like a mathematical subtlety, but it is not. If we use ordinary least squares to estimate Equation 4 when we have a randomly distributed independent variable that is a lagged value of the dependent variable, our statistical inference may be invalid. To make a valid statistical inference, we must make a key assumption in time-series analysis: We must assume that the time series we are modeling is **covariance stationary**.[1]

What does it mean for a time series to be covariance stationary? The basic idea is that a time series is covariance stationary if its properties, such as mean and variance, do not change over time. A covariance stationary series must satisfy three principal requirements. First, the expected value of the time series must be constant and finite in all periods: $E(y_t) = \mu$ and $|\mu| < \infty$, $t = 1, 2, \ldots, T$ (for this first requirement, we use the absolute value to rule out the case in which the mean is negative without limit—i.e., minus infinity). Second, the variance of the time series must be constant and finite in all periods. Third, the covariance of the time series with itself for a fixed number of periods in the past or future must be constant and finite in all periods. The second and third requirements can be summarized as follows:

$$\text{cov}(y_t, y_{t-s}) = \lambda_s; |\lambda_s| < \infty; t = 1, 2, \ldots, T; s = 0, \pm 1, \pm 2, \ldots, \pm T,$$

where λ signifies a constant. (Note that when s in this equation equals 0, this equation imposes the condition that the variance of the time series is finite, because the covariance of a random variable with itself is its variance: $\text{cov}(y_t, y_t) = \text{var}(y_t)$.) What happens if a time series is not covariance stationary but we model it using Equation 4? The estimation results will have no economic meaning. For a non-covariance-stationary time series, estimating the regression in Equation 4 will yield spurious results. In particular, the estimate of b_1 will be biased, and any hypothesis tests will be invalid.

How can we tell if a time series is covariance stationary? We can often answer this question by looking at a plot of the time series. If the plot shows roughly the same mean and variance over time without any significant seasonality, then we may want to assume that the time series is covariance stationary.

Some of the time series we looked at in the exhibits appear to be covariance stationary. For example, the inflation data shown in Exhibit 3 appear to have roughly the same mean and variance over the sample period. Many of the time series one encounters in business and investments, however, are not covariance stationary. For example, many time series appear to grow (or decline) steadily over time and thus have a mean that is nonconstant, which implies that they are nonstationary. As an example, the time series of quarterly sales in Exhibit 8 clearly shows the mean increasing as time passes. Thus, Starbucks' quarterly sales are not covariance stationary (in

---

1 "Weakly stationary" is a synonym for covariance stationary. Note that the terms "stationary" and "stationarity" are often used to mean "covariance-stationary" or "covariance stationarity," respectively. You may also encounter the more restrictive concept of "strictly" stationary, which has little practical application. For details, see Diebold (2008).

general, any time series accurately described with a linear or log-linear trend model is not covariance stationary, although a transformation of the original series might be covariance stationary). Macroeconomic time series such as those relating to income and consumption are often strongly trending as well. A time series with seasonality (regular patterns of movement with the year) also has a nonconstant mean, as do other types of time series that we discuss later (in particular, random walks are not covariance stationary).

Exhibit 2 showed that monthly retail sales (not seasonally adjusted) are also not covariance stationary. Sales in December are always much higher than sales in other months (these are the regular large peaks), and sales in January are always much lower (these are the regular large drops after the December peaks). On average, sales also increase over time, so the mean of sales is not constant.

Later we will show that we can often transform a nonstationary time series into a stationary time series. But whether a stationary time series is original or transformed, a warning is necessary: Stationarity in the past does not guarantee stationarity in the future. There is always the possibility that a well-specified model will fail when the state of the world changes and yields a different underlying model that generates the time series.

6 DETECTING SERIALLY CORRELATED ERRORS IN AN AR MODEL

☐ describe the structure of an autoregressive (AR) model of order p and calculate one- and two-period-ahead forecasts given the estimated coefficients

☐ explain how autocorrelations of the residuals can be used to test whether the autoregressive model fits the time series

We can estimate an autoregressive model using ordinary least squares if the time series is covariance stationary and the errors are uncorrelated. Unfortunately, our previous test for serial correlation, the Durbin–Watson statistic, is invalid when the independent variables include past values of the dependent variable. Therefore, for most time-series models, we cannot use the Durbin–Watson statistic. Fortunately, we can use other tests to determine whether the errors in a time-series model are serially correlated. One such test reveals whether the autocorrelations of the error term are significantly different from 0. This test is a *t*-test involving a residual autocorrelation and the standard error of the residual autocorrelation. As background for the test, we next discuss autocorrelation in general before moving to residual autocorrelation.

The **autocorrelations** of a time series are the correlations of that series with its own past values. The order of the correlation is given by k, where k represents the number of periods lagged. When $k = 1$, the autocorrelation shows the correlation of the variable in one period with its occurrence in the previous period. For example, the ***k*th-order autocorrelation** (ρ_k) is

$$\rho_k = \frac{\text{cov}\,(x_t, x_{t-k})}{\sigma_x^2} = \frac{E\left[\,(x_t - \mu)\,(x_{t-k} - \mu)\,\right]}{\sigma_x^2},$$

where E stands for the expected value. Note that we have the relationship cov(x_t, x_{t-k}) $\leq \sigma_x^2$, with equality holding when $k = 0$. This means that the absolute value of ρ_k is less than or equal to 1.

Of course, we can never directly observe the autocorrelations, ρ_k. Instead, we must estimate them. Thus, we replace the expected value of x_t, μ, with its estimated value, $\bar{x}$, to compute the estimated autocorrelations. The kth-order estimated autocorrelation of the time series x_t, which we denote $\hat{\rho}_k$, is

$$\hat{\rho}_k = \frac{\sum_{t=k+1}^{T} \left[(x_t - \bar{x}) \, (x_{t-k} - \bar{x}) \right]}{\sum_{t=1}^{T} (x_t - \bar{x})^2}.$$

Analogous to the definition of autocorrelations for a time series, we can define the autocorrelations of the error term for a time-series model as[2]

$$\rho_{\varepsilon,k} = \frac{\text{cov} \left(\varepsilon_t, \varepsilon_{t-k} \right)}{\sigma_\varepsilon^2}$$

$$= \frac{E \left[(\varepsilon_t - 0) \, (\varepsilon_{t-k} - 0) \right]}{\sigma_\varepsilon^2}$$

$$= \frac{E \left(\varepsilon_t \varepsilon_{t-k} \right)}{\sigma_\varepsilon^2}.$$

We assume that the expected value of the error term in a time-series model is 0.[3]

We can determine whether we are using the correct time-series model by testing whether the autocorrelations of the error term (**error autocorrelations**) differ significantly from 0. If they do, the model is not specified correctly. We estimate the error autocorrelation using the sample autocorrelations of the residuals (**residual autocorrelations**) and their sample variance.

A test of the null hypothesis that an error autocorrelation at a specified lag equals 0 is based on the residual autocorrelation for that lag and the standard error of the residual correlation, which is equal to $1/\sqrt{T}$, where T is the number of observations in the time series (Diebold 2008). Thus, if we have 100 observations in a time series, the standard error for each of the estimated autocorrelations is 0.1. We can compute the t-test of the null hypothesis that the error correlation at a particular lag equals 0 by dividing the residual autocorrelation at that lag by its standard error $\left(1/\sqrt{T} \right)$.

How can we use information about the error autocorrelations to determine whether an autoregressive time-series model is correctly specified? We can use a simple three-step method. First, estimate a particular autoregressive model—say, an AR(1) model. Second, compute the autocorrelations of the residuals from the model.[4] Third, test to see whether the residual autocorrelations differ significantly from 0. If significance tests show that the residual autocorrelations differ significantly from 0, the model is not correctly specified; we may need to modify it in ways that we will discuss shortly.[5] We now present an example to demonstrate how this three-step method works.

---

2 Whenever we refer to autocorrelation without qualification, we mean autocorrelation of the time series itself rather than autocorrelation of the error term or residuals.

3 This assumption is similar to the one made in earlier coverage of regression analysis about the expected value of the error term.

4 We can compute these residual autocorrelations easily with most statistical software packages. In Microsoft Excel, for example, to compute the first-order residual autocorrelation, we compute the correlation of the residuals from Observations 1 through $T - 1$ with the residuals from Observations 2 through T.

5 Often, econometricians use additional tests for the significance of residual autocorrelations. For example, the Box–Pierce Q-statistic is frequently used to test the joint hypothesis that all autocorrelations of the residuals are equal to 0. For further discussion, see Diebold (2008).

EXAMPLE 4

Predicting Gross Margins for Intel Corporation

1. Analyst Melissa Jones decides to use a time-series model to predict Intel Corporation's gross margin [(Sales – Cost of goods sold)/Sales] using quarterly data from the first quarter of 1999 through the second quarter of 2019. She does not know the best model for gross margin but believes that the current-period value will be related to the previous-period value. She decides to start out with a first-order autoregressive model, AR(1): Gross margin$_t$ = b_0 + b_1(Gross margin$_{t-1}$) + ε_t. Her observations on the dependent variable are 1Q 2003 through 2Q 2019. Exhibit 12 shows the results of estimating this AR(1) model, along with the autocorrelations of the residuals from that model.

Exhibit 12: Autoregression: AR(1) Model Gross Margin of Intel Quarterly Observations, January 2003–June 2019

Regression Statistics

R^2	0.5746
Standard error	0.03002
Observations	65
Durbin–Watson	1.743

	Coefficient	Standard Error	t-Statistic
Intercept	0.1513	0.0480	3.15
Gross margin$_{t-1}$	0.7462	0.0809	9.2236

Autocorrelations of the Residual

Lag	Autocorrelation	Standard Error	t-Statistic
1	0.1308	0.1240	1.0545
2	−0.2086	0.1240	−1.6818
3	0.0382	0.1240	0.3080
4	0.0608	0.1240	0.4903

Source: Bloomberg.

The first thing to note about Exhibit 12 is that both the intercept ($\hat{b}_0$ = 0.1513) and the coefficient on the first lag ($\hat{b}_1$ = 0.7462) of the gross margin are highly significant in the regression equation. The first lag of a time series is the value of the time series in the previous period. The *t*-statistic for the intercept is about 3.2, whereas the *t*-statistic for the first lag of the gross margin is more than 9. With 65 observations and two parameters, this model has 63 degrees of freedom. At the 0.05 significance level, the critical value for a *t*-statistic is about 2.0. Therefore, Jones must reject the null hypotheses that the intercept is equal to 0 (b_0 = 0) and the coefficient on the first lag is equal to 0 (b_1 = 0) in favor of the alternative hypothesis that the coefficients, individually, are not equal to 0. But are these statistics valid? Although the Durbin–Watson statistic is presented in Exhibit 12, it cannot be used to test serial correlation when the independent variables include past values of the dependent variable. The correct approach is to test whether the residuals from this model are serially correlated.

At the bottom of Exhibit 12, the first four autocorrelations of the residual are displayed along with the standard error and the t-statistic for each of those autocorrelations.[6] The sample has 65 observations, so the standard error for each of the autocorrelations is $1/\sqrt{65} = 0.1240$. Exhibit 12 shows that none of the first four autocorrelations has a t-statistic larger than 1.6818 in absolute value. Therefore, Jones can conclude that none of these autocorrelations differs significantly from 0. Consequently, she can assume that the residuals are not serially correlated and that the model is correctly specified, and she can validly use ordinary least squares to estimate the parameters and the parameters' standard errors in the autoregressive model (for other tests for serial correlation of residuals, see Diebold 2008).

Now that Jones has concluded that this model is correctly specified, how can she use it to predict Intel's gross margin in the next period? The estimated equation is Gross margin$_t$ = 0.1513 + 0.7462(Gross margin$_{t-1}$) + ε_t. The expected value of the error term is 0 in any period. Therefore, this model predicts that gross margin in period $t + 1$ will be Gross margin$_{t+1}$ = 0.1513 + 0.7462(Gross margin$_t$). For example, if gross margin is 55% in this quarter (0.55), the model predicts that in the next quarter gross margin will increase to 0.1513 + 0.7462(0.55) = 0.5617, or 56.17%. However, if gross margin is currently 65% (0.65), the model predicts that in the next quarter, gross margin will fall to 0.1513 + 0.7462(0.65) = 0.6363, or 63.63%. As we show in the following section, the model predicts that gross margin will increase if it is below a certain level (59.61%) and decrease if it is above that level.

MEAN REVERSION AND MULTIPERIOD FORECASTS

7

☐   explain mean reversion and calculate a mean-reverting level

☐   describe the structure of an autoregressive (AR) model of order p and calculate one- and two-period-ahead forecasts given the estimated coefficients

We say that a time series shows **mean reversion** if it tends to fall when its level is above its mean and rise when its level is below its mean. Much like the temperature in a room controlled by a thermostat, a mean-reverting time series tends to return to its long-term mean. How can we determine the value that the time series tends toward? If a time series is currently at its mean-reverting level, then the model predicts that the value of the time series will be the same in the next period. At its mean-reverting level, we have the relationship $x_{t+1} = x_t$. For an AR(1) model ($x_{t+1} = b_0 + b_1 x_t$), the equality $x_{t+1} = x_t$ implies the level $x_t = b_0 + b_1 x_t$ or that the mean-reverting level, x_t, is given by

---

6 For seasonally unadjusted data, analysts often compute the same number of autocorrelations as there are observations in a year (for example, four for quarterly data). The number of autocorrelations computed also often depends on sample size, as discussed in Diebold (2008).

$$x_t = \frac{b_0}{1 - b_1}.$$

So the AR(1) model predicts that the time series will stay the same if its current value is $b_0/(1 - b_1)$, increase if its current value is below $b_0/(1 - b_1)$, and decrease if its current value is above $b_0/(1 - b_1)$.

In the case of gross margins for Intel, the mean-reverting level for the model shown in Exhibit 12 is $0.1513/(1 - 0.7462) = 0.5961$. If the current gross margin is above 0.5961, the model predicts that the gross margin will fall in the next period. If the current gross margin is below 0.5961, the model predicts that the gross margin will rise in the next period. As we will discuss later, all covariance-stationary time series have a finite mean-reverting level.

Multiperiod Forecasts and the Chain Rule of Forecasting

Often, financial analysts want to make forecasts for more than one period. For example, we might want to use a quarterly sales model to predict sales for a company for each of the next four quarters. To use a time-series model to make forecasts for more than one period, we must examine how to make multiperiod forecasts using an AR(1) model. The one-period-ahead forecast of x_t from an AR(1) model is as follows:

$$\hat{x}_{t+1} = \hat{b}_0 + \hat{b}_1 x_t \tag{6}$$

If we want to forecast x_{t+2} using an AR(1) model, our forecast will be based on

$$\hat{x}_{t+2} = \hat{b}_0 + \hat{b}_1 x_{t+1} \tag{7}$$

Unfortunately, we do not know x_{t+1} in period t, so we cannot use Equation 7 directly to make a two-period-ahead forecast. We can, however, use our forecast of x_{t+1} and the AR(1) model to make a prediction of x_{t+2}. The **chain rule of forecasting** is a process in which the next period's value, predicted by the forecasting equation, is substituted into the equation to give a predicted value two periods ahead. Using the chain rule of forecasting, we can substitute the predicted value of x_{t+1} into Equation 7 to get $\hat{x}_{t+2} = \hat{b}_0 + \hat{b}_1 \hat{x}_{t+1}$. We already know $\hat{x}_{t+1}$ from our one-period-ahead forecast in Equation 6. Now we have a simple way of predicting x_{t+2}.

Multiperiod forecasts are more uncertain than single-period forecasts because each forecast period has uncertainty. For example, in forecasting x_{t+2}, we first have the uncertainty associated with forecasting x_{t+1} using x_t, and then we have the uncertainty associated with forecasting x_{t+2} using the forecast of x_{t+1}. In general, the more periods a forecast has, the more uncertain it is. Note that if a forecasting model is well specified, the prediction errors from the model will not be serially correlated. If the prediction errors for each period are not serially correlated, then the variance of a multiperiod forecast will be higher than the variance of a single-period forecast.

EXAMPLE 5

Multiperiod Prediction of Intel's Gross Margin

Suppose that at the beginning of 2020, we want to predict Intel's gross margin in two periods using the model shown in Exhibit 12. Assume that Intel's gross margin in the current period is 63%. The one-period-ahead forecast of Intel's gross margin from this model is 0.6214 = 0.1513 + 0.7462(0.63). By substituting the one-period-ahead forecast, 0.6214, back into the regression equation, we can derive the following two-period-ahead forecast: 0.6150 = 0.1513 + 0.7462(0.6214). Therefore, if the current gross margin for Intel is 63%, the model predicts that Intel's gross margin in two quarters will be 61.50%.

Modeling US CPI Inflation

Analyst Lisette Miller has been directed to build a time-series model for monthly US inflation. Inflation and expectations about inflation, of course, have a significant effect on bond returns. For a 24-year period beginning January 1995 and ending December 2018, she selects as data the annualized monthly percentage change in the CPI. Which model should Miller use?

The process of model selection parallels that of Example 4 relating to Intel's gross margins. The first model Miller estimates is an AR(1) model, using the previous month's inflation rate as the independent variable: $\text{Inflation}_t = b_0 + b_1(\text{Inflation}_{t-1}) + \varepsilon_t, t = 1, 2, \ldots, 359$. To estimate this model, she uses monthly CPI inflation data from January 1995 to December 2018 ($t = 1$ denotes February 1995). Exhibit 13 shows the results of estimating this model.

Exhibit 13: Monthly CPI Inflation at an Annual Rate: AR(1) Model— Monthly Observations, February 1995–December 2018

Regression Statistics	
R^2	0.1586
Standard error	2.9687
Observations	287
Durbin–Watson	1.8442

	Coefficient	Standard Error	t-Statistic
Intercept	1.3346	0.2134	6.2540
Inflation_{t-1}	0.3984	0.0544	7.3235

Autocorrelations of the Residual			
Lag	Autocorrelation	Standard Error	t-Statistic
1	0.0777	0.0590	1.3175
2	−0.1653	0.0590	−2.8013
3	−0.1024	0.0590	−1.7362
4	−0.0845	0.0590	1.4324

Source: US Bureau of Labor Statistics.

As Exhibit 13 shows, both the intercept ($\hat{b}_0 = 1.3346$) and the coefficient on the first lagged value of inflation ($\hat{b}_1 = 0.3984$) are highly statistically significant, with large t-statistics. With 287 observations and two parameters, this model has 285 degrees of freedom. The critical value for a t-statistic at the 0.05 significance level is about 1.97. Therefore, Miller can reject the individual null hypotheses that the intercept is equal to 0 ($b_0 = 0$) and the coefficient on the first lag is equal to 0 ($b_1 = 0$) in favor of the alternative hypothesis that the coefficients, individually, are not equal to 0.

Are these statistics valid? Miller will know when she tests whether the residuals from this model are serially correlated. With 287 observations in this sample, the standard error for each of the estimated autocorrelations is $1/\sqrt{287} = 0.0590$. The critical value for the t-statistic is 1.97. Because the second estimated autocorrelation has t-statistic larger than 1.97 in absolute value, Miller concludes that the autocorrelations are significantly different from 0. This model is thus misspecified because the residuals are serially correlated.

If the residuals in an autoregressive model are serially correlated, Miller can eliminate the correlation by estimating an autoregressive model with more lags of the dependent variable as explanatory variables. Exhibit 14 shows the result of estimating a second time-series model, an AR(2) model using the same data as in the analysis shown in Exhibit 13. With 286 observations and three parameters, this model has 283 degrees of freedom. Because the degrees of freedom are almost the same as those for the estimates shown in Exhibit 13, the critical value of the t-statistic at the 0.05 significance level also is almost the same (1.97). If she estimates the equation with two lags—Inflation$_t = b_0 + b_1$(Inflation$_{t-1}$) + b_2(Inflation$_{t-2}$) + ε_t—Miller finds that all three of the coefficients in the regression model (an intercept and the coefficients on two lags of the dependent variable) differ significantly from 0. The bottom portion of Exhibit 14 shows that none of the first four autocorrelations of the residual has a t-statistic greater in absolute value than the critical value of 1.97. Therefore, Miller fails to reject the hypothesis that the individual autocorrelations of the residual equal 0. She concludes that this model is correctly specified because she finds no evidence of serial correlation in the residuals.

Exhibit 14: Monthly CPI Inflation at an Annual Rate: AR(2) Model—Monthly Observations, March 1995–December 2018

Regression Statistics	
R^2	0.1907
Standard error	2.9208
Observations	286
Durbin–Watson	1.9934

	Coefficient	Standard Error	t-Statistic
Intercept	1.5996	0.2245	7.1252
Inflation$_{t-1}$	0.4759	0.0583	8.1636
Inflation$_{t-2}$	−0.1964	0.0583	−3.368

Autocorrelations of the Residual			
Lag	Autocorrelation	Standard Error	t-Statistic
1	0.0032	0.0591	0.0536
2	0.0042	0.0591	0.0707
3	−0.0338	0.0591	−0.5696
4	0.0155	0.0591	0.2623

Source: US Bureau of Labor Statistics.

1. The analyst selected an AR(2) model because the residuals from the AR(1) model were serially correlated. Suppose that in a given month, inflation had been 4% at an annual rate in the previous month and 3% in the month

before that. What would be the difference in the analyst forecast of inflation for that month if she had used an AR(1) model instead of the AR(2) model?

Solution

The AR(1) model shown in Exhibit 13 predicted that inflation in the next month would be 1.3346 + 0.3984(4) = 2.93%, approximately, whereas the AR(2) model shown in Exhibit 14 predicts that inflation in the next month will be 1.5996 + 0.4759(4) − 0.1964(3) = 2.91% approximately. If the analyst had used the incorrect AR(1) model, she would have predicted inflation to be 2 bps higher (2.93% versus 2.91%) than when using the AR(2) model. Although in this case the difference in the predicted inflation is actually very small, this kind of scenario illustrates that using an incorrect forecast could adversely affect the quality of her company's investment choices.

COMPARING FORECAST MODEL PERFORMANCE   8

☐ | contrast in-sample and out-of-sample forecasts and compare the forecasting accuracy of different time-series models based on the root mean squared error criterion

One way to compare the forecast performance of two models is to compare the variance of the forecast errors that the two models make. The model with the smaller forecast error variance will be the more accurate model, and it will also have the smaller standard error of the time-series regression. (This standard error usually is reported directly in the output for the time-series regression.)

In comparing forecast accuracy among models, we must distinguish between in-sample forecast errors and out-of-sample forecast errors. **In-sample forecast errors** are the residuals from a fitted time-series model. For example, when we estimated a linear trend with raw inflation data from January 1995 to December 2018, the in-sample forecast errors were the residuals from January 1995 to December 2018. If we use this model to predict inflation outside this period, the differences between actual and predicted inflation are **out-of-sample forecast errors**.

EXAMPLE 7

In-Sample Forecast Comparisons of US CPI Inflation

In Example 6, the analyst compared an AR(1) forecasting model of monthly US inflation with an AR(2) model of monthly US inflation and decided that the AR(2) model was preferable. Exhibit 13 showed that the standard error from the AR(1) model of inflation is 2.9687, and Exhibit 14 showed that the standard error from the AR(2) model is 2.9208. Therefore, the AR(2) model had a lower in-sample forecast error variance than the AR(1) model had, which is consistent with our belief that the AR(2) model was preferable. Its standard error is 2.9208/2.9687 = 98.39% of the forecast error of the AR(1) model.

Often, we want to compare the forecasting accuracy of different models after the sample period for which they were estimated. We wish to compare the out-of-sample forecast accuracy of the models. Out-of-sample forecast accuracy is important because the future is always out of sample. Although professional forecasters distinguish between out-of-sample and in-sample forecasting performance, many articles that analysts read contain only in-sample forecast evaluations. Analysts should be aware that out-of-sample performance is critical for evaluating a forecasting model's real-world contribution.

Typically, we compare the out-of-sample forecasting performance of forecasting models by comparing their **root mean squared error (RMSE)**, which is the square root of the average squared error. The model with the smallest RMSE is judged the most accurate. The following example illustrates the computation and use of RMSE in comparing forecasting models.

EXAMPLE 8

Out-of-Sample Forecast Comparisons of US CPI Inflation

1. Suppose we want to compare the forecasting accuracy of the AR(1) and AR(2) models of US inflation estimated over 1995 to 2018, using data on US inflation from January 2019 to September 2019.

Exhibit 15: Out-of-Sample Forecast Error Comparisons: January 2019–September 2019 US CPI Inflation (Annualized)

Date	Infl(t)	Infl($t-1$)	Infl($t-2$)	AR(1) Error	Squared Error	AR(2) Error	Squared Error
2019							
January	0.0000	0.0000	0.0000	0.1335	0.0178	−1.6000	2.5599
February	2.4266	0.0000	0.0000	−2.2931	5.2585	0.8266	0.6833
March	4.9070	2.4266	0.0000	−3.8068	14.4916	2.1522	4.6320
April	3.6600	4.9070	2.4266	−1.5716	2.4699	0.2014	0.0406
May	1.2066	3.6600	4.9070	0.3850	0.1482	−1.1714	1.3722
June	1.2066	1.2066	3.6600	−0.5924	0.3510	−0.2488	0.0619
July	3.6600	1.2066	1.2066	−3.0458	9.2770	1.7228	2.9680
August	1.2066	3.6600	1.2066	0.3850	0.1482	−1.8982	3.6030
September	0.0000	1.2066	3.6600	0.6142	0.3772	−1.4554	2.1181
				Average	3.6155	Average	2.0043
				RMSE	1.9014	RMSE	1.4157

Note: Any apparent discrepancies between error and squared error results are due to rounding.

Source: US Bureau of Labor Statistics.

Solution

For each month from January 2019 to September 2019, the first column of numbers in Exhibit 15 shows the actual annualized inflation rate during the month. The second and third columns show the rate of inflation in the previous two months. The fourth column shows the out-of-sample errors (Actual – Forecast) from the AR(1) model shown in Exhibit 13. The fifth column shows the squared errors from the AR(1) model. The sixth column shows the out-of-sample errors from the AR(2) model shown in Exhibit 14. The final column shows the squared errors from the AR(2) model. The bottom of the table displays the average squared error and the RMSE. According to these measures, the AR(2) model was slightly more accurate than the AR(1) model in its out-of-sample forecasts of inflation from January 2019 to September 2019. The RMSE from the AR(2) model was only 1.4157/1.9014

= 74.46% as large as the RMSE from the AR(1) model. Therefore, the AR(2) model was more accurate both in sample and out of sample. Of course, this was a small sample to use in evaluating out-of-sample forecasting performance. Sometimes, an analyst may have conflicting information about whether to choose an AR(1) or an AR(2) model. We must also consider regression coefficient stability. We will continue the comparison between these two models in the following section.

INSTABILITY OF REGRESSION COEFFICIENTS

9

☐ | explain the instability of coefficients of time-series models

One of the important issues an analyst faces in modeling a time series is the sample period to use. The estimates of regression coefficients of the time-series model can change substantially across different sample periods used for estimating the model. Often, the regression coefficient estimates of a time-series model estimated using an earlier sample period can be quite different from those of a model estimated using a later sample period. Similarly, the estimates can be different between models estimated using relatively shorter and longer sample periods. Further, the choice of model for a particular time series can also depend on the sample period. For example, an AR(1) model may be appropriate for the sales of a company in one particular sample period, but an AR(2) model may be necessary for an earlier or later sample period (or for a longer or shorter sample period). Thus, the choice of a sample period is an important decision in modeling a financial time series.

Unfortunately, there is usually no clear-cut basis in economic or financial theory for determining whether to use data from a longer or shorter sample period to estimate a time-series model. We can get some guidance, however, if we remember that our models are valid only for covariance-stationary time series. For example, we should not combine data from a period when exchange rates were fixed with data from a period when exchange rates were floating. The exchange rates in these two periods would not likely have the same variance because exchange rates are usually much more volatile under a floating-rate regime than when rates are fixed. Similarly, many US analysts consider it inappropriate to model US inflation or interest-rate behavior since the 1960s as a part of one sample period, because the Federal Reserve had distinct policy regimes during this period. A simple way to determine appropriate samples for time-series estimation is to look at graphs of the data to see whether the time series looks stationary before estimation begins. If we know that a government policy changed on a specific date, we might also test whether the time-series relation was the same before and after that date.

In the following example, we illustrate how the choice of a longer versus a shorter period can affect the decision of whether to use, for example, a first- or second-order time-series model. We then show how the choice of the time-series model (and the associated regression coefficients) affects our forecast. Finally, we discuss which sample period, and accordingly which model and corresponding forecast, is appropriate for the time series analyzed in the example.

EXAMPLE 9

Instability in Time-Series Models of US Inflation

In Example 6, the analyst Lisette Miller concluded that US CPI inflation should be modeled as an AR(2) time series. A colleague examined her results and questioned estimating one time-series model for inflation in the United States since 1984, given that the Federal Reserve responded aggressively to the financial crisis that emerged in 2007. He argues that the inflation time series from 1995 to 2018 has two **regimes** or underlying models generating the time series: one running from 1995 through 2007 and another starting in 2008. Therefore, the colleague suggests that Miller estimate a new time-series model for US inflation starting in 2008. Because of his suggestion, Miller first estimates an AR(1) model for inflation using data for a sample period from 2008 to 2018. Exhibit 16 shows her AR(1) estimates.

Exhibit 16: Autoregression: AR(1) Model Monthly CPI Inflation at an Annual Rate, January 2008–December 2018

Regression Statistics	
R^2	0.2536
Standard error	3.0742
Observations	132
Durbin–Watson	1.8164

	Coefficient	Standard Error	t-Statistic
Intercept	0.8431	0.2969	2.8397
Inflation$_{t-1}$	0.5036	0.0758	6.6438

Autocorrelations of the Residual			
Lag	Autocorrelation	Standard Error	t-Statistic
1	0.0999	0.087	1.1479
2	−0.1045	0.087	−1.2015
3	−0.1568	0.087	−1.8051
4	0.0500	0.087	0.5750

Source: US Bureau of Labor Statistics.

The bottom part of Exhibit 16 shows that the first four autocorrelations of the residuals from the AR(1) model are quite small. None of these autocorrelations has a *t*-statistic larger than 1.99, the critical value for significance. Consequently, Miller cannot reject the null hypothesis that the residuals are serially uncorrelated. The AR(1) model is correctly specified for the sample period from 2008 to 2018, so there is no need to estimate the AR(2) model. This conclusion is very different from that reached in Example 6 using data from 1995 to 2018. In that example, Miller initially rejected the AR(1) model because its residuals exhibited serial correlation. When she used a larger sample, an AR(2) model initially appeared to fit the data much better than did an AR(1) model.

How deeply does our choice of sample period affect our forecast of future inflation? Suppose that in a given month, inflation was 4% at an annual rate, and the month before that it was 3%. The AR(1) model shown in Exhibit 16 predicts that inflation in the next month will be 0.8431 + 0.5036(4) ≈ 2.86%. Therefore, the forecast of the next month's inflation using the 2008 to 2018 sample is 2.86%. Remember from the analysis following Example 6 that the AR(2) model for the 1995 to 2018 sample predicts inflation of 2.91% in the next month. Thus, using the correctly specified model for the shorter sample produces an inflation forecast 0.05 pps below the forecast made from the correctly specified model for the longer sample period. Such a difference might substantially affect a particular investment decision.

Which model is correct? Exhibit 17 suggests an answer. Monthly US inflation was so much more volatile during the middle part of the study period than in the earlier or later years that inflation is probably not a covariance-stationary time series from 1995 to 2018. Therefore, we can reasonably believe that the data have more than one regime and Miller should estimate a separate model for inflation from 2009 to 2018, as shown previously. In fact, the standard deviation of annualized monthly inflation rates is just 2.86% for 1995–2007 but 3.54% for 2008–2018, largely because of volatility during the 2008 crisis. As the example shows, experience (such as knowledge of government policy changes) and judgment play a vital role in determining how to model a time series. Simply relying on autocorrelations of the residuals from a time-series model cannot tell us the correct sample period for our analysis.

Exhibit 17: Monthly CPI Inflation

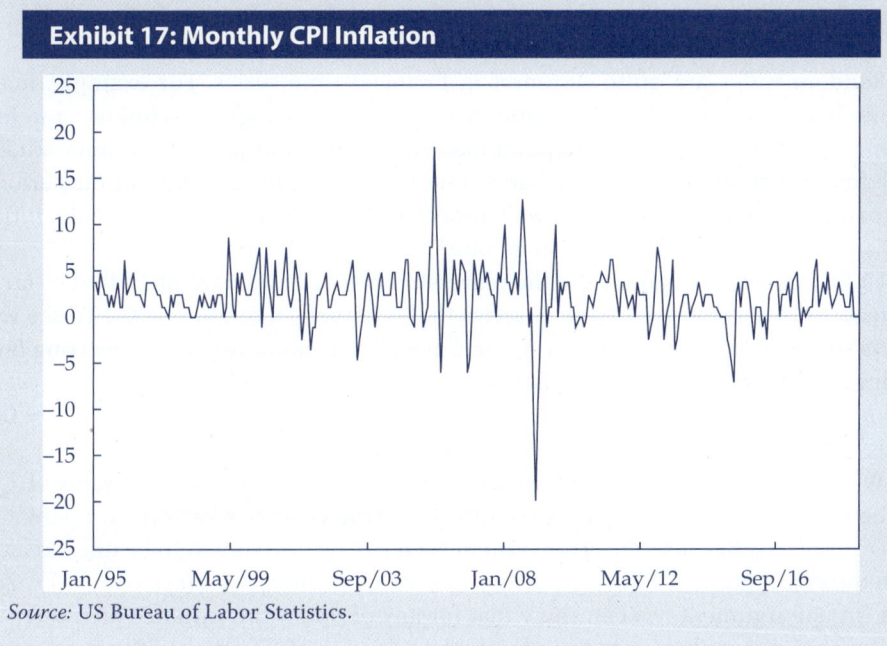

Source: US Bureau of Labor Statistics.

RANDOM WALKS

10

- [ ] describe characteristics of random walk processes and contrast them to covariance stationary processes
- [ ] explain mean reversion and calculate a mean-reverting level

So far, we have examined those time series in which the time series has a tendency to revert to its mean level as the change in a variable from one period to the next follows a mean-reverting pattern. In contrast, there are many financial time series in which the changes follow a random pattern. We discuss these "random walks" in the following section.

Random Walks

A random walk is one of the most widely studied time-series models for financial data. A **random walk** is a time series in which the value of the series in one period is the value of the series in the previous period plus an unpredictable random error. A random walk can be described by the following equation:

$$x_t = x_{t-1} + \varepsilon_t, \quad E(\varepsilon_t) = 0, \quad E(\varepsilon_t^2) = \sigma^2, \quad \text{cov}(\varepsilon_t, \varepsilon_s) = E(\varepsilon_t \varepsilon_s)$$
$$= 0 \text{ if } t \neq s. \tag{8}$$

Equation 8 means that the time series x_t is in every period equal to its value in the previous period plus an error term, ε_t, that has constant variance and is uncorrelated with the error term in previous periods. Note two important points. First, this equation is a special case of an AR(1) model with $b_0 = 0$ and $b_1 = 1$.[7] Second, the expected value of ε_t is zero. Therefore, the best forecast of x_t that can be made in period $t - 1$ is x_{t-1}. In fact, in this model, x_{t-1} is the best forecast of x in every period after $t - 1$.

Random walks are quite common in financial time series. For example, many studies have tested whether and found that currency exchange rates follow a random walk. Consistent with the second point made in the previous paragraph, some studies have found that sophisticated exchange rate forecasting models cannot outperform forecasts made using the random walk model and that the best forecast of the future exchange rate is the current exchange rate.

Unfortunately, we cannot use the regression methods we have discussed so far to estimate an AR(1) model on a time series that is actually a random walk. To see why this is so, we must determine why a random walk has no finite mean-reverting level or finite variance. Recall that if x_t is at its mean-reverting level, then $x_t = b_0 + b_1 x_t$, or $x_t = b_0/(1 - b_1)$. In a random walk, however, $b_0 = 0$ and $b_1 = 1$, so $b_0/(1 - b_1) = 0/0$. Therefore, a random walk has an undefined mean-reverting level.

What is the variance of a random walk? Suppose that in Period 1, the value of x_1 is 0. Then we know that $x_2 = 0 + \varepsilon_2$. Therefore, the variance of $x_2 = \text{var}(\varepsilon_2) = \sigma^2$. Now $x_3 = x_2 + \varepsilon_3 = \varepsilon_2 + \varepsilon_3$. Because the error term in each period is assumed to be uncorrelated with the error terms in all other periods, the variance of $x_3 = \text{var}(\varepsilon_2) + \text{var}(\varepsilon_3) = 2\sigma^2$. By a similar argument, we can show that for any period t, the variance of $x_t = (t - 1)\sigma^2$. But this means that as t grows large, the variance of x_t grows without an upper bound: It approaches infinity. This lack of upper bound, in turn, means that a random walk is not a covariance-stationary time series, because a covariance-stationary time series must have a finite variance.

What is the practical implication of these issues? *We cannot use standard regression analysis on a time series that is a random walk.* We can, however, attempt to convert the data to a covariance-stationary time series if we suspect that the time series is a random walk. In statistical terms, we can difference it.

We difference a time series by creating a new time series—say, y_t—that in each period is equal to the difference between x_t and x_{t-1}. This transformation is called **first-differencing** because it subtracts the value of the time series in the first prior

---

7 Equation 8 with a nonzero intercept added (as in Equation 9, given later) is sometimes referred to as a random walk with drift.

period from the current value of the time series. Sometimes the first difference of x_t is written as $\Delta x_t = x_t - x_{t-1}$. Note that the first difference of the random walk in Equation 8 yields

$$y_t = x_t - x_{t-1} = \varepsilon_t, \quad E\left(\varepsilon_t\right) = 0, \quad E\left(\varepsilon_t^2\right) = \sigma^2, \quad \text{cov}\left(\varepsilon_t, \varepsilon_s\right) = E\left(\varepsilon_t \varepsilon_s\right)$$
$$= 0 \text{ for } t \neq s.$$

The expected value of ε_t is 0. Therefore, the best forecast of y_t that can be made in period $t - 1$ is 0. This implies that the best forecast is that there will be no change in the value of the current time series, x_{t-1}.

The first-differenced variable, y_t, is covariance stationary. How is this so? First, note that this model ($y_t = \varepsilon_t$) is an AR(1) model with $b_0 = 0$ and $b_1 = 0$. We can compute the mean-reverting level of the first-differenced model as $b_0/(1 - b_1) = 0/1 = 0$. Therefore, a first-differenced random walk has a mean-reverting level of 0. Note also that the variance of y_t in each period is var(ε_t) = σ^2. Because the variance and the mean of y_t are constant and finite in each period, y_t is a covariance-stationary time series and we can model it using linear regression. Of course, modeling the first-differenced series with an AR(1) model does not help us predict the future, because $b_0 = 0$ and $b_1 = 0$. We simply conclude that the original time series is, in fact, a random walk.

Had we tried to estimate an AR(1) model for a time series that was a random walk, our statistical conclusions would have been incorrect because AR models cannot be used to estimate random walks or any time series that is not covariance stationary. The following example illustrates this issue with exchange rates.

THE YEN/US DOLLAR EXCHANGE RATE

1. Financial analysts often assume that exchange rates are random walks. Consider an AR(1) model for the Japanese yen/US dollar exchange rate (JPY/USD). Exhibit 18 shows the results of estimating the model using month-end observations from October 1980 through August 2019.

Exhibit 18: Yen/US Dollar Exchange Rate: AR(1) Model Month-End Observations, October 1980–August 2019

Regression Statistics

R^2	0.9897
Standard error	4.5999
Observations	467
Durbin–Watson	1.9391

	Coefficient	Standard Error	t-Statistic
Intercept	0.8409	0.6503	1.2931
JPY/USD$_{t-1}$	0.9919	0.0047	211.0426

Autocorrelations of the Residual

Lag	Autocorrelation	Standard Error	t-Statistic
1	0.0302	0.0465	0.6495
2	0.0741	0.0465	1.5935
3	0.0427	0.0465	0.9183

Autocorrelations of the Residual

Lag	Autocorrelation	Standard Error	t-Statistic
4	−0.0034	0.0465	0.0731

Source: US Federal Reserve Board of Governors.

The results in Exhibit 18 suggest that the yen/US dollar exchange rate is a random walk because the estimated intercept does not appear to be significantly different from 0 and the estimated coefficient on the first lag of the exchange rate is very close to 1. Can we use the *t*-statistics in Exhibit 18 to test whether the exchange rate is a random walk? Unfortunately, no, because the standard errors in an AR model are invalid if the model is estimated using a data series that is a random walk (remember, a random walk is not covariance stationary). If the exchange rate is, in fact, a random walk, we might come to an incorrect conclusion based on faulty statistical tests and then invest incorrectly. We can use a test presented in the next section to test whether the time series is a random walk.

Suppose the exchange rate is a random walk, as we now suspect. If so, the first-differenced series, $y_t = x_t - x_{t-1}$, will be covariance stationary. We present the results from estimating $y_t = b_0 + b_1 y_{t-1} + \varepsilon_t$ in Exhibit 19. If the exchange rate is a random walk, then $b_0 = 0$, $b_1 = 0$, and the error term will not be serially correlated.

Exhibit 19: First-Differenced Yen/US Dollar Exchange Rate: AR(1) Model Month-End Observations, November 1980–August 2019

Regression Statistics

R^2	0.0008
Standard error	4.6177
Observations	466
Durbin–Watson	2.0075

	Coefficient	Standard Error	t-Statistic
Intercept	−0.2185	0.2142	−1.0200
JPY/USD$_{t-1}$ − JPY/USD$_{t-2}$	0.0287	0.0464	0.6185

Autocorrelations of the Residual

Lag	Autocorrelation	Standard Error	t-Statistic
1	−0.0023	0.0463	−0.0501
2	0.0724	0.0463	1.5643
3	0.0387	0.0463	0.8361
4	−0.0062	0.0463	−0.1329

Source: US Federal Reserve Board of Governors.

In Exhibit 19, neither the intercept nor the coefficient on the first lag of the first-differenced exchange rate differs significantly from 0, and no residual autocorrelations differ significantly from 0. These findings are consistent with the yen/US dollar exchange rate being a random walk.

We have concluded that the differenced regression is the model to choose. Now we can see that we would have been seriously misled if we had based our model choice on an R^2 comparison. In Exhibit 18, the R^2 is 0.9897, whereas in Exhibit 19, the R^2 is 0.0008. How can this be, if we just concluded that the model in Exhibit 19 is the one that we should use? In Exhibit 18, the R^2 measures how well the exchange rate in one period predicts the exchange rate in the next period. If the exchange rate is a random walk, its current value will be an extremely good predictor of its value in the next period, and thus the R^2 will be extremely high. At the same time, if the exchange rate is a random walk, then changes in the exchange rate should be completely unpredictable. Exhibit 19 estimates whether changes in the exchange rate from one month to the next can be predicted by changes in the exchange rate over the previous month. If they cannot be predicted, the R^2 in Exhibit 19 should be very low. In fact, it is low (0.0008). This comparison provides a good example of the general rule that we cannot necessarily choose which model is correct solely by comparing the R^2 from the two models.

The exchange rate is a random walk, and changes in a random walk are by definition unpredictable. Therefore, we cannot profit from an investment strategy that predicts changes in the exchange rate.

To this point, we have discussed only simple random walks—that is, random walks without drift. In a random walk without drift, the best predictor of the time series in the next period is its current value. A random walk with drift, however, should increase or decrease by a constant amount in each period. The equation describing a random walk with drift is a special case of the AR(1) model:

$$x_t = b_0 + b_1 x_{t-1} + \varepsilon_t,$$
$$b_1 = 1, \quad b_0 \neq 0, \text{ or} \tag{9}$$
$$x_t = b_0 + x_{t-1} + \varepsilon_t, \quad E(\varepsilon_t) = 0.$$

A random walk with drift has $b_0 \neq 0$, compared to a simple random walk, which has $b_0 = 0$.

We have already seen that $b_1 = 1$ implies an undefined mean-reversion level and thus nonstationarity. Consequently, we cannot use an AR model to analyze a time series that is a random walk with drift until we transform the time series by taking first differences. If we first-difference Equation 9, the result is $y_t = x_t - x_{t-1}$, $y_t = b_0 + \varepsilon_t$, $b_0 \neq 0$.

THE UNIT ROOT TEST OF NONSTATIONARITY 11

- [ ] describe implications of unit roots for time-series analysis, explain when unit roots are likely to occur and how to test for them, and demonstrate how a time series with a unit root can be transformed so it can be analyzed with an AR model
- [ ] describe the steps of the unit root test for nonstationarity and explain the relation of the test to autoregressive time-series models

In this section, we discuss how to use random walk concepts to determine whether a time series is covariance stationary. This approach focuses on the slope coefficient in the random-walk-with-drift case of an AR(1) model in contrast with the traditional autocorrelation approach, which we discuss first.

The examination of the autocorrelations of a time series at various lags is a well-known prescription for inferring whether or not a time series is stationary. Typically, for a stationary time series, either autocorrelations at all lags are statistically indistinguishable from zero or the autocorrelations drop off rapidly to zero as the number of lags becomes large. Conversely, the autocorrelations of a nonstationary time series do not exhibit those characteristics. However, this approach is less definite than a currently more popular test for nonstationarity known as the Dickey–Fuller test for a unit root.

We can explain what is known as the unit root problem in the context of an AR(1) model. If a time series comes from an AR(1) model, then to be covariance stationary, the absolute value of the lag coefficient, b_1, must be less than 1.0. We could not rely on the statistical results of an AR(1) model if the absolute value of the lag coefficient were greater than or equal to 1.0 because the time series would not be covariance stationary. If the lag coefficient is equal to 1.0, the time series has a **unit root**: It is a random walk and is not covariance stationary (note that when b_1 is greater than 1 in absolute value, we say that there is an "explosive root"). By definition, all random walks, with or without a drift term, have unit roots.

How do we test for unit roots in a time series? If we believed that a time series, x_t, was a random walk with drift, it would be tempting to estimate the parameters of the AR(1) model $x_t = b_0 + b_1 x_{t-1} + \varepsilon_t$ using linear regression and conduct a t-test of the hypothesis that $b_1 = 1$. Unfortunately, if $b_1 = 1$, then x_t is not covariance stationary and the t-value of the estimated coefficient, $\hat{b}_1$, does not actually follow the t-distribution; consequently, a t-test would be invalid.

Dickey and Fuller (1979) developed a regression-based unit root test based on a transformed version of the AR(1) model $x_t = b_0 + b_1 x_{t-1} + \varepsilon_t$. Subtracting x_{t-1} from both sides of the AR(1) model produces

$$x_t - x_{t-1} = b_0 + (b_1 - 1)x_{t-1} + \varepsilon_t,$$

or

$$x_t - x_{t-1} = b_0 + g_1 x_{t-1} + \varepsilon_t, \ E(\varepsilon_t) = 0, \tag{10}$$

where $g_1 = (b_1 - 1)$. If $b_1 = 1$, then $g_1 = 0$ and thus a test of $g_1 = 0$ is a test of $b_1 = 1$. If there is a unit root in the AR(1) model, then g_1 will be 0 in a regression where the dependent variable is the first difference of the time series and the independent variable is the first lag of the time series. The null hypothesis of the Dickey–Fuller test is $H_0: g_1 = 0$—that is, that the time series has a unit root and is nonstationary—and the alternative hypothesis is $H_a: g_1 < 0$, that the time series does not have a unit root and is stationary.

To conduct the test, one calculates a t-statistic in the conventional manner for $\hat{g}_1$ but instead of using conventional critical values for a t-test, one uses a revised set of values computed by Dickey and Fuller; the revised critical values are larger in absolute value than the conventional critical values. A number of software packages incorporate Dickey–Fuller tests.

EXAMPLE 11

(Historical Example)

AstraZeneca's Quarterly Sales (1)

In January 2012, equity analyst Aron Berglin is building a time-series model for the quarterly sales of AstraZeneca, a British/Swedish biopharmaceutical company headquartered in London. He is using AstraZeneca's quarterly sales in US dollars for January 2000 to December 2011 and any lagged sales data that he may need prior to 2000 to build this model. He finds that a log-linear trend model seems better suited for modeling AstraZeneca's sales than does a linear trend model. However, the Durbin–Watson statistic from the log-linear regression is just 0.7064, which causes him to reject the hypothesis that the errors in the regression are serially uncorrelated. He concludes that he cannot model the log of AstraZeneca's quarterly sales using only a time trend line. He decides to model the log of AstraZeneca's quarterly sales using an AR(1) model. He uses $\ln \text{Sales}_t = b_0 + b_1(\ln \text{Sales}_{t-1}) + \varepsilon_t$.

Before he estimates this regression, the analyst should use the Dickey–Fuller test to determine whether there is a unit root in the log of AstraZeneca's quarterly sales. If he uses the sample of quarterly data on AstraZeneca's sales from the first quarter of 2000 through the fourth quarter of 2011, takes the natural log of each observation, and computes the Dickey–Fuller t-test statistic, the value of that statistic might cause him to fail to reject the null hypothesis that there is a unit root in the log of AstraZeneca's quarterly sales.

If a time series appears to have a unit root, how should we model it? One method that is often successful is to model the first-differenced series as an autoregressive time series. The following example demonstrates this method.

EXAMPLE 12

AstraZeneca's Quarterly Sales (2)

1. The plot of the log of AstraZeneca's quarterly sales is shown in Exhibit 20. By looking at the plot, Berglin is convinced that the log of quarterly sales is not covariance stationary (that it has a unit root).

Exhibit 20: Log of AstraZeneca's Quarterly Sales

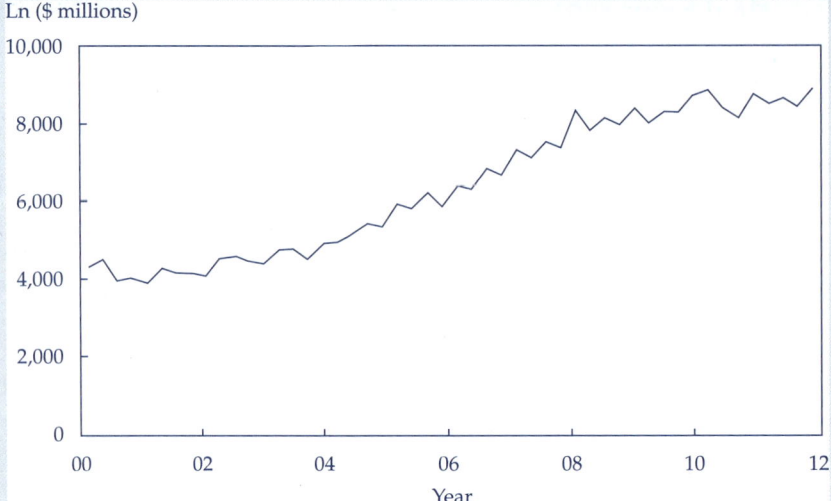

Source: Compustat.

So he creates a new series, y_t, that is the first difference of the log of Astra-Zeneca's quarterly sales. Exhibit 21 shows that series.

Berglin compares Exhibit 21 to Exhibit 20 and notices that first-differencing the log of AstraZeneca's quarterly sales eliminates the strong upward trend that was present in the log of AstraZeneca's sales. Because the first-differenced series has no strong trend, Berglin is better off assuming that the differenced series is covariance stationary rather than assuming that AstraZeneca's sales or the log of AstraZeneca's sales is a covariance-stationary time series.

Exhibit 21: Log Difference, AstraZeneca's Quarterly Sales

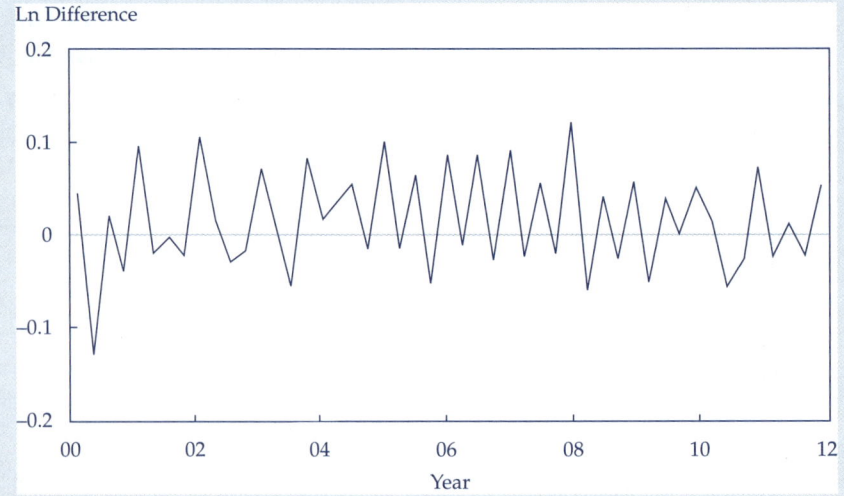

Source: Compustat.

Now suppose Berglin decides to model the new series using an AR(1) model. Berglin uses $\ln(\text{Sales}_t) - \ln(\text{Sales}_{t-1}) = b_0 + b_1[\ln(\text{Sales}_{t-1}) - \ln(\text{Sales}_{t-2})] + \varepsilon_t$. Exhibit 22 shows the results of that regression.

Exhibit 22: Log Differenced Sales: AR(1) Model of AstraZeneca Quarterly Observations, January 2000–December 2011

Regression Statistics

R^2	0.3005
Standard error	0.0475
Observations	48
Durbin–Watson	1.6874

	Coefficient	Standard Error	t-Statistic
Intercept	0.0222	0.0071	3.1268
ln Sales$_{t-1}$ – ln Sales$_{t-2}$	−0.5493	0.1236	−4.4442

Autocorrelations of the Residual

Lag	Autocorrelation	Standard Error	t-Statistic
1	0.2809	0.1443	1.9466
2	−0.0466	0.1443	−0.3229
3	0.0081	0.1443	0.0561
4	0.2647	0.1443	1.8344

Source: Compustat.

The lower part of Exhibit 22 suggests that the first four autocorrelations of residuals in this model are not statistically significant. With 48 observations and two parameters, this model has 46 degrees of freedom. The critical value for a *t*-statistic in this model is above 2.0 at the 0.05 significance level. None of the *t*-statistics for these autocorrelations has an absolute value larger than 2.0. Therefore, we fail to reject the null hypotheses that each of these autocorrelations is equal to 0 and conclude instead that no significant autocorrelation is present in the residuals.

This result suggests that the model is well specified and that we could use the estimates. Both the intercept ($\hat{b}_0 = 0.0222$) and the coefficient ($\hat{b}_1 = -0.5493$) on the first lag of the new first-differenced series are statistically significant.

1. Explain how to interpret the estimated coefficients in the model.

Solution

The value of the intercept (0.0222) implies that if sales have not changed in the current quarter ($y_t = \ln \text{Sales}_t - \ln \text{Sales}_{t-1} = 0$), sales will grow by 2.22% next quarter.[8] If sales have changed during this quarter, however, the model predicts that sales will grow by 2.22% minus 0.5493 times the sales growth in this quarter.

---

8 Note that 2.22 percent is the exponential growth rate, not [(Current quarter sales/Previous quarter sales) – 1]. The difference between these two methods of computing growth is usually small.

2. AstraZeneca's sales in the third and fourth quarters of 2011 were $8,405 million and $8,872 million, respectively. If we use the previous model soon after the end of the fourth quarter of 2011, what will be the predicted value of AstraZeneca's sales for the first quarter of 2012?

Solution

Let us say that t is the fourth quarter of 2011, so $t - 1$ is the third quarter of 2011 and $t + 1$ is the first quarter of 2012. Then we would have to compute $\hat{y}_{t+1} = 0.0222 - 0.5493y_t$. To compute $\hat{y}_{t+1}$, we need to know $y_t = \ln$ Sales$_t$ – ln Sales$_{t-1}$. In the third quarter of 2011, AstraZeneca's sales were $8,405 million, so ln Sales$_{t-1}$ = ln 8,405 = 9.0366. In the fourth quarter of 2011, AstraZeneca's sales were $8,872 million, so ln Sales$_t$ = ln 8,872 = 9.0907. Thus y_t = 9.0907 – 9.0366 = 0.0541. Therefore, $\hat{y}_{t+1}$ = 0.0222 – 0.5493(0.0541) = –0.0075. If $\hat{y}_{t+1}$ = –0.0075, then –0.0075 = ln Sales$_{t+1}$ – ln Sales$_t$ = ln(Sales$_{t+1}$/Sales$_t$). If we exponentiate both sides of this equation, the result is

$$e^{-0.0075} = \left(\frac{\text{Sales}_{t+1}}{\text{Sales}_t} \right).$$

$$\text{Sales}_{t+1} = \text{Sales}_t e^{-0.0075}$$
$$= \$8,872 \text{ million} \times 0.9925$$
$$= \$8,805 \text{ million}.$$

Thus, based on fourth quarter sales for 2011, this model would have predicted that AstraZeneca's sales in the first quarter of 2012 would be $8,805 million. This sales forecast might have affected our decision to buy AstraZeneca's stock at the time.

12   MOVING-AVERAGE TIME-SERIES MODELS

So far, many of the forecasting models we have used have been autoregressive models. Because most financial time series have the qualities of an autoregressive process, autoregressive time-series models are probably the most frequently used time-series models in financial forecasting. Some financial time series, however, seem to more closely follow another kind of time-series model, called a moving-average model. For example, as we will show, returns on the S&P BSE 100 Index can be better modeled as a moving-average process than as an autoregressive process.

In this section, we present the fundamentals of moving-average models so that you can ask the right questions when considering their use. We first discuss how to smooth past values with a moving average and then how to forecast a time series using a moving-average model. Even though both methods include the words "moving average" in the name, they are very different.

Smoothing Past Values with an *n*-Period Moving Average

Suppose you are analyzing the long-term trend in the past sales of a company. In order to focus on the trend, you may find it useful to remove short-term fluctuations or noise by smoothing out the time series of sales. One technique to smooth out period-to-period fluctuations in the value of a time series is an ***n*-period moving average**. An *n*-period moving average of the current and past $n - 1$ values of a time series, x_t, is calculated as

$$\frac{x_t + x_{t-1} + \cdots + x_{t-(n-1)}}{n}.$$

(11)

The following example demonstrates how to compute a moving average of AstraZeneca's quarterly sales.

EXAMPLE 13

AstraZeneca's Quarterly Sales (3)

Suppose we want to compute the four-quarter moving average of AstraZeneca's sales as of the beginning of the first quarter of 2012. AstraZeneca's sales in the previous four quarters were as follows: 1Q 2011, $8,490 million; 2Q 2011, $8,601 million; 3Q 2011, $8,405 million; and 4Q 2011, $8,872 million. The four-quarter moving average of sales as of the beginning of the first quarter of 2012 is thus (8,490 + 8,601 + 8,405 + 8,872)/4 = $8,592 million.

We often plot the moving average of a series with large fluctuations to help discern any patterns in the data. Exhibit 23 shows monthly retail sales for the United States from December 1995 to June 2019, along with a 12-month moving average of the data (data from January 1995 are used to compute the 12-month moving average).

Exhibit 23: Monthly US Real Retail Sales and 12-Month Moving Average of Retail Sales

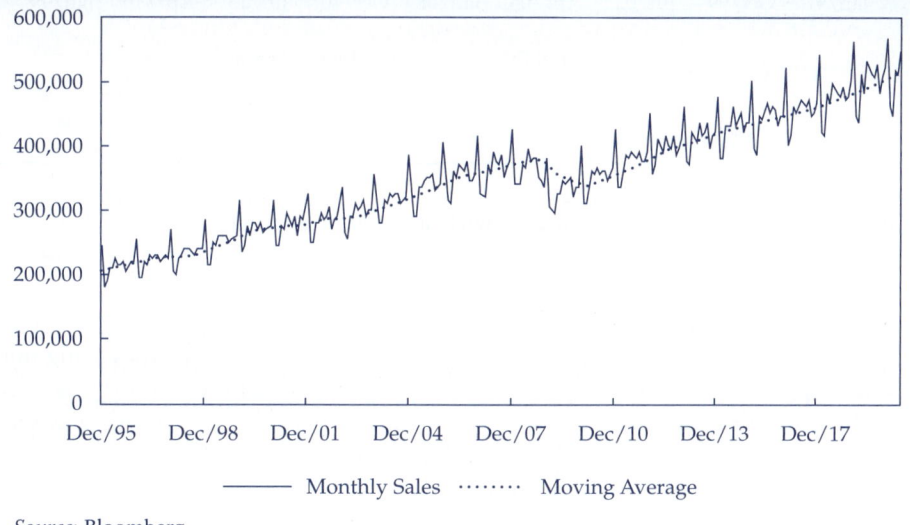

—— Monthly Sales ········ Moving Average

Source: Bloomberg.

As Exhibit 23 shows, each year has a very strong peak in retail sales (December) followed by a sharp drop in sales (January). Because of the extreme seasonality in the data, a 12-month moving average can help us focus on the long-term movements in retail sales instead of seasonal fluctuations. Note that the moving average does not have the sharp seasonal fluctuations of the original retail sales data. Rather, the moving average of retail sales grows steadily—for example, from 1995 through the second half of 2008—and then declines for about a year and grows steadily thereafter. We can see that trend more easily by looking at a 12-month moving average than by looking at the time series itself.

Exhibit 24 shows monthly Europe Brent Crude Oil spot prices along with a 12-month moving average of oil prices. Although these data do not have the same sharp regular seasonality displayed in the retail sales data in Exhibit 23, the moving average smooths out the monthly fluctuations in oil prices to show the longer-term movements.

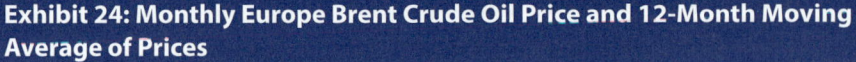

Exhibit 24: Monthly Europe Brent Crude Oil Price and 12-Month Moving Average of Prices

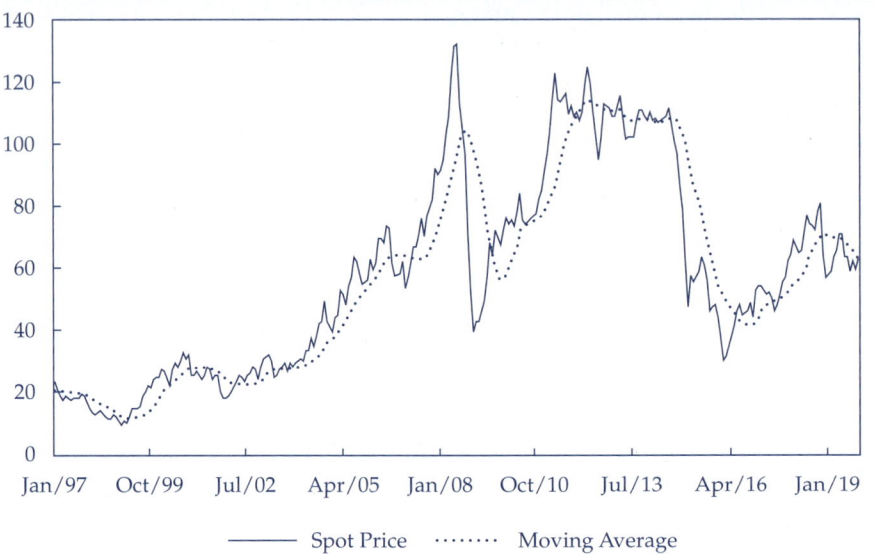

Source: US Energy Information Administration.

Exhibit 24 also shows one weakness with a moving average: It always lags large movements in the actual data. For example, when oil prices rose quickly in late 2007 and the first half of 2008, the moving average rose only gradually. When oil prices fell sharply toward the end of 2008, the moving average also lagged. Consequently, a simple moving average of the recent past, though often useful in smoothing out a time series, may not be the best predictor of the future. A main reason for this is that a simple moving average gives equal weight to all the periods in the moving average. In order to forecast the future values of a time series, it is often better to use a more sophisticated moving-average time-series model. We discuss such models below.

Moving-Average Time-Series Models for Forecasting

Suppose that a time series, x_t, is consistent with the following model:

$$x_t = \varepsilon_t + \theta\varepsilon_{t-1}, \quad E\left(\varepsilon_t\right) = 0, \quad E\left(\varepsilon_t^2\right) = \sigma^2,$$
$$\mathrm{cov}\left(\varepsilon_t, \varepsilon_s\right) = E\left(\varepsilon_t \varepsilon_s\right) = 0 \text{ for } t \neq s. \tag{12}$$

This equation is called a moving-average model of order 1, or simply an MA(1) model. Theta (θ) is the parameter of the MA(1) model.[9]

---

[9] Note that a moving-average time-series model is very different from a simple moving average, as discussed in Section 6.1. The simple moving average is based on observed values of a time series. In a moving-average time-series model, we never directly observe ε_t or any other ε_{t-j}, but we can infer how a particular moving-average model will imply a particular pattern of serial correlation for a time series, as we will discuss.

Equation 12 is a moving-average model because in each period, x_t is a moving average of ε_t and ε_{t-1}, two uncorrelated random variables that each have an expected value of zero. Unlike the simple moving-average model of Equation 11, this moving-average model places different weights on the two terms in the moving average (1 on ε_t, and θ on ε_{t-1}).

We can see if a time series fits an MA(1) model by looking at its autocorrelations to determine whether x_t is correlated only with its preceding and following values. First, we examine the variance of x_t in Equation 12 and its first two autocorrelations. Because the expected value of x_t is 0 in all periods and ε_t is uncorrelated with its own past values, the first autocorrelation is not equal to 0, but the second and higher autocorrelations are equal to 0. Further analysis shows that all autocorrelations except for the first will be equal to 0 in an MA(1) model. Thus for an MA(1) process, any value x_t is correlated with x_{t-1} and x_{t+1} but with no other time-series values; we could say that an MA(1) model has a memory of one period.

Of course, an MA(1) model is not the most complex moving-average model. A qth-order moving-average model, denoted MA(q) and with varying weights on lagged terms, can be written as

$$x_t = \varepsilon_t + \theta_1 \varepsilon_{t-1} + \cdots + \theta_q \varepsilon_{t-q}, \quad E(\varepsilon_t) = 0, \quad E(\varepsilon_t^2) = \sigma^2,$$
$$\operatorname{cov}(\varepsilon_t, \varepsilon_s) = E(\varepsilon_t \varepsilon_s) = 0 \text{ for } t \neq s. \tag{13}$$

How can we tell whether an MA(q) model fits a time series? We examine the autocorrelations. For an MA(q) model, the first q autocorrelations will be significantly different from 0, and all autocorrelations beyond that will be equal to 0; an MA(q) model has a memory of q periods. This result is critical for choosing the right value of q for an MA model. We discussed this result previously for the specific case of $q = 1$ that all autocorrelations except for the first will be equal to 0 in an MA(1) model.

How can we distinguish an autoregressive time series from a moving-average time series? Once again, we do so by examining the autocorrelations of the time series itself. The autocorrelations of most autoregressive time series start large and decline gradually, whereas the autocorrelations of an MA(q) time series suddenly drop to 0 after the first q autocorrelations. We are unlikely to know in advance whether a time series is autoregressive or moving average. Therefore, the autocorrelations give us our best clue about how to model the time series. Most time series, however, are best modeled with an autoregressive model.

EXAMPLE 14

(Historical Example)

A Time-Series Model for Monthly Returns on the S&P BSE 100 Index

The S&P BSE 100 Index is designed to reflect the performance of India's top 100 large-cap companies listed on the BSE Ltd. (formerly Bombay Stock Exchange). Are monthly returns on the S&P BSE 100 Index autocorrelated? If so, we may be able to devise an investment strategy to exploit the autocorrelation. What is an appropriate time-series model for S&P BSE 100 monthly returns?

Exhibit 25 shows the first six autocorrelations of returns to the S&P BSE 100 using monthly data from January 2000 through December 2013. Note that all of the autocorrelations are quite small. Do they reach significance? With 168 observations, the critical value for a t-statistic in this model is about 1.98 at the 0.05 significance level. None of the autocorrelations has a t-statistic larger in absolute value than the critical value of 1.98. Consequently, we fail to reject the null hypothesis that those autocorrelations, individually, do not differ significantly from 0.

Exhibit 25: Annualized Monthly Returns to the S&P BSE 100, January 2000–December 2013

Autocorrelations

Lag	Autocorrelation	Standard Error	*t*-Statistic
1	0.1103	0.0772	1.4288
2	−0.0045	0.0772	−0.0583
3	0.0327	0.0772	0.4236
4	0.0370	0.0772	0.4793
5	−0.0218	0.0772	−0.2824
6	0.0191	0.0772	0.2474
Observations	168		

Source: BSE Ltd.

If returns on the S&P BSE 100 were an MA(q) time series, then the first q autocorrelations would differ significantly from 0. None of the autocorrelations is statistically significant, however, so returns to the S&P BSE 100 appear to come from an MA(0) time series. An MA(0) time series in which we allow the mean to be nonzero takes the following form:[10]

$$x_t = \mu + \varepsilon_t, \quad E\left(\varepsilon_t\right) = 0, \quad E\left(\varepsilon_t^2\right) = \sigma^2,$$
$$\text{cov}\left(\varepsilon_t, \varepsilon_s\right) = E\left(\varepsilon_t \varepsilon_s\right) = 0 \text{ for } t \neq s, \tag{14}$$

which means that the time series is not predictable. This result should not be surprising, because most research suggests that short-term returns to stock indexes are difficult to predict.

We can see from this example how examining the autocorrelations allowed us to choose between the AR and MA models. If returns to the S&P BSE 100 had come from an AR(1) time series, the first autocorrelation would have differed significantly from 0 and the autocorrelations would have declined gradually. Not even the first autocorrelation is significantly different from 0, however. Therefore, we can be sure that returns to the S&P BSE 100 do not come from an AR(1) model—or from any higher-order AR model, for that matter. This finding is consistent with our conclusion that the S&P BSE 100 series is MA(0).

---

10 On the basis of investment theory and evidence, we expect that the mean monthly return on the S&P BSE 100 is positive ($\mu > 0$). We can also generalize Equation 13 for an MA(q) time series by adding a constant term, μ. Including a constant term in a moving-average model does not change the expressions for the variance and autocovariances of the time series. A number of early studies of weak-form market efficiency used Equation 14 as the model for stock returns. See Garbade (1982).

SEASONALITY IN TIME-SERIES MODELS

13

☐ explain how to test and correct for seasonality in a time-series model and calculate and interpret a forecasted value using an AR model with a seasonal lag

As we analyze the results of the time-series models in this reading, we encounter complications. One common complication is significant **seasonality**, a case in which the series shows regular patterns of movement within the year. At first glance, seasonality might appear to rule out using autoregressive time-series models. After all, autocorrelations will differ by season. This problem can often be solved, however, by using seasonal lags in an autoregressive model.

A seasonal lag is usually the value of the time series one year before the current period, included as an extra term in an autoregressive model. Suppose, for example, that we model a particular quarterly time series using an AR(1) model, $x_t = b_0 + b_1 x_{t-1} + \varepsilon_t$. If the time series had significant seasonality, this model would not be correctly specified. The seasonality would be easy to detect because the seasonal autocorrelation (in the case of quarterly data, the fourth autocorrelation) of the error term would differ significantly from 0. Suppose this quarterly model has significant seasonality. In this case, we might include a seasonal lag in the autoregressive model and estimate

$$x_t = b_0 + b_1 x_{t-1} + b_2 x_{t-4} + \varepsilon_t \qquad (15)$$

to test whether including the seasonal lag would eliminate statistically significant autocorrelation in the error term.

In Example 15 and Example 16, we illustrate how to test and adjust for seasonality in a time-series model. We also illustrate how to compute a forecast using an autoregressive model with a seasonal lag.

SEASONALITY IN SALES AT STARBUCKS

1. Earlier, we concluded that we could not model the log of Starbucks' quarterly sales using only a time-trend line (as shown in Example 3) because the Durbin–Watson statistic from the regression provided evidence of positive serial correlation in the error term. Based on methods presented in this reading, we might next investigate using the first difference of log sales to remove an exponential trend from the data to obtain a covariance-stationary time series.

   Using quarterly data from the last quarter of 2001 to the second quarter of 2019, we estimate the following AR(1) model using ordinary least squares: $(\ln \text{Sales}_t - \ln \text{Sales}_{t-1}) = b_0 + b_1(\ln \text{Sales}_{t-1} - \ln \text{Sales}_{t-2}) + \varepsilon_t$. Exhibit 26 shows the results of the regression.

Exhibit 26: Log Differenced Sales: AR(1) Model—Starbucks, Quarterly Observations, 2001–2019

Regression Statistics

R^2	0.2044
Standard error	0.0611
Observations	72

Regression Statistics			
Durbin–Watson			1.9904

	Coefficient	Standard Error	t-Statistic
Intercept	0.0469	0.0080	5.8625
ln Sales$_{t-1}$ – ln Sales$_{t-2}$	−0.4533	0.1069	−4.2404

Autocorrelations of the Residual			
Lag	Autocorrelation	Standard Error	t-Statistic
1	0.0051	0.1179	−0.0433
2	−0.1676	0.1179	−1.4218
3	−0.0130	0.1179	−0.1099
4	0.7630	0.1179	6.4720

Source: Bloomberg.

The first thing to note in Exhibit 26 is the strong seasonal autocorrelation of the residuals. The bottom portion of the table shows that the fourth autocorrelation has a value of 0.7630 and a t-statistic of 6. With 72 observations and two parameters, this model has 70 degrees of freedom.[11] The critical value for a t-statistic is about 1.99 at the 0.05 significance level. Given this value of the t-statistic, we must reject the null hypothesis that the fourth autocorrelation is equal to 0 because the t-statistic is larger than the critical value of 1.99.

In this model, the fourth autocorrelation is the seasonal autocorrelation because this AR(1) model is estimated with quarterly data. Exhibit 26 shows the strong and statistically significant seasonal autocorrelation that occurs when a time series with strong seasonality is modeled without taking the seasonality into account. Therefore, the AR(1) model is misspecified, and we should not use it for forecasting.

Suppose we decide to use an autoregressive model with a seasonal lag because of the seasonal autocorrelation. We are modeling quarterly data, so we estimate Equation 15: $(\ln \text{Sales}_t - \ln \text{Sales}_{t-1}) = b_0 + b_1(\ln \text{Sales}_{t-1} - \ln \text{Sales}_{t-2}) + b_2(\ln \text{Sales}_{t-4} - \ln \text{Sales}_{t-5}) + \varepsilon_t$. Adding the seasonal difference $\ln \text{Sales}_{t-4} - \ln \text{Sales}_{t-5}$ is an attempt to remove a consistent quarterly pattern in the data and could also eliminate a seasonal nonstationarity if one existed. The estimates of this equation appear in Exhibit 27.

---

11 In this example, we restrict the start of the sample period to the beginning of 2001, and we do not use prior observations for the lags. Accordingly, the number of observations decreases with an increase in the number of lags. In Exhibit 26, the first observation is for the third quarter of 2001 because we use up to two lags. In Exhibit 27, the first observation is for the second quarter of 2002 because we use up to five lags.

> ### Exhibit 27: Log Differenced Sales: AR(1) Model with Seasonal Lag— Starbucks, Quarterly Observations, 2005–2019
>
> | Regression Statistics | |
> |---|---|
> | R^2 | 0.7032 |
> | Standard error | 0.0373 |
> | Observations | 69 |
> | Durbin–Watson | 2.0392 |
>
> | | Coefficient | Standard Error | t-Statistic |
> |---|---|---|---|
> | Intercept | 0.0107 | 0.0059 | 1.8136 |
> | ln Sales$_{t-1}$ – ln Sales$_{t-2}$ | −0.1540 | 0.0729 | −2.1125 |
> | ln Sales$_{t-4}$ – ln Sales$_{t-5}$ | 0.7549 | 0.0720 | 10.4847 |
>
> | Autocorrelations of the Residual | | | |
> |---|---|---|---|
> | Lag | Autocorrelation | Standard Error | t-Statistic |
> | 1 | 0.0135 | 0.1204 | 0.1121 |
> | 2 | −0.0171 | 0.1204 | −0.1420 |
> | 3 | 0.1589 | 0.1204 | 1.3198 |
> | 4 | −0.1498 | 0.1204 | −1.2442 |

Source: Compustat.

Note the autocorrelations of the residual shown at the bottom of Exhibit 27. None of the *t*-statistics on the first four autocorrelations is now significant. Because the overall regression is highly significant (an *F*-test, not shown in the exhibit, is significant at the 0.01 level), we can take an AR(1) model with a seasonal lag as a reasonable working model for Starbucks sales. (A model having only a seasonal lag term was investigated and not found to improve on this model.)

How can we interpret the coefficients in this model? To predict the current quarter's sales growth at Starbucks, we need to know two things: sales growth in the previous quarter and sales growth four quarters ago. If sales remained constant in each of those two quarters, the model in Exhibit 27 would predict that sales will grow by 0.0107 (1.07%) in the current quarter. If sales grew by 1% last quarter and by 2% four quarters ago, then the model would predict that sales growth this quarter will be 0.0107 − 0.0154(0.01) + 0.7549(0.02) = 0.0256, or 2.56%. Note that all of these growth rates are exponential growth rates. Notice also that the R^2 in the model with the seasonal lag (0.7032 in Exhibit 27) was more than three times higher than the R^2 in the model without the seasonal lag (0.2044 in Exhibit 26). Again, the seasonal lag model does a much better job of explaining the data.

EXAMPLE 16

(Historical Example)

Retail Sales Growth

We want to predict the growth in monthly retail sales of Canadian furniture and home furnishing stores so that we can decide whether to recommend the shares of these stores. We decide to use non-seasonally adjusted data on retail sales. To begin with, we estimate an AR(1) model with observations on the annualized monthly growth in retail sales from January 1995 to December 2012. We estimate the following equation: Sales growth$_t$ = b_0 + b_1(Sales growth$_{t-1}$) + ε_t. Exhibit 28 shows the results from this model.

The autocorrelations of the residuals from this model, shown at the bottom of Exhibit 28, indicate that seasonality is extremely significant in this model. With 216 observations and two parameters, this model has 214 degrees of freedom. At the 0.05 significance level, the critical value for a t-statistic is about 1.97. The 12th-lag autocorrelation (the seasonal autocorrelation, because we are using monthly data) has a value of 0.7620 and a t-statistic of 11.21. The t-statistic on this autocorrelation is larger than the critical value (1.97), implying that we can reject the null hypothesis that the 12th autocorrelation is 0. Note also that many of the other t-statistics for autocorrelations shown in the table differ significantly from 0. Consequently, the model shown in Exhibit 28 is misspecified, so we cannot rely on it to forecast sales growth.

Suppose we add the seasonal lag of sales growth (the 12th lag) to the AR(1) model to estimate the equation Sales growth$_t$ = b_0 + b_1(Sales growth$_{t-1}$) + b_2(Sales growth$_{t-12}$) + ε_t. In this example, although we state that the sample period begins in 1995, we use prior observations for the lags. This results in the same number of observations irrespective of the number of lags. Exhibit 29 presents the results of estimating this equation. The estimated value of the seasonal autocorrelation (the 12th autocorrelation) has fallen to −0.1168. None of the first 12 autocorrelations has a t-statistic with an absolute value greater than the critical value of 1.97 at the 0.05 significance level. We can conclude that there is no significant serial correlation in the residuals from this model. Because we can reasonably believe that the model is correctly specified, we can use it to predict retail sales growth. Note that the R^2 in Exhibit 29 is 0.6724, much larger than the R^2 in Exhibit 28 (computed by the model without the seasonal lag).

Exhibit 28: Monthly Retail Sales Growth of Canadian Furniture and Home Furnishing Stores: AR(1) Model, January 1995–December 2012

Regression Statistics	
R^2	0.0509
Standard error	1.8198
Observations	216
Durbin–Watson	2.0956

	Coefficient	Standard Error	t-Statistic
Intercept	1.0518	0.1365	7.7055
Sales growth$_{t-1}$	−0.2252	0.0665	−3.3865

Autocorrelations of the Residual			
Lag	**Autocorrelation**	**Standard Error**	**t-Statistic**
1	−0.0109	0.0680	−0.1603
2	−0.1949	0.0680	−2.8662
3	0.1173	0.0680	1.7250
4	−0.0756	0.0680	−1.1118
5	−0.1270	0.0680	−1.8676
6	−0.1384	0.0680	−2.0353
7	−0.1374	0.0680	−2.0206
8	−0.0325	0.0680	−0.4779
9	0.1207	0.0680	1.7750
10	−0.2197	0.0680	−3.2309
11	−0.0342	0.0680	−0.5029
12	0.7620	0.0680	11.2059

Source: Statistics Canada (Government of Canada).

How can we interpret the coefficients in the model? To predict growth in retail sales in this month, we need to know last month's retail sales growth and retail sales growth 12 months ago. If retail sales remained constant both last month and 12 months ago, the model in Exhibit 29 would predict that retail sales will grow at an annual rate of about 23.7% this month. If retail sales grew at an annual rate of 10% last month and at an annual rate of 5% 12 months ago, the model in Exhibit 29 would predict that retail sales will grow in the current month at an annual rate of $0.2371 - 0.0792(0.10) + 0.7798(0.05) = 0.2682$, or 26.8%.

Exhibit 29: Monthly Retail Sales Growth of Canadian Furniture and Home Furnishing Stores: AR(1) Model with Seasonal Lag, January 1995–December 2012

Regression Statistics	
R^2	0.6724
Standard error	1.0717
Observations	216
Durbin–Watson	2.1784

	Coefficient	**Standard Error**	**t-Statistic**
Intercept	0.2371	0.0900	2.6344
Sales growth$_{t-1}$	−0.0792	0.0398	−1.9899
Sales growth$_{t-12}$	0.7798	0.0388	20.0979

Autocorrelations of the Residual			
Lag	**Autocorrelation**	**Standard Error**	**t-Statistic**
1	−0.0770	0.0680	−1.1324
2	−0.0374	0.0680	−0.5500

Autocorrelations of the Residual			
Lag	**Autocorrelation**	**Standard Error**	***t*-Statistic**
3	0.0292	0.0680	0.4294
4	−0.0358	0.0680	−0.5265
5	−0.0399	0.0680	−0.5868
6	0.0227	0.0680	0.3338
7	−0.0967	0.0680	−1.4221
8	0.1241	0.0680	1.8250
9	0.0499	0.0680	0.7338
10	−0.0631	0.0680	−0.9279
11	0.0231	0.0680	0.3397
12	−0.1168	0.0680	−1.7176

Source: Statistics Canada (Government of Canada).

14   AR MOVING-AVERAGE MODELS AND ARCH MODELS

☐   explain autoregressive conditional heteroskedasticity (ARCH) and describe how ARCH models can be applied to predict the variance of a time series

So far, we have presented autoregressive and moving-average models as alternatives for modeling a time series. The time series we have considered in examples have usually been explained quite well with a simple autoregressive model (with or without seasonal lags).[12] Some statisticians, however, have advocated using a more general model, the autoregressive moving-average (ARMA) model. The advocates of ARMA models argue that these models may fit the data better and provide better forecasts than do plain autoregressive (AR) models. However, as we discuss later in this section, there are severe limitations to estimating and using these models. Because you may encounter ARMA models, we next provide a brief overview.

An ARMA model combines both autoregressive lags of the dependent variable and moving-average errors. The equation for such a model with p autoregressive terms and q moving-average terms, denoted ARMA(p, q), is

$$x_t = b_0 + b_1 x_{t-1} + \cdots + b_p x_{t-p} + \varepsilon_t + \theta_1 \varepsilon_{t-1} + \cdots + \theta_q \varepsilon_{t-q},$$

$$E(\varepsilon_t) = 0, \quad E(\varepsilon_t^2) = \sigma^2, \quad \text{cov}(\varepsilon_t, \varepsilon_s) = E(\varepsilon_t \varepsilon_s) = 0 \text{ for } t \neq s,$$

(16)

where $b_1, b_2, \ldots, b_p$ are the autoregressive parameters and $\theta_1, \theta_2, \ldots, \theta_q$ are the moving-average parameters.

Estimating and using ARMA models has several limitations. First, the parameters in ARMA models can be very unstable. In particular, slight changes in the data sample or the initial guesses for the values of the ARMA parameters can result in very different final estimates of the ARMA parameters. Second, choosing the right ARMA model

---

12 For the returns on the S&P BSE 100 (see Example 14), we chose a moving-average model over an autoregressive model.

is more of an art than a science. The criteria for deciding on p and q for a particular time series are far from perfect. Moreover, even after a model is selected, that model may not forecast well.

To reiterate, ARMA models can be very unstable, depending on the data sample used and the particular ARMA model estimated. Therefore, you should be skeptical of claims that a particular ARMA model provides much better forecasts of a time series than any other ARMA model. In fact, in most cases, you can use an AR model to produce forecasts that are just as accurate as those from ARMA models without nearly as much complexity. Even some of the strongest advocates of ARMA models admit that these models should not be used with fewer than 80 observations, and they do not recommend using ARMA models for predicting quarterly sales or gross margins for a company using even 15 years of quarterly data.

Autoregressive Conditional Heteroskedasticity Models

Up to now, we have ignored any issues of heteroskedasticity in time-series models and have assumed homoskedasticity. **Heteroskedasticity** is the dependence of the error term variance on the independent variable; **homoskedasticity** is the independence of the error term variance from the independent variable. We have assumed that the error term's variance is constant and does not depend on the value of the time series itself or on the size of previous errors. At times, however, this assumption is violated and the variance of the error term is not constant. In such a situation, the standard errors of the regression coefficients in AR, MA, or ARMA models will be incorrect, and our hypothesis tests would be invalid. Consequently, we can make poor investment decisions based on those tests.

For example, suppose you are building an autoregressive model of a company's sales. If heteroskedasticity is present, then the standard errors of the regression coefficients of your model will be incorrect. It is likely that because of heteroskedasticity, one or more of the lagged sales terms may appear statistically significant when in fact they are not. Therefore, if you use this model for your decision making, you may make some suboptimal decisions.

In work responsible in part for his shared 2003 Nobel Prize in Economics, Robert F. Engle in 1982 first suggested a way of testing whether the variance of the error in a particular time-series model in one period depends on the variance of the error in previous periods. He called this type of heteroskedasticity "autoregressive conditional heteroskedasticity" (ARCH).

As an example, consider the ARCH(1) model

$$\varepsilon_t \sim N\left(0, a_0 + a_1 \varepsilon_{t-1}^2\right), \tag{17}$$

where the distribution of ε_t, conditional on its value in the previous period, ε_{t-1}, is normal, with mean 0 and variance $a_0 + a_1 \varepsilon_{t-1}^2$. If $a_1 = 0$, the variance of the error in every period is just a_0. The variance is constant over time and does not depend on past errors. Now suppose that $a_1 > 0$. Then the variance of the error in one period depends on how large the squared error was in the previous period. If a large error occurs in one period, the variance of the error in the next period will be even larger.

Engle showed that we can test whether a time series is ARCH(1) by regressing the squared residuals from a previously estimated time-series model (AR, MA, or ARMA) on a constant and one lag of the squared residuals. We can estimate the linear regression equation

$$\hat{\varepsilon}_t^2 = a_0 + a_1 \hat{\varepsilon}_{t-1}^2 + u_t, \tag{18}$$

where u_t is an error term. If the estimate of a_1 is statistically significantly different from zero, we conclude that the time series is ARCH(1). If a time-series model has ARCH(1) errors, then the variance of the errors in period $t + 1$ can be predicted in period t using the formula $\hat{\sigma}_{t+1}^2 = \hat{a}_0 + \hat{a}_1 \hat{\varepsilon}_t^2$.

EXAMPLE 17

Testing for ARCH(1) in Monthly Inflation

Analyst Lisette Miller wants to test whether monthly data on CPI inflation contain autoregressive conditional heteroskedasticity. She could estimate Equation 18 using the residuals from the time-series model. Based on the analyses in Examples 6 through 9, she has concluded that if she modeled monthly CPI inflation from 1995 to 2018, there would not be much difference in the performance of AR(1) and AR(2) models in forecasting inflation. The AR(1) model is clearly better for the period 2008–2018. She decides to further explore the AR(1) model for the entire period 1995 to 2018. Exhibit 30 shows the results of testing whether the errors in that model are ARCH(1). Because the test involves the first lag of residuals of the estimated time-series model, the number of observations in the test is one less than that in the model.

The t-statistic for the coefficient on the previous period's squared residuals is greater than 4.8. Therefore, Miller easily rejects the null hypothesis that the variance of the error does not depend on the variance of previous errors. Consequently, the test statistics she computed in Exhibits 13 and 14 are not valid, and she should not use them in deciding her investment strategy.

Exhibit 30: Test for ARCH(1) in an AR(1) Model: Residuals from Monthly CPI Inflation at an Annual Rate, March 1995–December 2018

Regression Statistics

R^2	0.0759
Standard error	23.7841
Observations	286
Durbin–Watson	2.0569

	Coefficient	Standard Error	t-Statistic
Intercept	6.3626	1.4928	4.2622
$\hat{\varepsilon}_{t-1}^2$	0.2754	0.0570	4.8316

Source: US Bureau of Labor Statistics.

It is possible Miller's conclusion—that the AR(1) model for monthly inflation has ARCH in the errors—may have been due to the sample period used (1995–2018). In Example 9, she used a shorter sample period, 2008–2018, and concluded that monthly CPI inflation follows an AR(1) process. (These results were shown in Exhibit 16.) Exhibit 30 shows that errors for a time-series model of inflation for the entire sample (1995–2018) have ARCH errors. Do the errors estimated with a shorter sample period (2008–2018) also display ARCH? For the shorter sample period, Miller estimated an AR(1) model using monthly inflation data. Now she tests to see whether the errors display ARCH. Exhibit 31 shows the results.

In this sample, the coefficient on the previous period's squared residual has a t-statistic of 4.0229. Consequently, Miller rejects the null hypothesis that the errors in this regression have no autoregressive conditional heteroskedasticity. The error variance appears to be heteroskedastic, and Miller cannot rely on the t-statistics.

Exhibit 31: Test for ARCH(1) in an AR(1) Model: Monthly CPI Inflation at an Annual Rate, February 2008–December 2018

Regression Statistics

R^2	0.1113
Standard error	24.64
Observations	131
Durbin–Watson	2.0385

	Coefficient	Standard Error	t-Statistic
Intercept	6.2082	2.2873	2.7142
$\hat{\varepsilon}_{t-1}^2$	0.3336	0.0830	4.0229

Source: US Bureau of Labor Statistics.

Suppose a model contains ARCH(1) errors. What are the consequences of that fact? First, if ARCH exists, the standard errors for the regression parameters will not be correct. We will need to use generalized least squares[13] or other methods that correct for heteroskedasticity to correctly estimate the standard error of the parameters in the time-series model. Second, if ARCH exists and we have it modeled—for example, as ARCH(1)—we can predict the variance of the errors. Suppose, for instance, that we want to predict the variance of the error in inflation using the estimated parameters from Exhibit 30: $\hat{\sigma}_t^2 = 6.3626 + 0.2754\hat{\varepsilon}_{t-1}^2$. If the error in one period were 0%, the predicted variance of the error in the next period would be $6.3626 + 0.2754(0) = 6.3626$. If the error in one period were 1%, the predicted variance of the error in the next period would be $6.3626 + 0.2754(1^2) = 6.6380$.

Engle and other researchers have suggested many generalizations of the ARCH(1) model, including ARCH(p) and generalized autoregressive conditional heteroskedasticity (GARCH) models. In an ARCH(p) model, the variance of the error term in the current period depends linearly on the squared errors from the previous p periods: $\sigma_t^2 = a_0 + a_1\varepsilon_{t-1}^2 + \cdots + a_p\varepsilon_{t-p}^2$. GARCH models are similar to ARMA models of the error variance in a time series. Just like ARMA models, GARCH models can be finicky and unstable: Their results can depend greatly on the sample period and the initial guesses of the parameters in the GARCH model. Financial analysts who use GARCH models should be well aware of how delicate these models can be, and they should examine whether GARCH estimates are robust to changes in the sample and the initial guesses about the parameters.[14]

---

13 See Greene (2018).

14 For more on ARCH, GARCH, and other models of time-series variance, see Hamilton (1994).

15   REGRESSIONS WITH MORE THAN ONE TIME SERIES

> ☐   explain how time-series variables should be analyzed for nonstationarity and/or cointegration before use in a linear regression; and

Up to now, we have discussed time-series models only for one time series. Although in the readings on correlation and regression and on multiple regression we used linear regression to analyze the relationship among different time series, in those readings we completely ignored unit roots. A time series that contains a unit root is not covariance stationary. If any time series in a linear regression contains a unit root, ordinary least squares estimates of regression test statistics may be invalid.

To determine whether we can use linear regression to model more than one time series, let us start with a single independent variable; that is, there are two time series, one corresponding to the dependent variable and one corresponding to the independent variable. We will then extend our discussion to multiple independent variables.

We first use a unit root test, such as the Dickey–Fuller test, for each of the two time series to determine whether either of them has a unit root.[15] There are several possible scenarios related to the outcome of these tests. One possible scenario is that we find that neither of the time series has a unit root. Then we can safely use linear regression to test the relations between the two time series. Otherwise, we may have to use additional tests, as we discuss later in this section.

EXAMPLE 18

Unit Roots and the Fisher Effect

Researchers at an asset management firm examined the Fisher effect by estimating the regression relation between expected inflation and US Treasury bill (T-bill) returns. They used 181 quarterly observations on expected inflation rates and T-bill returns from the sample period extending from the fourth quarter of 1968 through the fourth quarter of 2013. They used linear regression to analyze the relationship between the two time series. The results of this regression would be valid if both time series are covariance stationary; that is, neither of the two time series has a unit root. So, if they compute the Dickey–Fuller t-test statistic of the hypothesis of a unit root separately for each time series and find that they can reject the null hypothesis that the T-bill return series has a unit root and the null hypothesis that the expected inflation time series has a unit root, then they can use linear regression to analyze the relation between the two series. In that case, the results of their analysis of the Fisher effect would be valid.

A second possible scenario is that we reject the hypothesis of a unit root for the independent variable but fail to reject the hypothesis of a unit root for the dependent variable. In this case, the error term in the regression would not be covariance stationary. Therefore, one or more of the following linear regression assumptions would be violated: (1) that the expected value of the error term is 0, (2) that the variance of the error term is constant for all observations, and (3) that the error term is uncorrelated across observations. Consequently, the estimated regression coefficients and standard

---

15 For theoretical details of unit root tests, see Greene (2018) or Tsay (2010). Unit root tests are available in some econometric software packages, such as EViews.

errors would be inconsistent. The regression coefficients might appear significant, but those results would be spurious.[16] Thus we should not use linear regression to analyze the relation between the two time series in this scenario.

A third possible scenario is the reverse of the second scenario: We reject the hypothesis of a unit root for the dependent variable but fail to reject the hypothesis of a unit root for the independent variable. In this case also, like the second scenario, the error term in the regression would not be covariance stationary, and we cannot use linear regression to analyze the relation between the two time series.

EXAMPLE 19

(Historical Example)

Unit Roots and Predictability of Stock Market Returns by Price-to-Earnings Ratio

Johann de Vries is analyzing the performance of the South African stock market. He examines whether the percentage change in the Johannesburg Stock Exchange (JSE) All Share Index can be predicted by the price-to-earnings ratio (P/E) for the index. Using monthly data from January 1994 to December 2013, he runs a regression using $(P_t - P_{t-1})/P_{t-1}$ as the dependent variable and P_{t-1}/E_{t-2} as the independent variable, where P_t is the value of the JSE index at time t and E_t is the earnings on the index. De Vries finds that the regression coefficient is negative and statistically significant and the value of the R^2 for the regression is quite high. What additional analysis should he perform before accepting the regression as valid?

De Vries needs to perform unit root tests for each of the two time series. If one of the two time series has a unit root, implying that it is not stationary, the results of the linear regression are not meaningful and cannot be used to conclude that stock market returns are predictable by P/E.[17]

The next possibility is that both time series have a unit root. In this case, we need to establish whether the two time series are **cointegrated** before we can rely on regression analysis.[18] Two time series are cointegrated if a long-term financial or economic relationship exists between them such that they do not diverge from each other without bound in the long run. For example, two time series are cointegrated if they share a common trend.

In the fourth scenario, both time series have a unit root but are not cointegrated. In this scenario, as in the second and third scenarios, the error term in the linear regression will not be covariance stationary, some regression assumptions will be violated, the regression coefficients and standard errors will not be consistent, and we cannot use them for hypothesis tests. Consequently, linear regression of one variable on the other would be meaningless.

Finally, the fifth possible scenario is that both time series have a unit root but they are cointegrated. In this case, the error term in the linear regression of one time series on the other will be covariance stationary. Accordingly, the regression coefficients and standard errors will be consistent, and we can use them for hypothesis tests. However, we should be very cautious in interpreting the results of a regression with cointegrated variables. The cointegrated regression estimates the long-term relation between the

---

16 The problem of spurious regression for nonstationary time series was first discussed by Granger and Newbold (1974).

17 Barr and Kantor (1999) contains evidence that the P/E time series is nonstationary.

18 Engle and Granger (1987) first discussed cointegration.

two series but may not be the best model of the short-term relation between the two series. Short-term models of cointegrated series (error correction models) are discussed in Engle and Granger (1987) and Tsay (2010), but these are specialist topics.

Now let us look at how we can test for cointegration between two time series that each have a unit root, as in the fourth and fifth scenarios.[19] Engle and Granger suggested the following test. If y_t and x_t are both time series with a unit root, we should do the following:

1. Estimate the regression $y_t = b_0 + b_1 x_t + \varepsilon_t$.

2. Test whether the error term from the regression in Step 1 has a unit root using a Dickey–Fuller test. Because the residuals are based on the estimated coefficients of the regression, we cannot use the standard critical values for the Dickey–Fuller test. Instead, we must use the critical values computed by Engle and Granger, which take into account the effect of uncertainty about the regression parameters on the distribution of the Dickey–Fuller test.

3. If the (Engle–Granger) Dickey–Fuller test fails to reject the null hypothesis that the error term has a unit root, then we conclude that the error term in the regression is not covariance stationary. Therefore, the two time series are not cointegrated. In this case, any regression relation between the two series is spurious.

4. If the (Engle–Granger) Dickey–Fuller test rejects the null hypothesis that the error term has a unit root, then we may assume that the error term in the regression is covariance stationary and that the two time series are cointegrated. The parameters and standard errors from linear regression will be consistent and will let us test hypotheses about the long-term relation between the two series.

EXAMPLE 20

Testing for Cointegration between Intel Sales and Nominal GDP

Suppose we want to test whether the natural log of Intel's sales and the natural log of GDP are cointegrated (that is, whether there is a long-term relation between GDP and Intel sales). We want to test this hypothesis using quarterly data from the first quarter of 1995 through the fourth quarter of 2019. Here are the steps:

1. Test whether the two series each have a unit root. If we cannot reject the null hypothesis of a unit root for both series, implying that both series are nonstationary, we must then test whether the two series are cointegrated.

2. Having established that each series has a unit root, we estimate the regression ln Intel sales$_t = b_0 + b_1(\ln \text{GDP}_t) + \varepsilon_t$, then conduct the (Engle–Granger) Dickey–Fuller test of the hypothesis that there is a unit root in the error term of this regression using the residuals from the estimated regression. If we reject the null hypothesis of a unit root in the error term of the regression, we reject the null hypothesis of

---

19 Consider a time series, x_t, that has a unit root. For many such financial and economic time series, the first difference of the series, $x_t - x_{t-1}$, is stationary. We say that such a series, whose first difference is stationary, has a *single* unit root. However, for some time series, even the first difference may not be stationary and further differencing may be needed to achieve stationarity. Such a time series is said to have *multiple* unit roots. In this section, we consider only the case in which each nonstationary series has a single unit root (which is quite common).

no cointegration. That is, the two series would be cointegrated. If the two series are cointegrated, we can use linear regression to estimate the long-term relation between the natural log of Intel sales and the natural log of GDP.

We have so far discussed models with a single independent variable. We now extend the discussion to a model with two or more independent variables, so that there are three or more time series. The simplest possibility is that none of the time series in the model has a unit root. Then, we can safely use multiple regression to test the relation among the time series.

EXAMPLE 21

Unit Roots and Returns to the Fidelity Select Technology Fund

In earlier coverage of multiple regression, we used a multiple linear regression model to examine whether returns to either the S&P 500 Growth Index or the S&P 500 Value Index explain returns to the Fidelity Select Technology Portfolio using monthly observations between October 2015 and August 2019. Of course, if any of the three time series has a unit root, then the results of our regression analysis may be invalid. Therefore, we could use a Dickey–Fuller test to determine whether any of these series has a unit root.

If we reject the hypothesis of unit roots for all three series, we can use linear regression to analyze the relation among the series. In that case, the results of our analysis of the factors affecting returns to the Fidelity Select Technology Portfolio would be valid.

If at least one time series (the dependent variable or one of the independent variables) has a unit root while at least one time series (the dependent variable or one of the independent variables) does not, the error term in the regression cannot be covariance stationary. Consequently, we should not use multiple linear regression to analyze the relation among the time series in this scenario.

Another possibility is that each time series, including the dependent variable and each of the independent variables, has a unit root. If this is the case, we need to establish whether the time series are cointegrated. To test for cointegration, the procedure is similar to that for a model with a single independent variable. First, estimate the regression $y_t = b_0 + b_1 x_{1t} + b_2 x_{2t} + \ldots + b_k x_{kt} + \varepsilon_t$. Then conduct the (Engle–Granger) Dickey–Fuller test of the hypothesis that there is a unit root in the errors of this regression using the residuals from the estimated regression.

If we cannot reject the null hypothesis of a unit root in the error term of the regression, we cannot reject the null hypothesis of no cointegration. In this scenario, the error term in the multiple regression will not be covariance stationary, so we cannot use multiple regression to analyze the relationship among the time series.

If we can reject the null hypothesis of a unit root in the error term of the regression, we can reject the null hypothesis of no cointegration. However, modeling three or more time series that are cointegrated may be difficult. For example, an analyst may want to predict a retirement services company's sales based on the country's GDP and the total population over age 65. Although the company's sales, GDP, and the population over 65 may each have a unit root and be cointegrated, modeling the cointegration of the three series may be difficult, and doing so is beyond the scope of this volume. Analysts who have not mastered all these complex issues should avoid forecasting models with multiple time series that have unit roots; the regression coefficients may be inconsistent and may produce incorrect forecasts.

16   OTHER ISSUES IN TIME SERIES

☐ | determine an appropriate time-series model to analyze a given investment problem and justify that choice

Time-series analysis is an extensive topic and includes many highly complex issues. Our objective in this reading has been to present those issues in time series that are the most important for financial analysts and can also be handled with relative ease. In this section, we briefly discuss some of the issues that we have not covered but could be useful for analysts.

In this reading, we have shown how to use time-series models to make forecasts. We have also introduced the RMSE as a criterion for comparing forecasting models. However, we have not discussed measuring the uncertainty associated with forecasts made using time-series models. The uncertainty of these forecasts can be very large, and should be taken into account when making investment decisions. Fortunately, the same techniques apply to evaluating the uncertainty of time-series forecasts as apply to evaluating the uncertainty about forecasts from linear regression models. To accurately evaluate forecast uncertainty, we need to consider both the uncertainty about the error term and the uncertainty about the estimated parameters in the time-series model. Evaluating this uncertainty is fairly complicated when using regressions with more than one independent variable.

In this reading, we used the US CPI inflation series to illustrate some of the practical challenges analysts face in using time-series models. We used information on US Federal Reserve policy to explore the consequences of splitting the inflation series in two. In financial time-series work, we may suspect that a time series has more than one regime but lack the information to attempt to sort the data into different regimes. If you face such a problem, you may want to investigate other methods, especially switching regression models, to identify multiple regimes using only the time series itself.

If you are interested in these and other advanced time-series topics, you can learn more from Diebold (2008) and Tsay (2010).

Suggested Steps in Time-Series Forecasting

The following is a step-by-step guide to building a model to predict a time series.

1. Understand the investment problem you have, and make an initial choice of model. One alternative is a regression model that predicts the future behavior of a variable based on hypothesized causal relationships with other variables. Another is a time-series model that attempts to predict the future behavior of a variable based on the past behavior of the same variable.

2. If you have decided to use a time-series model, compile the time series and plot it to see whether it looks covariance stationary. The plot might show important deviations from covariance stationarity, including the following:

   - a linear trend,

   - an exponential trend,

   - seasonality, or

   - a significant shift in the time series during the sample period (for example, a change in mean or variance).

3. If you find no significant seasonality or shift in the time series, then perhaps either a linear trend or an exponential trend will be sufficient to model the time series. In that case, take the following steps:

   - Determine whether a linear or exponential trend seems most reasonable (usually by plotting the series).
   - Estimate the trend.
   - Compute the residuals.
   - Use the Durbin–Watson statistic to determine whether the residuals have significant serial correlation. If you find no significant serial correlation in the residuals, then the trend model is sufficient to capture the dynamics of the time series and you can use that model for forecasting.

4. If you find significant serial correlation in the residuals from the trend model, use a more complex model, such as an autoregressive model. First, however, reexamine whether the time series is covariance stationary. The following is a list of violations of stationarity, along with potential methods to adjust the time series to make it covariance stationary:

   - If the time series has a linear trend, first-difference the time series.
   - If the time series has an exponential trend, take the natural log of the time series and then first-difference it.
   - If the time series shifts significantly during the sample period, estimate different time-series models before and after the shift.
   - If the time series has significant seasonality, include seasonal lags (discussed in Step 7).

5. After you have successfully transformed a raw time series into a covariance-stationary time series, you can usually model the transformed series with a short autoregression.[20] To decide which autoregressive model to use, take the following steps:

   - Estimate an AR(1) model.
   - Test to see whether the residuals from this model have significant serial correlation.
   - If you find no significant serial correlation in the residuals, you can use the AR(1) model to forecast.

6. If you find significant serial correlation in the residuals, use an AR(2) model and test for significant serial correlation of the residuals of the AR(2) model.

   - If you find no significant serial correlation, use the AR(2) model.
   - If you find significant serial correlation of the residuals, keep increasing the order of the AR model until the residual serial correlation is no longer significant.

7. Your next move is to check for seasonality. You can use one of two approaches:

---

20 Most financial time series can be modeled using an autoregressive process. For a few time series, a moving-average model may fit better. To see whether this is the case, examine the first five or six autocorrelations of the time series. If the autocorrelations suddenly drop to 0 after the first q autocorrelations, a moving-average model (of order q) is appropriate. If the autocorrelations start large and decline gradually, an autoregressive model is appropriate.

- Graph the data and check for regular seasonal patterns.

- Examine the data to see whether the seasonal autocorrelations of the residuals from an AR model are significant (for example, the fourth autocorrelation for quarterly data) and whether the autocorrelations before and after the seasonal autocorrelations are significant. To correct for seasonality, add seasonal lags to your AR model. For example, if you are using quarterly data, you might add the fourth lag of a time series as an additional variable in an AR(1) or an AR(2) model.

8. Next, test whether the residuals have autoregressive conditional heteroskedasticity. To test for ARCH(1), for example, do the following:

- Regress the squared residual from your time-series model on a lagged value of the squared residual.

- Test whether the coefficient on the squared lagged residual differs significantly from 0.

- If the coefficient on the squared lagged residual does not differ significantly from 0, the residuals do not display ARCH and you can rely on the standard errors from your time-series estimates.

- If the coefficient on the squared lagged residual does differ significantly from 0, use generalized least squares or other methods to correct for ARCH.

9. Finally, you may also want to perform tests of the model's out-of-sample forecasting performance to see how the model's out-of-sample performance compares to its in-sample performance.

Using these steps in sequence, you can be reasonably sure that your model is correctly specified.

SUMMARY

- The predicted trend value of a time series in period t is $\hat{b}_0 + \hat{b}_1 t$ in a linear trend model; the predicted trend value of a time series in a log-linear trend model is $e^{\hat{b}_0+\hat{b}_1 t}$.

- Time series that tend to grow by a constant amount from period to period should be modeled by linear trend models, whereas time series that tend to grow at a constant rate should be modeled by log-linear trend models.

- Trend models often do not completely capture the behavior of a time series, as indicated by serial correlation of the error term. If the Durbin–Watson statistic from a trend model differs significantly from 2, indicating serial correlation, we need to build a different kind of model.

- An autoregressive model of order p, denoted AR(p), uses p lags of a time series to predict its current value: $x_t = b_0 + b_1 x_{t-1} + b_2 x_{t-2} + \ldots + b_p x_{t-p} + \varepsilon_t$.

- A time series is covariance stationary if the following three conditions are satisfied: First, the expected value of the time series must be constant and finite in all periods. Second, the variance of the time series must be constant and finite in all periods. Third, the covariance of the time-series with itself for a fixed number of periods in the past or future must be constant and finite in all periods. Inspection of a nonstationary time-series plot may reveal an upward or downward trend (nonconstant mean) and/or nonconstant variance. The use of linear regression to estimate an autoregressive time-series model is not valid unless the time series is covariance stationary.

- For a specific autoregressive model to be a good fit to the data, the autocorrelations of the error term should be 0 at all lags.

- A time series is mean reverting if it tends to fall when its level is above its long-run mean and rise when its level is below its long-run mean. If a time series is covariance stationary, then it will be mean reverting.

- The one-period-ahead forecast of a variable x_t from an AR(1) model made in period t for period $t + 1$ is $\hat{x}_{t+1} = \hat{b}_0 + \hat{b}_1 x_t$. This forecast can be used to create the two-period-ahead forecast from the model made in period t, $\hat{x}_{t+2} = \hat{b}_0 + \hat{b}_1 x_{t+1}$. Similar results hold for AR(p) models.

- In-sample forecasts are the in-sample predicted values from the estimated time-series model. Out-of-sample forecasts are the forecasts made from the estimated time-series model for a time period different from the one for which the model was estimated. Out-of-sample forecasts are usually more valuable in evaluating the forecasting performance of a time-series model than are in-sample forecasts. The root mean squared error (RMSE), defined as the square root of the average squared forecast error, is a criterion for comparing the forecast accuracy of different time-series models; a smaller RMSE implies greater forecast accuracy.

- Just as in regression models, the coefficients in time-series models are often unstable across different sample periods. In selecting a sample period for estimating a time-series model, we should seek to assure ourselves that the time series was stationary in the sample period.

- A random walk is a time series in which the value of the series in one period is the value of the series in the previous period plus an unpredictable random error. If the time series is a random walk, it is not covariance stationary. A random walk with drift is a random walk with a nonzero intercept term. All random walks have unit roots. If a time series has a unit root, then it will not be covariance stationary.

- If a time series has a unit root, we can sometimes transform the time series into one that is covariance stationary by first-differencing the time series; we may then be able to estimate an autoregressive model for the first-differenced series.

- An n-period moving average of the current and past $(n - 1)$ values of a time series, x_t, is calculated as $[x_t + x_{t-1} + \ldots + x_{t-(n-1)}]/n$.

- A moving-average model of order q, denoted MA(q), uses q lags of a random error term to predict its current value.

- The order q of a moving-average model can be determined using the fact that if a time series is a moving-average time series of order q, its first q autocorrelations are nonzero while autocorrelations beyond the first q are zero.

- The autocorrelations of most autoregressive time series start large and decline gradually, whereas the autocorrelations of an MA(q) time series suddenly drop to 0 after the first q autocorrelations. This helps in distinguishing between autoregressive and moving-average time series.

■ If the error term of a time-series model shows significant serial correlation at seasonal lags, the time series has significant seasonality. This seasonality can often be modeled by including a seasonal lag in the model, such as adding a term lagged four quarters to an AR(1) model on quarterly observations.

■ The forecast made in time t for time $t + 1$ using a quarterly AR(1) model with a seasonal lag would be $x_{t+1} = \hat{b}_0 + \hat{b}_1 x_t + \hat{b}_2 x_{t-3}$.

■ ARMA models have several limitations: The parameters in ARMA models can be very unstable; determining the AR and MA order of the model can be difficult; and even with their additional complexity, ARMA models may not forecast well.

■ The variance of the error in a time-series model sometimes depends on the variance of previous errors, representing autoregressive conditional heteroskedasticity (ARCH). Analysts can test for first-order ARCH in a time-series model by regressing the squared residual on the squared residual from the previous period. If the coefficient on the squared residual is statistically significant, the time-series model has ARCH(1) errors.

■ If a time-series model has ARCH(1) errors, then the variance of the errors in period $t + 1$ can be predicted in period t using the formula $\hat{\sigma}^2_{t+1} = \hat{a}_0 + \hat{a}_1 \hat{\varepsilon}^2_t$.

■ If linear regression is used to model the relationship between two time series, a test should be performed to determine whether either time series has a unit root:

  • If neither of the time series has a unit root, then we can safely use linear regression.

  • If one of the two time series has a unit root, then we should not use linear regression.

  • If both time series have a unit root and the time series are cointegrated, we may safely use linear regression; however, if they are not cointegrated, we should not use linear regression. The (Engle–Granger) Dickey–Fuller test can be used to determine whether time series are cointegrated.

REFERENCES

Barr, G. D. I., B. S. Kantor. 1999. "Price–Earnings Ratios on the Johannesburg Stock Exchange— Are They a Good Value?" SA Journal of Accounting Research 13 (1): 1–23.

Dickey, David A., Wayne A. Fuller. 1979. "Distribution of the Estimators for Autoregressive Time Series with a Unit Root." Journal of the American Statistical Association 74 (366): 427–31. 10.2307/2286348

Diebold, Francis X. 2008. Elements of Forecasting, 4th ed. Cincinnati: South-Western.

Engle, Robert F., Clive W. J. Granger. 1987. "Co-Integration and Error Correction: Representation, Estimation, and Testing." Econometrica 55 (2): 251–76. 10.2307/1913236

Garbade, Kenneth. 1982. Securities Markets. New York: McGraw-Hill.

Granger, Clive W. J., Paul Newbold. 1974. "Spurious Regressions in Econometrics." Journal of Econometrics 2 (2): 111–20. 10.1016/0304-4076(74)90034-7

Hamilton, James D. 1994. Time Series Analysis. Princeton, NJ: Princeton University Press.

Tsay, Ruey S. 2010. Analysis of Financial Time Series, 3rd ed. New York: Wiley.

PRACTICE PROBLEMS

The following information relates to questions 1-7

Angela Martinez, an energy sector analyst at an investment bank, is concerned about the future level of oil prices and how it might affect portfolio values. She is considering whether to recommend a hedge for the bank portfolio's exposure to changes in oil prices. Martinez examines West Texas Intermediate (WTI) monthly crude oil price data, expressed in US dollars per barrel, for the 181-month period from August 2000 through August 2015. The end-of-month WTI oil price was $51.16 in July 2015 and $42.86 in August 2015 (Month 181).

After reviewing the time-series data, Martinez determines that the mean and variance of the time series of oil prices are not constant over time. She then runs the following four regressions using the WTI time-series data.

- Linear trend model: Oil price$_t = b_0 + b_1 t + e_t$.
- Log-linear trend model: ln Oil price$_t = b_0 + b_1 t + e_t$.
- AR(1) model: Oil price$_t = b_0 + b_1$Oil price$_{t-1} + e_t$.
- AR(2) model: Oil price$_t = b_0 + b_1$Oil price$_{t-1} + b_2$Oil price$_{t-2} + e_t$.

Exhibit 1 presents selected data from all four regressions, and Exhibit 2 presents selected autocorrelation data from the AR(1) models.

Exhibit 1: Crude Oil Price per Barrel, August 2000–August 2015

	Regression Statistics (t-statistics for coefficients are reported in parentheses)			
	Linear	**Log-Linear**	**AR(1)**	**AR(2)**
R^2	0.5703	0.6255	0.9583	0.9656
Standard error	18.6327	0.3034	5.7977	5.2799
Observations	181	181	180	179
Durbin–Watson	0.10	0.08	1.16	2.08
RMSE			2.0787	2.0530
Coefficients:				
Intercept	28.3278	3.3929	1.5948	2.0017
	(10.1846)	(74.9091)	(1.4610)	(1.9957)
t (Trend)	0.4086	0.0075		
	(15.4148)	(17.2898)		
Oil price$_{t-1}$			0.9767	1.3946
			(63.9535)	(20.2999)
Oil price$_{t-2}$				–0.4249
				(–6.2064)

In Exhibit 1, at the 5% significance level, the lower critical value for the Durbin–Watson test statistic is 1.75 for both the linear and log-linear regressions.

Exhibit 2: Autocorrelations of the Residual from AR(1) Model

Lag	Autocorrelation	t-Statistic
1	0.4157	5.5768
2	0.2388	3.2045
3	0.0336	0.4512
4	−0.0426	−0.5712

Note: At the 5% significance level, the critical value for a *t*-statistic is 1.97.

After reviewing the data and regression results, Martinez draws the following conclusions.

Conclusion 1   The time series for WTI oil prices is covariance stationary.

Conclusion 2   Out-of-sample forecasting using the AR(1) model appears to be more accurate than that of the AR(2) model.

1. Based on Exhibit 1, the predicted WTI oil price for October 2015 using the linear trend model is *closest* to:

   A. $29.15.

   B. $74.77.

   C. $103.10.

2. Based on Exhibit 1, the predicted WTI oil price for September 2015 using the log-linear trend model is *closest* to:

   A. $29.75.

   B. $29.98.

   C. $116.50.

3. Based on the regression output in Exhibit 1, there is evidence of positive serial correlation in the errors in:

   A. the linear trend model but not the log-linear trend model.

   B. both the linear trend model and the log-linear trend model.

   C. neither the linear trend model nor the log-linear trend model.

4. Martinez's Conclusion 1 is:

   A. correct.

   B. incorrect because the mean and variance of WTI oil prices are not constant over time.

  C. incorrect because the Durbin–Watson statistic of the AR(2) model is greater than 1.75.

5. Based on Exhibit 1, the forecasted oil price in September 2015 based on the AR(2) model is *closest* to:

  A. $38.03.

  B. $40.04.

  C. $61.77.

6. Based on the data for the AR(1) model in Exhibits 1 and 2, Martinez can conclude that the:

  A. residuals are not serially correlated.

  B. autocorrelations do not differ significantly from zero.

  C. standard error for each of the autocorrelations is 0.0745.

7. Based on the mean-reverting level implied by the AR(1) model regression output in Exhibit 1, the forecasted oil price for September 2015 is *most likely* to be:

  A. less than $42.86.

  B. equal to $42.86.

  C. greater than $42.86.

8. You have been assigned to analyze automobile manufacturers, and as a first step in your analysis, you decide to model monthly sales of lightweight vehicles to determine sales growth in that part of the industry. Exhibit 3 gives lightweight vehicle monthly sales (annualized) from January 1992 to December 2000.

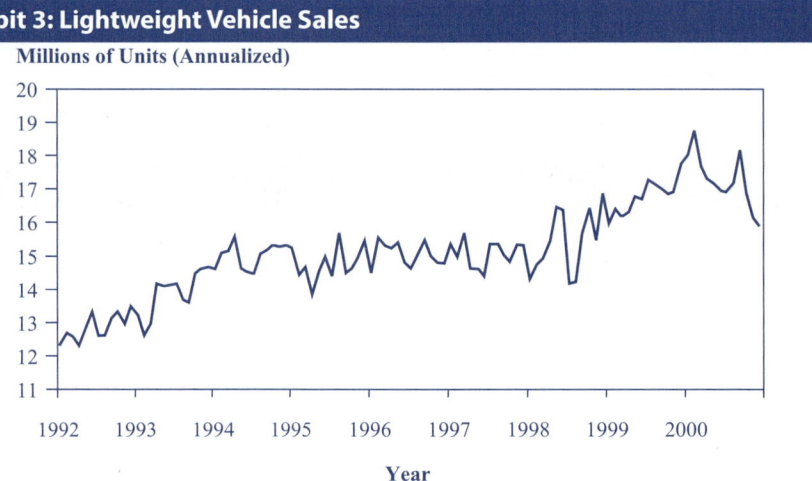

Exhibit 3: Lightweight Vehicle Sales

Millions of Units (Annualized)

Year

Monthly sales in the lightweight vehicle sector, $Sales_t$, have been increasing over time, but you suspect that the growth rate of monthly sales is relatively constant. Write the simplest time-series model for $Sales_t$ that is consistent with your perception.

The following information relates to questions 9-10

The civilian unemployment rate (UER) is an important component of many economic models. Exhibit 1 gives regression statistics from estimating a linear trend model of the unemployment rate: $\text{UER}_t = b_0 + b_1 t + \varepsilon_t$.

Exhibit 1: Estimating a Linear Trend in the Civilian Unemployment Rate: Monthly Observations, January 2013–August 2019

Regression Statistics

R^2	0.9316
Standard error	0.3227
Observations	80
Durbin–Watson	0.1878

	Coefficient	Standard Error	t-Statistic
Intercept	7.2237	0.0728	99.1704
Trend	−0.0510	0.0016	−32.6136

9. Using the regression output in the previous table, what is the model's prediction of the unemployment rate for July 2013?

10. How should we interpret the Durbin–Watson (DW) statistic for this regression? What does the value of the DW statistic say about the validity of a *t*-test on the coefficient estimates?

11. Exhibit 2 compares the predicted civilian unemployment rate (PRED) with the actual civilian unemployment rate (UER) from January 2013 to August 2019. The predicted results come from estimating the linear time trend model $\text{UER}_t = b_0 + b_1 t + \varepsilon_t$.
    What can we conclude about the appropriateness of this model?

Exhibit 1: Predicted and Actual Civilian Unemployment Rates

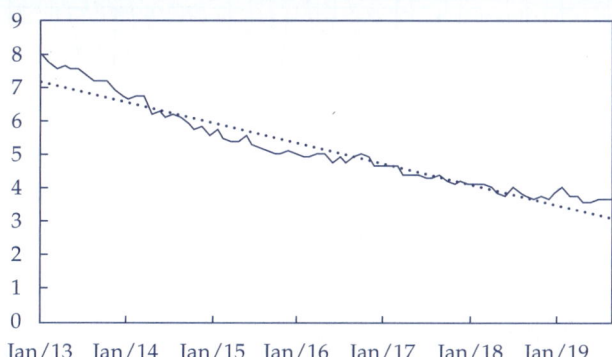

12. Exhibit 9 shows a plot of first differences in the log of monthly lightweight vehicle sales over the same period as in Problem 11. Has differencing the data made the resulting series, $\Delta\ln(\text{Sales}_t) = \ln(\text{Sales}_t) - \ln(\text{Sales}_{t-1})$, covariance stationary?

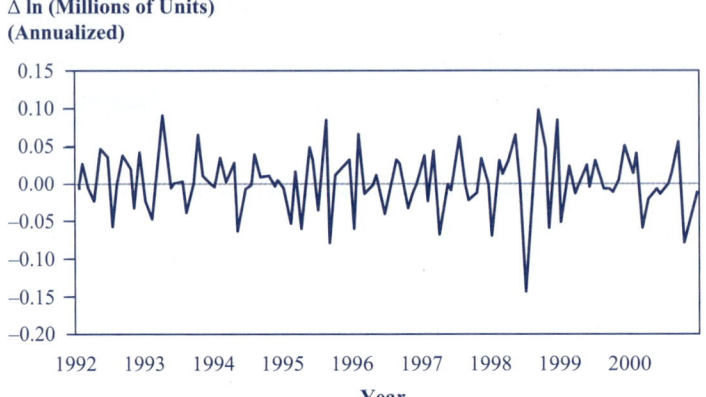

Exhibit 1: Change in Natural Log of Lightweight Vehicle Sales

The following information relates to questions 13-14

Exhibit 4 shows a plot of the first differences in the civilian unemployment rate (UER) between January 2013 and August 2019, $\Delta\text{UER}_t = \text{UER}_t - \text{UER}_{t-1}$.

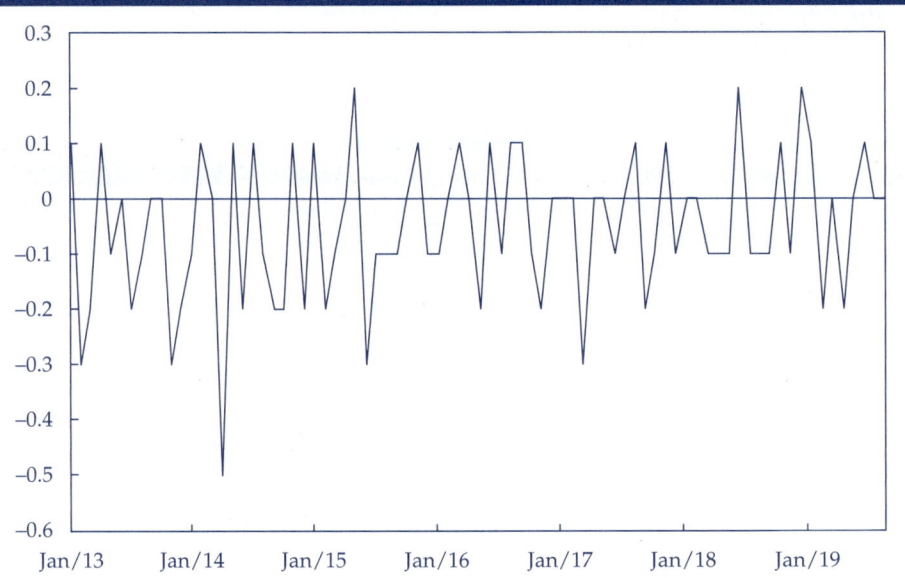

Exhibit 1: Change in Civilian Unemployment Rate

13. Has differencing the data made the new series, ΔUER_t, covariance stationary? Explain your answer.

14. Given the graph of the change in the unemployment rate shown in the figure, describe the steps we should take to determine the appropriate autoregressive time-series model specification for the series ΔUER_t.

15. Exhibit 5 gives the regression output of an AR(1) model on first differences in the unemployment rate. Describe how to interpret the DW statistic for this regression.

Exhibit 1: Estimating an AR(1) Model of Changes in the Civilian Unemployment Rate: Monthly Observations, February 2013–August 2019

Regression Statistics

R^2	0.0546
Standard error	0.1309
Observations	79
Durbin–Watson	2.0756

	Coefficient	Standard Error	t-Statistic
Intercept	−0.0668	0.0158	−4.2278
ΔUER_{t-1}	−0.2320	0.1100	−2.191

The following information relates to questions 16-17

Using monthly data from January 1992 to December 2000, we estimate the following equation for lightweight vehicle sales: $\Delta \ln(Sales_t) = 2.7108 + 0.3987\Delta \ln(Sales_{t-1}) + \varepsilon_t$. Exhibit 10 gives sample autocorrelations of the errors from this model.

Exhibit 1: Different Order Autocorrelations of Differences in the Logs of Vehicle Sales

Lag	Autocorrelation	Standard Error	t-Statistic
1	0.9358	0.0962	9.7247
2	0.8565	0.0962	8.9005
3	0.8083	0.0962	8.4001
4	0.7723	0.0962	8.0257
5	0.7476	0.0962	7.7696
6	0.7326	0.0962	7.6137
7	0.6941	0.0962	7.2138
8	0.6353	0.0962	6.6025
9	0.5867	0.0962	6.0968

Lag	Autocorrelation	Standard Error	t-Statistic
10	0.5378	0.0962	5.5892
11	0.4745	0.0962	4.9315
12	0.4217	0.0962	4.3827

16. Use the information in the table to assess the appropriateness of the specification given by the equation.

17. If the residuals from the AR(1) model above violate a regression assumption, how would you modify the AR(1) specification?

18. Assume that changes in the civilian unemployment rate are covariance stationary and that an AR(1) model is a good description for the time series of changes in the unemployment rate. Specifically, we have $\Delta UER_t = -0.0668 - 0.2320\Delta UER_{t-1}$ (using the coefficient estimates given in the previous problem). Given this equation, what is the mean-reverting level to which changes in the unemployment rate converge?

The following information relates to questions 19-21

Suppose the following model describes changes in the civilian unemployment rate: $\Delta UER_t = -0.0668 - 0.2320\Delta UER_{t-1}$. The current change (first difference) in the unemployment rate is 0.0300. Assume that the mean-reverting level for changes in the unemployment rate is −0.0542.

19. What is the best prediction of the next change?

20. What is the prediction of the change following the next change?

21. Explain your answer to Part B in terms of equilibrium.

22. Exhibit 1 gives the actual sales, log of sales, and changes in the log of sales of Cisco Systems for the period 1Q 2019 to 4Q 2019.

Exhibit 1			
Date	**Actual Sales ($ Millions)**	**Log of Sales**	**Changes in Log of Sales $\Delta\ln(Sales_t)$**
1Q 2019	13,072	9.4782	0.0176
2Q 2019	12,446	9.4292	−0.0491
3Q 2019	12,958	9.4695	0.403
4Q 2019	13,428	9.5051	0.0356
1Q 2020			
2Q 2020			

Forecast the first- and second-quarter sales of Cisco Systems for 2020 using the regression $\Delta\ln(Sales_t) = 0.0068 + 0.2633\Delta\ln(Sales_{t-1})$.

The following information relates to questions 23-24

Exhibit 1 gives the actual change in the log of sales of Cisco Systems from 1Q 2019 to 4Q 2019, along with the forecasts from the regression model $\Delta\ln(\text{Sales}_t)$ = 0.0068 + 0.2633$\Delta\ln(\text{Sales}_{t-1})$ estimated using data from 1Q 2001 to 4Q 2018. (Note that the observations after the fourth quarter of 2018 are out of sample.)

Exhibit 1		
Date	Actual Value of Changes in the Log of Sales $\Delta\ln(\text{Sales}_t)$	Forecast Value of Changes in the Log of Sales $\Delta\ln(\text{Sales}_t)$
1Q 2019	0.0176	0.0147
2Q 2019	−0.0491	0.0107
3Q 2019	0.4030	0.0096
4Q 2019	0.0356	0.0093

23. Calculate the RMSE for the out-of-sample forecast errors.

24. Compare the forecasting performance of the model given with that of another model having an out-of-sample RMSE of 2%.

The following information relates to questions 25-26

25. The AR(1) model for the civilian unemployment rate, $\Delta\text{UER}_t = -0.0405 - 0.4674\Delta\text{UER}_{t-1}$, was developed with five years of data. What would be the drawback to using the AR(1) model to predict changes in the civilian unemployment rate 12 months or more ahead, as compared with 1 month ahead?

26. For purposes of estimating a predictive equation, what would be the drawback to using 30 years of civilian unemployment data rather than only 5 years?

The following information relates to questions 27-35

Max Busse is an analyst in the research department of a large hedge fund. He was recently asked to develop a model to predict the future exchange rate between two currencies. Busse gathers monthly exchange rate data from the most recent 10-year period and runs a regression based on the following AR(1) model specification:

Regression 1: $x_t = b_0 + b_1x_{t-1} + \varepsilon_t$, where x_t is the exchange rate at time t.

Based on his analysis of the time series and the regression results, Busse reaches the following conclusions:

Conclusion 1   The variance of x_t increases over time.

Conclusion 2   The mean-reverting level is undefined.

Conclusion 3 b_0 does not appear to be significantly different from 0.

Busse decides to do additional analysis by first-differencing the data and running a new regression.

Regression 2: $y_t = b_0 + b_1 y_{t-1} + \varepsilon_t$, where $y_t = x_t - x_{t-1}$.

Exhibit 1 shows the regression results.

Exhibit 1: First-Differenced Exchange Rate AR(1) Model: Month-End Observations, Last 10 Years

Regression Statistics

R^2	0.0017
Standard error	7.3336
Observations	118
Durbin–Watson	1.9937

	Coefficient	Standard Error	t-Statistic
Intercept	−0.8803	0.6792	−1.2960
$x_{t-1} - x_{t-2}$	0.0412	0.0915	0.4504

Autocorrelations of the Residual

Lag	Autocorrelation	Standard Error	t-Statistic
1	0.0028	0.0921	0.0300
2	0.0205	0.0921	0.2223
3	0.0707	0.0921	0.7684
4	0.0485	0.0921	0.5271

Note: The critical *t*-statistic at the 5% significance level is 1.98.

Busse decides that he will need to test the data for nonstationarity using a Dickey–Fuller test. To do so, he knows he must model a transformed version of Regression 1.

Busse's next assignment is to develop a model to predict future quarterly sales for PoweredUP, Inc., a major electronics retailer. He begins by running the following regression:

Regression 3: $\ln \text{Sales}_t - \ln \text{Sales}_{t-1} = b_0 + b_1(\ln \text{Sales}_{t-1} - \ln \text{Sales}_{t-2}) + \varepsilon_t$.

Exhibit 2 presents the results of this regression.

Exhibit 2: Log Differenced Sales AR(1) Model: PoweredUP, Inc., Last 10 Years of Quarterly Sales

Regression Statistics

R^2	0.2011

Regression Statistics

Standard error	0.0651
Observations	38
Durbin–Watson	1.9677

	Coefficient	Standard Error	t-Statistic
Intercept	0.0408	0.0112	3.6406
ln Sales$_{t-1}$ – ln Sales$_{t-2}$	−0.4311	0.1432	−3.0099

Autocorrelations of the Residual

Lag	Autocorrelation	Standard Error	t-Statistic
1	0.0146	0.1622	0.0903
2	−0.1317	0.1622	−0.8119
3	−0.1123	0.1622	−0.6922
4	0.6994	0.1622	4.3111

Note: The critical t-statistic at the 5% significance level is 2.02.

Because the regression output from Exhibit 2 raises some concerns, Busse runs a different regression. These regression results, along with quarterly sales data for the past five quarters, are presented in Exhibits 3 and 4, respectively.

Exhibit 3: Log Differenced Sales AR(1) Model with Seasonal Lag: PoweredUP, Inc., Last 10 Years of Quarterly Sales

Regression Statistics

R^2	0.6788
Standard error	0.0424
Observations	35
Durbin–Watson	1.8799

	Coefficient	Standard Error	t-Statistic
Intercept	0.0092	0.0087	1.0582
ln Sales$_{t-1}$ – ln Sales$_{t-2}$	−0.1279	0.1137	−1.1252
ln Sales$_{t-4}$ – ln Sales$_{t-5}$	0.7239	0.1093	6.6209

Autocorrelations of the Residual

Lag	Autocorrelation	Standard Error	t-Statistic
1	0.0574	0.1690	0.3396
2	0.0440	0.1690	0.2604
3	0.1923	0.1690	1.1379
4	−0.1054	0.1690	−0.6237

Note: The critical t-statistic at the 5% significance level is 2.03.

Exhibit 4: Most Recent Quarterly Sales Data (in billions)	
Dec 2015 ($Sales_{t-1}$)	$3.868
Sep 2015 ($Sales_{t-2}$)	$3.780
June 2015 ($Sales_{t-3}$)	$3.692
Mar 2015 ($Sales_{t-4}$)	$3.836
Dec 2014 ($Sales_{t-5}$)	$3.418

After completing his work on PoweredUP, Busse is asked to analyze the relationship of oil prices and the stock prices of three transportation companies. His firm wants to know whether the stock prices can be predicted by the price of oil. Exhibit 5 shows selected information from the results of his analysis.

Exhibit 5: Analysis Summary of Stock Prices for Three Transportation Stocks and the Price of Oil					
	Unit Root?	Linear or Exponential Trend?	Serial Correlation of Residuals in Trend Model?	ARCH(1)?	Comments
Company 1	Yes	Exponential	Yes	Yes	Not cointegrated with oil price
Company 2	Yes	Linear	Yes	No	Cointegrated with oil price
Company 3	No	Exponential	Yes	No	Not cointegrated with oil price
Oil Price	Yes				

To assess the relationship between oil prices and stock prices, Busse runs three regressions using the time series of each company's stock prices as the dependent variable and the time series of oil prices as the independent variable.

27. Which of Busse's conclusions regarding the exchange rate time series is consistent with both the properties of a covariance-stationary time series and the properties of a random walk?

    A. Conclusion 1

    B. Conclusion 2

    C. Conclusion 3

28. Based on the regression output in Exhibit 1, the first-differenced series used to run Regression 2 is consistent with:

    A. a random walk.

    B. covariance stationarity.

    C. a random walk with drift.

29. Based on the regression results in Exhibit 1, the *original* time series of exchange rates:

    A. has a unit root.

    B. exhibits stationarity.

    C. can be modeled using linear regression.

30. In order to perform the nonstationarity test, Busse should transform the Regression 1 equation by:

    A. adding the second lag to the equation.

    B. changing the regression's independent variable.

    C. subtracting the independent variable from both sides of the equation.

31. Based on the regression output in Exhibit 2, what should lead Busse to conclude that the Regression 3 equation is not correctly specified?

    A. The Durbin–Watson statistic

    B. The t-statistic for the slope coefficient

    C. The t-statistics for the autocorrelations of the residual

32. Based on the regression output in Exhibit 3 and sales data in Exhibit 4, the forecasted value of quarterly sales for March 2016 for PoweredUP is *closest* to:

    A. $4.193 billion.

    B. $4.205 billion.

    C. $4.231 billion.

33. Based on Exhibit 5, Busse should conclude that the variance of the error terms for Company 1:

    A. is constant.

    B. can be predicted.

    C. is homoskedastic.

34. Based on Exhibit 5, for which company would the regression of stock prices on oil prices be expected to yield valid coefficients that could be used to estimate the long-term relationship between stock price and oil price?

    A. Company 1

    B. Company 2

    C. Company 3

35. Based on Exhibit 5, which single time-series model would *most likely* be appropriate for Busse to use in predicting the future stock price of Company 3?

    A. Log-linear trend model

    B. First-differenced AR(2) model

    C. First-differenced log AR(1) model

The following information relates to questions 36-37

Exhibit 1 shows monthly observations on the natural log of lightweight vehicle sales, $\ln(\text{Sales}_t)$, for January 1992 to December 2000.

Exhibit 1: Lightweight Vehicle Sales

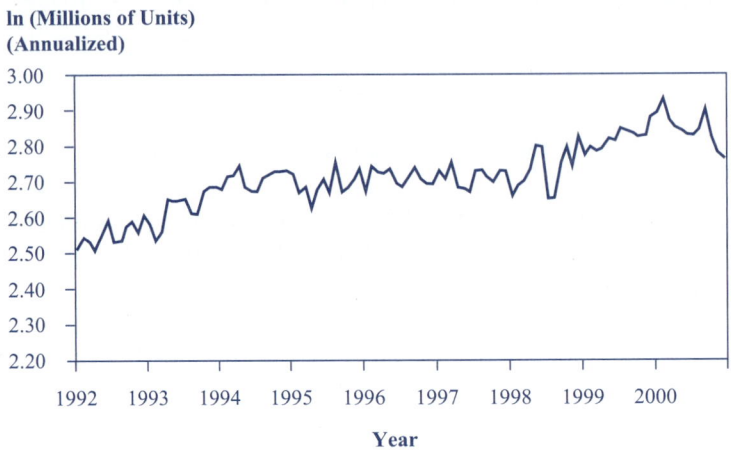

36. Using the figure, comment on whether the specification $\ln(\text{Sales}_t) = b_0 + b_1[\ln(\text{Sales}_{t-1})] + \varepsilon_t$ is appropriate.

37. State an appropriate transformation of the time series.

38. Suppose we want to predict the annualized return of the five-year T-bill using the annualized return of the three-month T-bill with monthly observations from January 1993 to December 2002. Our analysis produces the data shown in Exhibit 1.

Exhibit 1: Regression with Three-Month T-Bill as the Independent Variable and the Five-Year T-Bill as the Dependent Variable: Monthly Observations, January 1993–December 2002

Regression Statistics

R^2	0.5829
Standard error	0.6598
Observations	120
Durbin–Watson	0.1130

	Coefficient	Standard Error	t-Statistic
Intercept	3.0530	0.2060	14.8181
Three-month	0.5722	0.0446	12.8408

Can we rely on the regression model in Exhibit 1 to produce meaningful predictions? Specify what problem might be a concern with this regression.

39. Exhibit 2 shows the quarterly sales of Avon Products from 1Q 1992 to 2Q 2002. Describe the salient features of the data shown.

Exhibit 2: Quarterly Sales at Avon

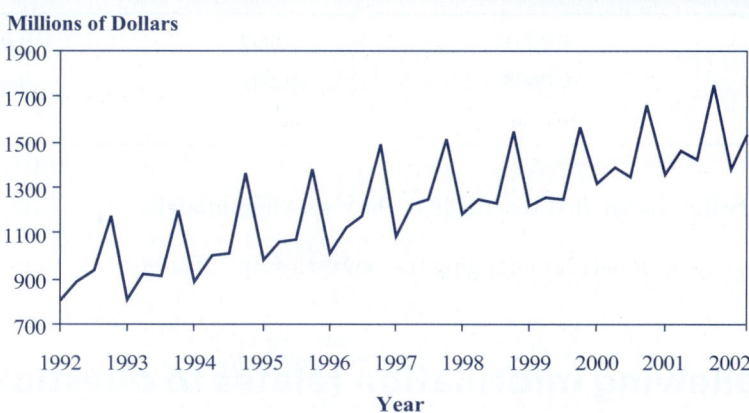

Millions of Dollars

The following information relates to questions 40–41

Exhibit 1 shows the autocorrelations of the residuals from an AR(1) model fit to the changes in the gross profit margin (GPM) of the Home Depot, Inc.

Exhibit 1: Autocorrelations of the Residuals from Estimating the Regression $\Delta GPM_t = 0.0006 - 0.3330\Delta GPM_{t-1} + \varepsilon_t$, 1Q 1992–4Q 2001 (40 Observations)

Lag	Autocorrelation
1	−0.1106
2	−0.5981
3	−0.1525
4	0.8496
5	−0.1099

Exhibit 2 shows the output from a regression on changes in the GPM for Home Depot, where we have changed the specification of the AR regression.

Exhibit 2: Change in Gross Profit Margin for Home Depot, 1Q 1992–4Q 2001

Regression Statistics

R^2	0.9155
Standard error	0.0057

Regression Statistics

Observations	40		
Durbin–Watson	2.6464		

	Coefficient	Standard Error	t-Statistic
Intercept	−0.0001	0.0009	−0.0610
ΔGPM_{t-1}	−0.0608	0.0687	−0.8850
ΔGPM_{t-4}	0.8720	0.0678	12.8683

40. Identify the change that was made to the regression model.

41. Discuss the rationale for changing the regression specification.

The following information relates to questions 42-43

Suppose we decide to use an autoregressive model with a seasonal lag because of the seasonal autocorrelation in the previous problem. We are modeling quarterly data, so we estimate Equation 15: $(\ln Sales_t - \ln Sales_{t-1}) = b_0 + b_1(\ln Sales_{t-1} - \ln Sales_{t-2}) + b_2(\ln Sales_{t-4} - \ln Sales_{t-5}) + \varepsilon_t$. Exhibit 1 shows the regression statistics from this equation.

Exhibit 1: Log Differenced Sales: AR(1) Model with Seasonal Lag Johnson & Johnson Quarterly Observations, January 1985–December 2001

Regression Statistics

R^2	0.4220		
Standard error	0.0318		
Observations	68		
Durbin–Watson	1.8784		

	Coefficient	Standard Error	t-Statistic
Intercept	0.0121	0.0053	2.3055
Lag 1	−0.0839	0.0958	−0.8757
Lag 4	0.6292	0.0958	6.5693

Autocorrelations of the Residual

Lag	Autocorrelation	Standard Error	t-Statistic
1	0.0572	0.1213	0.4720
2	−0.0700	0.1213	−0.5771
3	0.0065	0.1213	−0.0532
4	−0.0368	0.1213	−0.3033

42. Using the information in Exhibit 1, determine whether the model is correctly specified.

43. If sales grew by 1% last quarter and by 2% four quarters ago, use the model to predict the sales growth for this quarter.

44. Describe how to test for autoregressive conditional heteroskedasticity (ARCH) in the residuals from the AR(1) regression on first differences in the civilian unemployment rate, $\Delta UER_t = b_0 + b_1 \Delta UER_{t-1} + \varepsilon_t$.

The following information relates to questions 45-47

Exhibit 1 shows the quarterly sales of Cisco Systems from 3Q 2001 to 2Q 2019.

Exhibit 1: Quarterly Sales at Cisco

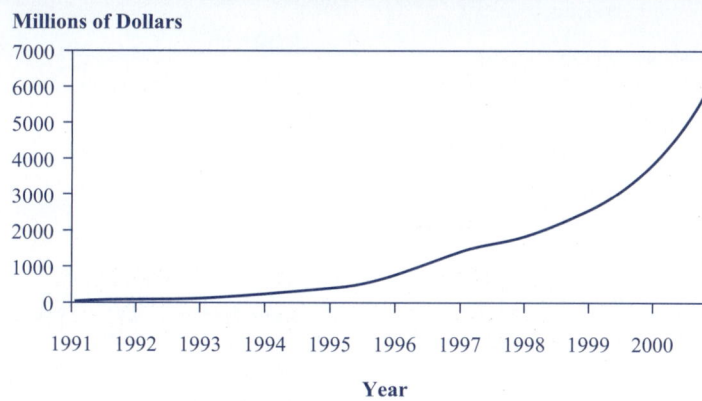

Exhibit 2 gives the regression statistics from estimating the model $\Delta \ln(Sales_t) = b_0 + b_1 \Delta \ln(Sales_{t-1}) + \varepsilon_t$.

Exhibit 2: Change in the Natural Log of Sales for Cisco Quarterly Observations, 3Q 1991–4Q 2000

Regression Statistics

R^2	0.2899
Standard error	0.0408
Observations	38
Durbin–Watson	1.5707

	Coefficient	Standard Error	t-Statistic
Intercept	0.0661	0.0175	3.7840
$\Delta \ln(Sales_{t-1})$	0.4698	0.1225	3.8339

45. Describe the salient features of the quarterly sales series.

46. Describe the procedures we should use to determine whether the AR(1) specification is correct.

47. Assuming the model is correctly specified, what is the long-run change in the log of sales toward which the series will tend to converge?

SOLUTIONS

1. C is correct. The predicted value for period t from a linear trend is calculated as $\hat{y}_t = \hat{b}_0 + \hat{b}_1(t)$.

   October 2015 is the second month out of sample, or $t = 183$. So, the predicted value for October 2015 is calculated as

   $\hat{y}_t = 28.3278 + 0.4086(183) = \$103.10$.

   Therefore, the predicted WTI oil price for October 2015 based on the linear trend model is $103.10.

2. C is correct. The predicted value for period t from a log-linear trend is calculated as $\ln\hat{y}_t = \hat{b}_0 + \hat{b}_1(t)$.

   September 2015 is the first month out of sample, or $t = 182$. So, the predicted value for September 2015 is calculated as follows:

   $\ln\hat{y}_t = 3.3929 + 0.0075(182)$.

   $\ln\hat{y}_t = 4.7579$.

   $\hat{y}_t = e^{4.7579} = \$116.50$.

   Therefore, the predicted WTI oil price for September 2015, based on the log-linear trend model, is $116.50.

3. B is correct. The Durbin–Watson statistic for the linear trend model is 0.10 and for the log-linear trend model is 0.08. Both of these values are below the critical value of 1.75. Therefore, we can reject the hypothesis of no positive serial correlation in the regression errors in both the linear trend model and the log-linear trend model.

4. B is correct. There are three requirements for a time series to be covariance stationary. First, the expected value of the time series must be constant and finite in all periods. Second, the variance of the time series must be constant and finite in all periods. Third, the covariance of the time series with itself for a fixed number of periods in the past or future must be constant and finite in all periods. Martinez concludes that the mean and variance of the time series of WTI oil prices are not constant over time. Therefore, the time series is not covariance stationary.

5. B is correct. The last two observations in the WTI time series are July and August 2015, when the WTI oil price was $51.16 and $42.86, respectively. Therefore, September 2015 represents a one-period-ahead forecast. The one-period-ahead forecast from an AR(2) model is calculated as

   $\hat{x}_{t+1} = \hat{b}_0 + \hat{b}_1 x_t + \hat{b}_2 x_{t-1}$.

   So, the one-period-ahead (September 2015) forecast is calculated as

   $\hat{x}_{t+1} = 2.0017 + 1.3946(\$42.86) - 0.4249(\$51.16) = \$40.04$.

   Therefore, the September 2015 forecast based on the AR(2) model is $40.04.

6. C is correct. The standard error of the autocorrelations is calculated as $\frac{1}{\sqrt{T}}$, where T represents the number of observations used in the regression. Therefore, the standard error for each of the autocorrelations is $\frac{1}{\sqrt{180}} = 0.0745$. Martinez can conclude that the residuals are serially correlated and are significantly different from zero because two of the four autocorrelations in Exhibit 2 have a t-statistic

in absolute value that is greater than the critical value of 1.97.

Choices A and B are incorrect because two of the four autocorrelations have a *t*-statistic in absolute value that is greater than the critical value of the *t*-statistic of 1.97.

7. C is correct. The mean-reverting level from the AR(1) model is calculated as

$$\hat{x}_t = \frac{b_0}{1 - b_1} = \frac{1.5948}{1 - 0.9767} = \$68.45.$$

Therefore, the mean-reverting WTI oil price from the AR(1) model is $68.45. The forecasted oil price in September 2015 will likely be greater than $42.86 because the model predicts that the price will rise in the next period from the August 2015 price of $42.86.

8. A log-linear model captures growth at a constant rate. The log-linear model $\ln(\text{Sales}_t) = b_0 + b_1 t + \varepsilon_t$ would be the simplest model consistent with a constant growth rate for monthly sales. Note that we would need to confirm that the regression assumptions are satisfied before accepting the model as valid.

9. The estimated forecasting equation is $\text{UER}_t = 5.5098 - 0.0294(t)$. The data begin in January 2013, and July 2013 is Period 7. Thus the linear trend model predicts the unemployment rate to be $\text{UER}_7 = 7.2237 - 0.0510(7) = 6.8667$, or approximately 6.9%.

10. The DW statistic is designed to detect positive serial correlation of the errors of a regression equation. Under the null hypothesis of no positive serial correlation, the DW statistic is 2.0. Positive serial correlation will lead to a DW statistic that is less than 2.0. From the table in Problem 1, we see that the DW statistic is 0.1878. To see whether this result is significantly less than 2.0, refer to the Durbin–Watson table in Appendix E at the end of this volume, in the column marked $k = 1$ (one independent variable) and the row corresponding to 60 observations. We see that $d_l = 1.61$. Because our DW statistic is clearly less than d_l, we reject the null hypothesis of no serial correlation at the 0.05 significance level.

The presence of serial correlation in the error term violates one of the regression assumptions. The standard errors of the estimated coefficients will be biased downward, so we cannot conduct hypothesis testing on the coefficients.

11. The difference between UER and its forecast value, PRED, is the forecast error. In an appropriately specified regression model, the forecast errors are randomly distributed around the regression line and have a constant variance. We can see that the errors from this model specification are persistent. The errors tend first to be above the regression line, and then, starting in 2014, they tend to be below the regression line until 2017, when they again are persistently above the regression line. This persistence suggests that the errors are positively serially correlated. Therefore, we conclude that the model is not appropriate for making estimates.

12. The plot of the series $\Delta\ln(\text{Sales}_t)$ appears to fluctuate around a constant mean; its volatility seems constant throughout the period. Differencing the data appears to have made the time series covariance stationary.

13. The plot of the series ΔUER_t seems to fluctuate around a constant mean; its volatility appears to be constant throughout the period. Our initial judgment is that the differenced series is covariance stationary.

14. The change in the unemployment rate seems covariance stationary, so we should first estimate an AR(1) model and test to see whether the residuals from this model have significant serial correlation. If the residuals do not display signifi-

cant serial correlation, we should use the AR(1) model. If the residuals do display significant serial correlation, we should try an AR(2) model and test for serial correlation of the residuals of the AR(2) model. We should continue this procedure until the errors from the final AR(p) model are serially uncorrelated.

15. The DW statistic cannot be appropriately used for a regression that has a lagged value of the dependent variable as one of the explanatory variables. To test for serial correlation, we need to examine the autocorrelations.

16. In a correctly specified regression, the residuals must be serially uncorrelated. We have 108 observations, so the standard error of the autocorrelation is $1/\sqrt{T}$, or in this case $1/\sqrt{108} = 0.0962$. The t-statistic for each lag is significant at the 0.01 level. We would have to modify the model specification before continuing with the analysis.

17. Because the residuals from the AR(1) specification display significant serial correlation, we should estimate an AR(2) model and test for serial correlation of the residuals of the AR(2) model. If the residuals from the AR(2) model are serially uncorrelated, we should then test for seasonality and ARCH behavior. If any serial correlation remains in the residuals, we should estimate an AR(3) process and test the residuals from that specification for serial correlation. We should continue this procedure until the errors from the final AR(p) model are serially uncorrelated. When serial correlation is eliminated, we should test for seasonality and ARCH behavior.

18. When a covariance-stationary series is at its mean-reverting level, the series will tend not to change until it receives a shock (ε_t). So, if the series ΔUER_t is at the mean-reverting level, $\Delta UER_t = \Delta UER_{t-1}$. This implies that $\Delta UER_t = -0.0668 - 0.2320\Delta UER_t$, so that $(1 + 0.2320)\Delta UER_t = -0.0668$ and $\Delta UER_t = -0.0668/(1 + 0.2320) = -0.0542$. The mean-reverting level is -0.0542. In an AR(1) model, the general expression for the mean-reverting level is $b_0/(1 - b_1)$.

19. The predicted change in the unemployment rate for next period is -7.38%, found by substituting 0.0300 into the forecasting model: $-0.0668 - 0.2320(0.03) = -0.0738$.

20. If we substitute our one-period-ahead forecast of -0.0738 into the model (using the chain rule of forecasting), we get a two-period-ahead forecast of -0.0497, or -4.97%.

21. The answer to Part B is quite close to the mean-reverting level of -0.0542. A stationary time series may need many periods to return to its equilibrium, mean-reverting level.

22. The forecast of sales is $13,647 million for the first quarter of 2020 and $13,800 million for the second quarter of 2002, as the following table shows.

Date	Sales ($ Millions)	Log of Sales	Actual Value of Changes in the Log of Sales $\Delta\ln(Sales_t)$	Forecast Value of Changes in the Log of Sales $\Delta\ln(Sales_t)$
1Q 2019	13,072	9.4782	0.0176	
2Q 2019	12,446	9.4292	−0.0491	
3Q 2019	12,958	9.4695	0.4030	
4Q 2019	13,428	9.5051	0.0356	
1Q 2020	13,647	9.5213		0.0162

Date	Sales ($ Millions)	Log of Sales	Actual Value of Changes in the Log of Sales $\Delta \ln(\text{Sales}_t)$	Forecast Value of Changes in the Log of Sales $\Delta \ln(\text{Sales}_t)$
2Q 2020	13,800	9.5324		0.0111

We find the forecasted change in the log of sales for the first quarter of 2020 by inputting the value for the change in the log of sales from the previous quarter into the equation $\Delta \ln(\text{Sales}_t) = 0.0068 + 0.2633\Delta \ln(\text{Sales}_{t-1})$. Specifically, $\Delta \ln(\text{Sales}_t) = 0.0068 + 0.2633(0.0356) = 0.0162$, which means that we forecast the log of sales in the first quarter of 2020 to be $9.5051 + 0.0162 = 9.5213$.

Next, we forecast the change in the log of sales for the second quarter of 2020 as $\Delta \ln(\text{Sales}_t) = 0.0068 + 0.2633(0.0162) = 0.0111$. Note that we have to use our first-quarter 2020 estimated value of the change in the log of sales as our input for $\Delta \ln(\text{Sales}_{t-1})$ because we are forecasting past the period for which we have actual data.

With a forecasted change of 0.0111, we forecast the log of sales in the second quarter of 2020 to be $9.5213 + 0.0111 = 9.5324$.

We have forecasted the log of sales in the first and second quarters of 2020 to be 9.5213 and 9.5324, respectively. Finally, we take the antilog of our estimates of the log of sales in the first and second quarters of 2020 to get our estimates of the level of sales: $e^{9.5213} = 13,647$ and $e^{9.5324} = 13,800$, respectively, for sales of $13,647 million and $13,800 million.

23. The RMSE of the out-of-sample forecast errors is approximately 3.6%. Out-of-sample error refers to the difference between the realized value and the forecasted value of $\Delta \ln(\text{Sales}_t)$ for dates beyond the estimation period. In this case, the out-of-sample period is 1Q 2019 to 4Q 2019. These are the four quarters for which we have data that we did not use to obtain the estimated model $\Delta \ln(\text{Sales}_t) = 0.0068 + 0.2633\Delta \ln(\text{Sales}_{t-1})$.

The steps to calculate RMSE are as follows:

i. Take the difference between the actual and the forecast values. This is the error.

ii. Square the error.

iii. Sum the squared errors.

iv. Divide by the number of forecasts.

v. Take the square root of the average.

We show the calculations for RMSE in the following table.

Actual Values of Changes in the Log of Sales $\Delta \ln(\text{Sales}_t)$	Forecast Values of Changes in the Log of Sales $\Delta \ln(\text{Sales}_t)$	Error (Column 1 – Column 2)	Squared Error (Column 3 Squared)
0.0176	0.0147	0.0029	0.0000
−0.0491	0.0107	−0.0598	0.0036
0.0403	0.0096	0.0307	0.0009
0.0356	0.0093	0.0263	0.0007
		Sum	0.0052
		Mean	0.0013
		RMSE	0.036

24. The lower the RMSE, the more accurate the forecasts of a model in forecasting. Therefore, the model with the RMSE of 2% has greater accuracy in forecasting than the model in Part A, which has an RMSE of 3.6%.

25. Predictions too far ahead can be nonsensical. For example, the AR(1) model we have been examining, $\Delta UER_t = -0.0405 - 0.4674\Delta UER_{t-1}$, taken at face value, predicts declining civilian unemployment into the indefinite future. Because the civilian unemployment rate will probably not go below 3% frictional unemployment and cannot go below 0% unemployment, this model's long-range forecasts are implausible. The model is designed for short-term forecasting, as are many time-series models.

26. Using more years of data for estimation may lead to nonstationarity even in the series of first differences in the civilian unemployment rate. As we go further back in time, we increase the risk that the underlying civilian unemployment rate series has more than one regime (or true model). If the series has more than one regime, fitting one model to the entire period would not be correct. Note that when we have good reason to believe that a time series is stationary, a longer series of data is generally desirable.

27. C is correct. A random walk can be described by the equation $x_t = b_0 + b_1 x_{t-1} + \varepsilon_t$, where $b_0 = 0$ and $b_1 = 1$. So $b_0 = 0$ is a characteristic of a random walk time series. A covariance-stationary series must satisfy the following three requirements:

    1. The expected value of the time series must be constant and finite in all periods.

    2. The variance of the time series must be constant and finite in all periods.

    3. The covariance of the time series with itself for a fixed number of periods in the past or future must be constant and finite in all periods.

    $b_0 = 0$ does not violate any of these three requirements and is thus consistent with the properties of a covariance-stationary time series.

28. B is correct. The critical t-statistic at a 5% confidence level is 1.98. As a result, neither the intercept nor the coefficient on the first lag of the first-differenced exchange rate in Regression 2 differs significantly from zero. Also, the residual autocorrelations do not differ significantly from zero. As a result, Regression 2 can be reduced to $y_t = \varepsilon_t$, with a mean-reverting level of $b_0/(1 - b_1) = 0/1 = 0$. Therefore, the variance of y_t in each period is $var(\varepsilon_t) = \sigma^2$. The fact that the residuals are not autocorrelated is consistent with the covariance of the times series with itself being constant and finite at different lags. Because the variance and the mean of y_t are constant and finite in each period, we can also conclude that y_t is covariance stationary.

29. A is correct. If the exchange rate series is a random walk, then the first-differenced series will yield $b_0 = 0$ and $b_1 = 0$ and the error terms will not be serially correlated. The data in Exhibit 1 show that this is the case: Neither the intercept nor the coefficient on the first lag of the first-differenced exchange rate in Regression 2 differs significantly from zero because the t-statistics of both coefficients are less than the critical t-statistic of 1.98. Also, the residual autocorrelations do not differ significantly from zero because the t-statistics of all autocorrelations are less than the critical t-statistic of 1.98. Therefore, because all random walks have unit roots, the exchange rate time series used to run Regression 1 has a unit root.

30. C is correct. To conduct the Dickey–Fuller test, one must subtract the independent variable, x_{t-1}, from both sides of the original AR(1) model. This results in a change of the dependent variable (from x_t to $x_t - x_{t-1}$) and a change in the regression's slope coefficient (from b_1 to $b_1 - 1$) but not a change in the independent variable.

31. C is correct. The regression output in Exhibit 2 suggests there is serial correlation in the residual errors. The fourth autocorrelation of the residual has a value of 0.6994 and a t-statistic of 4.3111, which is greater than the t-statistic critical value of 2.02. Therefore, the null hypothesis that the fourth autocorrelation is equal to zero can be rejected. This indicates strong and significant seasonal autocorrelation, which means the Regression 3 equation is misspecified.

32. C is correct. The quarterly sales for March 2016 are calculated as follows:

ln Sales$_t$ − ln Sales$_{t-1}$ = b_0 + b_1(ln Sales$_{t-1}$ − ln Sales$_{t-2}$) + b_2(ln Sales$_{t-4}$ − ln Sales$_{t-5}$).

ln Sales$_t$ − ln 3.868 = 0.0092 − 0.1279(ln 3.868 − ln 3.780) + 0.7239(ln 3.836 − ln 3.418).

ln Sales$_t$ − 1.35274 = 0.0092 − 0.1279(1.35274 − 1.32972) + 0.7239(1.34443 − 1.22906).

ln Sales$_t$ = 1.35274 + 0.0092 − 0.1279(0.02301) + 0.7239(0.11538).

ln Sales$_t$ = 1.44251.

Sales$_t$ = $e^{1.44251}$ = 4.231.

33. B is correct. Exhibit 5 shows that the time series of the stock prices of Company 1 exhibits heteroskedasticity, as evidenced by the fact that the time series is ARCH(1). If a time series is ARCH(1), then the variance of the error in one period depends on the variance of the error in previous periods. Therefore, the variance of the errors in period $t + 1$ can be predicted in period t using the formula

$$\hat{\sigma}_{t+1}^2 = \hat{a}_0 + \hat{a}_1 \hat{\varepsilon}_t^2.$$

34. B is correct. When two time series have a unit root but are cointegrated, the error term in the linear regression of one time series on the other will be covariance stationary. Exhibit 5 shows that the series of stock prices of Company 2 and the oil prices both contain a unit root and the two time series are cointegrated. As a result, the regression coefficients and standard errors are consistent and can be used for hypothesis tests. Although the cointegrated regression estimates the long-term relation between the two series, it may not be the best model of the short-term relationship.

35. C is correct. As a result of the exponential trend in the time series of stock prices for Company 3, Busse would want to take the natural log of the series and then first-difference it. Because the time series also has serial correlation in the residuals from the trend model, Busse should use a more complex model, such as an autoregressive (AR) model.

36. The graph of ln(Sales$_t$) appears to trend upward over time. A series that trends upward or downward over time often has a unit root and is thus not covariance stationary. Therefore, using an AR(1) regression on the undifferenced series is probably not correct. In practice, we need to examine regression statistics to confirm such visual impressions.

37. The most common way to transform a time series with a unit root into a covariance-stationary time series is to difference the data—that is, to create a new series: $\Delta\ln(Sales_t) = \ln(Sales_t) - \ln(Sales_{t-1})$.

38. To determine whether we can use linear regression to model more than one time series, we should first determine whether any of the time series has a unit root. If none of the time series has a unit root, then we can safely use linear regression to test the relations between the two time series. Note that if one of the two variables has a unit root, then our analysis would not provide valid results; if both of the variables have unit roots, then we would need to evaluate whether the variables are cointegrated.

39. The quarterly sales of Avon show an upward trend and a clear seasonal pattern, as indicated by the repeated regular cycle.

40. A second explanatory variable, the change in the gross profit margin lagged four quarters, ΔGPM_{t-4}, was added.

41. The model was augmented to account for seasonality in the time series (with quarterly data, significant autocorrelation at the fourth lag indicates seasonality). The standard error of the autocorrelation coefficient equals 1 divided by the square root of the number of observations: $1/\sqrt{40}$, or 0.1581. The autocorrelation at the fourth lag (0.8496) is significant: $t = 0.8496/0.1581 = 5.37$. This indicates seasonality, and accordingly we added ΔGPM_{t-4}. Note that in the augmented regression, the coefficient on ΔGPM_{t-4} is highly significant. (Although the autocorrelation at second lag is also significant, the fourth lag is more important because of the rationale of seasonality. Once the fourth lag is introduced as an independent variable, we might expect that the second lag in the residuals would not be significant.)

42. In order to determine whether this model is correctly specified, we need to test for serial correlation among the residuals. We want to test whether we can reject the null hypothesis that the value of each autocorrelation is 0 against the alternative hypothesis that each is not equal to 0. At the 0.05 significance level, with 68 observations and three parameters, this model has 65 degrees of freedom. The critical value of the t-statistic needed to reject the null hypothesis is thus about 2.0. The absolute value of the t-statistic for each autocorrelation is below 0.60 (less than 2.0), so we cannot reject the null hypothesis that each autocorrelation is not significantly different from 0. We have determined that the model is correctly specified.

43. If sales grew by 1% last quarter and by 2% four quarters ago, then the model predicts that sales growth this quarter will be $0.0121 - 0.0839[\ln(1.01)] + 0.6292[\ln(1.02)] = e^{0.02372} - 1 = 2.40\%$.

44. We should estimate the regression $\Delta UER_t = b_0 + b_1\Delta UER_{t-1} + \varepsilon_t$ and save the residuals from the regression. Then we should create a new variable, $\hat{\varepsilon}_t^2$, by squaring the residuals. Finally, we should estimate $\hat{\varepsilon}_t^2 = a_0 + a_1\hat{\varepsilon}_{t-1}^2 + u_t$ and test to see whether a_1 is statistically different from 0.

45. The series has a steady upward trend of growth, suggesting an exponential growth rate. This finding suggests transforming the series by taking the natural log and differencing the data.

46. First, we should determine whether the residuals from the AR(1) specification are serially uncorrelated. If the residuals are serially correlated, then we should try an AR(2) specification and then test the residuals from the AR(2) model for serial correlation. We should continue in this fashion until the residuals are se-

rially uncorrelated and then look for seasonality in the residuals. If seasonality is present, we should add a seasonal lag. If no seasonality is present, we should test for ARCH. If ARCH is not present, we can conclude that the model is correctly specified.

47. If the model $\Delta \ln(\text{Sales}_t) = b_0 + b_1[\Delta \ln(\text{Sales}_{t-1})] + \varepsilon_t$ is correctly specified, then the series $\Delta \ln(\text{Sales}_t)$ is covariance stationary. So, this series tends to its mean-reverting level, which is $b_0/(1 - b_1)$, or $0.0661/(1 - 0.4698) = 0.1247$.

6

Machine Learning

by Kathleen DeRose, CFA, Matthew Dixon, PhD, FRM, and Christophe Le Lannou.

Kathleen DeRose, CFA, is at New York University, Stern School of Business (USA). Matthew Dixon, PhD, FRM, is at Illinois Institute of Technology, Stuart School of Business (USA). Christophe Le Lannou is at dataLearning (United Kingdom).

LEARNING OUTCOMES	
Mastery	The candidate should be able to:
☐	describe supervised machine learning, unsupervised machine learning, and deep learning
☐	describe overfitting and identify methods of addressing it
☐	describe supervised machine learning algorithms—including penalized regression, support vector machine, k-nearest neighbor, classification and regression tree, ensemble learning, and random forest—and determine the problems for which they are best suited
☐	describe unsupervised machine learning algorithms—including principal components analysis, k-means clustering, and hierarchical clustering—and determine the problems for which they are best suited
☐	describe neural networks, deep learning nets, and reinforcement learning

INTRODUCTION   1

☐ | describe supervised machine learning, unsupervised machine learning, and deep learning

Investment firms are increasingly using technology at every step of the investment management value chain—from improving their understanding of clients to uncovering new sources of alpha and executing trades more efficiently. Machine learning techniques, a central part of that technology, are the subject of this reading. These techniques first appeared in finance in the 1990s and have since flourished with the explosion of data and cheap computing power.

This reading provides a high-level view of machine learning (ML). It covers a selection of key ML algorithms and their investment applications. Investment practitioners should be equipped with a basic understanding of the types of investment problems that machine learning can address, an idea of how the algorithms work, and the vocabulary to interact with machine learning and data science experts. While investment practitioners need not master the details and mathematics of machine learning, as domain experts in investments they can play an important role in the implementation of these techniques by being able to source appropriate model inputs, interpret model outputs, and translate outputs into appropriate investment actions.

Section 2 gives an overview of machine learning in investment management. Section 3 defines machine learning and the types of problems that can be addressed by supervised and unsupervised learning. Section 4 describes evaluating machine learning algorithm performance. Key supervised machine learning algorithms are covered in Section 5, and Section 6 describes key unsupervised machine learning algorithms. Neural networks, deep learning nets, and reinforcement learning are covered in Section 7. Section 8 provides a decision flowchart for selecting the appropriate ML algorithm. The reading concludes with a summary.

Machine Learning and Investment Management

The growing volume and exploding diversity of data, as well as the perceived increasing economic value of insights extracted from these data, have inspired rapid growth in data science. This newly emerging field combines mathematics, computer science, and business analytics. It also strikes out in a new direction that relies on learning—from basic learning functions that map relationships between variables to advanced neural networks that mimic physical processes that absorb, order, and adapt to information.

Machine learning has theoretical and practical implications for investment management. For example, machine learning could potentially reshape accepted wisdom about asset risk premiums and reconfigure investment management business processes. Large datasets and learning models are already affecting investment management practices—from client profiling to asset allocation, stock selection, portfolio construction and risk management, and trading.

Machine learning applications are at each step of the asset and wealth management value chain. Chatbots answer basic retirement savings questions, learning from their interactions with investors. Machine learning methods can be used to generate alpha signals used in security selection by creating a non-linear forecast for a single time series, by deriving a forecast from a suite of predefined factors, or even by choosing input signals from existing or newly found data. For example, researchers using textual analysis have found that year-over-year changes in annual (10-K) and quarterly (10-Q) filings, particularly negative changes in the management discussion and risk sections, can strongly predict equity returns.

Machine learning methods can help calculate target portfolio weights that incorporate client restrictions and then dynamically weight them to maximize a Sharpe ratio. Another use of machine learning methods is better estimation of the variance–covariance matrix via principal components analysis, which reduces the number of variables needed to explain the variation in the data. Research suggests that machine learning solutions outperform mean–variance optimization in portfolio construction. Machine learning techniques are already creating better order flow management tools with non-linear trading algorithms that reduce the costs of implementing portfolio decisions. These developments have caused an evolution in the automation of tools, processes, and businesses (such as robo-advising).

WHAT IS MACHINE LEARNING

2

☐ | describe supervised machine learning, unsupervised machine learning, and deep learning

We now discuss some fundamental concepts of machine learning, including a definition and an overview of key types of machine learning, such as supervised and unsupervised ML.

Defining Machine Learning

Statistical approaches and machine learning techniques both analyze observations to reveal some underlying process; however, they diverge in their assumptions, terminology, and techniques. Statistical approaches rely on foundational assumptions and explicit models of structure, such as observed samples that are assumed to be drawn from a specified underlying probability distribution. These a priori restrictive assumptions can fail in reality.

In contrast, machine learning seeks to extract knowledge from large amounts of data with fewer such restrictions. The goal of machine learning algorithms is to automate decision-making processes by generalizing (i.e., "learning") from known examples to determine an underlying structure in the data. The emphasis is on the ability of the algorithm to generate structure or predictions from data without any human help. An elementary way to think of ML algorithms is to "find the pattern, apply the pattern."

Machine learning techniques are better able than statistical approaches (such as linear regression) to handle problems with many variables (high dimensionality) or with a high degree of non-linearity. ML algorithms are particularly good at detecting change, even in highly non-linear systems, because they can detect the preconditions of a model's break or anticipate the probability of a regime switch.

Machine learning is broadly divided into three distinct classes of techniques: supervised learning, unsupervised learning, and deep learning/reinforcement learning.

Supervised Learning

Supervised learning involves ML algorithms that infer patterns between a set of inputs (the X's) and the desired output (Y). The inferred pattern is then used to map a given input set into a predicted output. Supervised learning requires a **labeled dataset**, one that contains matched sets of observed inputs and the associated output. Applying the ML algorithm to this dataset to infer the pattern between the inputs and output is called "training" the algorithm. Once the algorithm has been trained, the inferred pattern can be used to predict output values based on new inputs (i.e., ones not in the training dataset).

Multiple regression is an example of supervised learning. A regression model takes matched data (X's, Y) and uses it to estimate parameters that characterize the relationship between Y and the X's. The estimated parameters can then be used to predict Y on a new, different set of X's. The difference between the predicted and actual Y is used to evaluate how well the regression model predicts out-of-sample (i.e., using new data).

The terminology used with ML algorithms differs from that used in regression. Exhibit 1 provides a visual of the supervised learning model training process and a translation between regression and ML terminologies.

Exhibit 1: Overview of Supervised Learning

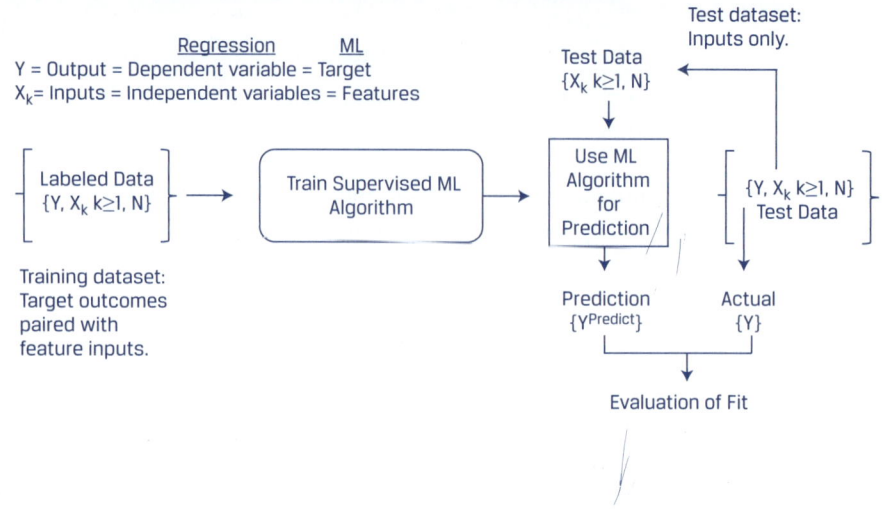

Regression   ML
Y = Output = Dependent variable = Target
X_k = Inputs = Independent variables = Features

Labeled Data
$\{Y, X_k\ k \geq 1, N\}$

Train Supervised ML Algorithm

Test Data
$\{X_k\ k \geq 1, N\}$

Use ML Algorithm for Prediction

Test dataset: Inputs only.

$\{Y, X_k\ k \geq 1, N\}$
Test Data

Training dataset: Target outcomes paired with feature inputs.

Prediction
$\{Y^{Predict}\}$

Actual
$\{Y\}$

Evaluation of Fit

In supervised machine learning, the dependent variable (Y) is the **target** and the independent variables (X's) are known as **features**. The labeled data (training dataset) is used to train the supervised ML algorithm to infer a pattern-based prediction rule. The fit of the ML model is evaluated using labeled test data in which the predicted targets ($Y^{Predict}$) are compared to the actual targets (Y^{Actual}).

An example of supervised learning is the case in which ML algorithms are used to predict whether credit card transactions are fraudulent or legitimate. In the credit card example, the target is a binary variable with a value of 1 for "fraudulent" or 0 for "non-fraudulent." The features are the transaction characteristics. The chosen ML algorithm uses these data elements to train a model to predict the likelihood of fraud more accurately in new transactions. The ML program "learns from experience" if the percentage of correctly predicted credit card transactions increases as the amount of input from a growing credit card database increases. One possible ML algorithm to use would be to fit a logistic regression model to the data to provide an estimate of the probability a transaction is fraudulent.

Supervised learning can be divided into two categories of problems—regression and classification—with the distinction between them being determined by the nature of the target (Y) variable. If the target variable is continuous, then the task is one of regression (even if the ML technique used is not "regression"; note this nuance of ML terminology). If the target variable is categorical or ordinal (i.e., a ranked category), then it is a classification problem. Regression and classification use different ML techniques.

Regression focuses on making predictions of continuous target variables. Most readers are already familiar with multiple linear regression (e.g., ordinary least squares) models, but other supervised learning techniques exist, including non-linear models. These non-linear models are useful for problems involving large datasets with large numbers of features, many of which may be correlated. Some examples of problems belonging to the regression category are using historical stock market returns to forecast stock price performance or using historical corporate financial ratios to forecast the probability of bond default.

Classification focuses on sorting observations into distinct categories. In a regression problem, when the dependent variable (target) is categorical, the model relating the outcome to the independent variables (features) is called a "classifier." You should already be familiar with logistic regression as a type of classifier. Many classification models are binary classifiers, as in the case of fraud detection for credit card transactions. Multi-category classification is not uncommon, as in the case of classifying firms into multiple credit rating categories. In assigning ratings, the outcome variable is ordinal, meaning the categories have a distinct order or ranking (e.g., from low to high creditworthiness). Ordinal variables are intermediate between categorical variables and continuous variables on a scale of measurement.

Unsupervised Learning

Unsupervised learning is machine learning that does not make use of labeled data. More formally, in unsupervised learning, we have inputs (X's) that are used for analysis without any target (Y) being supplied. In unsupervised learning, because the ML algorithm is not given labeled training data, the algorithm seeks to discover structure within the data themselves. As such, unsupervised learning is useful for exploring new datasets because it can provide human experts with insights into a dataset too big or too complex to visualize.

Two important types of problems that are well suited to unsupervised machine learning are reducing the dimension of data and sorting data into clusters, known as dimension reduction and clustering, respectively.

Dimension reduction focuses on reducing the number of features while retaining variation across observations to preserve the information contained in that variation. Dimension reduction may have several purposes. It may be applied to data with a large number of features to produce a lower dimensional representation (i.e., with fewer features) that can fit, for example, on a computer screen. Dimension reduction is also used in many quantitative investment and risk management applications where it is critical to identify the most predictive factors underlying asset price movements.

Clustering focuses on sorting observations into groups (clusters) such that observations in the same cluster are more similar to each other than they are to observations in other clusters. Groups are formed based on a set of criteria that may or may not be prespecified (such as the number of groups). Clustering has been used by asset managers to sort companies into groupings driven by data (e.g., based on their financial statement data or corporate characteristics) rather than conventional groupings (e.g., based on sectors or countries).

Deep Learning and Reinforcement Learning

More broadly in the field of artificial intelligence, additional categories of machine learning algorithms are distinguished. In **deep learning**, sophisticated algorithms address complex tasks, such as image classification, face recognition, speech recognition, and natural language processing. Deep learning is based on **neural networks** (NNs), also called artificial neural networks (ANNs)—highly flexible ML algorithms that have been successfully applied to a variety of supervised and unsupervised tasks characterized by large datasets, non-linearities, and interactions among features. In **reinforcement learning**, a computer learns from interacting with itself or data generated by the same algorithm. Deep learning and reinforcement learning principles have been combined to create efficient algorithms for solving a range of highly complex problems in robotics, health care, and finance.

Summary of ML Algorithms and How to Choose among Them

Exhibit 2 is a guide to the various machine learning algorithms organized by algorithm type (supervised or unsupervised) and by type of variables (continuous, categorical, or both). We will not cover linear or logistic regression since they are covered elsewhere in readings on quantitative methods. The extensions of linear regression, such as penalized regression and least absolute shrinkage and selection operator (LASSO), as well as the other ML algorithms shown in Exhibit 2, will be covered in this reading.

Exhibit 2: Guide to ML Algorithms

Variables	ML Algorithm Type	
	Supervised (Target Variable)	Unsupervised (No Target Variable)
Continuous	**Regression** • Linear; Penalized Regression/LASSO • Logistic • Classification and Regression Tree (CART) • Random Forest	**Dimension Reduction** • Principal Components Analysis (PCA) **Clustering** • *K*-Means • Hierarchical
Categorical	**Classification** • Logistic • Support Vector Machine (SVM) • *K*-Nearest Neighbor (KNN) • Classification and Regression Tree (CART)	**Dimension Reduction** • Principal Components Analysis (PCA) **Clustering** • *K*-Means • Hierarchical
Continuous or Categorical	Neural Networks Deep Learning Reinforcement Learning	Neural Networks Deep Learning Reinforcement Learning

EXAMPLE 1

Machine Learning Overview

1. Which of the following *best* describes machine learning? Machine learning:

   A. is a type of computer algorithm used just for linear regression.

   B. is a set of algorithmic approaches aimed at generating structure or predictions from data without human intervention by finding a pattern and then applying the pattern.

   C. is a set of computer-driven approaches adapted to extracting information from linear, labeled datasets.

Solution

B is correct. A is incorrect because machine learning algorithms are typically not used for linear regression. C is incorrect because machine learning is not limited to extracting information from linear, labeled datasets.

2. Which of the following statements is *most* accurate? When attempting to discover groupings of data without any target (*Y*) variable:

   A. an unsupervised ML algorithm is used.

   B. an ML algorithm that is given labeled training data is used.

   C. a supervised ML algorithm is used.

Solution

A is correct. B is incorrect because the term "labeled training data" means the target (Y) is provided. C is incorrect because a supervised ML algorithm is meant to predict a target (Y) variable.

3. Which of the following statements concerning supervised learning *best* distinguishes it from unsupervised learning? Supervised learning involves:

   A. training on labeled data to infer a pattern-based prediction rule.
   B. training on unlabeled data to infer a pattern-based prediction rule.
   C. learning from unlabeled data by discovering underlying structure in the data themselves.

Solution

A is correct. B is incorrect because supervised learning uses labeled training data. C is incorrect because it describes unsupervised learning.

4. Which of the following *best* describes dimension reduction? Dimension reduction:

   A. focuses on classifying observations in a dataset into known groups using labeled training data.
   B. focuses on clustering observations in a dataset into unknown groups using unlabeled data.
   C. focuses on reducing the number of features in a dataset while retaining variation across observations to preserve the information in that variation.

Solution

C is correct. A is incorrect because it describes classification, not dimension reduction. B is incorrect because it describes clustering, not dimension reduction.

EVALUATING ML ALGORITHM PERFORMANCE

3

☐ | describe overfitting and identify methods of addressing it

Machine learning algorithms promise several advantages relative to a structured statistical approach in exploring and analyzing the structure of very large datasets. ML algorithms have the ability to uncover complex interactions between feature variables and the target variable, and they can process massive amounts of data quickly. Moreover, many ML algorithms can easily capture non-linear relationships and may be able to recognize and predict structural changes between features and the target. These advantages mainly derive from the non-parametric and non-linear models that allow more flexibility when inferring relationships.

The flexibility of ML algorithms comes with a price, however. ML algorithms can produce overly complex models with results that are difficult to interpret, may be sensitive to noise or particulars of the data, and may fit the training data too well. An

ML algorithm that fits the training data too well will typically not predict well using new data. This problem is known as **overfitting**, and it means that the fitted algorithm does not **generalize** well to new data. A model that generalizes well is a model that retains its explanatory power when predicting using out-of-sample (i.e., new) data. An overfit model has incorporated the noise or random fluctuations in the training data into its learned relationship. The problem is that these aspects often do not apply to new data the algorithm receives and so will negatively impact the model's ability to generalize, therefore reducing its overall predictive value. The evaluation of any ML algorithm thus focuses on its prediction error on new data rather than on its goodness of fit on the data with which the algorithm was fitted (i.e., trained).

Generalization is an objective in model building, so the problem of overfitting is a challenge to attaining that objective. These two concepts are the focus of the discussion below.

Generalization and Overfitting

To properly describe generalization and overfitting of an ML model, it is important to note the partitioning of the dataset to which the model will be applied. The dataset is typically divided into three non-overlapping samples: (1) **training sample** used to train the model, (2) **validation sample** for validating and tuning the model, and (3) **test sample** for testing the model's ability to predict well on new data. The training and validation samples are often referred to as being "in-sample," and the test sample is commonly referred to as being "out-of-sample." We will return shortly to the topic of partitioning the dataset.

To be valid and useful, any supervised machine learning model must generalize well beyond the training data. The model should retain its explanatory power when tested out-of-sample. As mentioned, one common reason for failure to generalize is overfitting. Think of overfitting as tailoring a custom suit that fits only one person. Continuing the analogy, underfitting is similar to making a baggy suit that fits no one, whereas robust fitting, the desired result, is similar to fashioning a universal suit that fits all people of similar dimensions.

The concepts of underfitting, overfitting, and good (or robust) fitting are illustrated in Exhibit 3. Underfitting means the model does not capture the relationships in the data. The left graph shows four errors in this underfit model (three misclassified circles and one misclassified triangle). Overfitting means training a model to such a degree of specificity to the training data that the model begins to incorporate noise coming from quirks or spurious correlations; it mistakes randomness for patterns and relationships. The algorithm may have memorized the data, rather than learned from it, so it has perfect hindsight but no foresight. The main contributors to overfitting are thus high noise levels in the data and too much complexity in the model. The middle graph shows no errors in this overfit model. **Complexity** refers to the number of features, terms, or branches in the model and to whether the model is linear or non-linear (non-linear is more complex). As models become more complex, overfitting risk increases. A good fit/robust model fits the training (in-sample) data well and generalizes well to out-of-sample data, both within acceptable degrees of error. The right graph shows that the good fitting model has only one error, the misclassified circle.

Exhibit 3: Underfitting, Overfitting, and Good Fitting

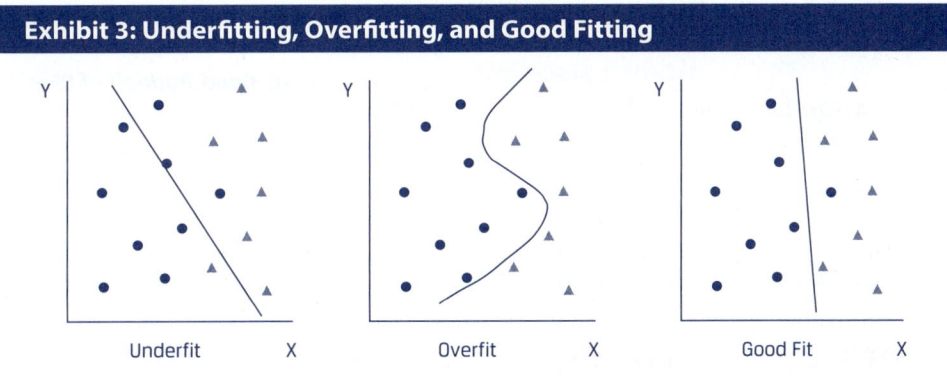

Errors and Overfitting

To capture these effects and calibrate degree of fit, data scientists compare error rates in- and out-of-sample as a function of both the data and the algorithm. Total in-sample errors (E_{in}) are generated by the predictions of the fitted relationship relative to actual target outcomes on the training sample. Total out-of-sample errors (E_{out}) are from either the validation or test samples. Low or no in-sample error but large out-of-sample error are indicative of poor generalization. Data scientists decompose the total out-of-sample error into three sources:

1. **Bias error**, or the degree to which a model fits the training data. Algorithms with erroneous assumptions produce high bias with poor approximation, causing underfitting and high in-sample error.

2. **Variance error**, or how much the model's results change in response to new data from validation and test samples. Unstable models pick up noise and produce high variance, causing overfitting and high out-of-sample error.

3. **Base error** due to randomness in the data.

A **learning curve** plots the accuracy rate (= 1 − error rate) in the validation or test samples (i.e., out-of-sample) against the amount of data in the training sample, so it is useful for describing under- and overfitting as a function of bias and variance errors. If the model is robust, out-of-sample accuracy increases as the training sample size increases. This implies that error rates experienced in the validation or test samples (E_{out}) and in the training sample (E_{in}) converge toward each other and toward a desired error rate (or, alternatively, the base error). In an underfitted model with high bias error, shown in the left panel of Exhibit 4, high error rates cause convergence below the desired accuracy rate. Adding more training samples will not improve the model to the desired performance level. In an overfitted model with high variance error, shown in the middle panel of Exhibit 4, the validation sample and training sample error rates fail to converge. In building models, data scientists try to simultaneously minimize both bias and variance errors while selecting an algorithm with good predictive or classifying power, as seen in the right panel of Exhibit 4.

Exhibit 4: Learning Curves: Accuracy in Validation and Training Samples

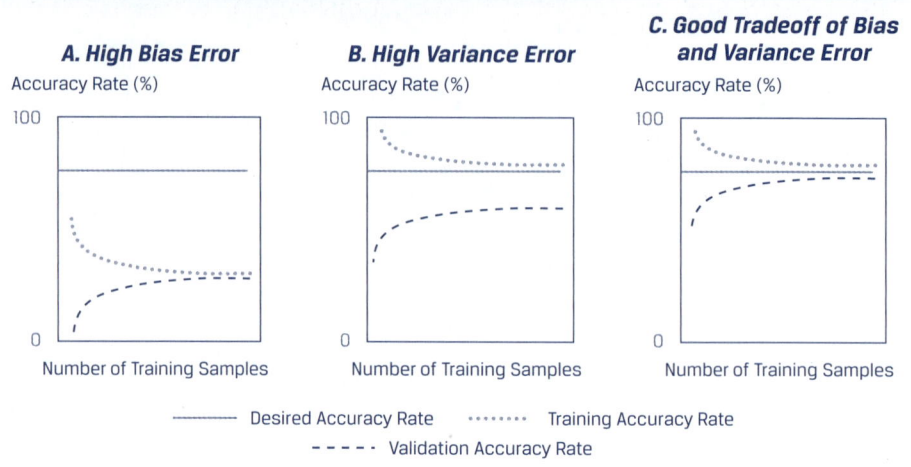

Out-of-sample error rates are also a function of model complexity. As complexity increases in the training set, error rates (E_{in}) fall and bias error shrinks. As complexity increases in the test set, however, error rates (E_{out}) rise and variance error rises. Typically, linear functions are more susceptible to bias error and underfitting, while non-linear functions are more prone to variance error and overfitting. Therefore, an optimal point of model complexity exists where the bias and variance error curves intersect and in- and out-of-sample error rates are minimized. A **fitting curve**, which shows in- and out-of-sample error rates (E_{in} and E_{out}) on the *y*-axis plotted against model complexity on the *x*-axis, is presented in Exhibit 5 and illustrates this trade-off.

Exhibit 5: Fitting Curve Shows Trade-Off between Bias and Variance Errors and Model Complexity

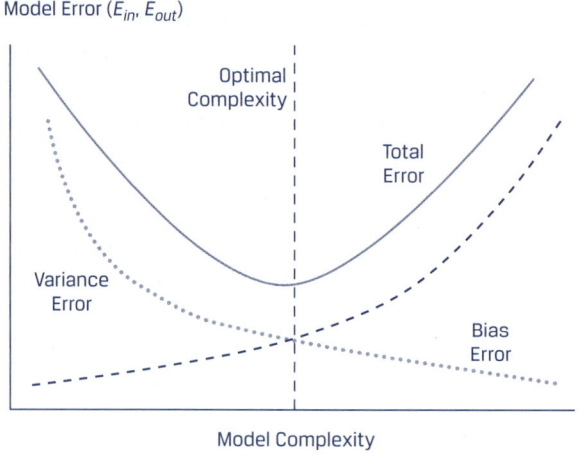

Finding the optimal point (managing overfitting risk)—the point just before the total error rate starts to rise (due to increasing variance error)—is a core part of the machine learning process and the key to successful generalization. Data scientists express the trade-off between overfitting and generalization as a trade-off between *cost* (the difference between in- and out-of-sample error rates) and *complexity*. They use the trade-off between cost and complexity to calibrate and visualize under- and overfitting and to optimize their models.

Preventing Overfitting in Supervised Machine Learning

We have seen that overfitting impairs generalization, but overfitting potential is endemic to the supervised machine learning process due to the presence of noise. So, how do data scientists combat this risk? Two common methods are used to reduce overfitting: (1) preventing the algorithm from getting too complex during selection and training, which requires estimating an overfitting penalty, and (2) proper data sampling achieved by using **cross-validation**, a technique for estimating out-of-sample error directly by determining the error in validation samples.

The first strategy comes from Occam's razor, the problem-solving principle that the simplest solution tends to be the correct one. In supervised machine learning, it means limiting the number of features and penalizing algorithms that are too complex or too flexible by constraining them to include only parameters that reduce out-of-sample error.

The second strategy comes from the principle of avoiding sampling bias. But sampling bias can creep into machine learning in many ways. The challenge is having a large enough dataset to make both training and testing possible on representative samples. An unrepresentative sample or reducing the training sample size too much could obscure its true patterns, thereby increasing bias. In supervised machine learning, the technique for reducing sampling bias is through careful partitioning of the dataset into three groups: (1) training sample, the set of labeled training data where the target variable (Y) is known;(2) validation sample, the set of data used for making structural choices on the degree of model complexity, comparing various solutions, and tuning the selected model, thereby validating the model; and (3) test sample, the set of data held aside for testing to confirm the model's predictive or classifying power. The goal, of course, is to deploy the tested model on fresh data from the same domain.

To mitigate the problem of such **holdout samples** (i.e., data samples not used to train the model) reducing the training set size too much, modelers use special cross-validation techniques. One such technique is **k-fold cross-validation**, in which the data (excluding test sample and fresh data) are shuffled randomly and then are divided into k equal sub-samples, with $k - 1$ samples used as training samples and one sample, the kth, used as a validation sample. Note that k is typically set at 5 or 10. This process is then repeated k times, which helps minimize both bias and variance by insuring that each data point is used in the training set $k - 1$ times and in the validation set once. The average of the k validation errors (mean E_{val}) is then taken as a reasonable estimate of the model's out-of-sample error (E_{out}). A limitation of k-fold cross-validation is that it cannot be used with time-series data, where only the most recent data can reasonably be used for model validation.

In sum, mitigating overfitting risk by avoiding excessive out-of-sample error is critical to creating a supervised machine learning model that generalizes well to fresh datasets drawn from the same distribution. The main techniques used to mitigate overfitting risk in model construction are complexity reduction (or regularization) and cross-validation.

EXAMPLE 2

Evaluating ML Algorithm Performance

Shreya Anand is a portfolio manager based in the Mumbai headquarters office of an investment firm, where she runs a high-dividend-yield fund for wealthy clients. Anand has some knowledge of data science from her university studies. She is interested in classifying companies in the NIFTY 200 Index—an index of large- and mid-cap companies listed on the National Stock Exchange of India—into two categories: dividend increase and no dividend increase. She assembles data for training, validating, and testing an ML-based model that consists of 1,000 observations of NIFTY 200 companies, each consisting of 25 features (fundamental and technical) and the labeled target (dividend increase or no dividend increase).

After training her model, Anand discovers that while it is good at correctly classifying using the training sample, it does not perform well on new data. In consulting her colleagues about this issue, Anand hears conflicting explanations about what constitutes good generalization in an ML model:

Statement 1   The model retains its explanatory power when predicting using new data (i.e., out-of-sample).

Statement 2   The model shows low explanatory power after training using in-sample data (i.e., training data).

Statement 3   The model loses its explanatory power when predicting using new data (i.e., out-of-sample).

1. Which statement made to Anand is *most* accurate?

   A. Statement 1
   B. Statement 2
   C. Statement 3

Solution

A, Statement 1, is correct. B, Statement 2, is incorrect because it describes a poorly fitting model with high bias. C, Statement 3, is incorrect because it describes an overfitted model with poor generalization.

2. Anand's model is *most likely* being impaired by which of the following?

   A. Underfitting and bias error
   B. Overfitting and variance error
   C. Overfitting and bias error

Solution

B is correct. Anand's model is good at correctly classifying using the training sample, but it does not perform well using new data. The model is overfitted, so it has high variance error.

3. By implementing which one of the following actions can Anand address the problem?

   A. Estimate and incorporate into the model a penalty that decreases in size with the number of included features.

> **B.** Use the *k*-fold cross-validation technique to estimate the model's out-of-sample error, and then adjust the model accordingly.
>
> **C.** Use an unsupervised learning model.
>
> ## Solution
>
> B is correct. A is incorrect because the penalty should increase in size with the number of included features. C is incorrect because Anand is using labeled data for classification, and unsupervised learning models do not use labeled data.

SUPERVISED ML ALGORITHMS: PENALIZED REGRESSION

4

☐ | describe supervised machine learning algorithms—including penalized regression, support vector machine, k-nearest neighbor, classification and regression tree, ensemble learning, and random forest—and determine the problems for which they are best suited

Supervised machine learning models are trained using labeled data, and depending on the nature of the target (*Y*) variable, they can be divided into two types: regression for a continuous target variable and classification for a categorical or ordinal target variable. As shown in Exhibit 2 under regression, we will now cover penalized regression and LASSO. Then, as shown under classification, we will introduce support vector machine (SVM), *k*-nearest neighbor (KNN), and classification and regression tree (CART) algorithms. Note that CART, as its name implies, can be used for both classification and regression problems.

In the following discussion, assume we have a number of observations of a target variable, *Y*, and *n* real valued features, $X_1, \ldots, X_n$, that we may use to establish a relationship (regression or classification) between X (a vector of the X_i) and *Y* for each observation in our dataset.

Penalized Regression

Penalized regression is a computationally efficient technique used in prediction problems. In practice, penalized regression has been useful for reducing a large number of features to a manageable set and for making good predictions in a variety of large datasets, especially where features are correlated (i.e., when classical linear regression breaks down).

In a large dataset context, we may have many features that potentially could be used to explain *Y*. When a model is fit to training data, the model may so closely reflect the characteristics of the specific training data that the model does not perform well on new data. Features may be included that reflect noise or randomness in the training dataset that will not be present in new or future data used for making predictions. That is the problem of overfitting, and penalized regression can be described as a technique to avoid overfitting. In prediction, out-of-sample performance is key, so relatively parsimonious models (that is, models in which each variable plays an essential role) tend to work well because they are less subject to overfitting.

Let us suppose that we standardize our data so the features have a mean of 0 and a variance of 1. Standardization of features will allow us to compare the magnitudes of regression coefficients for the feature variables. In ordinary linear regression (i.e., ordinary least squares, or OLS), the regression coefficients $\hat{b}_0, \hat{b}_1, \ldots, \hat{b}_K$ are chosen to *minimize* the sum of the squared residuals (i.e., the sum of the squared difference between the actual values, Y_i, and the predicted values, $\hat{Y}_i$), or

$$\sum_{i=1}^{n} \left(Y_i - \hat{Y}_i\right)^2.$$

Penalized regression includes a constraint such that the regression coefficients are chosen to minimize the sum of squared residuals *plus* a penalty term that increases in size with the number of included features. So, in a penalized regression, a feature must make a sufficient contribution to model fit to offset the penalty from including it. Therefore, only the more important features for explaining Y will remain in the penalized regression model.

In one popular type of penalized regression, **LASSO**, or least absolute shrinkage and selection operator, the penalty term has the following form, with $\lambda > 0$:

$$\text{Penalty term} = \lambda \sum_{k=1}^{K} |\hat{b}_k|.$$

In addition to minimizing the sum of the squared residuals, LASSO involves minimizing the sum of the absolute values of the regression coefficients (see the following expression). The greater the number of included features (i.e., variables with non-zero coefficients), the larger the penalty term. Therefore, penalized regression ensures that a feature is included only if the sum of squared residuals declines by more than the penalty term increases. All types of penalized regression involve a trade-off of this type. Also, since LASSO eliminates the least important features from the model, it automatically performs a type of feature selection.

$$\sum_{i=1}^{n} \left(Y_i - \hat{Y}_i\right)^2 + \lambda \sum_{k=1}^{K} |\hat{b}_k|.$$

Lambda (λ) is a **hyperparameter**—a parameter whose value must be set by the researcher before learning begins—of the regression model and will determine the balance between fitting the model versus keeping the model parsimonious. In practice, a hyperparameter is set by reviewing model performance repeatedly at different settings on the validation set, and hence the test set is also essential to avoid overfitting of hyperparameters to the validation data.

Note that in the case where $\lambda = 0$, the LASSO penalized regression is equivalent to an OLS regression. When using LASSO or other penalized regression techniques, the penalty term is added only during the model building process (i.e., when fitting the model to the training data). Once the model has been built, the penalty term is no longer needed, and the model is then evaluated by the sum of the squared residuals generated using the test dataset.

With today's availability of fast computation algorithms, investment analysts are increasingly using LASSO and other regularization techniques to remove less pertinent features and build parsimonious models. **Regularization** describes methods that reduce statistical variability in high-dimensional data estimation problems—in this case, reducing regression coefficient estimates toward zero and thereby avoiding complex models and the risk of overfitting. LASSO has been used, for example, for forecasting default probabilities in industrial sectors where scores of potential features, many collinear, have been reduced to fewer than 10 variables, which is important given the relatively small number (about 100) of observations of default.

Regularization methods can also be applied to non-linear models. A long-term challenge of the asset management industry in applying mean–variance optimization has been the estimation of stable covariance matrixes and asset weights for large portfolios. Asset returns typically exhibit strong multi-collinearity, making the estimation of the covariance matrix highly sensitive to noise and outliers, so the resulting optimized asset weights are highly unstable. Regularization methods have been used to address this problem. The relatively parsimonious models produced by applying penalized regression methods, such as LASSO, tend to work well because they are less subject to overfitting.

SUPPORT VECTOR MACHINE

5

☐ | describe supervised machine learning algorithms—including penalized regression, support vector machine, k-nearest neighbor, classification and regression tree, ensemble learning, and random forest—and determine the problems for which they are best suited

Support vector machine (SVM) is one of the most popular algorithms in machine learning. It is a powerful supervised algorithm used for classification, regression, and outlier detection. Despite its complicated-sounding name, the notion is relatively straightforward and best explained with a few pictures. The left panel in Exhibit 6 presents a simple dataset with two features (x and y coordinates) labeled in two groups (triangles and crosses). These binary labeled data are noticeably separated into two distinct regions, which could represent stocks with positive and negative returns in a given year. These two regions can be easily separated by an infinite number of straight lines; three of them are shown in the right panel of Exhibit 6. The data are thus linearly separable, and any of the straight lines shown would be called a **linear classifier**—a binary classifier that makes its classification decision based on a linear combination of the features of each data point.

Exhibit 6: Scatterplots and Linear Separation of Labeled Data

A. Data Labelled in Two Groups

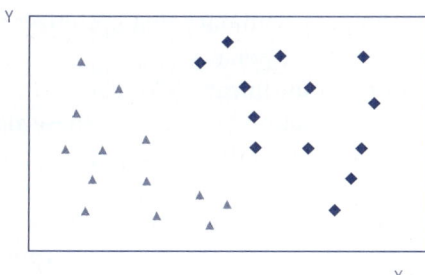

B. Data Is Linearly Separable

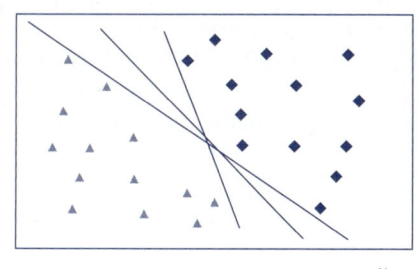

With two dimensions or features (x and y), linear classifiers can be represented as straight lines. Observations with n features can be represented in an n-dimension space, and the dataset would be linearly separable if the observations can be separated into two distinct regions by a linear space boundary. The general term for such a space boundary is an n-dimensional hyperplane, which with $n = 1$ is called a line and with $n = 2$ is called a plane.

Support vector machine is a linear classifier that determines the hyperplane that optimally separates the observations into two sets of data points. The intuitive idea behind the SVM algorithm is maximizing the probability of making a correct prediction (here, that an observation is a triangle or a cross) by determining the boundary that is the furthest away from all the observations. In Exhibit 7, SVM separates the data by the maximum margin, where the margin is the shaded strip that divides the observations into two groups. The straight line in the middle of the shaded strip is the discriminant boundary, or boundary, for short. We can see that the SVM algorithm produces the widest shaded strip (i.e., the one with the maximum margin on either side of the boundary). The margin is determined by the observations closest to the boundary (the circled points) in each set, and these observations are called support vectors. Adding more training data away from the support vectors will not affect the boundary. In our training datasets, however, adding data points which are close to the hyperplane may move the margin by changing the set of support vectors.

Exhibit 7: Linear Support Vector Machine Classifier

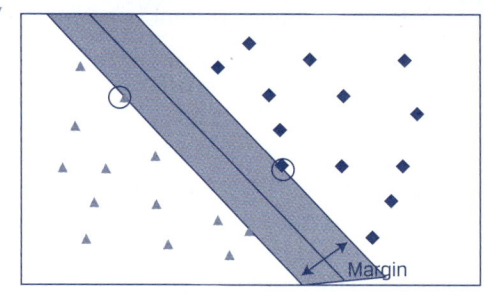

In Exhibit 7, SVM is classifying all observations perfectly. Most real-world datasets, however, are not linearly separable. Some observations may fall on the wrong side of the boundary and be misclassified by the SVM algorithm. The SVM algorithm handles this problem by an adaptation called **soft margin classification**, which adds a penalty to the objective function for observations in the training set that are misclassified. In essence, the SVM algorithm will choose a discriminant boundary that optimizes the trade-off between a wider margin and a lower total error penalty.

As an alternative to soft margin classification, a non-linear SVM algorithm can be run by introducing more advanced, non-linear separation boundaries. These algorithms may reduce the number of misclassified instances in the training datasets but are more complex and, so, are prone to overfitting.

SVM has many applications in investment management. It is particularly suited for small to medium-size but complex high-dimensional datasets, such as corporate financial statements or bankruptcy databases. Investors seek to predict company failures for identifying stocks to avoid or to short sell, and SVM can generate a binary classification (e.g., bankruptcy likely versus bankruptcy unlikely) using many fundamental and technical feature variables. SVM can effectively capture the characteristics of such data with many features while being resilient to outliers and correlated features. SVM can also be used to classify text from documents (e.g., news articles, company announcements, and company annual reports) into useful categories for investors (e.g., positive sentiment and negative sentiment).

K-NEAREST NEIGHBOR

6

☐ | describe supervised machine learning algorithms—including penalized regression, support vector machine, k-nearest neighbor, classification and regression tree, ensemble learning, and random forest—and determine the problems for which they are best suited

K-nearest neighbor (KNN) is a supervised learning technique used most often for classification and sometimes for regression. The idea is to classify a new observation by finding similarities ("nearness") between this new observation and the existing data. Going back to the scatterplot in Exhibit 6, let us assume we have a new observation: The diamond in Exhibit 8 needs to be classified as belonging to either the cross or the triangle category. If $k = 1$, the diamond will be classified into the same category as its nearest neighbor (i.e., the triangle in the left panel). The right panel in Exhibit 8 presents the case where $k = 5$, so the algorithm will look at the diamond's five nearest neighbors, which are three triangles and two crosses. The decision rule is to choose the classification with the largest number of nearest neighbors out of the five being considered. So, the diamond is again classified as belonging to the triangle category.

Exhibit 8: *K*-Nearest Neighbor Algorithm

A. KNN With New Observation, K=1

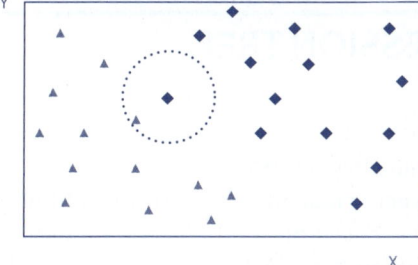

B. KNN With New Observation, K=5

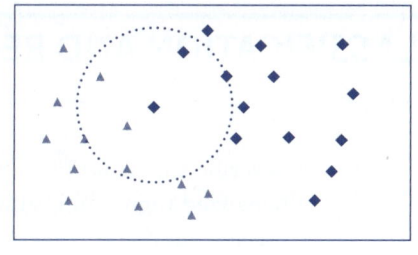

Let us suppose we have a database of corporate bonds classified by credit rating that also contains detailed information on the characteristics of these bonds. Such features would include those of the issuing company (e.g., asset size, industry, leverage ratios, cash flow ratios) and of the bond issue itself (e.g., tenor, fixed/floating coupon, embedded options). Now, assume a new bond is about to be issued with no credit rating. By nature, corporate bonds with similar issuer and issue characteristics should be given a similar credit rating. So, by using KNN, we can predict the implied credit rating of the new bond based on the similarities of its characteristics to those of the bonds in our database.

KNN is a straightforward, intuitive model that is still very powerful because it is non-parametric; the model makes no assumptions about the distribution of the data. Moreover, it can be used directly for multi-class classification. A critical challenge of KNN, however, is defining what it means to be "similar" (or near). Besides the selection of features, an important decision relates to the distance metric used to model similarity because an inappropriate measure will generate poorly performing models. The choice of a correct distance measure may be even more subjective for ordinal or categorical data. For example, if an analyst is looking at the similarities in market performance of various equities, he or she may consider using the correlation between the stocks' historical returns as an appropriate measure of similarity.

Knowledge of the data and understanding of the business objectives of the analysis are critical aspects in the process of defining similarity. KNN results can be sensitive to inclusion of irrelevant or correlated features, so it may be necessary to select features manually. By doing so, the analyst removes less valuable information to keep the most relevant and pertinent information. If done correctly, this process should generate a more representative distance measure. KNN algorithms tend to work better with a small number of features.

Finally, the number k, the hyperparameter of the model, must be chosen with the understanding that different values of k can lead to different conclusions. For predicting the credit rating of an unrated bond, for example, should k be the 3, 15, or 50 bonds most similar to the unrated bond? If k is an even number, there may be ties and no clear classification. Choosing a value for k that is too small would result in a high error rate and sensitivity to local outliers, but choosing a value for k that is too large would dilute the concept of nearest neighbors by averaging too many outcomes. In practice, several different techniques can be used to determine an optimal value for k, taking into account the number of categories and their partitioning of the feature space.

The KNN algorithm has many applications in the investment industry, including bankruptcy prediction, stock price prediction, corporate bond credit rating assignment, and customized equity and bond index creation. For example, KNN is useful for determining bonds that are similar and those that are dissimilar, which is critical information for creating a custom, diversified bond index.

7 CLASSIFICATION AND REGRESSION TREE

☐ | describe supervised machine learning algorithms—including penalized regression, support vector machine, k-nearest neighbor, classification and regression tree, ensemble learning, and random forest—and determine the problems for which they are best suited

Classification and regression tree (CART) is another common supervised machine learning technique that can be applied to predict either a categorical target variable, producing a classification tree, or a continuous target variable, producing a regression tree. CART is commonly applied to binary classification or regression.

CART will be discussed in the context of a simplified model for classifying companies by whether they are likely to increase their dividends to shareholders. Such a classification requires a binary tree: a combination of an initial root node, decision nodes, and terminal nodes. The root node and each decision node represent a single feature (f) and a cutoff value (c) for that feature. As shown in Panel A of Exhibit 9, we start at the initial root node for a new data point. In this case, the initial root node represents the feature investment opportunities growth (IOG), designated as X1, with a cutoff value of 10%. From the initial root node, the data are partitioned at decision nodes into smaller and smaller subgroups until terminal nodes that contain the predicted labels are formed. In this case, the predicted labels are either dividend increase (the cross) or no dividend increase (the dash).

Also shown in Panel A of Exhibit 9, if the value of feature IOG (X1) is greater than 10% (Yes), then we proceed to the decision node for free cash flow growth (FCFG), designated as X2, which has a cutoff value of 20%. Now, if the value of FCFG is not greater than 20% (No), then CART will predict that that data point belongs to the no dividend increase (dash) category, which represents a terminal node. Conversely, if the value of X2 is greater than 20% (Yes), then CART will predict that that data point belongs to the dividend increase (cross) category, which represents another terminal node.

It is important to note that the same feature can appear several times in a tree in combination with other features. Moreover, some features may be relevant only if other conditions have been met. For example, going back to the initial root node, if IOG is not greater than 10% (X1 ≤ 10%) and FCFG is greater than 10%, then IOG appears again as another decision node, but this time it is lower down in the tree and has a cutoff value of 5%.

Exhibit 9: Classification and Regression Tree—Decision Tree and Partitioning of the Feature Space

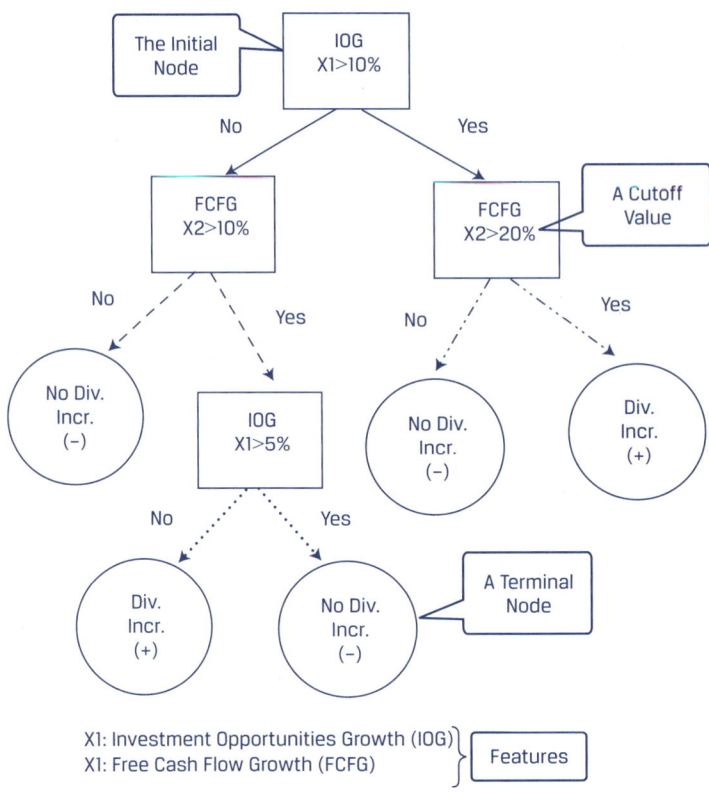

A. Decision Tree

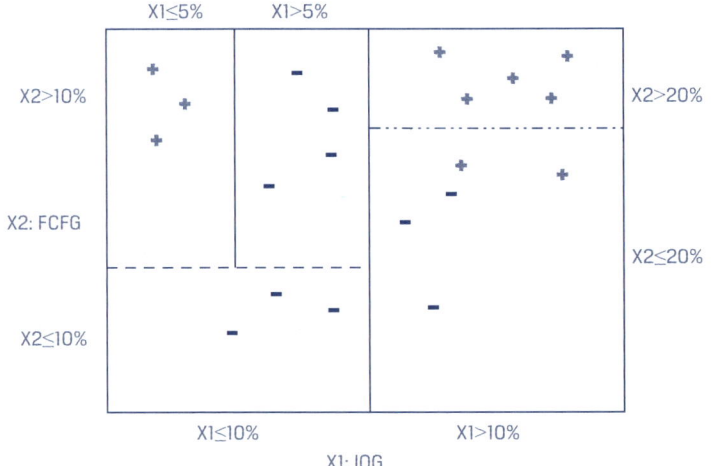

B. Partitioning of the Feature (X1, X2) Space

We now turn to how the CART algorithm selects features and cutoff values for them. Initially, the classification model is trained from the labeled data, which in this hypothetical case are 10 instances of companies having a dividend increase (the crosses) and 10 instances of companies with no dividend increase (the dashes). As shown in Panel B of Exhibit 9, at the initial root node and at each decision node, the feature space (i.e., the plane defined by X1 and X2) is split into two rectangles for values above and below the cutoff value for the particular feature represented at that node. This can be seen by noting the distinct patterns of the lines that emanate from the decision nodes in Panel A. These same distinct patterns are used for partitioning the feature space in Panel B.

The CART algorithm chooses the feature and the cutoff value at each node that generates the widest separation of the labeled data to minimize classification error (e.g., by a criterion, such as mean-squared error). After each decision node, the partition of the feature space becomes smaller and smaller, so observations in each group have lower within-group error than before. At any level of the tree, when the classification error does not diminish much more from another split (bifurcation), the process stops, the node is a terminal node, and the category that is in the majority at that node is assigned to it. If the objective of the model is classification, then the prediction of the algorithm at each terminal node will be the category with the majority of data points. For example, in Panel B of Exhibit 9, the top right rectangle of the feature space, representing IOG (X1) > 10% and FCFG (X2)> 20%, contains five crosses, the most data points of any of the partitions. So, CART would predict that a new data point (i.e., a company) with such features belongs to the dividend increase (cross) category. However, if instead the new data point had IOG (X1) > 10% and FCFG (X2) ≤ 20%, then it would be predicted to belong to the no dividend increase (dash) category—represented by the lower right rectangle, with two crosses but with three dashes. Finally, if the goal is regression, then the prediction at each terminal node is the mean of the labeled values.

CART makes no assumptions about the characteristics of the training data, so if left unconstrained, it potentially can perfectly learn the training data. To avoid such overfitting, regularization parameters can be added, such as the maximum depth of the tree, the minimum population at a node, or the maximum number of decision nodes. The iterative process of building the tree is stopped once the regularization criterion has been reached. For example, in Panel B of Exhibit 9, the upper left rectangle of the feature space (determined by X1 ≤ 10%, X2 > 10%, and X1 ≤ 5% with three crosses) might represent a terminal node resulting from a regularization criterion with minimum population equal to 3. Alternatively, regularization can occur via a **pruning** technique that can be used afterward to reduce the size of the tree. Sections of the tree that provide little classifying power are pruned (i.e., cut back or removed).

By its iterative structure, CART can uncover complex dependencies between features that other models cannot reveal. As demonstrated in Exhibit 9, the same feature can appear several times in combination with other features and some features may be relevant only if other conditions have been met.

As shown in Exhibit 10, high profitability is a critical feature for predicting whether a stock is an attractive investment or a value trap (i.e., an investment that, although apparently priced cheaply, is likely to be unprofitable). This feature is relevant only if the stock is cheap: For example, in this hypothetical case, if P/E is less than 15, leverage is high (debt to total capital > 50%) and sales are expanding (sales growth > 15%). Said another way, high profitability is irrelevant in this context if the stock is not cheap *and* if leverage is not high *and* if sales are not expanding. Multiple linear regression typically fails in such situations where the relationship between the features and the outcome is non-linear.

Exhibit 10: Stylized Decision Tree—Attractive Investment or Value Trap?

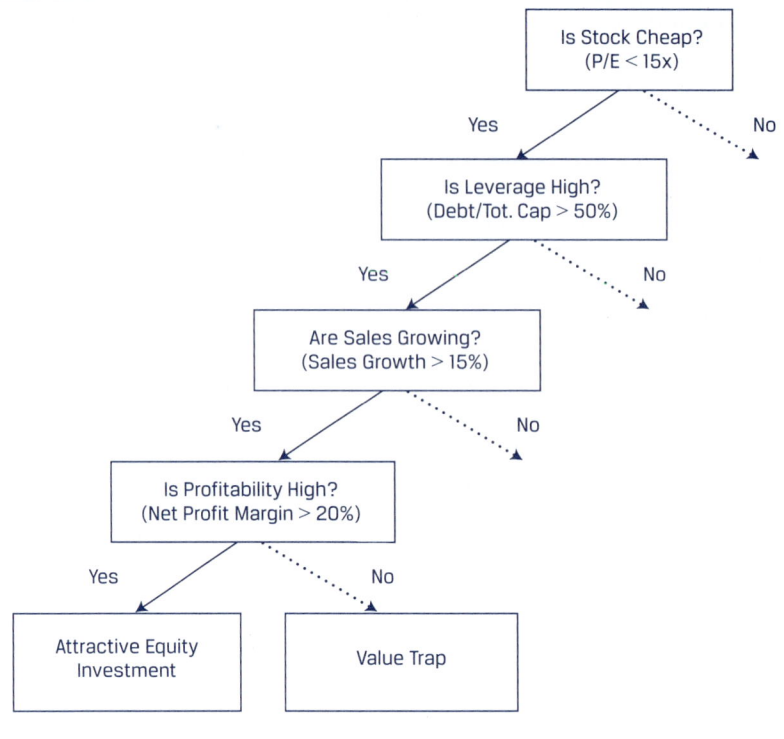

CART models are popular supervised machine learning models because the tree provides a visual explanation for the prediction. This contrasts favorably with other algorithms that are often considered to be "black boxes" because it may be difficult to understand the reasoning behind their outcomes and thus to place trust in them. CART is a powerful tool to build expert systems for decision-making processes. It can induce robust rules despite noisy data and complex relationships between high numbers of features. Typical applications of CART in investment management include, among others, enhancing detection of fraud in financial statements, generating consistent decision processes in equity and fixed-income selection, and simplifying communication of investment strategies to clients.

8   ENSEMBLE LEARNING AND RANDOM FOREST

☐ describe supervised machine learning algorithms—including penalized regression, support vector machine, k-nearest neighbor, classification and regression tree, ensemble learning, and random forest—and determine the problems for which they are best suited

Instead of basing predictions on the results of a single model as in the previous discussion, why not use the predictions of a group—or an ensemble—of models? Each single model will have a certain error rate and will make noisy predictions. But by taking the average result of many predictions from many models, we can expect to achieve a reduction in noise as the average result converges toward a more accurate prediction. This technique of combining the predictions from a collection of models is called **ensemble learning**, and the combination of multiple learning algorithms is known as the **ensemble method**. Ensemble learning typically produces more accurate and more stable predictions than the best single model. In fact, in many prestigious machine learning competitions, an ensemble method is often the winning solution.

Ensemble learning can be divided into two main categories: (1) aggregation of heterogeneous learners (i.e., different types of algorithms combined with a voting classifier) or (2) aggregation of homogeneous learners (i.e., a combination of the same algorithm using different training data that are based, for example, on a bootstrap aggregating, or bagging, technique, as discussed later).

Voting Classifiers

Suppose you have been working on a machine learning project for some time and have trained and compared the results of several algorithms, such as SVM, KNN, and CART. A **majority-vote classifier** will assign to a new data point the predicted label with the most votes. For example, if the SVM and KNN models are both predicting the category "stock outperformance" and the CART model is predicting the category "stock underperformance," then the majority-vote classifier will choose stock outperformance." The more individual models you have trained, the higher the accuracy of the aggregated prediction up to a point. There is an optimal number of models beyond which performance would be expected to deteriorate from overfitting. The trick is to look for diversity in the choice of algorithms, modeling techniques, and hypotheses. The (extreme) assumption here is that if the predictions of the individual models are independent, then we can use the law of large numbers to achieve a more accurate prediction.

Bootstrap Aggregating (Bagging)

Alternatively, one can use the same machine learning algorithm but with different training data. **Bootstrap aggregating (or bagging)** is a technique whereby the original training dataset is used to generate n new training datasets or bags of data. Each new bag of data is generated by random sampling with replacement from the initial training set. The algorithm can now be trained on n independent datasets that will generate n new models. Then, for each new observation, we can aggregate the n predictions using a majority-vote classifier for a classification or an average for a regression. Bagging is a very useful technique because it helps to improve the stability of predictions and protects against overfitting the model.

Random Forest

A **random forest classifier** is a collection of a large number of decision trees trained via a bagging method. For example, a CART algorithm would be trained using each of the n independent datasets (from the bagging process) to generate the multitude of different decision trees that make up the random forest classifier.

To derive even more individual predictions, added diversity can be generated in the trees by randomly reducing the number of features available during training. So, if each observation has n features, one can randomly select a subset of m features (where $m < n$) that will then be considered by the CART algorithm for splitting the dataset at each of the decision nodes. The number of subset features (m), the number of trees to use, the minimum size (population) of each node (or leaf), and the maximum depth of each tree are all hyperparameters that can be tuned to improve overall model prediction accuracy. For any new observation, we let all the classifier trees (the "random forest") undertake classification by majority vote—implementing a machine learning version of the "wisdom of crowds." The process involved in random forest construction tends to reduce variance and protect against overfitting on the training data. It also reduces the ratio of noise to signal because errors cancel out across the collection of slightly different classification trees. However, an important drawback of random forest is that it lacks the ease of interpretability of individual trees; as a result, it is considered a relatively black box type of algorithm.

Exhibit 11 presents three scatterplots of actual and predicted defaults by small and medium-sized businesses with respect to two features, X and Y—for example, firm profitability and leverage, respectively. The left plot shows the actual cases of default in light shade and no default in dark shade, while the middle and right plots present the predicted defaults and no defaults (also in light and dark shades, respectively). It is clear from the middle plot, which is based on a traditional linear regression model, that the model fails to predict the complex non-linear relationship between the features. Conversely, the right plot, which presents the prediction results of a random forest model, shows that this model performs very well in matching the actual distribution of the data.

Exhibit 11: Credit Defaults of Small- and Medium-Sized Borrowers

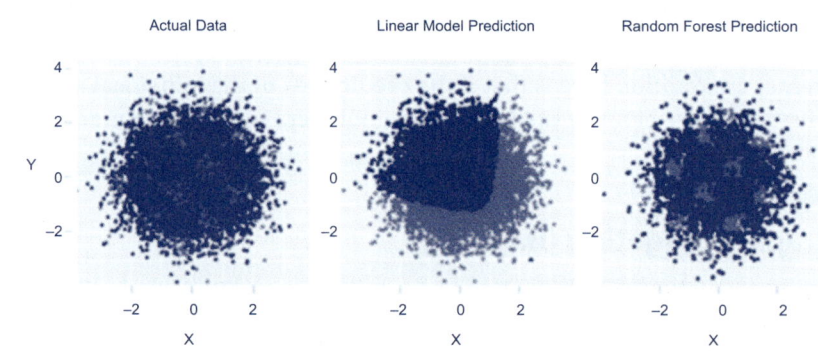

Source: Bacham and Zhao (2017).

ENSEMBLE LEARNING WITH RANDOM FOREST

In making use of voting across classifier trees, random forest is an example of ensemble learning: Incorporating the output of a collection of models produces classifications that have better signal-to-noise ratios than the individual classifiers. A good example is a credit card fraud detection problem that comes from an open source dataset on Kaggle.[1] Here, the data contained several anonymized features that might be used to explain which transactions were fraudulent. The difficulty in the analysis arises from the fact that the rate of fraudulent transactions is very low; in a sample of 284,807 transactions, only 492 were fraudulent (0.17%). This is akin to finding a needle in a haystack. Applying a random forest classification algorithm with an oversampling technique—which involves increasing the proportional representation of fraudulent data in the training set—does extremely well. Despite the lopsided sample, it delivers **precision** (the ratio of correctly predicted fraudulent cases to all predicted fraudulent cases) of 89% and **recall** (the ratio of correctly predicted fraudulent cases to all actual fraudulent cases) of 82%.

---

1 See www.kaggle.com/mlg-ulb/creditcardfraud (accessed 1 October 2018).

Despite its relative simplicity, random forest is a powerful algorithm with many investment applications. These include, for example, use in factor-based investment strategies for asset allocation and investment selection or use in predicting whether an IPO will be successful (e.g., percent oversubscribed, first trading day close/IPO price) given the attributes of the IPO offering and the corporate issuer. Later, in a mini-case study, Deep Neural Network–Based Equity Factor Model, we present further details of how supervised machine learning is used for fundamental factor modeling.

EXAMPLE 3

Support Vector Machine and *K*-Nearest Neighbor

Rachel Lee is a fixed-income portfolio manager with Zeta Investment Management Company. Zeta manages an investment-grade bond portfolio for small, conservative institutions and a non-investment-grade (i.e., high-yield) bond portfolio for yield-seeking, high-net-worth individuals. Both portfolios can hold unrated bonds if the characteristics of the unrated bonds closely match those of the respective portfolio's average holding.

Lee is discussing an upcoming straight, 10-year fixed-coupon bond issue with senior credit analyst Marc Watson. Watson comments that although the bond's issuer, Biotron Corporation, has not had this issue rated, his analysis of the company's profitability, cash flow, leverage, and coverage ratios places the issue near the borderline between low investment-grade (Baa3/BBB–) and high non-investment-grade (Ba1/BB+) bonds.

Lee decides to use machine learning methods to confirm the implied credit rating of Biotron Corporation.

Lee decides to apply the two identified ML algorithms. Both algorithms clearly support a high non-investment-grade rating. Watson states that because both ML algorithms agree on the rating, he has confidence in relying on the rating.

---

1. State the type of problem being addressed by Lee.

Solution

Lee is addressing a supervised learning classification problem because she must determine whether Biotron's upcoming bond issue would be classified as investment grade or non-investment grade.

---

2. State two ML algorithms that Lee could use to explore the implied credit rating of Biotron Corporation, and then describe how each algorithm could be applied.

Solution

One suitable ML algorithm is SVM. The SVM algorithm is a linear classifier that aims to find the optimal hyperplane—the one that separates observations into two distinct sets by the maximum margin. So, SVM is well suited to binary classification problems, such as the one facing Lee (investment grade versus non-investment grade). In this case, Lee could train the SVM algorithm on data—characteristics (features) and rating (target)—of low investment-grade (Baa3/BBB–) and high non-investment-grade (Ba1/BB+) bonds. Lee would then note on which side of the margin the new data point (Biotron's new bonds) lies.

The KNN algorithm is also well suited for classification problems because it classifies a new observation by finding similarities (or nearness) between the new observation and the existing data. Training the algorithm with data as for SVM, the decision rule for classifying Biotron's new bonds is which classification is in the majority among its k-nearest neighbors. Note that k (a hyperparameter) must be pre-specified by Lee.

3. State one argument in support of Watson's viewpoint.

Solution

If the ML algorithms disagreed on the classification, the classification would be more likely to be sensitive to the algorithm's approach to classifying data. Because the classification of Biotron's new issue appears robust to the choice of ML algorithm (i.e., both algorithms agree on the rating), the resulting classification will more likely be correct.

EXAMPLE 4

CART and Ensemble Learning

Laurie Kim is a portfolio manager at Hilux LLC, a high-yield bond investment firm. The economy has been in recession for several months, and high-yield bond prices have declined precipitously as credit spreads have widened in response to the weak macroeconomic environment. Kim, however, believes this is a good time to buy because she expects to profit as credit spreads narrow and high-yield bond prices rise in anticipation of economic recovery.

Based on her analysis, Kim believes that corporate high-yield bonds in the credit quality range of B/B2 to CCC/Caa2 are the most attractive. However, she must carefully select which bonds to buy and which bonds to avoid because of the elevated default risk caused by the currently weak economy.

To help with her bond selection, Kim turns to Hilux's data analytics team. Kim has supplied them with historical data consisting of 19 fundamental and 5 technical factors for several thousand high-yield bond issuers and issues labeled to indicate default or no default. Kim requests that the team develop an ML-based model using all the factors provided that will make accurate classifications in two categories: default and no default. Exploratory data analysis suggests considerable non-linearities among the feature set.

1. State the type of problem being addressed by Kim.

Solution

Kim is addressing a classification problem because she must determine whether bonds that she is considering purchasing in the credit quality range of B/B2 to CCC/Caa2 will default or not default.

2. Describe the dimensionality of the model that Kim requests her analytics team to develop.

Solution

With 19 fundamental and 5 technical factors (i.e., the features), the dimensionality of the model is 24.

3. Evaluate whether a CART model is appropriate for addressing her problem.

Solution

The CART model is an algorithm for addressing classification problems. Its ability to handle complex, non-linear relationships makes it a good choice to address the modeling problem at hand. An important advantage of CART is that its results are relatively straightforward to visualize and interpret, which should help Kim explain her recommendations based on the model to Hilux's investment committee and the firm's clients.

4. Describe how a CART model operates at each node of the tree.

Solution

At each node in the decision tree, the algorithm will choose the feature and the cutoff value for the selected feature that generates the widest separation of the labeled data to minimize classification error.

5. Describe how the team might avoid overfitting and improve the predictive power of a CART model.

Solution

The team can avoid overfitting and improve the predictive power of the CART model by adding regularization parameters. For example, the team could specify the maximum depth of the tree, the minimum population at a node, or the maximum number of decision nodes. The iterative process of building nodes will be stopped once the regularization criterion has been reached. Alternatively, a pruning technique can be used afterward to remove parts of the CART model that provide little power to correctly classify instances into default or no default categories.

6. Describe how ensemble learning might be used by the team to develop even better predictions for Kim's selection of corporate high-yield bonds.

Solution

The analytics team might use ensemble learning to combine the predictions from a collection of models, where the average result of many predictions leads to a reduction in noise and thus more accurate predictions. Ensemble learning can be achieved by an aggregation of either heterogeneous learners—different types of algorithms combined with a voting classifier—or homogeneous learners—a combination of the same algorithm but using different training data based on the bootstrap aggregating (i.e., bagging) technique. The team may also consider developing a random forest classifier (i.e., a collection of many decision trees) trained via a bagging method.

9 CASE STUDY: CLASSIFICATION OF WINNING AND LOSING FUNDS

☐ | describe unsupervised machine learning algorithms—including principal components analysis, k-means clustering, and hierarchical clustering—and determine the problems for which they are best suited

The following case study was developed and written by Matthew Dixon, PhD, FRM.

    A research analyst for a fund of funds has been tasked with identifying a set of attractive exchange-traded funds (ETFs) and mutual funds (MFs) in which to invest. She decides to use machine learning to identify the best (i.e., winners) and worst (i.e., losers) performing funds and the features which are most important in such an identification. Her aim is to train a model to correctly classify the winners and losers and then to use it to predict future outperformers. She is unsure of which type of machine learning classification model (i.e., classifier) would work best, so she reports and cross-compares her findings using several different well-known machine learning algorithms.

    The goal of this case is to demonstrate the application of machine learning classification to fund selection. Therefore, the analyst will use the following classifiers to identify the best and worst performing funds:

- classification and regression tree (CART),
- support vector machine (SVM),
- *k*-nearest neighbors (KNN), and
- random forests.

Data Description

In the following experiments, the performance of each fund is learned by the machine learning algorithms based on fund type and size, asset class composition, fundamentals (i.e., valuation multiples), and sector composition characteristics. To form a cross-sectional classifier, the sector composition and fund size reported on 15 February 2019 are assumed to be representative of the latest month over which the fund return is reported. Exhibit 12 presents a description of the dataset.

Exhibit 12: Dataset Description

Dataset: MF and ETF Data

There are two separate datasets, one for MFs and one for ETFs, consisting of fund type, size, asset class composition, fundamental financial ratios, sector weights, and monthly total return labeled to indicate the fund as being a winner, a loser, or neither. Number of observations: 6,085 MFs and 1,594 ETFs.
Features: Up to 21, as shown below:

General (six features):

1. cat investment*: Fund type, either "blend," "growth," or "value"
2. net assets: Total net assets in US dollars
3. cat size: Investment category size, either "small," "medium," or "large" market capitalization stocks

4. portfolio cash**: The ratio of cash to total assets in the fund

5. portfolio stocks: The ratio of stocks to total assets in the fund

6. portfolio bonds: The ratio of bonds to total assets in the fund

Fundamentals (four features):

7. price earnings: The ratio of price per share to earnings per share

8. price book: The ratio of price per share to book value per share

9. price sales: The ratio of price per share to sales per share

10. price cashflow: The ratio of price per share to cash flow per share

Sector weights (for 11 sectors) provided as percentages:

11. basic materials

12. consumer cyclical

13. financial services

14. real estate

15. consumer defensive

16. healthcare

17. utilities

18. communication services

19. energy

20. industrials

21. technology

Labels

Winning and losing ETFs or MFs are determined based on whether their returns are one standard deviation or more above or below the distribution of one-month fund returns across all ETFs or across all MFs, respectively. More precisely, the labels are:

1, if fund_return_1 month ≥ mean(fund_return_1 month) + one std.dev(-fund_return_1 month), indicating a winning fund;

-1, if fund_return_1 month ≤ mean(fund_return_1 month) − one std. dev(fund_return_1 month), indicating a losing fund; and

0, otherwise.

*Feature appears in the ETF dataset only.
**Feature appears in the MF dataset only.
Data sources: Kaggle, Yahoo Finance on 15 February 2019.

Methodology

The classification model is trained to determine whether a fund's performance is one standard deviation or more above the mean return (Label 1), within one standard deviation of the mean return (Label 0), or one standard deviation or more below the mean return (Label -1), where the mean return and standard deviation are either for all ETFs or all MFs, depending on the particular fund's type (ETF or MF). Performance is based on the one-month return of each fund as of 15 February 2019.

This procedure results in most of the funds being labeled as "0" (or average). After removing missing values in the dataset, there are 1,594 and 6,085 observations in the ETF and MF datasets, respectively. The data table is a 7,679 × 22 matrix, with 7,679 rows for each fund observation (1,594 for ETFs and 6,085 for MFs) and 22 columns for the 21 features plus the return label, and all data are recorded as of 15 February 2019.

The aim of the experiment is to identify not only winning and losing funds but also the features which are useful for distinguishing winners from losers. An important caveat, however, is that no claim is made that such features are causal.

A separate multi-classifier, with three classes, is run for each dataset. Four types of machine learning algorithms are used to build each classifier: (i) CART, (ii) SVM, (iii) KNN, and (iv) random forest. Random forest is an example of an ensemble method (based on bagging), whereas the other three algorithms do not use bagging.

A typical experimental design would involve using 70% of the data for training and holding 15% for tuning model hyperparameters and the remaining 15% of the data for testing. For simplicity, we shall not tune the hyperparameters but simply use the default settings without attempting to fine tune each one for best performance. So, in this case, we do not withhold 15% of the data for validation but instead train the classifier on a random split of 70% of the dataset, with the remaining 30% of the dataset used for testing. Crucially, for fairness of evaluation, each algorithm is trained and tested on identical data: The same 70% of observations are used for training each algorithm, and the same 30% are used for testing each one. The most important hyperparameters and settings for the algorithms are shown in Exhibit 13.

Exhibit 13: Parameter Settings for the Four Machine Learning Classifiers

1. CART: maximum tree depth: 5 levels
2. SVM: cost parameter: 1.0
3. KNN: number of nearest neighbors: 4
4. Random forest: number of trees: 100; maximum tree depth: 20 levels

---

The choices of hyperparameter values for the four machine learning classifiers are supported by theory, academic research, practice, and experimentation to yield a satisfactory bias–variance trade-off. For SVM, the cost parameter is a penalty on the margin of the decision boundary. A large cost parameter forces the SVM to use a thin margin, whereas a smaller cost parameter widens the margin. For random forests, recall that this is an ensemble method which uses multiple decision trees to classify, typically by majority vote. Importantly, no claim is made that these choices of hyperparameters are universally optimal for any dataset.

Results

The results of each classifier are evaluated separately on the test portion of the ETF and MF datasets. The evaluation metrics used are based on Type I and Type II classification errors, where a Type I error is a false positive (FP) and a Type II error is a false negative (FN). Correct classifications are true positive (TP) and true negative (TN).

- The first evaluation metric is **accuracy**, the percentage of correctly predicted classes out of total predictions. So, high accuracy implies low Type I and Type II errors.

- **F1 score**, the second evaluation metric, is the weighted average of precision and recall. Precision is the ratio of correctly predicted positive classes to all predicted positive classes, and recall is the ratio of correctly predicted positive classes to all actual positive classes.

F1 score is a more appropriate evaluation metric to use than accuracy when there is unequal class distribution ("class imbalance") in the dataset, as is the case here. As mentioned, most of the funds in the ETF and MF datasets are designated as "0," indicating average performers.

Exhibit 14 shows the comparative performance results for each algorithm applied to the ETF dataset. These results show the random forest model is the most accurate (0.812), but once class imbalance is accounted for using F1 score (0.770), random forest is about as good as CART. Generally, ensemble methods, such as random forest, are expected to be at least as good as their single-model counterparts because ensemble forecasts generalize better out-of-sample. Importantly, while the relative accuracies and F1 scores across the different methods provide a basis for comparison, they do not speak to the absolute performance. In this regard, values approaching 1 suggest an excellent model, whereas values of approximately 1/3 would indicate the model is useless: 1/3 is premised on three (+1, 0, -1) equally distributed labels. However, because the distribution of classes is often not balanced, this ratio typically requires some adjustment.

Exhibit 14: Comparison of Accuracy and F1 Score for Each Classifier Applied to the ETF Dataset

	CART	SVM	KNN	Random Forest
Accuracy	0.770	0.774	0.724	0.812
F1 score	0.769	0.693	0.683	0.770

Exhibit 15 shows that the random forest model outperforms all the other classifiers under both metrics when applied to the MF dataset. Overall, the accuracy and F1 score for the SVM and KNN methods are similar for each dataset, and these algorithms are dominated by CART and random forest, especially in the larger MF dataset. The difference in performance between the two datasets for all the algorithms is to be expected, since the MF dataset is approximately four times larger than the ETF dataset and a larger sample set generally leads to better model performance. Moreover, the precise explanation of why random forest and CART outperform SVM and KNN is beyond the scope of this case. Suffice it to say that random forests are well known to be more robust to noise than most other classifiers.

Exhibit 15: Comparison of Accuracy and F1 Score for Each Classifier Applied to the Mutual Fund Dataset

	CART	SVM	KNN	Random Forest
Accuracy	0.959	0.859	0.856	0.969
F1 score	0.959	0.847	0.855	0.969

Exhibit 16 presents results on the relative importance of the features in the random forest model for both the ETF (Panel A) and MF (Panel B) datasets. Relative importance is determined by **information gain**, which quantifies the amount of information that the feature holds about the response. Information gain can be regarded as a form of non-linear correlation between Y and X. Note the horizontal scale of Panel B (MF dataset) is more than twice as large as that of Panel A (ETF dataset), and the bar colors represent the feature rankings, not the features themselves.

Exhibit 16: Relative Importance of Features in the Random Forest Model

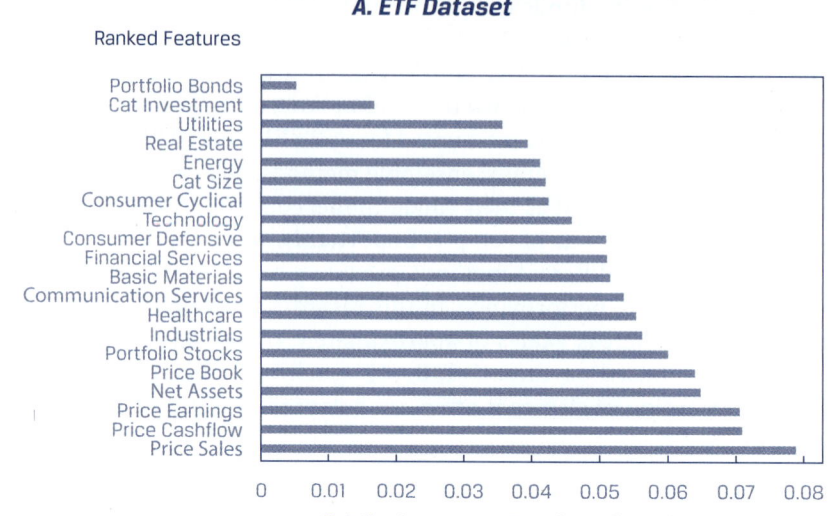

A. ETF Dataset

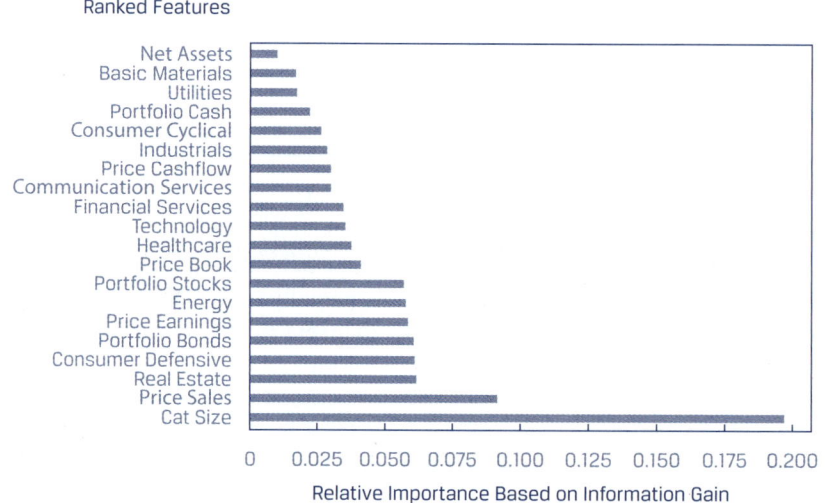

B. Mutual Fund Dataset

The prices-to-sales (price_sales) and prices-to-earnings (price_earnings) ratios are observed to be important indicators of performance, at about 0.08–0.09 and 0.06–0.07, respectively, in the random forest models for each dataset. The ratio of stocks to total assets (portfolio_stocks), at 0.06, is another key feature. Moreover, the industrials, health care, and communication services sector weightings are relatively important in the ETF dataset, while the real estate, consumer defensive, and energy sector weightings are key features in the MF dataset for differentiating between winning and losing funds.

Another important observation is that the category of the fund size (cat_size) is by far the most important feature in the model's performance for the MF dataset ($\approx$ 0.20), whereas it is of much less importance for model performance using the ETF dataset ($\approx$ 0.04). Conversely, net assets is a relatively important feature for model performance using the ETF dataset (0.065), while it is the least important feature when the random forest model is applied to the MF dataset (0.01).

Conclusion

The research analyst has trained and tested machine learning–based models that she can use to identify potential winning and losing ETFs and MFs. Her classification models use input features based on fund type and size, asset class composition, fundamentals, and sector composition characteristics. She is more confident in her assessment of MFs than of ETFs, owing to the substantially larger sample size of the former. She is also confident that any imbalance in class has not led to misinterpretation of her models' results, since she uses F1 score as her primary model evaluation metric. Moreover, she determines that the best performing model using both datasets is an ensemble-type random forest model. Finally, she concludes that while fundamental ratios, asset class ratios, and sector composition are important features for both models, net assets and category size also figure prominently in discriminating between winning and losing ETFs and MFs.

EXAMPLE 5

Classification of Funds

The research analyst from the previous case uses CART to generate the decision tree shown in Exhibit 17, which she will use to predict whether and explain why a new ETF is likely to be a winner (+1), an average performer (0), or a loser (-1). This ETF's fundamental valuation ratios are as follows: Price-to-sales = 2.29, price-to-earnings = 7.20, price-to-book = 1.41, and price-to-cash flow = 2.65. Note that the sample size is 1,067 ETFs and the CART model uses just valuation ratios, because these are deemed the most important features for ETF performance classification.

Exhibit 17: CART-Based Decision Tree for EFT Performance Classification

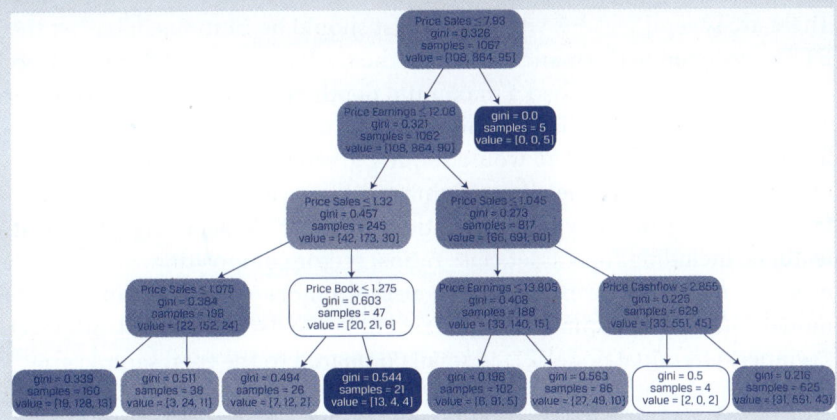

Legend:

Darkest shade, 5th (last) level: Winner (Class = +1)

Light to medium shade: Average Performer (Class = 0); note that the medium shade indicates more confidence in the classification.

Darkest shade, 2nd level: Loser (Class = -1)

White: Inconclusive, either because there is a tie with multiple categories or there are too few samples

Value: The number of sample cases in each of the three classes: Winner, Average Performer, or Loser

Path: Left path is True and right path is False.

1. Explain the CART model's prediction for performance of the new ETF: winner, loser, or average performer.

Solution

Based on its valuation ratios (P/S = 2.29; P/E = 7.20; P/B = 1.41), the new ETF is predicted to be a winner because the decision path leads to the dark shaded, 5th level ("winner") terminal node. The split criteria and decisions are as follows:

Initial node: P/S ≤ 7.93 and EFT P/S = 2.29, so True.
2nd-level node: P/E ≤ 12.08 and EFT P/E = 7.20, so True.
3rd-level node: P/S ≤ 1.32 and EFT P/S = 2.29, so False.
4th-level node: P/B ≤ 1.275 and EFT P/B = 1.41, so False.
5th-level (terminal) node: darkest shaded terminal node indicates "winner."

2. Calculate the probability that the fund will be in the class predicted by the CART model.

Solution

The output from the CART model in the darkest shaded, 5th level (winner) terminal node is [13, 4, 4], which indicates it includes 13 funds of Class +1 (winners), 4 funds of Class 0 (average performers), and 4 funds of Class -1 (losers). Thus, the probability predicted by the CART model that this ETF will be in the "winner" class is 13/21, or 62%. There are also equal probabilities of it being an average performer (19%) or a loser (19%).

3. Explain why the analyst should be cautious in basing the ETF's predicted performance solely on the CART-generated decision tree.

Solution

There are several reasons why the analyst should be cautious in basing the ETF's predicted performance solely on the CART-generated decision tree. First, this CART model had a maximum depth of just five levels. Truncating at five levels facilitates visualization, but a more realistic decision path is likely to be nuanced and so would require greater depth. Second, only some of the important variables (from Exhibit 16) were used in generating this tree, again for simplicity of visualization. A CART model using additional features, including fund asset class ratios, sector composition, and, especially, net assets would be expected to generate a more accurate (using F1 score) model. Finally, the number of funds reaching the darkest shaded, 5th level ("winner") terminal node (21) is small compared to the total sample size (1,067), so there may be too few clear winners (13) under this decision path from which to draw a statistically significant conclusion. Besides increasing the maximum tree depth and adding more features, another approach the analyst might take in this case for achieving a more accurate model is random forest; being an ensemble classifier, a random forest model would generalize out-of-sample better than any single CART model.

ESG DATA AS ALTERNATIVE DATA AND ML/AI FOR INTEGRATING ESG DATA INTO INVESTMENT DECISIONS

As an investment professional, how might you set about measuring the potential impact of climate change on a company's future prospects? Negative climate outcomes in coming years may include higher temperatures, more intense storms, melting glaciers, rising sea levels, shifting agricultural patterns, pressure on food and water, and new threats to human health. Assessing the likely severity of these future events and then quantifying the impact on companies is no easy task. Big Data techniques could be pivotal in generating usable information that could help investment professionals unlock long-term shareholder value.

Some fund managers, influenced by evolving investor preferences and increasing disclosure by companies on non-financial issues, have already incorporated ESG analysis into their investment processes. Governance ("G") data are generally objective: Investors are able to observe and measure corporate board actions, making governance comparable across companies and regions. Data on Environmental ("E") and Social ("S") impacts on listed companies, on the other hand, are more subjective, less reliable, and less comparable.

ESG data resemble alternative data in the sense that they have generally been poorly defined, are complex and unstructured, and need considerable due diligence before being used in investment decision making. Applying Machine Learning (ML) and Artificial Intelligence (AI) techniques can transform ESG data into meaningful information that is more useful for investment analysis.

Corporate sustainability reports often suffer from haphazard data collection and missing values. Equally, when data vendors acquire and combine raw ESG data into aggregate ESG scores, potential signals may be lost. ESG data and scoring across companies and data vendors can lack consistency and comparability; as a result, using simple summary scores in investment analysis is potentially flawed. Data analysts can apply data-science methods, such as data cleansing and data wrangling, to raw ESG data to create a structured dataset. Then, ML/AI techniques, such as natural language processing (NLP), can be applied to text-based, video, or audio ESG data. The foundation of NLP consists of supervised machine learning algorithms that typically include logistic regression, SVM, CART, random forests, or neural networks.

NLP can, for instance, search for key ESG words in corporate earnings calls. An increase in the number of mentions of, say, "human capital," employee "health and safety," or "flexible working" arrangements may indicate an increased focus on the "S" pillar of ESG. This would potentially raise the overall ESG score of a particular company. The results of such an application of NLP to corporate earnings calls are illustrated in the following exhibit:

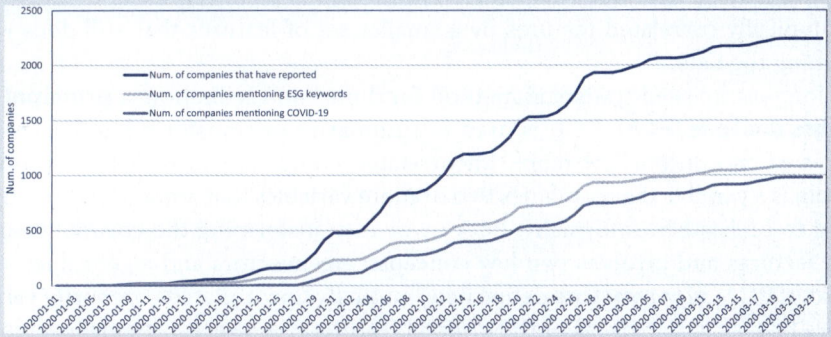

Source: "GS SUSTAIN: ESG—Neither Gone Nor Forgotten" by Evan Tylenda, Sharmini Chetwode, and Derek R. Bingham, Goldman Sachs Global Investment Research (2 April 2020).

ML/AI can help fund managers apply only those ESG factors that are relevant to a company and its sector. For example, "E" factors are important for mining and utility companies but less so for clothing manufacturers. Likewise, "S" factors are important for the global clothing manufacturing sector but less so for mining and utility companies.

ML/AI techniques are not used in isolation. ESG scoring systems tend to rely on cross-functional teams, with data scientists operating in tandem with economists, fundamental analysts, and portfolio managers to identify strengths and weaknesses of companies and sectors. Fundamental analysts, for instance, typically do not need to know the details of ML algorithms to make valuable contributions to the ESG investment workflow. The industry-specific knowledge of fundamental analysts can provide nuanced viewpoints that help to: 1) identify relevant raw data; 2) enable data scientists to incorporate ESG data into appropriate investment models; and 3) interpret model outputs and investment implications.

10   UNSUPERVISED ML ALGORITHMS AND PRINCIPAL COMPONENT ANALYSIS

☐   describe unsupervised machine learning algorithms—including principal components analysis, k-means clustering, and hierarchical clustering—and determine the problems for which they are best suited

Unsupervised learning is machine learning that does not use labeled data (i.e., no target variable); thus, the algorithms are tasked with finding patterns within the data themselves. The two main types of unsupervised ML algorithms shown in Exhibit 2 are dimension reduction, using principal components analysis, and clustering, which includes *k*-means and hierarchical clustering. These will now be described in turn.

Principal Components Analysis

Dimension reduction is an important type of unsupervised learning that is used widely in practice. When many features are in a dataset, representing the data visually or fitting models to the data may become extremely complex and "noisy" in the sense of reflecting random influences specific to a dataset. In such cases, dimension reduction may be necessary. Dimension reduction aims to represent a dataset with many typically correlated features by a smaller set of features that still does well in describing the data.

A long-established statistical method for dimension reduction is **principal components analysis (PCA)**. PCA is used to summarize or transform highly correlated features of data into a few main, uncorrelated composite variables. A **composite variable** is a variable that combines two or more variables that are statistically strongly related to each other. Informally, PCA involves transforming the covariance matrix of the features and involves two key concepts: eigenvectors and eigenvalues. In the context of PCA, **eigenvectors** define new, mutually uncorrelated composite variables that are linear combinations of the original features. As a vector, an eigenvector also represents a direction. Associated with each eigenvector is an eigenvalue. An **eigenvalue** gives the proportion of total variance in the initial data that is explained by each eigenvector. The PCA algorithm orders the eigenvectors from highest to lowest according to their eigenvalues—that is, in terms of their usefulness in explaining the total variance in the initial data (this will be shown shortly using a scree plot). PCA selects as the first principal component the eigenvector that explains the largest proportion of variation in the dataset (the eigenvector with the largest eigenvalue). The second principal component explains the next-largest proportion of variation remaining after the first principal component; this process continues for the third, fourth, and subsequent principal components. Because the principal components are linear combinations of the initial feature set, only a few principal components are typically required to explain most of the total variance in the initial feature covariance matrix.

Exhibit 18 shows a hypothetical dataset with three features, so it is plotted in three dimensions along the x-, y-, and z-axes. Each data point has a measurement (x, y, z), and the data should be standardized so that the mean of each series (x's, y's, and z's) is 0 and the standard deviation is 1. Assume PCA has been applied, revealing the first two principal components, PC1 and PC2. With respect to PC1, a perpendicular line dropped from each data point to PC1 shows the vertical distance between the data point and PC1, representing **projection error**. Moreover, the distance between each data point in the direction that is parallel to PC1 represents the spread or variation of the data along PC1. The PCA algorithm operates in such a way that it finds PC1 by selecting the line for which the sum of the projection errors for all data points is minimized and for which the sum of the spread between all the data is maximized. As a consequence of these selection criteria, PC1 is the unique vector that accounts for the largest proportion of the variance in the initial data. The next-largest portion of the remaining variance is best explained by PC2, which is at right angles to PC1 and thus is uncorrelated with PC1. The data points can now be represented by the first two principal components. This example demonstrates the effectiveness of the PCA algorithm in summarizing the variability of the data and the resulting dimension reduction.

Exhibit 18: First and Second Principal Components of a Hypothetical Three-Dimensional Dataset

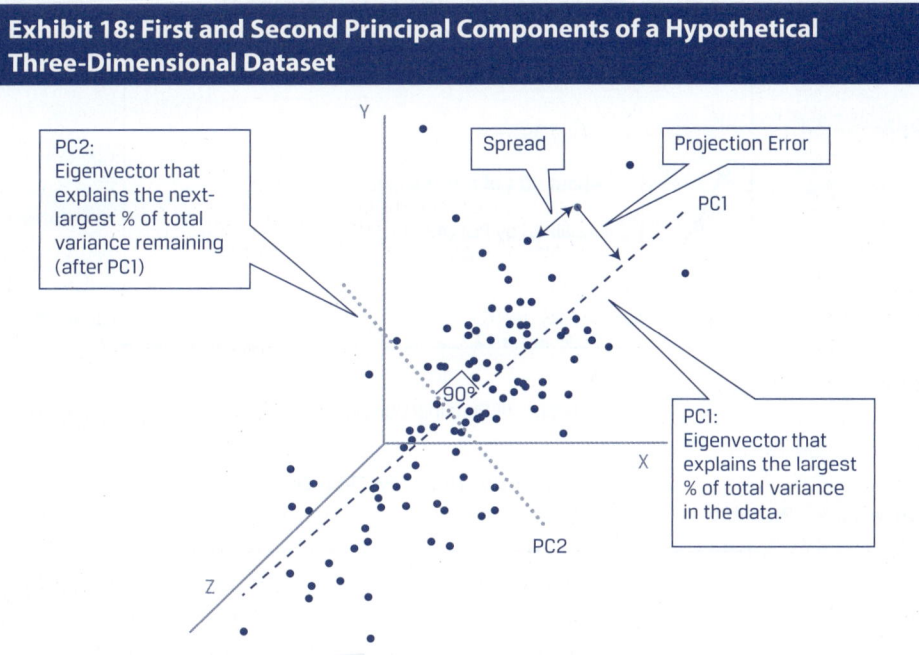

It is important to know how many principal components to retain because there is a trade-off between a lower-dimensional, more manageable view of a complex dataset when a few are selected and some loss of information. **Scree plots**, which show the proportion of total variance in the data explained by each principal component, can be helpful in this regard (see the accompanying sidebar). In practice, the smallest number of principal components that should be retained is that which the scree plot shows as explaining a desired proportion of total variance in the initial dataset (often 85% to 95%).

SCREE PLOTS FOR THE PRINCIPAL COMPONENTS OF RETURNS TO THE HYPOTHETICAL DLC 500 AND VLC 30 EQUITY INDEXES

In this illustration, researchers use scree plots and decide that three principal components are sufficient for explaining the returns to the hypothetical Diversified Large Cap (DLC) 500 and Very Large Cap (VLC) 30 equity indexes over the last 10-year period. The DLC 500 can be thought of as a diversified index of large-cap companies covering all economic sectors, while the VLC 30 is a more concentrated index of the 30 largest publicly traded companies. The dataset consists of index prices and more than 2,000 fundamental and technical features. Multi-collinearity among the features is a typical problem because that many features or combinations of features tend to have overlaps. To mitigate the problem, PCA can be used to capture the information and variance in the data. The following scree plots show that of the 20 principal components generated, the first 3 together explain about 90% and 86% of the variance in the value of the DLC 500 and VLC 30 indexes, respectively. The scree plots indicate that for each of these indexes, the incremental contribution to explaining the variance structure of the data is quite small after about the fifth principal component. Therefore, these less useful principal components can be ignored without much loss of information.

Scree Plots of Percent of Total Variance Explained by Each Principal Component for Hypothetical DLC 500 and VLC 30 Equity Indexes

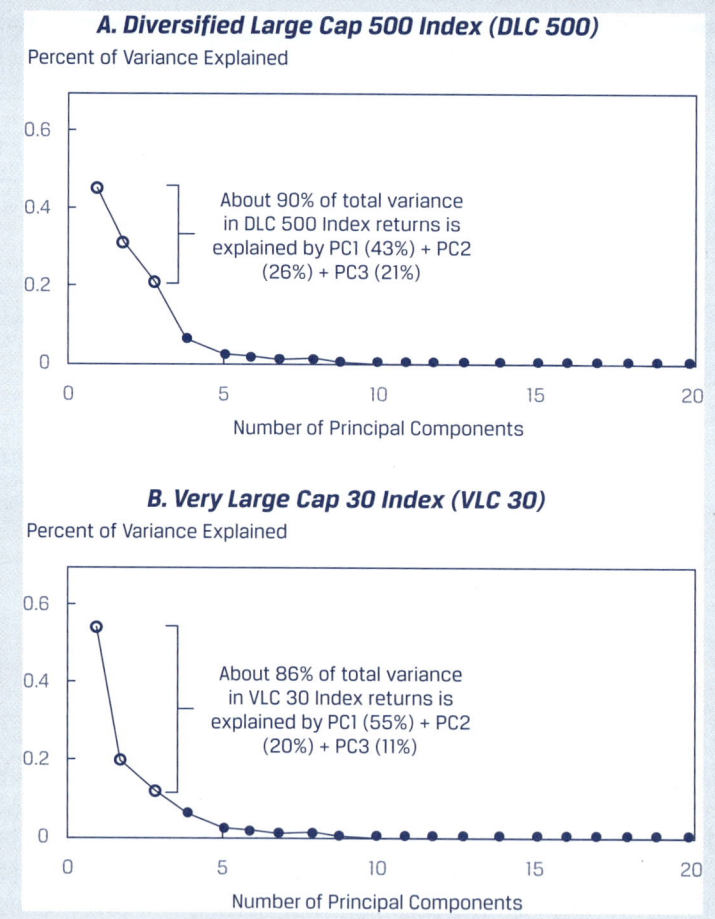

A. Diversified Large Cap 500 Index (DLC 500)

Percent of Variance Explained

About 90% of total variance in DLC 500 Index returns is explained by PC1 (43%) + PC2 (26%) + PC3 (21%)

Number of Principal Components

B. Very Large Cap 30 Index (VLC 30)

Percent of Variance Explained

About 86% of total variance in VLC 30 Index returns is explained by PC1 (55%) + PC2 (20%) + PC3 (11%)

Number of Principal Components

The main drawback of PCA is that since the principal components are combinations of the dataset's initial features, they typically cannot be easily labeled or directly interpreted by the analyst. Compared to modeling data with variables that represent well-defined concepts, the end user of PCA may perceive PCA as something of a "black box."

Reducing the number of features to the most relevant predictors is very useful, even when working with datasets having as few as 10 or so features. Notably, dimension reduction facilitates visually representing the data in two or three dimensions. It is typically performed as part of exploratory data analysis, before training another supervised or unsupervised learning model. Machine learning models are quicker to train, tend to reduce overfitting (by avoiding the curse of dimensionality), and are easier to interpret if provided with lower-dimensional datasets.

CLUSTERING

11

☐ describe unsupervised machine learning algorithms—including principal components analysis, k-means clustering, and hierarchical clustering—and determine the problems for which they are best suited

Clustering is another type of unsupervised machine learning, which is used to organize data points into similar groups called clusters. A **cluster** contains a subset of observations from the dataset such that all the observations within the same cluster are deemed "similar." The aim is to find a good clustering of the data—meaning that the observations inside each cluster are similar or close to each other (a property known as cohesion) and the observations in two different clusters are as far away from one another or are as dissimilar as possible (a property known as separation). Exhibit 19 depicts this intra-cluster cohesion and inter-cluster separation.

Exhibit 19: Evaluating Clustering—Intra-Cluster Cohesion and Inter-Cluster Separation

Bad Clustering
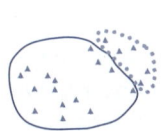

Good Clustering

(Maybe) Better Clustering

Clustering algorithms are particularly useful in the many investment problems and applications in which the concept of similarity is important. Applied to grouping companies, for example, clustering may uncover important similarities and differences among companies that are not captured by standard classifications of companies by industry and sector. In portfolio management, clustering methods have been used for improving portfolio diversification.

In practice, expert human judgment has a role in using clustering algorithms. In the first place, one must establish what it means to be "similar." Each company can be considered an observation with multiple features, including such financial statement items as total revenue and profit to shareholders, a wide array of financial ratios, or any other potential model inputs. Based on these features, a measure of similarity or "distance" between two observations (i.e., companies) can be defined. The smaller the distance, the more similar the observations; the larger the distance, the more dissimilar the observations.

A commonly used definition of distance is the Euclidian distance, the straight-line distance between two points. A closely related distance useful in portfolio diversification is correlation, which is the average Euclidian distance between a set of standardized points. Roughly a dozen different distance measures are used regularly in ML. In practice, the choice of the distance measures depends on the nature of the data (numerical or not) and the business problem being investigated. Once the relevant distance measure is defined, similar observations can be grouped together. We now introduce two of the more popular clustering approaches: k-means and hierarchical clustering.

12   K-MEANS CLUSTERING

☐   describe unsupervised machine learning algorithms—including principal components analysis, k-means clustering, and hierarchical clustering—and determine the problems for which they are best suited

K-means is an algorithm that repeatedly partitions observations into a fixed number, k, of non-overlapping clusters. The number of clusters, k, is a model hyperparameter. Each cluster is characterized by its **centroid** (i.e., center), and each observation is assigned by the algorithm to the cluster with the centroid to which that observation is closest. Notably, once the clusters are formed, there is no defined relationship between them.

The k-means algorithm follows an iterative process. It is illustrated in Exhibit 20 for $k = 3$ and a set of observations on a variable that can be described by two features. In Exhibit 20, the horizontal and vertical axes represent, respectively, the first and second features. For example, an investment analyst may want to group a set of firms into three groups according to two numerical measures of management quality. The algorithm groups the observations in the following steps:

1. K-means starts by determining the position of the k (here, 3) initial random centroids.

2. The algorithm then analyzes the features for each observation. Based on the distance measure that is used, k-means assigns each observation to its closest centroid, which defines a cluster.

3. Using the observations within each cluster, k-means then calculates the new (k) centroids for each cluster, where the centroid is the average value of their assigned observations.

4. K-means then reassigns the observations to the new centroids, redefining the clusters in terms of included and excluded observations.

5. The process of recalculating the new (k) centroids for each cluster is reiterated.

6. K-means then reassigns the observations to the revised centroids, again redefining the clusters in terms of observations that are included and excluded.

The k-means algorithm will continue to iterate until no observation is reassigned to a new cluster (i.e., no need to recalculate new centroids). The algorithm has then converged and reveals the final k clusters with their member observations. The k-means algorithm has minimized intra-cluster distance (thereby maximizing cohesion) and has maximized inter-cluster distance (thereby maximizing separation) under the constraint that $k = 3$.

Exhibit 20: Example of 3-Means Algorithm

A. Chooses Initial Random Centroids: C1, C2, C3

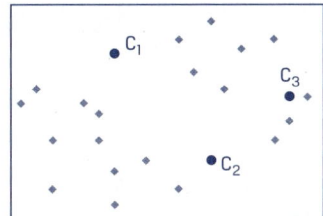

B. Assigns Each Observation to Nearest Centroid (defining initial 3 clusters)

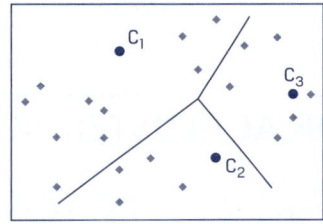

C. Calculates New Centroids as the Average Values of Observations in a Cluster

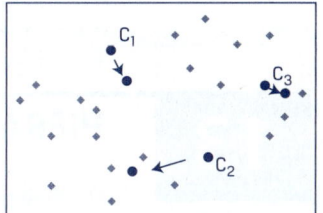

D. Reassigns Each Observation to the Nearest Centroid (from C)

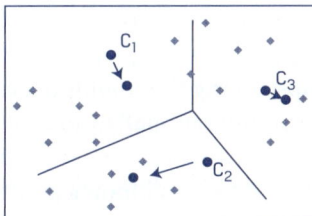

E. Reiterates the Process of Recalculating New Centroids

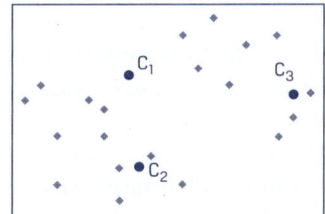

F. Reassigns Each Observation to the Nearest Centroid (from E), Completing Second Iteration

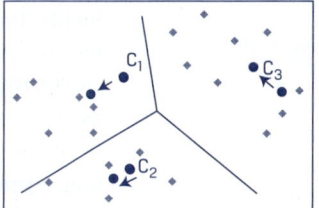

The k-means algorithm is fast and works well on very large datasets, those with hundreds of millions of observations. However, the final assignment of observations to clusters can depend on the initial location of the centroids. To address this problem, the algorithm can be run several times using different sets of initial centroids, and then one can choose the clustering that is most useful given the business purpose.

One limitation of this technique is that the hyperparameter, k, the number of clusters in which to partition the data, must be decided before k-means can be run. So, one needs to have a sense of how many clusters are reasonable for the problem under investigation and the dataset being analyzed. Alternatively, one can run the algorithm using a range of values for k to find the optimal number of clusters—the k that minimizes intra-cluster distance and thereby maximizes intra-cluster similarity (i.e., cohesion) and that maximizes inter-cluster distance (i.e., separation). However, note that the final results can be subjective and dependent on the context of the problem and the particular training set. In practice, it is common to make the final choice of k based on face validity, such that the clusters feel sensible and are interpretable. This decision is greatly assisted by using summary information about the centroids and ranges of values and naming example items in each cluster.

For example, consider the Russell 3000 Index, which tracks the 3,000 highest market capitalization stocks in the United States. These 3,000 stocks can be grouped in 10, 50, or even more clusters based on their financial characteristics (e.g., total assets, total revenue, profitability, leverage) and operating characteristics (e.g., employee headcount, R&D intensity). Because companies in the same standard industry classification can have very different financial and operating characteristics, using *k*-means to derive different clusters can provide insights and understanding into the nature of "peer" groups. As mentioned, the exact choice of the *k*, the number of clusters, will depend on the level of precision or segmentation desired. In a similar vein, clustering can be used to classify collective investment vehicles or hedge funds as an alternative to standard classifications. Clustering analysis can also help visualize the data and facilitate detecting trends or outliers.

In sum, the *k*-means algorithm is among the most used algorithms in investment practice, particularly in data exploration for discovering patterns in high-dimensional data or as a method for deriving alternatives to existing static industry classifications.

13   HIERARCHICAL CLUSTERING

☐ | describe neural networks, deep learning nets, and reinforcement learning

Hierarchical clustering is an iterative procedure used to build a hierarchy of clusters. In *k*-means clustering, the algorithm segments the data into a predetermined number of clusters; there is no defined relationship among the resulting clusters. In hierarchical clustering, however, the algorithms create intermediate rounds of clusters of increasing (in "agglomerative") or decreasing (in "divisive") size until a final clustering is reached. The process creates relationships among the rounds of clusters, as the word "hierarchical" suggests. Although more computationally intensive than *k*-means clustering, hierarchical clustering has the advantage of allowing the investment analyst to examine alternative segmentations of data of different granularity before deciding which one to use.

Agglomerative clustering (or bottom-up hierarchical clustering) begins with each observation being treated as its own cluster. Then, the algorithm finds the two closest clusters, defined by some measure of distance (similarity), and combines them into one new larger cluster. This process is repeated iteratively until all observations are clumped into a single cluster. A hypothetical example of how agglomerative clustering develops a hierarchical clustering scheme is depicted in the top part of Exhibit 21, where observations are lettered (A to K) and circles around observations denote clusters. The process begins with 11 individual clusters and then generates a sequence of groupings. The first sequence includes five clusters with two observations each and one cluster with a single observation, G, for a total of six clusters. It then generates two clusters—one cluster with six observations and the other with five observations. The final result is one large cluster containing all 11 observations. It is easily seen that this final large cluster includes the two main sub-clusters, with each containing three smaller sub-clusters.

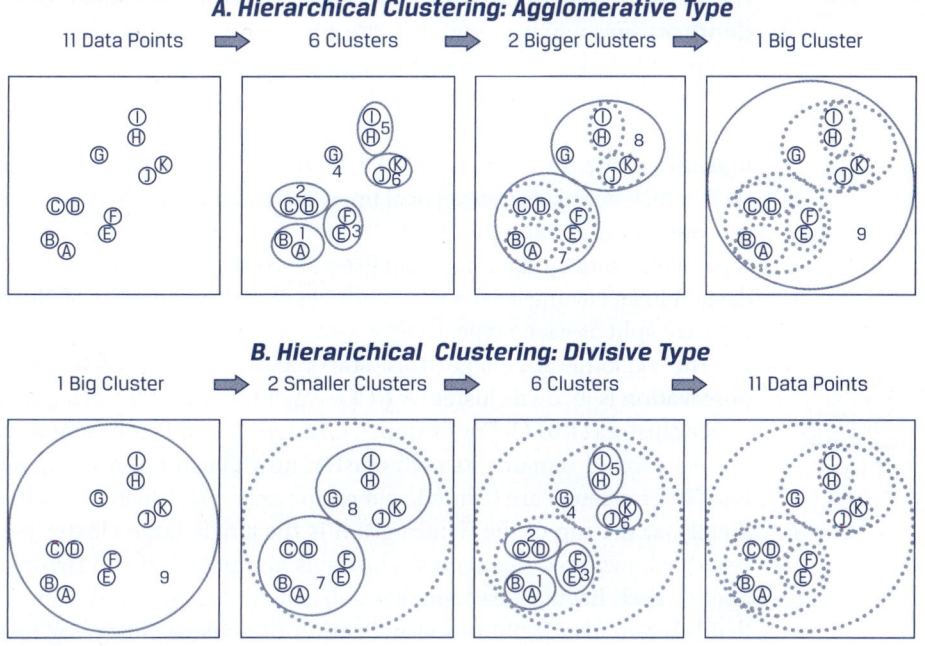

Exhibit 21: Agglomerative and Divisive Hierarchical Clustering

A. Hierarchical Clustering: Agglomerative Type

11 Data Points ➡ 6 Clusters ➡ 2 Bigger Clusters ➡ 1 Big Cluster

B. Hierarichical Clustering: Divisive Type

1 Big Cluster ➡ 2 Smaller Clusters ➡ 6 Clusters ➡ 11 Data Points

By contrast, **divisive clustering** (or top-down hierarchical clustering) starts with all the observations belonging to a single cluster. The observations are then divided into two clusters based on some measure of distance (similarity). The algorithm then progressively partitions the intermediate clusters into smaller clusters until each cluster contains only one observation. Divisive clustering is depicted in the bottom part of Exhibit 21, which begins with all 11 observations in one large cluster. Next, the algorithm generates two smaller clusters, one with six observations and the other with five observations, and then six clusters, with two observations each except for observation G, which is its own cluster. Finally, 11 clusters are generated, with each cluster containing only one observation.

Although this is not a typical outcome (because the two methods generally use different algorithms), in this hypothetical illustration, the agglomerative and divisive clustering methods produced the same result: two main sub-clusters each having three smaller sub-clusters. The analyst could decide between using a six- or a two-cluster representation of the data. The agglomerative method is the approach typically used with large datasets because of the algorithm's fast computing speed. The agglomerative clustering algorithm makes clustering decisions based on local patterns without initially accounting for the global structure of the data. As such, the agglomerative method is well suited for identifying small clusters. However, because the divisive method starts with a holistic representation of the data, the divisive clustering algorithm is designed to account for the global structure of the data and thus is better suited for identifying large clusters.

To decide on the closest clusters for combining in the agglomerative process or for dividing in the divisive process, an explicit definition for the distance between two clusters is required. Some commonly used definitions for the distance between two clusters involve finding the minimum, the maximum, or the average of the straight-line distances between all the pairs of observations in each cluster.

Dendrograms

A type of tree diagram for visualizing a hierarchical cluster analysis is known as a **dendrogram**, which highlights the hierarchical relationships among the clusters. Exhibit 22 shows a dendrogram representation for the clustering shown in Exhibit 21. First, a few technical points on dendrograms bear mentioning—although they may not all be apparent in Exhibit 22. The x-axis shows the clusters, and the y-axis indicates some distance measure. Clusters are represented by a horizontal line, the arch, which connects two vertical lines, called dendrites, where the height of each arch represents the distance between the two clusters being considered. Shorter dendrites represent a shorter distance (and greater similarity) between clusters. The horizontal dashed lines cutting across the dendrites show the number of clusters into which the data are split at each stage.

The agglomerative algorithm starts at the bottom of the dendrite, where each observation is its own cluster (A to K). Agglomerative clustering then generates the six larger clusters (1 to 6). For example, Clusters A and B combine to form Cluster 1, and Observation G remains its own cluster, now Cluster 4. Moving up the dendrogram, two larger clusters are formed, where, for example, Cluster 7 includes Clusters 1 to 3. Finally, at the top of the dendrogram is the single large cluster (9). The dendrogram readily shows how this largest cluster is composed of the two main sub-clusters (7 and 8), each having three smaller sub-clusters (1 to 3 and 4 to 6, respectively). The dendrogram also facilitates visualization of divisive clustering by starting at the top of the largest cluster and then working downward until the bottom is reached, where all 11 single-observation clusters are shown.

Exhibit 22: Dendrogram of Agglomerative Hierarchical Clustering

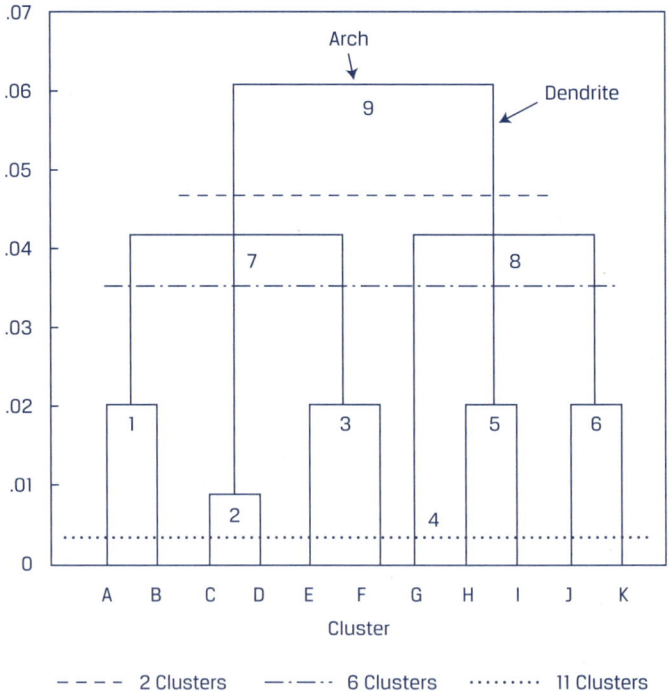

Clustering has many applications in investment management. For example, portfolio diversification can be approached as a clustering problem with the aim of optimally diversifying risks by investing in assets from multiple different clusters. Because the clusters have maximum inter-cluster separation, diversifying among them helps ensure that the portfolio reflects a wide diversity of characteristics with well-diversified risk. In contrast, information that investments are concentrated in a cluster indicates a high probability of concentrated risk. Finally, it is important to note that while the results of clustering algorithms are often difficult to evaluate (because the resulting clusters themselves are not explicitly defined), they are still very useful in practice for uncovering important underlying structure (namely, similarities among observations) in complex datasets.

EXAMPLE 6

Investment Uses of Clustering Algorithms

István Perényi is a portfolio manager of the Europe Diversified Equity Fund ("the Fund") within the Diversified Investment Management Company (DIMCO) fund family. The Fund is benchmarked to the STOXX Europe 600 Index, which spans 17 countries, 19 industry sectors, and three market capitalization groupings (large-, mid-, and small-cap).

Examining the Fund's most recent performance, Perényi is concerned that the Fund's holdings, although approximately aligned with the STOXX Europe 600 Index's country weights, may have unrecognized risk biases and concentrations. Perényi asks Elsa Lund, DIMCO's chief risk officer, to investigate the Fund's diversification. Lund asks her analysts for ideas on how Perényi's request can be addressed and receives three suggestions:

Suggestion 1   Estimate the country, industry, and market cap exposures of each Fund holding, aggregate them, and compare the aggregate exposures to the benchmark's exposures. Then, examine mismatches for evidence of unexpected biases or concentrations.

Suggestion 2   Identify inherent groupings among fund holdings based on a broad set of eight numerical (operating and financial) measures related to the holdings' characteristics. Then, examine the groupings for evidence of unexpected biases or concentrations.

Suggestion 3   Regress the return of the Fund on a set of country equity market indexes and sector indexes based on the Fund's benchmark. Then, examine the regression coefficients for evidence of unexpected biases or concentrations.

Lund has several questions for analyst Greg Kane about using one or more clustering machine learning algorithms in relation to addressing Perényi's request.

Lund asks whether any information needs to be specified for the ML clustering algorithms no matter which one is used. Kane replies that only the distance measure that the algorithm will use and the hyperparameter, k, for k-means clustering need to be specified.

Lund further asks whether there would be an advantage to using k-means clustering as opposed to hierarchical clustering. Kane replies that in his opinion, hierarchical clustering is the more appropriate algorithm.

---

1. Which analyst suggestion is *most likely* to be implemented using machine learning?

   A. Suggestion 1

B. Suggestion 2

C. Suggestion 3

Solution

B is correct. A machine learning clustering algorithm could be used to implement Suggestion 2. A and C are incorrect because Suggestions 1 and 3, respectively, can be addressed easily using traditional regression analysis.

---

2. Kane's reply to Lund's first question about specification of ML clustering models is:

A. correct.

B. not correct, because other hyperparameters must also be specified.

C. not correct, because the feature set for describing the measure used to group holdings must also be specified.

Solution

C is correct. Beyond specifying a distance measure and the k for k-means, whichever clustering algorithm is selected, the feature set used to group holdings by similarities must also be specified. Operating and financial characteristics of the companies represented in the Fund's portfolio are examples of such features.

---

3. The best justification for Kane's preference for hierarchical clustering in his reply to Lund's second question is that Kane is *most likely* giving consideration to:

A. the speed of the algorithms.

B. the dimensionality of the dataset.

C. the need to specify the hyperparameter, k, in using a k-means algorithm.

Solution

C is correct. The value of the hyperparameter, k, the number of distinct groups into which the STOXX Europe 600 Index can be segmented, is not known and needs to be specified in advance by the analyst. Using a hierarchical algorithm, the sorting of observations into clusters will occur without any prior input on the analyst's part.

---

14   CASE STUDY: CLUSTERING STOCKS BASED ON CO-MOVEMENT SIMILARITY

☐ | describe neural networks, deep learning nets, and reinforcement learning

The following case study was developed and written by Matthew Dixon, PhD, FRM.
An endowment fund's Investment Committee is seeking three "buy" recommendations for the fund's large-cap equity portfolio. An analyst working for the Investment Committee is given a subset of eight stocks from the S&P 500 Index and asked to

determine the co-movement similarity (i.e., correlation) of their returns. Specifically, for diversification purposes, the Investment Committee wants the correlation of returns between the recommended stocks to be low, so the analyst decides to use clustering to identify the most similar stocks and then choose one stock from each cluster. Although this case study focuses mainly on hierarchical agglomerative clustering, the analyst's results using other clustering algorithms (i.e., divisive clustering and k-means) are also briefly discussed. Exhibit 23 provides a description of the data used by the analyst.

Exhibit 23: Dataset of Eight Stocks from the S&P 500 Index

Description: Daily adjusted closing prices of eight S&P 500 member stocks

Trading Dates: 30 May 2017 to 24 May 2019

Number of Observations: 501

Stocks (Ticker Symbols): AAPL, F, FB, GM, GS, GOOG, JPM, and UBS

The following steps are taken by the analyst to perform the hierarchical agglomerative cluster analysis:

1. Collect panel data on adjusted closing prices for the stocks under investigation.

2. Calculate the daily log returns for each stock, where each time series of stock returns is an n-vector ($n = 500$).

3. Run the agglomerative hierarchical clustering algorithm.

    a. The algorithm calculates the pairwise distance (i.e., Euclidean distance) between vectors of any two stocks' returns. Each pairwise distance is an element of a distance matrix (i.e., dissimilarity matrix) with zero diagonals.

    b. The algorithm starts with each stock as its own cluster, finds the pair of clusters which are closest to each other, and then redefines them as a new cluster.

    c. The algorithm finds the distances from this new cluster to the remaining return clusters. Using a process called average (centroid) linkage, it determines the distances from the center of the new cluster to the centers of the remaining clusters. Note that there are several other linkage methods, but whichever method is selected, the algorithm proceeds in the same fashion: It combines the pair of clusters which are closest, redefines them as a new cluster, and recalculates the distances to the remaining clusters.

4. Repeat Step 3c until the data are aggregated into a single large cluster.

5. Plot the resulting dendrogram to visualize the hierarchical clusters and draw the highest horizontal line intersecting three (i.e., the desired number of clusters, since the Investment Committee wants three "buy" recommendations) vertical lines (or dendrites) to determine the appropriate cluster configuration.

Exhibit 24 shows for illustrative purposes a subset of the panel data on daily returns, calculated from the adjusted closing prices of the eight stocks collected in Step 1. The clustering is performed on the daily returns.

Exhibit 24: Subset of Stock Returns, Calculated from Adjusted Closing Prices, for Clustering

Date	JPM	UBS	GS	FB	AAPL	GOOG	GM	F
2017-05-31	−0.021	−0.007	−0.033	−0.006	−0.006	−0.011	0.012	0.004
2017-06-01	0.011	0.013	0.018	0.000	0.003	0.002	0.015	0.026
2017-06-02	−0.005	−0.002	−0.008	0.014	0.015	0.009	0.001	−0.005
2017-06-05	0.002	−0.007	0.003	0.000	−0.010	0.008	0.000	−0.009
2017-06-06	0.002	0.002	0.003	−0.005	0.003	−0.007	−0.001	−0.012

The results of the remaining steps are described using the distance matrix shown in Exhibit 25.

Exhibit 25: Distance Matrix for Hierarchical Agglomerative Clustering

	JPM	UBS	GS	FB	AAPL	GOOG	GM	F
JPM	0.000	0.243	0.215	0.456	0.364	0.332	0.358	0.348
UBS	0.243	0.000	0.281	0.460	0.380	0.338	0.384	0.385
GS	0.215	0.281	0.000	0.471	0.375	0.345	0.383	0.393
FB	0.456	0.460	0.471	0.000	0.437	0.357	0.491	0.480
AAPL	0.364	0.380	0.375	0.437	0.000	0.307	0.445	0.456
GOOG	0.332	0.338	0.345	0.357	0.307	0.000	0.405	0.422
GM	0.358	0.384	0.383	0.491	0.445	0.405	0.000	0.334
F	0.348	0.385	0.393	0.480	0.456	0.422	0.334	0.000

The distance matrix reveals the closest pair of stocks is JPM and GS, with a distance of 0.215. Therefore, this pair becomes the first combined cluster as shown in the dendrogram in Exhibit 26. Note that the vertical distance connecting the various clusters represents the Euclidean distance between clusters, so the arch between this pair has a height of 0.215. Now that JPM and GS are paired in a cluster (i.e., GS_JPM), we treat the mean of their two return vectors as a new point.

Exhibit 26: Dendrogram for Hierarchical Agglomerative Clustering

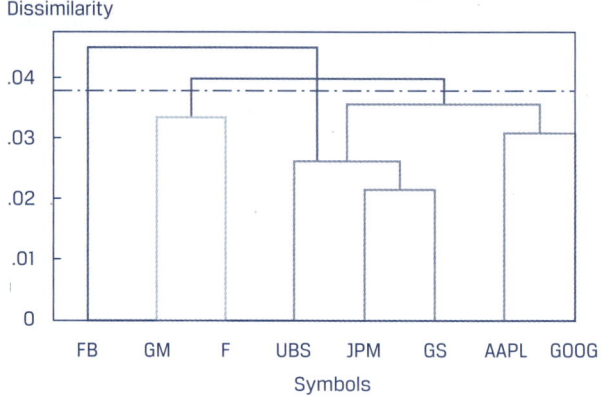

From the distance matrix, the average distance of UBS to the new cluster (i.e., GS_JPM) is the sum of the distance between UBS and JPM, 0.243, and the distance between UBS and GS, 0.281, divided by two, which is 0.262 (= (0.243 + 0.281)/2). Since this distance is smaller than the distance between any of the other unpaired stock clusters, UBS is merged with this cluster to create a new cluster (i.e., GS_JPM_UBS). The height of the arch in the dendrogram for this new cluster is 0.262, which is now observed to contain three banking sector stocks. Although not shown in the dendrogram, the cluster is identified by the return vector averaged over the three stocks.

The next closest pair of points, whether stock to stock or stock to cluster, is AAPL and GOOG, with a distance of 0.307, so the algorithm merges these two points into a second cluster (i.e., AAPL_GOOG), with an arch height of 0.307. Next, GM and F are paired into a third cluster (i.e., F_GM), with an arch height of 0.334. Finally, the first two clusters are merged to form a five-stock cluster (i.e., GS_JPM_UBS_AAPL_GOOG), with an arch height of 0.356. Note that this value is determined by taking the average distance between the three banks and AAPL and GOOG: 0.356 = (0.364 + 0.380 + 0.375 + 0.332 + 0.338 + 0.345)/6. The result is three separate clusters: the five-stock cluster, F_GM, and FB by itself. Also, note the horizontal dashed line that cuts the dendrogram into three distinct clusters, with FB as its own cluster.

This agglomerative hierarchical clustering analysis reveals some interesting preliminary results—largely grouping the stocks by their sectors but also uncovering some anomalies. In particular, FB is found to behave quite differently, in terms of return co-movement similarity, from the other technology stocks (AAPL and GOOG). Also, AAPL and GOOG are found to behave more like the bank stocks and less like the auto stocks (F and GM), which appear in their own cluster.

In contrast to agglomerative clustering, the divisive clustering algorithm starts with all stocks assigned to one large cluster and then splits the cluster into sub-clusters recursively, until each stock occupies its own cluster. Determining how to split the first cluster requires searching over all combinations of possible splits, so it is too numerically intensive to cover the details here. However, results of the first two splits for divisive clustering, into three clusters, are shown in Exhibit 27. Results for k-means, with $k = 3$, and agglomerative clustering are also presented.

Exhibit 27: Comparison of Results of Different Clustering Algorithms

	Agglomerative	K-means	Divisive
AAPL	3	2	2
F	2	1	1
FB	1	2	3
GM	2	1	1
GOOG	3	2	2
GS	3	3	1
JPM	3	3	1

	Agglomerative	K-means	Divisive
UBS	3	3	1

Whereas the assignment of the cluster number (1, 2, 3), shown in the upper panel, can be taken as arbitrary across each algorithm, the useful information is in the grouping of like stocks. As seen in the stylized clusters in the lower panel, all three clustering algorithms agree that bank stocks belong in the same cluster. Both hierarchical agglomerative and k-means algorithms also agree that auto stocks belong in their own separate cluster. K-means clusters the stocks precisely by industry sector, whereas hierarchical agglomerative and divisive clustering identify FB as an outlier and place it in its own cluster. In general, the most agreement is expected between the two hierarchical clustering algorithms, although their results are not guaranteed to match, even when using the same linkage process. K-means starts with three clusters (k = 3) and iteratively swaps points in and out of these clusters using a partitioning mechanism different from that of hierarchical clustering. Thus, k-means results are typically not expected to match those of hierarchical clustering.

In conclusion, based on the analyses of the co-movement similarity of returns among the eight stocks using the agglomerative clustering algorithm and the Investment Committee's requirement that the correlation of returns between the recommended stocks should be low, the analyst's recommendation should be as follows:

- buy FB,
- buy the most attractive of the two auto stocks (F or GM), and
- buy the most attractive of the three bank stocks (GS, JPM, or UBS).

EXAMPLE 7

Hierarchical Agglomerative Clustering

Assume the analyst is given the same set of stocks as previously excluding F and GM (i.e., no auto stocks)—so now, six stocks. Using the information from this mini-case study, answer the following questions:

1. Describe how the inputs to the hierarchical agglomerative clustering algorithm would differ from those in the mini-case study.

Solution

The panel data on closing prices and daily log returns would include the same stocks as before but without F and GM—so, AAPL, FB, GOOG, GS, JPM, and UBS. The distance matrix would also appear the same except without F, GM, or any of the pairwise distances between them and the remaining stocks.

2. Describe the three clusters that would now result from running the hierarchical agglomerative clustering algorithm.

Solution

The three clusters that would now result from running the agglomerative clustering algorithm are GS_JPM_UBS (i.e., one cluster of three bank stocks), AAPL_GOOG (i.e., one cluster of two technology stocks), and FB by itself.

3. Explain why these results differ from the previous case, with eight stocks (including the two auto stocks).

Solution

The agglomerative clustering algorithm now combines GS and JPM and then UBS, as before, to form a bank cluster. Next, and as previously, the algorithm combines AAPL and GOOG into a cluster. However, without the auto stocks, there is no need to combine AAPL_GOOG with the bank cluster. There are now three distinct clusters, since (as before) the algorithm treats FB as its own cluster, given the high degree of return co-movement dissimilarity between FB and the other clusters (i.e., AAPL_GOOG, and GS_JPM_UBS).

4. Describe the analyst's new recommendation to the Investment Committee.

Solution

The analyst's new recommendation to the Investment Committee would be to buy FB, buy the cheapest of AAPL or GOOG, and buy the most attractive of the three bank stocks (GS, JPM, or UBS).

NEURAL NETWORKS, DEEP LEARNING NETS, AND REINFORCEMENT LEARNING

15

☐ | describe neural networks, deep learning nets, and reinforcement learning

The artificial intelligence revolution has been driven in large part by advances in neural networks, deep learning algorithms, and reinforcement learning. These sophisticated algorithms can address highly complex machine learning tasks, such as image classification, face recognition, speech recognition, and natural language processing. These complicated tasks are characterized by non-linearities and interactions between large numbers of feature inputs. We now provide an overview of these algorithms and their investment applications.

Neural Networks

Neural networks (also called artificial neural networks, or ANNs) are a highly flexible type of ML algorithm that have been successfully applied to a variety of tasks characterized by non-linearities and complex interactions among features. Neural networks are commonly used for classification and regression in supervised learning but are also important in reinforcement learning, which does not require human-labeled training data.

Exhibit 28 shows the connection between multiple regression and neural networks. Panel A represents a hypothetical regression for data using four inputs, the features x_1 to x_4, and one output—the predicted value of the target variable y. Panel B shows a schematic representation of a basic neural network, which consists of nodes (circles) connected by links (arrows connecting nodes). Neural networks have three types of layers: an input layer (here with a node for each of the four features); hidden layers, where learning occurs in training and inputs are processed on trained nets; and an output layer (here consisting of a single node for the target variable y), which passes information outside the network.

Besides the network structure, another important difference between multiple regression and neural networks is that the nodes in the neural network's hidden layer transform the inputs in a non-linear fashion into new values that are then combined into the target value. For example, consider the popular rectified linear unit (ReLU) function, $f(x) = \max(0, x)$, which takes on a value of zero if there is a negative input and takes on the value of the input if it is positive. In this case, y will be equal to β_1 times z_1, where z_1 is the maximum of $(x_1 + x_2 + x_3)$ or 0, plus β_2 times z_2, the maximum of $(x_2 + x_4)$ or 0, plus β_3 times z_3, the maximum of $(x_2 + x_3 + x_4)$ or 0, plus an error term.

Exhibit 28: Regression and Neural Networks (Regression with Transformed Features)

A. Conceptual Illustration of Regression

B. Conceptual Illustration of Hypothetical Neural Network

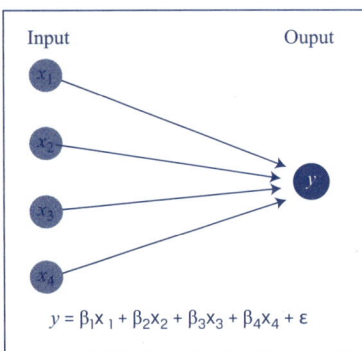

$$y = \beta_1 x_1 + \beta_2 x_2 + \beta_3 x_3 + \beta_4 x_4 + \varepsilon$$

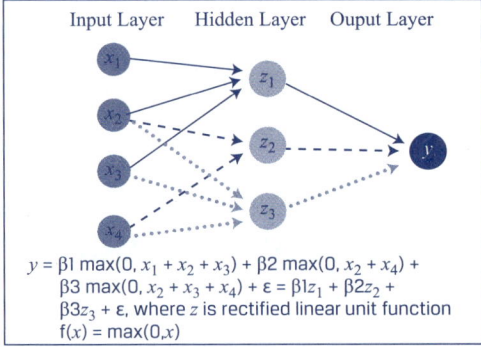

$y = \beta1 \max(0, x_1 + x_2 + x_3) + \beta2 \max(0, x_2 + x_4) + \beta3 \max(0, x_2 + x_3 + x_4) + \varepsilon = \beta1z_1 + \beta2z_2 + \beta3z_3 + \varepsilon$, where z is rectified linear unit function $f(x) = \max(0,x)$

Note that for neural networks, the feature inputs would be scaled (i.e., standardized) to account for differences in the units of the data. For example, if the inputs were positive numbers, each could be scaled by its maximum value so that their values lie between 0 and 1.

Exhibit 29 shows a more complex neural network, with an input layer consisting of four nodes (i.e., four features), one hidden layer consisting of five hidden nodes, and an output node. These three numbers—4, 5, and 1—for the neural network are hyperparameters that determine the structure of the neural network.

Exhibit 29: A More Complex Neural Network with One Hidden Layer

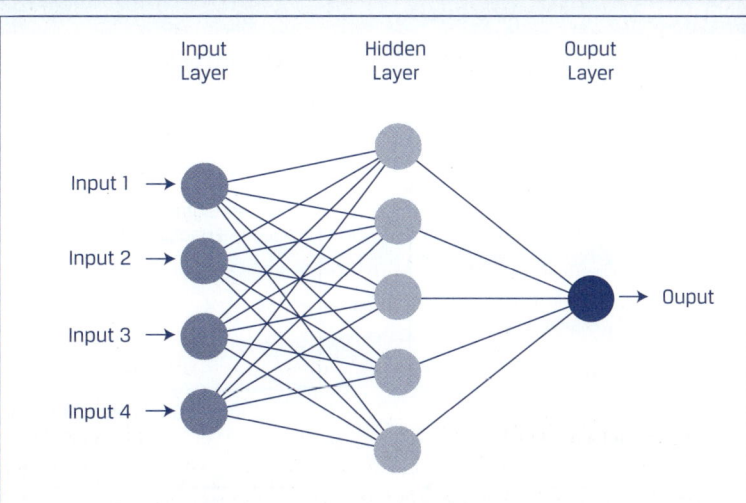

Now consider any of the nodes to the right of the input layer. These nodes are sometimes called "neurons" because they process information received. Take the topmost hidden node. Four links connect to that node from the inputs, so the node gets four values transmitted by the links. Each link has a weight meant to represent its importance (initially these weights may be assigned randomly). Each node has, conceptually, two functional parts: a summation operator and an activation function. Once the node receives the four input values, the **summation operator** multiplies each value by its respective weight and then sums the weighted values to form the total net input. The total net input is then passed to the **activation function**, which transforms this input into the final output of the node. Informally, the activation function operates like a light dimmer switch that decreases or increases the strength of the input. The activation function, which is chosen by the modeler (i.e., a hyperparameter), is characteristically non-linear, such as an S-shaped (sigmoidal) function (with output range of 0 to 1) or the rectified linear unit function shown in Panel B of Exhibit 28. Non-linearity implies that the rate of change of output differs at different levels of input.

This activation function is shown in Exhibit 30, where in the left graph a negative total net input is transformed via the S-shaped function into an output close to 0. This low output implies the node does not trigger, so there is nothing to pass to the next node. Conversely, in the right graph a positive total net input is transformed into an output close to 1, so the node does trigger. The output of the activation function is then transmitted to the next set of nodes if there is a second hidden layer or, as in this case, to the output layer node as the predicted value. The process of transmission just described (think of forward pointing arrows in Exhibit 29) is referred to as **forward propagation**.

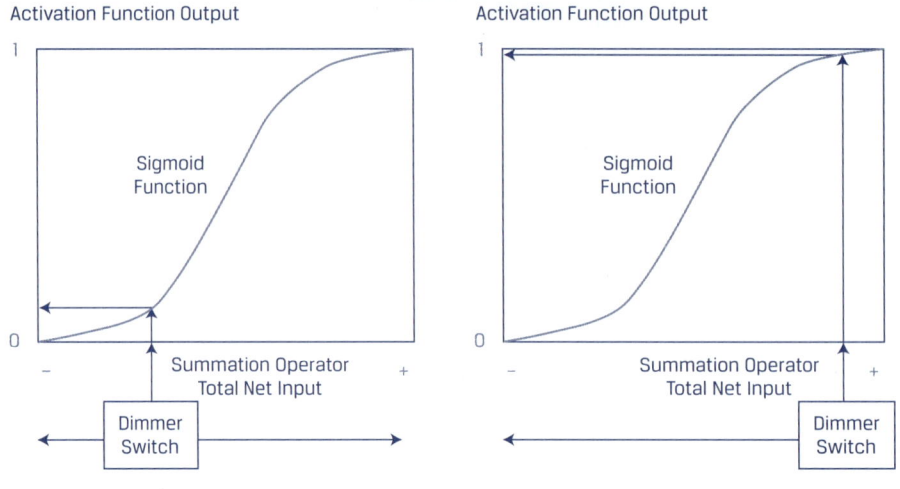

Exhibit 30: Activation Function as "Light Dimmer Switch" at Each Node in a Neural Network

Starting with an initialized set of random network weights (i.e., the weights assigned to each of the links), training a neural network in a supervised learning context is an iterative process in which predictions are compared to actual values of labeled data and evaluated by a specified performance measure (e.g., mean squared error). Then, the network weights are adjusted to reduce total error of the network. (If the process of adjustment works backward through the layers of the network, this process is called **backward propagation**). Learning takes place through this process of adjustment to the network weights with the aim of reducing total error. Without proliferating notation relating to nodes, the gist of the updating can be expressed informally as

New weight

= (Old weight) − (Learning rate) × (Partial derivative of the total error with respect to the old weight),

where partial derivative is a gradient or rate of change of the total error with respect to the change in the old weight and **learning rate** is a hyperparameter that affects the magnitude of adjustments. When learning is completed, all the network weights have assigned values; these are the parameters of the network.

The structure of a network in which all the features are interconnected with non-linear activation functions allows neural networks to uncover and approximate complex non-linear relationships among features. Broadly speaking, when more nodes and more hidden layers are specified, a neural network's ability to handle complexity tends to increase (but so does the risk of overfitting).

Asset pricing is a noisy, stochastic process with potentially unstable relationships that challenge modeling processes, so researchers are asking if machine learning can improve our understanding of how markets work. Research comparing statistical and machine learning methods' abilities to explain and predict equity prices so far indicates that simple neural networks produce models of equity returns at the individual stock and portfolio level that are superior to models built using traditional statistical methods due to their ability to capture dynamic and interacting variables. This suggests that ML-based models, such as neural networks, may simply be better able to cope with the non-linear relationships inherent in security prices. However, the trade-offs in using neural networks are their lack of interpretability (i.e., black box nature) and the large amounts of data and high computation intensity needed to train such models; thus, neural networks may not be a good choice in many investment applications.

DEEP NEURAL NETWORKS

16

The previous discussion of neural networks was limited to types of neural networks referred to as "shallow neural networks"—exhibiting just one hidden layer. Neural networks with many hidden layers—at least 2 but potentially more than 20—are known as **deep neural networks** (DNNs). DNNs are the foundation of deep learning and have proven to be successful across a wide range of artificial intelligence applications. Advances in DNNs have driven developments in many complex activities, such as image, pattern, and speech recognition. To state the operation of DNNs succinctly, they take a set of inputs x from a feature set (the input layer), which are then passed to a layer of non-linear mathematical functions (neurons) with weights w_{ij} (for neuron i and input j), each of which usually produces a scaled number in the range (0, 1) or (−1, 1). These numbers are then passed to another layer of functions and into another and so on until the final layer produces a set of probabilities of the observation being in any of the target categories (each represented by a node in the output layer). The DNN assigns the category based on the category with the highest probability. The DNN is trained on large datasets; during training, the weights, w_i, are determined to minimize a specified loss function.

In practice, while the number of nodes in the input and the output layers are typically determined by the characteristics of the features and predicted output, many model hyperparameters still must be decided, particularly the number of hidden layers, the number of nodes per hidden layer, and their connectivity and activation architecture. The objective is to choose them to achieve the best out-of-sample performance, but it is still a challenge with no simple solution. As such, a good starting point is a "reasonable" guess for hyperparameters based on experience and literature. The researcher can then observe the result and adjust the hyperparameters incrementally until the model performance goal is reached. In practice, DNNs require substantial time to train, and systematically varying the hyperparameters may not be feasible. So, for many problems with relatively small datasets, one can start with just two or three hidden layers and a few hundred nodes before tuning the parameters until a model with acceptable predictive power is achieved.

DNNs have been shown to be useful in general for pattern recognition problems (e.g., character and image recognition), credit card fraud detection, vision and control problems in autonomous cars, natural language processing (such as machine translation), and other applications. DNNs have become hugely successful because of a confluence of three developments: (1) the availability of large quantities of machine-readable data to train models, (2) advances in analytical methods for fitting these models, and (3) fast computers, especially new chips in the graphics processing unit (GPU) class, tailored for the type of calculations done on DNNs.

Several financial firms are experimenting with DNNs for trading as well as automating their internal processes. Culkin and Das (2017) described how they trained DNNs to price options, mimicking the Black–Scholes–Merton model. Their research used the same six input parameters for the model as input layer features—spot price, strike, time to maturity, dividend yield, risk-free interest rate, and volatility—with four hidden layers of 100 neurons each and one output layer. The predicted option prices out-of-sample were very close to the actual option prices: A regression of predicted option prices on actual prices had an R^2 of 99.8%.

Reinforcement Learning

Reinforcement learning (RL) made headlines in 2017 when DeepMind's AlphaGo program beat the reigning world champion at the ancient game of Go. The RL framework involves an agent that is designed to perform actions that will maximize its rewards over time, taking into consideration the constraints of its environment. In the case of AlphaGo, a virtual gamer (the agent) uses his or her console commands (the actions) with the information on the screen (the environment) to maximize his or her score (the reward). Unlike supervised learning, reinforcement learning has neither direct labeled data for each observation nor instantaneous feedback. With RL, the algorithm needs to observe its environment, learn by testing new actions (some of which may not be immediately optimal), and reuse its previous experiences. The learning subsequently occurs through millions of trials and errors. Academics and practitioners are applying RL in a similar way in investment strategies where the agent could be a virtual trader who follows certain trading rules (the actions) in a specific market (the environment) to maximize its profits (its reward). The success of RL in dealing with the complexities of financial markets is still an open question.

EXAMPLE 8

Deep Neural Networks

Glen Mitsui is the chief investment officer for a large Australian state's Public Employees' Pension Fund (PEPF), which currently has assets under management (AUM) of A\$20 billion. The fund manages one-quarter of its assets internally, with A\$5 billion mostly in domestic government and corporate fixed-income instruments and domestic equities. The remaining three-quarters of AUM, or A\$15 billion, is managed by nearly 100 mostly active external asset managers and is invested in a wide range of asset classes, including foreign fixed income and equities, domestic and foreign hedge funds, REITs, commodities, and derivatives.

PEPF has a small staff of four investment professionals tasked with selecting and monitoring these external managers to whom it pays more than A\$400 million in fees annually. Performance (compared to appropriate benchmarks) of many of PEPF's external managers has been lagging over the past several years. After studying the situation, Mitsui concludes that style drift may be an important factor in explaining such underperformance, for which PEPF is not happy to pay. Mitsui believes that machine learning may help and consults with Frank Monroe, professor of data analysis at Epsilon University.

Monroe suggests using a deep neural network model that collects and analyzes the real-time trading data of PEPF's external managers and compares them to well-known investment styles (e.g., high dividend, minimum volatility, momentum, growth, value) to detect potential style drift. Mitsui arranges for Monroe to meet with PEPF's investment committee (IC) to discuss the matter. As a junior data analyst working with Monroe, you must help him satisfy the following requests from the IC:

---

1. Define a deep neural network.

Solution

A deep neural network is a neural network (NN) with many hidden layers (at least 2 but often more than 20). NNs and DNNs have been successfully applied to a wide variety of complex tasks characterized by non-linearities and interactions among features, particularly pattern recognition problems.

2. Evaluate Monroe's opinion on the applicability of deep neural networks to Mitsui's problem.

Solution

Mitsui wants to detect patterns of potential style drift in the daily trading of nearly 100 external asset managers in many markets. This task will involve the processing of huge amounts of complicated data. Monroe is correct that a DNN is well suited to PEPF's needs.

3. Describe the functions of the three groups of layers of a deep neural network.

Solution

The input layer, the hidden layers, and the output layer constitute the three groups of layers of DNNs. The input layer receives the inputs (i.e., features) and has as many nodes as there are dimensions of the feature set. The hidden layers consist of nodes, each comprising a summation operator and an activation function that are connected by links. These hidden layers are, in effect, where the model is learned. The final layer, the output layer, produces a set of probabilities of an observation being in any of the target style categories (each represented by a node in the output layer). For example, if there are three target style categories, then three nodes in the output layer are activated to produce outputs that sum to one. So, output (Style Category I, 0.7; Style Category II, 0.2; Style Category III, 0.1) would indicate that the model assigns the greatest probability to an observation being in Style Category I and the least probability to Style Category III. The DNN assigns the observation to the style category with the highest probability.

CASE STUDY: DEEP NEURAL NETWORK–BASED EQUITY FACTOR MODEL

17

The following case study was developed and written by Matthew Dixon, PhD, FRM.

An investment manager wants to select stocks based on their predicted performance using a fundamental equity factor model. She seeks to capture superior performance from stocks with the largest excess return using a non-linear factor model and so chooses a deep neural network to predict the stock returns. The goal of this mini-case study is to demonstrate the application of deep neural networks to fundamental equity factor modeling. We shall focus on using feed-forward (i.e., forward propagation) network regression in place of ordinary least squares linear regression. Since neural networks are prone to over-fitting, we shall use LASSO penalization, the same penalty score–based approach used previously with regression, to mitigate this issue.

Introduction

Cross-sectional fundamental factor models are used extensively by investment managers to capture the effects of company-specific factors on individual securities. A fixed universe of N assets is first chosen, together with a set of K fundamental factors. Each asset's sensitivity (i.e., exposure or loading) to a fundamental factor is represented by beta, B, and the factors are represented by factor returns (f_t). There are two standard approaches to estimating a factor model: (i) adopt time-series regression (TSR) to recover loadings if factors are known or (ii) use cross-sectional regression (CSR) to recover factor returns from known loadings. We shall follow the CSR approach; the factor exposures are used to predict a stock's return (r_t) by estimating the factor returns using multivariate linear regression (where ε_t is the model error at time t):

$$r_t = Bf_t + \varepsilon_t.$$

However, this CSR model is too simplistic to capture non-linear relationships between stock returns and fundamental factors. So, instead we use a deep neural network to learn the non-linear relationships between the betas (B) and asset returns (r_t) at each time t. The goal of deep learning is to find the network weights which minimize the out-of-sample mean squared error (MSE) between the predicted stock returns, $\hat{r}$, and the observed stock returns, r. We shall see that simply increasing the number of neurons in the network will increase predictive performance using the in-sample data but to the detriment of out-of-sample performance; this phenomenon is the bias–variance trade-off. To mitigate this effect, we add a LASSO penalty term to the loss function to automatically shrink the number of non-zero weights in the network. In doing so, we shall see that this leads to better out-of-sample predictive performance.

Note that each weight corresponds to a link between a node in the previous and current layer. Reducing the number of weights generally means that the number of connections—not the number of nodes—is reduced. The exception is when all weights from the neurons in the previous layer are set to zero—in which case the number of nodes in the current layer would be reduced. In the special case when the previous layer is the input layer, the number of features is also reduced.

We shall illustrate the data preparation and the neural network fitting using six fundamental equity factors. This choice of number and type of fundamental factor is arbitrary, and an investment manager may use many more factors in her or his model, often representing industry sectors and sub-sectors using dummy variables.

Data Description

A description of the stock price and fundamental equity factor data used for training and evaluating the neural network is shown in Exhibit 31.

Exhibit 31: Dataset of S&P 500 Stocks and Fundamental Factors

Description:

A subset of S&P 500 Index stocks, historical monthly adjusted closing prices, and corresponding monthly fundamental factor loadings.

Time period: June 2010 to November 2018

Number of periods: 101

Number of stocks (N): 218 stocks

Number of features (K): 6

Features: Fundamental equity factors:

1. Current enterprise value (i.e., market values of equity + preferred stock + debt – cash – short-term investments)
2. Current enterprise value to trailing 12-month EBITDA
3. Price-to-sales ratio
4. Price-to-earnings ratio

5. Price-to-book ratio

6. Log of stock's market capitalization (i.e., share price × number of shares outstanding)

Output: Monthly return for each stock over the following month.

We define the universe as the top 250 stocks from the S&P 500, ranked by market capitalization as of June 2010. All stock prices and factor loadings are sourced from Bloomberg. An illustrative extract of the data is given in Exhibit 32. Note that after removing stocks with missing factor loadings, we are left with 218 stocks.

Exhibit 32: Extract of Six Factor Loadings and Return for Three Selected Stocks

TICKER	CURR_EV ($ Mil.)	CURR_EV_TO_ T12M_EBITDA (X)	PX_TO_ SALES (X)	PX_TO_ EARN (X)	PX_TO_ BOOK (X)	LOG_CAP ($ Mil.)	RETURN (%)
SWK	10,775.676	30.328	1.138	16.985	1.346	9.082970	−0.132996
STZ	7,433.553	15.653	1.052	10.324	1.480	8.142253	−0.133333
SRE	19,587.124	10.497	1.286	10.597	1.223	9.314892	−0.109589

Experimental Design

The method used to train the deep neural network is time-series cross-validation (i.e., walk-forward optimization), as depicted in Exhibit 33. At each time period, the investment manager fits a new model; each factor (f_1 to f_6) is a feature in the network, and the loadings of the factors for each stock is a feature vector observation (i.e., the set of observations for each stock for each period), leading to $N = 218$ observations of pairs of feature vectors and output (monthly return, r_t) in the training set per period. The network is initially trained at period t, and then it is tested over the next period, $t + 1$, which also has $N = 218$ observations of pairs of feature vectors and output. In the next iteration, the $t + 1$ data become the new training set and the revised model is tested on the $t + 2$ data. The walk-forward optimization of the neural network continues until the last iteration: model training with $t + 99$ data (from Period 100) and testing with $t + 100$ data (from the last period, 101).

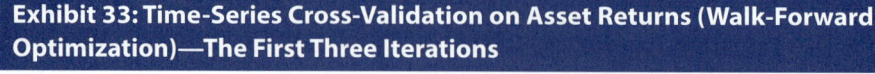

Exhibit 33: Time-Series Cross-Validation on Asset Returns (Walk-Forward Optimization)—The First Three Iterations

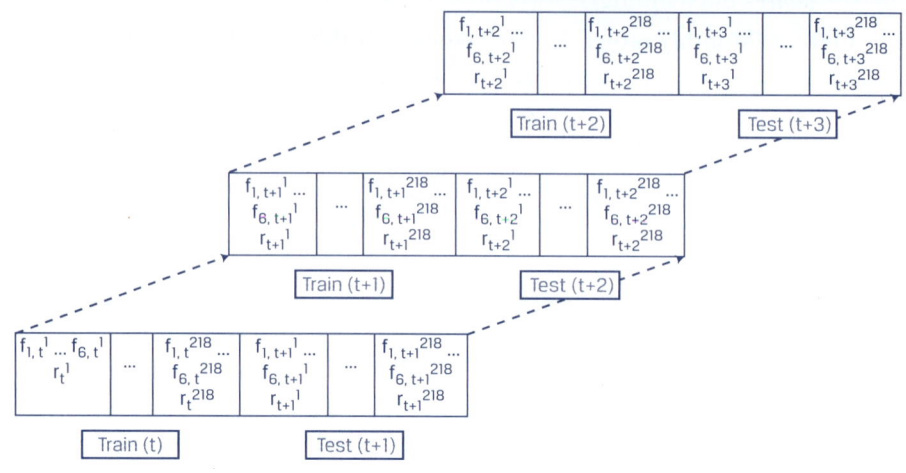

We use a feed-forward neural network with six input nodes (i.e., neurons), two hidden layers, and one output neuron. There are 50 neurons in each hidden layer to intentionally over-specify the number of parameters needed in the model, meaning bias (variance) is substantially lower (higher) than optimal. LASSO penalization is then used to automatically shrink the parameter set. Additionally, it is important for the number of nodes in each hidden layer not to exceed the number of observations in the training set (50 nodes per layer versus 218 observations). The model training in period t involves finding the optimal bias-versus-variance trade-off. Once fitted, we record the in-sample MSE and the out-of-sample MSE in addition to the optimal regularization parameter. This procedure is then repeated sequentially over the horizon of 100 remaining periods, tuning the hyperparameters at each stage using cross-validation. The end result of this procedure is a fitted model, trained monthly on the current cross-sectional data and for which hyperparameters have been tuned at each step.

Results

Exhibit 34 presents the results from model evaluation; it compares the in-sample and out-of-sample MSEs of the deep neural network over all 101 months. Note that the out-of-sample error (dotted line) is typically significantly larger than the in-sample error (solid line). However, as the time periods pass and the model is repeatedly trained and tested, the difference between the out-of-sample and in-sample MSEs narrows dramatically.

Exhibit 34: In-Sample and Out-of-Sample MSE for Each Training and Testing Period

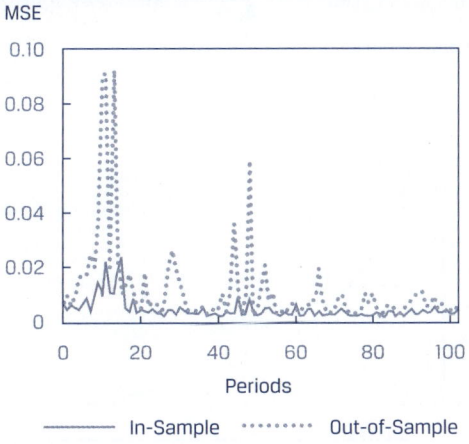

Exhibit 35 shows the effect of LASSO regularization on the in-sample MSE (lower panel, B) and the out-of-sample MSE (upper panel, A) for the first iteration of the time-series cross-validation (training with data from period t and testing with data from period $t + 1$). The degree of LASSO regularization needed is found by cross-validation using 50 neurons in each hidden layer. Increasing the LASSO regularization, which reduces the number of non-zero weights in the model, introduces more bias and hence increases the in-sample error. Conversely, increasing the LASSO regularization reduces the model's variance and thereby reduces the out-of-sample error. Overall, the amount of LASSO regularization needed is significant, at 0.10; typically the regularization hyperparameter is between 0.001 and 1.0. Also, the out-of-sample and in-sample MSEs have not yet converged. There is still a substantial gap, of roughly 0.0051 (= 0.01025 − 0.0052), and the slope of the curves in each plot suggests the optimal value of the regularization hyperparameter is significantly more than 0.10. Note that the value of the regularization hyperparameter is not interpretable and does not correspond to the number of weights eliminated. Suffice it to say, the larger the value of the regularization hyperparameter, the more the loss is being penalized.

Exhibit 35: LASSO Regularization for Optimizing Bias–Variance Trade-Off (First Iteration)

A.

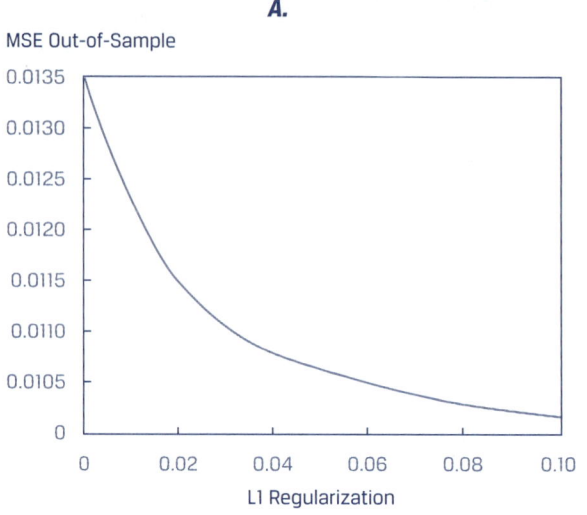

B.

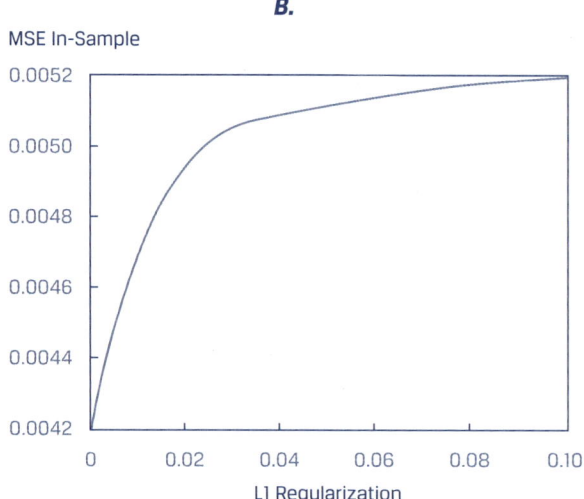

It is important to recognize that although the out-of-sample MSE of this deep learning neural network is key to characterizing its predictive performance, it does not necessarily follow that a stock selection strategy based on the neural network will be successful. This is because the neural network predicts the next month's expected (i.e., mean) asset returns and not the full distribution of returns. Hence a simple stock selection strategy—measured by information ratios (recall the information ratio, or IR, is alpha divided by nonsystematic risk, so it measures the abnormal return per unit of risk for a well-diversified portfolio) of the portfolio returns—that selects stocks ranked by predicted returns will not necessarily lead to positive information ratios.

Exhibit 36 presents the information ratios found by back-testing a simple stock selection strategy that picks the top performing stocks determined by the neural network's forecasted returns realized in month $t +1$ using features observed in month t. Note these IRs do not account for transaction costs, interest rates, or any other fees. The upper panel (A) shows the best-case scenario; the neural network in-sample prediction is used to select the n (where n is 10, 15, 20, or 25) top performing stocks. The IRs are shown for each of the different-sized portfolios; they range from 0.697

to 0.623. Note that as a rule of thumb, IRs in the range of 0.40–0.60 are considered quite good. The lower panel (B) shows the IRs from back-test results for the same strategy applied to the out-of-sample data. The out-of-sample IRs range from 0.260 to 0.315 and so are substantially smaller than in-sample IRs.

Exhibit 36: Information Ratios from Back-Testing a Stock Selection Strategy Using Top Performers from the Neural Network

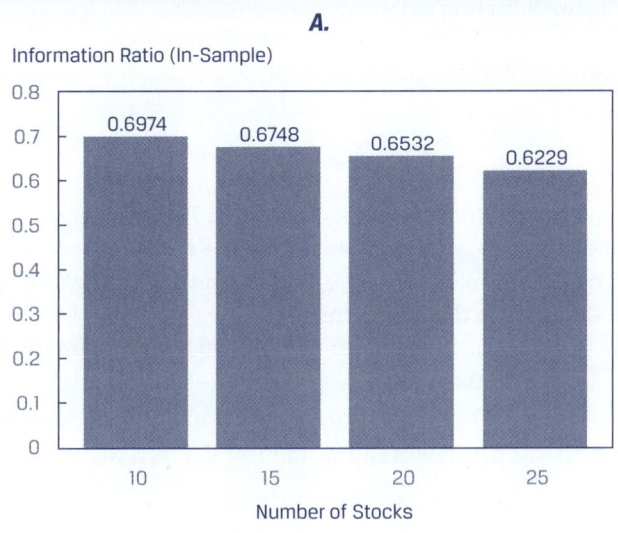

A.

Information Ratio (In-Sample)

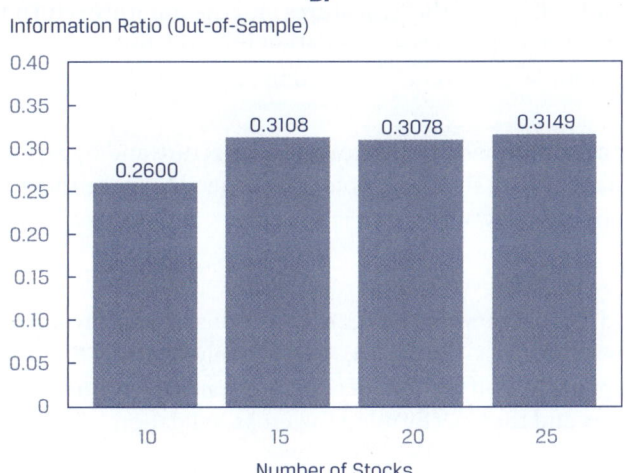

B.

Information Ratio (Out-of-Sample)

Importantly, the out-of-sample performance provides the most realistic assessment of the likely future investment performance from applying this deep learning neural network to stock selection. It is a baseline for further model refinements, including adding more fundamental and macroeconomic factors. With such refinements, it can be expected that the out-of-sample IRs should improve substantially.

EXAMPLE 9

Deep Learning–Based Fundamental Factor Model

A research analyst, Jane Hinton, has been tasked with further developing the deep learning–based fundamental factor model. She decides to refine the model by adding four more fundamental factors (such as debt leverage and R&D intensity) given by firm characteristics and by including dummy variables for 11 industrial sectors. Moreover, she additionally expands the universe of stocks to 420 from 218 by using a supplementary data source.

1. Describe how Jane would modify the inputs of the neural network architecture for this new dataset.

Solution

Jane adds four more fundamental factors and 11 dummy variables, to represent each industrial sector, for a total of 21 (= 4 + 11 + 6) features. Therefore, the refined neural network will have 21 input neurons. The output layer will remain the same. Note that concerns of collinearity of the features through the dummy variables or high correlation, which are problematic for linear regression, are not an issue for a deep learning–based model.

2. Describe the size of the new training and test datasets.

Solution

There are now data on 420 stocks, for each of the 101 time periods, consisting of factor loadings for the 21 features and the monthly return for each stock. Per the time-series cross-validation method, the test dataset in the current iteration will become the training dataset in the next iteration.

3. Describe any additional changes to the architecture and hyperparameters of the neural network that Jane would likely need to make to ensure good performance of the network.

Solution

Jane should find the new optimal LASSO regularization hyperparameter using time-series cross-validation. Alternatively, she may find the optimal bias–variance trade-off by first increasing the number of neurons in the hidden layers and then performing the cross-validation.

4. Explain how Jane should evaluate whether the new model leads to improved portfolio performance.

Solution

Once Jane has found the optimal LASSO hyperparameter and network architecture, she will use the model to forecast the out-of-sample monthly asset returns (i.e., the model forecasts from factor loadings which are not in the training set). She will then rank and select the top predicted performers and finally measure the realized monthly portfolio return. She will then repeat the experiment by moving forward one month in the dataset and repeating the out-of-sample forecast of the asset returns, until she has generated forecasts for all time periods. Finally, Jane will calculate the information ratios from the mean and standard deviation of the monthly portfolio excess returns.

EXAMPLE 10

Summing Up the Major Types of Machine Learning

1. As used in supervised machine learning, classification problems involve the following *except*:

   A. binary target variables.

   B. continuous target variables.

   C. categorical target variables.

Solution

B is correct. A and C are incorrect because when the target variable is binary or categorical (not continuous), the problem is a classification problem.

---

2. Which of the following *best* describes penalized regression? Penalized regression:

   A. is unrelated to multiple linear regression.

   B. involves a penalty term that is added to the predicted target variable.

   C. is a category of general linear models used when the number of features and overfitting are concerns.

Solution

C is correct. A is incorrect because penalized regression is related to multiple linear regression. B is incorrect because penalized regression involves adding a penalty term to the sum of the squared regression residuals.

---

3. CART is *best* described as:

   A. an unsupervised ML algorithm.

   B. a clustering algorithm based on decision trees.

   C. a supervised ML algorithm that accounts for non-linear relationships among the features.

Solution

C is correct. A is incorrect because CART is a supervised ML algorithm. B is incorrect because CART is a classification and regression algorithm, not a clustering algorithm.

---

4. A neural network is *best* described as a technique for machine learning that is:

   A. exactly modeled on the human nervous system.

   B. based on layers of nodes connected by links when the relationships among the features are usually non-linear.

   C. based on a tree structure of nodes when the relationships among the features are linear.

Solution

B is correct. A is incorrect because neural networks are not exactly modeled on the human nervous system. C is incorrect because neural networks are not based on a tree structure of nodes when the relationships among the features are linear.

5. Hierarchical clustering is *best* described as a technique in which:

   A. the grouping of observations is unsupervised.
   B. features are grouped into a pre-specified number, *k*, of clusters.
   C. observations are classified according to predetermined labels.

Solution

A is correct. B is incorrect because it refers to *k*-means clustering. C is incorrect because it refers to classification, which involves supervised learning.

6. Dimension reduction techniques are *best* described as a means to reduce a set of features to a manageable size:

   A. without regard for the variation in the data.
   B. while increasing the variation in the data.
   C. while retaining as much of the variation in the data as possible.

Solution

C is correct because dimension reduction techniques, such as PCA, are aimed at reducing the feature set to a manageable size while retaining as much of the variation in the data as possible.

18   CHOOSING AN APPROPRIATE ML ALGORITHM

Exhibit 37 presents a simplified decision flowchart for choosing among the machine learning algorithms which have been discussed. The dark-shaded ovals contain the supervised ML algorithms, the light-shaded ovals contain the unsupervised ML algorithms, and the key questions to consider are shown in the unshaded rounded rectangles.

Exhibit 37: Stylized Decision Flowchart for Choosing ML Algorithms

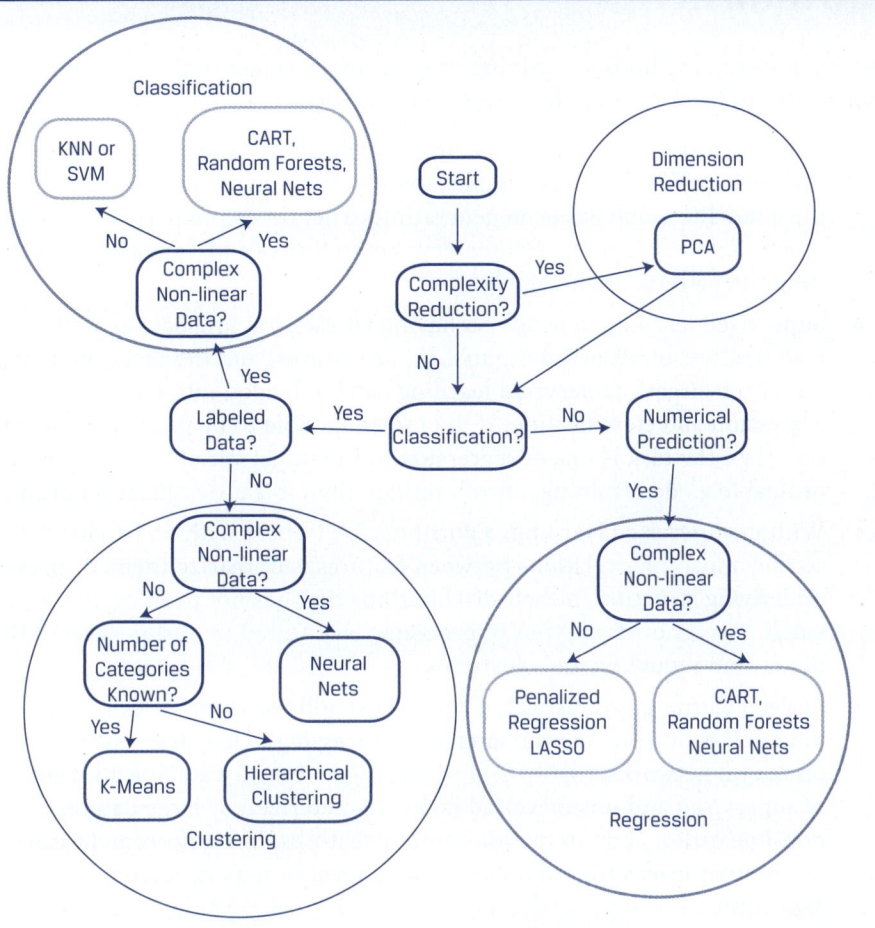

First, start by asking, Are the data complex, having many features that are highly correlated? If yes, then dimension reduction using principal components analysis is appropriate.

Next, is the problem one of classification or numerical prediction? If numerical prediction, then depending on whether the data have non-linear characteristics, the choice of ML algorithms is from a set of regression algorithms—either penalized regression/LASSO for linear data or CART, random forest, or neural networks for non-linear data.

If the problem is one of classification, then depending on whether the data are labeled, the choice is either from a set of classification algorithms using labeled data or from a set of clustering algorithms using unlabeled data.

If the data are labeled, then depending on whether the data have non-linear characteristics, the choice of classification algorithm would be K-nearest neighbor and support vector machine for linear data or CART, random forest, or neural networks (or deep neural networks) for non-linear data.

Finally, if the data are unlabeled, the choice of clustering algorithm depends on whether the data have non-linear characteristics. The choice of clustering algorithm would be neural networks (or deep neural networks) for non-linear data or for linear data, K-means with a known number of categories and hierarchical clustering with an unknown number of categories.

SUMMARY

Machine learning methods are gaining usage at many stages in the investment management value chain. Among the major points made are the following:

- Machine learning aims at extracting knowledge from large amounts of data by learning from known examples to determine an underlying structure in the data. The emphasis is on generating structure or predictions without human intervention. An elementary way to think of ML algorithms is to "find the pattern, apply the pattern."

- Supervised learning depends on having labeled training data as well as matched sets of observed inputs (X's, or features) and the associated output (Y, or target). Supervised learning can be divided into two categories: regression and classification. If the target variable to be predicted is continuous, then the task is one of regression. If the target variable is categorical or ordinal (e.g., determining a firm's rating), then it is a classification problem.

- With unsupervised learning, algorithms are trained with no labeled data, so they must infer relations between features, summarize them, or present underlying structure in their distributions that has not been explicitly provided. Two important types of problems well suited to unsupervised ML are dimension reduction and clustering.

- In deep learning, sophisticated algorithms address complex tasks (e.g., image classification, natural language processing). Deep learning is based on neural networks, highly flexible ML algorithms for solving a variety of supervised and unsupervised tasks characterized by large datasets, non-linearities, and interactions among features. In reinforcement learning, a computer learns from interacting with itself or data generated by the same algorithm.

- Generalization describes the degree to which an ML model retains its explanatory power when predicting out-of-sample. Overfitting, a primary reason for lack of generalization, is the tendency of ML algorithms to tailor models to the training data at the expense of generalization to new data points.

- Bias error is the degree to which a model fits the training data. Variance error describes how much a model's results change in response to new data from validation and test samples. Base error is due to randomness in the data. Out-of-sample error equals bias error plus variance error plus base error.

- K-fold cross-validation is a technique for mitigating the holdout sample problem (excessive reduction of the training set size). The data (excluding test sample and fresh data) are shuffled randomly and then divided into k equal sub-samples, with $k - 1$ samples used as training samples and one sample, the kth, used as a validation sample.

- Regularization describes methods that reduce statistical variability in high-dimensional data estimation or prediction problems via reducing model complexity.

- LASSO (least absolute shrinkage and selection operator) is a popular type of penalized regression where the penalty term involves summing the absolute values of the regression coefficients. The greater the number of included features, the larger the penalty. So, a feature must make a sufficient contribution to model fit to offset the penalty from including it.

- Support vector machine (SVM) is a classifier that aims to seek the optimal hyperplane—the one that separates the two sets of data points by the maximum margin (and thus is typically used for classification).

- *K*-nearest neighbor (KNN) is a supervised learning technique most often used for classification. The idea is to classify a new observation by finding similarities ("nearness") between it and its *k*-nearest neighbors in the existing dataset.

- Classification and regression tree (CART) can be applied to predict either a categorical target variable, producing a classification tree, or a continuous target variable, producing a regression tree.

- A binary CART is a combination of an initial root node, decision nodes, and terminal nodes. The root node and each decision node represent a single feature (*f*) and a cutoff value (*c*) for that feature. The CART algorithm iteratively partitions the data into sub-groups until terminal nodes are formed that contain the predicted label.

- Ensemble learning is a technique of combining the predictions from a collection of models. It typically produces more accurate and more stable predictions than any single model.

- A random forest classifier is a collection of many different decision trees generated by a bagging method or by randomly reducing the number of features available during training.

- Principal components analysis (PCA) is an unsupervised ML algorithm that reduces highly correlated features into fewer uncorrelated composite variables by transforming the feature covariance matrix. PCA produces eigenvectors that define the principal components (i.e., the new uncorrelated composite variables) and eigenvalues, which give the proportion of total variance in the initial data that is explained by each eigenvector and its associated principal component.

- *K*-means is an unsupervised ML algorithm that partitions observations into a fixed number (*k*) of non-overlapping clusters. Each cluster is characterized by its centroid, and each observation belongs to the cluster with the centroid to which that observation is closest.

- Hierarchical clustering is an unsupervised iterative algorithm that is used to build a hierarchy of clusters. Two main strategies are used to define the intermediary clusters (i.e., those clusters between the initial dataset and the final set of clustered data).

- Agglomerative (bottom-up) hierarchical clustering begins with each observation being its own cluster. Then, the algorithm finds the two closest clusters, defined by some measure of distance, and combines them into a new, larger cluster. This process is repeated until all observations are clumped into a single cluster.

- Divisive (top-down) hierarchical clustering starts with all observations belonging to a single cluster. The observations are then divided into two clusters based on some measure of distance. The algorithm then progressively partitions the intermediate clusters into smaller clusters until each cluster contains only one observation.

- Neural networks consist of nodes connected by links. They have three types of layers: an input layer, hidden layers, and an output layer. Learning takes place in the hidden layer nodes, each of which consists of a summation operator and an activation function. Neural networks have been successfully applied to a variety of investment tasks characterized by non-linearities and complex interactions among variables.

- Neural networks with many hidden layers (at least 2 but often more than 20) are known as deep neural networks (DNNs) and are the backbone of the artificial intelligence revolution.

- Reinforcement learning (RL) involves an agent that should perform actions that will maximize its rewards over time, taking into consideration the constraints of its environment.

REFERENCES

Bacham, Dinesh, Janet Zhao. 2017. "Machine Learning: Challenges, Lessons, and Opportunities in Credit Risk Modeling." Moody's Analytics Risk Perspectives 9:28–35.

Culkin, Robert, Sanjiv R. Das. 2017. "Machine Learning in Finance: The Case of Deep Learning for Option Pricing." Journal of Investment Management 15 (4): 92–100.

PRACTICE PROBLEMS

The following information relates to questions 1-10

Alef Associates manages a long-only fund specializing in global smallcap equities. Since its founding a decade ago, Alef maintains a portfolio of 100 stocks (out of an eligible universe of about 10,000 stocks). Some of these holdings are the result of screening the universe for attractive stocks based on several ratios that use readily available market and accounting data; others are the result of investment ideas generated by Alef's professional staff of five securities analysts and two portfolio managers.

Although Alef's investment performance has been good, its Chief Investment Officer, Paul Moresanu, is contemplating a change in the investment process aimed at achieving even better returns. After attending multiple workshops and being approached by data vendors, Moresanu feels that data science should play a role in the way Alef selects its investments. He has also noticed that much of Alef's past outperformance is due to stocks that became takeover targets. After some research and reflection, Moresanu writes the following email to the Alef's CEO.

Exhibit 1: Subject: Investment Process Reorganization

I have been thinking about modernizing the way we select stock investments. Given that our past success has put Alef Associates in an excellent financial position, now seems to be a good time to invest in our future. What I propose is that we continue managing a portfolio of 100 global small-cap stocks but restructure our process to benefit from machine learning (ML). Importantly, the new process will still allow a role for human insight, for example, in providing domain knowledge. In addition, I think we should make a special effort to identify companies that are likely to be acquired. Specifically, I suggest following the four steps which would be repeated every quarter.

Step 1	We apply ML techniques to a model including fundamental and technical variables (features) to predict next quarter's return for each of the 100 stocks currently in our portfolio. Then, the 20 stocks with the lowest estimated return are identified for replacement.
Step 2	We utilize ML techniques to divide our investable universe of about 10,000 stocks into 20 different groups, based on a wide variety of the most relevant financial and non-financial characteristics. The idea is to prevent unintended portfolio concentration by selecting stocks from each of these distinct groups.
Step 3	For each of the 20 different groups, we use labeled data to train a model that will predict the five stocks (in any given group) that are most likely to become acquisition targets in the next one year.

Step 4   Our five experienced securities analysts are each assigned four of the groups, and then each analyst selects their one best stock pick from each of their assigned groups. These 20 "high-conviction" stocks will be added to our portfolio (in replacement of the 20 relatively underperforming stocks to be sold in Step 1).

A couple of additional comments related to the above:

Comment 1   The ML algorithms will require large amounts of data. We would first need to explore using free or inexpensive historical datasets and then evaluate their usefulness for the ML-based stock selection processes before deciding on using data that requires subscription.

Comment 2   As time passes, we expect to find additional ways to apply ML techniques to refine Alef's investment processes.

What do you think?

Paul Moresanu

---

1. The machine learning techniques appropriate for executing Step 1 are *most* likely to be based on:

   A. regression

   B. classification

   C. clustering

2. Assuming regularization is utilized in the machine learning technique used for executing Step 1, which of the following ML models would be *least* appropriate:

   A. Regression tree with pruning.

   B. LASSO with lambda (λ) equal to 0.

   C. LASSO with lambda (λ) between 0.5 and 1.

3. Which of the following machine learning techniques is *most* appropriate for executing Step 2:

   A. K-Means Clustering

   B. Principal Components Analysis (PCA)

   C. Classification and Regression Trees (CART)

4. The hyperparameter in the ML model to be used for accomplishing Step 2 is?

   A. 100, the number of small-cap stocks in Alef's portfolio.

   B. 10,000, the eligible universe of small-cap stocks in which Alef can potentially invest.

   C. 20, the number of different groups (i.e. clusters) into which the eligible universe of small-cap stocks will be divided.

5. The target variable for the labelled training data to be used in Step 3 is *most* likely which one of the following?

   A. A continuous target variable.

    B. A categorical target variable.

    C. An ordinal target variable.

6. Comparing two ML models that could be used to accomplish Step 3, which statement(s) *best* describe(s) the advantages of using Classification and Regression Trees (CART) instead of K-Nearest Neighbor (KNN)?

Statement 1	For CART there is no requirement to specify an initial hyperparameter (like K).
Statement 2	For CART there is no requirement to specify a similarity (or distance) measure.
Statement 3	For CART the output provides a visual explanation for the prediction.

    A. Statement 1 only.

    B. Statement 3 only.

    C. Statements 1, 3 and 3.

7. Assuming a Classification and Regression Tree (CART) model is used to accomplish Step 3, which of the following is *most* likely to result in model overfitting?

    A. Using the k-fold cross validation method

    B. Including an overfitting penalty (i.e., regularization term).

    C. Using a fitting curve to select a model with low bias error and high variance error.

8. Assuming a Classification and Regression Tree (CART) model is initially used to accomplish Step 3, as a further step which of the following techniques is most likely to result in more accurate predictions?

    A. Discarding CART and using the predictions of a Support Vector Machine (SVM) model instead.

    B. Discarding CART and using the predictions of a K-Nearest Neighbor (KNN) model instead.

    C. Combining the predictions of the CART model with the predictions of other models – such as logistic regression, SVM, and KNN – via ensemble learning.

9. Regarding Comment #2, Moresanu has been thinking about the applications of neural networks (NNs) and deep learning (DL) to investment management. Which statement(s) *best* describe(s) the tasks for which NNs and DL are well-suited?

Statement 1	NNs and DL are well-suited for image and speech recognition, and natural language processing.
Statement 2	NNs and DL are well-suited for developing single variable ordinary least squares regression models.

Statement 3   NNs and DL are well-suited for modelling non-linearities and complex interactions among many features.

  A. Statement 2 only.

  B. Statements 1 and 3.

  C. Statements 1, 2 and 3.

10. Regarding neural networks (NNs) that Alef might potentially implement, which of the following statements is *least* accurate?

  A. NNs must have at least 10 hidden layers to be considered deep learning nets.

  B. The activation function in a node operates like a light dimmer switch since it decreases or increases the strength of the total net input.

  C. The summation operator receives input values, multiplies each by a weight, sums up the weighted values into the total net input, and passes it to the activation function.

SOLUTIONS

1. A is correct. The target variable (quarterly return) is continuous, hence this calls for a supervised machine learning based regression model.

    B is incorrect, since classification uses categorical or ordinal target variables, while in Step 1 the target variable (quarterly return) is continuous.

    C is incorrect, since clustering involves unsupervised machine learning so does not have a target variable.

2. B is correct. It is least appropriate because with LASSO, when $\lambda = 0$ the penalty (i.e., regularization) term reduces to zero, so there is no regularization and the regression is equivalent to an ordinary least squares (OLS) regression.

    A is incorrect. With Classification and Regression Trees (CART), one way that regularization can be implemented is via pruning which will reduce the size of the regression tree—sections that provide little explanatory power are pruned (i.e., removed).

    C is incorrect. With LASSO, when λ is between 0.5 and 1 the relatively large penalty (i.e., regularization) term requires that a feature makes a sufficient contribution to model fit to offset the penalty from including it in the model.

3. A is correct. K-Means clustering is an unsupervised machine learning algorithm which repeatedly partitions observations into a fixed number, k, of non-overlapping clusters (i.e., groups).

    B is incorrect. Principal Components Analysis is a long-established statistical method for dimension reduction, not clustering. PCA aims to summarize or reduce highly correlated features of data into a few main, uncorrelated composite variables.

    C is incorrect. CART is a supervised machine learning technique that is most commonly applied to binary classification or regression.

4. C is correct. Here, 20 is a hyperparameter (in the K-Means algorithm), which is a parameter whose value must be set by the researcher before learning begins.

    A is incorrect, because it is not a hyperparameter. It is just the size (number of stocks) of Alef's portfolio.

    B is incorrect, because it is not a hyperparameter. It is just the size (number of stocks) of Alef's eligible universe.

5. B is correct. To predict which stocks are likely to become acquisition targets, the ML model would need to be trained on categorical labelled data having the following two categories: "0" for "not acquisition target", and "1" for "acquisition target".

    A is incorrect, because the target variable is categorical, not continuous.

    C is incorrect, because the target variable is categorical, not ordinal (i.e., 1st, 2nd, 3rd, etc.).

6. C is correct. The advantages of using CART over KNN to classify companies into two categories ("not acquisition target" and "acquisition target"), include all of the following: For CART there are no requirements to specify an initial hyperparameter (like K) or a similarity (or distance) measure as with KNN, and CART provides a visual explanation for the prediction (i.e., the feature variables and their cut-off values at each node).

    A is incorrect, because CART provides all of the advantages indicated in Statements 1, 2 and 3.

B is incorrect, because CART provides all of the advantages indicated in Statements 1, 2 and 3.

7. C is correct. A fitting curve shows the trade-off between bias error and variance error for various potential models. A model with low bias error and high variance error is, by definition, overfitted.

    A is incorrect, because there are two common methods to reduce overfitting, one of which is proper data sampling and cross-validation. K-fold cross validation is such a method for estimating out-of-sample error directly by determining the errorin validation samples.

    B is incorrect, because there are two common methods to reduce overfitting, one of which is preventing the algorithm from getting too complex during selection and training, which requires estimating an overfitting penalty.

8. C is correct. Ensemble learning is the technique of combining the predictions from a collection of models, and it typically produces more accurate and more stable predictions than the best single model.

    A is incorrect, because a single model will have a certain error rate and will make noisy predictions. By taking the average result of many predictions from many models (i.e., ensemble learning) one can expect to achieve a reduction in noise as the average result converges towards a more accurate prediction.

    B is incorrect, because a single model will have a certain error rate and will make noisy predictions. By taking the average result of many predictions from many models (i.e., ensemble learning) one can expect to achieve a reduction in noise as the average result converges towards a more accurate prediction.

9. B is correct. NNs and DL are well-suited for addressing highly complex machine learning tasks, such as image classification, face recognition, speech recognition and natural language processing. These complicated tasks are characterized by non-linearities and complex interactions between large numbers of feature inputs.

    A is incorrect, because NNs and DL are well-suited for addressing highly complex machine learning tasks, not simple single variable OLS regression models.

    C is incorrect, because NNs and DL are well-suited for addressing highly complex machine learning tasks, not simple single variable OLS regression models.

10. A is correct. It is the least accurate answer because neural networks with many hidden layers—at least 3, but often more than 20 hidden layers—are known as deep learning nets.

    B is incorrect, because the node's activation function operates like a light dimmer switch which decreases or increases the strength of the (total net) input.

    C is incorrect, because the node's summation operator multiplies each (input) value by a weight and sums up the weighted values to form the total net input. The total net input is then passed to the activation function.

7

Big Data Projects

by Sreekanth Mallikarjun, PhD, and Ahmed Abbasi, PhD.

Sreekanth Mallikarjun, PhD, is at Reorg (USA) and the University of Virginia, School of Data Science (USA). Ahmed Abbasi, PhD, is at the University of Virginia, McIntire School of Commerce (USA).

LEARNING OUTCOMES

Mastery	The candidate should be able to:
☐	identify and explain steps in a data analysis project
☐	describe objectives, steps, and examples of preparing and wrangling data
☐	evaluate the fit of a machine learning algorithm
☐	describe objectives, methods, and examples of data exploration
☐	describe methods for extracting, selecting and engineering features from textual data
☐	describe objectives, steps, and techniques in model training
☐	describe preparing, wrangling, and exploring text-based data for financial forecasting

INTRODUCTION

1

Big data (also referred to as alternative data) encompasses data generated by financial markets (e.g., stock and bond prices), businesses (e.g., company financials, production volumes), governments (e.g., economic and trade data), individuals (e.g., credit card purchases, social media posts), sensors (e.g., satellite imagery, traffic patterns), and the Internet of Things, or IoT, (i.e., the network of interrelated digital devices that can transfer data among themselves without human interaction). A veritable explosion in big data has occurred over the past decade or so, especially in unstructured data generated from social media (e.g., posts, tweets, blogs), email and text communications, web traffic, online news sites, electronic images, and other electronic information sources. The prospects are for exponential growth in big data to continue.

Investment managers are increasingly using big data in their investment processes as they strive to discover signals embedded in such data that can provide them with an information edge. They seek to augment structured data with a plethora of unstructured data to develop improved forecasts of trends in asset prices, detect anomalies, etc. A typical example involves a fund manager using financial text data from 10-K reports for forecasting stock sentiment (i.e., positive or negative), which can then be used as an input to a more comprehensive forecasting model that includes corporate financial data.

Unlike structured data (numbers and values) that can be readily organized into data tables to be read and analyzed by computers, unstructured data typically require specific methods of preparation and refinement before being usable by machines (i.e., computers) and useful to investment professionals. Given the volume, variety, and velocity of available big data, it is important for portfolio managers and investment analysts to have a basic understanding of how unstructured data can be transformed into structured data suitable as inputs to machine learning (ML) methods (in fact, for any type of modeling methods) that can potentially improve their financial forecasts.

This reading describes the steps in using big data, both structured and unstructured, in financial forecasting. The concepts and methods are then demonstrated in a case study of an actual big data project. The project uses text-based data derived from financial documents to train an ML model to classify text into positive or negative sentiment classes for the respective stocks and then to predict sentiment.

Section 2 of the reading covers a description of the key characteristics of big data. Section 3 provides an overview of the steps in executing a financial forecasting project using big data. We then describe in Sections 4–6 key aspects of data preparation and wrangling, data exploration, and model training using structured data and unstructured (textual) data. In Section 7, we bring these pieces together by covering the execution of an actual big data project. A summary in Section 8 concludes the reading.

Big Data in Investment Management

Big data differs from traditional data sources based on the presence of a set of characteristics commonly referred to as the 3Vs: volume, variety, and velocity.

Volume refers to the quantity of data. The US Library of Congress, which is tasked with archiving both digital and physical information artifacts in the United States, has collected hundreds of terabytes of data (one terabyte equals 1,024 gigabytes, which are equal to 1,048,576 megabytes). Several years ago, one of the authors managed an archival project for the Library of Congress in which many terabytes of online content were collected—a copious amount of data at the time. However, in most US industry sectors today, the average company collects more data than the Library of Congress! In big data conversations, terabytes have been replaced with petabytes and exabytes (one exabyte equals 1,024 petabytes, which are equal to 1,048,576 terabytes). The classic grains of sand analogy puts these volumes into perspective: If a megabyte is a tablespoon of sand, then a petabyte is a 1.6-kilometer-long beach and an exabyte is a beach extending about 1,600 kilometers.

Variety pertains to the array of available data sources. Organizations are now dealing with structured, semi-structured, and unstructured data from within and outside the enterprise. Variety includes traditional transactional data; user-generated text, images, and videos; social media; sensor-based data; web and mobile clickstreams; and spatial-temporal data. Effectively leveraging the variety of available data presents both opportunities and challenges, including such legal and ethical issues as data privacy.

Velocity is the speed at which data are created. Many large organizations collect several petabytes of data every hour. With respect to unstructured data, more than one billion new tweets (i.e., a message of 280 characters or less posted on the social media website Twitter) are generated every three days; five billion search queries occur daily. Such information has important implications for real-time predictive analytics in various financial applications. Analyzing such "data-in-motion" poses challenges since relevant patterns and insights might be moving targets relative to situations of "data-at-rest."

When using big data for inference or prediction, there is a "fourth V": *Veracity relates to the credibility and reliability of different data sources.* Determining the credibility and reliability of data sources is an important part of any empirical investigation. The issue of veracity becomes critically important for big data, however, because of the varied sources of these large datasets. Big data amplifies the age-old challenge of disentangling quality from quantity. Social media, including blogs, forums, and social networking sites, are plagued with spam; by some estimates, as much as 10%–15% of such content is completely fake. Similarly, according to our research, web spam accounts for more than 20% of all content on the worldwide web. Clickstreams from website and mobile traffic are equally susceptible to noise. Furthermore, deriving deep semantic knowledge from text remains challenging in certain instances despite significant advances in natural language processing (NLP).

These Vs have numerous implications for financial technology (commonly referred to as "fintech") pertaining to investment management. Machine learning assessments of creditworthiness, which have traditionally relied on structured financial metrics, are being enhanced by incorporating text derived from financial statements, news articles, and call transcripts. Customers in the financial industry are being segmented based not only on their transactional data but also on their views and preferences expressed on social media (to the degree permissible under applicable privacy agreements). Big data also affords opportunities for enhanced fraud detection and risk management.

EXECUTING A DATA ANALYSIS PROJECT   **2**

☐ | identify and explain steps in a data analysis project

In the era of big data, firms treat data like they do important assets. However, effective big data analytics are critical to allow appropriate data monetization. Let us take financial forecasting as an application area. Numerous forecasting tasks in this domain can benefit from predictive analytics models built using machine learning methods. One common example is predicting whether stock prices (for an individual stock or a portfolio) will go up or down in value at some specific point in the future. Traditionally, financial forecasting relied on various financial and accounting numbers, ratios, and metrics coupled with statistical or mathematical models. More recently, machine learning models have been commonly utilized. However, with the proliferation of textual big data (e.g., online news articles, internet financial forums, social networking platforms), such unstructured data have been shown to offer insights faster (as they are real-time) and have enhanced predictive power.

Textual big data provides several valuable types of information, including topics and sentiment. Topics are what people are talking about (e.g., a firm, an industry, a particular event). Sentiment is how people feel about what they are discussing. For instance, they might express positive, negative, or neutral views (i.e., sentiments) toward a topic of discussion. One study conducted in the United States found that positive sentiment on Twitter could predict the trend for the Dow Jones Industrial Average up to three days later with nearly 87% accuracy.

Deriving such insights requires supplementing traditional data with textual big data. As depicted in Exhibit 1, the inclusion of big data has immediate implications for building the machine learning model as well as downstream implications for financial forecasting and analysis. We begin with the top half of Exhibit 1, which shows the traditional (i.e., with structured data) *ML Model Building Steps:*

1. *Conceptualization of the modeling task.* This crucial first step entails determining what the output of the model should be (e.g., whether the price of a stock will go up/down one week from now), how this model will be used and by whom, and how it will be embedded in existing or new business processes.

2. *Data collection.* The data traditionally used for financial forecasting tasks are mostly numeric data derived from internal and external sources. Such data are typically already in a structured tabular format, with columns of features, rows of instances, and each cell representing a particular value.

3. *Data preparation and wrangling.* This step involves cleansing and preprocessing of the raw data. Cleansing may entail resolving missing values, out-of-range values, and the like. Preprocessing may involve extracting, aggregating, filtering, and selecting relevant data columns.

4. *Data exploration.* This step encompasses exploratory data analysis, feature selection, and feature engineering.

5. *Model training.* This step involves selecting the appropriate ML method (or methods), evaluating performance of the trained model, and tuning the model accordingly.

Note that these steps are iterative because model building is an iterative process. The insights gained from one iteration may inform the next iteration, beginning with reconceptualization. In contrast with structured data sources, textual big data originating in online news articles, social media, internal/external documents (such as public financial statements), and other openly available data sources are unstructured.

The *TextML Model Building Steps* used for the unstructured data sources of big data are shown in the bottom half of Exhibit 1. They differ from those used for traditional data sources and are typically intended to create output information that is structured. The differences in steps between the text model and traditional model account for the characteristics of big data: volume, velocity, variety, and veracity. In this reading, we mostly focus on the variety and veracity dimensions of big data as they manifest themselves in text. The major differences in the *Text ML Model Building Steps* are in the first four steps:

1. *Text problem formulation.* Analysts begin by determining how to formulate the text classification problem, identifying the exact inputs and outputs for the model. Perhaps we are interested in computing sentiment scores (structured output) from text (unstructured input). Analysts must also decide how the text ML model's classification output will be utilized.

2. *Data (text) curation.* This step involves gathering relevant external text data via web services or **web spidering (scraping or crawling) programs** that extract raw content from a source, typically web pages. Annotation of the text data with high-quality, reliable target (dependent) variable labels might also be necessary for supervised learning and performance evaluation purposes. For instance, experts might need to label whether a given expert assessment of a stock is bearish or bullish.

3. *Text preparation and wrangling.* This step involves critical cleansing and preprocessing tasks necessary to convert streams of unstructured data into a format that is usable by traditional modeling methods designed for structured inputs.

4. *Text exploration.* This step encompasses text visualization through techniques, such as word clouds, and text feature selection and engineering.

The resulting output (e.g., sentiment prediction scores) can either be combined with other structured variables or used directly for forecasting and/or analysis.

Next, we describe two key steps from the *ML Model Building Steps* depicted in Exhibit 1 that typically differ for structured data versus textual big data: data/text preparation and wrangling and data/text exploration. We then discuss model training. Finally, we focus on applying these steps to a case study related to classifying and predicting stock sentiment from financial texts.

Exhibit 1: Model Building for Financial Forecasting Using Big Data: Structured (Traditional) vs. Unstructured (Text)

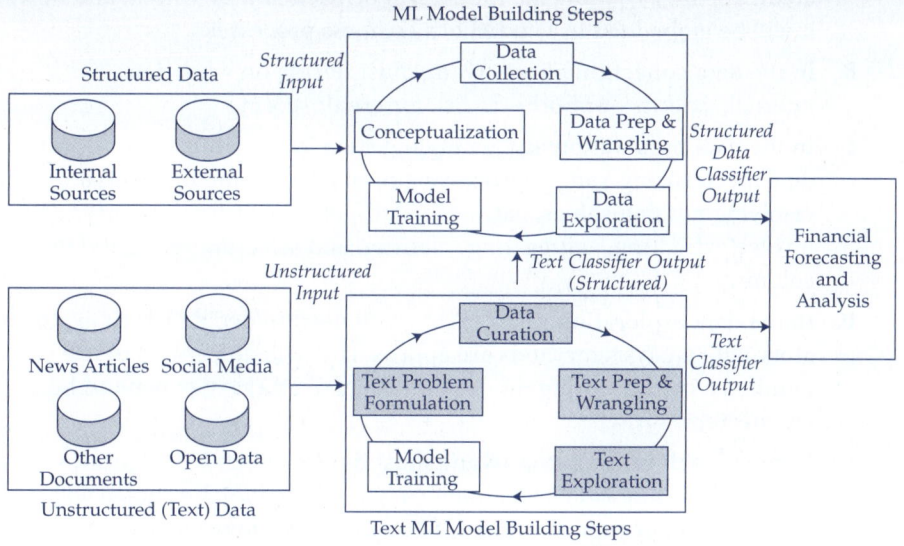

In a later phase of the project, LendALot attempts to improve its credit scoring processes by incorporating textual data in credit scoring. Wang tells his team, "Enhance the creditworthiness scoring model by incorporating insights from text provided by the prospective borrowers in the loan application free response fields."

1. State and explain one decision Wang will need to make related to:

   A. conceptualizing the modeling task.

   B. data collection.

   C. data preparation and wrangling.

   D. data exploration.

   E. model training.

Solution

   A. In the conceptualization step, Wang will need to decide how the output of the ML model will be specified (e.g., a binary classification of creditworthiness), how the model will be used and by whom, and how it will be embedded in LendALot's business processes.

   B. In the data collection phase, Wang must decide on what data—internal, external, or both—to use for credit scoring.

   C. In the data preparation and wrangling step, Wang will need to decide on data cleansing and preprocessing needs. Cleansing may entail resolving missing values, extreme values, etc. Preprocessing may involve extracting, aggregating, filtering, and selecting relevant data columns.

   D. In the data exploration phase, Wang will need to decide which exploratory data analysis methods are appropriate, which features to use in building a credit scoring model, and which features may need to be engineered.

   E. In the model training step, Wang must decide which ML algorithm(s) to use. Assuming labeled training data are available, the choice will be among supervised learning algorithms. Decisions will need to be made on how model fit is measured and how the model is validated and tuned.

2. Identify the process step that Wang's statement addresses.

Solution

Wang's statement relates to the initial step of text problem formulation.

3. State two potential needs of the LendAlot team in relation to text curation.

Solution

Related to text curation, the team will be using internal data (from loan applications). They will need to ensure that the text comment fields on the loan applications have been correctly implemented and enabled. If these fields are not required, they need to ensure there is a sufficient response rate to analyze.

4. State two potential needs of the LendAlot team in relation to text preparation and wrangling.

Solution

Related to text preparation and wrangling, the team will need to carry out the critical tasks of text cleansing and text preprocessing. These two tasks are necessary to convert an unstructured stream of data into structured values for use by traditional modeling methods.

DATA PREPARATION AND WRANGLING

3

☐ describe objectives, steps, and examples of preparing and wrangling data

☐ evaluate the fit of a machine learning algorithm

Data preparation and wrangling involve cleansing and organizing raw data into a consolidated format. The resulting dataset is suitable to use for further analyses and training a machine learning (ML) model. This is a critical stage, the foundation, in big data projects. Most of the project time is spent on this step, and the quality of the data affects the training of the selected ML model. Domain knowledge—that is, the involvement of specialists in the particular field in which the data are obtained and used—is beneficial and often necessary to successfully execute this step. Data preparation is preceded by data collection, so we discuss the data collection process first.

Before the data collection process even begins, it is important to state the problem, define objectives, identify useful data points, and conceptualize the model. Conceptualization is like a blueprint on a drawing board, a modifiable plan that is necessary to initiate the model building process. A project overview is established by determining the ML model type—supervised or unsupervised—and data sources/collection plans with respect to the needs of the project.

Data collection involves searching for and downloading the raw data from one or multiple sources. Data can be stored in different formats, sources, and locations. As databases are the most common primary sources, building necessary queries with the help of database administrators is critical. Database schemas are built with certain assumptions and exceptions, and it is safest to clarify the database architecture with an administrator or database architect before downloading the necessary data. Data also exist in the form of spreadsheets, comma-separated values (csv) files, text files, and other formats. Care must be taken before using such data, and documentation (often referred to as "Readme" files) must be referred to, if available. **Readme files** are text files provided with the raw data that contain information related to a data file. They are useful for understanding the data and how they can be interpreted correctly.

Alternatively, third-party data vendors can be sources of clean data. External data usually can be accessed through an **application programming interface (API)**—a set of well-defined methods of communication between various software components—or the vendors can deliver the required data in the form of csv files or other formats (as previously mentioned). Using external data can save time and resources that would otherwise go into data preparation and wrangling; however, vendor contracts come with a price. Depending on the big data project constraints, a decision must be made regarding the use of internal or external data based on the trade-offs between time, financial costs, and accuracy. For projects using internal user data, external data might not be suitable. For example, to understand user traffic on a company website, internally recorded site visits and click frequency may be captured and stored in the internal databases. External data are advantageous when a project requires generic data, such as demographics of a geographic area or traffic data of a public service. Another consideration in using external vendor provided data is that during the cleansing process, underlying trends in the data that are important for particular end-uses may be masked or even lost. This is where "alpha" is often found; so by simply buying a dataset from a vendor, you may lose your information edge. Of course, application of the data (e.g., merging and combining, putting through different types of models) will be different for everyone who uses it; there are always different ways to extract value.

Once the data are collected, the data preparation and wrangling stage begins. This stage involves two important tasks: cleansing and preprocessing, respectively. Exhibit 2 outlines data preparation and wrangling and defines the two component tasks. These tasks are explained in detail under the structured and unstructured sub-sections because the steps vary by the nature of data.

Exhibit 2: Data Preparation and Wrangling Stage

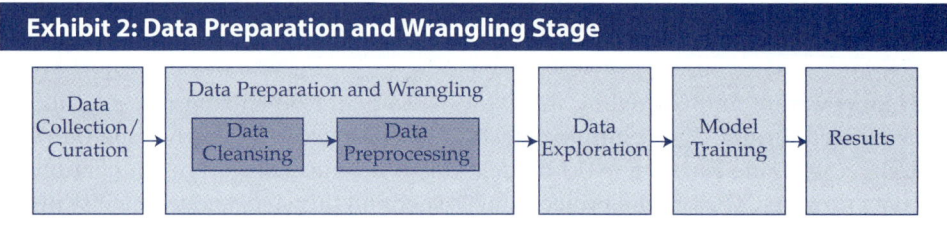

Data Preparation (Cleansing): This is the initial and most common task in data preparation that is performed on raw data. Data cleansing is the process of examining, identifying, and mitigating errors in raw data. Normally, the raw data are neither sufficiently complete nor sufficiently clean to directly train the ML model. Manually entered data can have incomplete, duplicated, erroneous, or inaccurate values. Automated data (recorded by systems) can have similar problems due to server failures and software bugs.

Data Wrangling (Preprocessing): This task performs transformations and critical processing steps on the cleansed data to make the data ready for ML model training. Raw data most commonly are not present in the appropriate format for model consumption. After the cleansing step, data need to be processed by dealing with outliers, extracting useful variables from existing data points, and scaling the data.

Structured Data

Data Preparation (Cleansing)

Structured data are organized in a systematic format that is readily searchable and readable by computer operations for processing and analyzing. In structured data, data errors can be in the form of incomplete, invalid, inaccurate, inconsistent, non-uniform, and duplicate data observations. The data cleansing process mainly deals with identifying and mitigating all such errors. Exhibit 3 shows a raw dataset before cleansing. The data have been collected from different sources and are organized in a data matrix (or data table) format. Each row contains observations of each customer of a US-based bank. Each column represents a variable (or feature) corresponding to each customer.

Exhibit 3: Raw Data Before Cleansing								
1	ID	Name	Gender	Date of Birth	Salary	Other Income	State	Credit Card
2	1	Mr. ABC	M	12/5/1970	$50,200	$5,000	VA	Y
3	2	Ms. XYZ	M	15 Jan, 1975	$60,500	$0	NY	Y
4	3	EFG		1/13/1979	$65,000	$1,000	CA	N
5	4	Ms. MNO	F	1/1/1900	—	—	FL	Don't Know
6	5	Ms. XYZ	F	15/1/1975	$60,500	$0		Y
7	6	Mr. GHI	M	9/10/1942	NA	$55,000	TX	N
8	7	Mr. TUV	M	2/27/1956	$300,000	$50,000	CT	Y
9	8	Ms. DEF	F	4/4/1980	$55,000	$0	British Columbia	N

The possible errors in a raw dataset include the following:

1. *Incompletenesserror* is where the data are not present, resulting in missing data. This can be corrected by investigating alternate data sources. Missing values and NAs (not applicable or not available values) must be either omitted or replaced with "NA" for deletion or substitution with imputed values during the data exploration stage. The most common imputations are mean, median, or mode of the variable or simply assuming zero. In Exhibit 3, rows 4 (ID 3), 5 (ID 4), 6 (ID 5), and 7 (ID 6) are incomplete due to missing values in either Gender, Salary, Other Income, Name (Salutation), and State columns.

2. *Invalidityerror* is where the data are outside of a meaningful range, resulting in invalid data. This can be corrected by verifying other administrative data records. In Exhibit 3, row 5 likely contains invalid data as the date of birth is out of the range of the expected human life span.

3. *Inaccuracyerror* is where the data are not a measure of true value. This can be rectified with the help of business records and administrators. In Exhibit 3, row 5 is inaccurate (it shows "Don't Know"); in reality, every person either has a credit card or does not.

4. *Inconsistencyerror* is where the data conflict with the corresponding data points or reality. This contradiction should be eliminated by clarifying with another source. In Exhibit 3, row 3 (ID 2) is likely to be inconsistent as the Name column contains a female title and the Gender column contains male.

5. *Non-uniformityerror* is where the data are not present in an identical format. This can be resolved by converting the data points into a preferable standard format. In Exhibit 3, the data under the Date of Birth column is present in various formats. The data under the Salary column may also be non-uniform as the monetary units are ambiguous; the dollar symbol can represent US dollar, Canadian dollar, or others.

6. *Duplicationerror* is where duplicate observations are present. This can be corrected by removing the duplicate entries. In Exhibit 3, row 6 is a duplicate as the data under Name and Date of Birth columns are identical to the ones in row 3, referring to the same customer.

Exhibit 4 shows the dataset after completion of the cleansing process.

| Exhibit 4: Data After Cleansing |

1	ID	Name	Gender	Date of Birth	Salary	Other Income	State	Credit Card
2	1	Mr. ABC	M	12/5/1970	USD 50200	USD 5000	VA	Y
3	2	Ms. XYZ	F	1/15/1975	USD 60500	USD 0	NY	Y
4	3	Mr. EFG	M	1/13/1979	USD 65000	USD 1000	CA	N
5	6	Mr. GHI	M	9/10/1942	USD 0	USD 55000	TX	N
6	7	Mr. TUV	M	2/27/1956	USD 300000	USD 50000	CT	Y
7	8	Ms. DEF	F	4/4/1980	CAD 55000	CAD 0	British Columbia	N

Data cleansing can be expensive and cumbersome because it involves the use of automated, rule-based, and pattern recognition tools coupled with manual human inspection to sequentially check for the aforementioned types of errors row by row and column by column. The process involves a detailed data analysis as an initial step in identifying various errors that are present in the data. In addition to a manual inspection and verification of the data, analysis software, such as SPSS, can be used to understand **metadata** (data that describes and gives information about other data) about the data properties to use as a starting point to investigate any errors in the data. The business value of the project determines the necessary quality of data cleansing and subsequently the amount of resources used in the cleansing process. In case the errors cannot be resolved due to lack of available resources, the data points with errors can simply be omitted depending on the size of the dataset. For instance, if a dataset is large with more than 10,000 rows, removing a few rows (approximately 100) may not have a significant impact on the project. If a dataset is small with less than 1,000 rows, every row might be important and deleting many rows thus harmful to the project.

Data Wrangling (Preprocessing)

To make structured data ready for analyses, the data should be preprocessed. Data preprocessing primarily includes transformations and scaling of the data. These processes are exercised on the cleansed dataset. The following transformations are common in practice:

1. *Extraction:* A new variable can be extracted from the current variable for ease of analyzing and using for training the ML model. In Exhibit 4, the Date of Birth column consists of dates that are not directly suitable for analyses. Thus, an additional variable called "Age" can be extracted by calculating the number of years between the present day and date of birth.

2. *Aggregation:* Two or more variables can be aggregated into one variable to consolidate similar variables. In Exhibit 4, the two forms of income, Salary and Other Income, can be summed into a single variable called Total Income.

3. *Filtration:* The data rows that are not needed for the project must be identified and filtered. In Exhibit 4, row 7 (ID 8) has a non-US state; however, this dataset is for the US-based bank customers where it is required to have a US address.

4. *Selection:* The data columns that are intuitively not needed for the project can be removed. This should not be confused with feature selection, which is explained later. In Exhibit 4, Name and Date of Birth columns are not

required for training the ML model. The ID column is sufficient to identify the observations, and the new extracted variable Age replaces the Date of Birth column.

5. *Conversion:* The variables can be of different types: nominal, ordinal, continuous, and categorical. The variables in the dataset must be converted into appropriate types to further process and analyze them correctly. This is critical for ML model training. Before converting, values must be stripped out with prefixes and suffixes, such as currency symbols. In Exhibit 4, Name is nominal, Salary and Income are continuous, Gender and Credit Card are categorical with 2 classes, and State is nominal. In case row 7 is not excluded, the Salary in row 7 must be converted into US dollars. Also, the conversion task applies to adjusting time value of money, time zones, and others when present.

Outliers may be present in the data, and domain knowledge is needed to deal with them. Any outliers that are present must first be identified. The outliers then should be examined and a decision made to either remove or replace them with values imputed using statistical techniques. In Exhibit 4, row 6 (ID 7) is an outlier because the Salary value is far above the upper quartile. Row 5 (ID 6) is also an outlier because the Salary value is far below the lower quartile. However, after the aggregation and formation of a new variable Total Income, as shown in Exhibit 5, row 5 (ID 6), it is no longer an outlier.

In practice, several techniques can be used to detect outliers in the data. Standard deviation can be used to identify outliers in normally distributed data. In general, a data value that is outside of 3 standard deviations from the mean may be considered an outlier. The interquartile range (IQR) can be used to identify outliers in data with any form of distribution. IQR is the difference between the 75th and the 25th percentile values of the data. In general, data values outside of the following are considered as outliers: +1.5 x IQR + 3rd Quartile Upper Bound; and -1.5 x IQR + 2nd Quartile Lower Bound. Using a multiple of 3.0 (instead of 1.5) times IQR would indicate extreme values.

There are several practical methods for handling outliers. When extreme values and outliers are simply removed from the dataset, it is known as **trimming** (also called truncation). For example, a 5% trimmed dataset is one for which the 5% highest and the 5% lowest values have been removed. When extreme values and outliers are replaced with the maximum (for large value outliers) and minimum (for small value outliers) values of data points that are not outliers, the process is known as **winsorization**.

Exhibit 5: Data After Applying Transformations

1	ID	Gender	Age	Total Income	State	Credit Card
2	1	M	48	55200	VA	Y
3	2	F	43	60500	NY	Y
4	3	M	39	66000	CA	N
5	6	M	76	55000	TX	N

Scaling is a process of adjusting the range of a feature by shifting and changing the scale of data. Variables, such as age and income, can have a diversity of ranges that result in a heterogeneous training dataset. For better ML model training when using such methods as support vector machines (SVMs) and artificial neural networks (ANNs), all variables should have values in the same range to make the dataset homogeneous. It is important to remove outliers before scaling is performed. Here are two of the most common ways of scaling:

1. *Normalization* is the process of rescaling numeric variables in the range of [0, 1]. To normalize variable X, the minimum value (X_{min}) is subtracted from each observation (X_i), and then this value is divided by the difference between the maximum and minimum values of X ($X_{max} - X_{min}$) as follows:

$$X_{i \text{ (normalized)}} = \frac{X_i - X_{min}}{X_{max} - X_{min}}. \tag{1}$$

2. *Standardization* is the process of both centering and scaling the variables. Centering involves subtracting the mean (μ) of the variable from each observation (X_i) so the new mean is 0. Scaling adjusts the range of the data by dividing the centered values ($X_i - \mu$) by the standard deviation (σ) of feature X. The resultant standardized variable will have an arithmetic mean of 0 and standard deviation of 1.

$$X_{i \text{ (standardized)}} = \frac{X_i - \mu}{\sigma} \tag{2}$$

Normalization is sensitive to outliers, so treatment of outliers is necessary before normalization is performed. Normalization can be used when the distribution of the data is not known. Standardization is relatively less sensitive to outliers as it depends on the mean and standard deviation of the data. However, the data must be normally distributed to use standardization.

EXAMPLE 2

Preparing and Wrangling Structured Data

Paul Wang's analytics team at LendALot Corporation is working to develop its first ML model for classifying prospective borrowers' creditworthiness. Wang has asked one of his data scientists, Lynn Lee, to perform a preliminary assessment of the data cleansing and preprocessing tasks the team will need to perform. As part of this assessment, Lee pulled the following sample of data for manual examination, which she brings to Wang to discuss.

1	ID	Name	Loan Outcome	Income (USD)	Loan Amount (USD)	Credit Score	Loan Type
2	1	Mr. Alpha	No Default	34,000	10,000	685	Mortgage
3	2	Ms. Beta	No Default	−63,050	49,000	770	Student Loan
4	3	Mr. Gamma	Defaulted	20,565	35,000	730	
5	4	Ms. Delta	No Default	50,021	unknown	664	Mortgage
6	5	Mr. Epsilon	Defaulted	100,350	129,000	705	Car Loan
7	6	Mr. Zeta	No Default	800,000	300,000	800	Boat Loan
8	6	Mr. Zeta	No Default	800,000	300,000	800	Boat Loan

After sharing a concern that the data should be thoroughly cleansed, Wang makes the following statements:

Statement 1   "Let's keep the ID column and remove the column for Name from the dataset."

Statement 2	"Let's create a new feature, "Loan Amount as a Percent of Income," to use as an additional feature."

1. The data shown for Ms. Beta contain what is *best described* as an:

    A. invalidity error.

    B. inaccuracy error.

    C. incompleteness error.

Solution

A is correct. This is an invalidity error because the data are outside of a meaningful range. Income cannot be negative.

2. The data shown for Mr. Gamma contain what is *best described* as an:

    A. invalidity error.

    B. duplication error.

    C. incompleteness error.

Solution

C is correct. This is an incompleteness error as the loan type is missing.

3. The data shown for Ms. Delta contain what is *best described* as an:

    A. invalidity error.

    B. inaccuracy error.

    C. duplication error.

Solution

B is correct. This is an inaccuracy error because LendALot must know how much they have lent to that particular borrower (who eventually repaid the loan as indicated by the loan outcome of no default).

4. The data shown for Mr. Zeta contain what is *best described* as an:

    A. invalidity error.

    B. inaccuracy error.

    C. duplication error.

Solution

C is correct. Row 8 duplicates row 7: This is a duplication error.

5. The process mentioned in Wang's first statement is *best described* as:

    A. feature selection.

    B. feature extraction.

    C. feature engineering

Solution

A is correct. The process mentioned involves selecting the features to use. The proposal makes sense; with "ID," "Name" is not needed to identify an observation.

6. Wang's second statement is *best described* as:

   A. feature selection.

   B. feature extraction.

   C. feature engineering.

Solution

B is correct. The proposed feature is a ratio of two existing features. *Feature extraction* is the process of creating (i.e., extracting) new variables from existing ones in the data.

4 | UNSTRUCTURED (TEXT) DATA

☐ | describe objectives, steps, and examples of preparing and wrangling data

Unstructured data are not organized into any systematic format that can be processed by computers directly. They are available in formats meant for human usage rather than computer processing. Unstructured data constitute approximately 80% of the total data available today. They can be in the form of text, images, videos, and audio files. Unlike in structured data, preparing and wrangling unstructured data are both more challenging. For analysis and use to train the ML model, the unstructured data must be transformed into structured data. In this section, text data will be used to demonstrate unstructured data preparation and wrangling. The cleansing and preprocessing of text data is called *text processing*. Text processing is essentially cleansing and transforming the unstructured text data into a structured format. Text processing can be divided into two tasks: cleansing and preprocessing. The following content is related to text data in the English language.

Text Preparation (Cleansing)

Raw text data are a sequence of characters and contain other non-useful elements, including html tags, punctuations, and white spaces (including tabs, line breaks, and new lines). It is important to clean the text data before preprocessing. Exhibit 6 shows a sample text from the home page for the hypothetical company Robots Are Us website. The text appears to be clean visually and is designed for human readability.

Exhibit 6: Sample Text from Robots Are Us Home Page

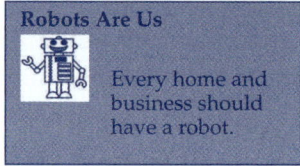

However, the source text that can be downloaded is not as clean. The raw text contains html tags and formatting elements along with the actual text. Exhibit 7 shows the raw text from the source.

Exhibit 7: Raw Text from the Source

```
<h1 class="text-left mb-3">Robots Are Us</h1>
<h2> Every home and business should have a robot    </h2>
```

The initial step in text processing is cleansing, which involves basic operations to clean the text by removing unnecessary elements from the raw text. Text operations often use regular expressions. A **regular expression (regex)** is a series that contains characters in a particular order. Regex is used to search for patterns of interest in a given text. For example, a regex "<.*?>" can be used to find all the html tags that are present in the form of <...> in text.[1] GREP (global regular expression print) is a commonly available utility in programming languages for searching patterns using regex. Once a pattern is found, it can be removed or replaced. Additionally, advanced html parsers and packages are available in the popular programming languages, such as R and Python, to deal with this task.

The following steps describe the basic operations in the text cleansing process.

1. *Remove html tags*: Most of the text data are acquired from web pages, and the text inherits html markup tags with the actual content. The initial task is to remove (or strip) the html tags that are not part of the actual text using programming functions or using regular expressions. In Exhibit 7, </h2> is an html tag that can be identified by a regex and be removed. Note that it is not uncommon to keep some generic html tags to maintain certain formatting meaning in the text.

2. *Remove Punctuations*: Most punctuations are not necessary for text analysis and should be removed. However, some punctuations, such as percentage signs, currency symbols, and question marks, may be useful for ML model training. These punctuations should be substituted with such annotations as /percentSign/, /dollarSign/, and /questionMark/ to preserve their grammatical meaning in the text. Such annotations preserve the semantic meaning of important characters in the text for further text processing and analysis stages. It is important to note that periods (dots) in the text need to be processed carefully. There are different circumstances for periods to be present in text—characteristically used for abbreviations, sentence boundaries, and decimal points. The periods and the context in which they are used need to be identified and must be appropriately replaced or removed. In general, periods after abbreviations can be removed, but the periods separating sentences should be replaced by the annotation /endSentence/. Some punctuations, such as hyphens and underscores, can be kept in the text to keep the consecutive words intact as a single term (e.g., e-mail). Regex are often used to remove or replace punctuations.

3. *Remove Numbers*: When numbers (or digits) are present in the text, they should be removed or substituted with an annotation /number/. This helps inform the computer that a number is present, but the actual value of the

---

1 A regex of the form "<.*?>" will identify all html tags with anything (*) of any length (?) between the brackets (< >).

number itself is not helpful for categorizing/analyzing the text. Such operations are critical for ML model training. Otherwise, the computers will treat each number as a separate word, which may complicate the analyses or add noise. Regex are often used to remove or replace numbers. However, the number and any decimals must be retained where the outputs of interest are the actual values of the number. One such text application is information extraction (IE), where the goal is to extract relevant information from a given text. An IE task could be extracting monetary values from financial reports, where the actual number values are critical.

4. *Remove white spaces*: It is possible to have extra white spaces, tab spaces, and leading and ending spaces in the text. The extra white spaces may be introduced after executing the previously mentioned operations. These should be identified and removed to keep the text intact and clean. Certain functions in programming languages can be used to remove unnecessary white spaces from the text. For example, the text mining package in R offers a *stripwhitespace* function.

Exhibit 8 uses a sample financial text to show the transformations occurring after applying each operation of the text cleansing process. The four steps are applied on a mock financial text after scraping from a source. As noted previously, scraping (or web scraping) is a technique to extract raw content from a source, typically web pages. It is important to note that the sequence and choice of cleansing operations does matter. For instance, after removing punctuation, the "1.2 million" becomes "12 million." This is acceptable here since a subsequent operation replaces all numbers with a "/number/" tag. However, if numbers were not replaced with such tags, the punctuation removal operation could affect the data.

Original text from a financial statement as shown on a webpage

CapEx on the normal operations remained stable on historicallylow levels, $800,000 compared to $1.2 million last year.

Quarter 3, so far, is 5% sales growth quarter-to-date, and year-to-date, we have a 4% local currency sales development.

Raw text after scraping from the source

\<p>\<font size = "4"> CapEx on the normal operations remained stable on historically low levels, $800,000 compared to $1.2 million last year. \<b/>\<b/> Quarter 3, so far, is 5% sales growth quarter-to-date, and year-to-date, we have a 4% local currency sales development.\</font>\</p>

Text after removing html tags

CapEx on the normal operations remained stable on historically low levels, $800,000 compared to $1.2 million last year.
Quarter 3, so far, is 5% sales growth quarter-to-date, and year-to-date, we have a 4% local currency sales development.

Text after removing and replacing punctuations

CapEx on the normal operations remained stable on historically low levels /dollarSign/800000 compared to /dollarSign/12 million last year /endSentence/ Quarter 3 so far is 5 /percentSign/ sales growth quarter-to-date and year-to-date we have a 4 /percentSign/ local currency sales development /endSentence/

Text after replacing numbers

CapEx on the normal operations remained stable on historically low levels /dollarSign//number / compared to/dollarSign//number/ million last year /endSentence/ Quarter/number/ so far is /number/ /percentSign/sales growth quarter-to-date and year-to-date we have a /number/ / percentSign/ local currency sales development /endSentence/

Text after removing extra white spaces

CapEx on the normal operations remained stable on historically low levels/dollarSign//number /compared to/dollarSign//number/million last year/endSentence/ Quarter/number/so far is /number//percentSign/sales growth quarter-to-date and year-to-date we have a/number// percentSign/local currency sales development/endSentence/

Text Wrangling (Preprocessing)

To further understand text processing, tokens and tokenization need to be defined. A **token** is equivalent to a word, and **tokenization** is the process of splitting a given text into separate tokens. In other words, a text is considered to be a collection of tokens. Tokenization can be performed at word or character level, but it is most commonly performed at word level. Exhibit 9 shows a sample dataset of four cleansed texts and their word tokens.

	Cleaned Texts	Tokens
Text 1	The man went to the market today	The man went to the market today
Text 2	Market values are increasing	Market values are increasing
Text 3	Increased marketing is needed	Increased marketing is needed
Text 4	There is no market for the product	There is no market for the product

Similar to structured data, text data also require normalization. The normalization process in text processing involves the following:

1. *Lowercasing* the alphabet removes distinctions among the same words due to upper and lower cases. This action helps the computers to process the same words appropriately (e.g., "The" and "the").

2. *Stop words* are such commonly used words as "the," "is," and "a." Stop words do not carry a semantic meaning for the purpose of text analyses and ML training. However, depending on the end-use of text processing, for advance text applications it may be critical to keep the stop words in the text in order to understand the context of adjacent words. For ML training purposes, stop words typically are removed to reduce the number of tokens involved in the training set. A predefined list of stop words is available in programming languages to help with this task. In some cases, additional stop words can be added to the list based on the content. For example, the word "exhibit" may occur often in financial filings, which in general is not a stop word but in the context of the filings can be treated as a stop word.

3. *Stemming* is the process of converting inflected forms of a word into its base word (known as stem). Stemming is a rule-based approach, and the results need not necessarily be linguistically sensible. Stems may not be the same as the morphological root of the word. Porter's algorithm is the most popular method for stemming. For example, the stem of the words "analyzed" and "analyzing" is "analyz." Similarly, the British English variant "analysing" would become "analys." Stemming is available in R and Python. The text mining package in R provides a *stemDocument* function that uses this algorithm.

4. *Lemmatization* is the process of converting inflected forms of a word into its morphological root (known as lemma). Lemmatization is an algorithmic approach and depends on the knowledge of the word and language structure. For example, the lemma of the words "analyzed" and "analyzing" is "analyze." Lemmatization is computationally more expensive and advanced.

Stemming or lemmatization will reduce the repetition of words occurring in various forms and maintain the semantic structure of the text data. Stemming is more common than lemmatization in the English language since it is simpler to perform. In text data, data sparseness refers to words that appear very infrequently, resulting in data consisting of many unique, low frequency tokens. Both techniques decrease data sparseness by aggregating many sparsely occurring words in relatively less sparse stems or lemmas, thereby aiding in training less complex ML models.

After the cleansed text is normalized, a bag-of-words is created. **Bag-of-words (BOW)** representation is a basic procedure used to analyze text. It is essentially a collection of a distinct set of tokens from all the texts in a sample dataset. BOW is simply a set of words and does not capture the position or sequence of words present in the text. However, it is memory efficient and easy to handle for text analyses.

Exhibit 10 shows the BOW and transformations occurring in each step of normalization on the cleansed texts from Exhibit 9. Note that the number of words decreases as the normalizing steps are applied, making the resulting BOW smaller and simpler.

Exhibit 10: Bag-of-Words Representation of Four Texts Before and After Normalization Process

BOW before normalizing

"The"	"man"	"went"	"to"	"the"	"market"
"today"	"Market"	"values"	"are"	"increasing"	"Increased"
"marketing"	"is"	"needed"	"There"	"no"	"for"
"product"					

BOW after removing uppercase letters

"the"	"man"	"went"	"to"	"market"	"today"
"values"	"are"	"increasing"	"increased"	"marketing"	"is"
"needed"	"there"	"no"	"for"	"product"	

BOW after removing stop words

"man"	"went"	"market"	"today"	"values"	"increasing"
"increased"	"marketing"	"needed"	"product"		

BOW after stemming

"man"	"went"	"market"	"today"	"valu"	"increas"	"need"	"product"

The last step of text preprocessing is using the final BOW after normalizing to build a **document term matrix (DTM)**. DTM is a matrix that is similar to a data table for structured data and is widely used for text data. Each row of the matrix belongs to a document (or text file), and each column represents a token (or term). The number of rows of DTM is equal to the number of documents (or text files) in a sample dataset. The number of columns is equal to the number of tokens from the BOW that is built using all the documents in a sample dataset. The cells can contain the counts of the number of times a token is present in each document. The matrix cells can be filled with other values that will be explained in the financial forecasting project section of this reading; a large dataset is helpful in understanding the concepts. At this point, the unstructured text data are converted to structured data that can be processed further and used to train the ML model. Exhibit 11 shows a DTM constructed from the resultant BOW of the four texts from Exhibit 10.

Exhibit 11: DTM of Four Texts and Using Normalized BOW Filled with Counts of Occurrence

	man	went	market	today	valu	increas	need	product
Text 1	1	1	1	1	0	0	0	0
Text 2	0	0	1	0	1	1	0	0
Text 3	0	0	1	0	0	1	1	0
Text 4	0	0	1	0	0	0	0	1

As seen in Exhibit 10, BOW does not represent the word sequences or positions, which limits its use for some advanced ML training applications. In the example, the word "no" is treated as a single token and has been removed during the normalization because it is a stop word. Consequently, this fails to signify the negative meaning ("no market") of the text (i.e., Text 4). To overcome such problems, a technique called n-grams can be employed. **N-grams** is a representation of word sequences. The length of a sequence can vary from 1 to n. When one word is used, it is a unigram; a two-word sequence is a bigram; and a 3-word sequence is a trigram; and so on. Exhibit 10, for example, shows a unigram ($n = 1$) BOW. The advantage of n-grams is that they can be used in the same way as unigrams to build a BOW. In practice, different n-grams can be combined to form a BOW and eventually be used to build a DTM. Exhibit 12 shows unigrams, bigrams, and trigrams. Exhibit 12 also shows a combined unigram-to-trigram BOW for the particular text. Stemming can be applied on the cleansed text before building n-grams and BOW (not shown in Exhibit 12).

Exhibit 12:   N-Grams and N-Grams BOW

Clean text

The man went to the market today

Unigrams

"The"   "man"   "went"   "to"   "the"   "market" "today"

Bigrams

"The_man"   "man_went"   "went_to"   "to_the"   "the_market"   "market_today"

Trigrams

"The_man_went" "man_went_to" "went_to_the" "to_the_market" "the_market_today"

BOW before normalizing

"The"   "man"   "went"   "to"   "the"   "market"   "today"
"The_man"   "man_went"   "went_to"   "to_the"   "the_market" "market_today" "The_man_went"
"man_went_to" "went_to_the" "to_the_market" "the_market_today"

BOW after removing upper case letters

"the"   "man"   "went"   "to"   "market"   "today"   "the_man"
"man_went"   "went_to"   "to_the"   "the_market" "market_today" "the_man_went" "man_went_to"
"went_to_the" "to_the_market" "the_market_today"

BOW after removing stop words

"man"   "went"   "market"   "today"   "the_man"   "man_went"   "went_to"
"to_the"   "the_market" "market_today" "the_man_went" "man_went_to" "went_to_the" "to_the_market"
"the_market_today"

The n-grams implementation will vary the impact of normalization on the BOW. Even after removing isolated stop words, stop words tend to persist when they are attached to their adjacent words. For instance, "to_the" (Exhibit 12) is a single bigram token consisting of stop words and will not be removed by the predetermined list of stop words.

EXAMPLE 3

Unstructured Data Preparation and Wrangling

1. The output produced by preparing and wrangling textual data is best described as a:

   A. data table.

   B. confusion matrix.

   C. document term matrix.

Solution

C is correct. The objective of data preparation and wrangling of textual data is to transform the unstructured data into structured data. The output of these processes is a document term matrix that can be read by computers. The document term matrix is similar to a data table for structured data.

2. In text cleansing, situations in which one may need to add an annotation include the removal of:

   A. html tags.
   B. white spaces.
   C. punctuations.

Solution

C is correct. Some punctuations, such as percentage signs, currency symbols, and question marks, may be useful for ML model training, so when such punctuations are removed annotations should be added.

3. A column of a document term matrix is *best* described as representing:

   A. a token.
   B. a regularization term.
   C. an instance.

Solution

A is correct. Each column of a document term matrix represents a token from the bag-of-words that is built using all the documents in a sample dataset.

4. A cell of a document term matrix is *best* described as containing:

   A. a token.
   B. a count of tokens.
   C. a count of instances.

Solution

B is correct. A cell in a document term matrix contains a count of the number of tokens of the kind indicated in the column heading.

5. Points to cover in normalizing textual data include:

   A. removing numbers.
   B. removing white spaces.
   C. lowercasing the alphabet.

Solution

C is correct. The other choices are related to text cleansing.

6. When some words appear very infrequently in a textual dataset, techniques that may address the risk of training highly complex models include:

   A. stemming.
   B. scaling.

C. data cleansing.

Solution

A is correct. Stemming, the process of converting inflected word forms into a base word (or stem), is one technique that can address the problem described.

7. Which of the following statements concerning tokenization is *most* accurate?

A. Tokenization is part of the text cleansing process.

B. Tokenization is most commonly performed at the character level.

C. Tokenization is the process of splitting a given text into separate tokens.

Solution

C is correct, by definition. The other choices are not true.

5 DATA EXPLORATION OBJECTIVES AND METHODS

☐ describe objectives, methods, and examples of data exploration

Data exploration is a crucial part of big data projects. The prepared data are explored to investigate and comprehend data distributions and relationships. The knowledge that is gained about the data in this stage is used throughout the project. The outcome and quality of exploration strongly affects ML model training results. Domain knowledge plays a vital role in exploratory analysis as this stage should involve cooperation between analysts, model designers, and experts in the particular data domain. Data exploration without domain knowledge can result in ascertaining spurious relationships among the variables in the data that can mislead the analyses. The data exploration stage follows the data preparation stage and leads to the model training stage.

Data exploration involves three important tasks: exploratory data analysis, feature selection, and feature engineering. These three tasks are outlined in Exhibit 13 and are defined and further explained under the structured and unstructured data subsections.

Exhibit 13: Data Exploration Stage

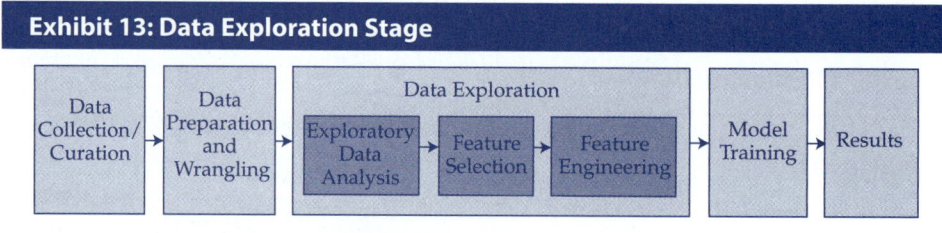

Exploratory data analysis (EDA) is the preliminary step in data exploration. Exploratory graphs, charts, and other visualizations, such as heat maps and word clouds, are designed to summarize and observe data. In practice, many exploratory graphs are made for investigation and can be made swiftly using statistical programming and generic spreadsheet software tools. Data can also be summarized and examined using quantitative methods, such as descriptive statistics and central tendency measures. An important objective of EDA is to serve as a communication medium among project stakeholders, including business users, domain experts, and analysts. Relatively quick and easy exploratory visualizations help stakeholders connect and ensure the prepared data are sensible. Other objectives of EDA include:

- understanding data properties,
- finding patterns and relationships in data,
- inspecting basic questions and hypotheses,
- documenting data distributions and other characteristics, and
- planning modeling strategies for the next steps.

Feature selection is a process whereby only pertinent features from the dataset are selected for ML model training. Selecting fewer features decreases ML model complexity and training time. **Feature engineering** is a process of creating new features by changing or transforming existing features. Model performance heavily depends on feature selection and engineering.

Structured Data

Exploratory Data Analysis

For structured data, each data table row contains an observation and each column contains a feature. EDA can be performed on a single feature (one-dimension) or on multiple features (multi-dimension). For high-dimension data with many features, EDA can be facilitated by using a dimension reduction technique, such as principal components analysis (PCA). Based on the number of dimensions, the exploratory techniques will vary.

For one-dimensional data, summary statistics, such as mean, median, quartiles, ranges, standard deviations, skewness, and kurtosis, of a feature can be computed. One-dimension visualization summarizes each feature in the dataset. The basic one-dimension exploratory visualizations are as follows:

- Histograms
- Bar charts
- Box plots
- Density plots

Histograms represent equal bins of data and their respective frequencies. They can be used to understand the high-level distribution of the data. Bar charts summarize the frequencies of categorical variables. Box plots show the distribution of continuous data by highlighting the median, quartiles, and outliers of a feature that is normally distributed. Density plots are another effective way to understand the distribution of continuous data. Density plots are smoothed histograms and are commonly laid on top of histograms, as shown in Exhibit 14. This histogram shows a hypothetical annual salary distribution (in £) of entry-level analyst positions at UK banks. The data represent a normal distribution with an approximate mean of £68,500.

Exhibit 14: Histogram with Superimposed Density Plot

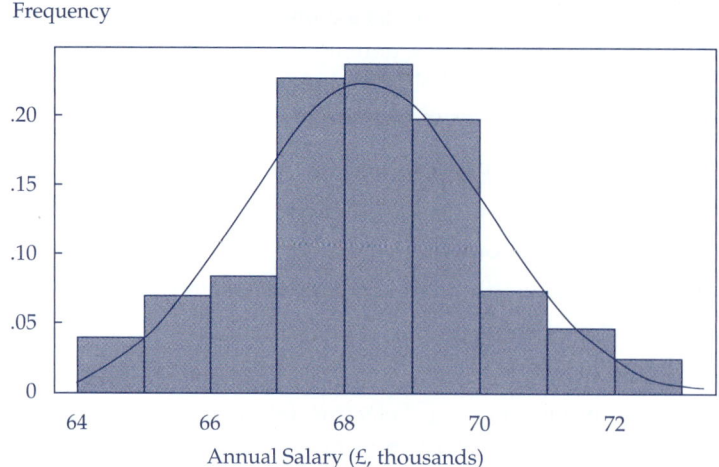

For data with two or more dimensions, summary statistics of relationships, such as a correlation matrix, can be calculated. Two- or more-dimensional visualization explores interactions between different features in the dataset. Common methods include scatterplots and line graphs. In multi-dimensional visualization, one-dimensional plots are overlaid to summarize each feature, thus enabling comparison between features. Additionally, attributes (e.g., color, shape, and size) and legends can be used creatively to pack more information about the data into fewer graphs.

For multivariate data, commonly utilized exploratory visualization designs include stacked bar and line charts, multiple box plots, and scatterplots showing multivariate data that use different colors or shapes for each feature. Multiple box plots can be arranged in a single chart, where each individual box plot represents a feature. Such a multi-box plot chart assesses the relationship between each feature (x-axis) in the dataset and the target variable of interest (y-axis). The multi-box plot chart in Exhibit 15 represents units of shares purchased versus stock price for a hypothetical stock. The x-axis shows the stock price in increments of $0.125, and the y-axis shows units of shares purchased. The individual box plots indicate the distribution of shares purchased at the different stock prices. When the stock price is $0.25, the median number of shares purchased is the highest; when the stock price is $0.625, the median number of shares purchased is the lowest. However, visually it appears that the number of shares purchased at different stock prices is not significantly different.

Exhibit 15: Multiple Box Plots in One Chart

Units of Shares Purchased

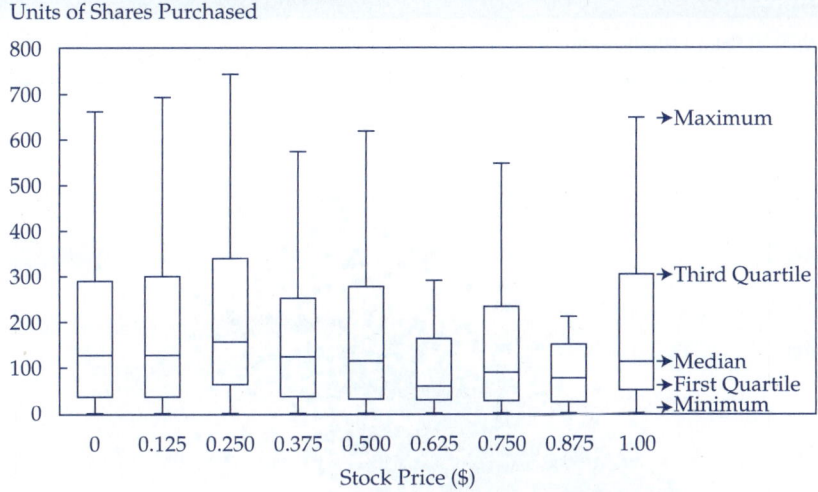

Two-dimensional charts can summarize and approximately measure relationships between two or more features. An example scatterplot in Exhibit 16 shows the interaction of two hypothetical features: age (x-axis) and annual salary (y-axis). The feature on the y-axis tends to increase as the feature on the x-axis increases. This pattern appears true visually; however, it may not be a statistically significant relationship. A scatterplot provides a starting point where relationships can be examined visually. These potential relationships should be tested further using statistical tests. Common parametric statistical tests include ANOVA, *t*-test, and Pearson correlation. Common non-parametric statistical tests include chi-square and the Spearman rank-order correlation.

Exhibit 16: Scatterplot Showing a Linear Relationship Between Two Features

Annual Salary (thousands)

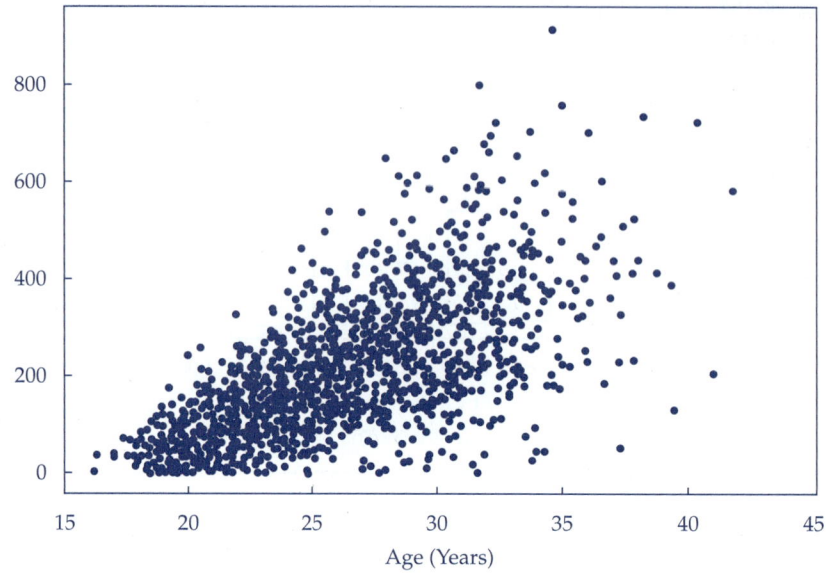

Age (Years)

In addition to visualization, descriptive statistics are a good means to summarize data. Central tendency measures as well as minimum and maximum values for continuous data are useful. Counts and frequencies for categorical data are commonly employed to gain insight regarding the distribution of possible values.

EDA is not only useful for revealing possible relationships among features or general trends in the data; it is also beneficial during the feature selection and engineering stages. These possible relationships and trends in the data may be used to suggest new features that, when incorporated into a model, may improve model training.

Feature Selection

Structured data consist of features, represented by different columns of data in a table or matrix. After using EDA to discover relevant patterns in the data, it is essential to identify and remove unneeded, irrelevant, and redundant features. Basic diagnostic testing should also be performed on features to identify redundancy, heteroscedasticity, and multi-collinearity. The objective of the feature selection process is to assist in identifying significant features that when used in a model retain the important patterns and complexities of the larger dataset while requiring fewer data overall. This last point is important since computing power is not free (i.e., explicit costs and processing time).

Typically, structured data even after the data preparation step can contain features that do not contribute to the accuracy of an ML model or that negatively affect the quality of ML training. The most desirable outcome is a parsimonious model with fewer features that provides the maximum predictive power out-of-sample.

Feature selection must not be confused with the data preprocessing steps during data preparation. Good feature selection requires an understanding of the data and statistics, and comprehensive EDA must be performed to assist with this step. Data preprocessing needs clarification only from data administrators and basic intuition (e.g., salary vs. income) during data preparation.

Feature selection on structured data is a methodical and iterative process. Statistical measures can be used to assign a score gauging the importance of each feature. The features can then be ranked using this score and either retained or eliminated from the dataset. The statistical methods utilized for this task are usually univariate and consider each feature independently or with regard to the target variable. Methods include chi-square test, correlation coefficients, and information-gain measures (i.e., R-squared values from regression analysis). All of these statistical methods can be combined in a manner that uses each method individually on each feature, automatically performing backward and forward passes over features to improve feature selection. Prebuilt feature selection functions are available in popular programming languages used to build and train ML models.

Dimensionality reduction assists in identifying the features in the data that account for the greatest variance between observations and allows for the processing of a reduced volume of data. Dimensionality reduction may be implemented to reduce a large number of features, which helps reduce the memory needed and speed up learning algorithms. Feature selection is different from dimensionality reduction, but both methods seek to reduce the number of features in the dataset. The dimensionality reduction method creates new combinations of features that are uncorrelated, whereas feature selection includes and excludes features present in the data without altering them.

Feature Engineering

After the appropriate features are selected, feature engineering helps further optimize and improve the features. The success of ML model training depends on how well the data are presented to the model. The feature engineering process attempts to produce good features that describe the structures inherent in the dataset. This process depends on the context of the project, domain of the data, and nature of the problem. Structured data are likely to contain quantities, which can be engineered to better present relevant patterns in the dataset. This action involves engineering an existing feature into a new feature or decomposing it into multiple features.

For continuous data, a new feature may be created—for example, by taking the logarithm of the product of two or more features. As another example, when considering a salary or income feature, it may be important to recognize that different salary brackets impose a different taxation rate. Domain knowledge can be used to decompose an income feature into different tax brackets, resulting in a new feature: "income_above_100k," with possible values 0 and 1. The value 1 under the new feature captures the fact that a subject has an annual salary of more than $100,000. By grouping subjects into income categories, assumptions about income tax can be made and utilized in a model that uses the income tax implications of higher and lower salaries to make financial predictions.

For categorical data, for example, a new feature can be a combination (e.g., sum or product) of two features or a decomposition of one feature into many. If a single categorical feature represents education level with five possible values—high school, associates, bachelor's, master's, and doctorate—then these values can be decomposed into five new features, one for each possible value (e.g., is_highSchool, is_doctorate) filled with 0s (for false) and 1s (for true). The process in which categorical variables are converted into binary form (0 or 1) for machine reading is called **one hot encoding**. It is one of the most common methods for handling categorical features in text data. When date-time is present in the data, such features as "second of the hour," "hour of the day," and "day of the date" can be engineered to capture critical information about temporal data attributes—which are important, for example, in modeling trading algorithms.

Feature engineering techniques systemically alter, decompose, or combine existing features to produce more meaningful features. More meaningful features allow an ML model to train more swiftly and easily. Different feature engineering strategies can lead to the generation of dramatically different results from the same ML model. The impact of feature selection and engineering on ML training is discussed further in the next section.

6   UNSTRUCTURED DATA: TEXT EXPLORATION

- [ ] describe objectives, methods, and examples of data exploration
- [ ] describe methods for extracting, selecting and engineering features from textual data

Exploratory Data Analysis

Just like with structured data, it is important to gain insight into existing patterns in the unstructured data for further analysis. In this section, text data will be discussed. Text analytics has various applications. The most common applications are text classification, topic modeling, fraud detection, and sentiment analysis. Text classification uses supervised ML approaches to classify texts into different classes. Topic modeling uses unsupervised ML approaches to group the texts in the dataset into topic clusters. Sentiment analysis predicts sentiment (negative, neutral, or positive) of the texts in a dataset using both supervised and unsupervised approaches.

Various statistics are used to explore, summarize, and analyze text data. Text data include a collection of texts (also known as a corpus) that are sequences of tokens. It is useful to perform EDA of text data by computing on the tokens such basic text statistics as **term frequency (TF)**, the ratio of the number of times a given token occurs in all the texts in the dataset to the total number of tokens in the dataset (e.g., word associations, average word and sentence length, and word and syllable counts).

Text statistics reveal patterns in the co-occurrence of words. There are many applications of text analytics, and necessary text statistics vary according to the context of the application. Topic modeling is a text data application in which the words that are most informative are identified by calculating the TF of each word. For example, the word "soccer" can be informative for the topic "sports." The words with high TF values are eliminated as they are likely to be stop words or other common vocabulary words, making the resulting BOW compact and more likely to be relevant to topics within the texts. In sentiment analysis and text classification applications, the chi-square measure of word association can be useful for understanding the significant word appearances in negative and positive sentences in the text or in different documents. The chi-square measure is further explained under feature selection. Such EDA plays a vital role in executing the feature selection step.

Text statistics can be visually comprehended by using the same methods as explained in the structured data section. For example, bar charts can be used to show word counts or frequency. Words clouds are common visualizations when working with text data as they can be made to visualize the most informative words and their TF values. The most commonly occurring words in the dataset can be shown by varying font size, and color is used to add more dimensions, such as frequency and length of words. Exhibit 17 shows a word cloud constructed from a sample dataset of generic financial news wires after text processing. Word cloud building functions and packages are available in several popular programming languages. A detailed demonstration of text data EDA will be presented in Section 7, where we work with actual text data in a financial forecasting project.

Exhibit 17: Word Cloud of Generic Financial Newsfeed Data Sample

Feature Selection

For text data, feature selection involves selecting a subset of the terms or tokens occurring in the dataset. The tokens serve as features for ML model training. Feature selection in text data effectively decreases the size of the vocabulary or BOW. This helps the ML model be more efficient and less complex. Another benefit is to eliminate noisy features from the dataset. Noisy features are tokens that do not contribute to ML model training and actually might detract from the ML model accuracy.

Noisy features are both the most frequent and most sparse (or rare) tokens in the dataset. On one end, noisy features can be stop words that are typically present frequently in all the texts across the dataset. On the other end, noisy features can be sparse terms that are present in only a few text cases. Text classification involves dividing text documents into assigned classes (a class is a category; examples include "relevant" and "irrelevant" text documents or "bearish" and "bullish" sentences). The *frequent* tokens strain the ML model to choose a decision boundary among the texts as the terms are present across all the texts, an example of model *underfitting*. The *rare* tokens mislead the ML model into classifying texts containing the rare terms into a specific class, an example of model *overfitting*. Identifying and removing noise features is very critical for text classification applications. The general feature selection methods in text data are as follows:

1. *Frequency* measures can be used for vocabulary pruning to remove noise features by filtering the tokens with very high and low TF values across all the texts. **Document frequency (DF)** is another frequency measure that helps to discard the noise features that carry no specific information about the text class and are present across all texts. The DF of a token is defined

as the number of documents (texts) that contain the respective token divided by the total number of documents. It is the simplest feature selection method and often performs well when many thousands of tokens are present.

2. *Chi-square* test can be useful for feature selection in text data. The chi-square test is applied to test the independence of two events: occurrence of the token and occurrence of the class. The test ranks the tokens by their usefulness to each class in text classification problems. Tokens with the highest chi-square test statistic values occur more frequently in texts associated with a particular class and therefore can be selected for use as features for ML model training due to higher discriminatory potential.

3. *Mutual information* (MI) measures how much information is contributed by a token to a class of texts. The **mutual information** value will be equal to 0 if the token's distribution in all text classes is the same. The MI value approaches 1 as the token in any one class tends to occur more often in only that particular class of text. Exhibit 18 shows a simple depiction of some tokens with high MI scores for their corresponding text classes. Note how the tokens (or features) with the highest MI values narrowly relate to their corresponding text class name.

Exhibit 18: Tokens with Mutual Information (MI) Values for Two Given Text Classes			
Text Classes: Sports or Politics			
Sports		**Politics**	
Token	**MI Value**	**Token**	**MI Value**
soccer	0.0781	election	0.0612
cup	0.0525	president	0.0511
match	0.0456	polls	0.0341
play	0.0387	vote	0.0288
game	0.0299	party	0.0202
team	0.0265	candidate	0.0201
win	0.0189	campaign	0.0201

Feature Engineering

As with structured data, feature engineering can greatly improve ML model training and remains a combination of art and science. The following are some techniques for feature engineering, which may overlap with text processing techniques.

1. *Numbers*: In text processing, numbers are converted into a token, such as "/number/." However, numbers can be of different lengths of digits representing different kinds of numbers, so it may be useful to convert different numbers into different tokens. For example, numbers with four digits may indicate years, and numbers with many digits could be an identification number. Four-digit numbers can be replaced with "/number4/," 10-digit numbers with "/number10/," and so forth.

2. *N-grams*: Multi-word patterns that are particularly discriminative can be identified and their connection kept intact. For example, "market" is a common word that can be indicative of many subjects or classes; the words "stock market" are used in a particular context and may be helpful to distinguish general texts from finance-related texts. Here, a bigram would be useful as it treats the two adjacent words as a single token (e.g., stock_market).

3. *Name entity recognition (NER)*: NER is an extensive procedure available as a library or package in many programming languages. The **name entity recognition** algorithm analyzes the individual tokens and their surrounding semantics while referring to its dictionary to tag an object class to the token. Exhibit 19 shows the NER tags of the text *"CFA Institute was formed in 1947 and is headquartered in Virginia."* Additional object classes are, for example, MONEY, TIME, and PERCENT, which are not present in the example text. The NER tags, when applicable, can be used as features for ML model training for better model performance. NER tags can also help identify critical tokens on which such operations as lowercasing and stemming then can be avoided (e.g., Institute here refers to an organization rather than a verb). Such techniques make the features more discriminative.

Exhibit 19: Name Entity Recognition and Parts of Speech (POS) on Example Text

Token	NER Tag	POS Tag	POS Description
CFA	ORGANIZATION	NNP	Proper noun
Institute	ORGANIZATION	NNP	Proper noun
was		VBD	Verb, past tense
formed		VBN	Verb, past participle
in		IN	Preposition
1947	DATE	CD	Cardinal number
and		CC	Coordinating conjunction
is		VBZ	Verb, 3rd person singular present
headquartered		VBN	Verb, past participle
in		IN	Preposition
Virginia	LOCATION	NNP	Proper noun

4. *Parts of speech (POS)*: Similar to NER, **parts of speech** uses language structure and dictionaries to tag every token in the text with a corresponding part of speech. Some common POS tags are noun, verb, adjective, and proper noun. Exhibit 19 shows the POS tags and descriptions of tags for the example text. POS tags can be used as features for ML model training and to identify the number of tokens that belong to each POS tag. If a given text contains many proper nouns, it means that it may be related to people and organizations and may be a business topic. POS tags can be useful for separating verbs and nouns for text analytics. For example, the word "market" can be a verb when used as "to market …" or noun when used as "in the market." Differentiating such tokens can help further clarify the meaning of the text. The use of "market" as a verb could indicate that the text relates to the topic of marketing and might discuss marketing a product or service. The use of "market" as a noun could suggest that the text relates

to a physical or stock market and might discuss stock trading. Also for POS tagging, such compound nouns as "CFA Institute" can be treated as a single token. POS tagging can be performed using libraries or packages in programming languages.

In addition, many more creative techniques convey text information in a structured way to the ML training process. The goal of feature engineering is to maintain the semantic essence of the text while simplifying and converting it into structured data for ML.

EXAMPLE 4

Data Exploration

Paul Wang's analytics team at LendALot Corporation has completed its initial data preparation and wrangling related to their creditworthiness classification ML model building efforts. As a next step, Wang has asked one of the team members, Eric Kim, to examine the available structured data sources to see what types of exploratory data analysis might make sense. Kim has been tasked with reporting to the team on high-level patterns and trends in the data and which variables seem interesting. Greater situational awareness about the data can inform the team's decisions regarding model training and whether (and how) to incorporate textual big data in conjunction with the structured data inputs. Use the following sample of columns and rows Kim pulled for manual examination to answer the next questions.

1	ID	Loan Outcome	Income (USD)	Loan Amount (USD)	Credit Score	Loan Type	Free Responses to "Explain Credit Score" (excerpts from full text)
2	1	No Default	34,000	10,000	685	Mortgage	I am embarrassed that my score is below 700, but it was due to mitigating circumstances. I have developed a plan to improve my score.
3	2	No Default	63,050	49,000	770	Student Loan	I have a good credit score and am constantly looking to further improve it...
4	3	Defaulted	20,565	35,000	730	Student Loan	I think I have great credit. I don't think there are any issues. Having to provide a written response to these questions is kind of annoying...
5	4	No Default	50,021	10,000	664	Mortgage	I have a decent credit score. I regret not being as responsible in the past but feel I have worked hard to improve my score recently...
6	5	Defaulted	100,350	129,000	705	Car Loan	Honestly, my score probably would have been higher if I had worked harder. But it is probably good enough...
7	6	No Default	800,000	300,000	800	Boat Loan	I have worked hard to maintain a good credit rating. I am very responsible. I maintain a payment schedule and always stick to the payment plan...

1. Evaluate whether data visualization techniques, such as histograms, box plots, and scatterplots, could be relevant to exploratory data analysis.

Solution

The data provided include structured features (ID, Loan Outcome, Income, Loan Amount, Credit Score) and unstructured data. Histograms, box plots, and scatterplots are relevant visualization methods for structured data features. Histograms and box plots could be used by Kim to see how income, loan amount, and credit score are distributed. Moreover, these visualizations can be performed across all historical borrowing instances in the dataset as well as within the sets of defaulted loans versus non-defaulted loans. Scatterplots of income versus loan amount, income versus credit score, and loan amount versus credit score, both overall and within defaulted and non-defaulted datasets, can shed light on relationships between potentially important continuous variables.

2. State one visualization technique that could be used in relation to the free responses.

Solution

For the text in the free response field, word clouds offer an appropriate starting point for exploratory analysis. A word cloud can enable a quick glimpse into the most frequently occurring words (i.e., term frequency). While some obvious words (e.g., "credit" and "score") may be valuable, other frequently occurring words (e.g., "worked," "hard," "probably," "embarrassed," "regret," "good," "decent," and "great") might have potential use for creditworthiness prediction.

3. Describe how ranking methods can be used to select potentially interesting features to report back to the team.

Solution

Kim can use feature selection methods to rank all features. Since the target variable of interest (loan outcome) is discrete in this case, such techniques as chi-square and information gain would be well suited. These are univariate techniques that can score feature variables individually. In addition to the structured features, these univariate ranking methods can also be applied to word count-related features, such as term frequency and document frequency, that are derived from the text using frequently occurring words. Such frequently occurring words (e.g., "worked" and "hard") can be identified from the word cloud.

4. State an example of a bigram from the free response texts that could be used to discriminate among loan outcomes.

Solution

The bigrams "credit_score" and "worked_hard" from the text in the free response section may have potential to discriminate among loan outcomes.

EXAMPLE 5

Textual Feature Representations for ML Model Building

Having completed their exploration of the data, Paul Wang's analytics team at LendALot Corporation recognizes the importance of incorporating features derived from text data in their ML models for classifying creditworthiness. Wang has asked his colleagues, Lynn Lee and Eric Kim, to propose textual feature representations that might be well suited to constructing features for their task. As a starting point, Lee and Kim review the following sample of data:

1	ID	Loan Outcome	Income (USD)	Loan Amount (USD)	Credit Score	Loan Type	Free Responses to "Explain Credit Score" (excerpts from full text)
2	1	No Default	34,000	10,000	685	Mortgage	I am embarrassed that my score is below 700, but it was due to mitigating circumstances. I have developed a plan to improve my score.
3	2	No Default	63,050	49,000	770	Student Loan	I have a good credit score and am constantly looking to further improve it…
4	3	Defaulted	20,565	35,000	730	Student Loan	I think I have great credit. I don't think there are any issues. Having to provide a written response to these questions is kind of annoying…
5	4	No Default	50,021	10,000	664	Mortgage	I have a decent credit score. I regret not being as responsible in the past but feel I have worked hard to improve my score recently…
6	5	Defaulted	100,350	129,000	705	Car Loan	Honestly, my score probably would have been higher if I had worked harder. But it is probably good enough…
7	6	No Default	800,000	300,000	800	Boat Loan	I have worked hard to maintain a good credit rating. I am very responsible. I maintain a payment schedule and always stick to the payment plan…

Based on the information given, address the following questions.

1. Describe three textual feature representations that Lee and Kim should consider for their text data.

Solution 1:

Lee and Kim should consider bag-of-words (BOW), n-grams, and parts-of-speech (POS) as key textual feature representations for their text data. Conversely, name entity recognition (NER) might not be as applicable in this context because the data on prospective borrowers does not include any explicit references to people, locations, dates, or organizations.

2. Describe a rationale for adopting each of the three textual feature representations identified in Question 1.

Solution 2:

All three textual feature representations have the potential to add value.

Bag-of-words (BOW) is typically applicable in most contexts involving text features derived from languages where token boundaries are explicitly present (e.g., English) or can be inferred through processing (e.g., a different language, such as Spanish). BOW is generally the best starting point for most projects exploring text feature representations.

N-grams, representations of word or token sequences, are also applicable. N-grams can offer invaluable contextual information that can complement and enrich a BOW. In this specific credit-worthiness context, we examine the BOW token "worked." It appears three times (rows 5–7), twice in no-default loan texts and once in a defaulted loan text. This finding suggests that "worked" is being used to refer to the borrower's work ethic and may be a good predictor of credit worthiness. Digging deeper and looking at several trigrams (i.e., three-token sequences) involving "worked," we see that "have_worked_hard" appears in the two no-default loan related texts (referring to borrower accomplishments and plans) and "had_worked_harder" appears in the defaulted loan text (referring to what could have been done). This example illustrates how n-grams can provide richer contextualization capabilities for the creditworthiness prediction ML models.

Parts-of-speech tags can add value because they identify the composition of the texts. For example, POS provides information on whether the prospective borrowers are including many action words (verbs) or descriptors (adjectives) and whether this is being done differently in instances of no-default versus instances of defaulted loans.

MODEL TRAINING, STRUCTURED VS. UNSTRUCTURED DATA, AND METHOD SELECTION

7

☐ | describe objectives, steps, and techniques in model training

Machine learning model training is a systematic, iterative, and recursive process. The number of iterations required to reach optimum results depends on:

- the nature of the problem and input data and
- the level of model performance needed for practical application.

Machine learning models combine multiple principles and operations to provide predictions. As seen in the last two sections, typical ML model building requires data preparation and wrangling (cleansing and preprocessing) and data exploration (exploratory data analysis as well as feature selection and engineering). In addition, domain knowledge related to the nature of the data is required for good model building and training. For instance, knowledge of investment management and securities trading is important when using financial data to train a model for predicting costs of trading stocks. It is crucial for ML engineers and domain experts to work together in building and training robust ML models.

The three tasks of ML model training are method selection, performance evaluation, and tuning. Exhibit 20 outlines model training and its three component tasks. Method selection is the art and science of deciding which ML method(s) to incorporate and is guided by such considerations as the classification task, type of data, and size of data. Performance evaluation entails using an array of complementary techniques and measures to quantify and understand a model's performance. Tuning is the process of undertaking decisions and actions to improve model performance. These steps may be repeated multiple times until the desired level of ML model performance is attained. Although no standard rulebook for training an ML model exists, having a fundamental understanding of domain-specific training data and ML algorithm principles plays a vital role in good model training.

Exhibit 20: Model Training Stage

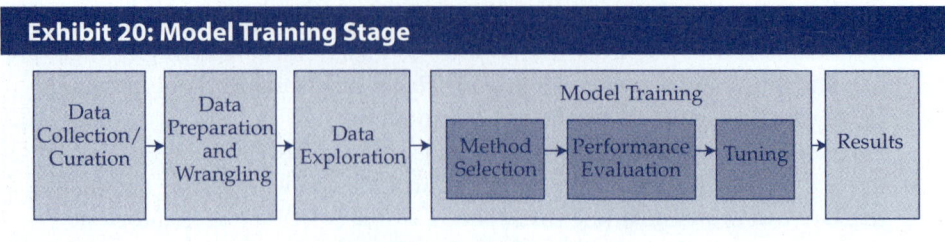

Before training a model, it is important to state the problem, define objectives, identify useful data points, and conceptualize the model. Conceptualization is like a blueprint on a drawing board, a modifiable plan that is necessary to initiate the model training process. Because modeling is an iterative process, many changes and refinements will be made to the model plan as the process evolves.

Structured and Unstructured Data

The ML model training process for structured and unstructured data is typically the same. Most ML models are intended to train on structured data, so unstructured data in the data preparation stage are processed and organized into a structured format. The systematic processing of unstructured text data so that they can be structured in the form of a data matrix has been previously covered. Similarly, other forms of unstructured data can also be prepared and formed into data matrixes or tables for ML training.

The fundamental idea of ML model training is fitting a system of rules on a training dataset to reveal a pattern in the data. In other words, fitting describes the degree to which (or how well) an ML model can be generalized to new data. A good model fit results in good model performance and can be validated using new data outside of the training dataset (i.e., out-of-sample). Exhibit 21 shows model decision boundaries in three possible model fitting scenarios for a classification task comprising two different classes of data (i.e., circles and triangles). The model on the left is underfit; it does not fit the training data well enough since it results in four misclassification errors (three circles and one triangle). Although the center model that generates the "S"-shaped line has the best accuracy (no errors) on the training data, it is overfit (i.e., fits the training data too well) and thus unlikely to perform well on future test cases. The model on the right (with one classification error, a circle) is a model with good fit (i.e., it fits the training data well but not so well that it cannot be generalized to out-of-sample data).

Exhibit 21: Model Fitting Scenarios: Underfit, Overfit, and Good Fit

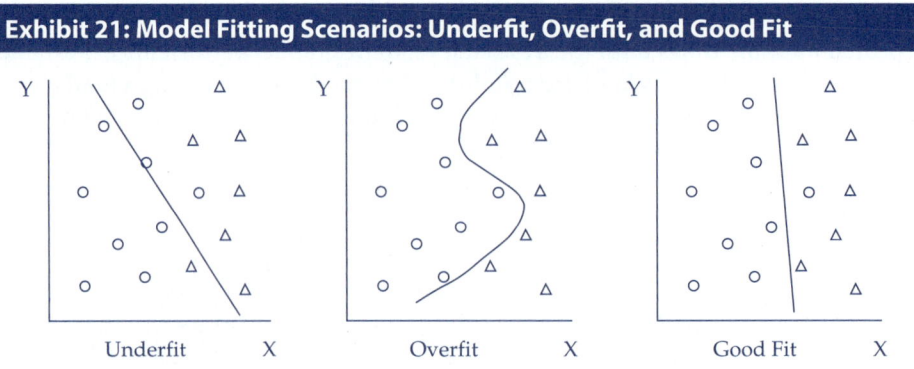

Model fitting errors are caused by several factors—the main ones being dataset size and number of features in the dataset.

- *Dataset Size*: Small datasets can lead to underfitting of the model since small datasets often are not sufficient to expose patterns in the data. Restricted by a small dataset, an ML model may not recognize important patterns.

- *Number of Features*: A dataset with a small number of features can lead to underfitting, and a dataset with a large number of features can lead to overfitting. As with small dataset size, a small number of features may not carry all the characteristics that explain relationships between the target variable and the features. Conversely, a large number of features can complicate the model and potentially distort patterns in the data due to low degrees of freedom, causing overfitting. Therefore, appropriate feature selection using the types of techniques described earlier (e.g., chi-square, mutual information) is a key factor in minimizing such model overfitting.

Feature engineering tends to prevent underfitting in the training of the model. New features, when engineered properly, can elevate the underlying data points that better explain the interactions of features. Thus, feature engineering can be critical to overcome underfitting. Method-related factors that affect model fitting are explained shortly under tuning.

Method Selection

ML model training is a craft (part art and part science); it has no strict guidelines. Selecting and applying a method or an algorithm is the first step of the training process. Method selection is governed by the following factors:

1. *Supervised or unsupervised learning.* The data for training and testing supervised ML models contain **ground truth**, the known outcome (i.e., target variable) of each observation in these datasets. Unsupervised ML modeling is relatively challenging because of the absence of ground truth (i.e., no target variable). Supervised models bring a structure that may or may not be supported by the data. Unsupervised models bring no structure beyond that which arises from the given data. For supervised learning (with labeled training data), typical methods of choice are regression, ensemble trees, support vector machines (SVMs), and neural networks (NNs). Supervised learning would be used, for example, for default prediction based on high-yield corporate bond issuer data. For unsupervised learning, common methods are dimensionality reduction, clustering, and anomaly detection. Unsupervised learning, for example, would be used for clustering financial institutions into different groups based on their financial attributes.

2. *Type of data.* For numerical data (e.g., predicting stock prices using historical stock market values), classification and regression tree (CART) methods may be suitable. For text data (for example, predicting the topic of a financial news article by reading the headline of the article), such methods as generalized linear models (GLMs) and SVMs are commonly used. For image data (e.g., identifying objects in a satellite image, such as tanker ships moving in and out of port), NNs and deep learning methods tend to perform better than others. For speech data (e.g., predicting financial sentiment from quarterly earnings' conference call recordings), deep learning methods can offer promising results.

3. *Size of data.* A typical dataset has two basic characteristics: number of instances (i.e., observations) and number of features. The combination of these two characteristics can govern which method is most suitable for model training. For instance, SVMs have been found to work well on

"wider" datasets with 10,000 to 100,000 features and with fewer instances. Conversely, NNs often work better on "longer" datasets, where the number of instances is much larger than the number of features.

Once a method is selected, certain method-related decisions (e.g., on hyperparameters) need to be made. These decisions include the number of hidden layers in a neural network and the number of trees in ensemble methods (discussed later in the sub-section on tuning). In practice, datasets can be a combination of numerical and text data. To deal with mixed data, the results from more than one method can be combined. Sometimes, the predictions from one method can be used as predictors (features) by another. For example, unstructured financial text data can be used with logistic regression to classify stock sentiment as either positive or negative. Then, this sentiment classification cam be used as a predictor in a larger model, say CART, that also uses structured financial data as predictors for the purpose of stock selection. Finally, more than one method can be used and the results combined with quantitative or subjective weighing to exploit the advantages of each method.

Before model training begins, in the case of supervised learning the master dataset is split into three subsets used for model training and testing purposes. The first subset, a training set used to train the model, should constitute approximately 60% of the master dataset. The second subset, a cross-validation set (or validation set) used to tune and validate the model, should constitute approximately 20% of the master dataset. The third subset is a test set for testing the model and uses the remaining data. The data are split using a random sampling technique, such as the k-fold method. A commonly recommended split ratio is 60:20:20, as detailed above; however, the split percentages can vary. For unsupervised learning, no splitting is needed due to the absence of labeled training data.

Class imbalance, where the number of instances for a particular class is significantly larger than for other classes, may be a problem for data used in supervised learning because the ML classification method's objective is to train a high-accuracy model. In a high-yield bond default prediction example, say for corporate issuers in the BB+/Ba1 to B+/B1 credit quality range, issuers who defaulted (positive or "1" class) would be very few compared to issuers who did not default (negative or "0" class). Hence, on such training data, a naive model that simply assumes no corporate issuer will default may achieve good accuracy—albeit with all default cases misclassified. Balancing the training data can help alleviate such problems. In cases of unbalanced data, the "0" class (majority class) can be randomly undersampled or the "1" class (minority class) randomly oversampled. The random sampling can be done with or without replacement because they both work the same in general probability theory. Exhibit 22 depicts the idea of undersampling of the majority class and oversampling of the minority class. In practice, the choice of whether to undersample or oversample depends on the specific problem context. Advanced techniques can also reproduce synthetic observations from the existing data, and the new observations can be added to the dataset to balance the minority class.

Exhibit 22: Undersampling and Oversampling

Undersampling Majority Class ("0" class)

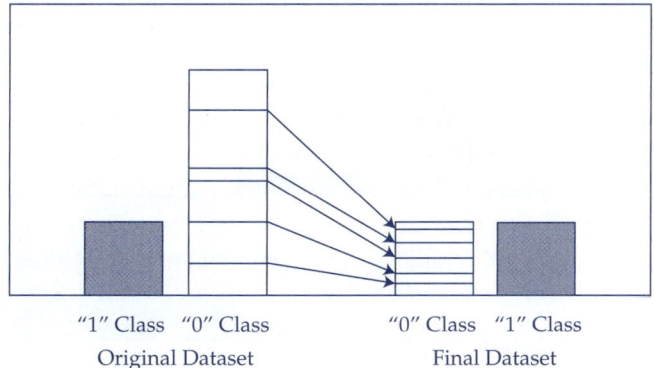

"1" Class   "0" Class   "0" Class   "1" Class
Original Dataset   Final Dataset

Oversampling Minority Class ("1" class)

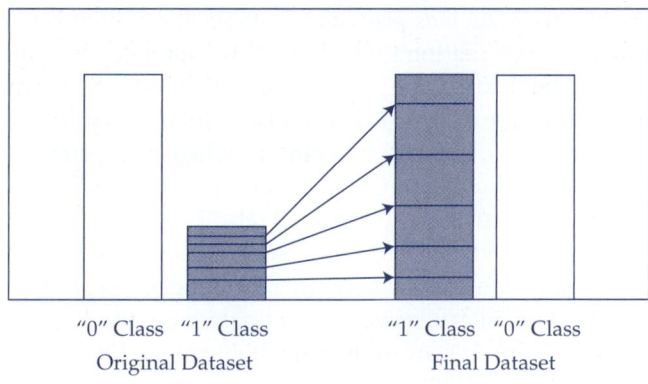

"0" Class   "1" Class   "1" Class   "0" Class
Original Dataset   Final Dataset

PERFORMANCE EVALUATION

8

☐ | describe objectives, steps, and techniques in model training

It is important to measure the model training performance or goodness of fit for validation of the model. We shall cover several techniques to measure model performance that are well suited specifically for binary classification models.

1. *Error analysis.* For classification problems, error analysis involves computing four basic evaluation metrics: true positive (TP), false positive (FP), true negative (TN), and false negative (FN) metrics. FP is also called a Type I error, and FN is also called a Type II error. Exhibit 23 shows a **confusion matrix**, a grid that is used to summarize values of these four metrics.

Exhibit 23: Confusion Matrix for Error Analysis

Actual Training Labels

	Class "1"	Class "0"
Class "1"	True Positives (TP)	False Positives (FP) Type I Error
Class "0"	False Negatives (FN) Type II Error	True Negatives (TN)

Predicted Results

Additional metrics, such as precision and recall, can be computed. Assume in the following explanation that Class "0" is "not defective" and Class "1" is "defective." **Precision** is the ratio of correctly predicted positive classes to all predicted positive classes. Precision is useful in situations where the cost of FP, or Type I error, is high—or example, when an expensive product fails quality inspection (predicted Class "1") and is scrapped, but it is actually perfectly good (actual Class "0"). **Recall** (also known as *sensitivity*) is the ratio of correctly predicted positive classes to all actual positive classes. Recall is useful in situations where the cost of FN or Type II error is high—for example, when an expensive product passes quality inspection (predicted Class "0") and is sent to the valued customer, but it is actually quite defective (actual Class "1"). The formulas for precision and recall are:

$$\text{Precision (P)} = TP/(TP + FP). \tag{3}$$

$$\text{Recall (R)} = TP/(TP + FN). \tag{4}$$

Trading off precision and recall is subject to business decisions and model application. Therefore, additional evaluation metrics that provide the overall performance of the model are generally used. The two overall performance metrics are accuracy and F1 score. **Accuracy** is the percentage of correctly predicted classes out of total predictions. **F1 score** is the harmonic mean of precision and recall. F1 score is more appropriate (than accuracy) when unequal class distribution is in the dataset and it is necessary to measure the equilibrium of precision and recall. High scores on both of these metrics suggest good model performance. The formulas for accuracy and F1 score are as follows:

$$\text{Accuracy} = (TP + TN)/(TP + FP + TN + FN). \tag{5}$$

$$\text{F1 score} = (2 * P * R)/(P + R). \tag{6}$$

Exhibit 24 illustrates computations of model evaluation metrics and performance scores on a sample dataset.

Exhibit 24: Performance Metrics and Scores Computation

Sample Dataset with Classification Results

Observation	Actual Training Labels	Predicted Results	Classification
1	1	1	TP
2	0	0	TN
3	1	1	TP
4	1	0	FN
5	1	1	TP
6	1	0	FN
7	0	0	TN
8	0	0	TN
9	0	0	TN
10	0	1	FP

Confusion Matrix

		Actual Training Labels	
		Class "1"	Class "0"
Predicted Results	Class "1"	3 (TP)	1 (FP)
	Class "0"	2 (FN)	4 (TN)

Performance Metrics

TP = 3, FP = 1, FN = 2, TN = 4

P = 3 / (3+1) = 0.75

R = 3 / (3+2) = 0.60

F1 Score = (2 × 0.75 × 0.60) / (0.75 + 0.60) = 0.67

Accuracy = (3 + 4) / (3 + 1 + 4 + 2) = 0.70

In Exhibit 24, if all "1" classes were predicted correctly (no FPs), the precision would have been equal to 1. If all "0" classes were predicted correctly (no FNs), the recall would have been equal to 1. Thus, the resulting F1 score would have been equal to 1. The precision of 0.75 and recall of 0.60 indicate that the model is better at minimizing FPs than FNs. To find the equilibrium between precision and recall, F1 score is calculated, which is equal to 0.67. The F1 score is closer to the smaller value among both precision and recall, giving the model a more appropriate score rather than just an arithmetic mean. Accuracy, the percentage of correct predictions (for both classes) made by the model, is equal to 0.70. Accuracy would be equal to 1 if all predictions were correct. As the number of "1" and "0" classes is equal in the dataset (i.e., a balanced dataset), accuracy can be considered an appropriate performance measure in this case. If the number of classes in a dataset is unequal; however, then F1 score should be used as the overall performance measure for the model.

2. *Receiver Operating Characteristic (ROC).* This technique for assessing model performance involves the plot of a curve showing the trade-off between the false positive rate (x-axis) and true positive rate (y-axis) for various cutoff points—for example, for the predicted probability (p) in a logistic regression. The formulas for false positive rate and true positive rate (note that true positive rate is the same as recall) are:

False positive rate (FPR) = FP/(TN + FP) and   (7)

True positive rate (TPR) = TP/(TP + FN).   (8)

If p from a logistic regression model for a given observation is greater than the cutoff point (or threshold), then the observation is classified as class = 1. Otherwise, the observation will be classified as class = 0.

The shape of the ROC curve provides insight into the model's performance. A more convex curve indicates better model performance. Area under the curve (AUC) is the metric that measures the area under the ROC curve. An AUC close to 1.0 indicates near perfect prediction, while an AUC of 0.5 signifies random guessing. Exhibit 25 displays three ROC curves and indicates their respective AUC values. It is clear from observing the shapes of the ROC curves and their AUCs that Model A—with the most convex ROC curve with AUC of more than 0.9 (or 90%)—is the best performing among the three models.

Exhibit 25: ROC Curves and AUCs

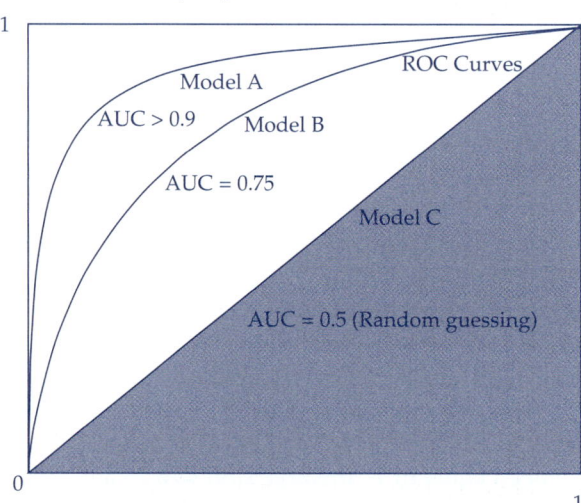

3. *Root Mean Squared Error (RMSE).* This measure is appropriate for continuous data prediction and is mostly used for regression methods. It is a single metric that captures all the prediction errors in the data (*n*). The root mean squared error is computed by finding the square root of the mean of the squared differences between the actual values and the model's predicted values (error). A small RMSE indicates potentially better model performance. The formula for RMSE is:

$$RMSE = \sqrt{\sum_{i=1}^{n} \frac{\left(\text{Predicted}_i - \text{Actual}_i\right)^2}{n}}.$$ (9)

TUNING

9

☐ | describe objectives, steps, and techniques in model training

Once the model is evaluated, certain decisions and actions must be taken based on the findings to improve the performance of the model. If the prediction error on the training set is high, the model is underfitting. If the prediction error on the cross-validation (CV) set is significantly higher than on the training set, the model is overfitting. Model fitting has two types of error: bias and variance. Bias error is associated with underfitting, and variance error is associated with overfitting. Bias error is high when a model is overly simplified and does not sufficiently learn from the patterns in the training data. Variance error is high when the model is overly complicated and memorizes the training data so much that it will likely perform poorly on new data. It is not possible to completely eliminate both types of errors. However, both errors can be minimized so the total aggregate error (bias error + variance error) is at a minimum. The bias–variance trade-off is critical to finding an optimum balance where a model neither underfits nor overfits.

1. *Parameters* are critical for a model and are dependent on the training data. Parameters are learned from the training data as part of the training process by an optimization technique. Examples of parameters include coefficients in regression, weights in NN, and support vectors in SVM.

2. *Hyperparameters* are used for estimating model parameters and are not dependent on the training data. Examples of hyperparameters include the regularization term (λ) in supervised models, activation function and number of hidden layers in NN, number of trees and tree depth in ensemble methods, k in k-nearest neighbor classification and k-means clustering, and p-threshold in logistic regression. Hyperparameters are manually set and tuned.

For example, if a researcher is using a logistic regression model to classify sentences from financial statements into positive or negative stock sentiment, the initial cutoff point for the trained model might be a p-threshold of 0.50 (50%). Therefore, any sentence for which the model produces a probability >50% is classified as having positive sentiment. The researcher can create a confusion matrix from the classification results (of running the CV dataset) to determine such model performance metrics as accuracy and F1 score. Next, the researcher can vary the logistic regression's p-threshold—say to 0.55 (55%), 0.60 (60%), or even 0.65 (65%)—and then re-run the CV set, create new confusion matrixes from the new classification results, and compare accuracy and F1 scores. Ultimately, the researcher would select the logistic regression model with a p-threshold value that produces classification results generating the highest accuracy and F1 scores. Note that the process just outlined will be demonstrated in Section 7.

There is no general formula to estimate hyperparameters. Thus, tuning heuristics and such techniques as grid search are used to obtain the optimum values of hyperparameters. **Grid search** is a method of systematically training an ML model by using various combinations of hyperparameter values, cross validating each model, and determining which combination of hyperparameter values ensures the best model performance. The model is trained using different combinations of hyperparameter values until the optimum set of values are found. Optimum values must result in similar performance of the model on training and CV datasets, meaning that the training error and CV error are close. This ensures that the model can be generalized to test data or to new data and thus is less likely to overfit. The plot of training errors for each value of a hyperparameter (i.e., changing model complexity) is called a fitting curve. Fitting curves provide visual insight on the model's performance (for the given hyperparameter and level of model complexity) on the training and CV datasets and are visually helpful to tune hyperparameters. Exhibit 26 shows the bias–variance error trade-off by plotting a generic fitting curve for a regularization hyperparameter (λ).

Exhibit 26: Fitting Curve for Regularization Hyperparameter (λ)

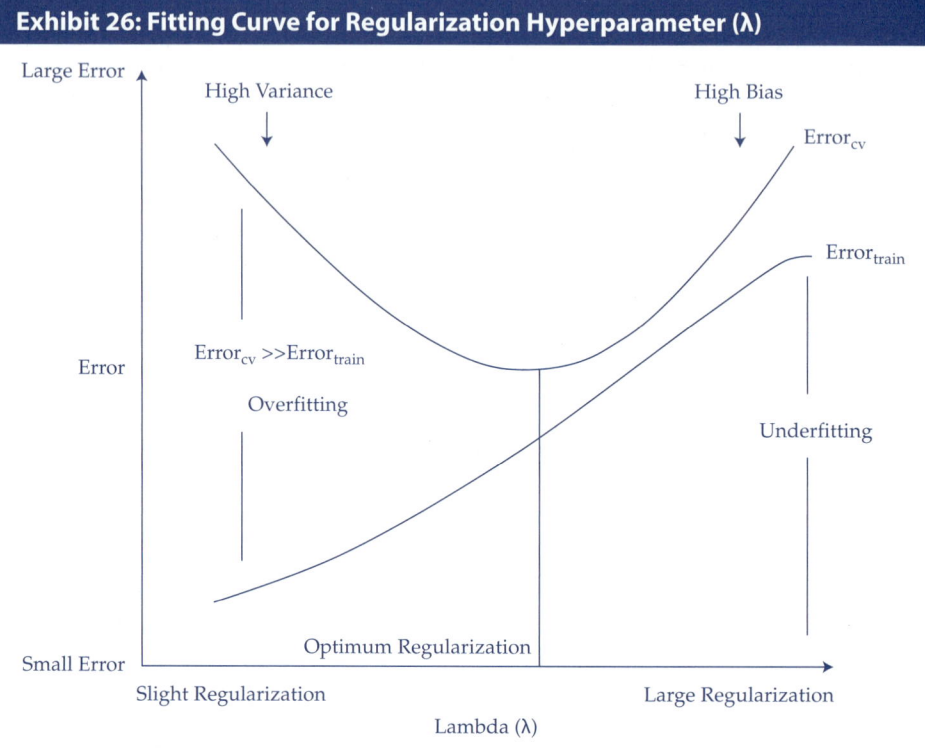

Slight regularization lightly penalizes model complexity, thereby allowing most or all of the features to be included in the model and thus potentially enabling the model to "memorize" the data. Typically with no or slight regularization, the prediction error on the training dataset is small while the prediction error on the CV dataset is significantly larger. This difference in error is variance. High variance error, which typically results from too many features and model complexity, results in model overfitting. When high variance error and low bias error exist, the model performs well on the training dataset but generates many FP and FN errors on the CV dataset; in other words, the model is overfitted and does not generalize to new data well.

Large regularization excessively penalizes model complexity, thereby allowing too few of the features to be included in the model and causing the model to learn less from the data. The model may lack the necessary predictor variables and complexity needed to discern underlying patterns in the data. Typically with large regularization, the prediction errors on the training and CV datasets are both large. Large prediction errors on the training dataset indicate high bias, and high bias error results from model underfitting. When high bias error exists, the model does not perform well on either training or CV datasets because it is typically lacking important predictor variables.

Optimum regularization minimizes both variance and bias errors in a balanced fashion. It penalizes model complexity just enough so that only the most important features are included in the model. This process prevents the model from memorizing the data while enabling the model to learn enough from the data to distinguish important patterns. This results in prediction errors in both training and CV datasets that are similar and also minimal. The range of optimum regularization values can be found heuristically using such techniques as grid search.

If high bias or variance exists after the tuning of hyperparameters, either a larger number of training examples (instances) may be needed or the number of features included in the model may need to be decreased (in the case of high variance) or increased (in the case of high bias). The model then needs to be re-trained and re-tuned using the new training dataset. In the case of a complex model, where a large model is comprised of sub-model(s), ceiling analysis can be performed. **Ceiling analysis** is a systematic process of evaluating different components in the pipeline of model building. It helps to understand what part of the pipeline can potentially improve in performance by further tuning. For example, a stock market prediction model needs historical data from the stock market and perhaps news articles related to the stocks. The sub-model will extract relevant information from the news articles or classify the sentiment of the news articles. The results of the sub-model will feed into the larger model as features. Thus, the performance of the larger model depends on performance of the sub-model(s). Ceiling analysis can help determine which sub-model needs to be tuned to improve the overall accuracy of the larger model.

FINANCIAL FORECASTING PROJECT 10

☐ | describe preparing, wrangling, and exploring text-based data for financial forecasting

Robo-readers are automated programs used to analyze large quantities of text, including news articles and social media. In the financial services space, robo-readers are being used by investors to examine how views expressed in text relate to future company performance. One important dimension that robo-readers look to analyze is sentiment polarity—which means how positive, negative, or neutral a particular phrase or statement is regarding a "target." For example, in the statement "XYZ Corporation is doing terrific things with its new product innovation," positive sentiment (i.e., the polarity) is being expressed regarding XYZ Corporation (i.e., the target of the sentiment). Such sentiment can provide invaluable predictive power, both alone and when coupled with structured financial data, for predicting stock price movements for individual firms and for portfolios of companies.

To provide a practical application, we use a financial forecasting project to examine how effectively sentiment—expressed in English news articles on LexisNexis (a searchable database of news articles) related to all companies listed on the NASDAQ OMX Helsinki (Finland)—can be classified. To accomplish this task, we followed the text ML model building steps presented in Sections 3 to 6 of this reading.

Text Curation, Preparation, and Wrangling

Text Curation

The text data used in this financial forecasting project are a collection of English language sentences from financial and economic news sources. The text data are acquired from the Financial Phrase Bank located on the website Researchgate.net.[2] The compressed folder contains six text files. The first two files are license and readme files. The other four files contain the text data. The data are presented in a text document format (.txt), which can be opened and viewed using any text editor. Note that this is cross-sectional data (not time series data).

A total of 14,780 sentences are in the four files. The sentiment of each sentence has already been labeled with one of three sentiment classes: positive, neutral, or negative. The sentiment classes are provided from an investor's perspective and may be useful for predicting whether a sentence may have a corresponding positive, neutral, or negative influence on the respective company's stock price.

This project uses sentences from two of the text files (Sentences_AllAgree and Sentences_75Agree), labeled as either in the positive or negative sentiment class, for a total of 2,180 sentences. There are 1,457 positive sentiment class sentences and 723 negative sentiment class sentences. A supervised ML model is trained, validated, and tested using these data. The final ML model can be used to predict the sentiment classes of sentences present in similar financial news statements. Exhibit 27 shows a sample of 10 rows of raw text from the Sentences_AllAgree text file. Note the sentiment annotations at the end of each sentence with prefix character "@."

Exhibit 27: Ten Sample Sentences and Sentiment from Raw Text File (Sentences_AllAgree.txt)

Profit before taxes amounted to EUR 56.5 mn , down from EUR 232.9 mn a year ago .@negative
Profit before taxes decreased by 9 % to EUR 187.8 mn in the first nine months of 2008 , compared to EUR 207.1 mn a year earlier .@negative
Profit before taxes decreased to EUR 31.6 mn from EUR 50.0 mn the year before .@negative
Profit before taxes was EUR 4.0 mn , down from EUR 4.9 mn .@negative
The company 's profit before taxes fell to EUR 21.1 mn in the third quarter of 2008 , compared to EUR 35.8 mn in the corresponding period in 2007 .@negative
In August-October 2010 , the company 's result before taxes totalled EUR 9.6 mn , up from EUR 0.5 mn in the corresponding period in 2009 .@positive
Finnish Bore that is owned by the Rettig family has grown recently through the acquisition of smaller shipping companies .@positive
The plan is estimated to generate some EUR 5 million (USD 6.5 m) in cost savings on an annual basis .@positive
Finnish pharmaceuticals company Orion reports profit before taxes of EUR 70.0 mn in the third quarter of 2010 , up from EUR 54.9 mn in the corresponding period in 2009 .@positive
Finnish Sampo Bank , of Danish Danske Bank group , reports profit before taxes of EUR 152.3 mn in 2010 , up from EUR 32.7 mn in 2009 .@positive

---

Text Preparation (Cleansing)

The raw text data (i.e., sentences) are initially organized into a data table. The data table contains two columns: The first column (sentence) is for the text, and the second column (sentiment) is for the corresponding sentiment class. The separator character, which is "@" in this case, is used to split the data into text and sentiment class columns. A collection of text data in any form, including list, matrix, or data table forms, is called a **corpus**. Exhibit 28 shows a sample of 10 sentences from the data table corpus.

Exhibit 28: Ten Sample Rows of the Data Table (Corpus)

Sentence	Sentiment
Profit before taxes amounted to EUR 56.5 mn , down from EUR 232.9 mn a year ago .	negative

---

2 https://www.researchgate.net/publication/251231364_FinancialPhraseBank-v10.

Sentence	Sentiment
Profit before taxes decreased by 9 % to EUR 187.8 mn in the first nine months of 2008 , compared to EUR 207.1 mn a year earlier .	negative
Profit before taxes decreased to EUR 31.6 mn from EUR 50.0 mn the year before .	negative
Profit before taxes was EUR 4.0 mn , down from EUR 4.9 mn .	negative
The company 's profit before taxes fell to EUR 21.1 mn in the third quarter of 2008 , compared to EUR 35.8 mn in the corresponding period in 2007 .	negative
In August-October 2010 , the company 's result before taxes totalled EUR 9.6 mn , up from EUR 0.5 mn in the corresponding period in 2009 .	positive
Finnish Bore that is owned by the Rettig family has grown recently through the acquisition of smaller shipping companies .	positive
The plan is estimated to generate some EUR 5 million (USD 6.5 m) in cost savings on an annual basis .	positive
Finnish pharmaceuticals company Orion reports profit before taxes of EUR 70.0 mn in the third quarter of 2010 , up from EUR 54.9 mn in the corresponding period in 2009 .	positive
Finnish Sampo Bank , of Danish Danske Bank group , reports profit before taxes of EUR 152.3 mn in 2010 , up from EUR 32.7 mn in 2009 .	positive

The raw text contains punctuations, numbers, and white spaces that may not be necessary for model training. Text cleansing involves removing, or incorporating appropriate substitutions for, potentially extraneous information present in the text. Operations to remove html tags are unnecessary because none are present in the text

Punctuations: Before stripping out punctuations, percentage and dollar symbols are substituted with word annotations to retain their essence in the financial texts. Such word annotation substitutions convey that percentage and currency-related tokens were involved in the text. As the sentences have already been identified within and extracted from the source text, punctuation helpful for identifying discrete sentences—such as periods, semi-colons, and commas—are removed. Some special characters, such as "+" and "©," are also removed. It is a good practice to implement word annotation substitutions before removing the rest of the punctuations.

Numbers: Numerical values of numbers in the text have no significant utility for sentiment prediction in this project because sentiment primarily depends on the words in a sentence. Here is an example sentence: *"Ragutis, which is based in Lithuania's second-largest city, Kaunas, boosted its sales last year 22.3 percent to 36.4 million litas."* The word "boosted" implies that there was growth in sales, so analysis of this sentiment does not need to rely on interpretation of numerical text data. Sentiment analysis typically does not involve extracting, interpreting, and calculating relevant numbers but instead seeks to understand the context in which the numbers are used. Other commonly occurring numbers are dates and years, which are also not required to predict sentence sentiment. Thus, all numbers present in the text are removed for this financial sentiment project. However, prior to removing numbers, abbreviations representing orders of magnitude, such as million (commonly represented by "m," "mln," or "mn"), billion, or trillion, are replaced with the complete word. Retaining these orders of magnitude-identifying words in the text preserves the original text meaning and can be useful in predicting sentence sentiment.

Whitespaces: White spaces are present in the raw text. Additional white spaces occur after performing the above operations to remove extraneous characters. The white spaces must be removed to keep the text intact. Exhibit 29 shows the sample text after cleansing. The cleansed text is free of punctuations and numbers, with useful substitutions.

Exhibit 29: Ten Sample Rows After Cleansing Process

Sentence	Sentiment
Profit before taxes amounted to EUR million down from EUR million a year ago	negative
Profit before taxes decreased by percentSign to EUR million in the first nine months of compared to EUR million a year earlier	negative
Profit before taxes decreased to EUR million from EUR million the year before	negative
Profit before taxes was EUR million down from EUR million	negative
The companys profit before taxes fell to EUR million in the third quarter of compared to EUR million in the corresponding period in	negative
In August October the companys result before taxes totalled EUR million up from EUR million in the corresponding period in	positive
Finnish Bore that is owned by the Rettig family has grown recently through the acquisition of smaller shipping companies	positive
The plan is estimated to generate some EUR million USD million in cost savings on an annual basis	positive
Finnish pharmaceuticals company Orion reports profit before taxes of EUR million in the third quarter of up from EUR million in the corresponding period in	positive
Finnish Sampo Bank of Danish Danske Bank group reports profit before taxes of EUR million in up from EUR million in	positive

Text Wrangling (Preprocessing)

The cleansed text needs to be normalized using the following normalization procedures:

1. *Lowercasing* of all text to consolidate duplicate words (example, "THE," "The," and "the").

2. *Stop words* are not removed because some stop words (e.g., not, more, very, and few) carry significant meaning in the financial texts that is useful for sentiment prediction. Some stop words, such as articles (a, an, the), may be removed. Nevertheless, to avoid confusion no words are removed at this point. This issue will be revisited during the data exploration stage, which will carefully examine the text using frequency analysis and find custom stop words (common words) for these particular text data.

3. *Stemming*, the converting of inflected forms of a word into its base word (stem), is performed on the text as it is simple to perform and is appropriate for training an ML model for sentiment prediction.

White spaces are stripped after performing these operations. As part of text normalization, different currency abbreviations, such as EUR and USD, can be converted into a single token, such as "currencysign." As we are dealing with financial domain text, the earlier substitution of dollarsign can be replaced with currencysign as well. This step will remove tokens that are different but redundant in nature while maintaining their meaning. Through careful examination of the text and use of domain knowledge, similar substitutions of redundant tokens can be performed. Exhibit 30 shows how the sample text appears after normalization.

Exhibit 30: Ten Sample Rows After Normalization Process

Sentence	Sentiment
profit befor tax amount to currencysign million down from currencysign million a year ago	negative
profit befor tax decreas by percentsign to currencysign million in the first nine month of compar to currencysign million a year earlier	negative
profit before tax decreas to currencysign million from currencysign million the year befor	negative
profit befor tax was currencysign million down from currencysign million	negative
the compani profit befor tax fell to currencysign million in the third quarter of compar to currencysign million in the correspond period in	negative
in august octob the compani result befor tax total currencysign million up from currencysign million in the correspond period in	positive
finnish bore that is own by the rettig famili has grown recent through the acquisit of smaller shipping company	positive
the plan is estim to generat some currencysign million currencysign million in cost save on an annual basi	positive
finnish pharmaceut compani orion report profit befor tax of currencysign million in the third quarter of up from currencysign million in the correspond period in	positive
finnish sampo bank of danish danske bank group report profit befor tax of currencysign million in up from currencysign million in	positive

The normalized text is tokenized, resulting in 2,673 unique tokens. Altogether, these unique tokens comprise the bag-of-words (BOW) of the text corpus. Exhibit 31 shows a sample of 100 tokens from the BOW. This preliminary unigram BOW can be used to construct a document term matrix (DTM) for ML training.

Exhibit 31: One Hundred Sample Tokens from Preliminary Unigram BOW

"for"	"foundri"	"quarter"	"shop"	"net"	"share"	"to"
"currencysign"	"nokia"	"same"	"plan"	"year"	"sanyo"	"it"
"move"	"nokian"	"tax"	"earn"	"in"	"expect"	"by"
"percentsign"	"director"	"rose"	"dividned"	"total"	"megafon"	"talentum"
"report"	"as"	"chain"	"number"	"consolid"	"accord"	"compar"
"prior"	"last"	"machin"	"componenta"	"afx"	"doubl"	"higher"
"led"	"from"	"announc"	"a"	"with"	"while"	"g"
"handset"	"pre"	"fourth"	"loss"	"analyst"	"increas"	"said"
"board"	"oper"	"propos"	"repres"	"paid"	"finnish"	"base"
"user"	"retail"	"market"	"is"	"late"	"amount"	"estim"
"the"	"divis"	"of"	"helsinki"	"sale"	"close"	
"million"	"after"	"period"	"team"	"earlier"	"manufactur"	
"zero"	"tyre"	"profit"	"beat"	"third"	"dealer"	
"and"	"will"	"correspond"	"per"	"up"	"subscrib"	
"cloth"	"decemb"	"sepp"	"custom"	"reach"	"teliasonera"	

The final DTM for ML model training will be prepared after the data exploration stage. Data exploration may reveal unnecessary tokens or anomalies in the data. Any unnecessary tokens that are not informative must be removed, which will also impact the creation of n-grams. Thus, the final DTM must be made after further analyses and operations, such as exploratory data analysis and feature selection.

# 11	DATA EXPLORATION

☐ | describe preparing, wrangling, and exploring text-based data for financial forecasting

Exploratory Data Analysis

Exploratory data analysis (EDA) performed on text data provides insights on word distribution in the text. Word counts from all the sentences are computed. These word counts can be used to examine outlier tokens—words that are most commonly and least commonly present in the texts. The most frequent word occurrences in all sentences from the dataset are shown in Exhibit 32. These common words will be removed during the feature selection step. Notably, the tokens "million" and "currencysign" occur frequently due to the financial nature of the data.

Exhibit 32: Most Frequently Used Tokens in the Corpus

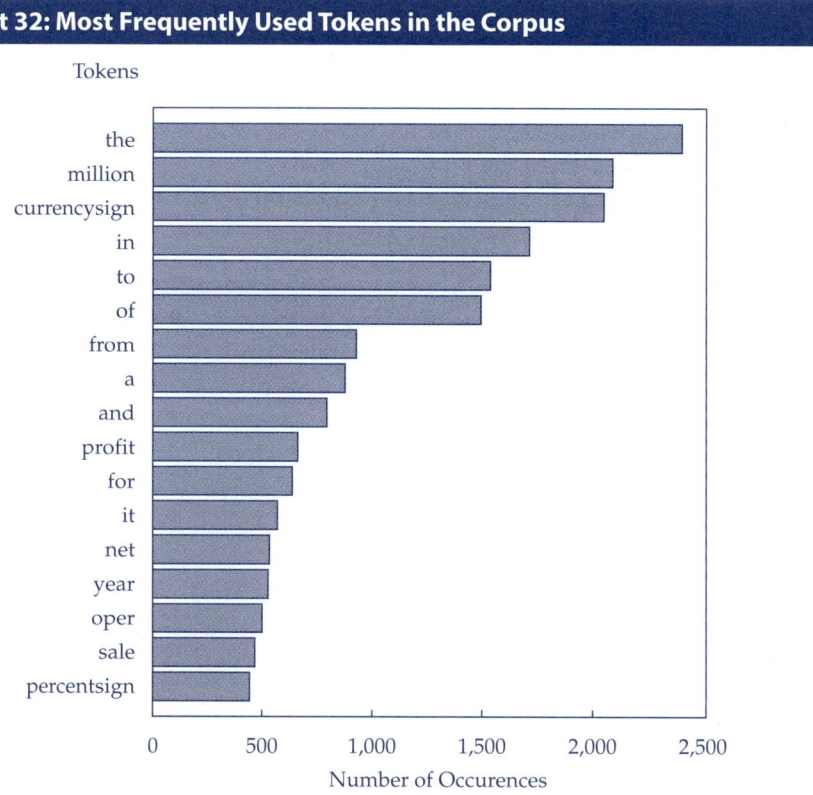

The most frequent word occurrences in the sentences in the negative sentiment and the positive sentiment classes are shown in Exhibit 33. The most commonly occurring words are similar for both sentiment classes, meaning that they are not useful in discriminating between the two sentiment classes. This finding demonstrates the utility of removing the most commonly used tokens from the BOW.

Exhibit 33: Most Frequently Used Tokens in Two Sentiment Classes of the Corpus

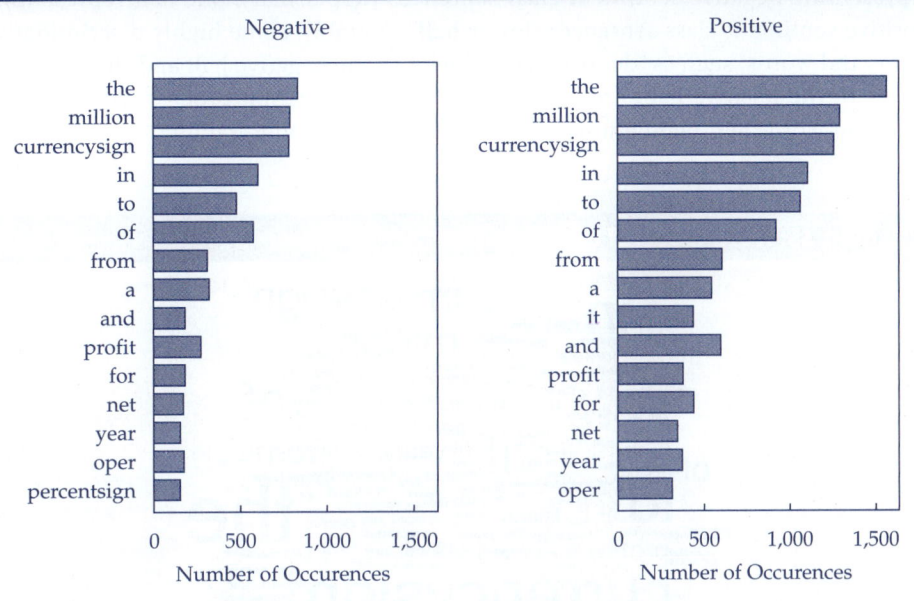

Exhibit 34 shows a histogram of sentence length distribution. **Sentence length** is defined as the number of characters, including spaces, in a sentence. The longest sentence has 273 characters; the shortest sentence has 26 characters; and the average number of characters is about 120 (indicated by the vertical line). Although this distribution does not have any direct impact on model training, this histogram visually demonstrates the range of sentence lengths and helps identify any extremely long or short sentences. This histogram does not appear unusual, so no outlier sentences need to be removed.

Exhibit 34: Histogram of Sentence Lengths with Mean Sentence Length

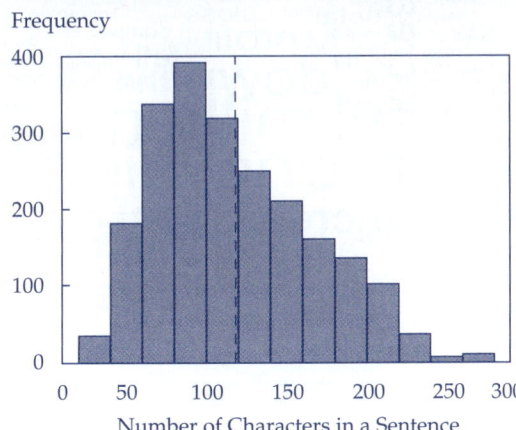

Word clouds are a convenient method of visualizing the text data because they enable rapid comprehension of a large number of tokens and their corresponding weights. Exhibit 35 shows a word cloud for all the sentences in the corpus. The font sizes of the words are proportionate to the number of occurrences of each word in the corpus. Similarly, Exhibit 36 shows the word cloud divided into two halves: one half representing negative sentiment class sentences (upper half); one half representing positive sentiment class sentences (lower half). Notably, some highly discriminative stems and words, such as "decreas" and "down" in the negative half and "increas" and "rose" in the positive half, are present. The feature selection process will eliminate common words and highlight useful words for better model training.

Exhibit 35: Word Cloud of Entire Corpus

Exhibit 36: Word Cloud Divided by Two Sub-Groups of the Corpus

Feature Selection

Exploratory data analysis revealed the most frequent tokens in the texts that could potentially add noise to this ML model training process. In addition to common tokens, many rarely occurring tokens, often proper nouns (i.e., names), are not informative for understanding the sentiment of the sentence. Further analyses must be conducted to decide which words to eliminate. Feature selection for text data involves keeping the useful tokens in the BOW that are informative and help to discriminate different classes of texts—those with positive sentiment and those with negative sentiment. At this point, a total of 44,151 non-unique tokens are in the 2,180 sentences.

Frequency analysis on the processed text data helps in filtering unnecessary tokens (or features) by quantifying how important tokens are in a sentence and in the corpus as a whole. Term frequency (TF) at the corpus level—also known as **collection frequency (CF)**—is the number of times a given word appears in the whole corpus (i.e., collection of sentences) divided by the total number of words in the corpus. Term frequency can be calculated and examined to identify outlier words. Exhibit 37 shows the descriptive statistics of term frequency for the words at the collection level. The statistics of TF range between 0 and 1 because TF values are ratios of total occurrences of a particular word to total number of words in the collection. A sample of words with the highest TF and lowest TF values is also shown to gain insight into what kinds of words occur at these extreme frequencies.

Exhibit 37: Summary Statistics of TF for Words at the Collection Level, Sample Words with High and Low TF Values, and Histogram of TF Values

Min.	1st Qu.	Median	Mean	3rd Qu.	Max.
2.265e-05	2.265e-05	4.530e-05	3.741e-04	1.585e-04	5.429e-02

word	TF	word	TF
<chr>	<dbl>	<chr>	<dbl>
the	0.05429096	yet	2.264954e-05
million	0.04722430	yihn	2.264954e-05
currencysign	0.04627302	young	2.264954e-05
in	0.03870807	zahariev	2.264954e-05
to	0.03476705	zone	2.264954e-05
of	0.03377047	zoo	2.264954e-05

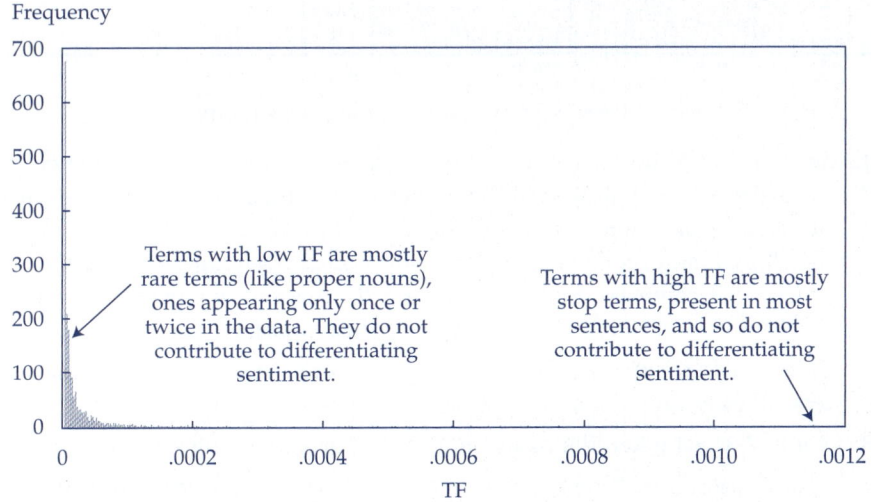

Calculating highest and lowest TFs at the collection level is a general strategy to identify noisy terms. The histogram in Exhibit 37 shows a long tail to the right, which represents common terms that must be removed. The high frequency bars on the left show that there are also many rare terms (e.g., ones appearing only once or twice across the data). Such rare terms do not appear enough to be used as meaningful features and are often removed. The words with the highest TF are mostly stop words that are not useful because they are present in most of the sentences and thus do not contribute to differentiating the sentiment embedded in the text. The words with the lowest TF values are mostly proper nouns or sparse terms that are also not important to the meaning of the text. In this example, after careful examination of words with extreme frequencies, the words with high TF values (>99.5th percentile, 14 words) and low TF values (<30th percentile, 714 words) are removed before forming the final document term matrix (DTM). Exhibit 38 shows the 14 words with the highest TF values (>99.5th percentile) that are the custom stop words for this project.

Exhibit 38: Fourteen Custom Stop Words for the Project

"the"	"million"	"currencysign"	"in"	"to"	"of"	"from"
"and"	"profit"	"for"	"it"	"not"	"year"	"a"

To construct a DTM for ML training, different TF measures need to be computed to fill in the cells of the DTM. Exhibit 39 displays part of a TF measures table that is computed for the text data before the removal of custom stop words.

Exhibit 39: Sample Output of Term Frequency (TF) Measures Table

SentenceNo	TotalWordsInSentence	Word	TotalWordCount	WordCountInSentence	SentenceCountWithWord	TF	DF	IDF	TFIDF
<int>	<int>	<chr>	<int>	<int>	<int>	<dbl>	<dbl>	<dbl>	<dbl>
624	34	a	873	6	687	0.1764706	0.3151376	1.1547459	0.20377868
701	39	the	2397	6	1453	0.1538462	0.6665138	0.4056945	0.06241454
1826	34	a	873	6	687	0.1764706	0.3151376	1.1547459	0.20377868
1963	39	the	2397	6	1453	0.1538462	0.6665138	0.4056945	0.06241454
128	30	of	1491	5	984	0.1666667	0.4513761	0.7954543	0.13257571
223	37	the	2397	5	1453	0.1351351	0.6665138	0.4056945	0.05482358

The columns of the term frequency measures table are as follows:

1. *SentenceNo*: A unique identification number assigned to each sentence in the order they are present in the original dataset. For example, sentence number 701 is a sentence in row 701 from the data table: "*the airlin estim that the cancel of it flight due to the closur of european airspac and the process of recommenc traffic have caus a the compani a loss of currencysign million includ the cost of strand passeng accommod.*"

2. *TotalWordsInSentence*: Count of total number of words present in the sentence. For example, sentence number 701 has a total of 39 words.

3. *Word*: A word token that is present in the corresponding sentence.

4. *TotalWordCount*: Total number of occurrences of the word in the entire corpus or collection. For example, the token "the" occurs 2,397 times in the whole collection of sentences. The following equation can be used to compute TF at the collection level:

TF (Collection Level)

$=$

TotalWordCount/Total number of words in collection.

(10)

The TF of the word "the" at the collection level is calculated as 2,397/44,151 = 0.05429096. Note that this result was seen previously in Exhibit 37.

5. *WordCountInSentence*: Number of times the token is present in the corresponding sentence. For example, token "the" is present six times in sentence number 701.

6. *SentenceCountWithWord*: Number of sentences in which the word is present. For example, the token "the" is present in 1,453 sentences.

7. *TF (Term Frequency) at Sentence Level*: Number of times a word is present in a sentence divided by the total number of words in that sentence. The following equation can be used to compute TF at the sentence level:

TF (Sentence Level)

$=$

WordCountInSentence/TotalWordsInSentence.

(11)

For example, TF at the sentence level for the word "the" in sentences number 701 and 223 is calculated as 6/39 = 0.1538462 and 5/37 = 0.1351351, respectively.

8. *DF (Document Frequency)*: Defined as the number of documents (i.e., sentences) that contain a given word divided by the total number of sentences (here, 2,180). Document frequency is important since words frequently occurring across sentences provide no differentiating information in each sentence. The following equation can be used to compute DF:

DF = SentenceCountWithWord/Total number of sentences.   (12)

For example, DF of the word "the" is 1,453/2,180 = 0.6665138; so, 66.7% of the sentences contain the word "the." A high DF indicates high word frequency in the text.

9. *IDF (Inverse Document Frequency)*: A relative measure of how unique a term is across the entire corpus. Its meaning is not directly related to the size of the corpus. The following equation can be used to compute IDF:

IDF = log(1/DF).   (13)

For example, IDF of the word "the" is log(1/0.6665138) = 0.4056945. A low IDF indicates high word frequency in the text.

10. *TF–IDF*: To get a complete representation of the value of each word, TF at the *sentence level* is multiplied by the IDF of a word across the entire dataset. Higher TF–IDF values indicate words that appear more frequently within a smaller number of documents. This signifies relatively more unique terms that are important. Conversely, a low TF–IDF value indicates terms that appear in many documents. TF–IDF values can be useful in measuring the key terms across a compilation of documents and can serve as word feature values for training an ML model. The following equation can be used to compute TF–IDF:

TF–IDF = TF × IDF.   (14)

For example, TF–IDF of the token "of" is calculated as $0.1666667 \times 0.7954543 = 0.13257571$.

Similarly, Exhibit 40 shows high TF–IDF words for the text data before the removal of custom stop words.

Exhibit 40: Sample Output of High TF–IDF Words

SentenceNo	TotalWordsInSentence	Word	TotalWordCount	WordCountInSentence	SentenceCountWithWord	TF	DF	IDF	TFIDF
<int>	<int>	<chr>	<int>	<int>	<int>	<dbl>	<dbl>	<dbl>	<dbl>
28	7	risen	3	1	3	0.1428571	0.0013761468	6.588468	0.9412097
830	7	diminish	2	1	2	0.1428571	0.0009174312	6.993933	0.9991333
1368	9	great	4	1	4	0.1111111	0.0018348624	6.300786	0.7000873
1848	8	injuri	1	1	1	0.1250000	0.0004587156	7.687080	0.9608850
1912	7	cheaper	1	1	1	0.1428571	0.0004587156	7.687080	1.0981543
1952	6	argument	1	1	1	0.1666667	0.0004587156	7.687080	1.2811800

TF or TF–IDF values are placed at the intersection of sentences (rows) and terms (columns) of the document term matrix. For this project, TF values are used for the DTM as the texts are sentences rather than paragraphs or other larger bodies of text. TF–IDF values vary by the *number* of documents in the dataset; therefore, the model performance can vary when applied to a dataset with just a few documents. In addition to removing custom stop words and sparse terms, single character letters are also eliminated because they do not add any value to the sentiment significance.

Feature Engineering

N-grams are used as a feature engineering process in this project. Use of n-grams helps to understand the sentiment of a sentence as a whole. As mentioned previously, the objective of this project is to predict sentiment class (positive and negative) from financial texts. Both unigram and bigrams are implemented, and the BOW is created from them. Bigram tokens are helpful for keeping negations intact in the text, which is vital for sentiment prediction. For example, the tokens "not" and "good" or "no" and "longer" can be formed into single tokens, now bigrams, such as "not_good" and "no_longer." These and similar tokens can be useful during ML model training and can improve model performance. Exhibit 41 shows a sample of 100 words from the BOW containing both unigram and bigram tokens after removal of custom stop words, sparse terms, and single characters. Note that the BOW contains such tokens as increas, loss, loss_prior, oper_rose, tax_loss, and sale_increas. Such tokens are informative about the embedded sentiment in the texts and are useful for training an ML model. The corresponding word frequency measures for the document term matrix are computed based on this new BOW.

Exhibit 41: One-Hundred Sample Tokens from Final BOW of Entire Corpus

"last"	"last_quarter"	"quarter"	"quarter_componenta"	"componenta"
"componenta_sale"	"sale"	"sale_doubl"	"doubl"	"doubl_same"
"same"	"same_period"	"period"	"period_earlier"	"earlier"
"earlier_while"	"while"	"while_move"	"move"	"move_zero"
"zero"	"zero_pre"	"pre"	"pre_tax"	"tax"
"tax_pre"	"tax_loss"	"loss"	"third"	"third_quarter"
"quarter_sale"	"sale_increas"	"increas"	"increas_by"	"by"
"by_percentsign"	"percentsign"	"percentsign_oper"	"oper"	"oper_by"
"oper_rose"	"rose"	"rose_correspond"	"correspond"	"correspond_period"
"period_repres"	"repres"	"repres_percentsign"	"percentsign_sale"	"oper_total"
"total"	"total_up"	"up"	"up_repres"	"finnish"
"finnish_talentum"	"talentum"	"talentum_report"	"report"	"report_oper"
"oper_increas"	"increas_sale"	"sale_total"	"cloth"	"cloth_retail"
"retail"	"retail_chain"	"chain"	"chain_sepp"	"sepp"
"sepp_ls"	"ls"	"ls_sale"	"consolid"	"consolid_sale"
"incres_percentsign"	"percentsign_reach"	"reach"	"reach_while"	"while_oper"
"oper_amount"	"amount"	"amount_compar"	"compar"	"compar_loss"
"loss_prior"	"prior"	"prior_period"	"foundri"	"foundri_divis"
"divis"	"divis_report"	"report_sale"	"percentsign_correspond"	"period_sale"
"sale_machin"	"machin"	"machin_shop"	"shop"	"shop_divis"

EXAMPLE 6

Calculating and Interpreting Term Frequency Measures

Data scientists Jack and Jill are using financial text data to develop sentiment indicators for forecasting future stock price movements. They have assembled a BOW from the corpus of text being examined and have pulled the following abbreviated term frequency measures tables.

Exhibit 42: Term Frequency Measures Table 1

SentenceNo	TotalWordsInSentence	Word	TotalWordCount	WordCountInSentence	SentenceCountWithWord
<int>	<int>	<chr>	<int>	<int>	<int>
624	34	a	873	6	687
701	39	the	2397	6	1453
1826	34	a	873	6	687
1963	39	the	2397	6	1453
128	30	of	1491	5	984
223	37	the	2397	5	1453

Exhibit 43: Term Frequency Measures Table 2

SentenceNo	TotalWordsInSentence	Word	TotalWordCount	WordCountInSentence	SentenceCountWithWord
<int>	<int>	<chr>	<int>	<int>	<int>
28	7	risen	3	1	3
830	7	diminish	2	1	2
1368	9	great	4	1	4
1848	8	injuri	1	1	1
1912	7	cheaper	1	1	1
1952	6	argument	1	1	1

1. Determine and interpret term frequency (TF) at the collection level and at the sentence level for the word (i.e., token) "a" in sentence 1,826 in term

frequency measures Table 1 and then for the token "great" in sentence 1,368 in term frequency measures Table 2.

Solution

TF at the collection level is calculated using Equation 10:

TF (Collection Level) = TotalWordCount/Total number of words in collection.

For token "a" in sentence 1,826 (Table 1), TF (Collection Level) is 873/44,151 = 0.019773 or 1.977%.For token "great" in sentence 1,368 (Table 2), TF (Collection Level) is 4/44,151 = 0.000091 or 0.009%.TF at the collection level is an indicator of the frequency, in percentage terms, that a token is used throughout the whole collection of texts (here, 44,151). It is useful for identifying outlier words: Tokens with highest TF values are mostly stop words that do not contribute to differentiating the sentiment embedded in the text (such as "a"), and tokens with lowest TF values are mostly proper nouns or sparse terms that are also not important to the meaning of the text. Conversely, tokens with intermediate TF values potentially carry important information useful for differentiating the sentiment embedded in the text.TF at the sentence level is calculated using Equation 11:

TF (Sentence Level) = WordCountInSentence/TotalWordsInSentence.

For token "a" in sentence 1,826, TF (Sentence Level) is 6/34 = 0.176471 or 17.647%.
For token "great" in sentence 1,368, TF (Sentence Level) is 1/9 = 0.111111 or 11.111%.
TF at the sentence level is an indicator of the frequency, in percentage terms, that a token is used in a particular sentence (i.e., instance). Therefore, it is useful for understanding the importance of the specific token in a given sentence.

2. Determine and interpret TF–IDF (term frequency–inverse document frequency) for the word "a" in sentence 1,826 in term frequency measures Table 1 and then for the token "great" in sentence 1,368 in term frequency measures Table 2.

Solution

To calculate TF–IDF, besides TF at the sentence level, document frequency (DF) and inverse document frequency (IDF) are also required.

DF is the number of documents (i.e., sentences) that contain a given word divided by the total number of sentences in the corpus (here, 2,180). DF is calculated using Equation 12:

DF = SentenceCountWithWord/Total number of sentences.

For token "a" in sentence 1,826, DF is 687/2,180 = 0.315138 or 31.514%.
For token "great" in sentence 1,368, DF is 4/2,180 = 0.001835 or 0.184%.
Document frequency is important since tokens occurring frequently across sentences (such as "a") provide no differentiating information in each sentence. Tokens occurring less frequently across sentences (such as "great"), however, may provide useful differentiating information.
IDF is a relative measure of how important a term is across the entire corpus (i.e., collection of texts/sentences). IDF is calculated using Equation 13:

IDF = log(1/DF).

For token "a" in sentence 1,826, IDF is log(1/0.315138) = 1.154746.
For token "great" in sentence 1,368, IDF is log(1/0.001835) = 6.300786.
Using TF and IDF, TF–IDF can now be calculated using Equation 14:

TF–IDF = TF × IDF.

For token "a" in sentence 1,826, TF–IDF = 0.176471 × 1.154746 = 0.203779,
or 20.378%.
For token "great" in sentence 1,368, TF–IDF = 0.111111 × 6.300786 =
0.700087, or 70.009%.
As TF–IDF combines TF at the *sentence level* with IDF across the entire
corpus, it provides a complete representation of the value of each word. A
high TF–IDF value indicates the word appears many times within a small
number of documents, signifying an important yet unique term within a
sentence (such as "great"). A low TF–IDF value indicates tokens that appear
in most of the sentences and are not discriminative (such as "a"). TF–IDF
values are useful in extracting the key terms in a document for use as features for training an ML model.

MODEL TRAINING

12

☐ | describe preparing, wrangling, and exploring text-based data for
financial forecasting

The sentiment class labels (positive and negative) constitute the target variable (*y*) for
model training. They are relabeled as 1 (for positive) and 0 (for negative) to enable
calculating the performance metrics, such as receiver operating characteristic (ROC)
curve and area under the curve (AUC) from the trained model results. The master
dataset that has been cleansed and preprocessed is partitioned into three separate
sets: 1) training set; 2) cross-validation (CV) set; and 3) test set. These are in the ratio
of 60:20:20, respectively (following common practice). For splitting, simple random
sampling is applied within levels of the target variable to balance the class distributions within the splits. The final DTM is built using the sentences (rows), which are
the instances, and resulting tokens (columns), which are the feature variables, from
the BOW of the training dataset. The final BOW consists of unigram and bigram
tokens from the sentences in the training corpus only. The DTM is then filled in with
resultant TF values of the tokens from the training corpus.

Similarly, the DTMs for the CV set and the test set are built using tokens from the
final training BOW for tuning, validating, and testing of the model. To be clear, the
final BOW from the training corpus is used for building DTMs across all the splits
because the model has been trained on that final BOW. Thus, the columns (think,
features) of all three DTMs are the same, but the number of rows varies because a
different number of sentences are in each split. The DTMs are filled with resultant
term frequency values calculated using sentences in the corpuses of the respective
splits—sentences from the CV set corpus and sentences from the test set corpus.
Exhibit 44 tabulates the summary of dimensions of the data splits and their uses in
the model training process. As mentioned, the columns of DTMs for the splits are
the same, equal to the number of unique tokens (i.e., features) from the final training

corpus BOW, which is 9,188. Note that this number of unique tokens (9,188) differs from that in the master corpus (11,501) based on the sentences that are included in the training corpus after the random sampling.

Exhibit 44: Summary of the Three Data Splits

Corpus	Split %	Number of Sentences	DTM Dimensions	Purpose
Master	100%	2180	2180 × 11501	Used for data exploration
Training	60%	1309	1309 × 9188	Used for ML model training
CV	20%	435	435 × 9188	Used for tuning and validating the trained model
Test	20%	436	436 × 9188	Used for testing the trained, tuned, and validated model

Method Selection

Alternative ML methods, including SVM, decision trees, and logistic regression, were examined because these techniques are all considered potentially suitable for this particular task (i.e., supervised learning), type of data (i.e., text), and size of data (i.e., wider data with many potential variables). The SVM and logistic regression methods appeared to offer better performance than decision trees. For brevity, we discuss logistic regression in the remainder of the chapter. Logistic regression was used to train the model, using the training corpus DTM containing 1,309 sentences. As a reminder, in this project texts are the sentences and the classifications are positive and negative sentiment classes (labeled 1 and 0, respectively). The tokens are feature variables, and the sentiment class is the target variable. Text data typically contain thousands of tokens. These result in sparse DTMs because each column represents a token feature and the values are mostly zeros (i.e., not all the tokens are present in every text). Logistic regression can deal with such sparse training data because the regression coefficients will be close to zero for tokens that are not present in a significant number of sentences. This allows the model to ignore a large number of minimally useful features. Regularization further helps lower the coefficients when the features rarely occur and do not contribute to the model training.

Logistic regression is applied on the final training DTM for model training. As this method uses maximum likelihood estimation, the output of the logistic model is a probability value ranging from 0 to 1. However, because the target variable is binary, coefficients from the logistic regression model are not directly used to predict the value of the target variable. Rather, a mathematical function uses the logistic regression coefficient (β) to calculate probability (p) of sentences having positive sentiment ($y =$ 1).[3] If p for a sentence is 0.90, there is a 90% likelihood that the sentence has positive sentiment. Theoretically, the sentences with $p > 0.50$ likely have positive sentiment. Because this is not always true in practice, however, it is important to find an ideal threshold value of p. We elaborate on this point in a subsequent example. The threshold value is a cutoff point for p values, and the ideal threshold p value is influenced by the dataset and model training. When the p values (i.e., probability of sentences having positive sentiment) of sentences are above this ideal threshold p value, then

---

3 This mathematical function is an exponential function of the form: $P\ (y = 1) = \frac{1}{1\ +\ \exp^{-\ (\beta_0 + \beta_1 x_1 + \beta_2 x_2 + \cdots + \beta_n x_n)}}$ where the βs are the logistic regression coefficients.

the sentences are *highly* likely to have positive sentiment ($y = 1$). The ideal threshold p value is estimated heuristically using performance metrics and ROC curves, as will be demonstrated shortly.

Performance Evaluation and Tuning

The trained ML model is used to predict the sentiments of the sentences in the training and CV DTMs. Exhibit 45 displays the ROC curves for the training (Panel A) and CV (Panel B) data. Remember that the x-axis is false positive rate, FP/(TN + FP), and the y-axis is true positive rate, TP/(TP + FN). As the model is trained using the training DTM, it clearly performs well on the same training data (so there is no concern about underfitting) but does not perform as well on the CV data. This is apparent as the ROC curves are significantly different between the training and CV datasets. The AUC is 96.5% on training data and 86.2% on CV data. This finding suggests that the model performs comparatively poorly (with a higher rate of error or misclassification) on the CV data when compared to training data. Thus, the implication is that the model is overfitted.

Exhibit 45: ROC Curves of Model Results for Training and CV Data Before Regularization

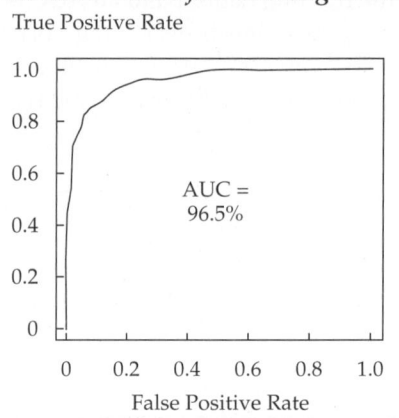
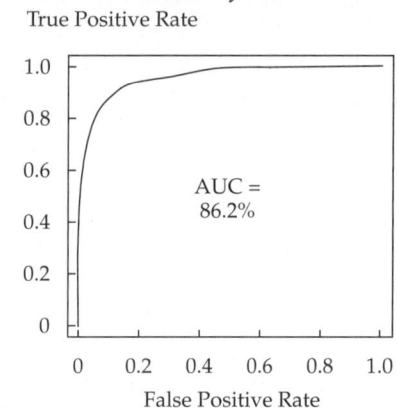

As the model is overfitted, least absolute shrinkage and selection operator (LASSO) regularization is applied to the logistic regression. LASSO regularization penalizes the coefficients of the logistic regression to prevent overfitting of the model. The penalized regression will select the tokens (features) that have statistically significant (i.e., non-zero) coefficients and that contribute to the model fit; LASSO does this while disregarding the other tokens. Exhibit 46 shows the ROC curves for the new model that uses regularized logistic regression. The ROC curves look similar for model performance on both datasets, with an AUC of 95.7% on the training dataset (Panel A) and 94.8% on the CV dataset (Panel B). These findings suggest that the model performs similarly on both training and CV data and thus indicate a good fitting model (one that is not overfitted).

Exhibit 46: ROC Curves of Model Results for Training and CV Data After Regularization

A. ROC Curve for Training Data
True Positive Rate

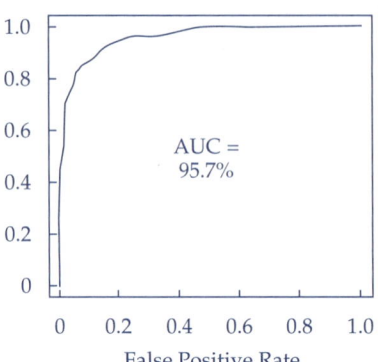

AUC = 95.7%

False Positive Rate

B. ROC Curve for CV Data
True Positive Rate

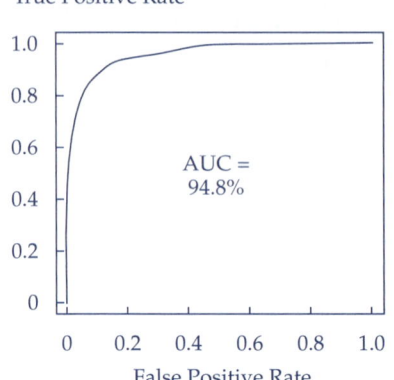

AUC = 94.8%

False Positive Rate

Regularization along with careful feature selection help to prevent overfitting in logistic regression models. Another model was trained using all token features, including stop words, sparse terms, and single characters, with no regularization. That model showed an AUC of 99.1% when applied on the training dataset and an AUC of 89.4% when applied on the CV dataset, suggesting that the model is overfitting. As the AUC values in all of the models discussed are not far from 100%, these models are clearly not underfitting. In sum, the final ML model for this project uses logistic regression with LASSO regularization.

To further evaluate the model, error analysis is conducted by calculating a confusion matrix using the ML model results from the cross-validation dataset. The threshold p value of 0.5 is used as a cutoff point. When target value p > 0.5, the prediction is assumed to be $y = 1$ (meaning, positive sentiment). Otherwise, the prediction is assumed to be $y = 0$ (negative sentiment). A confusion matrix, with performance metrics and overall scores for the model results using the CV data, is shown in Exhibit 47.

Exhibit 47: Confusion Matrix of Model Results for CV Data with Threshold p Value = 0.50

Confusion Matrix for CV Data with Threshold = 0.5

		Actual Training Labels	
		Class "1"	Class "0"
Predicted Results	Class "1"	284 (TP)	38 (FP)
	Class "0"	7 (FN)	106 (TN)

Performance Metrics

TP = 284, FP = 38, FN = 7, TN = 106

P = 284 / (284+38) = 0.88

R = 284 / (284+7) = 0.98

F1 Score = (2 × 0.88 × 0.98) / (0.88 + 0.98) = 0.93

Accuracy = (284 + 106) / (284 + 38 + 106 + 7) = 0.90

The model accuracy is 90% with a theoretically suggested (default) threshold p value of 0.5. The CV data are used to tune the threshold value for best model performance. Various p values from 0.01 to 0.99 are systematically evaluated individually, and confusion matrixes and performance metrics are calculated using each of these p values. Based on these metrics, the p value resulting in the highest model accuracy is selected as the ideal threshold p value. However, there are often trade-offs: Minimizing false positives (FPs) comes at a cost of increasing false negatives (FNs), and vice versa. Prioritizing various performance statistics (e.g., precision versus recall) depends on the context and relative consequences of FP and FN on the project applications. In this project, the values of negative sentiment and positive sentiment sentences are assumed to be equal, thus the impacts of FP and FN are also equal. It is common practice to simulate many model results using different threshold p values and to search for maximized accuracy and F1 statistics that minimize these trade-offs. As noted earlier, accuracy and F1 scores are overall performance measures that give equal weight to FP and FN.

Exhibit 48 shows the overall performance measures (i.e., F1 score and accuracy) for various threshold p values. The threshold p value that results in the highest accuracy and F1 score can now be identified. From the charts in Exhibit 47, the ideal threshold p value appears to be around 0.60. To investigate further, a table of performance measures (i.e., precision, recall, F1 score, and accuracy) is generated for a series of threshold p values ranging from 0.45 to 0.75. The table in Exhibit 49 demonstrates that threshold p values between 0.60 and 0.63 result in the highest accuracy and F1 score for the CV dataset. As a result of this analysis, a final threshold p value of 0.60 is selected.

Exhibit 48: Threshold Values Versus Overall Performance Measures

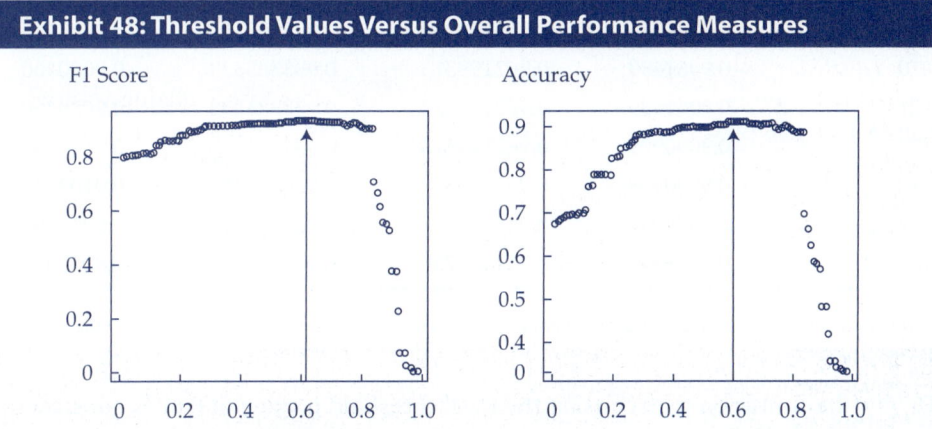

Exhibit 49: Performance Measures of the Model for a Series of Threshold Values

Threshold	Precision	Recall	F1	Accuracy
0.45	0.8750000	0.986254296	0.927302100	0.8965517
0.46	0.8827160	0.982817869	0.930081301	0.9011494
0.47	0.8827160	0.982817869	0.930081301	0.9011494
0.48	0.8819876	0.975945017	0.926590538	0.8965517

Threshold	Precision	Recall	F1	Accuracy
0.49	0.8819876	0.975945017	0.926590538	0.8965517
0.50	0.8819876	0.975945017	0.926590538	0.8965517
0.51	0.8819876	0.975945017	0.926590538	0.8965517
0.52	0.8819876	0.975945017	0.926590538	0.8965517
0.53	0.8902821	0.975945017	0.931147541	0.9034483
0.54	0.8930818	0.975945017	0.932676519	0.9057471
0.55	0.8930818	0.975945017	0.932676519	0.9057471
0.56	0.8958991	0.975945017	0.934210526	0.9080460
0.57	0.8958991	0.975945017	0.934210526	0.9080460
0.58	0.8958991	9.975945017	0.934210526	0.9080460
0.59	0.9015873	0.975945017	0.937293729	0.9126437
0.60	0.9044586	0.975945017	0.938842975	0.9149425
0.61	0.9044586	0.975945017	0.938842975	0.9149425
0.62	0.9044586	0.975945017	0.938842975	0.9149425
0.63	0.9041534	0.972508591	0.937086093	0.9126437
0.64	0.9041534	0.972508591	0.937086093	0.9126537
0.65	0.9041534	0.972508591	0.937086093	0.9126437
0.66	0.9035370	0.965635739	0.933554817	0.9080460
0.67	0.9035370	0.965635739	0.933554817	0.9080460
0.68	0.9064516	0.965635739	0.935108153	0.9103448
0.69	0.9064516	0.965635739	0.935108153	0.9103448
0.70	0.9061489	0.962199313	0.933333333	0.9080460
0.71	0.9061489	0.962199313	0.933333333	0.9080460
0.72	0.9090909	0.962199313	0.934891486	0.9103448
0.73	0.9090909	0.962199313	0.934891486	0.9103448
0.74	0.9078947	0.948453608	0.927731092	0.9011494
0.75	0.9072848	0.941580756	0.924114671	0.8965517

* *The shaded row shows the selected threshold p value (0.60) and the performance metrics for the selected model.*

Finally, the confusion matrix using the ideal threshold p value of 0.60 is constructed to observe the performance of the final model. When target value p > 0.60, the prediction is assumed to be $y = 1$ (indicating positive sentiment); otherwise, the prediction is assumed to be $y = 0$ (negative sentiment). The confusion matrix for the CV data is shown in Exhibit 50. It is clear that the model performance metrics have improved in the final model compared to the earliest case when the threshold p value was 0.50. Now, accuracy and F1 score have both increased by one percentage point to 91% and 94%, respectively, while precision has increased by two percentage points to 90%.

Confusion Matrix for CV Data with Threshold = 0.6

		Actual Training Labels	
		Class "1"	Class "0"
Predicted Results	Class "1"	284 (TP)	30 (FP)
	Class "0"	7 (FN)	114 (TN)

Performance Metrics

TP = 284, FP = 30, FN = 7, TN = 114

$P = 284 / (284+30) = 0.90$

$R = 284 / (284+7) = 0.98$

F1 Score $= (2 \times 0.90 \times 0.98) / (0.90 + 0.98) = 0.94$

Accuracy $= (284 + 114) / (284 + 30 + 114 + 7) = 0.91$

RESULTS AND INTERPRETATION

13

☐ describe preparing, wrangling, and exploring text-based data for financial forecasting

The final ML model with the appropriate threshold p value has been validated and is now ready for use. The model can be used to predict the sentiment of new sentences from the test data corpus as well as new sentences from similar financial text data sources, such as news wires, earnings call transcripts, and quarterly financial reports. The final model is a collection of penalized regression coefficients for unigram and bigram tokens from the BOW of the training corpus. To use the model to predict the sentiment of new sentences, tokenization and identical cleansing and preprocessing operations must be performed on the new sentences. All the processes performed on the training data must be performed on the new data to which the model will be applied (as was done for the test dataset). The model will use the trained penalized regression coefficients on the term frequency (TF) values of the tokens in the document term matrix (DTM) of the new sentences and will determine the target value (p). The columns of the DTM of the new sentences are the same as those of the training DTM, but the TF values are calculated based on the test corpus. Using the threshold p value of 0.60, the sentiment class for each sentence in the test corpus will be predicted.

The model is now applied on the test data that contains 436 sentences. Note that the test data were not used to train or validate/tune the model and are new to the model. The test data were preprocessed identically to the training and CV data while a part of the master corpus. The model is then applied to the test DTM, and the results are obtained. Exhibit 51 displays 30 sample results from the test corpus. The results table contains cleansed and preprocessed sentences, actual sentiment, target p values from the model, and predicted sentiment. Note that this sample contains three cases of misclassification: the 10th sentence (text), where p = 0.46; the 26th text, where p = 0.77; and the 30th text, where p = 0.71. Therefore, accuracy of this 30-text sample is 27/30 = 90%.

Exhibit 51: Thirty Sample Results of Test Data

Sentence	Sentiment	p	Predicted Sentiment
exclude non recur item pre tax surg percentsign	1	0.81	1
adp news feb finnish retail kesko oyj hel kesbv said today total sale exclud valu ad tax vat stood at januari down percentsign on yea	0	0.12	0
india trade with russia current stand at four billion dollar grow per cent fiscal	1	0.83	1
refin margin was bbl combar bbl prior	1	0.81	1
scania morgan Stanley lift share target on swedish heavi duti truck bus maker scania ab crown euro crown euro	1	0.83	1
deal is like bring save	1	0.83	1
will also strengthen ruukki offshore busi	1	0.83	1
last week finnish metl technolog group announc plan sell more than percent technolog unit further compani strategy goal becom world largest stainless steel maker	1	0.83	1
nest oil board propos dividend full compar with ago	1	0.81	1
pre tax loss total compar loss first quarter	1	0.46	0
pretax total compar loss fourth quarter	1	0.74	1
re use back into pet bottle has also steadili increas rate use strap tape has pick up again after dip pector said previous	1	0.95	1
satama sale would be higher than befor	1	0.83	1
octob finnish wood product technolog supplier raut oyj hel rutav said today swung first nine month versus loss same period earlier	1	0.79	1
ebit total compar loss correspond period	1	0.74	1
finnish consum packag manufactur huhtamaki oyj said swung euro first nine month loss euro same period	1	0.77	1
finnish dental care group oral hammaslaakarit oyj post total euro first nine month versus loss euro same period	1	0.79	1
finnish silicon water manufactur okmet oyj said swung euro first nine month loss euro earlier	1	0.77	1
adp news feb finnish print circuit board pcb maker aspocomp group oyj hel acg said today swung versus loss	1	0.79	1
mn pretax third quarter	1	0.83	1
oper total compar correspond period	1	0.81	1
raut post euro third quarter compar loss euro correspond period	1	0.74	1
russian export duti will active harvest finland sale russia will increas also	1	0.91	1
compani expect sale signific increas	1	0.91	1
compani amount ee which was percentsign more than	1	0.81	1
third quarter fiscal efor swung loss versus correspond period fiscal	0	0.77	1
acando ab acanb ss fell percent kronor lowest close sinc dec	0	0.20	0
compani oper loss total compar	0	0.27	0
last paseng flew airlin down percent	0	0.12	0
loss after financi item total compar correspond period	0	0.71	1

Exhibit 52 shows the confusion matrix for the test data. Accuracy and F1 score are 90% and 93%, respectively, while precision and recall are 89% and 98%, respectively. Therefore, it is apparent that the model performs similarly on the training, CV, and test datasets. These findings suggest that the model is robust and is not overfitting. They also suggest that the model should generalize well out-of-sample and can thus be used to predict the sentiment classes for new sentences from similar financial text data sources. Of course, these new text data must first be subjected to identical tokenization, cleansing, and preprocessing as done for the training dataset.

Exhibit 52: Confusion Matrix of Model Results for Test Data with Threshold p Value = 0.60

Confusion Matrix for Test Data

		Actual Training Labels	
		Class "1"	Class "0"
Predicted Results	Class "1"	284 (TP)	35 (FP)
	Class "0"	7 (FN)	110 (TN)

Performance Metrics

TP = 284, FP = 35, FN = 7, TN = 110

$P = 284 / (284+35) = 0.89$

$R = 284 / (284+7) = 0.98$

$\text{F1 Score} = (2 \times 0.89 \times 0.98) / (0.89 + 0.98) = 0.93$

$\text{Accuracy} = (284 + 110) / (284 + 35 + 110 + 7) = 0.90$

To recap, this project involves converting unstructured data (i.e., text data from financial data sources) into structured data (i.e., tokens, sentences, and term frequency values) in a document term matrix that is used as input for training, validating, and testing machine learning-based models (here, logistic regression) for predicting classification (here, sentiment classes). Similar models can be built and used in different contexts to understand the sentiment embedded in larger texts. The derived sentiment classification can be useful as a visualization tool to provide insight about the text without reading large documents. These sentiment classifications can also be used as structured input data for larger ML models that have a specific purpose, such as to predict future stock price movements.

EXAMPLE 7

Comparing Performance Metrics for Confusion Matrixes with Different Threshold p Values

In the previous analysis using the cross-validation dataset, performance measures for the sentiment classification ML model were calculated for a wide range (from 0.45 to 0.75) of threshold p values. The threshold value of 0.60 was determined to be the p value that maximizes model accuracy and F1 score; the confusion matrix for this model is shown in Exhibit 48. Use the following confusion matrixes with threshold p values of 0.75 and 0.45, A and B, respectively, to answer the following questions.

Confusion Matrix A			
Confusion Matrix for CV, Threshold = 0.75			
N = 436		Actual Training Labels	
		Class "1"	Class "0"
Predicted Results	Class "1"	281	28
	Class "0"	17	110

Confusion Matrix B			
Confusion Matrix for CV, Threshold = 0.45			
N = 436		Actual Training Labels	
		Class "1"	Class "0"
Predicted Results	Class "1"	281	41
	Class "0"	4	110

Performance Metrics

TP = 281, FP = 28, FN = 17, TN = 110
Precision = TP/(TP + FP) = 0.91
Recall = TP/(TP + FN) = 0.94
F1 Score = HMean: Prec. & Recall = 0.93
Accuracy = (TP + TN)/N = 0.90

Performance Metrics

TP = 281, FP = 41, FN = 4, TN = 110
Precision = TP/(TP + FP) = 0.87
Recall = TP/(TP + FN) = 0.99
F1 Score = HMean: Prec. & Recall = 0.93
Accuracy = (TP + TN)/N = 0.90

1. Compare the performance metrics of confusion matrix A (using a threshold p value of 0.75) with the confusion matrix in Exhibit 48 (using a threshold p value of 0.60).

Solution

Since confusion matrix A has fewer true positives (TPs) and fewer true negatives (TNs) than the confusion matrix in Exhibit 48 (281 vs. 284 and 110 vs. 114, respectively), confusion matrix A has lower accuracy and a lower F1 score compared to the one in Exhibit 48 (0.90 vs. 0.91 and 0.93 vs. 0.94, respectively). Also, although confusion matrix A has slightly better precision, 0.91 vs. 0.90, due to a few less false positives (FPs), it has significantly lower recall, 0.94 vs. 0.98, due to having many more false negatives (FNs), 17 vs. 7, than the confusion matrix in Exhibit 48. On balance, the ML model using the threshold p value of 0.60 is the superior model for this sentiment classification problem.

2. Compare the performance metrics of confusion matrix B (using a threshold p value of 0.45) with the confusion matrix in Exhibit 48 (using a threshold p value of 0.60).

Solution

Confusion matrix B has the same number of TPs (281) and TNs (110) as confusion matrix A. Therefore, confusion matrix B also has lower accuracy (0.90) and a lower F1 score (0.93) compared to the one in Exhibit 48. Although confusion matrix B has slightly better recall, 0.99 vs. 0.98, due to fewer FNs, it has somewhat lower precision, 0.87 vs. 0.90, due to having many more FPs, 41 vs. 30, than the confusion matrix in Exhibit 48. Again, it is apparent that the ML model using the threshold p value of 0.60 is the better model in this sentiment classification context.

3. Contrast the performance metrics of confusion matrixes A and B, and explain the trade-offs implied between them.

Solution

The main differences in performance metrics between confusion matrixes A and B are in precision and recall. Confusion matrix A has higher precision, at 0.91 vs. 0.87, but confusion matrix B has higher recall, at 0.99 vs. 0.94. These differences highlight the trade-off between FP (Type I error) and FN (Type II error). Precision is useful when the cost of FP is high, such as when an expensive product that is fine mistakenly fails quality inspection and is scrapped; in this case, FP should be minimized. Recall is useful when the cost of FN is high, such as when an expensive product is defective but mistakenly passes quality inspection and is sent to the customer; in this case, FN should be minimized. In the context of sentiment classification, FP might result in buying a stock for which sentiment is incorrectly classified as positive when it is actually negative. Conversely, FN might result in avoiding (or even shorting) a stock for which the sentiment is incorrectly classified as negative when it is actually positive. The model behind the confusion matrix in Exhibit 48 strikes a balance in the trade-off between precision and recall.

SUMMARY

In this reading, we have discussed the major steps in big data projects involving the development of machine learning (ML) models—namely, those combining textual big data with structured inputs.

- Big data—defined as data with volume, velocity, variety, and potentially lower veracity—has tremendous potential for various fintech applications, including several related to investment management.

- The main steps for traditional ML model building are conceptualization of the problem, data collection, data preparation and wrangling, data exploration, and model training.

- For textual ML model building, the first four steps differ somewhat from those used in the traditional model: Text problem formulation, text curation, text preparation and wrangling, and text exploration are typically necessary.

- For structured data, data preparation and wrangling entail data cleansing and data preprocessing. Data cleansing typically involves resolving incompleteness errors, invalidity errors, inaccuracy errors, inconsistency errors, non-uniformity errors, and duplication errors.

- Preprocessing for structured data typically involves performing the following transformations: extraction, aggregation, filtration, selection, and conversion.

- Preparation and wrangling text (unstructured) data involves a set of text-specific cleansing and preprocessing tasks. Text cleansing typically involves removing the following: html tags, punctuations, most numbers, and white spaces.

- Text preprocessing requires performing normalization that involves the following: lowercasing, removing stop words, stemming, lemmatization, creating bag-of-words (BOW) and n-grams, and organizing the BOW and n-grams into a document term matrix (DTM).

- Data exploration encompasses exploratory data analysis, feature selection, and feature engineering. Whereas histograms, box plots, and scatterplots are common techniques for exploring structured data, word clouds are an effective way to gain a high-level picture of the composition of textual content. These visualization tools help share knowledge among the team (business subject matter experts, quants, technologists, etc.) to help derive optimal solutions.

- Feature selection methods used for text data include term frequency, document frequency, chi-square test, and a mutual information measure. Feature engineering for text data includes converting numbers into tokens, creating n-grams, and using name entity recognition and parts of speech to engineer new feature variables.

- The model training steps (method selection, performance evaluation, and model tuning) often do not differ much for structured versus unstructured data projects.

- Model selection is governed by the following factors: whether the data project involves labeled data (supervised learning) or unlabeled data (unsupervised learning); the type of data (numerical, continuous, or categorical; text data; image data; speech data; etc.); and the size of the dataset.

- Model performance evaluation involves error analysis using confusion matrixes, determining receiver operating characteristics, and calculating root mean square error.

- To carry out an error analysis for each model, a confusion matrix is created; true positives (TPs), true negatives (TNs), false positives (FPs), and false negatives (FNs) are determined. Then, the following performance metrics are calculated: accuracy, F1 score, precision, and recall. The higher the accuracy and F1 score, the better the model performance.

- To carry out receiver operating characteristic (ROC) analysis, ROC curves and area under the curve (AUC) of various models are calculated and compared. The more convex the ROC curve and the higher the AUC, the better the model performance.

- Model tuning involves managing the trade-off between model bias error, associated with underfitting, and model variance error, associated with overfitting. A fitting curve of in-sample (training sample) error and out-of-sample (cross-validation sample) error on the y-axis versus model complexity on the x-axis is useful for managing the bias vs. variance error trade-off.

- In a real-world big data project involving text data analysis for classifying and predicting sentiment of financial text for particular stocks, the text data are transformed into structured data for populating the DTM, which is then used as the input for the ML algorithm.

- To derive term frequency (TF) at the sentence level and TF–IDF, both of which can be inputs to the DTM, the following frequency measures should be used to create a term frequency measures table: TotalWordsInSentence; TotalWordCount; TermFrequency (Collection Level); WordCountInSentence; SentenceCountWithWord; Document Frequency; and Inverse Document Frequency.

PRACTICE PROBLEMS

The following information relates to questions 1-15

Aaliyah Schultz is a fixed-income portfolio manager at Aries Investments. Schultz supervises Ameris Steele, a junior analyst.

A few years ago, Schultz developed a proprietary machine learning (ML) model that aims to predict downgrades of publicly-traded firms by bond rating agencies. The model currently relies only on structured financial data collected from different sources. Schultz thinks the model's predictive power may be improved by incorporating sentiment data derived from textual analysis of news articles and Twitter content relating to the subject companies.

Schultz and Steele meet to discuss plans for incorporating the sentiment data into the model. They discuss the differences in the steps between building ML models that use traditional structured data and building ML models that use textual big data. Steele tells Schultz:

Statement 1   The second step in building text-based ML models is text preparation and wrangling, whereas the second step in building ML models using structured data is data collection.

Statement 2   The fourth step in building both types of models encompasses data/text exploration.

Steele expresses concern about using Twitter content in the model, noting that research suggests that as much as 10%–15% of social media content is from fake accounts. Schultz tells Steele that she understands her concern but thinks the potential for model improvement outweighs the concern.

Steele begins building a model that combines the structured financial data and the sentiment data. She starts with cleansing and wrangling the raw structured financial data. Exhibit 1 presents a small sample of the raw dataset before cleansing: Each row represents data for a particular firm.

Exhibit 1: Sample of Raw Structured Data Before Cleansing

ID	Ticker	IPO Date	Industry (NAICS)	EBIT	Interest Expense	Total Debt
1	ABC	4/6/17	44	9.4	0.6	10.1
2	BCD	November 15, 2004	52	5.5	0.4	6.2
3	HIJ	26-Jun-74	54	8.9	1.2	15.8
4	KLM	14-Mar-15	72	5.7	1.5	0.0

After cleansing the data, Steele then preprocesses the dataset. She creates two new variables: an "Age" variable based on the firm's IPO date and an "Interest Coverage Ratio" variable equal to EBIT divided by interest expense. She also deletes the "IPO Date" variable from the dataset. After applying these transformations, Steele scales the financial data using normalization. She notes that over the full sample dataset, the "Interest Expense" variable ranges from a minimum of 0.2

and a maximum of 12.2, with a mean of 1.1 and a standard deviation of 0.4.

Steele and Schultz then discuss how to preprocess the raw text data. Steele tells Schultz that the process can be completed in the following three steps:

Step 1   Cleanse the raw text data.

Step 2   Split the cleansed data into a collection of words for them to be normalized.

Step 3   Normalize the collection of words from Step 2 and create a distinct set of tokens from the normalized words.

With respect to Step 1, Steele tells Schultz:

"I believe I should remove all html tags, punctuations, numbers, and extra white spaces from the data before normalizing them."

After properly cleansing the raw text data, Steele completes Steps 2 and 3. She then performs exploratory data analysis. To assist in feature selection, she wants to create a visualization that shows the most informative words in the dataset based on their term frequency (TF) values. After creating and analyzing the visualization, Steele is concerned that some tokens are likely to be noise features for ML model training; therefore, she wants to remove them.

Steele and Schultz discuss the importance of feature selection and feature engineering in ML model training. Steele tells Schultz:

"Appropriate feature selection is a key factor in minimizing model overfitting, whereas feature engineering tends to prevent model underfitting."

Once satisfied with the final set of features, Steele selects and runs a model on the training set that classifies the text as having positive sentiment (Class "1" or negative sentiment (Class "0"). She then evaluates its performance using error analysis. The resulting confusion matrix is presented in Exhibit 2.

Exhibit 2: Confusion Matrix

		Actual Training Results	
		Class "1"	Class "0"
Predicted Results	Class "1"	TP = 182	FP = 52
	Class "0"	FN = 31	TN = 96

1. Which of Steele's statements relating to the steps in building structured data-based and text-based ML models is correct?

    A. Only Statement 1 is correct.

    B. Only Statement 2 is correct.

    C. Statement 1 and Statement 2 are correct.

2. Steele's concern about using Twitter data in the model *best* relates to:

    A. volume.

    B. velocity.

    C. veracity.

3. What type of error appears to be present in the IPO Date column of Exhibit 1?

    A. invalidity error.

    B. inconsistency error.

    C. non-uniformity error.

4. What type of error is most likely present in the last row of data (ID #4) in Exhibit 1?

    A. Inconsistency error

    B. Incompleteness error

    C. Non-uniformity error

5. During the preprocessing of the data in Exhibit 1, what type of data transformation did Steele perform during the data preprocessing step?

    A. Extraction

    B. Conversion

    C. Aggregation

6. Based on Exhibit 1, for the firm with ID #3, Steele should compute the scaled value for the "Interest Expense" variable as:

    A. 0.008.

    B. 0.083.

    C. 0.250.

7. Is Steele's statement regarding Step 1 of the preprocessing of raw text data correct?

    A. Yes.

    B. No, because her suggested treatment of punctuation is incorrect.

    C. No, because her suggested treatment of extra white spaces is incorrect.

8. Steele's Step 2 can be *best* described as:

    A. tokenization.

    B. lemmatization.

    C. standardization.

9. The output created in Steele's Step 3 can be *best* described as a:

    A. bag-of-words.

    B. set of n-grams.

    C. document term matrix.

10. Given her objective, the visualization that Steele should create in the exploratory

data analysis step is a:

A. scatter plot.

B. word cloud.

C. document term matrix.

11. To address her concern in her exploratory data analysis, Steele should focus on those tokens that have:

A. low chi-square statistics.

B. low mutual information (ML) values.

C. very low and very high term frequency (TF) values.

12. Is Steele's statement regarding the relationship between feature selection/feature engineering and model fit correct?

A. Yes.

B. No, because she is incorrect with respect to feature selection.

C. No, because she is incorrect with respect to feature engineering.

13. Based on Exhibit 2, the model's precision metric is *closest* to:

A. 78%.

B. 81%.

C. 85%.

14. Based on Exhibit 2, the model's F1 score is *closest* to:

A. 77%.

B. 81%.

C. 85%.

15. Based on Exhibit 2, the model's accuracy metric is *closest* to:

A. 77%.

B. 81%.

C. 85%.

The following information relates to questions 16-24

Bernadette Rivera is a portfolio manager at Voxkor, a private equity company that provides financing to early-stage start-up businesses. Rivera is working with a data analyst, Tim Achler, on a text-based machine-learning (ML) model to enhance Voxkor's predictive ability to identify successful start-ups.

Voxkor currently uses ML models based only on traditional, structured financial data but would like to develop a new ML model that analyzes textual big data gathered from the internet. The model will classify text information into positive or negative sentiment classes for each respective start-up. Rivera wants to confirm her understanding of any differences in the ML model building steps between data analysis projects that use traditional structured data and projects that involve unstructured, text-based data. Rivera makes the following statements:

Statement 1   Some of the methods used in the exploration step are different for structured and unstructured data, but for both types of data, the step involves feature selection and feature engineering.

Statement 2   A major difference when developing a text-based ML model is the curation step, which involves cleansing, preprocessing, and converting the data into a structured format usable for model training.

Achler uses a web spidering program to obtain the data for the text-based model. The program extracts raw content from social media webpages, which contains English language sentences and special characters. After curating the text, Achler removes unnecessary elements from the raw text using regular expression software and completes additional text cleansing and preprocessing tasks.

Next, Achler and Rivera discuss remaining text wrangling tasks—specifically, which tokens to include in the document term matrix (DTM). Achler divides unique tokens into three groups; a sample of each group is shown in Exhibit 1.

Exhibit 1: Summary of Sample Tokens

Token Group 1	Token Group 2	Token Group 3
"not_increas_market"	"not_increased_market"	"not," "increased," "market"
"currencysign"	"currencysign"	"EUR"
"sale_decreas"	"sale_decreased"	"Sales," "decreased"

The dataset is now ready for the text exploration step. At this point in the process, Rivera wants to better comprehend the collection of unique words. Achler recommends an exploratory data analysis technique that visualizes words by varying their font size proportionately to the number of occurrences of each word in the corpus.

As an additional part of the text exploration step, Achler conducts a term frequency analysis to identify outliers. Achler summarizes the analysis in Exhibit 2.

Exhibit 2: Words with Highest and Lowest Frequency Value

Group 1		Group 2	
Word	Frequency	Word	Frequency
the	0.04935	naval	1.0123e-05
and	0.04661	stereotype	1.5185e-05
to	0.04179	till	1.5185e-05
that	0.03577	ribbon	2.0247e-05

	Group 1		Group 2	
Word	**Frequency**	**Word**	**Frequency**
in	0.03368	deposit	2.5308e-05

Note: "e-05" represents 10^{-5}.

Achler has the data ready for the model training process. Rivera asks Achler to include start-up failure rates as a feature. Achler notices that the number of start-ups that fail (majority class) is significantly larger than the number of the start-ups that are successful (minority class). Achler is concerned that because of class imbalance, the model will not be able to discriminate between start-ups that fail and start-ups that are successful.

Achler splits the DTM into training, cross-validation, and test datasets. Achler uses a supervised learning approach to train the logistic regression model in predicting sentiment. Applying the receiver operating characteristics (ROC) technique and area under the curve (AUC) metrics, Achler evaluates model performance on both the training and the cross-validation datasets. The trained model performance for three different logistic regressions' threshold p-values is presented in Exhibit 3.

Exhibit 3: AUC for Different Threshold p-values

Threshold p-Value	Training Set	Cross-Validation Set
$p = 0.57$	56.7%	57.3%
$p = 0.79$	91.3%	89.7%
$p = 0.84$	98.4%	87.1%

Rivera suggests adjusting the model's hyperparameters to improve performance. Achler runs a grid search that compares the difference between the prediction error on both the training and the cross-validation datasets for various combinations of hyperparameter values. For the current values of hyperparameters, Achler observes that the prediction error on the training dataset is small, whereas the prediction error on the cross-validation dataset is significantly larger.

16. Which of Rivera's statements about differences in ML model building steps is correct?

   A. Only Statement 1

   B. Only Statement 2

   C. Both Statement 1 and Statement 2

17. Based on the source of the data, as part of the data cleansing and wrangling process, Achler *most likely* needs to remove:

   A. html tags and perform scaling.

   B. numbers and perform lemmatization.

   C. white spaces and perform winsorization.

18. Based on Exhibit 1, which token group has *most likely* undergone the text prepa-

ration and wrangling process?

A. Token Group 1

B. Token Group 2

C. Token Group 3

19. The visual text representation technique that Achler recommends to Rivera is a:

A. word cloud.

B. bag of words.

C. collection frequency.

20. Based on Exhibit 2, Achler should exclude from further analysis words in:

A. only Group 1.

B. only Group 2.

C. both Group 1 and Group 2.

21. Achler's model training concern related to the model's ability to discriminate could be addressed by randomly:

A. oversampling the failed start-up data.

B. oversampling the successful start-up data.

C. undersampling the successful start-up data.

22. Based on Exhibit 3, which threshold p-value indicates the *best* fitting model?

A. 0.57

B. 0.79

C. 0.84

23. Based on Exhibit 3, if Achler wants to improve model performance at the threshold p-value of 0.84, he should:

A. tune the model to lower the AUC.

B. adjust model parameters to decrease ROC convexity.

C. apply LASSO regularization to the logistic regression.

24. Based on Achler's grid search analysis, the current model can be characterized as:

A. underfitted.

B. having low variance.

C. exhibiting slight regularization.

The following information relates to questions 25-31

Iesha Azarov is a senior analyst at Ganymede Moon Partners (Ganymede), where he works with junior analyst Pàola Bector. Azarov would like to incorporate machine learning (ML) models into the company's analytical process. Azarov asks Bector to develop ML models for two unstructured stock sentiment datasets, Dataset ABC and Dataset XYZ. Both datasets have been cleaned and preprocessed in preparation for text exploration and model training.

Following an exploratory data analysis that revealed Dataset ABC's most frequent tokens, Bector conducts a collection frequency analysis. Bector then computes TF–IDF (term frequency–inverse document frequency) for several words in the collection and tells Azarov the following:

Statement 1	IDF is equal to the inverse of the document frequency measure.
Statement 2	TF at the collection level is multiplied by IDF to calculate TF–IDF.
Statement 3	TF–IDF values vary by the number of documents in the dataset, and therefore, model performance can vary when applied to a dataset with just a few documents.

Bector notes that Dataset ABC is characterized by the absence of ground truth.

Bector turns his attention to Dataset XYZ, containing 84,000 tokens and 10,000 sentences. Bector chooses an appropriate feature selection method to identify and remove unnecessary tokens from the dataset and then focuses on model training. For performance evaluation purposes, Dataset XYZ is split into a training set, cross-validation (CV) set, and test set. Each of the sentences has already been labeled as either a positive sentiment (Class "1") or a negative sentiment (Class "0") sentence. There is an unequal class distribution between the positive sentiment and negative sentiment sentences in Dataset XYZ. Simple random sampling is applied within levels of the sentiment class labels to balance the class distributions within the splits. Bector's view is that the false positive and false negative evaluation metrics should be given equal weight. Select performance data from the cross-validation set confusion matrices is presented in Exhibit 1:

Exhibit 1: Performance Metrics for Dataset XYZ

Confusion Matrix	CV Data (threshold p-value)	Performance Metrics			
		Precision	Recall	F1 Score	Accuracy
A	0.50	0.95	0.87	0.91	0.91
B	0.35	0.93	0.90	0.91	0.92
C	0.65	0.86	0.97	0.92	0.91

Azarov and Bector evaluate the Dataset XYZ performance metrics for Confusion Matrices A, B, and C in Exhibit 1. Azarov says, "For Ganymede's purposes, we should be most concerned with the cost of Type I errors."

Azarov requests that Bector apply the ML model to the test dataset for Dataset XYZ, assuming a threshold p-value of 0.65. Exhibit 2 contains a sample of results from the test dataset corpus.

Exhibit 2: 10 Sample Results of Test Data for Dataset XYZ

Sentence #	Actual Sentiment	Target p-Value
1	1	0.75
2	0	0.45
3	1	0.64
4	1	0.81
5	0	0.43
6	1	0.78
7	0	0.59
8	1	0.60
9	0	0.67
10	0	0.54

Bector makes the following remarks regarding model training:

Remark 1: Method selection is governed by such factors as the type of data and the size of data.

Remark 2: In the performance evaluation stage, model fitting errors, such as bias error and variance error, are used to measure goodness of fit.

25. Based on the text exploration method used for Dataset ABC, tokens that potentially carry important information useful for differentiating the sentiment embedded in the text are *most likely* to have values that are:

   A. low.

   B. intermediate.

   C. high.

26. Which of Bector's statements regarding TF, IDF, and TF–IDF is correct?

   A. Statement 1

   B. Statement 2

   C. Statement 3

27. What percentage of Dataset ABC should be allocated to a training subset?

   A. 0%

   B. 20%

   C. 60%

28. Based only on Dataset XYZ's composition and Bector's view regarding false positive and false negative evaluation metrics, which performance measure is *most appropriate*?

   A. Recall

   B. F1 score

C. Precision

29. Based on Exhibit 1, which confusion matrix demonstrates the *most* favorable value of the performance metric that *best* addresses Azarov's concern?

    A. Confusion Matrix A

    B. Confusion Matrix B

    C. Confusion Matrix C

30. Based on Exhibit 2, the accuracy metric for Dataset XYZ's test set sample is *closest to*:

    A. 0.67.

    B. 0.70.

    C. 0.75.

31. Which of Bector's remarks related to model training is correct?

    A. Only Remark 1

    B. Only Remark 2

    C. Both Remark 1 and Remark 2

SOLUTIONS

1. B is correct. The five steps in building structured data-based ML models are: 1) conceptualization of the modeling task, 2) data collection, 3) data preparation and wrangling, 4) data exploration, and 5) model training. The five steps in building text-based ML models are: 1) text problem formulation, 2) data (text) curation, 3) text preparation and wrangling, 4) text exploration, and 5) model training. Statement 1 is incorrect: Text preparation and wrangling is the third step in building text ML models and occurs after the second data (text) curation step. Statement 2 is correct: The fourth step in building both types of models encompasses data/text exploration.

2. C is correct. Veracity relates to the credibility and reliability of different data sources. Steele is concerned about the credibility and reliability of Twitter content, noting that research suggests that as much as 10%–15% of social media content is from fake accounts.

3. C is correct. A non-uniformity error occurs when the data are not presented in an identical format. The data in the "IPO Date" column represent the IPO date of each firm. While all rows are populated with valid dates in the IPO Date column, the dates are presented in different formats (e.g., mm/dd/yyyy, dd/mm/yyyy).

4. A is correct. There appears to be an inconsistency error in the last row (ID #4). An inconsistency error occurs when a data point conflicts with corresponding data points or reality. In the last row, the interest expense data item has a value of 1.5, and the total debt item has a value of 0.0. This appears to be an error: Firms that have interest expense are likely to have debt in their capital structure, so either the interest expense is incorrect or the total debt value is incorrect. Steele should investigate this issue by using alternative data sources to confirm the correct values for these variables.

5. A is correct. During the data preprocessing step, Steele created a new "Age" variable based on the firm's IPO date and then deleted the "IPO Date" variable from the dataset. She also created a new "Interest Coverage Ratio" variable equal to EBIT divided by interest expense. Extraction refers to a data transformation where a new variable is extracted from a current variable for ease of analyzing and using for training an ML model, such as creating an age variable from a date variable or a ratio variable. Steele also performed a selection transformation by deleting the IPO Date variable, which refers to deleting the data columns that are not needed for the project.

6. B is correct. Steele uses normalization to scale the financial data. Normalization is the process of rescaling numeric variables in the range of [0, 1]. To normalize variable X, the minimum value (X_{min}) is subtracted from each observation (X_i), and then this value is divided by the difference between the maximum and minimum values of X ($X_{max} - X_{min}$):

$$X_{i \text{ (normalized)}} = \frac{X_i - X_{min}}{X_{max} - X_{min}}.$$

The firm with ID #3 has an interest expense of 1.2. So, its normalized value is calculated as:

$$X_{i \text{ (normalized)}} = \frac{1.2 - 0.2}{12.2 - 0.2} = 0.083.$$

7. B is correct. Although most punctuations are not necessary for text analysis and

should be removed, some punctuations (e.g., percentage signs, currency symbols, and question marks) may be useful for ML model training. Such punctuations should be substituted with annotations (e.g., /percentSign/, /dollarSign/, and /questionMark/) to preserve their grammatical meaning in the text. Such annotations preserve the semantic meaning of important characters in the text for further text processing and analysis stages.

8. A is correct. Tokenization is the process of splitting a given text into separate tokens. This step takes place after cleansing the raw text data (removing html tags, numbers, extra white spaces, etc.). The tokens are then normalized to create the bag-of-words (BOW).

9. A is correct. After the cleansed text is normalized, a bag-of-words is created. A bag-of-words (BOW) is a collection of a distinct set of tokens from all the texts in a sample dataset.

10. B is correct. Steele wants to create a visualization for Schultz that shows the most informative words in the dataset based on their term frequency (TF, the ratio of the number of times a given token occurs in the dataset to the total number of tokens in the dataset) values. A word cloud is a common visualization when working with text data as it can be made to visualize the most informative words and their TF values. The most commonly occurring words in the dataset can be shown by varying font size, and color is used to add more dimensions, such as frequency and length of words.

11. C is correct. Frequency measures can be used for vocabulary pruning to remove noise features by filtering the tokens with very high and low TF values across all the texts. Noise features are both the most frequent and most sparse (or rare) tokens in the dataset. On one end, noise features can be stop words that are typically present frequently in all the texts across the dataset. On the other end, noise features can be sparse terms that are present in only a few text files. Text classification involves dividing text documents into assigned classes. The frequent tokens strain the ML model to choose a decision boundary among the texts as the terms are present across all the texts (an example of underfitting). The rare tokens mislead the ML model into classifying texts containing the rare terms into a specific class (an example of overfitting). Thus, identifying and removing noise features are critical steps for text classification applications.

12. A is correct. A dataset with a small number of features may not carry all the characteristics that explain relationships between the target variable and the features. Conversely, a large number of features can complicate the model and potentially distort patterns in the data due to low degrees of freedom, causing overfitting. Therefore, appropriate feature selection is a key factor in minimizing such model overfitting. Feature engineering tends to prevent underfitting in the training of the model. New features, when engineered properly, can elevate the underlying data points that better explain the interactions of features. Thus, feature engineering can be critical to overcome underfitting.

13. A is correct. Precision, the ratio of correctly predicted positive classes (true positives) to all predicted positive classes, is calculated as:

Precision (P) = TP/(TP + FP) = 182/(182 + 52) = 0.7778 (78%).

14. B is correct. The model's F1 score, which is the harmonic mean of precision and recall, is calculated as:

F1 score = $(2 \times P \times R)/(P + R)$.

F1 score = (2 × 0.7778 × 0.8545)/(0.7778 + 0.8545) = 0.8143 (81%).

15. A is correct. The model's accuracy, which is the percentage of correctly predicted classes out of total predictions, is calculated as:

Accuracy = (TP + TN)/(TP + FP + TN + FN).

Accuracy = (182 + 96)/(182 + 52 + 96 + 31) = 0.7701 (77%).

16. A is correct. Statement 1 is correct because some of the methods used in the fourth step of ML model building (data/text exploration) are different for structured and unstructured data, and for both structured and unstructured data, the exploration step encompasses feature selection and feature engineering. Statement 2 is incorrect because Rivera described the text preparation and wrangling step, not the text curation step. The data (text) curation step involves gathering relevant external text data via web services or programs that extract raw content from a source.

B and C are incorrect because Statement 2 is incorrect. Rivera described the text preparation and wrangling step, not the text curation step. The data (text) curation step involves gathering relevant external text data via web services or programs that extract raw content from a source.

17. B is correct. Achler uses a web spidering program that extracts unstructured raw content from social media webpages. Raw text data are a sequence of characters and contain other non-useful elements including html tags, punctuation, and white spaces (including tabs, line breaks, and new lines). Removing numbers is one of the basic operations in the text cleansing/preparation process for unstructured data. When numbers (or digits) are present in the text, they should be removed or substituted with the annotation "/number/." Lemmatization, which takes places during the text wrangling/preprocessing process for unstructured data, is the process of converting inflected forms of a word into its morphological root (known as lemma). Lemmatization reduces the repetition of words occurring in various forms while maintaining the semantic structure of the text data, thereby aiding in training less complex ML models.

A is incorrect because although html tag removal is part of text cleansing/preparation for unstructured data, scaling is a data wrangling/preprocessing process applied to structured data. Scaling adjusts the range of a feature by shifting and changing the scale of data; it is performed on numeric variables, not on text data.

C is incorrect because although raw text contains white spaces (including tabs, line breaks, and new lines) that need to be removed as part of the data cleansing/preparation process for unstructured data, winsorization is a data wrangling/preprocessing task performed on values of data points, not on text data. Winsorization is used for structured numerical data and replaces extreme values and outliers with the maximum (for large-value outliers) and minimum (for small-value outliers) values of data points that are not outliers.

18. A is correct. Data preparation and wrangling involve cleansing and organizing raw data into a consolidated format. Token Group 1 includes n-grams ("not_increas_market," "sale_decreas") and the words that have been converted from their inflected forms into their base word ("increas," "decreas"), and the currency symbol has been replaced with a "currencysign" token. N-gram tokens are helpful for keeping negations intact in the text, which is vital for sentiment prediction. The process of converting inflected forms of a word into its base word is called stemming and helps decrease data sparseness, thereby aiding in training less

complex ML models.

B is incorrect because Token Group 2 includes inflected forms of words ("increased," "decreased") before conversion into their base words (known as stems). Stemming (along with lemmatization) decreases data sparseness by aggregating many sparsely occurring words in relatively less sparse stems or lemmas, thereby aiding in training less complex ML models.

C is incorrect because Token Group 3 includes inflected forms of words ("increased," "decreased") before conversion into their base words (known as stems). In addition, the "EUR" currency symbol has not been replaced with the "currencysign" token and the word "Sales" has not been lowercased.

19. A is correct. Achler recommends creating a word cloud, which is a common text visualization technique at the data exploration phase in ML model building. The most commonly occurring words in the dataset can be visualized by varying font size, and color is used to add more dimensions, such as frequency and length of words.

   B is incorrect because Achler recommends creating a word cloud and not a bag of words (BOW). A BOW is a collection of a distinct set of tokens from all the texts in a sample dataset. A BOW representation is a basic procedure used primarily to analyze text during Step 3 (text wrangling/preprocessing), although it may also be used in Step 4 during the feature engineering process. In contrast to a word cloud, which visually varies font size and color, BOW is simply a set of words (typically displayed in table).

   C is incorrect because Achler recommends creating a word cloud and not a collection frequency. Collection frequency (or term frequency) is the ratio of the number of times a given token occurs in all the texts in the dataset to the total number of tokens in the dataset. Collection frequency can be calculated and examined to identify outlier words, but it is not a visual text representation tool.

20. C is correct. Achler should remove words that are in both Group 1 and Group 2. Term frequency values range between 0 and 1. Group 1 consists of the highest frequency values (e.g., "the" = 0.04935), and Group 2 consists of the lowest frequency values (e.g., "naval" = 1.0123e–05). Frequency analysis on the processed text data helps in filtering unnecessary tokens (or features) by quantifying how important tokens are in a sentence and in the corpus as a whole. The most frequent tokens (Group 1) strain the machine-learning model to choose a decision boundary among the texts as the terms are present across all the texts, which leads to model underfitting. The least frequent tokens (Group 2) mislead the machine-learning model into classifying texts containing the rare terms into a specific class, which leads to model overfitting. Identifying and removing noise features is critical for text classification applications.

   A is incorrect because words in both Group 1 and Group 2 should be removed. The words with high term frequency value are mostly stop words, present in most sentences. Stop words do not carry a semantic meaning for the purpose of text analyses and ML training, so they do not contribute to differentiating sentiment.

   B is incorrect because words in both Group 1 and Group 2 should be removed. Terms with low term frequency value are mostly rare terms, ones appearing only once or twice in the data. They do not contribute to differentiating sentiment.

21. B is correct. Achler is concerned about class imbalance, which can be resolved by balancing the training data. The majority class (the failed start-up data) can be randomly undersampled, or the minority class (the successful start-up data) can be randomly oversampled.

22. B is correct. The higher the AUC, the better the model performance. For the

threshold p-value of 0.79, the AUC is 91.3% on the training dataset and 89.7% on the cross-validation dataset, and the ROC curves are similar for model performance on both datasets. These findings suggest that the model performs similarly on both training and CV data and thus indicate a good fitting model.

A is incorrect because for the threshold p-value of 0.57, the AUC is 56.7% on the training dataset and 57.3% on the cross-validation dataset. The AUC close to 50% signifies random guessing on both the training dataset and the cross-validation dataset. The implication is that for the threshold p-value of 0.57, the model is randomly guessing and is not performing well.

C is incorrect because for the threshold p-value of 0.84, there is a substantial difference between the AUC on the training dataset (98.4%) and the AUC on the cross-validation dataset (87.1%). This suggests that the model performs comparatively poorly (with a higher rate of error or misclassification) on the cross-validation dataset when compared with training data. Thus, the implication is that the model is overfitted.

23. C is correct. At the threshold p-value of 0.84, the AUC is 98.4% for the training dataset and 87.1% for the cross-validation dataset, which suggests that the model is currently overfitted. Least absolute shrinkage and selection operator (LASSO) regularization can be applied to the logistic regression to prevent overfitting of logistic regression models.

   A is incorrect because the higher the AUC, the better the model performance.

   B is incorrect because the more convex the ROC curve and the higher the AUC, the better the model performance. Adjusting model parameters with the aim of achieving lower ROC convexity would result in worse model performance on the cross-validation dataset.

24. C is correct. Slight regularization occurs when the prediction error on the training dataset is small, while the prediction error on the cross-validation data set is significantly larger. This difference in error is variance. High variance error, which typically is due to too many features and model complexity, results in model overfitting.

   A is incorrect. The current model has high variance which results in model overfitting, not underfitting.

   B is incorrect. The difference between the prediction error on the training dataset and the prediction error on the cross-validation dataset is high, which means that the current model has high variance, not low.

25. B is correct. When analyzing term frequency at the corpus level, also known as collection frequency, tokens with intermediate term frequency (TF) values potentially carry important information useful for differentiating the sentiment embedded in the text. Tokens with the highest TF values are mostly stop words that do not contribute to differentiating the sentiment embedded in the text, and tokens with the lowest TF values are mostly proper nouns or sparse terms that are also not important to the meaning of the text.

   A is incorrect because tokens with the lowest TF values are mostly proper nouns or sparse terms (noisy terms) that are not important to the meaning of the text.

   C is incorrect because tokens with the highest TF values are mostly stop words (noisy terms) that do not contribute to differentiating the sentiment embedded in the text.

26. C is correct. Statement 3 is correct. TF–IDF values vary by the number of documents in the dataset, and therefore, the model performance can vary when

applied to a dataset with just a few documents.

Statement 1 is incorrect because IDF is calculated as the log of the inverse, or reciprocal, of the document frequency measure. Statement 2 is incorrect because TF at the sentence (not collection) level is multiplied by IDF to calculate TF–IDF.

A is incorrect because Statement 1 is incorrect. IDF is calculated as the log of the inverse, or reciprocal, of the document frequency (DF) measure.

B is incorrect because Statement 2 is incorrect. TF at the sentence (not collection) level is multiplied by IDF to calculate TF–IDF.

27. A is correct; 0% of the master dataset of Dataset ABC should be allocated to a training subset. Dataset ABC is characterized by the absence of ground truth (i.e., no known outcome or target variable) and is therefore an unsupervised ML model. For unsupervised learning models, no splitting of the master dataset is needed, because of the absence of labeled training data. Supervised ML datasets (with labeled training data) contain ground truth, the known outcome (target variable) of each observation in the dataset.

    B is incorrect because 20% is the commonly recommended split for the cross-validation set and test set in supervised training ML datasets. Dataset ABC is an unsupervised ML dataset, for which no splitting (0%) of the master dataset is needed, because of the absence of labeled training data. In supervised ML models (which contain labeled training data), the master dataset is split into three subsets (a training set, cross-validation set, and test set), which are used for model training and testing purposes.

    C is incorrect because 60% is the commonly recommended split for the training set in supervised training ML datasets. Dataset ABC is an unsupervised ML dataset, for which no splitting (0%) of the master dataset is needed, because of the absence of labeled training data. In supervised ML models (which contain labeled training data), the master dataset is split into three subsets (a training set, cross-validation set, and test set), which are used for model training and testing purposes.

28. B is correct. F1 score is the most appropriate performance measure for Dataset XYZ. Bector gives equal weight to false positives and false negatives. Accuracy and F1 score are overall performance measures that give equal weight to false positives and false negatives. Accuracy is considered an appropriate performance measure for balanced datasets, where the number of "1" and "0" classes are equal. F1 score is considered more appropriate than accuracy when there is unequal class distribution in the dataset and it is necessary to measure the equilibrium of precision and recall. Since Dataset XYZ contains an unequal class distribution between positive and negative sentiment sentences, F1 score is the most appropriate performance measure.

    Precision is the ratio of correctly predicted positive classes to all predicted positive classes and is useful in situations where the cost of false positives or Type I errors is high. Recall is the ratio of correctly predicted positive classes to all actual positive classes and is useful in situations where the cost of false negatives or Type II errors is high.

    A is incorrect because Bector gives equal weight to false positives and false negatives. Accuracy and F1 score are overall performance measures that give equal weight to false positives and false negatives. Recall is the ratio of correctly predicted positive classes to all actual positive classes and is useful in situations where the cost of false negatives or Type II errors is high.

    C is incorrect because Bector gives equal weight to false positive and false negatives. Accuracy and F1 score are overall performance measures that give equal weight to false positives and false negatives. Precision is the ratio of correctly predicted positive classes to all predicted positive classes and is useful in situations where the cost of false positives or Type-I error is high.

29. A is correct. Precision is the ratio of correctly predicted positive classes to all predicted positive classes and is useful in situations where the cost of false positives or Type I errors is high. Confusion Matrix A has the highest precision and therefore demonstrates the most favorable value of the performance metric that best addresses Azarov's concern about the cost of Type I errors. Confusion Matrix A has a precision score of 0.95, which is higher than the precision scores of Confusion Matrix B (0.93) and Confusion Matrix C (0.86).

B is incorrect because precision, not accuracy, is the performance measure that best addresses Azarov's concern about the cost of Type I errors. Confusion Matrix B demonstrates the most favorable value for the accuracy score (0.92), which is higher than the accuracy scores of Confusion Matrix A (0.91) and Confusion Matrix C (0.91). Accuracy is a performance measure that gives equal weight to false positives and false negatives and is considered an appropriate performance measure when the class distribution in the dataset is equal (a balanced dataset). However, Azarov is most concerned with the cost of false positives, or Type I errors, and not with finding the equilibrium between precision and recall. Furthermore, Dataset XYZ has an unequal (unbalanced) class distribution between positive sentiment and negative sentiment sentences.

C is incorrect because precision, not recall or F1 score, is the performance measure that best addresses Azarov's concern about the cost of Type I errors. Confusion Matrix C demonstrates the most favorable value for the recall score (0.97), which is higher than the recall scores of Confusion Matrix A (0.87) and Confusion Matrix B (0.90). Recall is the ratio of correctly predicted positive classes to all actual positive classes and is useful in situations where the cost of false negatives, or Type II errors, is high. However, Azarov is most concerned with the cost of Type I errors, not Type II errors.

F1 score is more appropriate (than accuracy) when there is unequal class distribution in the dataset and it is necessary to measure the equilibrium of precision and recall. Confusion Matrix C demonstrates the most favorable value for the F1 score (0.92), which is higher than the F1 scores of Confusion Matrix A (0.91) and Confusion Matrix B (0.91). Although Dataset XYZ has an unequal class distribution between positive sentiment and negative sentiment sentences, Azarov is most concerned with the cost of false positives, or Type I errors, and not with finding the equilibrium between precision and recall.

30. B is correct. Accuracy is the percentage of correctly predicted classes out of total predictions and is calculated as (TP + TN)/(TP + FP + TN + FN).

In order to obtain the values for true positive (TP), true negative (TN), false positive (FP), and false negative (FN), predicted sentiment for the positive (Class "1") and the negative (Class "0") classes are determined based on whether each individual target p-value is greater than or less than the threshold p-value of 0.65. If an individual target p-value is greater than the threshold p-value of 0.65, the predicted sentiment for that instance is positive (Class "1"). If an individual target p-value is less than the threshold p-value of 0.65, the predicted sentiment for that instance is negative (Class "0"). Actual sentiment and predicted sentiment are then classified as follows:

Actual Sentiment	Predicted Sentiment	Classification
1	1	TP
0	1	FP
1	0	FN

Actual Sentiment	Predicted Sentiment	Classification
0	0	TN

Exhibit 2, with added "Predicted Sentiment" and "Classification" columns, is presented below:

10 Sample Results of Test Data for Dataset XYZ

Sentence #	Actual Sentiment	Target p-Value	Predicted Sentiment	Classification
1	1	0.75	1	TP
2	0	0.45	0	TN
3	1	0.64	0	FN
4	1	0.81	1	TP
5	0	0.43	0	TN
6	1	0.78	1	TP
7	0	0.59	0	TN
8	1	0.60	0	FN
9	0	0.67	1	FP
10	0	0.54	0	TN

Based on the classification data obtained from Exhibit 2, a confusion matrix can be generated:

Confusion Matrix for Dataset XYZ Sample Test Data with Threshold p-Value = 0.65

	Actual Training Labels	
Predicted Results	Class "1"	Class "0"
Class "1"	TP = 3	FP = 1
Class "0"	FN = 2	TN = 4

Using the data in the confusion matrix above, the accuracy metric is computed as follows:

Accuracy = (TP + TN)/(TP + FP + TN + FN).

Accuracy = (3 + 4)/(3 + 1 + 4 + 2) = 0.70.

A is incorrect because 0.67 is the F1 score, not accuracy metric, for the sample of the test set for Dataset XYZ, based on Exhibit 2. To calculate the F1 score, the precision (P) and the recall (R) ratios must first be calculated. Precision and recall for the sample of the test set for Dataset XYZ, based on Exhibit 2, are calculated as follows:

Precision (P) = TP/(TP + FP) = 3/(3 + 1) = 0.75.

Recall (R) = TP/(TP + FN) = 3/(3 + 2) = 0.60.

The F1 score is calculated as follows:

F1 score = $(2 \times P \times R)/(P + R) = (2 \times 0.75 \times 0.60)/(0.75 + 0.60)$

= 0.667, or 0.67.

C is incorrect because 0.75 is the precision ratio, not the accuracy metric, for the sample of the test set for Dataset XYZ, based on Exhibit 2. The precision score is calculated as follows:

Precision (P) = $TP/(TP + FP) = 3/(3 + 1) = 0.75$.

31. A is correct. Only Remark 1 is correct. Method selection is the first task of ML model training and is governed by the following factors: (1) supervised or unsupervised learning, (2) the type of data, and (3) the size of data. The second and third tasks of model training, respectively, are performance evaluation and tuning.

    Remark 2 is incorrect because model fitting errors (bias error and variance error) are used in tuning, not performance evaluation. The techniques used in performance evaluation, which measure the goodness of fit for validation of the model, include (1) error analysis, (2) receiver operating characteristic (ROC) plots, and (3) root mean squared error (RMSE) calculations.

    B and C are incorrect because Remark 2 is incorrect. Model fitting errors (bias error and variance error) are used in tuning, not performance evaluation. The techniques used in performance evaluation, which measure the goodness of fit for validation of the model, include (1) error analysis, (2) receiver operating characteristic plots, and (3) root mean squared error calculations.

Appendices

Appendix A
Cumulative Probabilities for a Standard Normal Distribution
$P(Z \leq x) = N(x)$ for $x \geq 0$ or $P(Z \leq z) = N(z)$ for $z \geq 0$

x or z	0	0.01	0.02	0.03	0.04	0.05	0.06	0.07	0.08	0.09
0.00	0.5000	0.5040	0.5080	0.5120	0.5160	0.5199	0.5239	0.5279	0.5319	0.5359
0.10	0.5398	0.5438	0.5478	0.5517	0.5557	0.5596	0.5636	0.5675	0.5714	0.5753
0.20	0.5793	0.5832	0.5871	0.5910	0.5948	0.5987	0.6026	0.6064	0.6103	0.6141
0.30	0.6179	0.6217	0.6255	0.6293	0.6331	0.6368	0.6406	0.6443	0.6480	0.6517
0.40	0.6554	0.6591	0.6628	0.6664	0.6700	0.6736	0.6772	0.6808	0.6844	0.6879
0.50	0.6915	0.6950	0.6985	0.7019	0.7054	0.7088	0.7123	0.7157	0.7190	0.7224
0.60	0.7257	0.7291	0.7324	0.7357	0.7389	0.7422	0.7454	0.7486	0.7517	0.7549
0.70	0.7580	0.7611	0.7642	0.7673	0.7704	0.7734	0.7764	0.7794	0.7823	0.7852
0.80	0.7881	0.7910	0.7939	0.7967	0.7995	0.8023	0.8051	0.8078	0.8106	0.8133
0.90	0.8159	0.8186	0.8212	0.8238	0.8264	0.8289	0.8315	0.8340	0.8365	0.8389
1.00	0.8413	0.8438	0.8461	0.8485	0.8508	0.8531	0.8554	0.8577	0.8599	0.8621
1.10	0.8643	0.8665	0.8686	0.8708	0.8729	0.8749	0.8770	0.8790	0.8810	0.8830
1.20	0.8849	0.8869	0.8888	0.8907	0.8925	0.8944	0.8962	0.8980	0.8997	0.9015
1.30	0.9032	0.9049	0.9066	0.9082	0.9099	0.9115	0.9131	0.9147	0.9162	0.9177
1.40	0.9192	0.9207	0.9222	0.9236	0.9251	0.9265	0.9279	0.9292	0.9306	0.9319
1.50	0.9332	0.9345	0.9357	0.9370	0.9382	0.9394	0.9406	0.9418	0.9429	0.9441
1.60	0.9452	0.9463	0.9474	0.9484	0.9495	0.9505	0.9515	0.9525	0.9535	0.9545
1.70	0.9554	0.9564	0.9573	0.9582	0.9591	0.9599	0.9608	0.9616	0.9625	0.9633
1.80	0.9641	0.9649	0.9656	0.9664	0.9671	0.9678	0.9686	0.9693	0.9699	0.9706
1.90	0.9713	0.9719	0.9726	0.9732	0.9738	0.9744	0.9750	0.9756	0.9761	0.9767
2.00	0.9772	0.9778	0.9783	0.9788	0.9793	0.9798	0.9803	0.9808	0.9812	0.9817
2.10	0.9821	0.9826	0.9830	0.9834	0.9838	0.9842	0.9846	0.9850	0.9854	0.9857
2.20	0.9861	0.9864	0.9868	0.9871	0.9875	0.9878	0.9881	0.9884	0.9887	0.9890
2.30	0.9893	0.9896	0.9898	0.9901	0.9904	0.9906	0.9909	0.9911	0.9913	0.9916
2.40	0.9918	0.9920	0.9922	0.9925	0.9927	0.9929	0.9931	0.9932	0.9934	0.9936
2.50	0.9938	0.9940	0.9941	0.9943	0.9945	0.9946	0.9948	0.9949	0.9951	0.9952
2.60	0.9953	0.9955	0.9956	0.9957	0.9959	0.9960	0.9961	0.9962	0.9963	0.9964
2.70	0.9965	0.9966	0.9967	0.9968	0.9969	0.9970	0.9971	0.9972	0.9973	0.9974
2.80	0.9974	0.9975	0.9976	0.9977	0.9977	0.9978	0.9979	0.9979	0.9980	0.9981
2.90	0.9981	0.9982	0.9982	0.9983	0.9984	0.9984	0.9985	0.9985	0.9986	0.9986
3.00	0.9987	0.9987	0.9987	0.9988	0.9988	0.9989	0.9989	0.9989	0.9990	0.9990
3.10	0.9990	0.9991	0.9991	0.9991	0.9992	0.9992	0.9992	0.9992	0.9993	0.9993
3.20	0.9993	0.9993	0.9994	0.9994	0.9994	0.9994	0.9994	0.9995	0.9995	0.9995
3.30	0.9995	0.9995	0.9995	0.9996	0.9996	0.9996	0.9996	0.9996	0.9996	0.9997
3.40	0.9997	0.9997	0.9997	0.9997	0.9997	0.9997	0.9997	0.9997	0.9997	0.9998
3.50	0.9998	0.9998	0.9998	0.9998	0.9998	0.9998	0.9998	0.9998	0.9998	0.9998
3.60	0.9998	0.9998	0.9999	0.9999	0.9999	0.9999	0.9999	0.9999	0.9999	0.9999
3.70	0.9999	0.9999	0.9999	0.9999	0.9999	0.9999	0.9999	0.9999	0.9999	0.9999
3.80	0.9999	0.9999	0.9999	0.9999	0.9999	0.9999	0.9999	0.9999	0.9999	0.9999
3.90	1.0000	1.0000	1.0000	1.0000	1.0000	1.0000	1.0000	1.0000	1.0000	1.0000
4.00	1.0000	1.0000	1.0000	1.0000	1.0000	1.0000	1.0000	1.0000	1.0000	1.0000

For example, to find the *z*-value leaving 2.5 percent of the area/probability in the upper tail, find the element 0.9750 in the body of the table. Read 1.90 at the left end of the element's row and 0.06 at the top of the element's column, to give 1.90 + 0.06 = 1.96. *Table generated with Excel.*

Quantitative Methods for Investment Analysis, Second Edition, by Richard A. DeFusco, CFA, Dennis W. McLeavey, CFA, Jerald E. Pinto, CFA, and David E. Runkle, CFA. Copyright © 2004 by CFA Institute.

Appendix A (continued)
Cumulative Probabilities for a Standard Normal Distribution
$P(Z \leq x) = N(x)$ for $x \leq 0$ or $P(Z \leq z) = N(z)$ for $z \leq 0$

x or z	0	0.01	0.02	0.03	0.04	0.05	0.06	0.07	0.08	0.09
0.0	0.5000	0.4960	0.4920	0.4880	0.4840	0.4801	0.4761	0.4721	0.4681	0.4641
−0.10	0.4602	0.4562	0.4522	0.4483	0.4443	0.4404	0.4364	0.4325	0.4286	0.4247
−0.20	0.4207	0.4168	0.4129	0.4090	0.4052	0.4013	0.3974	0.3936	0.3897	0.3859
−0.30	0.3821	0.3783	0.3745	0.3707	0.3669	0.3632	0.3594	0.3557	0.3520	0.3483
−0.40	0.3446	0.3409	0.3372	0.3336	0.3300	0.3264	0.3228	0.3192	0.3156	0.3121
−0.50	0.3085	0.3050	0.3015	0.2981	0.2946	0.2912	0.2877	0.2843	0.2810	0.2776
−0.60	0.2743	0.2709	0.2676	0.2643	0.2611	0.2578	0.2546	0.2514	0.2483	0.2451
−0.70	0.2420	0.2389	0.2358	0.2327	0.2296	0.2266	0.2236	0.2206	0.2177	0.2148
−0.80	0.2119	0.2090	0.2061	0.2033	0.2005	0.1977	0.1949	0.1922	0.1894	0.1867
−0.90	0.1841	0.1814	0.1788	0.1762	0.1736	0.1711	0.1685	0.1660	0.1635	0.1611
−1.00	0.1587	0.1562	0.1539	0.1515	0.1492	0.1469	0.1446	0.1423	0.1401	0.1379
−1.10	0.1357	0.1335	0.1314	0.1292	0.1271	0.1251	0.1230	0.1210	0.1190	0.1170
−1.20	0.1151	0.1131	0.1112	0.1093	0.1075	0.1056	0.1038	0.1020	0.1003	0.0985
−1.30	0.0968	0.0951	0.0934	0.0918	0.0901	0.0885	0.0869	0.0853	0.0838	0.0823
−1.40	0.0808	0.0793	0.0778	0.0764	0.0749	0.0735	0.0721	0.0708	0.0694	0.0681
−1.50	0.0668	0.0655	0.0643	0.0630	0.0618	0.0606	0.0594	0.0582	0.0571	0.0559
−1.60	0.0548	0.0537	0.0526	0.0516	0.0505	0.0495	0.0485	0.0475	0.0465	0.0455
−1.70	0.0446	0.0436	0.0427	0.0418	0.0409	0.0401	0.0392	0.0384	0.0375	0.0367
−1.80	0.0359	0.0351	0.0344	0.0336	0.0329	0.0322	0.0314	0.0307	0.0301	0.0294
−1.90	0.0287	0.0281	0.0274	0.0268	0.0262	0.0256	0.0250	0.0244	0.0239	0.0233
−2.00	0.0228	0.0222	0.0217	0.0212	0.0207	0.0202	0.0197	0.0192	0.0188	0.0183
−2.10	0.0179	0.0174	0.0170	0.0166	0.0162	0.0158	0.0154	0.0150	0.0146	0.0143
−2.20	0.0139	0.0136	0.0132	0.0129	0.0125	0.0122	0.0119	0.0116	0.0113	0.0110
−2.30	0.0107	0.0104	0.0102	0.0099	0.0096	0.0094	0.0091	0.0089	0.0087	0.0084
−2.40	0.0082	0.0080	0.0078	0.0075	0.0073	0.0071	0.0069	0.0068	0.0066	0.0064
−2.50	0.0062	0.0060	0.0059	0.0057	0.0055	0.0054	0.0052	0.0051	0.0049	0.0048
−2.60	0.0047	0.0045	0.0044	0.0043	0.0041	0.0040	0.0039	0.0038	0.0037	0.0036
−2.70	0.0035	0.0034	0.0033	0.0032	0.0031	0.0030	0.0029	0.0028	0.0027	0.0026
−2.80	0.0026	0.0025	0.0024	0.0023	0.0023	0.0022	0.0021	0.0021	0.0020	0.0019
−2.90	0.0019	0.0018	0.0018	0.0017	0.0016	0.0016	0.0015	0.0015	0.0014	0.0014
−3.00	0.0013	0.0013	0.0013	0.0012	0.0012	0.0011	0.0011	0.0011	0.0010	0.0010
−3.10	0.0010	0.0009	0.0009	0.0009	0.0008	0.0008	0.0008	0.0008	0.0007	0.0007
−3.20	0.0007	0.0007	0.0006	0.0006	0.0006	0.0006	0.0006	0.0005	0.0005	0.0005
−3.30	0.0005	0.0005	0.0005	0.0004	0.0004	0.0004	0.0004	0.0004	0.0004	0.0003
−3.40	0.0003	0.0003	0.0003	0.0003	0.0003	0.0003	0.0003	0.0003	0.0003	0.0002
−3.50	0.0002	0.0002	0.0002	0.0002	0.0002	0.0002	0.0002	0.0002	0.0002	0.0002
−3.60	0.0002	0.0002	0.0001	0.0001	0.0001	0.0001	0.0001	0.0001	0.0001	0.0001
−3.70	0.0001	0.0001	0.0001	0.0001	0.0001	0.0001	0.0001	0.0001	0.0001	0.0001
−3.80	0.0001	0.0001	0.0001	0.0001	0.0001	0.0001	0.0001	0.0001	0.0001	0.0001
−3.90	0.0000	0.0000	0.0000	0.0000	0.0000	0.0000	0.0000	0.0000	0.0000	0.0000
−4.00	0.0000	0.0000	0.0000	0.0000	0.0000	0.0000	0.0000	0.0000	0.0000	0.0000

For example, to find the z-value leaving 2.5 percent of the area/probability in the lower tail, find the element 0.0250 in the body of the table. Read −1.90 at the left end of the element's row and 0.06 at the top of the element's column, to give −1.90 − 0.06 = −1.96. *Table generated with Excel.*

Appendix B
Table of the Student's *t*-Distribution (One-Tailed Probabilities)

df	p = 0.10	p = 0.05	p = 0.025	p = 0.01	p = 0.005
1	3.078	6.314	12.706	31.821	63.657
2	1.886	2.920	4.303	6.965	9.925
3	1.638	2.353	3.182	4.541	5.841
4	1.533	2.132	2.776	3.747	4.604
5	1.476	2.015	2.571	3.365	4.032
6	1.440	1.943	2.447	3.143	3.707
7	1.415	1.895	2.365	2.998	3.499
8	1.397	1.860	2.306	2.896	3.355
9	1.383	1.833	2.262	2.821	3.250
10	1.372	1.812	2.228	2.764	3.169
11	1.363	1.796	2.201	2.718	3.106
12	1.356	1.782	2.179	2.681	3.055
13	1.350	1.771	2.160	2.650	3.012
14	1.345	1.761	2.145	2.624	2.977
15	1.341	1.753	2.131	2.602	2.947
16	1.337	1.746	2.120	2.583	2.921
17	1.333	1.740	2.110	2.567	2.898
18	1.330	1.734	2.101	2.552	2.878
19	1.328	1.729	2.093	2.539	2.861
20	1.325	1.725	2.086	2.528	2.845
21	1.323	1.721	2.080	2.518	2.831
22	1.321	1.717	2.074	2.508	2.819
23	1.319	1.714	2.069	2.500	2.807
24	1.318	1.711	2.064	2.492	2.797
25	1.316	1.708	2.060	2.485	2.787
26	1.315	1.706	2.056	2.479	2.779
27	1.314	1.703	2.052	2.473	2.771
28	1.313	1.701	2.048	2.467	2.763
29	1.311	1.699	2.045	2.462	2.756
30	1.310	1.697	2.042	2.457	2.750

df	p = 0.10	p = 0.05	p = 0.025	p = 0.01	p = 0.005
31	1.309	1.696	2.040	2.453	2.744
32	1.309	1.694	2.037	2.449	2.738
33	1.308	1.692	2.035	2.445	2.733
34	1.307	1.691	2.032	2.441	2.728
35	1.306	1.690	2.030	2.438	2.724
36	1.306	1.688	2.028	2.434	2.719
37	1.305	1.687	2.026	2.431	2.715
38	1.304	1.686	2.024	2.429	2.712
39	1.304	1.685	2.023	2.426	2.708
40	1.303	1.684	2.021	2.423	2.704
41	1.303	1.683	2.020	2.421	2.701
42	1.302	1.682	2.018	2.418	2.698
43	1.302	1.681	2.017	2.416	2.695
44	1.301	1.680	2.015	2.414	2.692
45	1.301	1.679	2.014	2.412	2.690
46	1.300	1.679	2.013	2.410	2.687
47	1.300	1.678	2.012	2.408	2.685
48	1.299	1.677	2.011	2.407	2.682
49	1.299	1.677	2.010	2.405	2.680
50	1.299	1.676	2.009	2.403	2.678
60	1.296	1.671	2.000	2.390	2.660
70	1.294	1.667	1.994	2.381	2.648
80	1.292	1.664	1.990	2.374	2.639
90	1.291	1.662	1.987	2.368	2.632
100	1.290	1.660	1.984	2.364	2.626
110	1.289	1.659	1.982	2.361	2.621
120	1.289	1.658	1.980	2.358	2.617
200	1.286	1.653	1.972	2.345	2.601
∞	1.282	1.645	1.960	2.326	2.576

To find a critical *t*-value, enter the table with df and a specified value for α, the significance level. For example, with 5 df, $\alpha = 0.05$ and a one-tailed test, the desired probability in the tail would be $p = 0.05$ and the critical *t*-value would be $t(5, 0.05) = 2.015$. With $\alpha = 0.05$ and a two-tailed test, the desired probability in each tail would be $p = 0.025 = \alpha/2$, giving $t(0.025) = 2.571$. *Table generated using Excel.*

Quantitative Methods for Investment Analysis, Second Edition, by Richard A. DeFusco, CFA, Dennis W. McLeavey, CFA, Jerald E. Pinto, CFA, and David E. Runkle, CFA. Copyright © 2004 by CFA Institute.

Appendix C
Values of χ^2 (Degrees of Freedom, Level of Significance)

Degrees of Freedom	Probability in Right Tail								
	0.99	0.975	0.95	0.9	0.1	0.05	0.025	0.01	0.005
1	0.000157	0.000982	0.003932	0.0158	2.706	3.841	5.024	6.635	7.879
2	0.020100	0.050636	0.102586	0.2107	4.605	5.991	7.378	9.210	10.597
3	0.1148	0.2158	0.3518	0.5844	6.251	7.815	9.348	11.345	12.838
4	0.297	0.484	0.711	1.064	7.779	9.488	11.143	13.277	14.860
5	0.554	0.831	1.145	1.610	9.236	11.070	12.832	15.086	16.750
6	0.872	1.237	1.635	2.204	10.645	12.592	14.449	16.812	18.548
7	1.239	1.690	2.167	2.833	12.017	14.067	16.013	18.475	20.278
8	1.647	2.180	2.733	3.490	13.362	15.507	17.535	20.090	21.955
9	2.088	2.700	3.325	4.168	14.684	16.919	19.023	21.666	23.589
10	2.558	3.247	3.940	4.865	15.987	18.307	20.483	23.209	25.188
11	3.053	3.816	4.575	5.578	17.275	19.675	21.920	24.725	26.757
12	3.571	4.404	5.226	6.304	18.549	21.026	23.337	26.217	28.300
13	4.107	5.009	5.892	7.041	19.812	22.362	24.736	27.688	29.819
14	4.660	5.629	6.571	7.790	21.064	23.685	26.119	29.141	31.319
15	5.229	6.262	7.261	8.547	22.307	24.996	27.488	30.578	32.801
16	5.812	6.908	7.962	9.312	23.542	26.296	28.845	32.000	34.267
17	6.408	7.564	8.672	10.085	24.769	27.587	30.191	33.409	35.718
18	7.015	8.231	9.390	10.865	25.989	28.869	31.526	34.805	37.156
19	7.633	8.907	10.117	11.651	27.204	30.144	32.852	36.191	38.582
20	8.260	9.591	10.851	12.443	28.412	31.410	34.170	37.566	39.997
21	8.897	10.283	11.591	13.240	29.615	32.671	35.479	38.932	41.401
22	9.542	10.982	12.338	14.041	30.813	33.924	36.781	40.289	42.796
23	10.196	11.689	13.091	14.848	32.007	35.172	38.076	41.638	44.181
24	10.856	12.401	13.848	15.659	33.196	36.415	39.364	42.980	45.558
25	11.524	13.120	14.611	16.473	34.382	37.652	40.646	44.314	46.928
26	12.198	13.844	15.379	17.292	35.563	38.885	41.923	45.642	48.290
27	12.878	14.573	16.151	18.114	36.741	40.113	43.195	46.963	49.645
28	13.565	15.308	16.928	18.939	37.916	41.337	44.461	48.278	50.994
29	14.256	16.047	17.708	19.768	39.087	42.557	45.722	49.588	52.335
30	14.953	16.791	18.493	20.599	40.256	43.773	46.979	50.892	53.672
50	29.707	32.357	34.764	37.689	63.167	67.505	71.420	76.154	79.490
60	37.485	40.482	43.188	46.459	74.397	79.082	83.298	88.379	91.952
80	53.540	57.153	60.391	64.278	96.578	101.879	106.629	112.329	116.321
100	70.065	74.222	77.929	82.358	118.498	124.342	129.561	135.807	140.170

To have a probability of 0.05 in the right tail when df = 5, the tabled value is $\chi^2(5, 0.05) = 11.070$.

Quantitative Methods for Investment Analysis, Second Edition, by Richard A. DeFusco, CFA, Dennis W. McLeavey, CFA, Jerald E. Pinto, CFA, and David E. Runkle, CFA. Copyright © 2004 by CFA Institute.

Appendix D
Table of the *F*-Distribution

Panel A. Critical values for right-hand tail area equal to 0.05

Numerator: df_1 and Denominator: df_2

df2:1	1	2	3	4	5	6	7	8	9	10	11	12	15	20	21	22	23	24	25	30	40	60	120	∞
1	161	200	216	225	230	234	237	239	241	242	243	244	246	248	248	249	249	249	249	250	251	252	253	254
2	18.5	19.0	19.2	19.2	19.3	19.3	19.4	19.4	19.4	19.4	19.4	19.4	19.4	19.4	19.4	19.5	19.5	19.5	19.5	19.5	19.5	19.5	19.5	19.5
3	10.1	9.55	9.28	9.12	9.01	8.94	8.89	8.85	8.81	8.79	8.76	8.74	8.70	8.66	8.65	8.65	8.64	8.64	8.63	8.62	8.59	8.57	8.55	8.53
4	7.71	6.94	6.59	6.39	6.26	6.16	6.09	6.04	6.00	5.96	5.94	5.91	5.86	5.80	5.79	5.79	5.78	5.77	5.77	5.75	5.72	5.69	5.66	5.63
5	6.61	5.79	5.41	5.19	5.05	4.95	4.88	4.82	4.77	4.74	4.70	4.68	4.62	4.56	4.55	4.54	4.53	4.53	4.52	4.50	4.46	4.43	4.40	4.37
6	5.99	5.14	4.76	4.53	4.39	4.28	4.21	4.15	4.10	4.06	4.03	4.00	3.94	3.87	3.86	3.86	3.85	3.84	3.83	3.81	3.77	3.74	3.70	3.67
7	5.59	4.74	4.35	4.12	3.97	3.87	3.79	3.73	3.68	3.64	3.60	3.57	3.51	3.44	3.43	3.43	3.42	3.41	3.40	3.38	3.34	3.30	3.27	3.23
8	5.32	4.46	4.07	3.84	3.69	3.58	3.50	3.44	3.39	3.35	3.31	3.28	3.22	3.15	3.14	3.13	3.12	3.12	3.11	3.08	3.04	3.01	2.97	2.93
9	5.12	4.26	3.86	3.63	3.48	3.37	3.29	3.23	3.18	3.14	3.10	3.07	3.01	2.94	2.93	2.92	2.91	2.90	2.89	2.86	2.83	2.79	2.75	2.71
10	4.96	4.10	3.71	3.48	3.33	3.22	3.14	3.07	3.02	2.98	2.94	2.91	2.85	2.77	2.76	2.75	2.75	2.74	2.73	2.70	2.66	2.62	2.58	2.54
11	4.84	3.98	3.59	3.36	3.20	3.09	3.01	2.95	2.90	2.85	2.82	2.79	2.72	2.65	2.64	2.63	2.62	2.61	2.60	2.57	2.53	2.49	2.45	2.40
12	4.75	3.89	3.49	3.26	3.11	3.00	2.91	2.85	2.80	2.75	2.72	2.69	2.62	2.54	2.53	2.52	2.51	2.51	2.50	2.47	2.43	2.38	2.34	2.30
13	4.67	3.81	3.41	3.18	3.03	2.92	2.83	2.77	2.71	2.67	2.63	2.60	2.53	2.46	2.45	2.44	2.43	2.42	2.41	2.38	2.34	2.30	2.25	2.21
14	4.60	3.74	3.34	3.11	2.96	2.85	2.76	2.70	2.65	2.60	2.57	2.53	2.46	2.39	2.38	2.37	2.36	2.35	2.34	2.31	2.27	2.22	2.18	2.13
15	4.54	3.68	3.29	3.06	2.90	2.79	2.71	2.64	2.59	2.54	2.51	2.48	2.40	2.33	2.32	2.31	2.30	2.29	2.28	2.25	2.20	2.16	2.11	2.07
16	4.49	3.63	3.24	3.01	2.85	2.74	2.66	2.59	2.54	2.49	2.46	2.42	2.35	2.28	2.26	2.25	2.24	2.24	2.23	2.19	2.15	2.11	2.06	2.01
17	4.45	3.59	3.20	2.96	2.81	2.70	2.61	2.55	2.49	2.45	2.41	2.38	2.31	2.23	2.22	2.21	2.20	2.19	2.18	2.15	2.10	2.06	2.01	1.96
18	4.41	3.55	3.16	2.93	2.77	2.66	2.58	2.51	2.46	2.41	2.37	2.34	2.27	2.19	2.18	2.17	2.16	2.15	2.14	2.11	2.06	2.02	1.97	1.92
19	4.38	3.52	3.13	2.90	2.74	2.63	2.54	2.48	2.42	2.38	2.34	2.31	2.23	2.16	2.14	2.13	2.12	2.11	2.11	2.07	2.03	1.98	1.93	1.88
20	4.35	3.49	3.10	2.87	2.71	2.60	2.51	2.45	2.39	2.35	2.31	2.28	2.20	2.12	2.11	2.10	2.09	2.08	2.07	2.04	1.99	1.95	1.90	1.84
21	4.32	3.47	3.07	2.84	2.68	2.57	2.49	2.42	2.37	2.32	2.28	2.25	2.18	2.10	2.08	2.07	2.06	2.05	2.05	2.01	1.96	1.92	1.87	1.81
22	4.30	3.44	3.05	2.82	2.66	2.55	2.46	2.40	2.34	2.30	2.26	2.23	2.15	2.07	2.06	2.05	2.04	2.03	2.02	1.98	1.94	1.89	1.84	1.78
23	4.28	3.42	3.03	2.80	2.64	2.53	2.44	2.37	2.32	2.27	2.24	2.20	2.13	2.05	2.04	2.02	2.01	2.01	2.00	1.96	1.91	1.86	1.81	1.76
24	4.26	3.40	3.01	2.78	2.62	2.51	2.42	2.36	2.30	2.25	2.22	2.18	2.11	2.03	2.01	2.00	1.99	1.98	1.97	1.94	1.89	1.84	1.79	1.73
25	4.24	3.39	2.99	2.76	2.60	2.49	2.40	2.34	2.28	2.24	2.20	2.16	2.09	2.01	2.00	1.98	1.97	1.96	1.96	1.92	1.87	1.82	1.77	1.71
30	4.17	3.32	2.92	2.69	2.53	2.42	2.33	2.27	2.21	2.16	2.13	2.09	2.01	1.93	1.92	1.91	1.90	1.89	1.88	1.84	1.79	1.74	1.68	1.62
40	4.08	3.23	2.84	2.61	2.45	2.34	2.25	2.18	2.12	2.08	2.04	2.00	1.92	1.84	1.83	1.81	1.80	1.79	1.78	1.74	1.69	1.64	1.58	1.51
60	4.00	3.15	2.76	2.53	2.37	2.25	2.17	2.10	2.04	1.99	1.95	1.92	1.84	1.75	1.73	1.72	1.71	1.70	1.69	1.65	1.59	1.53	1.47	1.39
120	3.92	3.07	2.68	2.45	2.29	2.18	2.09	2.02	1.96	1.91	1.87	1.83	1.75	1.66	1.64	1.63	1.62	1.61	1.60	1.55	1.50	1.43	1.35	1.25
Infinity	3.84	3.00	2.60	2.37	2.21	2.10	2.01	1.94	1.88	1.83	1.79	1.75	1.67	1.57	1.56	1.54	1.53	1.52	1.51	1.46	1.39	1.32	1.22	1.00

Appendix D (continued)
Table of the F-Distribution

Panel B. Critical values for right-hand tail area equal to 0.025

Numerator: df_1 and Denominator: df_2

df2:	1	2	3	4	5	6	7	8	9	10	11	12	15	20	21	22	23	24	25	30	40	60	120	∞
1	648	799	864	900	922	937	948	957	963	969	973	977	985	993	994	995	996	997	998	1001	1006	1010	1014	1018
2	38.51	39.00	39.17	39.25	39.30	39.33	39.36	39.37	39.39	39.40	39.41	39.41	39.43	39.45	39.45	39.45	39.45	39.46	39.46	39.46	39.47	39.48	39.49	39.50
3	17.44	16.04	15.44	15.10	14.88	14.73	14.62	14.54	14.47	14.42	14.37	14.34	14.25	14.17	14.16	14.14	14.13	14.12	14.12	14.08	14.04	13.99	13.95	13.90
4	12.22	10.65	9.98	9.60	9.36	9.20	9.07	8.98	8.90	8.84	8.79	8.75	8.66	8.56	8.55	8.53	8.52	8.51	8.50	8.46	8.41	8.36	8.31	8.26
5	10.01	8.43	7.76	7.39	7.15	6.98	6.85	6.76	6.68	6.62	6.57	6.52	6.43	6.33	6.31	6.30	6.29	6.28	6.27	6.23	6.18	6.12	6.07	6.02
6	8.81	7.26	6.60	6.23	5.99	5.82	5.70	5.60	5.52	5.46	5.41	5.37	5.27	5.17	5.15	5.14	5.13	5.12	5.11	5.07	5.01	4.96	4.90	4.85
7	8.07	6.54	5.89	5.52	5.29	5.12	4.99	4.90	4.82	4.76	4.71	4.67	4.57	4.47	4.45	4.44	4.43	4.41	4.40	4.36	4.31	4.25	4.20	4.14
8	7.57	6.06	5.42	5.05	4.82	4.65	4.53	4.43	4.36	4.30	4.24	4.20	4.10	4.00	3.98	3.97	3.96	3.95	3.94	3.89	3.84	3.78	3.73	3.67
9	7.21	5.71	5.08	4.72	4.48	4.32	4.20	4.10	4.03	3.96	3.91	3.87	3.77	3.67	3.65	3.64	3.63	3.61	3.60	3.56	3.51	3.45	3.39	3.33
10	6.94	5.46	4.83	4.47	4.24	4.07	3.95	3.85	3.78	3.72	3.66	3.62	3.52	3.42	3.40	3.39	3.38	3.37	3.35	3.31	3.26	3.20	3.14	3.08
11	6.72	5.26	4.63	4.28	4.04	3.88	3.76	3.66	3.59	3.53	3.47	3.43	3.33	3.23	3.21	3.20	3.18	3.17	3.16	3.12	3.06	3.00	2.94	2.88
12	6.55	5.10	4.47	4.12	3.89	3.73	3.61	3.51	3.44	3.37	3.32	3.28	3.18	3.07	3.06	3.04	3.03	3.02	3.01	2.96	2.91	2.85	2.79	2.72
13	6.41	4.97	4.35	4.00	3.77	3.60	3.48	3.39	3.31	3.25	3.20	3.15	3.05	2.95	2.93	2.92	2.91	2.89	2.88	2.84	2.78	2.72	2.66	2.60
14	6.30	4.86	4.24	3.89	3.66	3.50	3.38	3.29	3.21	3.15	3.09	3.05	2.95	2.84	2.83	2.81	2.80	2.79	2.78	2.73	2.67	2.61	2.55	2.49
15	6.20	4.77	4.15	3.80	3.58	3.41	3.29	3.20	3.12	3.06	3.01	2.96	2.86	2.76	2.74	2.73	2.71	2.70	2.69	2.64	2.59	2.52	2.46	2.40
16	6.12	4.69	4.08	3.73	3.50	3.34	3.22	3.12	3.05	2.99	2.93	2.89	2.79	2.68	2.67	2.65	2.64	2.63	2.61	2.57	2.51	2.45	2.38	2.32
17	6.04	4.62	4.01	3.66	3.44	3.28	3.16	3.06	2.98	2.92	2.87	2.82	2.72	2.62	2.60	2.59	2.57	2.56	2.55	2.50	2.44	2.38	2.32	2.25
18	5.98	4.56	3.95	3.61	3.38	3.22	3.10	3.01	2.93	2.87	2.81	2.77	2.67	2.56	2.54	2.53	2.52	2.50	2.49	2.44	2.38	2.32	2.26	2.19
19	5.92	4.51	3.90	3.56	3.33	3.17	3.05	2.96	2.88	2.82	2.76	2.72	2.62	2.51	2.49	2.48	2.46	2.45	2.44	2.39	2.33	2.27	2.20	2.13
20	5.87	4.46	3.86	3.51	3.29	3.13	3.01	2.91	2.84	2.77	2.72	2.68	2.57	2.46	2.45	2.43	2.42	2.41	2.40	2.35	2.29	2.22	2.16	2.09
21	5.83	4.42	3.82	3.48	3.25	3.09	2.97	2.87	2.80	2.73	2.68	2.64	2.53	2.42	2.41	2.39	2.38	2.37	2.36	2.31	2.25	2.18	2.11	2.04
22	5.79	4.38	3.78	3.44	3.22	3.05	2.93	2.84	2.76	2.70	2.65	2.60	2.50	2.39	2.37	2.36	2.34	2.33	2.32	2.27	2.21	2.14	2.08	2.00
23	5.75	4.35	3.75	3.41	3.18	3.02	2.90	2.81	2.73	2.67	2.62	2.57	2.47	2.36	2.34	2.33	2.31	2.30	2.29	2.24	2.18	2.11	2.04	1.97
24	5.72	4.32	3.72	3.38	3.15	2.99	2.87	2.78	2.70	2.64	2.59	2.54	2.44	2.33	2.31	2.30	2.28	2.27	2.26	2.21	2.15	2.08	2.01	1.94
25	5.69	4.29	3.69	3.35	3.13	2.97	2.85	2.75	2.68	2.61	2.56	2.51	2.41	2.30	2.28	2.27	2.26	2.24	2.23	2.18	2.12	2.05	1.98	1.91
30	5.57	4.18	3.59	3.25	3.03	2.87	2.75	2.65	2.57	2.51	2.46	2.41	2.31	2.20	2.18	2.16	2.15	2.14	2.12	2.07	2.01	1.94	1.87	1.79
40	5.42	4.05	3.46	3.13	2.90	2.74	2.62	2.53	2.45	2.39	2.33	2.29	2.18	2.07	2.05	2.03	2.02	2.01	1.99	1.94	1.88	1.80	1.72	1.64
60	5.29	3.93	3.34	3.01	2.79	2.63	2.51	2.41	2.33	2.27	2.22	2.17	2.06	1.94	1.93	1.91	1.90	1.88	1.87	1.82	1.74	1.67	1.58	1.48
120	5.15	3.80	3.23	2.89	2.67	2.52	2.39	2.30	2.22	2.16	2.10	2.05	1.94	1.82	1.81	1.79	1.77	1.76	1.75	1.69	1.61	1.53	1.43	1.31
Infinity	5.02	3.69	3.12	2.79	2.57	2.41	2.29	2.19	2.11	2.05	1.99	1.94	1.83	1.71	1.69	1.67	1.66	1.64	1.63	1.57	1.48	1.39	1.27	1.00

Appendix D (continued)
Table of the F-Distribution

Panel C. Critical values for right-hand tail area equal to 0.01

Numerator: df_1 and Denominator: df_2

df2:\df1:	1	2	3	4	5	6	7	8	9	10	11	12	15	20	21	22	23	24	25	30	40	60	120	∞
1	4052	5000	5403	5625	5764	5859	5928	5982	6023	6056	6083	6106	6157	6209	6216	6223	6229	6235	6240	6261	6287	6313	6339	6366
2	98.5	99.0	99.2	99.2	99.3	99.3	99.4	99.4	99.4	99.4	99.4	99.4	99.4	99.4	99.5	99.5	99.5	99.5	99.5	99.5	99.5	99.5	99.5	99.5
3	34.1	30.8	29.5	28.7	28.2	27.9	27.7	27.5	27.3	27.2	27.1	27.1	26.9	26.7	26.7	26.6	26.6	26.6	26.6	26.5	26.4	26.3	26.2	26.1
4	21.2	18.0	16.7	16.0	15.5	15.2	15.0	14.8	14.7	14.5	14.5	14.4	14.2	14.0	14.0	14.0	13.9	13.9	13.9	13.8	13.7	13.7	13.6	13.5
5	16.3	13.3	12.1	11.4	11.0	10.7	10.5	10.3	10.2	10.1	10.0	9.89	9.72	9.55	9.53	9.51	9.49	9.47	9.45	9.38	9.29	9.20	9.11	9.02
6	13.7	10.9	9.78	9.15	8.75	8.47	8.26	8.10	7.98	7.87	7.79	7.72	7.56	7.40	7.37	7.35	7.33	7.31	7.30	7.23	7.14	7.06	6.97	6.88
7	12.2	9.55	8.45	7.85	7.46	7.19	6.99	6.84	6.72	6.62	6.54	6.47	6.31	6.16	6.13	6.11	6.09	6.07	6.06	5.99	5.91	5.82	5.74	5.65
8	11.3	8.65	7.59	7.01	6.63	6.37	6.18	6.03	5.91	5.81	5.73	5.67	5.52	5.36	5.34	5.32	5.30	5.28	5.26	5.20	5.12	5.03	4.95	4.86
9	10.6	8.02	6.99	6.42	6.06	5.80	5.61	5.47	5.35	5.26	5.18	5.11	4.96	4.81	4.79	4.77	4.75	4.73	4.71	4.65	4.57	4.48	4.40	4.31
10	10.0	7.56	6.55	5.99	5.64	5.39	5.20	5.06	4.94	4.85	4.77	4.71	4.56	4.41	4.38	4.36	4.34	4.33	4.31	4.25	4.17	4.08	4.00	3.91
11	9.65	7.21	6.22	5.67	5.32	5.07	4.89	4.74	4.63	4.54	4.46	4.40	4.25	4.10	4.08	4.06	4.04	4.02	4.01	3.94	3.86	3.78	3.69	3.60
12	9.33	6.93	5.95	5.41	5.06	4.82	4.64	4.50	4.39	4.30	4.22	4.16	4.01	3.86	3.84	3.82	3.80	3.78	3.76	3.70	3.62	3.54	3.45	3.36
13	9.07	6.70	5.74	5.21	4.86	4.62	4.44	4.30	4.19	4.10	4.02	3.96	3.82	3.66	3.64	3.62	3.60	3.59	3.57	3.51	3.43	3.34	3.25	3.17
14	8.86	6.51	5.56	5.04	4.70	4.46	4.28	4.14	4.03	3.94	3.86	3.80	3.66	3.51	3.48	3.46	3.44	3.43	3.41	3.35	3.27	3.18	3.09	3.00
15	8.68	6.36	5.42	4.89	4.56	4.32	4.14	4.00	3.89	3.80	3.73	3.67	3.52	3.37	3.35	3.33	3.31	3.29	3.28	3.21	3.13	3.05	2.96	2.87
16	8.53	6.23	5.29	4.77	4.44	4.20	4.03	3.89	3.78	3.69	3.62	3.55	3.41	3.26	3.24	3.22	3.20	3.18	3.16	3.10	3.02	2.93	2.84	2.75
17	8.40	6.11	5.19	4.67	4.34	4.10	3.93	3.79	3.68	3.59	3.52	3.46	3.31	3.16	3.14	3.12	3.10	3.08	3.07	3.00	2.92	2.83	2.75	2.65
18	8.29	6.01	5.09	4.58	4.25	4.01	3.84	3.71	3.60	3.51	3.43	3.37	3.23	3.08	3.05	3.03	3.02	3.00	2.98	2.92	2.84	2.75	2.66	2.57
19	8.19	5.93	5.01	4.50	4.17	3.94	3.77	3.63	3.52	3.43	3.36	3.30	3.15	3.00	2.98	2.96	2.94	2.92	2.91	2.84	2.76	2.67	2.58	2.49
20	8.10	5.85	4.94	4.43	4.10	3.87	3.70	3.56	3.46	3.37	3.29	3.23	3.09	2.94	2.92	2.90	2.88	2.86	2.84	2.78	2.69	2.61	2.52	2.42
21	8.02	5.78	4.87	4.37	4.04	3.81	3.64	3.51	3.40	3.31	3.24	3.17	3.03	2.88	2.86	2.84	2.82	2.80	2.79	2.72	2.64	2.55	2.46	2.36
22	7.95	5.72	4.82	4.31	3.99	3.76	3.59	3.45	3.35	3.26	3.18	3.12	2.98	2.83	2.81	2.78	2.77	2.75	2.73	2.67	2.58	2.50	2.40	2.31
23	7.88	5.66	4.76	4.26	3.94	3.71	3.54	3.41	3.30	3.21	3.14	3.07	2.93	2.78	2.76	2.74	2.72	2.70	2.69	2.62	2.54	2.45	2.35	2.26
24	7.82	5.61	4.72	4.22	3.90	3.67	3.50	3.36	3.26	3.17	3.09	3.03	2.89	2.74	2.72	2.70	2.68	2.66	2.64	2.58	2.49	2.40	2.31	2.21
25	7.77	5.57	4.68	4.18	3.86	3.63	3.46	3.32	3.22	3.13	3.06	2.99	2.85	2.70	2.68	2.66	2.64	2.62	2.60	2.53	2.45	2.36	2.27	2.17
30	7.56	5.39	4.51	4.02	3.70	3.47	3.30	3.17	3.07	2.98	2.91	2.84	2.70	2.55	2.53	2.51	2.49	2.47	2.45	2.39	2.30	2.21	2.11	2.01
40	7.31	5.18	4.31	3.83	3.51	3.29	3.12	2.99	2.89	2.80	2.73	2.66	2.52	2.37	2.35	2.33	2.31	2.29	2.27	2.20	2.11	2.02	1.92	1.80
60	7.08	4.98	4.13	3.65	3.34	3.12	2.95	2.82	2.72	2.63	2.56	2.50	2.35	2.20	2.17	2.15	2.13	2.12	2.10	2.03	1.94	1.84	1.73	1.60
120	6.85	4.79	3.95	3.48	3.17	2.96	2.79	2.66	2.56	2.47	2.40	2.34	2.19	2.03	2.01	1.99	1.97	1.95	1.93	1.86	1.76	1.66	1.53	1.38
Infinity	6.63	4.61	3.78	3.32	3.02	2.80	2.64	2.51	2.41	2.32	2.25	2.18	2.04	1.88	1.85	1.83	1.81	1.79	1.77	1.70	1.59	1.47	1.32	1.00

Appendix D (continued)
Table of the F-Distribution

Panel D. Critical values for right-hand tail area equal to 0.005

Numerator: df_1, and Denominator: df_2

df2: \ df1:	1	2	3	4	5	6	7	8	9	10	11	12	15	20	21	22	23	24	25	30	40	60	120	∞
1	16211	20000	21615	22500	23056	23437	23715	23925	24091	24222	24334	24426	24630	24836	24863	24892	24915	24940	24959	25044	25146	25253	25359	25464
2	198.5	199.0	199.2	199.2	199.3	199.3	199.4	199.4	199.4	199.4	199.4	199.4	199.4	199.4	199.4	199.4	199.4	199.4	199.4	199.5	199.5	199.5	199.5	200
3	55.55	49.80	47.47	46.20	45.39	44.84	44.43	44.13	43.88	43.68	43.52	43.39	43.08	42.78	42.73	42.69	42.66	42.62	42.59	42.47	42.31	42.15	41.99	41.83
4	31.33	26.28	24.26	23.15	22.46	21.98	21.62	21.35	21.14	20.97	20.82	20.70	20.44	20.17	20.13	20.09	20.06	20.03	20.00	19.89	19.75	19.61	19.47	19.32
5	22.78	18.31	16.53	15.56	14.94	14.51	14.20	13.96	13.77	13.62	13.49	13.38	13.15	12.90	12.87	12.84	12.81	12.78	12.76	12.66	12.53	12.40	12.27	12.14
6	18.63	14.54	12.92	12.03	11.46	11.07	10.79	10.57	10.39	10.25	10.13	10.03	9.81	9.59	9.56	9.53	9.50	9.47	9.45	9.36	9.24	9.12	9.00	8.88
7	16.24	12.40	10.88	10.05	9.52	9.16	8.89	8.68	8.51	8.38	8.27	8.18	7.97	7.75	7.72	7.69	7.67	7.64	7.62	7.53	7.42	7.31	7.19	7.08
8	14.69	11.04	9.60	8.81	8.30	7.95	7.69	7.50	7.34	7.21	7.10	7.01	6.81	6.61	6.58	6.55	6.53	6.50	6.48	6.40	6.29	6.18	6.06	5.95
9	13.61	10.11	8.72	7.96	7.47	7.13	6.88	6.69	6.54	6.42	6.31	6.23	6.03	5.83	5.80	5.78	5.75	5.73	5.71	5.62	5.52	5.41	5.30	5.19
10	12.83	9.43	8.08	7.34	6.87	6.54	6.30	6.12	5.97	5.85	5.75	5.66	5.47	5.27	5.25	5.22	5.20	5.17	5.15	5.07	4.97	4.86	4.75	4.64
11	12.23	8.91	7.60	6.88	6.42	6.10	5.86	5.68	5.54	5.42	5.32	5.24	5.05	4.86	4.83	4.80	4.78	4.76	4.74	4.65	4.55	4.45	4.34	4.23
12	11.75	8.51	7.23	6.52	6.07	5.76	5.52	5.35	5.20	5.09	4.99	4.91	4.72	4.53	4.50	4.48	4.45	4.43	4.41	4.33	4.23	4.12	4.01	3.90
13	11.37	8.19	6.93	6.23	5.79	5.48	5.25	5.08	4.94	4.82	4.72	4.64	4.46	4.27	4.24	4.22	4.19	4.17	4.15	4.07	3.97	3.87	3.76	3.65
14	11.06	7.92	6.68	6.00	5.56	5.26	5.03	4.86	4.72	4.60	4.51	4.43	4.25	4.06	4.03	4.01	3.98	3.96	3.94	3.86	3.76	3.66	3.55	3.44
15	10.80	7.70	6.48	5.80	5.37	5.07	4.85	4.67	4.54	4.42	4.33	4.25	4.07	3.88	3.86	3.83	3.81	3.79	3.77	3.69	3.59	3.48	3.37	3.26
16	10.58	7.51	6.30	5.64	5.21	4.91	4.69	4.52	4.38	4.27	4.18	4.10	3.92	3.73	3.71	3.68	3.66	3.64	3.62	3.54	3.44	3.33	3.22	3.11
17	10.38	7.35	6.16	5.50	5.07	4.78	4.56	4.39	4.25	4.14	4.05	3.97	3.79	3.61	3.58	3.56	3.53	3.51	3.49	3.41	3.31	3.21	3.10	2.98
18	10.22	7.21	6.03	5.37	4.96	4.66	4.44	4.28	4.14	4.03	3.94	3.86	3.68	3.50	3.47	3.45	3.42	3.40	3.38	3.30	3.20	3.10	2.99	2.87
19	10.07	7.09	5.92	5.27	4.85	4.56	4.34	4.18	4.04	3.93	3.84	3.76	3.59	3.40	3.37	3.35	3.33	3.31	3.29	3.21	3.11	3.00	2.89	2.78
20	9.94	6.99	5.82	5.17	4.76	4.47	4.26	4.09	3.96	3.85	3.76	3.68	3.50	3.32	3.29	3.27	3.24	3.22	3.20	3.12	3.02	2.92	2.81	2.69
21	9.83	6.89	5.73	5.09	4.68	4.39	4.18	4.01	3.88	3.77	3.68	3.60	3.43	3.24	3.22	3.19	3.17	3.15	3.13	3.05	2.95	2.84	2.73	2.61
22	9.73	6.81	5.65	5.02	4.61	4.32	4.11	3.94	3.81	3.70	3.61	3.54	3.36	3.18	3.15	3.12	3.10	3.08	3.06	2.98	2.88	2.77	2.66	2.55
23	9.63	6.73	5.58	4.95	4.54	4.26	4.05	3.88	3.75	3.64	3.55	3.47	3.30	3.12	3.09	3.06	3.04	3.02	3.00	2.92	2.82	2.71	2.60	2.48
24	9.55	6.66	5.52	4.89	4.49	4.20	3.99	3.83	3.69	3.59	3.50	3.42	3.25	3.06	3.04	3.01	2.99	2.97	2.95	2.87	2.77	2.66	2.55	2.43
25	9.48	6.60	5.46	4.84	4.43	4.15	3.94	3.78	3.64	3.54	3.45	3.37	3.20	3.01	2.99	2.96	2.94	2.92	2.90	2.82	2.72	2.61	2.50	2.38
30	9.18	6.35	5.24	4.62	4.23	3.95	3.74	3.58	3.45	3.34	3.25	3.18	3.01	2.82	2.80	2.77	2.75	2.73	2.71	2.63	2.52	2.42	2.30	2.18
40	8.83	6.07	4.98	4.37	3.99	3.71	3.51	3.35	3.22	3.12	3.03	2.95	2.78	2.60	2.57	2.55	2.52	2.50	2.48	2.40	2.30	2.18	2.06	1.93
60	8.49	5.79	4.73	4.14	3.76	3.49	3.29	3.13	3.01	2.90	2.82	2.74	2.57	2.39	2.36	2.33	2.31	2.29	2.27	2.19	2.08	1.96	1.83	1.69
120	8.18	5.54	4.50	3.92	3.55	3.28	3.09	2.93	2.81	2.71	2.62	2.54	2.37	2.19	2.16	2.13	2.11	2.09	2.07	1.98	1.87	1.75	1.61	1.43
Infinity	7.88	5.30	4.28	3.72	3.35	3.09	2.90	2.74	2.62	2.52	2.43	2.36	2.19	2.00	1.97	1.95	1.92	1.90	1.88	1.79	1.67	1.53	1.36	1.00

With 1 degree of freedom (df) in the numerator and 3 df in the denominator, the critical F-value is 10.1 for a right-hand tail area equal to 0.05.

Quantitative Methods for Investment Analysis, Second Edition, by Richard A. DeFusco, CFA, Dennis W. McLeavey, CFA, Jerald E. Pinto, CFA, and David E. Runkle, CFA. Copyright © 2004 by CFA Institute.

Appendix E
Critical Values for the Durbin-Watson Statistic (α = .05)

	K = 1		K = 2		K = 3		K = 4		K = 5	
n	d_l	d_u	d_l	d_u	d_l	d_u	d_l	d_u	d_l	d_u
15	1.08	1.36	0.95	1.54	0.82	1.75	0.69	1.97	0.56	2.21
16	1.10	1.37	0.98	1.54	0.86	1.73	0.74	1.93	0.62	2.15
17	1.13	1.38	1.02	1.54	0.90	1.71	0.78	1.90	0.67	2.10
18	1.16	1.39	1.05	1.53	0.93	1.69	0.82	1.87	0.71	2.06
19	1.18	1.40	1.08	1.53	0.97	1.68	0.86	1.85	0.75	2.02
20	1.20	1.41	1.10	1.54	1.00	1.68	0.90	1.83	0.79	1.99
21	1.22	1.42	1.13	1.54	1.03	1.67	0.93	1.81	0.83	1.96
22	1.24	1.43	1.15	1.54	1.05	1.66	0.96	1.80	0.86	1.94
23	1.26	1.44	1.17	1.54	1.08	1.66	0.99	1.79	0.90	1.92
24	1.27	1.45	1.19	1.55	1.10	1.66	1.01	1.78	0.93	1.90
25	1.29	1.45	1.21	1.55	1.12	1.66	1.04	1.77	0.95	1.89
26	1.30	1.46	1.22	1.55	1.14	1.65	1.06	1.76	0.98	1.88
27	1.32	1.47	1.24	1.56	1.16	1.65	1.08	1.76	1.01	1.86
28	1.33	1.48	1.26	1.56	1.18	1.65	1.10	1.75	1.03	1.85
29	1.34	1.48	1.27	1.56	1.20	1.65	1.12	1.74	1.05	1.84
30	1.35	1.49	1.28	1.57	1.21	1.65	1.14	1.74	1.07	1.83
31	1.36	1.50	1.30	1.57	1.23	1.65	1.16	1.74	1.09	1.83
32	1.37	1.50	1.31	1.57	1.24	1.65	1.18	1.73	1.11	1.82
33	1.38	1.51	1.32	1.58	1.26	1.65	1.19	1.73	1.13	1.81
34	1.39	1.51	1.33	1.58	1.27	1.65	1.21	1.73	1.15	1.81
35	1.40	1.52	1.34	1.58	1.28	1.65	1.22	1.73	1.16	1.80
36	1.41	1.52	1.35	1.59	1.29	1.65	1.24	1.73	1.18	1.80
37	1.42	1.53	1.36	1.59	1.31	1.66	1.25	1.72	1.19	1.80
38	1.43	1.54	1.37	1.59	1.32	1.66	1.26	1.72	1.21	1.79
39	1.43	1.54	1.38	1.60	1.33	1.66	1.27	1.72	1.22	1.79
40	1.44	1.54	1.39	1.60	1.34	1.66	1.29	1.72	1.23	1.79
45	1.48	1.57	1.43	1.62	1.38	1.67	1.34	1.72	1.29	1.78
50	1.50	1.59	1.46	1.63	1.42	1.67	1.38	1.72	1.34	1.77
55	1.53	1.60	1.49	1.64	1.45	1.68	1.41	1.72	1.38	1.77
60	1.55	1.62	1.51	1.65	1.48	1.69	1.44	1.73	1.41	1.77
65	1.57	1.63	1.54	1.66	1.50	1.70	1.47	1.73	1.44	1.77
70	1.58	1.64	1.55	1.67	1.52	1.70	1.49	1.74	1.46	1.77
75	1.60	1.65	1.57	1.68	1.54	1.71	1.51	1.74	1.49	1.77
80	1.61	1.66	1.59	1.69	1.56	1.72	1.53	1.74	1.51	1.77
85	1.62	1.67	1.60	1.70	1.57	1.72	1.55	1.75	1.52	1.77
90	1.63	1.68	1.61	1.70	1.59	1.73	1.57	1.75	1.54	1.78
95	1.64	1.69	1.62	1.71	1.60	1.73	1.58	1.75	1.56	1.78
100	1.65	1.69	1.63	1.72	1.61	1.74	1.59	1.76	1.57	1.78

Note: K = the number of slope parameters in the model.

Source: From J. Durbin and G. S. Watson, "Testing for Serial Correlation in Least Squares Regression, II." *Biometrika* 38 (1951): 159–178.

Economics

Currency Exchange Rates: Understanding Equilibrium Value

by Michael R. Rosenberg, and William A. Barker, PhD, CFA.

Michael R. Rosenberg (USA). William A. Barker, PhD, CFA (Canada).

LEARNING OUTCOMES

Mastery	*The candidate should be able to:*
☐	calculate and interpret the bid–offer spread on a spot or forward currency quotation and describe the factors that affect the bid–offer spread
☐	identify a triangular arbitrage opportunity and calculate its profit, given the bid–offer quotations for three currencies
☐	explain spot and forward rates and calculate the forward premium/discount for a given currency
☐	calculate the mark-to-market value of a forward contract
☐	explain international parity conditions (covered and uncovered interest rate parity, forward rate parity, purchasing power parity, and the international Fisher effect)
☐	describe relations among the international parity conditions
☐	evaluate the use of the current spot rate, the forward rate, purchasing power parity, and uncovered interest parity to forecast future spot exchange rates
☐	explain approaches to assessing the long-run fair value of an exchange rate
☐	describe the carry trade and its relation to uncovered interest rate parity and calculate the profit from a carry trade
☐	explain how flows in the balance of payment accounts affect currency exchange rates
☐	explain the potential effects of monetary and fiscal policy on exchange rates
☐	describe objectives of central bank or government intervention and capital controls and describe the effectiveness of intervention and capital controls
☐	describe warning signs of a currency crisis

1   INTRODUCTION

Exchange rates are well known to follow a random walk, whereby fluctuations from one day to the next are unpredictable. The business of currency forecasting can be a humbling experience. Alan Greenspan, former chair of the US Federal Reserve Board, famously noted that "having endeavored to forecast exchange rates for more than half a century, I have understandably developed significant humility about my ability in this area."

Hence, our discussion is not about predicting exchange rates but about the tools the reader can use to better understand long-run equilibrium value. This outlook helps guide the market participant's decisions with respect to risk exposures, as well as whether currency hedges should be implemented and, if so, how they should be managed. After discussing the basics of exchange rate transactions, we present the main theories for currency determination—starting with the international parity conditions—and then describe other important influences, such as current account balances, capital flows, and monetary and fiscal policy.

Although these fundamentals-based models usually perform poorly in predicting future exchange rates in the short run, they are crucial for understanding long-term currency value. Thus, we proceed as follows:

- We review the basic concepts of the foreign exchange market covered in the CFA Program Level I curriculum and expand this previous coverage to incorporate more material on bid–offer spreads.

- We then begin to examine determinants of exchange rates, starting with longer-term interrelationships among exchange rates, interest rates, and inflation rates embodied in the international parity conditions. These parity conditions form the key building blocks for many long-run exchange rate models.

- We also examine the foreign exchange (FX) carry trade, a trading strategy that exploits deviations from uncovered interest rate parity and discuss the relationship between a country's exchange rate and its balance of payments.

- We then examine how monetary and fiscal policies can *indirectly* affect exchange rates by influencing the various factors described in our exchange rate model.

- The subsequent section focuses on *direct* public sector actions in foreign exchange markets, both through capital controls and by foreign exchange market intervention (buying and selling currencies for policy purposes).

- The last section examines historical episodes of currency crisis and some leading indicators that may signal the increased likelihood of a crisis.

2   FOREIGN EXCHANGE MARKET CONCEPTS

☐   calculate and interpret the bid–offer spread on a spot or forward currency quotation and describe the factors that affect the bid–offer spread

We begin with a brief review of some of the basic conventions of the FX market that were covered in the CFA Program Level I curriculum. In this section, we cover (1) the basics of exchange rate notation and pricing, (2) arbitrage pricing constraints on spot rate foreign exchange quotes, and (3) forward rates and covered interest rate parity.

An exchange rate is the price of the *base* currency expressed in terms of the *price* currency. For example, a USD/EUR rate of 1.1650 means the euro, the base currency, costs 1.1650 US dollars (an appendix defines the three-letter currency codes). The exact notation used to represent exchange rates can vary widely between sources, and occasionally the same exchange rate notation will be used by different sources to mean completely different things. *The reader should be aware that the notation used here may not be the same as that encountered elsewhere.* To avoid confusion, we will identify exchange rates using the convention of "P/B," referring to the price of the base currency, "B," expressed in terms of the price currency, "P."

> ### NOTATION CONVENTIONS
>
> Notation is generally not standardized in global foreign exchange markets, and there are several common ways of expressing the same currency pair (e.g., JPY/USD, USD:JPY, $/¥). What is common in FX markets, however, is the concept of a "base" and a "price" currency when setting exchange rates. We will sometimes switch to discussing a "domestic" and a "foreign" currency, quoted as foreign/domestic (f/d). This is only an illustrative device for more easily explaining various theoretical concepts. The candidate should be aware that currency pairs are not described in terms of "foreign" and "domestic" currencies in professional FX markets. This is because what is the "foreign" and what is the "domestic" currency depend on where one is located, which can lead to confusion. For instance, what is "foreign" and what is "domestic" for a Middle Eastern investor trading CHF against GBP with the New York branch of a European bank, with the trade ultimately booked at the bank's headquarters in Paris?

The spot exchange rate is usually used for settlement on the second business day after the trade date, referred to as $T + 2$ settlement (the exception being CAD/USD, for which standard spot settlement is $T + 1$). In foreign exchange markets—as in other financial markets—market participants are presented with a two-sided price in the form of a bid price and an offer price (also called an ask price) quoted by potential counterparties. The bid price is the price, defined in terms of the price currency, at which the counterparty is willing to buy one unit of the base currency. Similarly, the offer price is the price, in terms of the price currency, at which that counterparty is willing to sell one unit of the base currency. For example, given a price request from a client, a dealer might quote a two-sided price on the spot USD/EUR exchange rate of 1.1648/1.1652. This means that the dealer is willing to pay USD 1.1648 to buy one EUR and that the dealer is willing to sell one EUR for USD 1.1652.

There are two points to bear in mind about bid–offer quotes:

1. *The offer price is always higher than the bid price.* The bid–offer spread—the difference between the offer price and the bid price—is the compensation that counterparties seek for providing foreign exchange to other market participants.

2. *The party in the transaction who requests a two-sided price quote has the option (but not the obligation) to deal at either the bid (to sell the base currency) or the offer (to buy the base currency) quoted by the dealer.* If the party chooses to trade at the quoted prices, the party is said to have either "*hit the bid*" or "*paid the offer.*" If the base currency is being sold, the party is said to have hit the bid. If the base currency is being bought, the party is said to have paid the offer.

We will distinguish here between the bid–offer pricing *a client receives from a dealer* and the pricing *a dealer receives from the interbank market.* Dealers buy and sell foreign exchange among themselves in what is called the interbank market. This global network for exchanging currencies among professional market participants allows dealers to adjust their inventories and risk positions, distribute foreign currencies to end users who need them, and transfer foreign exchange rate risk to market participants who are willing to bear it. The interbank market is typically for dealing sizes of at least 1 million units of the base currency. Of course, the dealing amount can be larger than 1 million units; indeed, interbank market trades generally are measured in terms of multiples of a million units of the base currency. Please note that many non-bank entities can now access the interbank market. They include institutional asset managers and hedge funds.

The bid–offer spread a dealer provides to most clients typically is slightly wider than the bid–offer spread observed in the interbank market. Most currencies, except for the yen, are quoted to four decimal places. The fourth decimal place (0.0001) is referred to as a "pip." The yen is typically quoted to just two decimal places; in yen quotes, the second decimal place (0.01) is referred to as a pip.

For example, if the quote in the interbank USD/EUR spot market is 1.1649/1.1651 (two pips wide), the dealer might quote a client a bid–offer of 1.1648/1.1652 (four pips wide) for a spot USD/EUR transaction. When the dealer buys (sells) the base currency from (to) a client, the dealer is typically expecting to quickly turn around and sell (buy) the base currency in the interbank market. This offsetting transaction allows the dealer to divest the risk exposure assumed by providing a two-sided price to the client and to hopefully make a profit. Continuing our example, suppose the dealer's client hits the dealer's bid and sells EUR to the dealer for USD 1.1648. The dealer is now long EUR (and short USD) and wants to cover this position in the interbank market. To do this, the dealer sells the EUR in the interbank market by hitting the interbank bid. As a result, the dealer *bought* EUR from the client at USD 1.1648 and then *sold* the EUR in the interbank for USD 1.1649. This gives the dealer a profit of USD 0.0001 (one pip) for every EUR transacted. This one pip translates into a profit of USD 100 per EUR million bought from the client. If, instead of hitting his bid, the client paid the offer (1.1652), then the dealer could pay the offer in the interbank market (1.1651), earning a profit of one pip.

The size of the bid–offer spread quoted to dealers' clients in the FX market can vary widely across exchange rates and is not constant over time, even for a single exchange rate. The size of this spread depends primarily on three factors:

- the bid–offer spread in the interbank foreign exchange market for the two currencies involved,
- the size of the transaction, and
- the relationship between the dealer and the client.

We examine each factor in turn.

The size of the bid–offer spread quoted in the interbank market depends on the liquidity in this market. Liquidity is influenced by several factors:

1. *The currency pair involved.* Market participation is greater for some currency pairs than for others. Liquidity in the major currency pairs—for example, USD/EUR, JPY/USD, and USD/GBP—can be quite high. These markets are almost always deep, with multiple bids and offers from market participants around the world. In other currency pairs, particularly some of the more obscure currency cross rates (e.g., MXN/CHF), market participation is much thinner and consequently the bid–offer spread in the interbank market will be wider.

2. *The time of day.* The interbank FX markets are most liquid when the major FX trading centers are open. Business hours in London and New York—the two largest FX trading centers—overlap from approximately 8:00 a.m. to 11:00 a.m. New York time. The interbank FX market for most currency pairs is typically most liquid during these hours. After London closes, liquidity is thinner through the New York afternoon. The Asian session starts when dealers in Tokyo, Singapore, and Hong Kong SAR open for business, typically by 7:00 p.m. New York time. For most currency pairs, however, the Asian session is not as liquid as the London and New York sessions. Although FX markets are open 24 hours a day on business days, between the time New York closes and the time Asia opens, liquidity in interbank markets can be very thin because Sydney, Australia, tends to be the only active trading center during these hours. For reference, the chart below shows a 24-hour period from midnight (00:00) to midnight (24:00) London time, corresponding standard times in Tokyo and New York, and, shaded in grey, the *approximate* hours of the most liquid trading periods in each market.

Standard Time and Approximate FX Trading Hours in Major Markets: Midnight to Midnight (London Time)

Tokyo	09:00	13:00	17:00	21:00	01:00 Day+1	05:00 Day+1	09:00 Day+1
London	00:00	04:00	08:00	12:00	16:00	20:00	24:00
New York	19:00 Day−1	23:00 Day−1	03:00	07:00	11:00	15:00	19:00

3. *Market volatility.* As in any financial market, when major market participants have greater uncertainty about the factors influencing market pricing, they will attempt to reduce their risk exposures and/or charge a higher price for taking on risk. In the FX market, this response implies wider bid–offer spreads in both the interbank and broader markets. Geopolitical events (e.g., war, civil strife), market crashes, and major data releases (e.g., US non-farm payrolls) are among the factors that influence spreads and liquidity.

The size of the transaction can also affect the bid–offer spread shown by a dealer to clients. Typically, the larger the transaction, the further away from the current spot exchange rate the dealing price will be. Hence, a client who asks a dealer for a two-sided spot CAD/USD price on, for example, USD 50 million will be shown a wider bid–offer spread than a client who asks for a price on USD 1 million. The wider spread reflects the greater difficulty the dealer faces in offsetting the foreign exchange risk of the position in the interbank FX market. Smaller dealing sizes can also affect the bid–offer quote shown to clients. "Retail" quotes are typically for dealing sizes smaller than 1 million units of the base currency and can range all the way down to foreign exchange transactions conducted by individuals. The bid–offer spreads for these retail transactions can be very large compared with those in the interbank market.

The relationship between the dealer and the client can also affect the size of the bid–offer spread shown by the dealer. For many clients, the spot foreign exchange business is only one business service among many that a dealer provides to that client. For example, the dealer firm might also transact in bond and/or equity securities with the same client. In a competitive business environment, in order to win the client's business for these other services, the dealer might provide a tighter (i.e., smaller) bid–offer spot exchange rate quote. The dealer might also give tighter bid–offer quotes in order to win repeat FX business. A client's credit risk can also be a factor. A client with a poor credit profile may be quoted a wider bid–offer spread than one with good credit. Given the short settlement cycle for spot FX transactions (typically two business days), however, credit risk is not the most important factor in determining the client's bid–offer spread on spot exchange rates.

3 ARBITRAGE CONSTRAINTS ON SPOT EXCHANGE RATE QUOTES

> ☐ | identify a triangular arbitrage opportunity and calculate its profit, given the bid–offer quotations for three currencies

The bid–offer quotes a dealer shows in the interbank FX market must respect two arbitrage constraints; otherwise the dealer creates riskless arbitrage opportunities for other interbank market participants. We will confine our attention to the interbank FX market because arbitrage presumes the ability to deal simultaneously with different market participants and in different markets, the ability to access "wholesale" bid–offer quotes, and the market sophistication to spot arbitrage opportunities.

First, the bid shown by a dealer in the interbank market cannot be higher than the current interbank offer, and the offer shown by a dealer cannot be lower than the current interbank bid. If the bid–offer quotes shown by a dealer are inconsistent with the then-current interbank market quotes, other market participants will buy from the cheaper source and sell to the more expensive source. This arbitrage will eventually bring the two prices back into line. For example, suppose that the current spot USD/EUR price in the interbank market is 1.1649/1.1651. If a dealer showed a misaligned price quote of 1.1652/1.1654, then other market participants would pay the offer in the interbank market, *buying* EUR at a price of USD 1.1651, and then *sell* the EUR to the dealer by hitting the dealer's bid at USD 1.1652—thereby making a riskless profit of one pip on the trade. This arbitrage would continue as long as the dealer's bid–offer quote violated the arbitrage constraint.

Second, the cross-rate bids (offers) posted by a dealer must be lower (higher) than the implied cross-rate offers (bids) available in the interbank market. A currency dealer located in a given country typically provides exchange rate quotations between that country's currency and various foreign currencies. If a particular currency pair is not explicitly quoted, it can be inferred from the quotes for each currency in terms of the exchange rate with a third nation's currency. For example, given exchange rate quotes for the currency pairs A/B and C/B, we can back out the implied cross rate of A/C. This implied A/C cross rate must be consistent with the A/B and C/B rates. This again reflects the basic principle of arbitrage: If identical financial products are priced differently, then market participants will buy the cheaper one and sell the more expensive one until the price difference is eliminated. In the context of FX cross rates, there are two ways to trade currency A against currency C: (1) using the cross rate A/C or (2) using the A/B and C/B rates. Because, in the end, both methods involve selling (buying) currency C in order to buy (sell) currency A, the exchange rates for these two approaches must be consistent. If the exchange rates are not consistent, the arbitrageur will buy currency C from a dealer if it is undervalued (relative to the cross rate) and sell currency A. If currency C is overvalued by a dealer (relative to the cross rate), it will be sold and currency A will be bought.

To illustrate this **triangular arbitrage** among three currencies, suppose that the interbank market bid–offer in USD/EUR is 1.1649/1.1651 and that the bid–offer in JPY/USD is 105.39/105.41. We need to use these two interbank bid–offer quotes to calculate the market-implied bid–offer quote on the JPY/EUR cross rate.

Begin by considering the transactions required to *sell* JPY and *buy* EUR, going through the JPY/USD and USD/EUR currency pairs. We can view this process intuitively as follows:

Sell JPY		Sell JPY		Sell USD
Buy EUR	=	Buy USD	then	Buy EUR

Note that "Buy USD" and "Sell USD" in the expressions on the right-hand side of the equal sign will cancel out to give the JPY/EUR cross rate. In equation form, we can represent this relationship as follows:

$$\left(\frac{JPY}{EUR}\right) = \left(\frac{JPY}{\cancel{USD}}\right)\left(\frac{\cancel{USD}}{EUR}\right).$$

Now, let's incorporate the bid–offer rates in order to do the JPY/EUR calculation. A rule of thumb is that when we speak of a bid or offer exchange rate, we are referring to the bid or offer for the currency in the denominator (the base currency).

  i.   The left-hand side of the above equal sign is "Sell JPY, Buy EUR." In the JPY/EUR price quote, the EUR is in the denominator (it is the base currency). Because we want to buy the currency in the denominator, we need an exchange rate that is an offer rate. Thus, we will be calculating the *offer* rate for JPY/EUR.

 ii.   The first term on the right-hand side of the equal sign is "Sell JPY, Buy USD." Because we want to buy the currency in the denominator of the quote, we need an exchange rate that is an offer rate. Thus, we need the *offer* rate for JPY/USD.

iii.   The second term on the right-hand side of the equal sign is "Sell USD, Buy EUR." Because we want to buy the currency in the denominator of the quote, we need an exchange rate that is an offer rate. Thus, we need the *offer* rate for USD/EUR.

Combining all of this conceptually and putting in the relevant offer rates leads to a JPY/EUR offer rate of

$$\left(\frac{JPY}{EUR}\right)_{offer} = \left(\frac{JPY}{\boxed{USD}}\right)_{offer}\left(\frac{\boxed{USD}}{EUR}\right)_{offer} = 105.41 \times 1.1651 = 122.81.$$

Perhaps not surprisingly, calculating the implied JPY/EUR *bid* rate uses the same process as above but with "Buy JPY, Sell EUR" for the left-hand side of the equation, which leads to

$$\left(\frac{JPY}{EUR}\right)_{bid} = \left(\frac{JPY}{\boxed{USD}}\right)_{bid}\left(\frac{\boxed{USD}}{EUR}\right)_{bid} = 105.39 \times 1.1649 = 122.77.$$

As one would expect, the implied cross-rate bid (122.77) is less than the offer (122.81).

This simple formula seems relatively straightforward: To get the implied *bid* cross rate, simply multiply the *bid* rates for the other two currencies. However, depending on the quotes provided, it may be necessary to *invert* one of the quotes in order to complete the calculation.

This is best illustrated with an example. Consider the case of calculating the implied GBP/EUR cross rate if you are given USD/GBP and USD/EUR quotes. Simply using the provided quotes will not generate the desired GBP/EUR cross rate:

$$\frac{GBP}{EUR} \neq \left(\frac{USD}{GBP}\right)\left(\frac{USD}{EUR}\right).$$

Instead, because the USD is in the numerator in both currency pairs, we will have to invert one of the pairs to derive the GBP/EUR cross rate.

The following equation represents the cross-rate relationship we are trying to derive:

$$\frac{GBP}{EUR} = \left(\frac{GBP}{USD}\right)\left(\frac{USD}{EUR}\right).$$

But we don't have the GBP/USD quote. We can, however, invert the USD/GBP quote and use that in our calculation. Let's assume the bid–offer quote provided is for USD/GBP and is 1.2302/1.2304. With this quote, if we want to *buy* GBP (the currency in the denominator), we will buy GBP at the offer and the relevant quote is 1.2304. We can invert this quote to arrive at the needed GBP/USD quote: 1 ÷ 1.2304 = 0.81274. Note that, in this example, when we buy the GBP, we are also selling the USD. When we invert the provided USD/GBP offer quote, we obtain 0.81274 GBP/USD. This is the price at which we sell the USD—that is, the GBP/USD *bid*. It may help here to remember our rule of thumb from above: When we speak of a bid or offer exchange rate, we are referring to the bid or offer for the currency in the denominator (the base currency).

Similarly, to get a GBP/USD *offer*, we use the inverse of the USD/GBP *bid* of 1.2302: 1 ÷ 1.2302 = 0.81288. (Note that we extended the calculated GBP/USD 0.81274/0.81288 quotes to five decimal places to avoid truncation errors in subsequent calculations.)

We can now finish the calculation of the bid and offer cross rates for GBP/EUR. Using the previously provided 1.1649/1.1651 as the bid–offer in USD/EUR, we calculate the GBP/EUR *bid* rate as follows:

$$\left(\frac{GBP}{EUR}\right)_{bid} = \left(\frac{GBP}{\boxed{USD}}\right)_{bid}\left(\frac{\boxed{USD}}{EUR}\right)_{bid} = 0.81274 \times 1.1649 = 0.9468.$$

Similarly, the implied GBP/EUR *offer* rate is

$$\left(\frac{GBP}{EUR}\right)_{offer} = \left(\frac{GBP}{\boxed{USD}}\right)_{offer}\left(\frac{\boxed{USD}}{EUR}\right)_{offer} = 0.81288 \times 1.1651 = 0.9471.$$

Note that the implied *bid* rate is less than the implied *offer* rate, as it must be to prevent arbitrage.

We conclude this section on arbitrage constraints with some simple observations:

- The arbitrage constraint on implied cross rates is similar to that for spot rates (posted bid rates cannot be higher than the market's offer; posted offer rates cannot be lower than the market's bid). The only difference is that this second arbitrage constraint is applied *across* currency pairs instead of involving a *single* currency pair.

- In reality, any violations of these arbitrage constraints will quickly disappear. Both human traders and automatic trading algorithms are constantly on alert for any pricing inefficiencies and will arbitrage them away almost instantly. If Dealer 1 is buying a currency at a price higher than the price at which Dealer 2 is selling it, the arbitrageur will buy the currency from Dealer 2 and resell it to Dealer 1. As a result of buying and selling pressures, Dealer 2 will raise his offer prices and Dealer 1 will reduce her bid prices to the point where arbitrage profits are no longer available.

- Market participants do not need to calculate cross rates *manually* because electronic dealing machines (which are essentially just specialized computers) will automatically calculate cross bid–offer rates given any two underlying bid–offer rates.

EXAMPLE 1

Bid–Offer Rates

The following are spot rate quotes in the interbank market:

USD/EUR	1.1649/1.1651
JPY/USD	105.39/105.41
CAD/USD	1.3199/1.3201
SEK/USD	9.6300/9.6302

1. What is the bid–offer on the SEK/EUR cross rate implied by the interbank market?

   A. 0.1209/0.1211

   B. 8.2656/8.2668

   C. 11.2180/11.2201

   Solution

   C is correct. Using the provided quotes and setting up the equations so that the cancellation of terms results in the SEK/EUR quote,

   $$\frac{SEK}{EUR} = \frac{SEK}{USD} \times \frac{USD}{EUR}.$$

   Hence, to calculate the SEK/EUR bid (offer) rate, we multiply the SEK/USD and USD/EUR bid (offer) rates to get the following:

Bid:	11.2180 = 9.6300 × 1.1649.
Offer:	11.2201 = 9.6302 × 1.1651.

2. What is the bid–offer on the JPY/CAD cross rate implied by the interbank market?

   A. 78.13/78.17

   B. 79.85/79.85

   C. 79.84/79.86

   Solution

   C is correct. Using the intuitive equation-based approach,

   $$\frac{JPY}{CAD} = \frac{JPY}{USD} \times \left(\frac{CAD}{USD}\right)^{-1} = \frac{JPY}{\cancel{USD}} \times \frac{\cancel{USD}}{CAD}.$$

   This equation shows that we have to invert the CAD/USD quotes to get the USD/CAD bid–offer rates of 0.75752/0.75763. That is, given the CAD/USD quotes of 1.3199/1.3201, we take the inverse of each and interchange bid and offer, so that the USD/CAD quotes are (1/1.3201)/(1/1.3199), or 0.75752/0.75763. Multiplying the JPY/USD and USD/CAD bid–offer rates then leads to the following:

Bid:	79.84 = 105.39 × 0.75752.
Offer:	79.86 = 105.41 × 0.75763.

3. If a dealer quoted a bid–offer rate of 79.81/79.83 in JPY/CAD, then a triangular arbitrage would involve buying:

   A. CAD in the interbank market and selling it to the dealer, for a profit of JPY 0.01 per CAD.

   B. JPY from the dealer and selling it in the interbank market, for a profit of CAD 0.01 per JPY.

   C. CAD from the dealer and selling it in the interbank market, for a profit of JPY 0.01 per CAD.

   Solution

   C is correct. The implied interbank cross rate for JPY/CAD is 79.84/79.86 (the answer to Question 2). Hence, the dealer is offering to sell the CAD (the base currency in the quote) too cheaply, at an offer rate that is below the interbank bid rate (79.83 versus 79.84, respectively). Triangular arbitrage would involve buying CAD from the dealer (paying the dealer's offer) and selling CAD in the interbank market (hitting the interbank bid), for a profit of JPY 0.01 (79.84 – 79.83) per CAD transacted.

4. If a dealer quoted a bid–offer of 79.82/79.87 in JPY/CAD, then you could:

   A. not make any arbitrage profits.

   B. make arbitrage profits buying JPY from the dealer and selling it in the interbank market.

   C. make arbitrage profits buying CAD from the dealer and selling it in the interbank market.

   Solution

   A is correct. The arbitrage relationship is not violated: The dealer's bid (offer) is not above (below) the interbank market's offer (bid). The implied interbank cross rate for JPY/CAD is 79.84/79.86 (the solution to Question 2).

5. A market participant is considering the following transactions:

Transaction 1	Buy CAD 100 million against the USD at 15:30 London time.
Transaction 2	Sell CAD 100 million against the KRW at 21:30 London time.
Transaction 3	Sell CAD 10 million against the USD at 15:30 London time.

   Given the proposed transactions, what is the *most likely* ranking of the bid–offer spreads, from tightest to widest, under normal market conditions?

   A. Transactions 1, 2, 3

   B. Transactions 2, 1, 3

   C. Transactions 3, 1, 2

   Solution

   C is correct. The CAD/USD currency pair is most liquid when New York and London are both in their most liquid trading periods at the same time (approximately 8:00 a.m. to 11:00 a.m. New York time, or about 13:00 to 16:00 London time). Transaction 3 is for a smaller amount than Transaction 1. Transaction 2 is for a less liquid currency pair (KRW/CAD is traded less than CAD/USD) and occurs outside of normal dealing hours in all three

> major centers (London, North America, and Asia); the transaction is also for
> a large amount.

FORWARD MARKETS

4

☐ | explain spot and forward rates and calculate the forward premium/
    discount for a given currency

Outright forward contracts (often referred to simply as forwards) are agreements to
exchange one currency for another on a future date at an exchange rate agreed upon
today. Any exchange rate transaction that has a settlement date longer than $T + 2$ is
a forward contract.

Forward exchange rates must satisfy an arbitrage relationship that equates the
investment return on two alternative but equivalent investments. To simplify the explanation of this arbitrage relationship and to focus on the intuition behind forward rate
calculations, we will ignore the bid–offer spread on exchange rates and money market
instruments. In addition, we will alter our exchange rate notation from price/base
currency (P/B) to "foreign/domestic currency" (*f/d*), making the assumption that the
domestic currency for an investor is the base currency in the exchange rate quotation.
Using this (*f/d*) notation will make it easier to illustrate the choice an investor faces
between domestic and foreign investments, as well as the arbitrage relationships that
equate the returns on these investments when their risk characteristics are equivalent.

Consider an investor with one unit of domestic currency to invest for one year.
The investor faces two alternatives:

A. One alternative is to invest cash for one year at the domestic risk-free rate
(i_d). At the end of the year, the investment would be worth $(1 + i_d)$.

B. The other alternative is to convert the domestic currency to foreign currency at the spot rate of $S_{f/d}$ and invest for one year at the foreign risk-free
rate (i_f). At the end of the period, the investor would have $S_{f/d}(1 + i_f)$ units of
foreign currency. These funds then must be converted back to the investor's
domestic currency. If the exchange rate to be used for this end-of-year conversion is set at the start of the period using a one-year forward contract,
then the investor will have eliminated the foreign exchange risk associated
with converting at an unknown future spot rate. If we let $F_{f/d}$ denote the forward rate, the investor would obtain ($1/F_{f/d}$) units of the domestic currency
for each unit of foreign currency sold forward. Hence, in domestic currency,
at the end of the year, the investment would be worth $S_{f/d}(1 + i_f)(1/F_{f/d})$.

The two investment alternatives above (A and B) are risk free and therefore must
offer the same return. If they did not offer the same return, investors could earn a
riskless arbitrage profit by borrowing in one currency, lending in the other, and using
the spot and forward exchange markets to eliminate currency risk. Equating the
returns on these two investment alternatives—that is, putting investments A and B
on opposite sides of the equal sign—leads to the following relationship:

$$(1 + i_d) = S_{f/d}(1 + i_f)\left(\frac{1}{F_{f/d}}\right).$$

To see the intuition behind forward rate calculations, note that the right-hand side of the expression (for investment B) also shows the chronological order of this investment: Convert from domestic to foreign currency at the spot rate ($S_{f/d}$); invest this foreign currency amount at the foreign risk-free interest rate ($1 + i_f$); and then at maturity, convert the foreign currency investment proceeds back into the domestic currency using the forward rate ($1/F_{f/d}$).

For simplicity, we assumed a one-year horizon in the preceding example. However, the argument holds for any investment horizon. The risk-free assets used in this arbitrage relationship are typically bank deposits quoted using the appropriate Market Reference Rate for each currency involved. The day count convention MRR deposits may be Actual/360 or Actual/365. The notation Actual/360 means that interest is calculated as if there were 360 days in a year. The notation Actual/365 means interest is calculated as if there were 365 days in a year. The main exception to the Actual/360 day count convention is the GBP, for which the convention is Actual/365. For the purposes of our discussion, we will use Actual/360 consistently in order to avoid complication. Incorporating this day count convention into our arbitrage formula leads to

$$\left(1 + i_d\left[\frac{Actual}{360}\right]\right) = S_{f/d}\left(1 + i_f\left[\frac{Actual}{360}\right]\right)\left(\frac{1}{F_{f/d}}\right).$$

This equation can be rearranged to isolate the forward rate:

$$F_{f/d} = S_{f/d}\left(\frac{1 + i_f\left[\frac{Actual}{360}\right]}{1 + i_d\left[\frac{Actual}{360}\right]}\right). \tag{1}$$

Equation 1 describes **covered interest rate parity**. Our previous work shows that covered interest rate parity is based on an arbitrage relationship among risk-free interest rates and spot and forward exchange rates. Because of this arbitrage relationship between investment alternatives, Equation 1 can also be described as saying that the covered (i.e., currency-hedged) interest rate differential between the two markets is zero.

The covered interest rate parity equation can also be rearranged to give an expression for the forward premium or discount:

$$F_{f/d} - S_{f/d} = S_{f/d}\left(\frac{\left[\frac{Actual}{360}\right]}{1 + i_d\left[\frac{Actual}{360}\right]}\right)(i_f - i_d).$$

The domestic currency will trade at a forward premium ($F_{f/d} > S_{f/d}$) if, and only if, the foreign risk-free interest rate exceeds the domestic risk-free interest rate ($i_f > i_d$). Equivalently, in this case, the foreign currency will trade at a lower rate in the forward contract (relative to the spot rate), and we would say that the foreign currency trades at a forward discount. In other words, if it is possible to earn more interest in the foreign market than in the domestic market, then the forward discount for the foreign currency will offset the higher foreign interest rate. Otherwise, covered interest rate parity would not hold and arbitrage opportunities would exist.

When the foreign currency is at a higher rate in the forward contract, relative to the spot rate, we say that the foreign currency trades at a forward premium. In the case of a forward premium for the foreign currency, the foreign risk-free interest rate will be less than the domestic risk-free interest rate. Additionally, as can be seen in the equation above, the premium or discount is proportional to the spot exchange rate ($S_{f/d}$), proportional to the interest rate differential ($i_f - i_d$) between the markets, and approximately proportional to the time to maturity (Actual/360).

Although we have illustrated the covered interest rate parity equation (Equation 1) in terms of foreign and domestic currencies (using the notation f/d), this equation can also be expressed in our more standard exchange rate quoting convention of price and base currencies (P/B):

$$F_{P/B} = S_{P/B}\left(\frac{1 + i_P\left[\frac{\text{Actual}}{360}\right]}{1 + i_B\left[\frac{\text{Actual}}{360}\right]}\right).$$

When dealing in professional FX markets, it may be more useful to think of the covered interest rate parity equation and the calculation of forward rates in this P/B notation rather than in foreign/domestic (*f/d*) notation. Domestic and foreign are relative concepts that depend on where one is located, and because of the potential for confusion, these terms are not used for currency quotes in professional FX markets.

EXAMPLE 2

Calculating the Forward Premium (Discount)

The following table shows the mid-market rate (i.e., the average of the bid and offer) for the current CAD/AUD spot exchange rate as well as for AUD and CAD 270-day MRR (annualized):

Spot (CAD/AUD)	0.9000
270-day MRR (AUD)	1.47%
270-day MRR (CAD)	0.41%

1. The forward premium (discount) for a 270-day forward contract for CAD/AUD would be *closest* to:

   A. −0.0094.

   B. −0.0071.

   C. +0.0071.

   Solution

   B is correct. The equation to calculate the forward premium (discount) is as follows:

   $$F_{P/B} - S_{P/B} = S_{P/B}\left(\frac{\left[\frac{\text{Actual}}{360}\right]}{1 + i_B\left[\frac{\text{Actual}}{360}\right]}\right)(i_P - i_B).$$

   Because AUD is the base currency in the CAD/AUD quote, putting in the information from the table gives us

   $$F_{P/B} - S_{P/B} = 0.9000\left(\frac{\left[\frac{270}{360}\right]}{1 + 0.0147\left[\frac{270}{360}\right]}\right)(0.0041 - 0.0147) = -0.0071.$$

In professional FX markets, forward exchange rates are typically quoted in terms of points—the difference between the forward exchange rate quote and the spot exchange rate quote, scaled so that the points can be directly related to the last decimal place in the spot quote. Thus, the forward rate quote is typically shown as the bid–offer on the spot rate and the number of forward points at each maturity, as shown in Exhibit 1 ("Maturity" is defined in terms of the time between spot settlement—usually T + 2—and the settlement of the forward contract).

Exhibit 1: Sample Spot and Forward Quotes (Bid–Offer)	
Maturity	**Spot Rate**
Spot (USD/EUR)	1.1649/1.1651
	Forward Points
1 month	−5.6/−5.1
3 months	−15.9/−15.3
6 months	−37.0/−36.3
12 months	−94.3/−91.8

Note the following:

- As always, the offer in the bid–offer quote is larger than the bid. In this example, the forward points are negative (i.e., the forward rate for the EUR is at a discount to the spot rate) but the bid is a smaller number (−5.6 versus −5.1 at the one-month maturity).

- The absolute number of forward points is a function of the term of the forward contract: A longer contract term results in a larger number of points.

- Because this is an OTC market, a client is not restricted to dealing *only* at the dates/maturities shown. Dealers typically quote standard forward dates, but forward deals can be arranged for any forward date the client requires. The forward points for these non-standard (referred to as "broken") forward dates will typically be interpolated on the basis of the points shown for the standard settlement dates.

- The quoted points are already scaled to each maturity—they are not annualized—so there is no need to adjust them.

To convert any of these quoted forward points into a forward rate, divide the number of points by 10,000 (to scale it down to the same four decimal places in the USD/EUR spot quote) and then add the result to the spot exchange rate quote (because the JPY/USD exchange rate is quoted to only two decimal places, forward points for the dollar–yen currency pair are divided by 100). Be careful, however, about which side of the market (bid or offer) is being quoted. For example, suppose a market participant is *selling* the EUR forward against the USD and is given a USD/EUR quote. The EUR is the base currency; thus, the market participant must use the *bid* rates (i.e., hit the bid). Using the data in Exhibit 1, the three-month forward *bid* rate in this case would be based on the spot bid and the forward points bid and hence would be

$$1.1649 + (-15.9/10,000) = 1.16331.$$

The market participant would be selling EUR three months forward at a price of USD 1.16331 per EUR.

5   THE MARK-TO-MARKET VALUE OF A FORWARD CONTRACT

☐ | calculate the mark-to-market value of a forward contract

Next, we consider the mark-to-market value of forward contracts. As with other financial instruments, the mark-to-market value of forward contracts reflects the profit (or loss) that would be realized from closing out the position at current market prices. To close out a forward position, we must offset it with an equal and opposite forward position using the spot exchange rate and forward points available in the market when the offsetting position is created. When a forward contract is initiated, the mark-to-market value of the contract is zero, and no cash changes hands. From that moment onward, however, the mark-to-market value of the forward contract will change as the spot exchange rate changes and as interest rates change in either of the two currencies.

Let's look at an example. Suppose that a market participant bought GBP 10 million for delivery against the AUD in six months at an "all-in" forward rate of 1.8100 AUD/GBP. (The all-in forward rate is simply the sum of the spot rate and the scaled forward points.) Three months later, the market participant wants to close out this forward contract. This would require selling GBP 10 million three months forward using the AUD/GBP spot exchange rate and forward points in effect at that time. Before looking at this exchange rate, note that the offsetting forward contract is defined in terms of the original position taken. The original position in this example was "long GBP 10 million," so the offsetting contract is "short GBP 10 million." However, there is ambiguity here: To be long GBP 10 million at 1.8100 AUD/GBP is equivalent to being short AUD 18,100,000 (10,000,000 × 1.8100) at the same forward rate. To avoid this ambiguity, for the purposes of this discussion, we will state what the relevant forward position is for mark-to-market purposes. The net gain or loss from the transaction will be reflected in the alternate currency.

Assume the bid–offer quotes for spot and forward points three months prior to the settlement date are as follows:

Spot rate (AUD/GBP)	1.8210/1.8215
Three-month points	130/140

To sell GBP (the base currency in the AUD/GBP quote), we will be calculating the *bid* side of the market. Hence, the appropriate all-in three-month forward rate to use is

$$1.8210 + 130/10,000 = 1.8340.$$

This means that the market participant originally bought GBP 10 million at an AUD/GBP rate of 1.8100 and subsequently sold that amount at a rate of 1.8340. These GBP amounts will net to zero at the settlement date (GBP 10 million both bought and sold), but the AUD amounts will not, because the forward rate has changed. The AUD cash flow at the settlement date will be

$$(1.8340 - 1.8100) \times 10,000,000 = +AUD\ 240,000.$$

This is a cash *inflow* because the market participant was long the GBP with the original forward position and the GBP subsequently appreciated (the AUD/GBP rate increased).

This cash flow will be paid at the settlement day, which is still three months away. To calculate the mark-to-market value of the dealer's position, we must discount this cash flow to the present. The present value of this amount is found by discounting the settlement day cash flow by the three-month discount rate. Because this amount is in AUD, we use the three-month AUD discount rate. Suppose that three-month AUD MRR is 2.40% (annualized). The present value of this future AUD cash flow is then

$$\frac{AUD\ 240,000}{1 + 0.024\left(\frac{90}{360}\right)} = AUD\ 238,569.$$

This result is the mark-to-market value of the original long GBP 10 million six-month forward when it is closed out three months prior to settlement.

To summarize, the process for marking to market a forward position is relatively straightforward:

1. Create an offsetting forward position that is equal to the original forward position. (In the example above, the market participant was long GBP 10 million forward, so the offsetting forward contract would be to sell GBP 10 million.)

2. Determine the appropriate all-in forward rate for this new, offsetting forward position. If the base currency of the exchange rate quote is being sold (bought), then use the bid (offer) side of the market.

3. Calculate the cash flow at the settlement day. This amount will be based on the original contract size times the difference between the original forward rate and that calculated in Step 2. If the currency the market participant was originally long (short) subsequently appreciated (depreciated), then there will be a cash *inflow* (*outflow*). (In the above example, the market participant was long the GBP, which subsequently appreciated, leading to a cash inflow at the settlement day.)

4. Calculate the present value of this cash flow at the future settlement date. The currency of the cash flow and the discount rate must match. (In the example above, the cash flow at the settlement date was in AUD, so an AUD MRR was used to calculate the present value.)

The factors that affect the bid–offer spread for forward points are the same as those we discussed for spot bid–offer rates: the interbank market liquidity of the underlying currency pair, the size of the transaction, and the relationship between the client and the dealer. For forward bid–offer spreads, we can also add a fourth factor: the term of the forward contract. Generally, the longer the term of the forward contract, the wider the bid–offer spread. This relationship holds because as the term of the contract increases,

- liquidity in the forward market tends to decline,
- the exposure to counterparty credit risk increases, and
- the interest rate risk of the contract increases (forward rates are based on interest rate differentials, and a longer duration means greater price sensitivity to movements in interest rates).

EXAMPLE 3

Forward Rates and the Mark-to-Market Value of Forward Positions

A dealer is contemplating trade opportunities in the CHF/GBP currency pair. The following are the current spot rates and forward points being quoted for the CHF/GBP currency pair:

Spot rate (CHF/GBP)	1.2939/1.2941
One month	−8.3/−7.9
Two months	−17.4/−16.8
Three months	−25.4/−24.6
Four months	−35.4/−34.2
Five months	−45.9/−44.1
Six months	−56.5/−54.0

1. The current all-in bid rate for delivery of GBP against the CHF in three months is *closest* to:

    A. 1.29136.

    B. 1.29150.

    C. 1.29164.

    Solution

    A is correct. The current all-in three-month bid rate for GBP (the base currency) is equal to $1.2939 + (-25.4/10,000) = 1.29136$.

2. The all-in rate that the dealer will be quoted today by another dealer to sell the CHF six months forward against the GBP is *closest* to:

    A. 1.28825.

    B. 1.28835.

    C. 1.28870.

    Solution

    C is correct. The dealer will sell CHF against the GBP, which is equivalent to buying GBP (the base currency) against the CHF. Hence, the *offer* side of the market will be used for forward points. The all-in forward price will be $1.2941 + (-54.0/10,000) = 1.28870$.

3. Some time ago, Laurier Bay Capital, an investment fund based in Los Angeles, hedged a long exposure to the New Zealand dollar by selling NZD 10 million forward against the USD; the all-in forward price was 0.7900 (USD/ NZD). Three months prior to the settlement date, Laurier Bay wants to mark this forward position to market. The bid–offer for the USD/NZD spot rate, the three-month forward points, and the three-month MRRs (annualized) are as follows:

Spot rate (USD/NZD)	0.7825/0.7830
Three-month points	−12.1/−10.0
Three-month MRR (NZD)	3.31%
Three-month MRR (USD)	0.31%

    The mark-to-market value for Laurier Bay's forward position is *closest* to:

    A. −USD 87,100.

    B. +USD 77,437.

    C. +USD 79,938.

    Solution

    C is correct. Laurier Bay sold NZD 10 million forward to the settlement date at an all-in forward rate of 0.7900 (USD/NZD). To mark this position to market, the fund would need an offsetting forward transaction involving buying NZD 10 million three months forward to the settlement date. The NZD amounts on the settlement date net to zero. For the offsetting forward contract, because the NZD is the base currency in the USD/NZD quote, buying NZD forward means paying the offer for both the spot rate and the forward points. This scenario leads to an all-in three-month forward rate of $0.7830 - 0.0010 = 0.7820$. On the settlement day, Laurier Bay will receive

USD 7,900,000 (NZD 10,000,000 × 0.7900 USD/NZD) from the original forward contract and pay out USD 7,820,000 (NZD 10,000,000 × 0.7820 USD/NZD) based on the offsetting forward contract. The result is a net cash flow on the settlement day of 10,000,000 × (0.7900 − 0.7820) = +USD 80,000. This is a cash inflow because Laurier Bay sold the NZD forward and the NZD depreciated against the USD. This USD cash inflow will occur in three months. To calculate the mark-to-market value of the original forward position, we need to calculate the present value of this USD cash inflow using the three-month USD discount rate (we use USD MRR for this purpose):

$$\frac{\text{USD } 80,000}{1 + 0.0031\left(\frac{90}{360}\right)} = +\text{USD } 79,938.$$

4. Now, suppose that instead of having a long exposure to the NZD, Laurier Bay Capital had a long forward exposure to the USD, which it hedged by selling USD 10 million forward against the NZD at an all-in forward rate of 0.7900 (USD/NZD). Three months prior to settlement date, it wants to close out this short USD forward position.

Using the above table, the mark-to-market value for Laurier Bay's short USD forward position is *closest* to:

   A. −NZD 141,117.

   B. −NZD 139,959.

   C. −NZD 87,100.

Solution

B is correct. Laurier Bay initially sold USD 10 million forward, and it will have to buy USD 10 million forward to the same settlement date (i.e., in three months' time) in order to close out the initial position. Buying USD using the USD/NZD currency pair is the same as selling the NZD. Because the NZD is the base currency in the USD/NZD quote, selling the NZD means calculating the *bid* rate:

0.7825 + (−12.1/10,000) = 0.78129.

At settlement, the USD amounts will net to zero (USD 10 million both bought and sold). The NZD amounts will not net to zero, however, because the all-in forward rate changed between the time Laurier Bay initiated the original position and the time it closed out this position. At initiation, Laurier Bay contracted to sell USD 10 million and receive NZD 12,658,228 (i.e., 10,000,000/0.7900) on the settlement date. To close out the original forward contract, Laurier Bay entered into an offsetting forward contract to receive USD 10 million and pay out NZD 12,799,345 (i.e., 10,000,000/0.78129) at settlement. The difference between the NZD amounts that Laurier Bay will receive and pay out on the settlement date equals

NZD 12,658,228 − NZD 12,799,345 = −NZD 141,117.

This is a cash *outflow* for Laurier Bay because the fund was *short* the USD in the original forward position and the USD subsequently *appreciated* (i.e., the NZD subsequently depreciated, because the all-in forward rate in USD/NZD dropped from 0.7900 to 0.78129). This NZD cash outflow occurs in three months' time, and we must calculate its present value using the three-month NZD MRR:

$$\frac{-\text{NZD } 141,117}{1 + 0.0331\left(\frac{90}{360}\right)} = -\text{NZD } 139,959.$$

INTERNATIONAL PARITY CONDITIONS

6

☐ | explain international parity conditions (covered and uncovered interest rate parity, forward rate parity, purchasing power parity, and the international Fisher effect)

Having reviewed the basic tools of the FX market, we now turn our focus to how they are used in practice. At the heart of the trading decision in FX markets lies a view on equilibrium market prices. An understanding of equilibrium pricing will assist the investor in framing decisions regarding risk exposures and how they should be managed.

In this and the following sections, we lay out a framework for developing a view on equilibrium exchange rates. We begin by examining international parity conditions, which describe the inter-relationships that jointly determine *long-run* movements in exchange rates, interest rates, and inflation. These parity conditions are the basic building blocks for describing long-term equilibrium levels for exchange rates. In subsequent sections, we expand beyond the parity conditions by discussing other factors that influence a currency's value.

Always keep in mind that exchange rate movements reflect complex interactions among multiple forces. In trying to untangle this complex web of interactions, we must clearly delineate the following concepts:

1. Long run versus short run: Many of the factors that determine exchange rate movements exert subtle but persistent influences over long periods of time. Although a poor guide for short-term prediction, longer-term equilibrium values act as an anchor for exchange rate movements.

2. Expected versus unexpected changes: In reasonably efficient markets, prices will adjust to reflect market participants' expectations of future developments. When a key factor—say, inflation—is trending gradually in a particular direction, market pricing will eventually come to reflect expectations that this trend will continue. In contrast, large, unexpected movements in a variable (for example, a central bank intervening in the foreign exchange market) can lead to immediate, discrete price adjustments. This concept is closely related to risk. For example, a moderate but steady rate of inflation will not have the same effect on market participants as an inflation rate that is very unpredictable. The latter clearly describes a riskier financial environment. Market pricing will reflect risk premiums—that is, the compensation that traders and investors demand for being exposed to unpredictable outcomes. Whereas expectations of long-run equilibrium values tend to evolve slowly, risk premiums—which are closely related to confidence and reputation—can change quickly in response to unexpected developments.

3. Relative movements: An exchange rate represents the relative price of one currency in terms of another. Hence, for exchange rate determination, the level or variability of key factors in any particular country is typically much less important than the *differences* in these factors across countries. For

example, knowing that inflation is increasing in Country A may not give much insight into the direction of the A/B exchange rate without also knowing what is happening with the inflation rate in Country B.

As a final word of caution—and this cannot be emphasized enough—*there is no simple formula, model, or approach that will allow market participants to precisely forecast exchange rates.* Models that work well in one period may fail in others. Models that work for one set of exchange rates may fail to work for others.

Nonetheless, market participants must have a market view to guide their decisions, even if this view requires significant revision as new information becomes available. The following sections provide a framework for understanding FX markets, a guide for thinking through the complex forces driving exchange rates. As with all theory, however, it does not eliminate the need for insightful analysis of actual economic and market conditions.

International Parity Conditions

International parity conditions form the building blocks of most models of exchange rate determination. The key international parity conditions are as follows:

1. covered interest rate parity,
2. uncovered interest rate parity,
3. forward rate parity,
4. purchasing power parity, and
5. the international Fisher effect.

Parity conditions show how expected inflation differentials, interest rate differentials, forward exchange rates, current spot exchange rates, and expected future spot exchange rates would be linked in an ideal world. These conditions typically make simplifying assumptions, such as zero transaction costs, perfect information that is available to all market participants, risk neutrality, and freely adjustable market prices.

Although empirical studies have found that the parity conditions rarely hold in the short term, they do help form a broadly based, long-term view of exchange rates and accompanying risk exposures. The exception to the rule that parity conditions do not hold in the short term is covered interest rate parity, which is the only parity condition that is enforced by arbitrage. We examine this parity condition first.

7   COVERED AND UNCOVERED INTEREST RATE PARITY AND FORWARD RATE PARITY

☐	explain international parity conditions (covered and uncovered interest rate parity, forward rate parity, purchasing power parity, and the international Fisher effect)
☐	describe relations among the international parity conditions
☐	evaluate the use of the current spot rate, the forward rate, purchasing power parity, and uncovered interest parity to forecast future spot exchange rates

We have already discussed covered interest rate parity in our examination of forward exchange rates. Under this parity condition, *an investment in a foreign money market instrument that is completely hedged against exchange rate risk should yield exactly the same return as an otherwise identical domestic money market investment.* Given the spot exchange rate and the domestic and foreign yields, the forward exchange rate must equal the rate that gives these two alternative investment strategies—invest either in a domestic money market instrument or in a fully currency-hedged foreign money market instrument—exactly the same holding period return. If one strategy gave a higher holding period return than the other, then an investor could short-sell the lower-yielding approach and invest the proceeds in the higher-yielding approach, earning riskless arbitrage profits in the process. In real-world financial markets, such a disparity will be quickly arbitraged away so that no further arbitrage profits are available. Covered interest rate parity is thus said to be a no-arbitrage condition.

For covered interest rate parity to hold exactly, it must be assumed that there are zero transaction costs and that the underlying domestic and foreign money market instruments being compared are identical in terms of liquidity, maturity, and default risk. Where capital is permitted to flow freely, spot and forward exchange markets are liquid, and financial market conditions are relatively stress free, covered interest rate differentials are generally found to be close to zero and covered interest rate parity holds.

Uncovered Interest Rate Parity

According to the **uncovered interest rate parity** condition, the *expected* return on an uncovered (i.e., unhedged) foreign currency investment should equal the return on a comparable domestic currency investment. Uncovered interest rate parity states that *the change in spot rate over the investment horizon should, on average, equal the differential in interest rates between the two countries. That is, the expected appreciation/depreciation of the exchange rate will just offset the yield differential.*

To explain the intuition behind this concept, let's switch, as we did with the examples for covered interest rate parity, from the standard price/base currency notation (P/B) to foreign/domestic currency notation (*f/d*) in order to emphasize the choice between foreign and domestic investments. As before, we also will assume that for the investor, the base currency is the domestic currency. (In *covered* interest rate parity, we assumed the investor transacted at a forward rate that was locked in at strategy initiation. In *uncovered* interest rate parity, the investor is assumed to transact at a future spot rate that is unknown at the time the strategy is initiated and the investor's currency position in the future is not hedged—that is, uncovered.)

For our example, assume that this investor has a choice between a one-year domestic money market instrument and an unhedged one-year foreign-currency-denominated money market investment. Under the assumption of uncovered interest rate parity, the investor will compare the *known* return on the domestic investment with the *expected* all-in return on the unhedged foreign-currency-denominated investment (which includes the foreign yield as well as any movements in the exchange rate, in $S_{f/d}$ terms). The choice between these two investments will depend on which market offers the higher expected return on an unhedged basis.

For example, assume that the return on the one-year foreign money market instrument is 10% while the return on the one-year domestic money market instrument is 4%. From the investor's perspective, the 4% expected return on the one-year domestic investment in domestic currency terms is known with complete certainty. This is not the case for the uncovered investment in the foreign currency money market instrument. In domestic currency terms, the investment return on an uncovered (or unhedged) foreign-currency-denominated investment is equal to $(1 + i_f)(1 - \%\Delta S_{f/d}) - 1$.

Intuitively, the formula says that the investor's return on a foreign investment is a function of both the foreign interest rate and the change in the spot rate, whereby a depreciation in the foreign currency reduces the investor's return. The percentage change in $S_{f/d}$ enters with a minus sign because an *increase* in $S_{f/d}$ means the foreign currency *declines* in value, thereby reducing the all-in return from the domestic currency perspective of our investor. This all-in return depends on *future* movements in the $S_{f/d}$ rate, which cannot be known until the end of the period. This return can be approximated by $\cong i_f - \%\Delta S_{f/d}$.

Note that this approximate formula holds because the product ($i \times \%\Delta S$) is small compared with the interest rate (i) and the percentage change in the exchange rate ($\%\Delta S$). For simplicity of exposition, we will use the $\cong$ symbol when we introduce an approximation but will subsequently treat the relationship as an equality (=) unless the distinction is important for the issue being discussed.

Using the previous example, consider three cases:

1. The $S_{f/d}$ rate is expected to remain unchanged.
2. The domestic currency is expected to appreciate by 10%.
3. The domestic currency is expected to appreciate by 6%.

In the first case, the investor would prefer the foreign-currency-denominated money market investment because it offers a 10% (= 10% – 0%) expected return, while the comparable domestic investment offers only 4%. In the second case, the investor would prefer the domestic investment because the expected return on the foreign-currency-denominated investment is 0% (= 10% – 10%). In the third case, uncovered interest rate parity holds because both investments offer a 4% (for the foreign investment, 10% – 6%) expected return. In this case, the risk-neutral investor is assumed to be indifferent between the alternatives.

Note that in the third case, in which uncovered interest rate parity holds, while the *expected* return over the one-year investment horizon is the same for both instruments, that expected return is *just a point on the distribution* of possible total return outcomes. The all-in return on the foreign money market instrument is uncertain because the *future* $S_{f/d}$ rate is uncertain. Hence, when we say that the investor would be indifferent between owning domestic and foreign investments because they both offer the same *expected* return (4%), we are assuming that the investor is *risk neutral* (risk-neutral investors base their decisions solely on the expected return and are indifferent to the investments' risk). Thus, uncovered interest rate parity assumes that there are enough risk-neutral investors to force equality of expected returns.

Using our example's foreign/domestic (f/d) notation, uncovered interest rate parity says the expected change in the spot exchange rate over the investment horizon should be reflected in the interest rate differential:

$$\%\Delta S_{f/d}^e = i_f - i_d, \tag{2}$$

where ΔS^e indicates the change in the spot rate expected for *future* periods. Note that Equation 2 cannot hold simultaneously for $S_{f/d}$ and $S_{d/f} (= 1/S_{f/d})$ because their percentage changes are not of exactly equal magnitude. This reflects our earlier approximation. Using the exact return on the unhedged foreign instrument would alleviate this issue but would produce a less intuitive equation.

In our example, if the yield spread between the foreign and domestic investments is 6% ($i_f - i_d = 6\%$), then this spread implicitly reflects the expectation that the domestic currency will strengthen versus the foreign currency by 6%.

Uncovered interest rate parity assumes that the country with the *higher* interest rate or money market yield will see its currency *depreciate*. The depreciation of the currency offsets the initial higher yield so that the (expected) all-in return on the two investment choices is the same. Hence, if the uncovered interest rate parity condition held consistently in the real world, it would rule out the possibility of earning excess returns from going long a high-yield currency and going short a low-yield currency: The depreciation of the high-yield currency would exactly offset the yield advantage that the high-yield currency offers. Taking this scenario to its logical conclusion, if uncovered interest rate parity held at all times, investors would have no incentive to shift capital from one currency to another because expected returns on otherwise identical money market investments would be equal across markets and risk-neutral investors would be indifferent among them.

Most studies have found that over short- and medium-term periods, the rate of depreciation of the high-yield currency is less than what would be implied by uncovered interest rate parity. In many cases, high-yield currencies have been found to *strengthen*, not weaken. There is, however, evidence that uncovered interest rate parity works better over very long-term horizons.

Such findings have significant implications for foreign exchange investment strategies. If high-yield currencies do not depreciate in line with the path predicted by the uncovered interest rate parity condition, then high-yield currencies should exhibit a tendency to outperform low-yield currencies over time. If so, investors could adopt strategies that overweight high-yield currencies at the expense of low-yield currencies and generate attractive returns in the process. Such approaches are known as FX carry trade strategies. We will discuss them in greater detail later.

Forward Rate Parity

Forward rate parity states that the forward exchange rate will be an unbiased predictor of the future spot exchange rate. It does not state that the forward rate will be a perfect forecast, just an unbiased one; the forward rate may overestimate or underestimate the future spot rate from time to time, but on average, it will equal the future spot rate. Forward rate parity builds upon two other parity conditions, covered interest rate parity and uncovered interest rate parity.

The covered interest rate parity condition describes the relationship among the spot exchange rate, the forward exchange rate, and interest rates. Let's keep using the foreign/domestic exchange rate notation (f/d) to simplify the explanation. The arbitrage condition that underlies covered interest rate parity (illustrated earlier) can be rearranged to give an expression for the forward premium or discount:

$$F_{f/d} - S_{f/d} = S_{f/d}\left(\frac{\left[\frac{\text{Actual}}{360}\right]}{1 + i_d\left[\frac{\text{Actual}}{360}\right]}\right)(i_f - i_d).$$

The domestic currency will trade at a forward premium $(F_{f/d} > S_{f/d})$ if, and only if, the foreign risk-free interest rate exceeds the domestic risk-free interest rate $(i_f > i_d)$.

For the sake of simplicity, we assume that the investment horizon is one year, so that

$$F_{f/d} - S_{f/d} = S_{f/d}\left(\frac{i_f - i_d}{1 + i_d}\right).$$

Because the $1 + i_d$ denominator will be close to 1, we can approximate the above equation as follows:

$$F_{f/d} - S_{f/d} \cong S_{f/d}(i_f - i_d).$$

This covered interest rate parity equation can be rearranged to show the forward discount or premium as a percentage of the spot rate:

$$\frac{F_{f/d} - S_{f/d}}{S_{f/d}} \cong i_f - i_d.$$

We have also shown that if uncovered interest rate parity holds, then the expected change in the spot rate is equal to the interest rate differential:

$$\%\Delta S^e_{f/d} = i_f - i_d.$$

We can link the covered interest rate parity and uncovered interest rate parity equations as follows:

$$\frac{F_{f/d} - S_{f/d}}{S_{f/d}} = \%\Delta S^e_{f/d} = i_f - i_d.$$

Thus, the forward premium (discount) on a currency, expressed in percentage terms, equals the expected percentage appreciation (depreciation) of the domestic currency (assuming that the uncovered interest rate parity condition holds).

In theory, then, *the forward exchange rate will be an unbiased forecast of the future spot exchange rate if both covered and uncovered interest rate parity hold:*

$$F_{f/d} = S^e_{f/d}.$$

This condition is often referred to as **forward rate parity**.

We know covered interest rate parity must hold because it is enforced by arbitrage. *The question of whether forward rate parity holds is thus dependent upon whether uncovered interest rate parity holds.*

How might uncovered interest rate parity be enforced? It is not enforced by arbitrage because there is no combination of trades that will lock in a (riskless) profit. It could, however, hold if speculators willing to take risk enter the market. If the forward rate is above (below) speculators' expectations of the future spot rate, then risk-neutral speculators will buy the domestic currency in the spot (forward) market and simultaneously sell it in the forward (spot) market. These transactions would push the forward premium into alignment with the consensus expectation of the future spot rate. If the speculators' expectations are correct, they will make a profit.

Note, however, that spot exchange rates are volatile and determined by a complex web of influences: Interest rate differentials are only one among many factors. So, speculators can also lose. Because speculators are rarely, if ever, truly risk neutral and without an arbitrage relationship to enforce it, uncovered interest rate parity is often violated. *As a result, we can conclude that forward exchange rates are typically poor predictors of future spot exchange rates in the short run.* Over the longer term, uncovered interest rate parity and forward rate parity have more empirical support.

EXAMPLE 4

Covered and Uncovered Interest Rate Parity: Predictors of Future Spot Rates

An Australia-based fixed-income asset manager is deciding how to allocate money between Australia and Japan. Note that the base currency in the exchange rate quote (AUD) is the domestic currency for the asset manager.

JPY/AUD spot rate (mid-market)	71.78
One-year forward points (mid-market)	−139.4
One-year Australian deposit rate	3.00%
One-year Japanese deposit rate	1.00%

1. Based on uncovered interest rate parity, over the next year, the expected change in the JPY/AUD rate is *closest* to a(n):

   A. decrease of 6%.

   B. decrease of 2%.

    C. increase of 2%.

Solution

B is correct. The expected depreciation of the Australian dollar (decline in the JPY/AUD rate) is equal to the interest rate differential between Australia and Japan (3% − 1%).

2. The *best* explanation of why this prediction may not be very accurate is that:

    A. covered interest rate parity does hold in this case.

    B. the forward points indicate that a riskless arbitrage opportunity exists.

    C. there is no arbitrage condition that forces uncovered interest rate parity to hold.

Solution

C is correct. There is no arbitrage condition that forces uncovered interest rate parity to hold. In contrast, arbitrage virtually always ensures that covered interest rate parity holds. This is the case for our table, where the −139 point discount is calculated from the covered interest rate parity equation.

3. Using the forward points to forecast the future JPY/AUD spot rate one year ahead assumes that:

    A. investors are risk neutral.

    B. spot rates follow a random walk.

    C. it is not necessary for uncovered interest rate parity to hold.

Solution

A is correct. Using forward rates (i.e., adding the forward points to the spot rate) to forecast future spot rates assumes that uncovered interest rate parity and forward rate parity hold. Uncovered interest rate parity assumes that investors are risk neutral. If these conditions hold, then movements in the spot exchange rate, although they *approximate* a random walk, will not actually be a random walk because current interest spreads will determine expected exchange rate movements.

4. Forecasting that the JPY/AUD spot rate one year from now will equal 71.78 assumes that:

    A. investors are risk neutral.

    B. spot rates follow a random walk.

    C. it is necessary for uncovered interest rate parity to hold.

Solution

B is correct. Assuming that the current spot exchange rate is the best predictor of future spot rates assumes that exchange rate movements follow a random walk. If uncovered interest rate parity holds, the current exchange rate will not be the best predictor unless the interest rate differential happens to be zero. Risk neutrality is needed to enforce uncovered interest rate parity, but it will not make the current spot exchange rate the best predictor of future spot rates.

5. If the asset manager completely hedged the currency risk associated with a one-year Japanese deposit using a forward rate contract, the one-year all-in holding return, in AUD, would be *closest* to:

    A. 0%.

B. 1%.

C. 3%.

Solution

C is correct. A fully hedged JPY investment would provide the same return as the AUD investment: 3%. This represents covered interest rate parity, an arbitrage condition.

---

6. The fixed-income manager collects the following information and uses it, along with the international parity conditions, to estimate investment returns and future exchange rate movements.

	Today's One-Year MRR	Currency Pair	Spot Rate Today
JPY	0.10%	JPY/USD	105.40
USD	0.10%	USD/GBP	1.2303
GBP	3.00%	JPY/GBP	129.67

If covered interest rate parity holds, the all-in one-year investment return to a Japanese investor whose currency exposure to the GBP is fully hedged is *closest* to:

A. 0.10%.

B. 0.17%.

C. 3.00%.

Solution

A is correct. If covered interest rate parity holds (and it very likely does, because this is a pure arbitrage relationship), then the all-in investment return to a Japanese investor in a one-year, fully hedged GBP MRR position would be identical to a one-year JPY MRR position: 0.10%. No calculations are necessary.

---

7. If uncovered interest rate parity holds, today's expected value for the JPY/GBP currency pair one year from now would be *closest* to:

A. 126.02.

B. 129.67.

C. 130.05.

Solution

A is correct. If uncovered interest rate parity holds, then forward rate parity will hold and the expected spot rate one year forward is equal to the one-year forward exchange rate. This forward rate is calculated in the usual manner, given the spot exchange rates and MRRs:

$$S^e = F = 129.67(1.001/1.03) = 126.02.$$

---

8. If uncovered interest rate parity holds, between today and one year from now, the expected movement in the JPY/USD currency pair is *closest* to:

A. −1.60%.

B. +0.00%.

C. +1.63%.

Solution

B is correct. Given uncovered interest rate parity, the expected change in a spot exchange rate is equal to the interest rate differential. At the one-year term, there is no difference between USD MRR and JPY MRR.

PURCHASING POWER PARITY

8

☐ explain international parity conditions (covered and uncovered interest rate parity, forward rate parity, purchasing power parity, and the international Fisher effect)

☐ describe relations among the international parity conditions

☐ evaluate the use of the current spot rate, the forward rate, purchasing power parity, and uncovered interest parity to forecast future spot exchange rates

So far, we have looked at the relationship between exchange rates and interest rate differentials. Now, we turn to examining the relationship between exchange rates and inflation differentials. The basis for this relationship is known as **purchasing power parity (PPP)**.

Various versions of PPP exist. The foundation for all of the versions is the law of one price. According to the **law of one price**, identical goods should trade at the same price across countries when valued in terms of a common currency. To simplify the explanation, as we did with our examples for covered and uncovered interest rate parity, let's continue to use the foreign/domestic currency quote convention (f/d) and the case where the base currency in the P/B notation is the domestic currency for the investor in the f/d notation.

The law of one price asserts that the foreign price of good x, P_f^x, should equal the exchange rate–adjusted price of the identical good in the domestic country, P_d^x:

$$P_f^x = S_{f/d} \times P_d^x.$$

For example, for a euro-based consumer, if the price of good x in the euro area is EUR 100 and the nominal exchange rate stands at 1.15 USD/EUR, then the price of good x in the United States should equal USD 115.

The **absolute version of PPP** simply extends the law of one price to the broad range of goods and services that are consumed in different countries. Expanding our example above to include all goods and services, not just good x, the broad price level of the foreign country (P_f) should equal the currency-adjusted broad price level in the domestic country (P_d):

$$P_f = (S_{f/d})(P_d).$$

This equation implicitly assumes that all domestic and foreign goods are tradable and that the domestic and foreign price indexes include the same bundle of goods and services with the same exact weights in each country. Rearranging this equation and solving for the nominal exchange rate ($S_{f/d}$), the absolute version of PPP states that the nominal exchange rate will be determined by the ratio of the foreign and domestic broad price indexes:

$$S_{f/d} = P_f/P_d.$$

The absolute version of PPP asserts that the equilibrium exchange rate between two countries is determined entirely by the ratio of their national price levels. However, it is highly unlikely that this relationship actually holds in the real world. The absolute version of PPP assumes that goods arbitrage will equate the prices of all goods and service across countries, but if transaction costs are significant and/or not all goods and services are tradable, then goods arbitrage will be incomplete. Hence, sizable and persistent departures from absolute PPP are likely.

However, if it is assumed that transaction costs and other trade impediments are constant over time, it might be possible to show that *changes* in exchange rates and *changes* in national price levels are related, even if the relationship between exchange rate *levels* and national price *levels* does not hold. According to the **relative version of PPP**, the percentage change in the spot exchange rate ($\%\Delta S_{f/d}$) will be completely determined by the difference between the foreign and domestic inflation rates ($\pi_f - \pi_d$):

$$\%\Delta S_{f/d} \cong \pi_f - \pi_d. \tag{3}$$

Intuitively, the relative version of PPP implies that the exchange rate changes to offset changes in competitiveness arising from inflation differentials. For example, if the foreign inflation rate is assumed to be 9% while the domestic inflation rate is assumed to be 5%, then the $S_{f/d}$ exchange rate must rise by 4% ($\%\Delta S_{f/d} = 9\% - 5\% = 4\%$) in order to maintain the relative competitiveness of the two regions: The currency of the high-inflation country should depreciate relative to the currency of the low-inflation country. If the $S_{f/d}$ exchange rate remained unchanged, the higher foreign inflation rate would erode the competitiveness of foreign companies relative to domestic companies.

Conversion from Absolute Levels to a Rate of Change

We will occasionally need to convert from a relationship expressed in levels of the relevant variables to a relationship among rates of change. If $X = (Y \times Z)$, then

$$(1 + \%\Delta X) = (1 + \%\Delta Y)(1 + \%\Delta Z)$$

and

$$\%\Delta X \approx \%\Delta Y + \%\Delta Z$$

because ($\%\Delta Y \times \%\Delta Z$) is "small." Similarly, it can be shown that if $X = (Y/Z)$, then

$$(1 + \%\Delta X) = (1 + \%\Delta Y)/(1 + \%\Delta Z)$$

and

$$\%\Delta X \approx \%\Delta Y - \%\Delta Z.$$

Applying this conversion to the equation for absolute PPP gives Equation 3.

Whereas the relative version of PPP focuses on *actual* changes in exchange rates being driven by *actual* differences in national inflation rates, the ***ex ante* version of PPP** asserts that the *expected* changes in the spot exchange rate are entirely driven by *expected* differences in national inflation rates. *Ex ante* PPP tells us that countries that are expected to run *persistently* high inflation rates should expect to see their currencies depreciate over time, while countries that are expected to run relatively low inflation rates on a sustainable basis should expect to see their currencies appreciate over time. *Ex ante* PPP can be expressed as

$$\%\Delta S_{f/d}^e = \pi_f^e - \pi_d^e, \tag{4}$$

where it is understood that the use of expectations (the superscript e) indicates that we are now focused on *future* periods. That is, $\%\Delta S^e_{f/d}$ represents the expected percentage change in the spot exchange rate, while π^e_d and π^e_f represent the expected domestic and foreign inflation rates over the same period.

Studies have found that while *over shorter horizons nominal exchange rate movements may appear random, over longer time horizons nominal exchange rates tend to gravitate toward their long-run PPP equilibrium values.*

Exhibit 2 illustrates the success, or lack thereof, of the relative version of PPP at different time horizons: 1 year, 5 years, 10 years, and 15 years for a selection of countries over the period 1990-2020. Each chart plots the inflation differential (horizontal axis) against the percentage change in the exchange rate (vertical axis). If PPP holds, the points should fall along an upward-sloping diagonal line. The first panel of Exhibit 2 indicates no clear relationship between changes in exchange rates and inflation differentials at the one-year time horizon. As the time horizon is lengthened to five years and beyond, however, a strong positive relationship becomes apparent. Hence, *PPP appears to be a valid framework for assessing long-run fair value in the FX markets, even though the path to PPP equilibrium may be slow.*

Exhibit 2: Effect of Relative Inflation Rates on Exchange Rates at Different Time Horizons

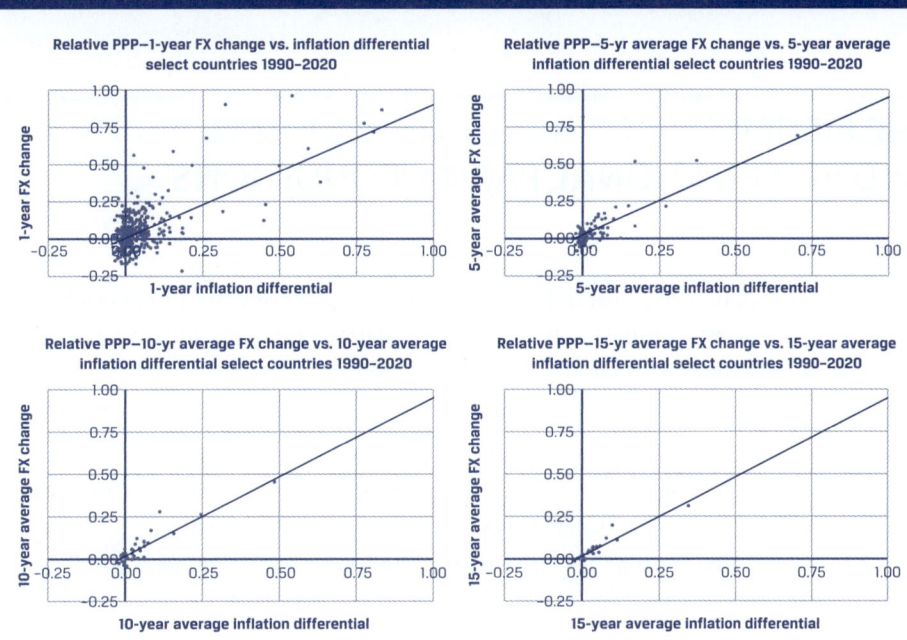

Exhibit 3 illustrates the success of the relative version of PPP even in the short run when differences in inflation rates between countries are large. Note that the Brazilian Real-USD exchange rate changes rapidly in the period 1990-1993, mirroring the very large differences in relative inflation between hyperinflationary Brazil and low inflation rate United States. It also indicates that the majority countries did not have large inflation differentials with the United States, and so 1-year changes in exchange rates cluster near the origin. This mirrors the upper left panel in Exhibit 2 above, which excludes Brazil from the sample of countries.

Exhibit 3: Effect of Large Differences in Inflation Rates on Exchange Rates over 1-Year Time Horizons

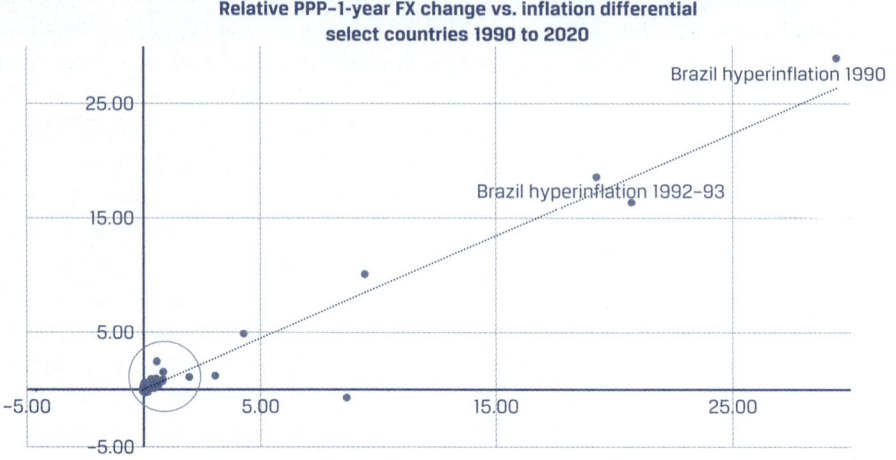

Relative PPP–1-year FX change vs. inflation differential
select countries 1990 to 2020

---

9   THE FISHER EFFECT, REAL INTEREST RATE PARITY, AND INTERNATIONAL PARITY CONDITIONS

☐   explain international parity conditions (covered and uncovered interest rate parity, forward rate parity, purchasing power parity, and the international Fisher effect)

☐   describe relations among the international parity conditions

☐   evaluate the use of the current spot rate, the forward rate, purchasing power parity, and uncovered interest parity to forecast future spot exchange rates

☐   explain approaches to assessing the long-run fair value of an exchange rate

So far, we have examined the relationships between exchange rates and interest rate differentials and between exchange rates and inflation differentials. Now, we will begin to bring these concepts together by examining how exchange rates, interest rates, and inflation rates interact.

According to what economists call the Fisher effect, one can break down the nominal interest rate (i) in a given country into two parts: (1) the real interest rate (r) in that particular country and (2) the expected inflation rate (π^e) in that country:

$$i = r + \pi^e.$$

To relate this concept to exchange rates, we can write the Fisher equation for both the domestic country and a foreign country. If the Fisher effect holds, the nominal interest rates in both countries will equal the sum of their respective real interest rates and expected inflation rates:

$$i_d = r_d + \pi_d^e.$$
$$i_f = r_f + \pi_f^e.$$

Let's take a closer look at the macroeconomic forces that drive the trend in nominal yield spreads. Subtracting the top equation from the bottom equation shows that the nominal yield spread between the foreign and domestic countries $(i_f - i_d)$ equals the sum of two parts: (1) the foreign–domestic real yield spread $(r_f - r_d)$ and (2) the foreign–domestic expected inflation differential $(\pi_f^e - \pi_d^e)$:

$$i_f - i_d = (r_f - r_d) + \left(\pi_f^e - \pi_d^e\right).$$

We can rearrange this equation to solve for the *real* interest rate differential instead of the *nominal* interest rate differential:

$$(r_f - r_d) = \left(i_f - i_d\right) - \left(\pi_f^e - \pi_d^e\right).$$

To tie this material to our previous work on exchange rates, recall our expression for uncovered interest rate parity:

$$\%\Delta S_{f/d}^e = i_f - i_d.$$

The nominal interest rate spread $(i_f - i_d)$ equals the expected change in the exchange rate $(\%\Delta S_{f/d}^e)$.

Recall also the expression for *ex ante* PPP:

$$\%\Delta S_{f/d}^e = \pi_f^e - \pi_d^e.$$

The difference in expected inflation rates equals the expected change in the exchange rate. Combining these two expressions, we derive the following:

$$i_f - i_d = \pi_f^e - \pi_d^e.$$

The nominal interest rate spread is equal to the difference in expected inflation rates. We can therefore conclude that if uncovered interest rate parity and *ex ante* PPP hold,

$$(r_f - r_d) = 0.$$

The real yield spread between the domestic and foreign countries $(r_f - r_d)$ will be zero, and the level of real interest rates in the domestic country will be identical to the level of real interest rates in the foreign country.

The proposition that real interest rates will converge to the same level across different markets is known as the **real interest rate parity** condition.

Finally, if real interest rates are equal across markets, then it also follows that the foreign–domestic nominal yield spread is determined solely by the foreign–domestic expected inflation differential:

$$i_f - i_d = \pi_f^e - \pi_d^e.$$

This is known as the **international Fisher effect**. The reader should be aware that some authors refer to uncovered interest rate parity as the "international Fisher effect." We reserve this term for the relationship between nominal interest rate differentials and expected inflation differentials because the original (domestic) Fisher effect is a relationship between interest rates and expected inflation.

The international Fisher effect and, by extension, real interest rate parity assume that currency risk is the same throughout the world. However, not all currencies carry the same risk. For example, an emerging country may have a high level of indebtedness, which could result in an elevated level of currency risk (i.e., likelihood of currency depreciation). In this case, because the emerging market currency has higher risk, subtracting the expected inflation rate from the nominal interest rate will result in a calculated real interest rate that is higher than in other countries. Economists typically separate the nominal interest rate into the real interest rate, an inflation premium, and a risk premium. The emerging country's investors will require a risk premium for holding the currency, which will be reflected in nominal and real interest rates that are higher than would be expected under the international Fisher effect and real interest rate parity conditions.

EXAMPLE 5

PPP and the International Fisher Effect

An Australia-based fixed-income investment manager is deciding how to allocate her portfolio between Australia and Japan. (As before, the AUD is the domestic currency.) Australia's one-year deposit rate is 3%, considerably higher than Japan's 1% rate, but the Australian dollar is estimated to be roughly 10% overvalued relative to the Japanese yen based on purchasing power parity. Before making her asset allocation, the investment manager considers the implications of interest rate differentials and PPP imbalances.

---

1. All else equal, which of the following events would restore the Australian dollar to its PPP value?

    A. The Japanese inflation rate increases by 2%.

    B. The Australian inflation rate decreases by 10%.

    C. The JPY/AUD exchange rate declines by 10%.

    Solution

    C is correct. If the Australian dollar is overvalued by 10% on a PPP basis, with all else held equal, a depreciation of the JPY/AUD rate by 10% would move the Australian dollar back to equilibrium.

---

2. If real interest rates in Japan and Australia were equal, then under the international Fisher effect, the inflation rate differential between Japan and Australia would be *closest* to:

    A. 0%.

    B. 2%.

    C. 10%.

    Solution

    B is correct. If the real interest rates were equal, then the difference in nominal yields would be explained by the difference in inflation rates (3% − 1%).

---

3. According to the theory and empirical evidence of purchasing power parity, which of the following would *not* be true if PPP holds in the long run?

    A. An exchange rate's equilibrium path should be determined by the long-term trend in domestic price levels relative to foreign price levels.

    B. Deviations from PPP might occur over short- and medium-term periods, but fundamental forces should eventually work to push exchange rates toward their long-term PPP path.

    C. High-inflation countries should tend to see their currencies appreciate over time.

    Solution

    C is correct. According to PPP, high-inflation countries should see their currencies depreciate (at least, over the longer term) in order to re-equilibrate real purchasing power between countries.

4. Which of the following would *best* explain the failure of the absolute version of PPP to hold?

    A. Inflation rates vary across countries.

    B. Real interest rates are converging across countries.

    C. Trade barriers exist, and different product mixes are consumed across countries.

Solution

C is correct. The absolute version of PPP assumes that all goods and services are tradable and that the domestic and foreign price indexes include the same bundle of goods and services with the same exact weights in each country.

International Parity Conditions: Tying All the Pieces Together

As noted above, the various parity relationships usually do not hold over short time horizons. However, studies show that over longer time periods, there is a discernible interaction among nominal interest rates, exchange rates, and inflation rates across countries, such that the international parity conditions serve as an anchor for longer-term exchange rate movements. We now summarize the key international parity conditions and describe how they are all linked.

1. According to covered interest rate parity, arbitrage ensures that nominal interest rate spreads equal the percentage forward premium (or discount).

2. According to uncovered interest rate parity, the expected percentage change of the spot exchange rate should, on average, be reflected in the nominal interest rate spread.

3. If both covered and uncovered interest rate parity hold—that is, the nominal yield spread equals both the forward premium (or discount) and the expected percentage change in the spot exchange rate—then the forward exchange rate will be an unbiased predictor of the future spot exchange rate.

4. According to the *ex ante* PPP approach to exchange rate determination, the expected change in the spot exchange rate should equal the expected difference between domestic and foreign inflation rates.

5. Assuming the Fisher effect holds in all markets—that is, the nominal interest rate in each market equals the real interest rate plus the expected inflation rate—and also assuming that real interest rates are broadly the same across all markets (real interest rate parity), then the nominal yield spread between domestic and foreign markets will equal the domestic–foreign expected inflation differential, which is the international Fisher effect.

6. If *ex ante* PPP and the international Fisher effect hold, then expected inflation differentials should equal both the expected change in the exchange rate and the nominal interest rate differential. This relationship implies that the expected change in the exchange rate equals the nominal interest rate differential, which is uncovered interest rate parity.

In sum, if all the key international parity conditions held at all times, then the expected percentage change in the *spot* exchange rate would equal

- the forward premium or discount (expressed in percentage terms),
- the nominal yield spread between countries, and
- the difference between expected national inflation rates.

In other words, *if all these parity conditions held, it would be impossible for a global investor to earn consistent profits on currency movements.* If forward exchange rates accurately predicted the future path of spot exchange rates, there would be no way to make money in forward exchange speculation. If high-yield currencies fell in value versus low-yield currencies exactly in line with the path implied by nominal interest rate spreads, all markets would offer the same currency-adjusted total returns over time. Investors would have no incentive to shift funds from one market to another based solely on currency considerations.

EXAMPLE 6

The Relationships among the International Parity Conditions

1. Which of the following is a no-arbitrage condition?

    A. Real interest rate parity

    B. Covered interest rate parity

    C. Uncovered interest rate parity

    Solution

    B is correct. Covered interest rate parity is enforced by equating the investment return on two riskless investments (domestic and currency-hedged foreign).

---

2. Forward rates are unbiased predictors of future spot rates if two parity conditions hold. Which of the following is *not* one of these conditions?

    A. Real interest rate parity

    B. Covered interest rate parity

    C. Uncovered interest rate parity

    Solution

    A is correct. Both covered and uncovered interest rate parity must hold for the forward rate to be an unbiased predictor of the future spot rate. Real interest rate parity is not required.

---

3. The international Fisher effect requires all but which of the following to hold?

    A. *Ex ante* PPP

    B. Absolute PPP

    C. Real interest rate parity

    Solution

    B is correct. The international Fisher effect is based on real interest rate parity and *ex ante* PPP (not absolute PPP).

---

4. The forward premium/discount is determined by nominal interest rate differentials because of:

    A. the Fisher effect.

    B. covered interest parity.

C. real interest rate parity.

Solution

B is correct. The forward premium/discount is determined by covered interest rate arbitrage.

5. If all of the key international parity conditions held at all times, then the expected percentage change in the spot exchange rate would equal all *except* which of the following?

   A. The real yield spread

   B. The nominal yield spread

   C. The expected inflation spread

Solution

A is correct. If all the international parity conditions held, the real yield spread would equal zero, regardless of expected changes in the spot exchange rate.

THE CARRY TRADE

10

☐ | describe the carry trade and its relation to uncovered interest rate parity and calculate the profit from a carry trade

According to uncovered interest rate parity, high-yield currencies are expected to depreciate in value, while low-yield currencies are expected to appreciate in value. If uncovered interest rate parity held at all times, investors would not be able to profit from a strategy that undertook long positions in high-yield currencies and short positions in low-yield currencies. The change in spot rates over the tenor of the forward contracts would cancel out the interest rate differentials locked in at the inception of the position.

Uncovered interest rate parity is one of the most widely tested propositions in international finance. The evidence suggests that uncovered interest rate parity does *not* hold over short and medium time periods. Studies have generally found that *high-yield currencies, on average, have not depreciated and low-yield currencies have not appreciated to the levels predicted by interest rate differentials.*

These findings underscore the potential profitability of a trading strategy known as the **FX carry trade**, which involves taking long positions in high-yield currencies and short positions in low-yield currencies. The latter are often referred to as "funding currencies." As a simplified example of the carry trade, assume a trader can borrow Canadian dollars at 1% and earn 9% on an investment in Brazilian reals for one year. To execute the trade to earn 8% from the interest rate differential, the trader will do the following:

1. Borrow Canadian dollars at $t = 0$.

2. Sell the dollars and buy Brazilian reals at the spot rate at $t = 0$.

3. Invest in a real-denominated investment at $t = 0$.

4. Liquidate the Brazilian investment at $t = 1$.

5. Sell the reals and buy dollars at the spot rate at $t = 1$.

6. Pay back the dollar loan.

If the real appreciates, the trader's profits will be greater than 8% because the stronger real will buy more dollars in one year. If the real depreciates, the trader's profits will be less than 8% because the weaker real will buy fewer dollars in the future. If the real falls in value by more than 8%, the trader will experience losses. The carry trader's return consists of the intermarket yield spread, the currency appreciation/depreciation, and the foreign investment appreciation/depreciation. Typically, a carry trade is executed using an investment in highly rated government debt so as to mitigate credit risk. In this simplified example, we use an additive approach to determine the trader's returns (i.e., we ignore the currency gain or loss on the 8% interest rate differential).

Historical evidence shows that carry trade strategies have generated positive returns over extended periods (see for example Dimson, Marsh, McGinnie, Staunton, and Wilmot 2012). One argument for the persistence of the carry trade is that the yields in higher interest rate countries reflect a risk premium due to a more unstable economy, while low-yield currencies represent less risky markets. Although small increases in financial market and/or FX volatility are unlikely to materially affect carry strategy profits, elevated levels of volatility and/or perceived risk in the financial markets can quickly turn these profits into substantial losses. That is, during turbulent periods, the returns on long high-yield currency positions will tend to decline dramatically, while the losses on short low-yield currency positions will tend to rise dramatically.

To understand why, we need to understand the nature of the risk and reward in the carry trade. The reward is the gradual accrual of the interest rate differential—income that is unrelated to exchange rate volatility. The risk arises from the potential for sudden adverse exchange rate movements that result in instantaneous capital losses. During periods of low turbulence, investors may feel relatively confident that exchange rate movements will not jeopardize the gradual accrual of the interest rate differential. Because low-volatility regimes have tended to be the norm and often last for extended periods, investors can become complacent, taking on larger carry trade positions in a search for yield but increasing their risk exposures. When volatility in the currency markets spikes, however, the risk of an adverse exchange rate movement rises sharply relative to the gradual flow of income. As the trade moves toward unprofitability, investors may rush to unwind the carry trade, selling high-yielding currencies and re-purchasing low-yielding currencies. These carry trades are often large-scale trades initiated by trading firms and other opportunistic investors, such as hedge funds. Traders often have stop-loss orders in place that are triggered when price declines reach a certain level. When they all attempt to unwind the trades at once, the selling pressure adds to the losses on the long position currency and the buying pressure on the short position currency drives that currency higher, exacerbating the loss. The "flight to quality" during turbulent times and the leverage inherent in the carry trade further compound the losses. The upshot is that *during periods of low volatility, carry trades tend to generate positive returns, but they are prone to significant crash risk in turbulent times.*

The tendency for carry trades to experience periodic crashes results in a non-normal distribution of returns for both developed and emerging market (EM) carry trades. Relative to a normal distribution, the distributions tend to be more peaked, with fatter tails and negative skewness. The more peaked distribution around the mean implies that carry trades have typically generated a larger number of trades with small gains/losses than would occur with the normal distribution. Although carry trades have generated positive returns on average in the past, the negative skew and fat tails indicate that carry trades have tended to have more frequent and larger losses than would have been experienced had the return distribution been normal.

EXAMPLE 7

Carry Trade Strategies

A currency fund manager is considering allocating a portion of her FX portfolio to carry trade strategies. The fund's investment committee asks the manager a number of questions about why she has chosen to become involved in FX carry trades and how she will manage the risk of potentially large downside moves associated with the unwinding of carry trades. Which of the following would be her *best* responses to the investment committee's questions?

1. Carry trades can be profitable when:

   A. covered interest rate parity does not hold.

   B. uncovered interest rate parity does not hold.

   C. the international Fisher effect does not hold.

   Solution

   B is correct. The carry trade is based on the supposition that uncovered interest rate parity does not hold.

2. Over time, the return distribution of the fund's FX carry trades is *most* likely to resemble a:

   A. normal distribution with fat tails.

   B. distribution with fat tails and a negative skew.

   C. distribution with thin tails and a positive skew.

   Solution

   B is correct. The "crash risk" of carry trades implies a fat-tailed distribution skewed toward a higher probability of large losses (compared with a normal distribution).

3. The volatility of the fund's returns relative to its equity base is *best* explained by:

   A. leverage.

   B. low deposit rates in the funding currency.

   C. the yield spread between the high- and low-yielding currencies.

   Solution

   A is correct. Carry trades are leveraged trades (borrow in the funding currency, invest in the high-yield currency), and leverage increases the volatility in the investor's return on equity.

4. A Tokyo-based asset manager enters into a carry trade position based on borrowing in yen and investing in one-year Australian MRR.

Today's One-Year MRR		Currency Pair	Spot Rate Today	Spot Rate One Year Later
JPY	0.10%	JPY/USD	105.40	104.60
AUD	1.70%	USD/AUD	0.6810	0.6850

   After one year, the all-in return to this trade, measured in JPY terms, would be *closest* to:

A. +0.03%.

B. +1.53%.

C. +1.63%.

Solution

B is correct. To calculate the all-in return for a Japanese investor in a one-year AUD MRR deposit, we must first calculate the current and one-year-later JPY/AUD cross rates. Because USD 1.0000 buys JPY 105.40 today and AUD 1.0000 buys USD 0.6810 today, today's JPY/AUD cross rate is the product of these two numbers: 105.40 × 0.6810 = 71.78 (rounded to two decimal places). Similarly, one year later, the observed cross rate is 104.60 × 0.6850 = 71.65 (rounded to two decimal places).

Accordingly, measured in yen, the investment return for the unhedged Australian MRR deposit is

$$(1/71.78)(1 + 1.70\%)71.65 - 1 = 0.0152.$$

Against this 1.52% *gross* return, however, the manager must charge the borrowing costs to fund the carry trade investment (one-year JPY MRR was 0.10%). Hence, the *net* return on the carry trade is 1.52% – 0.10% = 1.42%. We can also calculate the profit using a transactional approach. Assuming an initial position of, for example, 100 yen (JPY 100), the investor will obtain JPY 100 × 1/JPY 71.78 = AUD 1.3931. After one year, the investment will be worth AUD 1.3931 × 1.017 = AUD 1.4168. Converting back to yen in one year results in AUD 1.4168 × JPY 71.65/AUD = JPY 101.51. Paying off the yen loan results in a profit of JPY 101.51 – (JPY 100 × 1.001) = JPY 1.41. This is equivalent to the 1.42% profit calculated previously (slight difference arising due to rounding).

11   THE IMPACT OF BALANCE OF PAYMENTS FLOWS

☐ | explain how flows in the balance of payment accounts affect currency exchange rates

As noted earlier, the parity conditions may be appropriate for assessing fair value for currencies over long horizons, but they are of little use as a real-time gauge of value. There have been many attempts to find a better framework for determining a currency's short- or long-run equilibrium value. In this section, we examine the influence of trade and capital flows.

A country's balance of payments consists of its current account as well as its capital and financial account. The official balance of payments accounts make a distinction between the "capital account" and the "financial account" based on the nature of the assets involved. For simplicity, we will use the term "capital account" here to reflect all investment/financing flows. Loosely speaking, the current account reflects flows in the real economy, which refers to that part of the economy engaged in the actual production of goods and services (as opposed to the financial sector). The capital account reflects financial flows. Decisions about trade flows (the current account) and investment/financing flows (the capital account) are typically made by different entities with different perspectives and motivations. Their decisions are brought into alignment by changes in market prices and/or quantities. One of the key prices—perhaps *the* key price—in this process is the exchange rate.

Countries that import more than they export will have a negative current account balance and are said to have current account deficits. Those with more exports than imports will have a current account surplus. A country's current account balance must be matched by an equal and opposite balance in the capital account. Thus, countries with current account deficits must attract funds from abroad in order to pay for the imports (i.e., they must have a capital account surplus).

When discussing the effect of the balance of payments components on a country's exchange rate, one must distinguish between short- and intermediate-term influences on the one hand and longer-term influences on the other. Over the long term, countries that run persistent current account deficits (net borrowers) often see their currencies depreciate because they finance their acquisition of imports through the continued use of debt. Similarly, countries that run persistent current account surpluses (net lenders) often see their currencies appreciate over time.

However, investment/financing decisions are usually the dominant factor in determining exchange rate movements, at least in the short to intermediate term. There are four main reasons for this:

- Prices of real goods and services tend to adjust much more slowly than exchange rates and other asset prices.

- Production of real goods and services takes time, and demand decisions are subject to substantial inertia. In contrast, liquid financial markets allow virtually instantaneous redirection of financial flows.

- Current spending/production decisions reflect only purchases/sales of current production, while investment/financing decisions reflect not only the financing of current expenditures but also the reallocation of existing portfolios.

- *Expected* exchange rate movements can induce very large short-term capital flows. This tends to make the *actual* exchange rate very sensitive to the currency views held by owners/managers of liquid assets.

In this section, we first examine the impact of current account imbalances on exchange rates. Then, we take a closer look at capital flows.

Current Account Imbalances and the Determination of Exchange Rates

Current account trends influence the path of exchange rates over time through several mechanisms:

- The flow supply/demand channel
- The portfolio balance channel
- The debt sustainability channel

We briefly discuss each of these mechanisms next.

The Flow Supply/Demand Channel

The flow supply/demand channel is based on a fairly simple model that focuses on the fact that purchases and sales of internationally traded goods and services require the exchange of domestic and foreign currencies in order to arrange payment for those goods and services. For example, if a country sold more goods and services than it purchased (i.e., the country was running a current account surplus), then the demand for its currency should rise, and vice versa. Such shifts in currency demand should exert upward pressure on the value of the surplus nation's currency and downward pressure on the value of the deficit nation's currency.

Hence, countries with persistent current account surpluses should see their currencies appreciate over time, and countries with persistent current account deficits should see their currencies depreciate over time. A logical question, then, would be whether such trends can go on indefinitely. At some point, domestic currency strength should contribute to deterioration in the trade competitiveness of the surplus nation, while domestic currency weakness should contribute to an improvement in the trade competitiveness of the deficit nation. Thus, the exchange rate responses to these surpluses and deficits should eventually help eliminate—in the medium to long run—the source of the initial imbalances.

The amount by which exchange rates must adjust to restore current accounts to balanced positions depends on a number of factors:

- The initial gap between imports and exports
- The response of import and export prices to changes in the exchange rate
- The response of import and export demand to changes in import and export prices

If a country imports significantly more than it exports, export growth would need to far outstrip import growth in percentage terms in order to narrow the current account deficit. A large initial deficit may require a substantial depreciation of the currency to bring about a meaningful correction of the trade imbalance.

A depreciation of a deficit country's currency should result in an increase in import prices in domestic currency terms and a decrease in export prices in foreign currency terms. However, empirical studies often find limited pass-through effects of exchange rate changes on traded goods prices. For example, many studies have found that for every 1% decline in a currency's value, import prices rise by only 0.5%—and in some cases by even less—because foreign producers tend to lower their profit margins in an effort to preserve market share. In light of the limited pass-through of exchange rate changes into traded goods prices, the exchange rate adjustment required to narrow a trade imbalance may be far larger than would otherwise be the case.

Many studies have found that the response of import and export demand to changes in traded goods prices is often quite sluggish, and as a result, relatively long lags, lasting several years, can occur between (1) the onset of exchange rate changes, (2) the ultimate adjustment in traded goods prices, and (3) the eventual impact of those price changes on import demand, export demand, and the underlying current account imbalance.

The Portfolio Balance Channel

The second mechanism through which current account trends influence exchange rates is the so-called portfolio balance channel. Current account imbalances shift financial wealth from deficit nations to surplus nations. Countries with trade deficits will finance their trade with increased borrowing. This behavior may lead to shifts in global asset preferences, which in turn could influence the path of exchange rates. For example, nations running large current account surpluses versus the United States might find that their holdings of US dollar–denominated assets exceed the amount they desire to hold in a portfolio context. Actions they might take to reduce their dollar holdings to desired levels could then have a profound negative impact on the dollar's value.

The Debt Sustainability Channel

The third mechanism through which current account imbalances can affect exchange rates is the so-called debt sustainability channel. According to this mechanism, there should be some upper limit on the ability of countries to run persistently large current account deficits. If a country runs a large and persistent current account deficit over time, eventually it will experience an untenable rise in debt owed to foreign investors. If such investors believe that the deficit country's external debt is rising to unsustainable levels, they are likely to reason that a major depreciation of the deficit country's currency will be required at some point to ensure that the current account deficit narrows significantly and that the external debt stabilizes at a level deemed sustainable.

The existence of persistent current account imbalances will tend to alter the market's notion of what exchange rate level represents the true, long-run equilibrium value. For deficit nations, ever-rising net external debt levels as a percentage of GDP should give rise to steady (but not necessarily smooth) downward revisions in market expectations of the currency's long-run equilibrium value. For surplus countries, ever-rising net external asset levels as a percentage of GDP should give rise to steady upward revisions of the currency's long-run equilibrium value. Hence, one would expect currency values to move broadly in line with trends in debt and/or asset accumulation.

PERSISTENT CURRENT ACCOUNT DEFICITS: THE US CURRENT ACCOUNT AND THE US DOLLAR

The historical record indicates that the trend in the US current account has been an important determinant of the long-term swings in the US dollar's value but also that there can be rather long lags between the onset of a deterioration in the current account balance and an eventual decline in the dollar's value. For example, the US current account balance deteriorated sharply in the first half of the 1980s, yet the dollar soared over that period. The reason for the dollar's strength over that period was that high US real interest rates attracted large inflows of capital from abroad, which pushed the dollar higher despite the large US external imbalance. Eventually, however, concerns regarding the sustainability of the ever-widening US current account deficit triggered a major dollar decline in the second half of the 1980s.

History repeated itself in the second half of the 1990s, with the US current account balance once again deteriorating while the dollar soared over the same period. This time, the dollar's strength was driven by strong foreign direct investment, as well as both debt- and equity-related flows into the United States. Beginning in 2001, however, the ever-widening US current account deficit, coupled with a decline in US interest rates, made it more difficult for the United States to attract the foreign private capital needed to finance its current account deficit. The dollar eventually succumbed to the weight of ever-larger trade and current account deficits and began a multi-year slide, starting in 2002–2003. Interestingly, the US dollar has undergone three major downward cycles since the advent of floating exchange rates: 1977–1978, 1985–1987, and 2002–2008. In each of those downward cycles, the dollar's slide was driven in large part by concerns over outsized US current account deficits coupled with relatively low nominal and/or real short-term US interest rates, which made it difficult to attract sufficient foreign capital to the United States to finance those deficits.

EXCHANGE RATE ADJUSTMENT IN SURPLUS NATIONS: JAPAN AND CHINA

Japan and, for a number of years, China represent examples of countries with large current account surpluses and illustrate the pressure that those surpluses can bring to bear on currencies. In the case of Japan, its rising current account surplus has exerted persistent upward pressure on the yen's value versus the dollar over time. Part of this upward pressure simply reflected the increase in demand for yen to pay for Japan's merchandise exports. But some of the upward pressure on the yen might also have stemmed from rising commercial tensions between the United States and Japan.

Protectionist sentiment in the United States rose steadily with the rising bilateral trade deficit that the United States ran with Japan in the postwar period. US policymakers contended that the yen was undervalued and needed to appreciate. With the increasing trade imbalance between the two countries contributing to more heated protectionist rhetoric, Japan felt compelled to tolerate steady upward pressure on the yen. As a result, the yen's value versus the dollar has tended to move in sync with the trend in Japan's current account surplus.

12   CAPITAL FLOWS

☐ | explain how flows in the balance of payment accounts affect currency exchange rates

Greater financial integration of the world's capital markets and greater freedom of capital to flow across national borders have increased the importance of global financial flows in determining exchange rates, interest rates, and broad asset price trends. One can cite many examples in which global financial flows either caused or contributed to extremes in exchange rates, interest rates, or asset prices.

In numerous cases, global capital flows have helped fuel boom-like conditions in emerging market economies for a while before, suddenly and often without adequate warning, those flows reversed. The reversals often caused a major economic downturn, sovereign default, a serious banking crisis, and/or significant currency depreciation. Excessive emerging market capital inflows often plant the seeds of a crisis by contributing to:

1. an unwarranted appreciation of the emerging market currency,
2. a huge buildup in external indebtedness,
3. an asset bubble,
4. a consumption binge that contributes to explosive growth in domestic credit and/or the current account deficit, or
5. an overinvestment in risky projects and questionable activities.

Governments in emerging markets often resist currency appreciation from excessive capital inflows by using capital controls or selling their currency in the FX market. An example of capital controls is the Brazilian government 2016 tax on foreign exchange transactions to control capital flows and raise government revenue. In general, government control of the exchange rate will not be completely effective because even if a government prohibits investment capital flows, some capital flows will be needed for international trade. In addition, the existence or emergence of black markets for the country's currency will inhibit the ability of the government to fully control the exchange rates for its own currency.

Sometimes, capital flows due to interest rate spreads have little impact on the trend in exchange rates. Consider the case of the Turkish lira. The lira attracted a lot of interest on the part of global fund managers over the 2002–10 period, in large part because of its attractive yields. Turkish–US short-term yield spreads averaged over 1,000 bps during much of this period. As capital flowed into Turkey, the Turkish authorities intervened in the foreign exchange market in an attempt to keep the lira from appreciating. The result was that international investors were not able to reap the anticipated currency gains over this period. While the return from the movement in the spot exchange rate was fairly small, a long Turkish lira/short US dollar carry trade position generated significant long-run returns, mostly from the accumulated yield spread.

One-sided capital flows can persist for long periods. Consider the case of a high-yield, inflation-prone emerging market country that wants to promote price stability and long-term sustainable growth. To achieve price stability, policymakers in the high-yield economy will initiate a tightening in monetary policy by gradually raising the level of domestic interest rates relative to yield levels in the rest of the world. If the tightening in domestic monetary policy is sustained, inflation expectations for the high-yield economy relative to other economies should gradually decline. The combination of sustained wide nominal yield spreads and a steady narrowing in relative inflation expectations should exert upward pressure on the high-yield currency's value, resulting in carry trade profits over long periods.

Policymakers in high-yield markets can also pursue policies which attract foreign investment; such policies might include tighter fiscal policies, liberalization of financial markets, fewer capital flow restrictions, privatization, and/or a better business environment. Such policies should encourage investors to gradually require a lower risk premium to hold the high-yield currency's assets and revise upward their assessment of the long-run equilibrium value of that country's currency.

The historical evidence suggests that the impact of nominal interest rate spreads on the exchange rate tends to be gradual. Monetary policymakers tend to adjust their official lending rates slowly over time—in part because of the uncertainty that policymakers face and in part because the authorities do not want to disrupt the financial markets. This very gradual change in rates implies a very gradual narrowing of the spread between high-yield and low-yield countries. Similarly, the downward trends in inflation expectations and risk premiums in the higher-yield market also tend to unfold gradually. It often takes several years to determine whether structural economic changes will take root and boost the long-run competitiveness of the higher-yield country. Because these fundamental drivers tend to reinforce each other over time, there may be persistence in capital flows and carry trade returns.

Equity Market Trends and Exchange Rates

Increasing equity prices can also attract foreign capital. Although exchange rates and equity market returns sometimes exhibit positive correlation, the relationship between equity market performance and exchange rates is not stable. The long-run correlation between the US equity market and the dollar, for example, is very close to zero, but over short to medium periods, correlations tend to swing from being highly positive to being highly negative, depending on market conditions. For instance, between 1990 and 1995, the US dollar fell while the US equity market was strong and the Japanese yen soared while Japanese stocks were weak. In contrast, between 1995 and early 2000, the US dollar soared in tandem with a rising US equity market while the yen weakened in tandem with a decline in the Japanese equity market. *Such instability in the correlation between exchange rates and equity markets makes it difficult to form judgments on possible future currency moves based solely on expected equity market performance.*

Since the global financial crisis, there has been a decidedly negative correlation between the US dollar and the US equity market. Market observers attribute this behavior of the US dollar to its role as a safe haven asset. When investors' appetite for risk is high—that is, when the market is in "risk-on" mode—investor demand for risky assets, such as equities, tends to rise, which drives up their prices. At the same time, investor demand for safe haven assets, such as the dollar, tends to decline, which drives their values lower. The opposite has occurred when the market has been in "risk-off" mode.

EXAMPLE 8

Capital Flows and Exchange Rates

Monique Kwan, a currency strategist at a major foreign exchange dealer, is responsible for formulating trading strategies for the currencies of both developed market (DM) and emerging market (EM) countries. She examines two countries—one DM and one EM—and notes that the DM country has what is considered a low-yield safe haven currency while the EM country has a high-yield currency whose value is more exposed to fluctuations in the global economic growth rate. Kwan is trying to form an opinion about movements in the exchange rate for the EM currency.

1. All else equal, the exchange rate for the EM currency will *most likely* depreciate if the:

    A. long-run equilibrium value of the high-yield currency is revised upward.

    B. nominal yield spread between the EM and DM countries increases over time.

    C. expected inflation differential between the EM and DM countries is revised upward.

    Solution

    C is correct. All else equal, an increase in the expected inflation differential should lead to depreciation of the EM currency.

2. An increase in safe haven demand would *most likely*:

    A. increase the risk premium demanded by international investors to hold assets denominated in the EM currency.

    B. raise the return earned on carry trade strategies.

    C. exert upward pressure on the value of the EM currency.

    Solution

    A is correct. During times of intense risk aversion, investors will crowd into the safe haven currency. This tendency implies an increased risk premium demanded by investors to hold the EM currency.

3. Kwan notes that the DM country is running a persistent current account deficit with the EM country. To isolate the influence of this chronic imbalance on exchange rates, she focuses only on the bilateral relationship between the EM and DM countries and makes the simplifying assumption that the external accounts of these two countries are otherwise balanced (i.e., there are no other current account deficits).

    Over time and all else equal, the persistent current account deficit with the EM country would *most likely* lead to:

    A. a large buildup of the EM country's assets held by the DM country.

    B. an increase in the trade competitiveness of the EM country.

C. an upward revision in the long-run equilibrium EM currency value.
Solution

C is correct. Over time, the DM country will see its level of external debt rise as a result of the chronic current account imbalance. Eventually, this trend should lead to a downward revision of the DM currency's long-run equilibrium level (via the debt sustainability channel). This is equivalent to an *increase* in the EM currency's long-run exchange rate. A is incorrect because the DM country's current account deficit is likely to lead to a build-up in DM country assets held by the EM country. B is incorrect because, at some point, the currency strength should contribute to deterioration in the trade competitiveness of the country with the trade surplus (the EM country).

4. Kwan notes that because of the high yield on the EM country's bonds, international investors have recently been reallocating their portfolios more heavily toward this country's assets. As a result of these capital inflows, the EM country has been experiencing boom-like conditions.

   Given the current boom-like conditions in the EM economy, in the *near term*, these capital inflows are *most likely* to lead to:

   A. a decrease in inflation expectations in the EM.
   B. an increase in the risk premium for the EM.
   C. an increase in the EM currency value.
   Solution

   C is correct. Given the current investor enthusiasm for the EM country's assets and the boom-like conditions in the country, it is most likely that in the near term, the EM currency will appreciate. At the same time, expected inflation in the EM country is also likely increasing and—given the enthusiasm for EM assets—the risk premium is likely decreasing.

5. If these capital inflows led to an unwanted appreciation in the real value of its currency, the EM country's government would *most likely*:

   A. impose capital controls.
   B. decrease taxes on consumption and investment.
   C. buy its currency in the foreign exchange market.
   Solution

   A is correct. To reduce unwanted appreciation of its currency, the EM country would be most likely to impose capital controls to counteract the surging capital inflows. Because these inflows are often associated with overinvestment and consumption, the EM government would not be likely to encourage these activities through lower taxes. Nor would the EM country be likely to encourage further currency appreciation by intervening in the market to *buy* its own currency.

6. If government actions were ineffective and the EM country's bubble eventually burst, this would *most likely* be reflected in an increase in:

   A. the risk premium for the EM.
   B. the EM currency value.

    C. the long-run equilibrium EM currency value.

Solution

A is correct. Episodes of surging capital flows into EM countries have often ended badly (with a rapid reversal of these inflows as the bubble bursts). This is most likely to be reflected in an increase in the EM risk premium. It is much less likely that a bursting bubble would be reflected in an increase in either the EM currency value or its long-term equilibrium value.

7. Finally, Kwan turns to examining the link between the value of the DM country's currency and movements in the DM country's main stock market index. One of her research associates tells her that, in general, the correlation between equity market returns and changes in exchange rates has been found to be highly positive over time.

The statement made by the research associate is:

    A. correct.

    B. incorrect, because the correlation is highly negative over time.

    C. incorrect, because the correlation is not stable and tends to converge toward zero in the long run.

Solution

C is correct. Correlations between equity returns and exchange rates are unstable in the short term and tend toward zero in the long run.

---

13   MONETARY AND FISCAL POLICIES

☐ | explain the potential effects of monetary and fiscal policy on exchange rates

As the foregoing discussion indicates, government policies can have a significant impact on exchange rate movements. We now examine the channels through which government monetary and fiscal policies are transmitted.

The Mundell–Fleming Model

The Mundell–Fleming model describes how changes in monetary and fiscal policy within a country affect interest rates and economic activity, which in turn leads to changes in capital flows and trade and ultimately to changes in the exchange rate. The model focuses only on aggregate demand and assumes there is sufficient slack in the economy to allow increases in output without price level increases.

In this model, expansionary monetary policy affects growth, in part, by reducing interest rates and thereby increasing investment and consumption spending. Given flexible exchange rates and expansionary monetary policy, downward pressure on domestic interest rates will induce capital to flow to higher-yielding markets, putting downward pressure on the domestic currency. The more responsive capital flows are to interest rate differentials, the greater the depreciation of the currency.

Expansionary fiscal policy—either directly through increased spending or indirectly via lower taxes—typically exerts upward pressure on interest rates because larger budget deficits must be financed. With flexible exchange rates and mobile capital, the rising domestic interest rates will attract capital from lower-yielding markets, putting upward pressure on the domestic currency. If capital flows are highly sensitive to interest rate differentials, then the domestic currency will tend to appreciate substantially. If, however, capital flows are immobile and very insensitive to interest rate differentials, the policy-induced increase in aggregate demand will increase imports and worsen the trade balance, creating downward pressure on the currency with no offsetting capital inflows to provide support for the currency.

The specific mix of monetary and fiscal policies in a country can have a profound effect on its exchange rate. Consider first the case of high capital mobility. With floating exchange rates and high capital mobility, a domestic currency will appreciate given a restrictive domestic monetary policy and/or an expansionary fiscal policy. Similarly, a domestic currency will depreciate given an expansionary domestic monetary policy and/or a restrictive fiscal policy. In Exhibit 4, we show that the combination of a restrictive monetary policy and an expansionary fiscal policy is extremely bullish for a currency when capital mobility is high; likewise, the combination of an expansionary monetary policy and a restrictive fiscal policy is bearish for a currency. The effect on the currency of monetary and fiscal policies that are both expansionary or both restrictive is indeterminate under conditions of high capital mobility.

Exhibit 4: Monetary–Fiscal Policy Mix and the Determination of Exchange Rates under Conditions of High Capital Mobility

	Expansionary Monetary Policy	Restrictive Monetary Policy
Expansionary Fiscal Policy	Indeterminate	Domestic currency appreciates
Restrictive Fiscal Policy	Domestic currency depreciates	Indeterminate

Source: Rosenberg (1996, p. 132).

When capital mobility is low, the effects of monetary and fiscal policy on exchange rates will operate primarily through trade flows rather than capital flows. The combination of expansionary monetary *and* fiscal policy will be bearish for a currency. Earlier we said that expansionary fiscal policy will increase imports and hence the trade deficit, creating downward pressure on the currency. Layering on an expansive monetary policy will further boost spending and imports, worsening the trade balance and exacerbating the downward pressure on the currency.

The combination of restrictive monetary *and* fiscal policy will be bullish for a currency. This policy mix will tend to reduce imports, leading to an improvement in the trade balance.

The impact of expansionary monetary and restrictive fiscal policies (or restrictive monetary and expansionary fiscal policies) on aggregate demand and the trade balance, and hence on the exchange rate, is indeterminate under conditions of low capital mobility. Exhibit 5 summarizes these results.

Exhibit 5: Monetary–Fiscal Policy Mix and the Determination of Exchange Rates under Conditions of Low Capital Mobility

	Expansionary Monetary Policy	Restrictive Monetary Policy
Expansionary Fiscal Policy	Domestic currency depreciates	Indeterminate
Restrictive Fiscal Policy	Indeterminate	Domestic currency appreciates

Source: Adapted from Rosenberg (1996, p. 133).

Exhibit 4 is more relevant for the G–10 countries because capital mobility tends to be high in developed economies. Exhibit 5 is more relevant for emerging market economies that restrict capital movement.

A classic case in which a dramatic shift in the policy mix caused dramatic changes in exchange rates was that of Germany in 1990–1992. During that period, the German government pursued a highly expansionary fiscal policy to help facilitate German unification. At the same time, the Bundesbank pursued an extraordinarily restrictive monetary policy to combat the inflationary pressures associated with unification. The expansive fiscal/restrictive monetary policy mix drove German interest rates sharply higher, eventually causing the German currency to appreciate.

Monetary Models of Exchange Rate Determination

In the Mundell–Fleming model, monetary policy is transmitted to the exchange rate through its impact on interest rates and output. Changes in the price level and/or the inflation rate play no role. Monetary models of exchange rate determination generally take the opposite perspective: Output is fixed and monetary policy affects exchange rates primarily through the price level and the rate of inflation. In this section, we briefly describe two variations of the monetary approach to exchange rate determination.

The monetary approach asserts that an X percent rise in the domestic money supply will produce an X percent rise in the domestic price level. Assuming that purchasing power parity holds—that is, that changes in exchange rates reflect changes in relative inflation rates—a money supply–induced increase (decrease) in domestic prices relative to foreign prices should lead to a proportional decrease (increase) in the domestic currency's value.

One of the major shortcomings of the pure monetary approach is the assumption that purchasing power parity holds in both the short and long runs. Because purchasing power parity rarely holds in either the short or medium run, the pure monetary model may not provide a realistic explanation of the impact of monetary forces on the exchange rate.

To rectify that problem, Dornbusch (1976) constructed a modified monetary model that assumes prices have limited flexibility in the short run but are fully flexible in the long run. The long-run flexibility of the price level ensures that any increase in the domestic money supply will give rise to a proportional increase in domestic prices and thus contribute to a depreciation of the domestic currency in the long run, which is consistent with the pure monetary model. If the domestic price level is assumed to be inflexible in the short run, however, the model implies that the exchange rate is likely to overshoot its long-run PPP path in the short run. With inflexible domestic prices in the short run, any increase in the nominal money supply results in a decline in the domestic interest rate. Assuming that capital is highly mobile, the decline in domestic interest rates will precipitate a capital outflow, which in the short run will cause the domestic currency to depreciate below its new long-run equilibrium level. In the long run, once domestic nominal interest rates rise, the currency will appreciate and move into line with the path predicted by the conventional monetary approach.

Monetary Policy and Exchange Rates: The Historical Evidence

Historically, changes in monetary policy have had a profound impact on exchange rates. In the case of the US dollar, the Federal Reserve's policy of quantitative easing after the global financial crisis resulted in dollar depreciation from mid-2009 to 2011. The subsequent ending of quantitative easing in 2014, along with the anticipation that the United States would raise interest rates before many other countries, played a key role in driving the dollar higher.

Beginning in 2013, Abenomics—fiscal stimulus, monetary easing, and structural reforms—and the use of quantitative easing in Japan led to a steady decline in interest rates and eventually to negative interest rates in 2016. From 2013 to 2015, the value of the yen changed from roughly JPY 90/USD to JPY 120/USD. Likewise, the use of quantitative easing by the European Central Bank in 2015 led to declines in the value of the euro.

Excessively expansionary monetary policies by central banks in emerging markets have often planted the seeds of speculative attacks on their currencies. In the early 1980s, exchange rate crises in Argentina, Brazil, Chile, and Mexico were all preceded by sharp accelerations in domestic credit expansions. In 2012, Venezuela began a period of triple-digit inflation, followed by a massive currency depreciation and an economic crisis.

EXAMPLE 9

Monetary Policy and Exchange Rates

Monique Kwan, the currency strategist at a major foreign exchange dealer, is preparing a report on the outlook for several currencies that she follows. She begins by considering the outlook for the currency of a developed market country with high capital mobility across its borders and a flexible exchange rate. This DM country also has low levels of public and private debt.

Given these conditions, Kwan tries to assess the impact of each of the following policy changes.

1. For the DM currency, increasing the degree of monetary easing (reducing interest rates and increasing money supply) will *most likely*:

   A. cause the currency to appreciate.

   B. cause the currency to depreciate.

   C. have an indeterminate effect on the currency.

   Solution

   B is correct. A decrease in the policy rate would most likely cause capital to re-allocate to higher-yielding markets. This would lead to currency depreciation.

2. The pursuit of an expansionary domestic fiscal policy by the DM country will, in the short run, *most likely*:

   A. cause the domestic currency's value to appreciate.

   B. cause the domestic currency's value to depreciate.

   C. have an indeterminate effect on the domestic currency's value.

   Solution

   A is correct. An expansionary fiscal policy will lead to higher levels of government debt and interest rates, which will attract international capital flows. (In the long run, however, an excessive buildup in debt may eventually cause downward pressure on the domestic currency.)

3. Next, Kwan turns her attention to an emerging market country that has low levels of public and private debt. Currently, the EM country has a fixed exchange rate but no controls over international capital mobility. However, the country is considering replacing its fixed exchange rate policy with a policy based on capital controls. These proposed controls are meant to reduce international capital mobility by limiting short-term investment flows ("hot money") in and out of its domestic capital markets.

   To maintain the exchange rate peg while increasing the degree of monetary easing, the EM country will *most likely* have to:

   A. tighten fiscal policy.

   B. decrease interest rates.

   C. buy its own currency in the FX market.

   Solution

   C is correct. The looser monetary policy will lead to exchange rate depreciation. To counter this effect and maintain the currency peg, the central bank will have to intervene in the FX market, buying the country's own currency.

> A is incorrect because tighter fiscal policy is associated with lower interest rates and is therefore likely to increase rather than mitigate the downward pressure on the domestic currency. Similarly, B is incorrect because a move to lower interest rates would exacerbate the downward pressure on the currency and hence the pressure on the peg.

> 4. After the EM country replaces its currency peg with capital controls, would its exchange rate be unaffected by a tightening in monetary policy?
>
>   **A.** Yes.
>
>   **B.** No, the domestic currency would appreciate.
>
>   **C.** No, the domestic currency would depreciate.
>
>   **Solution**
>
>   B is correct. In general, capital controls will not completely eliminate capital flows but will limit their magnitude and responsiveness to investment incentives such as interest rate differentials. At a minimum, flows directly related to financing international trade will typically be allowed. The exchange rate will still respond to monetary policy. With limited capital mobility, however, monetary policy's main influence is likely to come through the impact on aggregate demand and the trade balance. A tighter domestic monetary policy will most likely lead to higher interest rates and less domestic demand, including less demand for imported goods. With fewer imports and with exports held constant, there will be modest upward pressure on the currency.

> 5. After the EM country replaces its currency peg with capital controls, the simultaneous pursuit of a tight monetary policy and a highly expansionary fiscal policy by the EM country will *most likely*:
>
>   **A.** cause the currency to appreciate.
>
>   **B.** cause the currency to depreciate.
>
>   **C.** have an indeterminate effect on the currency.
>
>   **Solution**
>
>   C is correct because (1) capital mobility is low, so the induced increase in interest rates is likely to exert only weak upward pressure on the currency; (2) the combined impact on aggregate demand is indeterminate; and (3) if aggregate demand increases, the downward pressure on the currency due to a worsening trade balance may or may not fully offset the upward pressure exerted by capital flows.

The Portfolio Balance Approach

In this section, we re-examine the role fiscal policy plays in determining exchange rates. The Mundell–Fleming model is essentially a short-run model of exchange rate determination. It makes no allowance for the long-term effects of budgetary imbalances that typically arise from sustained fiscal policy actions. The portfolio balance approach to exchange rate determination remedies this limitation. In our previous discussion of the portfolio balance channel, we stated that the currencies of countries with trade deficits will decline over time. We expand that discussion here to more closely examine how exchange rates change over the long term.

In the **portfolio balance approach**, global investors are assumed to hold a diversified portfolio of domestic and foreign assets, including bonds. The desired allocation is assumed to vary in response to changes in expected return and risk considerations.

In this framework, a growing government budget deficit leads to a steady increase in the supply of domestic bonds outstanding. These bonds will be willingly held only if investors are compensated in the form of a higher expected return. Such a return could come from (1) higher interest rates and/or a higher risk premium, (2) immediate *depreciation of the currency to a level sufficient to generate anticipation of gains from subsequent currency appreciation*, or (3) some combination of these two factors. The currency adjustments required in the second mechanism are the core of the portfolio balance approach.

One of the major insights one should draw from the portfolio balance model is that *in the long run, governments that run large budget deficits on a sustained basis could eventually see their currencies decline in value.*

The Mundell–Fleming and portfolio balance models can be combined into a single integrated framework in which expansionary fiscal policy under conditions of high capital mobility may be positive for a currency in the short run but negative in the long run. Exhibit 6 illustrates this concept. A domestic currency may rise in value when the expansionary fiscal policy is first put into place. As deficits mount over time and the government's debt obligations rise, however, market participants will begin to wonder how that debt will be financed. If the volume of debt rises to levels that are believed to be unsustainable, market participants may believe that the central bank will eventually be pressured to "monetize" the debt—that is, to buy the government's debt with newly created money. Such a scenario would clearly lead to a rapid reversal of the initial currency appreciation. Alternatively, the market may believe that the government will eventually have to shift toward significant restraint to implement a more restrictive, sustainable fiscal policy over the longer term.

Exhibit 6: The Short- and Long-Run Response of Exchange Rates to Changes in Fiscal Policy

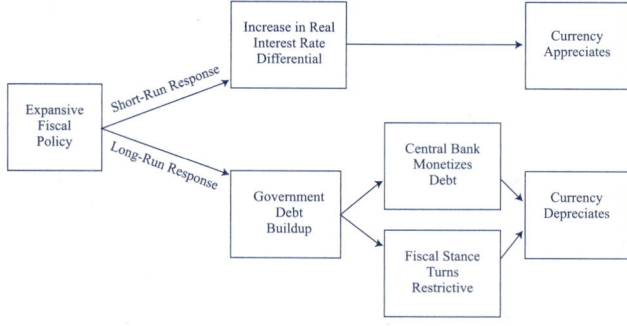

Source: Rosenberg (2003).

EXAMPLE 10

Fiscal Policy and Exchange Rates

Monique Kwan is continuing her analysis of the foreign exchange rate outlook for selected countries. She examines a DM country that has a high degree of capital mobility and a floating-rate currency regime. Kwan notices that although the current outstanding volume of government debt is low, as a percentage of

GDP, it is rising sharply as a result of expansionary fiscal policy. Moreover, projections for the government debt-to-GDP ratio point to further increases well into the future.

Kwan uses the Mundell–Fleming and portfolio balance models to form an opinion about both the short-run and long-run implications for the DM country's exchange rate.

1. Over the short run, Kwan is *most likely* to expect:

   A. appreciation of the DM's currency.

   B. an increase in the DM's asset prices.

   C. a decrease in the DM's risk premium.

   Solution

   A is correct. The DM country currently has a low debt load (as a percentage of GDP), and in the short run, its expansionary fiscal policy will lead to higher interest rates and higher real rates relative to other countries. This path should lead to currency appreciation. The higher domestic interest rates will (all else equal) depress local asset prices (so B is incorrect), and the rising debt load is likely to increase rather than decrease the risk premium (so C is incorrect).

2. Over the medium term, as the DM country's government debt becomes harder to finance, Kwan would be *most likely* to expect that:

   A. fiscal policy will turn more accommodative.

   B. the mark-to-market value of the debt will increase.

   C. monetary policy will become more accommodative.

   Solution

   C is correct. As government debt becomes harder to finance, the government will be tempted to monetize the debt through an accommodative monetary policy. A is incorrect because an inability to finance the debt will make it hard for fiscal policy to become more accommodative. B is incorrect because as investors demand a higher risk premium (a higher return) for holding the DM country's debt, the mark-to-market value of the debt will decline (i.e., bond prices will decrease and bond yields will increase).

3. Assuming that the DM country's government debt becomes harder to finance and there is no change in monetary policy, Kwan is *most likely* to expect that over the longer term, there will be a fiscal policy response that will lead to:

   A. currency appreciation as yields rise.

   B. currency depreciation as yields decline.

   C. an indeterminate impact on the currency, depending on which effect prevails.

   Solution

   B is correct. As the DM country's debt ratio deteriorates, foreign investors will demand a higher rate of return to compensate them for the increased risk. Assuming that the central bank will not accommodate (monetize) the rising government debt, the most likely fiscal response is an eventual move toward fiscal consolidation—reducing the public deficit and debt levels that were causing the debt metrics to deteriorate. This policy adjustment would involve issuing fewer government bonds. All else equal, bond yields would decrease, leading to a weaker domestic currency over the longer term. A is incorrect because currency appreciation is not likely to accompany rising yields when the government is having difficulty financing its deficit. There would be a rising risk premium (a deteriorating investor appetite) for holding DM assets, and hence a currency appreciation would be unlikely despite high DM yields. To avoid paying these high yields on its debt, the DM government would eventually have to take measures to reduce its deficit spending. This approach would eventually help reduce investor risk aversion and DM yields. C is incorrect because given the deterioration in the DM's debt metrics, a depreciation of its exchange rate is likely to be an important part of the restoration of financial market equilibrium.

14   EXCHANGE RATE MANAGEMENT: INTERVENTION AND CONTROLS

☐   describe objectives of central bank or government intervention and capital controls and describe the effectiveness of intervention and capital controls

Capital flows can be both a blessing and a curse. Capital inflows can be a blessing when they increase domestic investment, thereby increasing a country's economic growth and asset values. Currency appreciation often follows, which increases returns to global investors. Capital inflows can be a curse, however, if they fuel boom-like conditions, asset price bubbles, and overvaluation of a country's currency. If capital inflows then reverse, the result may be a major economic downturn, a significant decline in asset prices, and a large depreciation of the currency. Capital inflows often are driven by a combination of "pull" and "push" factors. Pull factors represent a favorable set of developments that encourage foreign capital inflows. These factors may stem from both the public and private sectors. Examples of better economic management by a government include

- a decrease in inflation and inflation volatility,
- more-flexible exchange rate regimes,
- improved fiscal positions,
- privatization of state-owned entities,
- liberalization of financial markets, and
- lifting of foreign exchange regulations and controls.

Ideally, these changes will facilitate strong economic growth in the private sector, which will attract further foreign investment. A healthy export sector will generate improvement in the current account balance and an increase in FX reserves, which can be used by the government as a buffer against future speculative attacks. The returns from the currency and assets should increase, increasing the foreign investor's return.

Push factors driving foreign capital inflows are not determined by the domestic policies but arise from the primary sources of internationally mobile capital, notably the investor base in industrial countries. For example, the pursuit of low interest rate policies in industrial countries since the 2008 financial crisis has encouraged global investors to seek higher returns abroad.

Another important push factor is the long-run trend in asset allocation by industrial country investors. For example, many fund managers have traditionally had underweight exposures to emerging market assets, but with the weight of emerging market equities in broad global equity market indexes on the rise (as of 2019 the EM share of world GDP at current prices is over 40%, up from 17% in the 1960s, according to the IMF), capital flows to EM countries, in the form of increased allocations to EM equities, are likely to rise.

Private capital inflows to emerging markets go through significant changes over time. For example, they rose steadily between 2003 and 2007, posting nearly a six-fold increase over the period. Both push and pull factors contributed to that surge in capital flows. Net private capital flows to emerging markets tumbled in 2008 and 2009 as heightened risk aversion during the global financial crisis prompted investors to unwind some of their EM exposures in favor of US assets. In 2010, capital flows to emerging markets rose as many EM economies weathered the global financial crisis better than many industrial economies. In addition, the pursuit of ultra-low interest rate policies in the United States, the euro area, and Japan encouraged global investors to invest in higher-yielding EM assets.

However beneficial foreign capital is, policymakers must guard against excessive capital inflows that could quickly be reversed. Capital flow surges planted the seeds of three major currency crises in the 1990s—the European Exchange Rate Mechanism (ERM) crisis in 1992–1993, the Mexican peso crisis in late 1994, and the Asian currency and financial crisis in 1997–1998. Each crisis episode was preceded by a surge in capital inflows and a buildup of huge, highly leveraged speculative positions by local as well as international investors in currencies that eventually came under heavy speculative attack. In the run-up to the ERM crisis, investors—believing that European yield convergence would occur as European monetary union approached—took on highly leveraged long positions in the higher-yielding European currencies financed by short positions in the lower-yielding European currencies. Likewise, in the run-up to the Mexican peso crisis, investors and banks were highly leveraged and made extensive use of derivative products in taking on speculative long Mexican peso/short US dollar positions. And in the run-up to the Asian financial crisis, Asian companies and banks were highly leveraged as they took on a huge volume of short-term dollar- and yen-denominated debt to fund local activities. In each case, the sudden unwinding of those leveraged long speculative positions triggered the attacks on the currencies.

Governments resist excessive inflows and currency bubbles by using capital controls and direct intervention (selling their currency) in the foreign exchange market. Capital controls can take many forms. In the Asian financial crisis, many countries, such as Malaysia, prevented their banks from offering currency transactions in which their currency was sold. As mentioned earlier, Brazil has used a tax to limit currency transactions. In 2006, Thailand required a one-year, non-interest-bearing deposit of 30% of an investment's value to reduce new foreign inflows, which had been appreciating the Thai baht. Vietnam has limited the foreign ownership of local financial institutions. In 2015, Ukraine was removed from the MSCI Frontier Markets equity index after its central bank prevented foreign investors from repatriating funds from the sale of Ukrainian stocks. By 2016, Venezuela had instituted capital controls in the form of four different exchange rates, whereby the rate for selling Venezuelan bolivars for US dollars depended on what the dollars were used for. As a result, many Venezuelans used the black market to obtain dollars. Venezuela's capital controls were subsequently loosened in 2018 and 2019.

At one time, capital controls were frowned on as a policy tool for curbing undesired surges in capital inflows. It was generally felt that such controls tended to generate distortions in global trade and finance and that, in all likelihood, market participants would eventually find ways to circumvent the controls. Furthermore, many thought that capital controls imposed by one country could deflect capital flows to other countries, which could complicate monetary and exchange rate policies in those economies. Despite such concerns, the IMF has said that the benefits associated with capital controls may exceed the associated costs. Given the painful lessons that EM policymakers have learned from previous episodes of capital flow surges, some believe that under certain circumstances, capital controls may be needed to prevent exchange rates from overshooting, asset bubbles from forming, and future financial conditions from deteriorating.

Although a case can be made for government intervention and capital controls to limit the potential damage associated with unrestricted inflows of overseas capital, the key issue for policymakers is whether intervention and capital controls will actually work in terms of (1) preventing currencies from appreciating too strongly, (2) reducing the aggregate volume of capital inflows, and (3) enabling monetary authorities to pursue independent monetary policies without having to worry about whether changes in policy rates might attract too much capital from overseas. As an example of the last issue, if a central bank increases interest rates to slow inflation, then capital controls might prevent foreign capital inflows from subsequently depressing interest rates.

Evidence on the effectiveness of direct government intervention suggests that, in the case of industrial countries, the volume of intervention is often quite small relative to the average daily turnover of G–10 currencies in the foreign exchange market. Hence, most studies have concluded that the effect of intervention in developed market economies is limited. For most developed market countries, the ratio of official FX reserves held by the respective central banks to the average daily turnover of foreign exchange trading in that currency is negligible. Most industrial countries hold insufficient reserves to significantly affect the supply of and demand for their currency. Note that if a central bank is intervening in an effort to weaken, rather than strengthen, its own currency, it could (at least in principle) create and sell an unlimited amount of its currency and accumulate a correspondingly large quantity of FX reserves. However, persistent intervention in the FX market can undermine the efficacy of domestic monetary policy.

The evidence on the effectiveness of government intervention in emerging market currencies is more mixed. Intervention appears to contribute to lower EM exchange rate volatility, but no statistically significant relationship has emerged between the level of EM exchange rates and intervention. Some studies have found, however, that EM policymakers might have greater success in controlling exchange rates than their industrial country counterparts because the ratio of EM central bank FX reserve holdings to average daily FX turnover in their domestic currencies is actually quite sizable. With considerably greater firepower in their reserve arsenals, emerging market central banks appear to be in a stronger position than their developed market counterparts to influence the level and path of their exchange rates. What's more, with emerging market central banks' FX reserve holdings expanding at a near-record clip in the past decade, the effectiveness of intervention may be greater now than in the past.

15   WARNING SIGNS OF A CURRENCY CRISIS

☐ | describe warning signs of a currency crisis

If capital inflows come to a sudden stop, the result may be a financial crisis, in which the economy contracts, asset values plummet, and the currency sharply depreciates. History is filled with examples of currencies that have come under heavy selling pressure within short windows of time. For example, between August 2008 and February

2009, 23 currencies dropped by 25% or more against the US dollar. These included the developed market currencies of Australia, Sweden, and the United Kingdom, which dropped by 35% or more, and the emerging market currencies of Brazil, Russia, and South Korea, which fell by more than 50%.

Currency crises often occur suddenly, with many investors caught by surprise. Once a wave of selling begins, investors and borrowers must immediately reposition their portfolios to avoid excessive capital losses. For example, assume a carry trader had gone long the Brazilian real and borrowed US dollars. Upon an initial depreciation of the real, the trader would be inclined to exit the trade by selling reals and buying dollars. Or consider a Brazilian public or private borrower that had financed in US dollars. The borrower would also be selling reals to buy dollars in order to cover future repayment of the dollar debt. Either of these actions will intensify selling pressure on the depreciated currency. It is this massive liquidation of vulnerable positions, often reinforced by speculative offshore selling, that is largely responsible for the excessive exchange rate movements that occur during currency crises.

Because most crisis episodes have not been adequately anticipated, a great deal of effort has been spent developing early warning systems. One of the problems in developing an early warning system is that views on the underlying causes of currency crises differ greatly. One school of thought contends that currency crises tend to be precipitated by deteriorating economic fundamentals, while a second school contends that currency crises can occur out of the blue, with little evidence of deteriorating fundamentals preceding them.

If, according to the first school of thought, deteriorating economic fundamentals often precede crises and if those economic fundamentals tend to deteriorate steadily and predictably, then it should be possible to construct an early warning system to anticipate when a currency might be vulnerable.

The second school of thought argues that, although evidence of deteriorating economic fundamentals might explain a relatively large number of currency collapses, there might be cases in which economies with relatively sound fundamentals have their currencies come under attack. Clearly, these currency crises would be more difficult to predict. Events that are largely unrelated to domestic economic fundamentals include sudden adverse shifts in market sentiment that become self-fulfilling prophecies and contagion from crises in other markets. A crisis may spread to a country when, for example, the country devalues its currency to keep its exports competitive with those of another country that devalued.

Recognizing that no single model can correctly anticipate the onset of all crisis episodes, an early warning system might nevertheless be useful in assisting investors in structuring and/or hedging their global portfolios. An ideal early warning system would need to incorporate a number of important features. First, it should have a strong record of predicting actual crises but also should not issue false alarms. Second, it should include macroeconomic indicators whose data are available on a timely basis. If data arrive with a long lag, a crisis could be under way before the early warning system starts flashing red. Third, because currency crises tend to be triggered in countries with a number of economic problems, not just one, an ideal early warning system should be broad based, incorporating a wide range of symptoms that crisis-prone currencies might exhibit.

Many studies have been conducted to develop an early warning system for currency crises, typically by constructing a model in which a number of variables constitute the early warning system. Various definitions of currency crises have been used. Although the variables and methodologies differ from one study to the next, the following conditions were identified in one or more studies (Babecký, Havránek, Matějů, Rusnák, Šmídková, and Vašíček 2013 and 2014; Daniels and VanHoose 2018):

1. Prior to a currency crisis, the capital markets have been liberalized to allow the free flow of capital.

2. There are large inflows of foreign capital (relative to GDP) in the period leading up to a crisis, with short-term funding denominated in a foreign currency being particularly problematic.

3. Currency crises are often preceded by (and often coincide with) banking crises.

4. Countries with fixed or partially fixed exchange rates are more susceptible to currency crises than countries with floating exchange rates.

5. Foreign exchange reserves tend to decline precipitously as a crisis approaches.

6. In the period leading up to a crisis, the currency has risen substantially relative to its historical mean.

7. The ratio of exports to imports (known as "the terms of trade") often deteriorates before a crisis.

8. Broad money growth and the ratio of M2 (a measure of money supply) to bank reserves tend to rise prior to a crisis.

9. Inflation tends to be significantly higher in pre-crisis periods compared with tranquil periods.

These factors are usually interrelated and often feed off one another. For example, in the case of the first five factors, large inflows of foreign capital occur because the financial markets have been liberalized and domestic banks have borrowed abroad. If the borrowing is denominated in a foreign currency and the domestic currency initially depreciates, the bank may have trouble servicing its debt, especially when the debt is of shorter maturity. This scenario may cause foreign investors to withdraw capital and speculators to short the currency, with their actions causing further declines in the currency. If the government is trying to maintain the currency's value, it could increase interest rates to stem capital outflows or defend its currency using direct intervention. The former action may worsen the banking industry's condition and slow down the economy. In the latter approach, the government will have to spend down its foreign currency reserves to buy its own currency in the foreign exchange markets. If the government appears unwilling or unable to defend its currency, then capital outflows and speculative attacks will increase.

The fifth through seventh factors are related because an overvalued currency may make the country's exports less competitive. With fewer exports, the country is not able to earn as much foreign currency. Other interrelationships occur because these factors often coincide.

Models cannot predict every crisis, and they sometimes generate false alarms. Nevertheless, an early warning system can be useful in assessing and preparing for potential negative tail risks. As with any analytical tool, the implementation of an early warning system requires integration with other analysis and judgment that cannot be easily quantified or conceptualized.

ICELAND'S CURRENCY CRISIS OF 2008

Iceland, a country with a population of 320,000, had traditionally relied on the fishing, energy, and aluminum industries for economic growth. That began to change in 2001, when the banking industry was liberalized. Three banks dominated the Icelandic banking industry: Glitnir, Kaupthing, and Landsbanki. Given Iceland's small population, these banks sought growth by offering short-term, internet-based deposit accounts to foreign investors. These accounts offered attractive interest rates and were denominated in foreign currencies. In particular, many of the depositors were British, Dutch, and other European citizens who held deposit accounts denominated in pounds and euros.

With government guarantees on their deposit accounts, the banking industry grew rapidly. The largest bank, Kaupthing, experienced asset growth of 30 times between 2000 and 2008. The three banks increased lending rapidly, with many of their loans being long term, resulting in a maturity mismatch of assets and liabilities. The banks' assets were more than 14 times the country's GDP, while foreign debt was five times GDP. The three banks constituted more than 70% of the national stock market capitalization.

The economy expanded at a real growth rate above 20% annually between 2002 and 2005, and many Icelanders left traditional industries to work in the banks. Iceland earned the nickname "Nordic Tiger" as per capita GDP approached USD 70,000 in 2007. The Icelandic krona increased in value against the US dollar by 40% between 2001 and 2007. By 2007, the unemployment rate was less than 1%. Icelanders went on a shopping spree for consumer goods, in part by using loans tied to the value of foreign currencies, motivated by lower interest rates abroad. A 2002 trade surplus turned into a trade deficit in the years 2003–2007. Iceland's external debt in 2008 was more than 7 times its GDP and 14 times its export revenue. Broad-based monetary aggregates grew at a rate of 14%–35% annually from 2002 to 2007. By the fall of 2008, inflation had reached 14%.

As the global financial crisis unfolded in 2008, interbank lending declined and Icelandic banks were unable to roll over their short-term debt. Anxious foreign depositors began withdrawing their funds. In the first half of 2008, the krona depreciated by more than 40% against the euro. As the Icelandic currency declined in value, it became more difficult for the banks to meet depositors' liquidity demands, while at the same time the banks' depreciating krona-denominated assets could not be used for collateral financing. The three banks collapsed in 2008. Unfortunately for foreign depositors, because of the relative size of the banks, the government guaranteed only domestic deposits. Iceland's central bank became technically insolvent, as its EUR 2 billion in assets was dwarfed by Iceland's debt to foreign banks of EUR 50 billion. Trading in the stock market was suspended in October 2008. When it reopened several days later, the Icelandic Stock Market Index fell by more than 77% as a result of the elimination of the three banks' equity value. The government attempted to peg the krona to the euro in October 2008 but abandoned the peg one day later. When trading in the currency was resumed later that month, the currency value fell by more than 60% and trading was eventually suspended. Iceland increased interest rates to 18% to stem outflows of krona and imposed capital controls on the selling of krona for foreign currency. The Icelandic economy contracted, and per capita GDP fell 9.2% in 2009. By the spring of 2009, unemployment was 9%. The country subsequently required a bailout from the IMF and its neighbors of USD 4.6 billion.

Source: Federal Reserve Bank of St. Louis database; Bekaert and Hodrick 2018; Matsangou 2015; Daniels and VanHoose 2017.

EXAMPLE 11

Currency Crises

Monique Kwan now turns her attention to the likelihood of crises in various emerging market currencies. She discusses this matter with a research associate, who tells her that the historical record of currency crises shows that most of these episodes were not very well anticipated by investors (in terms of their positioning), by the bond markets (in terms of yield spreads between countries), or by major credit rating agencies and economists (in terms of the sovereign credit ratings and forecasts, respectively).

1. The research associate is *most likely*:

   A. correct.

   B. incorrect, because most credit rating agencies and economists typically change their forecasts prior to a crisis.

   C. incorrect, because investor positioning and international yield differentials typically shift prior to a crisis.

   Solution

   A is correct. Currency crises often catch most market participants and analysts by surprise.

2. Kwan delves further into the historical record of currency crises. She concludes that even countries with relatively sound economic fundamentals can fall victim to these crisis episodes and that these attacks can occur when sentiment shifts for reasons unrelated to economic fundamentals.

   Kwan's conclusion is *most likely*:

   A. correct.

   B. incorrect, because there are few historical crises involving currencies of countries with sound economic fundamentals.

   C. incorrect, because there are few historical episodes in which a sudden adverse shift in market sentiment occurs that is unrelated to economic fundamentals.

   Solution

   A is correct. Even countries with sound economic fundamentals can be subject to a currency crisis, including instances when market sentiment shifts for non-economic reasons.

3. To better advise the firm's clients on the likelihood of currency crises, Kwan tries to formulate an early warning system for these episodes. She recognizes that a typical currency crisis tends to be triggered by a number of economic problems, not just one.

   Kwan's early warning system is *least likely* to indicate an impending crisis when there is:

   A. an expansionary monetary policy.

   B. an overly appreciated exchange rate.

   C. a rising level of foreign exchange reserves at the central bank.

   Solution

   C is correct. A high level of foreign exchange reserves held by a country typically decreases the likelihood of a currency crisis.

4. Kwan's early warning system would *most likely* be better if it:

   A. had a strong record of predicting actual crises, even if it generates a lot of false signals.

   B. included a wide variety of economic indicators, including those for which data are available only with a significant lag.

C. started flashing well in advance of an actual currency crisis to give market participants time to adjust or hedge their portfolios before the crisis hits.

Solution

C is correct. Early warnings are a positive factor in judging the effectiveness of the system, whereas false signals and the use of lagged data would be considered negative factors.

APPENDIX

Currency Codes Used	
USD	US dollar
EUR	euro
GBP	UK pound
JPY	Japanese yen
MXN	Mexican peso
CHF	Swiss franc
CAD	Canadian dollar
SEK	Swedish krona
AUD	Australian dollar
KRW	Korean won
NZD	New Zealand dollar

SUMMARY

Exchange rates are among the most difficult financial market prices to understand and therefore to value. There is no simple, robust framework that investors can rely on in assessing the appropriate level and likely movements of exchange rates.

Most economists believe that there is an equilibrium level or a path to that equilibrium value that a currency will gravitate toward in the long run. Although short- and medium-term cyclical deviations from the long-run equilibrium path can be sizable and persistent, fundamental forces should eventually drive the currency back toward its long-run equilibrium path. Evidence suggests that misalignments tend to build up gradually over time. As these misalignments build, they are likely to generate serious economic imbalances that will eventually lead to correction of the underlying exchange rate misalignment.

We have described how changes in monetary policy, fiscal policy, current account trends, and capital flows affect exchange rate trends, as well as what role government intervention and capital controls can play in counteracting potentially undesirable exchange rate movements. We have made the following key points:

- Spot exchange rates apply to trades for the next settlement date (usually $T + 2$) for a given currency pair. Forward exchange rates apply to trades to be settled at any longer maturity.

- Market makers quote bid and offer prices (in terms of the *price currency*) at which they will buy or sell the *base currency*.

  - The offer price is always higher than the bid price.
  - The counterparty that asks for a two-sided price quote has the option (but not the obligation) to deal at either the bid or offer price quoted.
  - The bid–offer spread depends on (1) the currency pair involved, (2) the time of day, (3) market volatility, (4) the transaction size, and (5) the relationship between the dealer and the client. Spreads are tightest in highly liquid currency pairs, when the key market centers are open, and when market volatility is relatively low.

- Absence of arbitrage requires the following:

  - The bid (offer) shown by a dealer in the interbank market cannot be higher (lower) than the current interbank offer (bid) price.
  - The cross-rate bids (offers) posted by a dealer must be lower (higher) than the implied cross-rate offers (bids) available in the interbank market. If they are not, then a triangular arbitrage opportunity arises.

- Forward exchange rates are quoted in terms of points to be added to the spot exchange rate. If the points are positive (negative), the base currency is trading at a forward premium (discount). The points are proportional to the interest rate differential and approximately proportional to the time to maturity.

- International parity conditions show us how expected inflation, interest rate differentials, forward exchange rates, and expected future spot exchange rates are linked. In an ideal world,

  - relative expected inflation rates should determine relative nominal interest rates,
  - relative interest rates should determine forward exchange rates, and

- forward exchange rates should correctly anticipate the path of the future spot exchange rate.

- International parity conditions tell us that countries with high (low) expected inflation rates should see their currencies depreciate (appreciate) over time, that high-yield currencies should depreciate relative to low-yield currencies over time, and that forward exchange rates should function as unbiased predictors of future spot exchange rates.

- With the exception of covered interest rate parity, which is enforced by arbitrage, the key international parity conditions rarely hold in either the short or medium term. However, the parity conditions tend to hold over relatively long horizons.

- According to the theory of covered interest rate parity, a foreign-currency-denominated money market investment that is completely hedged against exchange rate risk in the forward market should yield exactly the same return as an otherwise identical domestic money market investment.

- According to the theory of uncovered interest rate parity, the expected change in a domestic currency's value should be fully reflected in domestic–foreign interest rate spreads. Hence, an unhedged foreign-currency-denominated money market investment is expected to yield the same return as an otherwise identical domestic money market investment.

- According to the *ex ante* purchasing power parity condition, expected changes in exchange rates should equal the difference in expected national inflation rates.

- If both *ex ante* purchasing power parity and uncovered interest rate parity held, real interest rates across all markets would be the same. This result is real interest rate parity.

- The international Fisher effect says that the nominal interest rate differential between two currencies equals the difference between the expected inflation rates. The international Fisher effect assumes that risk premiums are the same throughout the world.

- If both covered and uncovered interest rate parity held, then forward rate parity would hold and the market would set the forward exchange rate equal to the expected spot exchange rate: The forward exchange rate would serve as an unbiased predictor of the future spot exchange rate.

- Most studies have found that high-yield currencies do not depreciate and low-yield currencies do not appreciate as much as yield spreads would suggest over short to medium periods, thus violating the theory of uncovered interest rate parity.

- Carry trades overweight high-yield currencies at the expense of low-yield currencies. Historically, carry trades have generated attractive returns in benign market conditions but tend to perform poorly (i.e., are subject to crash risk) when market conditions are highly volatile.

- According to a balance of payments approach, countries that run persistent current account deficits will generally see their currencies weaken over time. Similarly, countries that run persistent current account surpluses will tend to see their currencies appreciate over time.

- Large current account imbalances can persist for long periods of time before they trigger an adjustment in exchange rates.

- Greater financial integration of the world's capital markets and greater freedom of capital to flow across national borders have increased the importance of global capital flows in determining exchange rates.

- Countries that institute relatively tight monetary policies, introduce structural economic reforms, and lower budget deficits will often see their currencies strengthen over time as capital flows respond positively to relatively high nominal interest rates, lower inflation expectations, a lower risk premium, and an upward revision in the market's assessment of what exchange rate level constitutes long-run fair value.

- Monetary policy affects the exchange rate through a variety of channels. In the Mundell–Fleming model, it does so primarily through the interest rate sensitivity of capital flows, strengthening the currency when monetary policy is tightened and weakening it when monetary policy is eased. The more sensitive capital flows are to the change in interest rates, the greater the exchange rate's responsiveness to the change in monetary policy.

- In the monetary model of exchange rate determination, monetary policy is deemed to have a direct impact on the actual and expected path of inflation, which, via purchasing power parity, translates into a corresponding impact on the exchange rate.

- Countries that pursue overly easy monetary policies will see their currencies depreciate over time.

- In the Mundell–Fleming model, an expansionary fiscal policy typically results in a rise in domestic interest rates and an increase in economic activity. The rise in domestic interest rates should induce a capital inflow, which is positive for the domestic currency, but the rise in economic activity should contribute to a deterioration of the trade balance, which is negative for the domestic currency. The more mobile capital flows are, the greater the likelihood that the induced inflow of capital will dominate the deterioration in trade.

- Under conditions of high capital mobility, countries that simultaneously pursue expansionary fiscal policies and relatively tight monetary policies should see their currencies strengthen over time.

- The portfolio balance model of exchange rate determination asserts that increases in government debt resulting from a rising budget deficit will be willingly held by investors only if they are compensated in the form of a higher expected return. The higher expected return could come from (1) higher interest rates and/or a higher risk premium, (2) depreciation of the currency to a level sufficient to generate anticipation of gains from subsequent currency appreciation, or (3) some combination of the two.

- Surges in capital inflows can fuel boom-like conditions, asset price bubbles, and currency overvaluation.

- Many consider capital controls to be a legitimate part of a policymaker's toolkit. The IMF believes that capital controls may be needed to prevent exchange rates from overshooting, asset price bubbles from forming, and future financial conditions from deteriorating.

- The evidence indicates that government policies have had a significant impact on the course of exchange rates. Relative to developed countries, emerging markets may have greater success in managing their exchange rates because of their large foreign exchange reserve holdings, which appear sizable relative to the limited turnover of FX transactions in many emerging markets.

- Although each currency crisis is distinct in some respects, the following factors were identified in one or more studies:

  1. Prior to a currency crisis, the capital markets have been liberalized to allow the free flow of capital.

  2. There are large inflows of foreign capital (relative to GDP) in the period leading up to a crisis, with short-term funding denominated in a foreign currency being particularly problematic.

  3. Currency crises are often preceded by (and often coincide with) banking crises.

  4. Countries with fixed or partially fixed exchange rates are more susceptible to currency crises than countries with floating exchange rates.

  5. Foreign exchange reserves tend to decline precipitously as a crisis approaches.

  6. In the period leading up to a crisis, the currency has risen substantially relative to its historical mean.

  7. The terms of trade (exports relative to imports) often deteriorate before a crisis.

  8. Broad money growth and the ratio of M2 (a measure of money supply) to bank reserves tend to rise prior to a crisis.

  9. Inflation tends to be significantly higher in pre-crisis periods compared with tranquil periods.

REFERENCES

Babecký, Jan, Tomáš Havránek, Jakub Matějů, Marek Rusnák, Kateřina Šmídková, Bořek Vašíček. 2013. "Leading Indicators of Crisis Incidence: Evidence from Developed Countries." Journal of International Money and Finance35 (June): 1–19. 10.1016/j.jimonfin.2013.01.001

Babecký, Jan, Tomáš Havránek, Jakub Matějů, Marek Rusnák, Kateřina Šmídková, Bořek Vašíček. 2014. "Banking, Debt, and Currency Crises in Developed Countries: Stylized Facts and Early Warning Indicators." Journal of Financial Stability15 (December): 1–17. 10.1016/j.jfs.2014.07.001

Bekaert, Geert, Robert Hodrick. 2018. International Financial Management. 3rd ed.Cambridge, UK: Cambridge University Press.

Daniels, Joseph P., David D. VanHoose. 2017. Global Economic Issues and Policies. 4th ed.London: Routledge.

Dimson, Elroy, Paul Marsh, Paul McGinnie, Mike Staunton, Jonathan Wilmot. 2012. Credit Suisse Global Investment Returns Yearbook 2012. Zurich: Credit Suisse Research Institute.

Dornbusch, Rudiger. 1976. "Expectations and Exchange Rate Dynamics." Journal of Political Economy84 (6): 1161–76. 10.1086/260506

Matsangou, Elizabeth. 2015. "Failing Banks, Winning Economy: The Truth about Iceland's Recovery." *World Finance* (15 September).

Rosenberg, Michael R. 1996. Currency Forecasting: A Guide to Fundamental and Technical Models of Exchange Rate Determination. Chicago: Irwin Professional Publishing.

Rosenberg, Michael R. 2003. Exchange Rate Determination: Models and Strategies for Exchange Rate Forecasting. New York: McGraw-Hill.

PRACTICE PROBLEMS

The following information relates to questions 1-5

Ed Smith is a new trainee in the foreign exchange (FX) services department of a major global bank. Smith's focus is to assist senior FX trader Feliz Mehmet, CFA. Mehmet mentions that an Indian corporate client exporting to the United Kingdom wants to estimate the potential hedging cost for a sale closing in one year. Smith is to determine the premium/discount for an annual (360-day) forward contract using the exchange rate data presented in Exhibit 1.

Exhibit 1: Select Currency Data for GBP and INR	
Spot (INR/GBP)	79.5093
Annual (360-day) MRR (GBP)	5.43%
Annual (360-day) MRR (INR)	7.52%

Mehmet is also looking at two possible trades to determine their profit potential. The first trade involves a possible triangular arbitrage trade using the Swiss, US, and Brazilian currencies, to be executed based on a dealer's bid/offer rate quote of 0.2355/0.2358 in CHF/BRL and the interbank spot rate quotes presented in Exhibit 2.

Exhibit 2: Interbank Market Quotes	
Currency Pair	**Bid/Offer**
CHF/USD	0.9799/0.9801
BRL/USD	4.1699/4.1701

Mehmet is also considering a carry trade involving the USD and the EUR. He anticipates it will generate a higher return than buying a one-year domestic note at the current market quote due to low US interest rates and his predictions of exchange rates in one year. To help Mehmet assess the carry trade, Smith provides Mehmet with selected current market data and his one-year forecasts in Exhibit 3.

Exhibit 3: Spot Rates and Interest Rates for Proposed Carry Trade				
Today's One-Year MRR		Currency Pair (Price/ Base)	Spot Rate Today	Projected Spot Rate in One Year
USD	0.80%	CAD/USD	1.3200	1.3151
CAD	1.71%	EUR/CAD	0.6506	0.6567
EUR	2.20%			

Finally, Mehmet asks Smith to assist with a trade involving a US multinational customer operating in Europe and Japan. The customer is a very cost-conscious industrial company with an AA credit rating and strives to execute its currency trades at the most favorable bid–offer spread. Because its Japanese subsidiary is about to close on a major European acquisition in three business days, the client wants to lock in a trade involving the Japanese yen and the euro as early as possible the next morning, preferably by 8:05 a.m. New York time.

At lunch, Smith and other FX trainees discuss how best to analyze currency market volatility from ongoing financial crises. The group agrees that a theoretical explanation of exchange rate movements, such as the framework of the international parity conditions, should be applicable across all trading environments. They note such analysis should enable traders to anticipate future spot exchange rates. But they disagree on which parity condition best predicts exchange rates, voicing several different assessments. Smith concludes the discussion on parity conditions by stating to the trainees,

I believe that in the current environment both covered and uncovered interest rate parity conditions are in effect.

1. Based on Exhibit 1, the forward premium (discount) for a 360-day INR/GBP forward contract is *closest* to:

    A. −1.546.

    B. 1.546.

    C. 1.576.

2. Based on Exhibit 2, the *most* appropriate recommendation regarding the triangular arbitrage trade is to:

    A. decline the trade, because no arbitrage profits are possible.

    B. execute the trade, buy BRL in the interbank market, and sell BRL to the dealer.

    C. execute the trade, buy BRL from the dealer, and sell BRL in the interbank market.

3. Based on Exhibit 3, the potential all-in USD return on the carry trade is *closest* to:

    A. 0.83%.

    B. 1.23%.

    C. 1.63%.

4. The factor *least likely* to lead to a narrow bid–offer spread for the industrial company's needed currency trade is the:

    A. timing of its trade.

    B. company's credit rating.

    C. pair of currencies involved.

5. If Smith's statement on parity conditions is correct, future spot exchange rates are *most likely* to be forecast by:

    A. current spot rates.

    B. forward exchange rates.

    C. inflation rate differentials.

The following information relates to questions 6-13

Anna Goldsworthy is the chief financial officer of a manufacturing firm headquartered in the United Kingdom. She is responsible for overseeing exposure to price risk in both the commodity and currency markets. Goldsworthy is settling her end-of-quarter transactions and creating reports. Her intern, Scott Underwood, assists her in this process.

The firm hedges input costs using forward contracts that are priced in US dollars (USD) and Mexican pesos (MXN). Processed goods are packaged for sale under licensing agreements with firms in foreign markets. Goldsworthy is expecting to receive a customer payment of JPY 225,000,000 (Japanese yen) that she wants to convert to pounds sterling (GBP). Underwood gathers the exchange rates from Dealer A in Exhibit 1.

Exhibit 1: Dealer A's Spot Exchange Rates

Currency Pair (Price/Base)	Spot Exchange Rates		
	Bid	Offer	Midpoint
JPY/GBP	129.65	129.69	129.67
MXN/USD	20.140	20.160	20.150
GBP/EUR	0.9467	0.9471	0.9469
USD/EUR	1.1648	1.1652	1.1650
USD/GBP	1.2301	1.2305	1.2303

The firm must also buy USD to pay a major supplier. Goldsworthy calls Dealer A with specific details of the transaction and asks to verify the USD/GBP quote. Dealer A calls her back later with a revised USD/GBP bid–offer quote of 1.2299/1.2307.

Goldsworthy must purchase MXN 27,000,000 to pay an invoice at the end of the quarter. In addition to the quotes from Dealer A, Underwood contacts Dealer B, who provides a bid–offer price of GBP/MXN 0.0403/0.0406. To check whether the dealer quotes are reflective of an efficient market, Underwood examines whether the prices allow for an arbitrage profit.

In three months, the firm will receive EUR 5,000,000 from another customer. Six months ago, the firm sold EUR 5,000,000 against the GBP using a nine-month forward contract at an all-in price of GBP/EUR 0.9526. To mark the position to market, Underwood collects the GBP/EUR forward rates in Exhibit 2.

Exhibit 2: GBP/EUR Forward Rates

Maturity	Forward Points
One month	4.40/4.55

Maturity	Forward Points
Three months	14.0/15.0
Six months	29.0/30.0

Goldsworthy also asks for the current 90-day MRRs for the major currencies. Selected three-month MRRs (annualized) are shown in Exhibit 3. Goldsworthy studies Exhibit 3 and says, "We have the spot rate and the 90-day forward rate for GBP/EUR. As long as we have the GBP 90-day MRR, we will be able to calculate the implied EUR 90-day MRR."

Exhibit 3: 90-Day MRR	
Currency	**Annualized Rate**
GBP	0.5800%
JPY	0.0893%
USD	0.3300%

After reading a draft report, Underwood notes, "We do not hedge the incoming Japanese yen cash flow. Your report asks for a forecast of the JPY/GBP exchange rate in 90 days. We know the JPY/GBP spot exchange rate." He asks, "Does the information we have collected tell us what the JPY/GBP exchange rate will be in 90 days?"

Goldsworthy replies, "The JPY/GBP exchange rate in 90 days would be a valuable piece of information to know. An international parity condition can be used to provide an estimate of the future spot rate."

6. Using the quotes in Exhibit 1, the amount received by Goldsworthy from converting JPY 225,000,000 will be *closest* to:

   A. GBP 1,734,906.

   B. GBP 1,735,174.

   C. GBP 1,735,442.

7. Using Exhibit 1, which of the following would be the *best* reason for the revised USD/GBP dealer quote of 1.2299/1.2307?

   A. A request for a much larger transaction

   B. A drop in volatility in the USD/GBP market

   C. A request to trade when both New York and London trading centers are open

8. Using the quotes from Dealer A and B, the triangular arbitrage profit on a transaction of MXN 27,000,000 would be *closest* to:

   A. GBP 0.

   B. GBP 5,400.

   C. GBP 10,800.

9. Based on Exhibits 1, 2, and 3, the mark-to-market gain for Goldsworthy's forward position is *closest* to:

    A. GBP 19,971.

    B. GBP 20,500.

    C. GBP 21,968.

10. Based on Exhibit 2, Underwood should conclude that three-month EUR MRR is:

    A. below three-month GBP MRR.

    B. equal to three-month GBP MRR.

    C. above three-month GBP MRR.

11. Based on the exchange rate midpoint in Exhibit 1 and the rates in Exhibit 3, the 90-day forward premium (discount) for the USD/GBP would be *closest* to:

    A. −0.0040.

    B. −0.0010.

    C. +0.0010.

12. Using Exhibits 1, 2, and 3, which international parity condition would Goldsworthy *most likely* use to calculate the EUR MRR?

    A. Real interest rate parity

    B. Covered interest rate parity

    C. Uncovered interest rate parity

13. The international parity condition Goldsworthy will use to provide the estimate of the future JPY/GBP spot rate is *most likely*:

    A. covered interest rate parity.

    B. uncovered interest rate parity.

    C. relative purchasing power parity.

The following information relates to questions 14-20

Connor Wagener, a student at the University of Canterbury in New Zealand, has been asked to prepare a presentation on foreign exchange rates for his international business course. Wagener has a basic understanding of exchange rates but would like a practitioner's perspective, and he has arranged an interview with currency trader Hannah McFadden. During the interview, Wagener asks McFadden,

Could you explain what drives exchange rates? I'm curious as to why our New Zealand dollar was affected by the European debt crisis in 2011 and what other factors impact it.

In response, McFadden begins with a general discussion of exchange rates. She notes that international parity conditions illustrate how exchange rates are linked to expected inflation, interest rate differences, and forward exchange rates as well as current and expected future spot rates. McFadden makes the following statement:

Statement 1: "Fortunately, the international parity condition most relevant for FX carry trades does not always hold."

McFadden continues her discussion:

FX carry traders go long (i.e., buy) high-yield currencies and fund their position by shorting—that is, borrowing in—low-yield currencies. Unfortunately, crashes in currency values can occur which create financial crises as traders unwind their positions. For example, in 2008, the New Zealand dollar was negatively impacted when highly leveraged carry trades were unwound. In addition to investors, consumers and business owners can also affect currency exchange rates through their impact on their country's balance of payments. For example, if New Zealand consumers purchase more goods from China than New Zealand businesses sell to China, New Zealand will run a trade account deficit with China.

McFadden further explains,

Statement 2:   "A trade surplus will tend to cause the currency of the country in surplus to appreciate, while a deficit will cause currency depreciation. Exchange rate changes will result in immediate adjustments in the prices of traded goods as well as in the demand for imports and exports. These changes will immediately correct the trade imbalance."

McFadden next addresses the influence of monetary and fiscal policy on exchange rates:

Countries also exert significant influence on exchange rates both through the initial mix of their fiscal and monetary policies and by subsequent adjustments to those policies. Various models have been developed to identify how these policies affect exchange rates. The Mundell–Fleming model addresses how changes in both fiscal and monetary policies affect interest rates and ultimately exchange rates in the short term.

McFadden describes monetary models by stating,

Statement 3:   "Monetary models of exchange rate determination focus on the effects of inflation, price level changes, and risk premium adjustments."

McFadden continues her discussion:

So far, we've touched on balance of payments and monetary policy. The portfolio balance model addresses the impacts of sustained fiscal policy on exchange rates. I must take a client call but will return shortly. In the meantime, here is some relevant literature on the models I mentioned along with a couple of questions for you to consider:

Question 1:   Assume an emerging market (EM) country has restrictive monetary and fiscal policies under low capital mobility conditions. Are these policies likely to lead to currency appreciation or currency depreciation or to have no impact?

Question 2:   Assume a developed market (DM) country has an expansive fiscal policy under high capital mobility conditions. Why is its currency most likely to depreciate in the long run under an integrated Mundell–Fleming and portfolio balance approach?

Upon her return, Wagener and McFadden review the questions. McFadden notes that capital flows can have a significant impact on exchange rates and have contributed to currency crises in both EM and DM countries. She explains that central banks, such as the Reserve Bank of New Zealand, use FX market intervention as a tool to manage exchange rates. McFadden states,

Statement 4: "Some studies have found that EM central banks tend to be more effective in using exchange rate intervention than DM central banks, primarily because of one important factor."

McFadden continues her discussion:

Statement 5: "I mentioned that capital inflows could cause a currency crisis, leaving fund managers with significant losses. In the period leading up to a currency crisis, I would predict that an affected country's:

Prediction 1: foreign exchange reserves will increase.

Prediction 2: broad money growth will increase.

Prediction 3: exchange rate will be substantially higher than its mean level during tranquil periods."

After the interview, McFadden agrees to meet the following week to discuss more recent events on the New Zealand dollar.

14. The international parity condition McFadden is referring to in Statement 1 is:

   A. purchasing power parity.

   B. covered interest rate parity.

   C. uncovered interest rate parity.

15. In Statement 2, McFadden is *most likely* failing to consider the:

   A. initial gap between the country's imports and exports.

   B. effect of an initial trade deficit on a country's exchange rates.

   C. lag in the response of import and export demand to price changes.

16. The *least* appropriate factor used to describe the type of models mentioned in Statement 3 is:

   A. inflation.

   B. price level changes.

   C. risk premium adjustments.

17. The best response to Question 1 is that the policies will:

   A. have no impact.

   B. lead to currency appreciation.

   C. lead to currency depreciation.

18. The most likely response to Question 2 is a(n):

   A. increase in the price level.

    B. decrease in risk premiums.

    C. increase in government debt.

19. The factor that McFadden is *most likely* referring to in Statement 4 is:

    A. FX reserve levels.

    B. domestic demand.

    C. the level of capital flows.

20. Which of McFadden's predictions in Statement 5 is *least likely to be correct*?

    A. Prediction 1

    B. Prediction 2

    C. Prediction 3

SOLUTIONS

1. C is correct. The equation to calculate the forward premium (discount) is:

$$F_{f/d} - S_{f/d} = S_{f/d}\left(\frac{\left[\frac{Actual}{360}\right]}{1 + i_d\left[\frac{Actual}{360}\right]}\right)(i_f - i_d).$$

$S_{f/d}$ is the spot rate with GBP the base currency or d and INR the foreign currency or f. $S_{f/d}$ per Exhibit 1 is 79.5093, i_f is equal to 7.52%, and i_d is equal to 5.43%. With GBP as the base currency (i.e., the "domestic" currency) in the INR/GBP quote, substituting in the relevant base currency values from Exhibit 1 yields the following:

$$F_{f/d} - S_{f/d} = 79.5093\left(\frac{\left[\frac{360}{360}\right]}{1 + 0.0543\left[\frac{360}{360}\right]}\right)(0.0752 - 0.0543).$$

$$F_{f/d} - S_{f/d} = 79.5093\left(\frac{1}{1.0543}\right)(0.0752 - 0.0543).$$

$$F_{f/d} - S_{f/d} = 1.576.$$

2. B is correct. The dealer is posting a bid rate to buy BRL at a price that is too high. This overpricing is determined by calculating the interbank implied cross rate for the CHF/BRL using the intuitive equation-based approach:

   CHF/BRL = CHF/USD × (BRL/USD)⁻¹, or

   CHF/BRL = CHF/USD × USD/BRL.

   Inverting the BRL/USD given the quotes in Exhibit 2 determines the USD/BRL bid–offer rates of 0.23980/0.23982. (The bid of 0.23980 is the inverse of the BRL/USD offer, calculated as 1/4.1702; the offer of 0.23982 is the inverse of the BRL/USD bid, calculated as 1/4.1698.) Multiplying the CHF/USD and USD/BRL bid–offer rates then leads to the interbank implied CHF/BRL cross rate:

   Bid: 0.9799 × 0.23980 = 0.2349.

   Offer: 0.9801 × 0.23982 = 0.23505.

   Since the dealer is willing to buy BRL at 0.2355 but BRL can be purchased from the interbank market at 0.23505, there is an arbitrage opportunity to buy BRL in the interbank market and sell BRL to the dealer for a profit of 0.0045 CHF (0.2355 − 0.23505) per BRL transacted.

3. A is correct. The carry trade involves borrowing in a lower-yielding currency to invest in a higher-yielding one and netting any profit after allowing for borrowing costs and exchange rate movements. The relevant trade is to borrow USD and lend in EUR. To calculate the all-in USD return from a one-year EUR MRR deposit, first determine the current and one-year-later USD/EUR exchange rates. Because one USD buys CAD 1.3200 today and one CAD buys EUR 0.6506 today, today's EUR/USD rate is the product of these two numbers: 1.3200 × 0.6506 = 0.8588. The projected rate one year later is 1.3151 × 0.6567 = 0.8636. Accordingly, measured in dollars, the investment return for the unhedged EUR MRR deposit is equal to

$(1.3200 \times 0.6506) \times (1 + 0.022) \times [1/(1.3151 \times 0.6567)] - 1$
$= 0.8588 \times (1.022)(1/0.8636) - 1 = 1.01632 - 1$

$= 1.632\%.$

However, the borrowing costs must be charged against this *gross* return to fund the carry trade investment (one-year USD MRR was 0.80%). The *net* return on the carry trade is therefore 1.632% − 0.80% = 0.832%.

4. B is correct. While credit ratings can affect spreads, the trade involves spot settlement (i.e., two business days after the trade date), so the spread quoted to this highly rated (AA) firm is not likely to be much tighter than the spread that would be quoted to a somewhat lower-rated (but still high-quality) firm. The relationship between the bank and the client, the size of the trade, the time of day the trade is initiated, the currencies involved, and the level of market volatility are likely to be more significant factors in determining the spread for this trade.

5. B is correct. By rearranging the terms of the equation defining covered interest rate parity and assuming that uncovered interest rate parity is in effect, the forward exchange rate is equal to the expected future spot exchange rate—$F_{f/d} = S^e_{f/d}$—with the expected percentage change in the spot rate equal to the interest rate differential. Thus, the forward exchange rate is an unbiased forecast of the future spot exchange rate.

6. A is correct. Goldsworthy has been given a bid–offer spread. Because she is buying the base currency—in this case, GBP—she must pay the offer price of JPY 129.69 per GBP.

$$\frac{\text{JPY } 225,000,000}{129.69 \text{ JPY/GBP}} = \text{GBP } 1,734,906.$$

7. A is correct. Posted quotes are typically for transactions in 1 million units of the base currency. Larger transactions may be harder for the dealer to sell in the interbank market and would likely require the dealer to quote a wider spread (lower bid price and higher offer price).

8. A is correct. Using quotes from Dealer A, she can find

$$\frac{\text{MXN}}{\text{GBP}} = \frac{\text{MXN}}{\text{USD}} \times \frac{\text{USD}}{\text{GBP}}.$$

The bid from Dealer A for MXN/GBP is effectively

$$\left(\frac{\text{MXN}}{\text{GBP}}\right)_{bid} = \left(\frac{\text{MXN}}{\text{USD}}\right)_{bid} \times \left(\frac{\text{USD}}{\text{GBP}}\right)_{bid}$$
$$= 20.140 \times 1.2301 = 24.7742.$$

The offer from Dealer A is

$$\left(\frac{\text{MXN}}{\text{GBP}}\right)_{offer} = \left(\frac{\text{MXN}}{\text{USD}}\right)_{offer} \times \left(\frac{\text{USD}}{\text{GBP}}\right)_{offer}$$
$$= 20.160 \times 1.2305 = 24.8069.$$

To compare with Dealer B's quote, she must take the inverse of MXN/GBP, so she has an offer to sell MXN at a rate of 1/24.7742 = GBP 0.0404 and a bid to purchase MXN at a rate of 1/24.8069 = GBP 0.0403. Dealer A is effectively quoting MXN/GBP at 0.0403/0.0404. Although she can effectively buy MXN more cheaply from Dealer A (GBP 0.0404 from Dealer A, versus GBP 0.0406 from Dealer B), she cannot resell them to Dealer B for a higher price than GBP 0.0403. There is no profit from triangular arbitrage.

9. A is correct. Marking her nine-month contract to market six months later requires buying GBP/EUR three months forward. The GBP/EUR spot rate

is 0.9467/0.9471, and the three-month forward points are 14.0/15.0. The three-month forward rate to use is 0.9471 + (15/10000) = 0.9486. Goldsworthy sold EUR 5,000,000 at 0.9526 and bought at 0.9486. The net cash flow at the settlement date will equal EUR 5,000,000 × (0.9526 − 0.9486) GBP/EUR = GBP 20,000. This cash flow will occur in three months, so we discount at the three-month GBP MRR of 58 bps:

$$\frac{GBP\ 20{,}000}{1 + 0.0058\left(\frac{90}{360}\right)} = GBP\ 19{,}971.04.$$

10. A is correct. The positive forward points for the GBP/EUR pair shown in Exhibit 2 indicate that the EUR trades at a forward premium at all maturities, including three months. Covered interest rate parity,

$$F_{f/d} = S_{f/d}\left(\frac{1 + i_f\left[\frac{Actual}{360}\right]}{1 + i_d\left[\frac{Actual}{360}\right]}\right),$$

suggests a forward rate greater than the spot rate requires a non-domestic risk-free rate (in this case, the GBP MRR) greater than the domestic risk-free rate (EUR MRR). When covered interest rate parity is violated, traders can step in and conduct arbitrage.

11. B is correct. Using covered interest rate parity, the forward rate is

$$F_{f/d} = S_{f/d}\left(\frac{1 + i_f\left[\frac{Actual}{360}\right]}{1 + i_d\left[\frac{Actual}{360}\right]}\right)$$

$$= 1.2303\left(\frac{1 + 0.0033\left[\frac{90}{360}\right]}{1 + 0.0058\left[\frac{90}{360}\right]}\right) = 1.2295.$$

Because the domestic MRR is higher than the non-domestic MRR, the forward rate will be less than the spot rate, giving a forward discount of

$$F_{f/d} - S_{f/d} = 1.2295 - 1.2303 = -0.0008.$$

12. B is correct. The covered interest rate parity condition,

$$F_{f/d} = S_{f/d}\left(\frac{1 + i_f\left[\frac{Actual}{360}\right]}{1 + i_d\left[\frac{Actual}{360}\right]}\right), \text{(Equation 1)}$$

specifies the forward exchange rate that must hold to prevent arbitrage given the spot exchange rate and the risk-free rates in both countries. If the forward and spot exchange rates, as well as one of the risk-free rates, are known, the other risk-free rate can be calculated.

13. B is correct. According to uncovered interest rate parity,

$$\%\Delta S^e_{f/d} = i_f - i_d, \text{(Equation 2)}$$

the expected change in the spot exchange rate should reflect the interest rate spread between the two countries, which can be found in Exhibit 3. Given the spot exchange rate (from Exhibit 1) and the expected future change, she should be able to estimate the future spot exchange rate.

14. C is correct. The carry trade strategy is dependent on the fact that uncovered interest rate parity does not hold in the short or medium term. If uncovered interest rate parity held, it would mean that investors would receive identical returns from either an unhedged foreign currency investment or a domestic currency

investment because the appreciation/depreciation of the exchange rate would offset the yield differential. However, during periods of low volatility, evidence shows that high-yield currencies do not depreciate enough and low-yield currencies do not appreciate enough to offset the yield differential.

15. C is correct. McFadden states that exchange rates will *immediately* correct the trade imbalance. She is describing the flow supply/demand channel, which assumes that trade imbalances will be corrected as the deficit country's currency depreciates, causing its exports to become more competitive and its imports to become more expensive. Studies indicate that there can be long lags between exchange rate changes, changes in the prices of traded goods, and changes in the trade balance. In the short run, exchange rates tend to be more responsive to investment and financing decisions.

16. C is correct. Risk premiums are more closely associated with the portfolio balance approach. The portfolio balance approach addresses the impact of a country's net foreign asset/liability position. Under the portfolio balance approach, investors are assumed to hold a diversified portfolio of assets including foreign and domestic bonds. Investors will hold a country's bonds as long as they are compensated appropriately. Compensation may come in the form of higher interest rates and/or higher risk premiums.

17. B is correct. The currency is likely to appreciate. The emerging market country has both a restrictive monetary policy and a restrictive fiscal policy under conditions of low capital mobility. Low capital mobility indicates that interest rate changes induced by monetary and fiscal policy will not cause large changes in capital flows. Implementation of restrictive policies should result in an improvement in the trade balance, which will result in currency appreciation.

18. C is correct. Expansionary fiscal policies result in currency depreciation in the long run. Under a portfolio balance approach, the assumption is that investors hold a mix of domestic and foreign assets including bonds. Fiscal stimulus policies result in budget deficits, which are often financed by debt. As the debt level rises, investors become concerned as to how the ongoing deficit will be financed. The country's central bank may need to create more money in order to purchase the debt, which would cause the currency to depreciate. Or the government could adopt a more restrictive fiscal policy, which would also depreciate the currency.

19. A is correct. EM countries are better able to influence their exchange rates because their reserve levels as a ratio of average daily FX turnover are generally much greater than those of DM countries. This means that EM central banks are in a better position to affect currency supply and demand than DM countries, where the ratio is negligible. EM policymakers use their foreign exchange reserves as a kind of insurance to defend their currencies, as needed.

20. A is correct. Prediction 1 is least likely to be correct. Foreign exchange reserves tend to decline precipitously, not increase, as a currency crisis approaches. Broad money growth tends to rise in the period leading up to a currency crisis, and the exchange rate is substantially higher than its mean level during tranquil periods.

Economic Growth

by Paul R. Kutasovic, PhD, CFA.

Paul R. Kutasovic, PhD, CFA, is at New York Institute of Technology (USA).

LEARNING OUTCOMES

Mastery	The candidate should be able to:
☐	compare factors favoring and limiting economic growth in developed and developing economies
☐	describe the relation between the long-run rate of stock market appreciation and the sustainable growth rate of the economy
☐	explain why potential GDP and its growth rate matter for equity and fixed income investors
☐	contrast capital deepening investment and technological progress and explain how each affects economic growth and labor productivity
☐	demonstrate forecasting potential GDP based on growth accounting relations
☐	explain how natural resources affect economic growth and evaluate the argument that limited availability of natural resources constrains economic growth
☐	explain how demographics, immigration, and labor force participation affect the rate and sustainability of economic growth
☐	explain how investment in physical capital, human capital, and technological development affects economic growth
☐	compare classical growth theory, neoclassical growth theory, and endogenous growth theory
☐	explain and evaluate convergence hypotheses
☐	describe the economic rationale for governments to provide incentives to private investment in technology and knowledge
☐	describe the expected impact of removing trade barriers on capital investment and profits, employment and wages, and growth in the economies involved

AN INTRODUCTION TO GROWTH IN THE GLOBAL ECONOMY

Forecasts of long-run economic growth are important for global investors. Equity prices reflect expectations of the future stream of earnings, which depend on expectations of future economic activity. This dynamic means that in the long term, the same factors that drive economic growth will be reflected in equity values. Similarly, the expected long-run growth rate of real income is a key determinant of the average real interest rate level in the economy, and therefore the level of real returns in general. In the shorter term, the relationship between actual and potential growth (i.e., the degree of slack in the economy) is a key driver of fixed-income returns. Therefore, in order to develop global portfolio strategies and investment return expectations, investors must be able to identify and forecast the factors that drive long-term sustainable growth trends. Based on a country's long-term economic outlook, investors can then evaluate the long-term investment potential and risk of investing in the securities of companies located or operating in that country.

In contrast to the short-run fluctuations of the business cycle, the study of economic growth focuses on the long-run trend in aggregate output as measured by potential GDP. Over long periods, the actual growth rate of GDP should equal the rate of increase in potential GDP because, by definition, output in excess of potential GDP requires employing labor and capital beyond their optimum levels. Thus, the growth rate of potential GDP acts as an upper limit to growth and determines the economy's sustainable rate of growth. Increasing the growth rate of potential GDP is the key to raising the level of income, the level of profits, and the living standard of the population. Even small differences in the growth rate translate into large differences in the level of income over time.

What drives long-run growth? What distinguishes the "winners" from the "losers" in the long-run growth arena? Will poor countries catch up with rich countries over time? Can policies have a permanent effect on the sustainable growth rate? If so, how? If not, why not? These and other key questions are addressed in detail in this reading.

We first examine the long-term growth record, focusing on the extent of growth variation across countries and across decades. We then discuss the importance of economic growth to global investors and examine the relationship between investment returns and economic growth. We next turn to the factors that determine long-run economic growth before presenting the classical, neoclassical, and endogenous growth models. We also discuss whether poorer countries are converging to the higher income levels of the richer countries. Finally, we look at the impact of international trade on economic growth.

Growth in the Global Economy: Developed vs. Developing Economies

The first step in our study of long-term growth is to compare the economic performance of countries. GDP and per capita GDP are the best indicators economists have for measuring a country's standard of living and its level of economic development. Economic growth is calculated as the annual percentage change in real GDP or in real per capita GDP. Growth in real GDP measures how rapidly the total economy is expanding. Real per capita GDP reflects the average standard of living in each country—essentially the average level of material well-being. Growth in real GDP per capita (i.e., real GDP growing faster than the population) implies a rising standard of living.

Exhibit 1 presents data on the level of per capita GDP and the growth rate of GDP for a selection of economies. Because each economy reports its data in its own currency, each one's data must be converted into a common currency, usually the US dollar. One can convert the GDP data into dollars using either current market exchange rates or the exchange rates implied by **purchasing power parity (PPP)**. Purchasing power parity is the idea that exchange rates move to equalize the purchasing power of different currencies. At the exchange rates implied by PPP, the cost of a typical basket of goods and services is the same across all economies. In other words, exchange rates should be at a level where you can buy the same goods and services with the equivalent amount of any economy's currency.

Exhibit 1: Divergent Real GDP Growth among Selected Economies and Real GDP per Capita, in US$

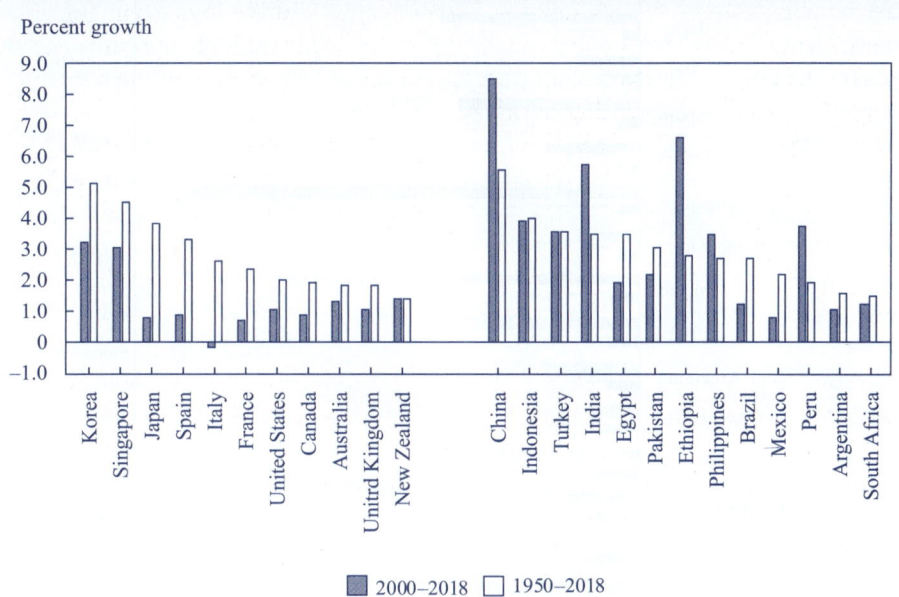

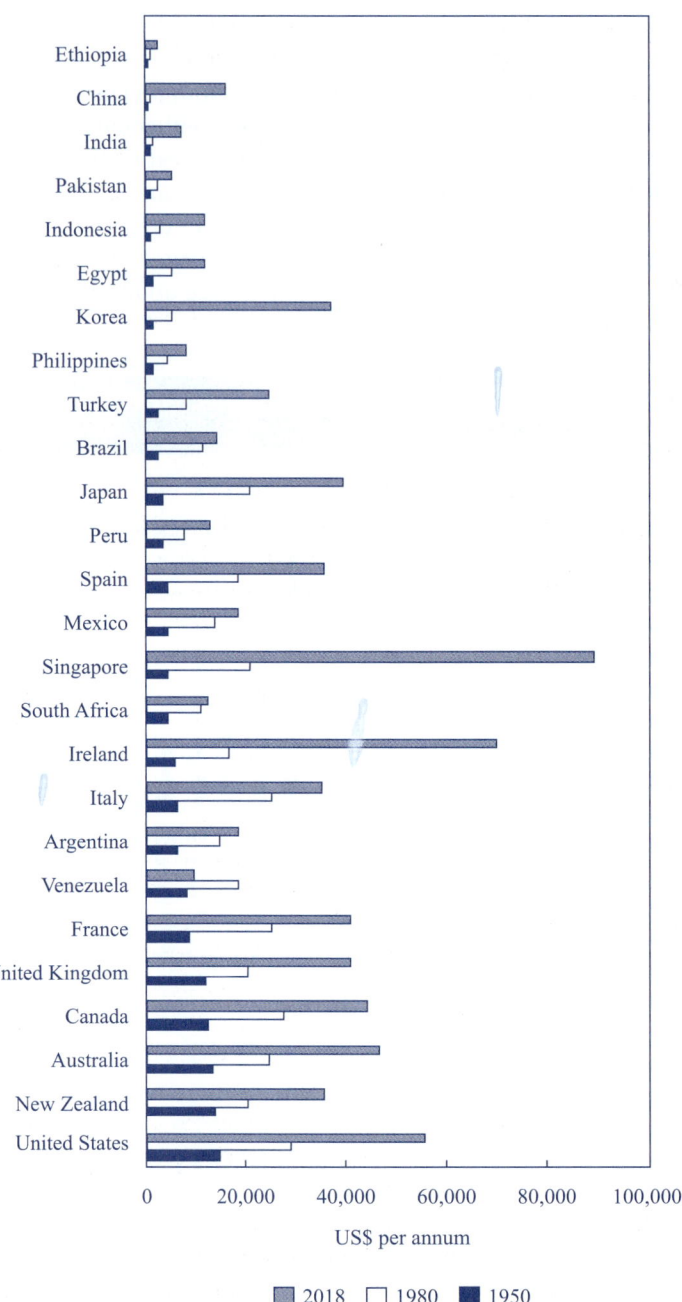

US$ per annum

■ 2018   □ 1980   ■ 1950

Note: The measure of GDP per capita is in constant US dollar market prices for 2011 and adjusted for cross-economy differences in the relative prices of goods and services using PPP.
Sources: International Monetary Fund, World Economic Outlook database for growth rates, and Conference Board, Total Economy Database (September 2019).

In general, the simple method of taking a country's GDP measured in its own currency and then multiplying by the current exchange rate to express it in another currency is not appropriate. Using market exchange rates has two problems. First, market exchange rates are very volatile. Changes in the exchange rate could result in large swings in measured GDP even if there is little or no growth in the country's economy. Second, market exchange rates are determined by financial flows and flows in tradable goods and services. This dynamic ignores the fact that much of global consumption is for non-tradable goods and services. Prices of non-traded goods and services differ by country. In particular, non-traded goods are generally less expensive in developing countries than in developed countries. For example, because labor is cheaper in Mexico City than in London, the prices of labor-intensive products, such as haircuts or taxi rides, are lower in Mexico City than in London. Failing to account for differences in the prices of non-traded goods and services across countries tends to understate the standard of living of consumers in developing countries. To compare standards of living across time or across countries, we need to use a common set of prices among a wide range of goods and services. Thus, cross-country comparisons of GDP should be based on purchasing power parity rather than current market exchange rates.

The economies in Exhibit 1 are divided into two categories: developed (or advanced) economies and developing economies. Developed economies tend to be those with high per capita GDP. There are no universally agreed-upon criteria, however, for classifying economies as advanced or developing. The International Monetary Fund (IMF) classifies 39 economies as advanced and 155 as developing. It says that "this classification is not based on strict criteria, economic or otherwise, and has evolved over time" (IMF 2019). Developed countries include the United States, Canada, Australia, Japan, and major economies in Europe. Growth in the large, developed economies generally slowed over the last few decades, with US growth exceeding that of Europe and Japan. Also included in this group are countries such as Singapore, Ireland, and Spain, which were poor in the 1950s but now have relatively high per capita real GDPs because of high growth rates over the past 50 years.

The second group of countries is the developing countries of Africa, Asia, and Latin America. Per capita GDP in these countries is lower than in the advanced countries, but GDP is generally growing faster than in the developed countries. Although the growth rates of the developing countries exceed those of the advanced countries, there is significant variation in economic performance among the developing countries. China and India have been growing at a rapid rate. Meanwhile, growth in Latin America, Africa, and the Middle East has lagged behind Asia.

What explains the diverse experiences among the developing countries and between the developed and developing ones? Singapore, for example, had less than half the per capita GDP of the United States in 1970 but now has per capita GDP that exceeds that of the United States. In contrast, such countries as Ethiopia and Kenya have remained poor, with little growth in per capita GDP. The literature on economic growth focuses primarily on the role of capital and labor resources and the use of technology as sources of growth. In addition to these purely economic drivers, developed and developing countries differ with respect to the presence or absence of appropriate institutions that support growth. These institutions enable developing countries to raise their standards of living and eventually move into the ranks of the developed countries. We now examine some of the key institutions and requirements for growth.

FACTORS FAVORING AND LIMITING ECONOMIC GROWTH

2

☐ | compare factors favoring and limiting economic growth in developed and developing economies

One of the major problems for some of the developing countries is a low level of capital per worker. Countries accumulate capital through private and public sector (e.g., infrastructure) investment. But increasing the investment rate may be difficult in developing countries because low levels of disposable income can make it difficult to generate significant saving. The low saving rate contributes to a vicious cycle of poverty: Low savings lead to low levels of investment, which leads to slow GDP growth, which implies persistently low income and savings. Therefore, it is very difficult to design policies to increase domestic saving and investment rates in developing countries. The good news is that the savings of domestic residents are not the only source of investment funds. A developing country can break out of the cycle of low savings by attracting foreign investment.

Financial Markets and Intermediaries

In addition to the saving rate, growth depends on how efficiently saving is allocated within the economy. A role of the financial sector in any economy is to channel funds from savers to investment projects. Financial markets and intermediaries, such as banks, can promote growth in at least three ways.

- By screening those who seek funding and monitoring those who obtain funding, the financial sector channels financial capital (savings) to projects that are likely to generate the highest risk-adjusted returns.

- The financial sector may encourage savings and assumption of risk by creating attractive investment instruments that facilitate risk transfer and diversification and enhance liquidity.

- The existence of well-developed financial markets and intermediaries can mitigate the credit constraints that companies might otherwise face in financing capital investments. For example, banks can aggregate small amounts of savings into a larger pool enabling them to finance larger projects that can exploit economies of scale.

Evidence suggests that countries with better-functioning financial markets and intermediaries grow at a faster rate (Levine, 2005). Not all financial sector developments promote economic growth, however. Financial sector intermediation that results in declining credit standards and/or increasing leverage will increase risk and not necessarily increase long-run growth.

Political Stability, Rule of Law, and Property Rights

Stable and effective government, a well-developed legal and regulatory system, and respect for property rights are key ingredients for economic growth. Property rights are the legal arrangements that govern the protection of private property, including intellectual property. Clearly established property rights create the incentive for domestic households and companies to invest and save. A legal system—substantive and procedural laws—is needed to establish and protect these rights. Substantive law focuses on the rights and responsibilities of entities and relationships among entities, and procedural law focuses on the protection and enforcement of the substantive laws. In developed countries these rights and arrangements are well established, but they may be lacking or ineffective in developing countries.

In addition, economic uncertainty increases when wars, military coups, corruption, and other sources of political instability are widespread. These factors raise investment risk, discourage foreign investment, and weaken growth. In many developing countries, especially those in Africa, the first priority in trying to enhance growth is to enact a legal system that establishes, protects, and enforces property rights.

Education and Health Care Systems

Inadequate education at all levels is a major impediment to growth for many developing countries. Many workers are illiterate, and few workers have the skills needed to use the latest technology. At the same time, many developing countries also suffer from a "brain drain," in which the most highly educated individuals leave the developing country for more-advanced countries. Basic education raises the skill level of the workforce and thus contributes to the country's potential for growth. In addition, because physical capital and human capital are often complementary, education can raise growth by increasing the productivity of existing physical capital. Thus, improving education, through both formal schooling and on-the-job training, is an important component of a sustainable growth strategy for a developing country. China and India are investing large amounts in education and have successfully graduated large numbers of students majoring in engineering and technology-related areas of study. This effort is significantly improving the quality of their workforces.

Empirical studies show that the allocation of education spending among different types and levels (primary, secondary, and post-secondary) of education is a key determinant of growth, especially in comparing growth in developed countries with growth in developing ones. The impact of education spending depends on whether the country is on the leading edge of technology and fostering innovation or simply relying on imitation as a source of growth. Typically, developed countries, such as the United States, Japan, and western European nations, are on the leading edge of technology and need to invest in post-secondary education to encourage innovation and growth. For these countries, incremental spending on primary and secondary education will have a relatively small impact on growth. In contrast, the developing countries, which largely apply technology developed elsewhere, should emphasize primary and secondary education. Such spending will improve growth by improving the countries' ability to absorb new technologies and to organize existing tasks more efficiently.

Poor health is another obstacle to growth in the developing countries. Life expectancy rates are substantially lower in many developing countries than in developed ones. In Africa, tropical diseases are rampant and AIDS has had a devastating impact. The GDP growth rate in Botswana, a huge success story in the 1970s and 1980s, slowed dramatically during the following two decades as a result, at least in part, of the AIDS epidemic.

Tax and Regulatory Systems

Tax and regulatory policies have an important impact on growth and productivity, especially at the company level. Analysis suggests that limited regulations encourage entrepreneurial activity and the entry of new companies. There is also a strong positive correlation between the entry of new companies and average productivity levels. Studies by the Organisation for Economic Co-Operation and Development (OECD) indicate that low administrative startup cost is a key factor encouraging entrepreneurship (OECD 2003).

Free Trade and Unrestricted Capital Flows

Opening an economy to capital and trade flows has a major impact on economic growth. In an open economy, world savings can finance domestic investment. As a potential source of funds, foreign investment can break the vicious cycle of low income, low domestic savings, and low investment. Foreign investment can occur in two ways:

- Foreign companies can invest directly in a domestic economy (so-called foreign direct investment, or FDI) by building or buying property, plant, and equipment.

- Foreign companies and individuals can invest indirectly in a domestic economy by purchasing securities (equity and fixed income) issued by domestic companies.

Both of these forms of foreign investment will potentially increase the developing economy's physical capital stock, leading to higher productivity, employment, and wages, and perhaps even increased domestic savings. This suggests that developing countries would benefit from policies that encourage investment from abroad, such as eliminating high tariffs on imports (especially capital goods) and removing restrictions on foreign direct and indirect investments.

Brazil and India are examples of developing countries that have benefited from foreign investment. Foreign companies directly invested $48.5 billion in Brazil in 2010, an important source of investment spending for the Brazilian economy (see Exhibit 19). Foreign direct investment also provides developing countries with access to advanced technology developed and used in the advanced countries. In 1999, India enacted new regulations that liberalized direct and indirect foreign investments in Indian companies. Foreign institutional and venture capital investors were given greater flexibility to invest directly in Indian entities as well as in the Indian capital markets. These changes also made it easier for foreign companies to invest in plant and equipment. These developments contributed to the acceleration in India's economic growth over the last decade (see Exhibit 1).

Capital flows are just one way that the international economy affects economic growth. The other is through trade in goods and services. In general, free trade benefits an economy by providing its residents with more goods at lower costs. With free trade, domestic companies face increased competition, which limits their price discretion, but they also obtain access to larger markets. The evidence of the benefits of open markets is discussed later in the reading.

Summary of Factors Limiting Growth in Developing Countries

Developing countries differ significantly from developed countries in terms of their institutional structure and their legal and political environments. Lack of appropriate institutions and poor legal and political environments restrain growth in the developing economies and partially explain why these countries are poor and experience slow growth. Factors limiting growth include the following:

- Low rates of saving and investment
- Poorly developed financial markets
- Weak, or even corrupt, legal systems and failure to enforce laws
- Lack of property rights and political instability
- Poor public education and health services
- Tax and regulatory policies discouraging entrepreneurship
- Restrictions on international trade and flows of capital

Although these factors are not necessarily absent in developed countries, they tend to be more prevalent in developing countries. Policies that correct these issues, or mitigate their impact, enhance the potential for growth. In addition to these institutional restraints, as we will see later, growth in developing countries may be limited by a lack of physical, human, and public capital, as well as little or no innovation.

EXAMPLE 1

Why Growth Rates Matter

In 1950, Argentina and Venezuela were relatively wealthy countries with per capita GDP levels of $6,164 and $8,104, respectively. Per capita GDPs in these Latin American countries were well above those of Japan, South Korea, and Singapore, which had per capita GDPs of $3,048, $1,185, and $4,299, respectively. By 2018, however, a dramatic change occurred in the relative GDPs per capita of these countries.

Real GDP Per Capita in US Dollars					
	Venezuela	Argentina	Singapore	Japan	South Korea
1950	$8,104	$6,164	$4,299	$3,048	$1,185
2018	$9,487	$18,255	$66,189	$39,313	$36,756

1. Calculate the annual growth rate in per capita GDP for each of the five countries over the period 1950–2018.

   Solution

   The annual growth rates for the five countries are calculated as follows:

Argentina	$[(\$18{,}255/\$6{,}164)^{1/68}] - 1 = 1.6\%$
Venezuela	$[(\$9{,}487/\$8{,}104)^{1/68}] - 1 = 0.2\%$
Japan	$[(\$39{,}313/\$3{,}048)^{1/68}] - 1 = 3.8\%$
Singapore	$[(\$66{,}189/\$4{,}299)^{1/68}] - 1 = 4.6\%$
South Korea	$[(\$36{,}756/\$1{,}185)^{1/68}] - 1 = 5.2\%$

2. Explain the implication of the growth rates for these countries.

   Solution

   Differences in GDP growth rates sustained over a number of decades will significantly alter the relative incomes of countries. Nations that experience sustained periods of high growth will eventually become high-income countries and move up the income ladder. In contrast, countries with slow growth will experience relative declines in living standards. This dynamic is well illustrated in this example by a historical comparison of growth in Argentina and Venezuela with Japan, Singapore, and South Korea. In 1950, Argentina and Venezuela were relatively wealthy countries with per capita GDP levels well above those of Japan, South Korea, and Singapore. Over the next 60 years, however, the rate of growth in per capita GDP was significantly slower in Venezuela and Argentina in comparison to the three Asian countries. This disparity resulted in a dramatic change in these countries' relative incomes. The per capita GDP of the three Asian countries rose sharply as each joined the ranks of developed countries. In contrast, Argentina and Venezuela stagnated and moved from the ranks of developed countries to developing country status. By 2018, per capita income in Singapore was more than seven times higher than in Venezuela.

Over the long run, the economic growth rate is an extremely important variable. Even small differences in growth rates matter because of the power of compounding. Thus, policy actions that affect the long-term growth rate even by a small amount will have a major economic impact.

3. Suppose that GDP per capita in Argentina had grown at the same rate as in Japan from 1950 to 2018. How much larger would real per capita GDP have been in Argentina in 2018?

Solution:

Assuming Argentina had grown at the same rate as Japan since 1950, its GDP per capita in 2018 would have been $(\$6,164)(1+0.038)^{68} = (\$6,164)$ $(12.63) = \$77,854$, versus \$18,255 from Exhibit 1.

If Argentina had grown at the same rate as Japan, it would have had one of the highest standards of living in the world in 2018. The question is why the growth rates in Argentina and Venezuela diverged so much from the three Asian countries.

4. Venezuela plans to stimulate growth in its economy by substantially increasing spending on infrastructure, education, and health care. Nevertheless, foreign investment is discouraged, and reforms such as strengthening the legal system and encouraging private ownership have been largely ignored. Explain whether the measures described here could lead to faster economic growth.

Solution

The preconditions for economic growth are well-functioning financial markets, clearly defined property rights and rule of law, open international trade and flows of capital, an educated and healthy population, and tax and regulatory policies that encourage entrepreneurship. Investment in infrastructure would increase Venezuela's stock of physical capital, which would raise labor productivity and growth. Better education and health care would increase human capital and also increase productivity and growth. These measures would raise Venezuela's growth prospects. Missing, however, are a legal system that could better enforce property rights, openness to international trade and foreign investment, and well-functioning capital markets. Without changes in these preconditions, a significant improvement in Venezuela's growth is unlikely to occur. The following table summarizes these preconditions:

Preconditions for Growth	Impact of Planned Policy Action in Venezuela
Saving and investment	Improve growth potential
Developed financial markets	No impact
Legal systems	No impact
Property rights and political stability	No impact
Education and health	Improve growth potential
Tax and regulatory polices discouraging entrepreneurship	No impact

Preconditions for Growth	Impact of Planned Policy Action in Venezuela
Restrictions on international trade and flows of capital	No impact

It should be noted that the global economy is evolving rapidly and past trends may or may not be sustained. Nonetheless, in order to provide concrete answers that do not require the reader to bring in additional information, our exercise solutions must assume past patterns are indicative of the future.

WHY POTENTIAL GROWTH MATTERS TO INVESTORS

3

- ☐ describe the relation between the long-run rate of stock market appreciation and the sustainable growth rate of the economy
- ☐ explain why potential GDP and its growth rate matter for equity and fixed income investors

The valuations of both equity and fixed-income securities are closely related to the growth rate of economic activity. Anticipated growth in aggregate earnings is a fundamental driver of the equity market. Growth in an economy's productive capacity, measured by **potential GDP**, places a limit on how fast the economy can grow. The idea is that potential GDP is the maximum amount of output an economy can sustainably produce without inducing an increase in the inflation rate. A key question for equity investors, therefore, is whether earnings growth is also bounded or limited by the growth rate of potential GDP.

For earnings growth to exceed GDP growth, the ratio of corporate profits to GDP must trend upward over time. It should be clear that the share of profits in GDP cannot rise forever. At some point, stagnant labor income would make workers unwilling to work and would also undermine demand, making further profit growth unsustainable. Thus, in the long run, real earnings growth cannot exceed the growth rate of potential GDP.

The relationship between economic growth and the return on equities is not straightforward. One way to capture the relationship of equity returns and economic growth is to use the Grinold-Kroner (2002) decomposition of the return to equity.

$E(R_e)$ = dividend yield + expected capital gain

= dividend yield + expected repricing + earnings growth per share

= *dividend yield + expected repricing*

+ inflation rate + real economic growth + change in shares outstanding

$= dy + \Delta(P/E) + i + g + \Delta S$

Over time, the dividend yield, dy, has been found to be fairly stable and a significant contributor to equity market returns. The expected repricing term, $\Delta(P/E)$, relates to changes to the P/E ratios in the market. There is some evidence that with increasing GDP growth rates, P/E ratios trend higher as investors perceive the country and its economy to be less risky and are willing to pay a higher price for earnings. However, the primary impact of this repricing term is the volatility in the market's P/E ratio over market cycles.

Earnings growth per share is the primary channel through which economic growth can impact equity returns. Earnings growth per share can be expressed as a function of inflation, real economic growth, and change in the number of shares traded in the market.

When the number of shares outstanding in a market is constant, real economic growth translates into higher expected returns on equity. The empirical evidence on the existence of a direct relationship between economic growth and equity returns is conflicting and suggests that the change in shares outstanding, ΔS, termed the dilution effect, plays an important role in determining expected equity returns. These dilution effects vary significantly across countries for a variety of reasons, including the level of development of the economy and the sophistication of the financial markets.

This wedge between economic growth and equity returns arises for at least two reasons. The first reason is that publicly traded companies either buy back their shares and increase equity returns by decreasing shares outstanding, or issue new shares and dilute existing shareholder returns. Net buybacks, or *nbb*, captures the net result of buybacks and new equity issuance at the national stock market level. The second effect is due to some part of economic growth coming from small- and medium-sized entrepreneurial firms that are not traded publicly on the stock market. The greater this effect, termed the relative dynamism of the economy, *rd*, the greater the divergence between economic growth in the economy as a whole and the earnings growth of companies listed on the stock market. Expanding the ΔS dilution effect term to focus on both components:

$$\Delta S = nbb + rd$$

Exhibit 2 illustrates the divergence possible between real economic growth and equity returns across a variety of markets, highlighting the differences in *nbb* and *rd* that are observed across markets.

Exhibit 2: Indexes with Significant Dilution Effects, 1997–2017

Country	Real Return in Local Currency, *r*	Real per Capita GDP Growth, *g*	Net Buybacks, *nbb*	Relative Dynamism, *rd*	Comments
Chile	4.8	2.9	1.1	0.0	Privatization of Telefoncia Chile with reduction in number of companies in index from 32 (1997) to 19 (2017).
China	0.7	8.2	−26.5	14.9	Privatization of large state-owned enterprises. Change in number of companies in index from 28 (1997) to 152 (2017).

Country	Real Return in Local Currency, r	Real per Capita GDP Growth, g	Net Buybacks, nbb	Relative Dynamism, rd	Comments
Czech Repub.	6.3	2.2	6.0	−11.7	Reduction in number of companies in index from 19 (1997) to 4 (2017). Loss of 38% of initial market cap.
Egypt	9.4	2.3	5.5	−3.9	Delistings. Reduction in number of companies in index from 13 (1997) to 3 (2017).
Greece	−8.7	0.5	−12.7	0.2	Privatizations, reclassification to emerging market, and bank recapitalizations.
Ireland	−0.8	3.8	−7.6	−1.9	Privatization of telecom operator Elrcom, secondary equity offerings in 1996−1997
Poland	1.9	3.9	−11.9	7.1	Privatizations in 1997−1998 of state-owned commodity firm and state-owned bank.
United States	6.1	1.4	−1.8	2.4	For comparison purposes.

Note: All percent figures expressed in log form.
Source: Table derived from data presented in L'Her, Masmoudi, and Krishnamoorthy, "Net Buybacks and the Seven Dwarfs," *Financial Analysts Journal* 74, no. 4 (2018).

Exhibit 2 illustrates the complexity in the relationship between economic growth and equity returns. China has the highest real economic growth rate over the period (8.2% annual) but a relatively low real return to equity (0.7%), because of significant dilution effects arising from the privatization of large state-owned enterprises. In contrast, Egypt experienced much lower economic growth (2.3%) but had a much higher real return to equity (9.4%), primarily because of a reduction of listed companies in the market index. Exhibit 2 illustrates how diverse the experience with net buybacks and relative dynamism is across countries and serves as evidence that this dispersion weakens the observed relationship between economic growth and equity returns.

The relationship between economic growth and returns to equity is thus a complex question. All else equal, higher economic growth should be associated with higher equity returns. It is clear, however, that all else is seldom equal and that equity returns are significantly influenced by dilution—coming from the need to raise new capital to support growth, changes in equity market composition such as large-scale privatizations, merger waves, and share buybacks. In addition, the companies traded on equity markets represent only one part of the economy. Outside of these firms, economic growth creates new firms, brings in new investors, and reshapes market valuations. Economic growth in and of itself does not guarantee that existing equity investors capture the new wealth created.

Estimates of potential GDP and its growth rate are widely available. Both the OECD and the International Monetary Fund (IMF) include these estimates in their intermediate-term and long-term economic growth forecasts for each country. Simply extrapolating past GDP growth into the future can produce incorrect forecasts because a country's GDP growth rate can, and frequently does, change over time. The rapid pace of economic transformation, privatizations, and increased economic liberalization in several Latin American and European countries in the late 1990s spurred brisk economic growth that translated into sizable stock market returns. For many of these countries, however, this high-growth period was followed by much lower long-run growth.

Factors or policies that cause potential growth to increase or decrease by even a small amount will have a large compounded impact on living standards, economic conditions, and the future level of economic activity. This reality has implications for long-run stock market returns, as shown earlier. Being able to recognize changes in economic factors and policies is critical for global equity investors.

Estimates of an economy's growth potential are also relevant for global fixed-income investors. Potential GDP forecasts can gauge inflationary pressures in the economy that arise from cyclical variations in actual output growth relative to the economy's long-term potential growth rate. Specifically, actual GDP growth above (below) the potential GDP growth rate puts upward (downward) pressure on inflation, which puts corresponding pressure on nominal interest rates and bond prices.

The growth rate of potential GDP is also an important factor for the level of real interest rates and, therefore, real asset returns in general. Faster growth in potential GDP translates into higher real interest rates and higher expected real asset returns in general. Higher real interest rates are required to induce savings to fund capital accumulation, which in turn can fuel higher potential GDP growth rates.

Potential GDP and its growth rate enter into fixed-income analysis in other ways as well. Among them are the following:

1. A higher rate of potential GDP growth improves the general credit quality of fixed-income securities. Credit rating agencies use the growth rate of potential GDP in evaluating the credit risk of sovereign debt. All else equal, slower estimated potential GDP growth raises the perceived risk of these bonds.

2. Monetary policy decisions are affected by the difference between an economy's estimated potential output and its actual operating level (referred to as the output gap) and by the growth of actual GDP relative to the long-term sustainable growth rate. Thus, fixed-income investors need to closely monitor the output gap and growth rates of actual and potential GDP to assess the likelihood of a change in central bank policy.

3. Government budget deficits typically increase during recessions and decrease during expansions. In examining fiscal policy, actual fiscal positions are often judged relative to structural or cyclically adjusted deficits, a theoretical budgetary balance that would exist if the economy were operating at its potential GDP.

EXAMPLE 2

Impact on Equity and Fixed Income Investors

Your firm subscribes to asset class risk and return estimates generated by a vendor. The equity market return estimates are based primarily on long-term average index returns. Following a multi-year period of very high equity returns driven by unusually high earnings growth and expanding P/E multiples, capital's share of total income as well as valuation multiples are near all-time highs. Based on the latest data, the vendor projects that over the long run, your domestic equity market will return 13.5% per year—11% annual appreciation and 2.5% dividend yield—forever.

Your firm also subscribes to a macroeconomic forecasting service that provides, in addition to shorter-term projections, estimates of the long-term growth rate of potential GDP and the long-term inflation rate. This service forecasts 3.25% real growth in the future and 3.75% inflation, down from 4.0% and 5.0%, respectively, over the last 75 years.

1. Why might you have greater confidence in the macroeconomic service's forecasts than in the vendor's equity market return forecast?

   Solution

   High volatility makes equity returns very hard to predict based on their own history. Extrapolating historical equity returns does not factor in changes in economic conditions, valuation changes, and the potential for economic growth.

   Long-term real GDP growth rates tend to be far less volatile, especially for developed economies such as the United States or the euro area, because long-term potential growth is driven by slowly evolving fundamental economic forces. Similarly, for countries with prudent monetary policies, inflation rates are much less volatile than stock prices. Thus, one could reasonably place much higher confidence in forecasts of long-term real and nominal (real growth plus inflation) GDP growth than in equity market return forecasts based on historical equity returns.

2. Assuming the macroeconomic forecasts are accurate, what implicit assumptions underlie the vendor's forecast of 11% equity market appreciation?

   Solution

   Using the Grinold-Kroner framework, equity market returns can be attributed to (1) dividend yield, (2) expansion/contraction of the price-to-earnings ratio, (3) nominal GDP growth, and (4) change in shares outstanding. The macroeconomic forecast indicates that nominal GDP will grow at 7% (3.25% real + 3.75% inflation). So, the vendor's forecast of 11% equity market appreciation implies a 4% annual combined contribution from expansion in the P/E multiple and/or change in shares outstanding of GDP over the long run, an assumption that cannot hold.

3. Assuming the macroeconomic forecasts are accurate, what would be a more reasonable forecast for long-term equity returns?

   Solution

   Neither the P/E nor the profit share of GDP can grow at a high rate forever. A much more reasonable forecast of long-term equity market returns would be the projected 7% growth rate of nominal GDP plus the 2.5% dividend yield. A projected equity return of 9.5% over the long run is much more reasonable, subject to variability in dividend yields and price-to-earnings ratios.

4. In addition to its long-term potential GDP forecast, the macroeconomic forecasting service estimates sluggish 1.5% GDP growth for the next year. Based on this short-term GDP forecast, the bond analyst at your firm

recommends that the firm increase its fixed-income investments. What assumptions underlie the bond analyst's forecast?

Solution

With forecasted actual GDP growth well below the growth in potential GDP, the bond analyst assumes a growing output gap or slack in the economy (i.e., there may be a slowdown in the economic cycle). This slack may place downward pressure on inflation and reduce inflationary expectations. To close this gap, the central bank may need to lower short-term interest rates and ease policy. In such an environment, bond prices should rise.

4   PRODUCTION FUNCTION AND GROWTH ACCOUNTING

☐   contrast capital deepening investment and technological progress and explain how each affects economic growth and labor productivity

☐   demonstrate forecasting potential GDP based on growth accounting relations

What are the forces driving long-run economic growth? The following sections discuss labor, physical and human capital, technology, and other factors, such as natural resources and public infrastructure, as inputs to economic growth and production functions and how changes in such inputs affect growth. We begin the discussion by presenting one of the simplest useful models of the production function.

Production Function

A production function is a model of the quantitative link between the inputs (factors of production), technology, and output. A two-factor aggregate production function with labor and capital as the inputs can be represented as

$$Y = AF(K,L), \tag{1}$$

where Y denotes the level of aggregate output in the economy, L is the quantity of labor or number of workers or hours worked in the economy, and K is an estimate of the capital services provided by the stock of equipment and structures used to produce goods and services. The function $F(\ )$ embodies the fact that capital and labor can be used in various combinations to produce output.

In the production function above, A is a multiplicative scale factor referred to as **total factor productivity (TFP)**. Note that an increase in TFP implies a proportionate increase in output for any combination of inputs. Hence, TFP reflects the general level of productivity or technology in the economy. The state of technology embodies the cumulative effects of scientific advances, applied research and development, improvements in management methods, and ways of organizing production that raise the productive capacity of factories and offices.

It is worth noting that both the function $F(\ )$ and the scale factor A reflect technology. An innovation that makes it possible to produce the same output with the same amount of capital but fewer workers would be reflected in a change in the function $F(\ )$ because the relative productivity of labor and capital has been altered. In contrast, an increase in TFP does not affect the relative productivity of the inputs. As is standard in the analysis of economic growth, *unless stated otherwise, the level of "technology" should be interpreted as referring to TFP.*

To obtain concrete results, it is useful to use a specific functional form for the production function. The **Cobb–Douglas production function**, given by

$$F(K,L) = K^\alpha L^{1-\alpha}, \qquad\qquad (2)$$

is widely used because it is easy to analyze and does a good job of fitting the historic data relating inputs and output. The parameter α determines the shares of output (factor shares) paid by companies to capital and labor and is assumed to have a value between 0 and 1. The reason for this follows from basic microeconomics. In a competitive economy, factors of production are paid their marginal product. Profit maximization requires that the marginal product of capital equal the **rental price of capital** and the marginal product of labor equal the (real) wage rate. In the case of capital, the marginal product of capital (MPK) for the Cobb–Douglas production function is[1]

$$MPK = \alpha A K^{\alpha-1}L^{1-\alpha} = \alpha Y/K.$$

Setting the MPK equal to the rental price (r) of capital,

$$\alpha Y/K = r.$$

If we solve this equation for α, we find that it equals the ratio of capital income, rK, to output or GDP, Y. Thus, α *is the share of GDP paid out to the suppliers of capital.* A similar calculation shows that $1 - \alpha$ is the share of income paid to labor. This result is important because it is easy to estimate α for an economy by simply looking at capital's share of income in the national income accounts.

The Cobb–Douglas production function exhibits two important properties that explain the relationship between the inputs and the output. First, the Cobb–Douglas production function exhibits **constant returns to scale**. This means that if all the inputs into the production process are increased by the same percentage, then output rises by that percentage. Under the assumption of constant returns to scale, we can modify the production function (Equation 1) and examine the determinants of the quantity of output per worker. Multiplying the production function by $1/L$ gives

$$Y/L = AF(K/L,L/L) = AF(K/L,1).$$

Defining $y = Y/L$ as the output per worker or (average) **labor productivity** and $k = K/L$ as the capital-to-labor ratio, the expression becomes

$$y = AF(k,1).$$

Specifying the Cobb–Douglas production function in output per worker terms, where again lower case letters denote variables measured on a per capita basis, we get

$$y = Y/L = A(K/L)^\alpha(L/L)^{1-\alpha} = Ak^\alpha. \qquad\qquad (3)$$

This equation tells us that the amount of goods a worker can produce (labor productivity) depends on the amount of capital available for each worker (capital-to-labor ratio), technology or TFP, and the share of capital in GDP (α). It is important to note that this equation contains two different measures of productivity or efficiency. Labor productivity measures the output produced by a unit of labor, dividing the output (GDP) by the labor input used to produce that output ($y = Y/L$). TFP is a scale factor that multiplies the impact of the capital and labor inputs. Changes in TFP are estimated using a growth accounting method discussed in the next section.

---

1 The marginal product of capital is simply the derivative of output with respect to capital. This relationship can be approximated as $\Delta Y/\Delta K \approx [A(K + \Delta K)^\alpha L^{1-\alpha} - AK^\alpha L^{1-\alpha}]/\Delta K \approx [A\alpha K^{\alpha-1}\Delta K L^{1-\alpha}]/\Delta K = A\alpha K^{\alpha-1}L^{1-\alpha}$ $= \alpha Y/K$. The approximation becomes exact for very small increments, ΔK.

A second important property of the model is the relation between an individual input and the level of output produced. The Cobb–Douglas production function exhibits **diminishing marginal productivity** with respect to each individual input. Marginal productivity is the extra output produced from a one-unit increase in an input keeping the other inputs unchanged. It applies to any input as long as the other inputs are held constant. For example, if we have a factory of a fixed size and we add more workers to the factory, the marginal productivity of labor measures how much additional output each additional worker will produce. Diminishing marginal productivity means that at some point, the extra output obtained from each additional unit of the input will decline. To continue our example, if we hire more workers at the existing factory (fixed capital input in this case), each additional worker adds less to output than the previously hired worker does, and average labor productivity (y) falls.

The significance of diminishing marginal returns in the Cobb–Douglas production function depends on the value of α. *A value of α close to zero means diminishing marginal returns to capital are very significant and the extra output made possible by additional capital declines quickly as capital increases.* In contrast, a value of α close to one means that the next unit of capital increases output almost as much as the previous unit of capital. In this case, diminishing marginal returns still occur but the impact is relatively small. Note that the exponents on the K and L variables in the Cobb–Douglas production function sum to one, indicating constant returns to scale—that is, there are no diminishing marginal returns if both inputs are increased proportionately.

Growth Accounting

Since the publication of Solow's seminal work (Solow 1957), growth accounting has been used to analyze the performance of economies. The growth accounting equation is essentially the production function written in the form of growth rates. It starts with the Cobb–Douglas production function and decomposes the percentage change in output into components attributable to capital, labor, and technology:

$$\Delta Y/Y = \Delta A/A + \alpha \Delta K/K + (1 - \alpha)\Delta L/L \tag{4}$$

The **growth accounting equation** states that the growth rate of output equals the rate of technological change plus α times the growth rate of capital plus $(1 - \alpha)$ multiplied by the growth rate of labor. Because a 1% increase in capital leads to an α% increase in output, α is the elasticity of output with respect to capital. Similarly, $(1 - \alpha)$ is the elasticity of output with respect to labor. Thus, in the Cobb–Douglas production function, the exponents α and $(1 - \alpha)$ play dual roles as both output elasticities and the shares of income paid to each factor. Note that the impact of any unspecified inputs (e.g., natural resources) is subsumed into the TFP component.

Data on output, capital, labor, and the elasticities of capital and labor are available for most developed countries. The rate of technological change is not directly measured and must therefore be estimated. The elasticities of capital and labor in the growth accounting equation are the relative shares of capital (α) and labor ($1 - \alpha$) in national income and are estimated from the GDP accounts. For the United States, the relative shares of labor and capital are approximately 0.7 and 0.3, respectively. This means that an increase in the growth rate of labor will have a significantly larger impact—roughly double—on potential GDP growth than will an equivalent increase in the growth rate of capital, holding all else equal. For example, because capital's share in GDP in the US economy is 0.3, a 1% increase in the amount of capital available for each worker increases output by only 0.3%. An equivalent increase in the labor input would boost growth by 0.7%.

The growth accounting equation has a number of uses in studying an economy. First, Solow used the equation to estimate the contribution of technological progress to economic growth. Solow estimated the growth in TFP as a residual in the preceding equation by plugging in $\Delta Y/Y$, $\Delta K/K$, $\Delta L/L$, and α and solving for $\Delta A/A$. This residual measures the amount of output that cannot be explained by growth in capital or labor and can thus be regarded as progress in TFP.

Second, the growth accounting equation is used to empirically measure the sources of growth in an economy. In such studies, the growth accounting equation is used to quantify the contribution of each factor to long-term growth in an economy and answer such questions as the following: How important are labor and demographic factors to growth? What is the contribution of capital, and how important is capital deepening as a source of growth? What is the impact of TFP? The growth accounting equation can be expanded by considering different forms of capital and labor inputs, such as human capital and knowledge capital, and by considering the quality of the inputs as well.

Finally, the growth accounting equation is used to measure potential output. Potential GDP is estimated using Equation 4 with trend estimates of labor and capital and α estimated as one minus the labor share of GDP. The difficult task is estimating the growth rate of TFP, which, by definition, is a residual in the growth accounting equation TFP is computed as the growth in output less the growth in the factor inputs. These inputs include labor and capital in the traditional Solow two-factor production model. If the production function is expanded by including more inputs, the weighted growth rates of these inputs would also be subtracted from the growth in output. The standard methodology treats TFP as exogenous and estimates its growth rate using various time-series models.

An alternative method of measuring potential GDP is the **labor productivity growth accounting equation**. It is very similar to the Solow approach but is simpler and models potential GDP as a function of the labor input and the productivity of the labor input. It avoids the need to estimate the capital input and the difficulty associated with computing total factor productivity. The disadvantage is that it incorporates both capital deepening and TFP progress in the productivity term in a way that can be difficult to analyze and to predict over long periods. Under this approach, the equation for estimating potential GDP is

$$\begin{aligned}
\text{Growth rate in potential GDP} \; &= \; \text{Long-term growth rate of labor force} \\
&+ \; \text{Long-term growth rate in labor productivity}
\end{aligned} \qquad (5)$$

Thus, potential GDP growth is a combination of the long-term growth rate of the labor force and the long-term growth rate of labor productivity. If the labor force is growing at 1% per year and productivity per worker is rising at 2% per year, then potential GDP is rising at 3% per year.

Extending the Production Function

As a simplification, the production function in Equation 1 focused on only the labor and capital inputs. A more complete specification of the production function expands the list of inputs to include the following:

- Raw materials: natural resources such as oil, lumber, and available land (N)
- Quantity of labor: the number of workers in the country (L)
- Human capital: education and skill level of these workers (H)
- Information, computer, and telecommunications (ICT) capital: computer hardware, software, and communication equipment (K_{IT})

- Non-ICT capital: transport equipment, metal products and plant machinery other than computer hardware and communications equipment, and non-residential buildings and other structures (K_{NT})

- Public capital: infrastructure owned and provided by the government (K_P)

- Technological knowledge: the production methods used to convert inputs into final products, reflected by total factor productivity (A)

The expanded production function is expressed mathematically as

$$Y = AF(N,L,H,K_{IT},K_{NT},K_P).$$

The impact of each of these inputs on economic growth is addressed in the following sections.

5   CAPITAL DEEPENING VS. TECHNOLOGICAL PROGRESS

The property of diminishing marginal returns plays an important role in assessing the contribution of capital and technology to economic growth. Exhibit 3 shows the relationship between per capita output and the capital-to-labor ratio. It shows that adding more and more capital to a fixed number of workers increases per capita output but at a decreasing rate. Looking at Equation 3 and Exhibit 3, we can think of growth in per capita output coming from two sources: capital deepening and an improvement in technology, often referred to as technological progress.

Exhibit 3: Per Capita Production Function Capital Deepening vs. Technological (TFP) Progress

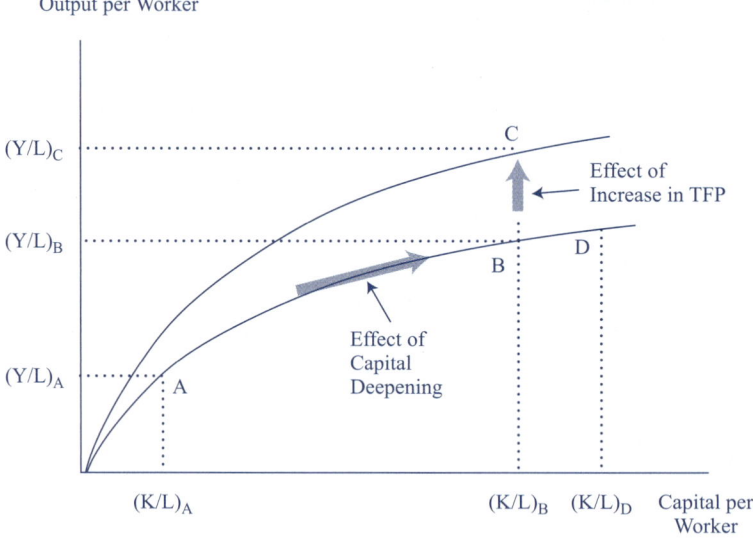

Capital deepening, an increase in the capital-to-labor ratio, is reflected in the exhibit by a move along the production function from point A to point B. The increase in the capital-to-labor ratio reflects rising investment in the economy. The ratio will increase as long as the growth rate of capital (net investment) exceeds the growth rate of labor.

Once the capital-to-labor ratio becomes very high, however, as at point B, further additions to capital have relatively little impact on per capita output (e.g., moving to point D). This dynamic occurs because the marginal product of capital declines as more capital is added to the labor input.

At the point at which the marginal product of capital equals its marginal cost, profit maximizing producers will stop adding capital (i.e., stop increasing the capital-to-labor ratio). As we will discuss later, this point is very significant in the neoclassical model of growth because per capita growth in the economy will come to a halt. Once the economy reaches this steady state, capital deepening cannot be a source of sustained growth in the economy. Only when the economy is operating below the steady state and when the marginal product of capital exceeds its marginal cost can capital deepening raise per capita growth. Note that once technological progress (TFP growth) is introduced, the capital-to-labor ratio will have to keep increasing just to keep the marginal productivity of capital equal to its marginal cost. But the point remains: Once that equality is attained, companies will not increase the capital-to-labor ratio faster than is necessary to maintain that equality.

The neoclassical model's stark implication that more-rapid capital accumulation—that is, higher rates of investment—cannot result in a permanently higher rate of per capita growth is somewhat disappointing. As we will see in our discussion of endogenous growth, capital accumulation can result in a permanently higher growth rate if the investment results not just in *more* capital (i.e., pure capital deepening) but also in new, innovative products and processes. That is, if the additional capital embodies new, more efficient methods of production or previously unavailable products, then more rapid capital accumulation can result in a permanently higher growth rate of per capita output.

In contrast to moves along a given production function, an improvement in TFP causes a proportional upward shift in the entire production function. As a result, the economy can produce higher output per worker for a given level of capital per worker. This dynamic is shown in Exhibit 3 by the move from B to C. Technological progress also increases the marginal product of capital relative to its marginal cost. This increase makes additional capital investments profitable and tends to mitigate the limits imposed on growth by diminishing marginal returns. In addition, continued growth in per capita output is possible even in the steady state as long as there is ongoing technological progress (increases in TFP). In summary, *sustained growth in per capita output requires progress in TFP.*

EXAMPLE 3

Capital Deepening vs. Technological Progress

One of main differences between developed and developing countries is the amount of capital available for each worker. Country A is an advanced economy with $100,000 of capital available for each worker and thus a high capital-to-labor ratio. In contrast, Country B is a developing country with only $5,000 of capital available for each worker.

What impact will the following developments have on the growth rate of potential GDP?

---

1. An increase in business investment in both countries

   Solution

   An increase in business investment will raise the capital-to-labor ratio in both countries. It results in capital deepening and a movement along the per worker production function. The impact on growth, however, will be significantly different for the two countries. Country B will experience an increase in output per worker and thus in the growth rate of potential GDP. This is because Country B operates at a low level of capital per worker, at a point like A in Exhibit 3. Diminishing returns to capital are small, so any addition to capital has a major impact on growth. Country A operates at a point like B in Exhibit 3, so additions to capital have little impact on growth because of diminishing returns.

2. An increase in the amount of spending on university research in both countries

Solution

An increase in spending on university research will increase TFP and cause an upward shift in the production function in both countries. This can be seen in the move from point B to point C in Exhibit 3. The shift in the production function will raise growth in both countries and offset the negative impact of diminishing returns. This result shows that developing countries have the potential to grow through both capital deepening and technological progress, whereas improvement in potential GDP growth in developed countries is largely driven by technological progress.

3. An elimination of restrictions in Country B on the inflow of foreign investment

Solution

The elimination of restrictions will result in higher foreign investment, which has the same impact as an increase in domestic business investment. This is again a movement along the production function such as from point A to B in Exhibit 3. With diminishing returns insignificant at low levels of capital to labor, the higher level of foreign investment will boost growth of potential GDP in Country B.

6   NATURAL RESOURCES

☐ explain how natural resources affect economic growth and evaluate the argument that limited availability of natural resources constrains economic growth

Raw materials, including everything from available land to oil to water, are an essential input to growth. There are two categories of natural resources:

1. **Renewable resources** are those that can be replenished, such as a forest. For example, if a tree is cut, a seedling can be planted and a new forest harvested in the future.
2. **Non-renewable resources** are finite resources that are depleted once they are consumed. Oil and coal are examples.

Although it seems intuitive that countries with more natural resources will be wealthier, the relation between resource endowment and growth is not so straightforward. Natural resources do account for some of the differences in growth among countries. Today, Middle Eastern countries and such countries as Brazil and Australia have relatively high per capita incomes because of their resource base. Countries in the Middle East have large pools of oil. Brazil has an abundance of land suitable for large-scale agricultural production, allowing it to be a major exporter of coffee, soybeans, and beef.

Even though *access* to natural resources (e.g., via trade) is important, *ownership and production of natural resources is not necessary for a country to achieve a high level of income.* Countries in East Asia, such as South Korea, have experienced rapid economic growth but have few natural resources. In contrast, both Venezuela and Saudi Arabia have large oil reserves and are major producers of oil, yet both countries have experienced subpar growth compared with the natural-resource-poor countries of Singapore and South Korea. As was examined earlier, economic growth in Venezuela over the last 60 years was well below that of Singapore, Japan, and South Korea.

For some countries, the presence of natural resources may even restrain growth, resulting in a "resource curse." Venezuela and Nigeria are two examples of countries blessed with resources yet with sluggish economic growth. There are two main reasons why this may occur. First, countries rich in natural resources may fail to develop the economic institutions necessary for growth. Second, countries rich in resources may suffer the **Dutch disease**, where currency appreciation driven by strong export demand for resources makes other segments of the economy, in particular manufacturing, globally uncompetitive. The name for this phenomenon comes from the experience of the Netherlands: Following the discovery of large natural gas fields in the Netherlands, the Dutch guilder (the nation's currency at that time) appreciated and the manufacturing sector contracted. Because of this contraction, the resource-rich country does not participate in the TFP progress that occurs in countries with more vigorous manufacturing sectors.

In contrast, there is a longstanding concern that non-renewable natural resources will eventually limit growth. The idea is that a combination of rapid economic growth and a fixed stock of resources will cause resource depletion as the available pool of resources is used up. These concerns are probably overstated. Technological progress (TFP from all sources) enables the economy to use fewer resources per unit of output and to develop substitutes. The growing scarcity of specific resources will increase their price and encourage a shift toward more plentiful substitutes. Finally, the share of national income going to land and resources has been declining for most countries, especially as the composition of output in the global economy shifts toward the use of more services.

EXAMPLE 4

Impact of Natural Resources

The table below shows the share of world proved oil reserves as of 1990 for a selection of countries, along with the growth rate of real per capita GDP from 1990 to 2018. The simple correlation between the share of oil reserves and subsequent growth is not statistically different from zero.

	Percentage of World Proved Oil Reserves, 1990	Avg. Real Per Capita GDP Growth (%) 1990–2018		Percentage of World Proved Oil Reserves, 1990	Avg. Real Per Capita GDP Growth (%) 1990–2018
Saudi Arabia	25.75	0.4	Germany	0.04	1.4
Venezuela	5.85	2.8	France	0.02	1.1
Mexico	5.64	1.3	New Zealand	0.01	1.6
United States	2.62	1.5	Pakistan	0.01	2.1
China	2.40	9.1	Japan	0.01	0.9

	Percentage of World Proved Oil Reserves, 1990	Avg. Real Per Capita GDP Growth (%) 1990–2018		Percentage of World Proved Oil Reserves, 1990	Avg. Real Per Capita GDP Growth (%) 1990–2018
Nigeria	1.60	2.1	Spain	0.00	1.6
Indonesia	0.82	3.7			
India	0.75	5.2	Botswana	0.00	2.5
Canada	0.61	1.3	Ethiopia	0.00	4.6
Egypt	0.45	2.1	Ireland	0.00	4.6
United Kingdom	0.43	1.5	Kenya	0.00	0.9
Brazil	0.28	1.1	Singapore	0.00	3.7
Argentina	0.23	2.0	South Africa	0.00	2.7
Australia	0.17	1.8	South Korea	0.00	4.4

Sources: US Energy Information Administration (www.eia.gov) and IMF.

1. What might account for the fact that real per capita GDP growth appears to be unrelated to oil reserves, perhaps the single most economically important natural resource (aside from water)?

Solution

Energy is a vital input for any economy. Thus, *access* to energy resources is critical. *Ownership* of raw energy resources, however, is not. Countries that are not self-sufficient in oil or other resources acquire what they need through trade. It should be noted that countries that lack oil may possess other types of energy resources, such as natural gas, coal, hydropower, or geothermal energy. In addition, countries can grow by emphasizing less energy intensive products, especially services, and adopting more energy efficient production methods. In sum, natural resources are important but not necessary for growth.

7   LABOR SUPPLY

☐ | explain how demographics, immigration, and labor force participation affect the rate and sustainability of economic growth

As noted earlier, economic growth is affected by increases in inputs, mainly labor and capital. Growth in the number of people available for work (quantity of workforce) is an important source of economic growth and partially accounts for the superior growth performance of the United States among the advanced economies—in particular, relative to Europe and Japan. Most developing countries, such as China, India, and Mexico, have a large potential labor supply. We can measure the potential size of the labor input as the total number of hours available for work. This, in turn, equals the labor force times the average hours worked per worker. The **labor force** is defined as the working age population (ages 16 to 64) that is either employed or available for work but not working (i.e., unemployed). Thus, growth in the labor input depends on four factors: population growth, labor force participation, net migration, and average hours worked.

Population Growth

Long-term projections of the labor supply are largely determined by the growth of the working age population. Population growth is determined by fertility rates and mortality rates. Population growth rates are significantly lower in the developed countries than in the developing countries. As a result, there is an ongoing decline in the developed countries' share of the world's population. Note that although population growth may increase the growth rate of the overall economy, it has no impact on the rate of increase in *per capita* GDP.

The age mix of the population is also important. The percentage of the population over the age of 65 and the percentage below the age of 16 are key considerations. Some of the developed countries, especially European countries, Japan, and South Korea, are facing a growing demographic burden as the portion of non-working elders (over 65) grows as a share of the population. In contrast, growth in many developing countries will receive a demographic boost as the fraction of the population below the age of 16 begins to decline. Interestingly, China is similar to the advanced economies, with a growing proportion of the population over age 65.

Exhibit 4: Population Data for Selected Countries (in millions, except growth rate)				
	2000	**2009**	**2018**	**Annual Growth (%), 2000–2018**
France	59.1	64.4	66.9	0.69
Germany	82.2	81.9	82.9	0.05
Ireland	3.8	4.5	4.9	1.42
Spain	40.3	46.4	46.7	0.82
United Kingdom	58.9	62.3	66.4	0.67
Russia	146.7	141.9	144.5	−0.08
Japan	126.9	128.0	126.4	-0.02
United States	282.2	306.8	327.2	0.83
Mexico	98.4	112.1	125.3	1.35
China	1,267.4	1,352.1	1,415.0	0.61
India	1,024.3	1,214.3	1,354.1	1.56

Source: OECD.Stat.

Labor Force Participation

In the short run, the labor force growth rate may differ from population growth because of changes in the participation rate. The **labor force participation rate** is defined as the percentage of the working age population in the labor force. It has trended upward in most countries over the last few decades because of rising participation rates among women. In contrast to population, an increase in the participation rate may raise the growth of per capita GDP. In many southern European countries, such as Greece and Italy, the participation rate among women is well below the rates in the United States and northern European countries (see Exhibit 5). Thus, rising participation rates among women in these countries could increase growth in the labor force and in potential GDP. This has been the case for Spain, where the female labor force participation rate rose from 52.0% in 2000 to 67.9% in 2018. It should be noted, however, that rising or falling labor force participation is likely to represent a transition to a new higher or lower level of participation rather than a truly permanent rate of change. Thus, although trends in participation may contribute to or detract from potential growth for substantial periods, one should be cautious in extrapolating such trends indefinitely.

Exhibit 5: Labor Force Data for Selected Countries (2018)

	Percentage of Population under Age 15	Percentage of Population over Age 65	Participation Rate: Male	Participation Rate: Female
France	18.0%	19.9%	75.4%	69.7%
Germany	13.5	21.5	83.1	76.5
Greece	14.4	21.8	75.6	59.7
Ireland	20.8	13.6	77.3	66.6
Italy	13.2	22.7	73.9	55.6
Spain	14.5	19.3	77.7	67.9
Sweden	17.8	19.9	84.9	83.2
United Kingdom	17.9	18.3	81.9	74.2
Japan	12.2	28.1	71.2	51.4
United States	18.6	16.0	76.2	68.3
Mexico	26.5	7.2	81.8	47.3
Turkey	23.5	8.6	78.6	38.4

Source: OECD Stat Extracts.

EXAMPLE 5

Impact of the Age Distribution on Growth: Mexico vs. Germany

Exhibit 4 and Exhibit 5 provide population data for selected countries. The data show that the rate of population growth and the age composition vary significantly among countries. Thus, demographic factors can be expected to have a significant impact on relative growth rates across countries. This effect is very clear in the cases of Mexico and Germany. There was essentially zero growth in Germany's population from 2000 to 2018, while Mexico's population increased by 1.35% annually. The age composition of the two countries is also very different.

1. How will the age distribution impact growth over the next decade?

   Solution

   What is important for growth is the number of workers available to enter the workforce. Over the next decade, Mexico will receive a demographic benefit because of the high percentage of young people entering the workforce. This is because 26.5% of the population in 2018 was below the age of 15. In contrast, only 13.5% of the German population was below the age of 15. In addition, Germany is facing a demographic challenge given the high and growing share of its population over the age of 65. In Mexico, only 7.2% of the population is above the age of 65, compared with 21.5% in Germany. In sum, the lack of population growth and a rapidly aging population in Germany will limit its potential rate of growth. Germany must rely on high labor productivity growth, increase its workforce participation rate, or encourage immigration if it is to increase its near-term potential rate of growth. Meanwhile, potential GDP growth in Mexico should receive a boost from its favorable population trends.

Net Migration

Another factor increasing economic and population growth, especially among the developed countries, is immigration. Heightened immigration is a possible solution to the slowing labor force growth being experienced by many developed countries with low birthrates within the native population. The growth rate of the labor force in Ireland, Spain, the United Kingdom, and the United States has increased between 2000 and 2010 because of immigration, although it slowed substantially in the 2010–2018 period. Focusing on the decade starting in 2000, Exhibit 4 shows the population growth rates for Ireland and Spain at 1.71% and 1.35%, respectively. The population growth rates were well above the population growth rates in other European countries. As shown in Exhibit 6, this is because of the impact of immigration. The open-border policies of both countries led to a significant population of immigrants that contributed to a large increase in labor input for both countries. As a consequence, both countries experienced GDP growth above the European average during this period (see Exhibit 1).

Exhibit 6: Ireland and Spain: Net Migration

	2000–2007	2008	2009	2010	Total 2000–2010	Total 2011–2016
Ireland	357,085	38,502	−7,800	−12,200	375,587	186,724
Spain	4,222,813	460,221	181,073	111,249	4,975,356	1,243,375

Source: OECD Stat Extracts

EXAMPLE 6

Potential Growth in Spain: Labor Input

The scenario below is set in early 2011. The Investment Policy Committee of Global Invest Inc. reviewed a report on the growth prospects for Spain and noted that, with total hours worked growing at a 1.2% annual rate between 2000 and 2010, labor input had been a major source of growth for the economy. Some members expect the growth rate of labor to slow considerably given projection from the OECD and IMF that immigration into Spain will fall to essentially zero over the next few years. A research assistant at the firm gathered demographic data on Spain from Exhibit 4–Exhibit 6 and other sources. The data are presented in the following table:

	2000	2010	Annual Growth (2000–2010)
Population (millions)	40.3	46.1	1.35%
Immigration since 2000 (millions)		4.975	
Percentage of population under 15		15.0%	
Percentage of population over 65		17.0%	
Male labor force participation rate		80.4%	
Female labor force participation rate		66.1%	
Unemployment rate		20.1%	

Using this information for Spain and Exhibit 4 and Exhibit 5 for relevant comparison data, determine the following:

1. Whether a change in the trend growth rate of the labor input is likely over the next few years.

   Solution

   The growth in the labor input depends on a number of factors, including the population growth rate, the labor force participation rate, and the percentage of the population below the age of 15. The labor force in Spain expanded sharply between 2000 and 2010, mainly because of a population increase of 5.8 million, going from 40.3 million in 2000 to 46.1 million in 2010. Looking ahead, growth in the labor force is set to slow substantially for a number of reasons:

   - The population increase between 2000 and 2010 is very misleading because it is not likely to be repeated in the future. Between 2000 and 2010, immigration raised the population of Spain by nearly 5 million people. Without the immigrants, the population would have grown by only about 825,000 people during this period, or at an annual rate of 0.2%. With immigration, the population growth rate was 1.35%. The pace of immigration that occurred between 2000 and 2010 is not sustainable and is likely to slow, which will result in slower growth in both the population and the labor force.

   - In the short run, the growth rate of the labor force may differ from population growth because of changes in the participation rate. Looking at the data, the male participation rate in Spain, at 80.4%, is very high and, as shown in Exhibit 5, is above the male participation rates in France, Greece, and Italy and slightly below that of Germany. The female participation rate is low in comparison to northern European countries, such as Sweden. But it is higher than in Italy, which is probably a better comparison. Thus, little increase is likely in the male or female participation rates.

   - Only 15% of the Spanish population is below the age of 15. The comparable figure from Exhibit 5 for the United Kingdom is 17.9%, for France 18.0%, for the United States 18.6%, and for Mexico 26.5%. Thus, Spain does not appear poised for a notable surge in young adults entering the labor force.

   In summary, growth in the labor input in Spain should slow over the next few years, and the growth rate of potential GDP should do the same.

2. How the high unemployment rate of 20.1% is likely to affect the growth rate of the labor force.

Solution

Reducing the unemployment rate would mitigate some of the negative demographic factors because a reduction in the number of unemployed workers would boost utilization of the existing labor supply. This shift would represent a transition to a higher level of employment rather than a permanent increase in the potential growth rate. Nonetheless, it could boost potential growth for a substantial period.

Average Hours Worked

The contribution of labor to overall output is also affected by changes in the average hours worked per worker. Average hours worked is highly sensitive to the business cycle. The long-term trend in average hours worked, however, has been toward a shorter work week in the advanced countries. This development is the result of legislation, collective bargaining agreements, the growth of part-time and temporary work, and the impact of both the "wealth effect" and high tax rates on labor income, which cause workers in high-income countries to value leisure time relatively more highly than labor income.

Exhibit 7 provides data on average hours worked per year per person in the labor force for selected years since 1995. For most countries, the average number of hours worked per year has been declining. There is also a significant difference in hours worked across countries. In 2018, average hours worked per year in South Korea, at 1,993 hours, were 46.1% more than the 1,363 average hours worked per year in Germany. The increase in female labor force participation rates may be contributing to the shorter average workweek because female workers disproportionately take on part-time, rather than full-time, jobs.

Exhibit 7: Average Hours Worked per Year per Person in Selected Countries			
	1995	**2005**	**2018**
France	1,651	1,559	1,520
Germany	1,534	1,435	1,363
Greece	2,123	2,081	1,956
Ireland	1,875	1,654	1,782
Italy	1,859	1,819	1,723
Spain	1,733	1,688	1,701
Sweden	1,609	1,607	1,474
United Kingdom	1,743	1,676	1,538
Japan	1,884	1,775	1,680
South Korea	2,658	2,364	1,993
Canada	1,761	1,738	1,708
United States	1,840	1,795	1,786
Mexico	1,857	1,909	2,148
Turkey	1,876	1,918	1,832

Source: OECD data.

Labor Quality: Human Capital

In addition to the quantity of labor, the quality of the labor force is an important source of growth for an economy. **Human capital** is the accumulated knowledge and skills that workers acquire from education, training, or life experience. In general, better-educated and more-skilled workers will be more productive and more adaptable to changes in technology or other shifts in market demand and supply.

An economy's human capital is increased through investment in education and on-the-job training. Like physical capital, investment in education is costly, but studies show that there is a significant return on that investment. That is, people with more education earn higher wages. In addition, education may also have a spillover or externality impact. Increasing the educational level of one person raises not only the output of that person but also the output of those around that person. The spillover effect operates through the link between education and advances in technology. Education not only improves the quality of the labor force, and thus the stock of human capital, but also encourages growth through innovation. Importantly, increased education, obtained both formally and via on-the-job training, could result in a permanent increase in the growth rate of an economy if the more educated workforce results in more innovations and a faster rate of technological progress. Investment in the population's health is also a major contributor to human capital, especially in developing countries.

8 ICT, NON-ICT, AND TECHNOLOGY AND PUBLIC INFRASTRUCTURE

☐ | explain how investment in physical capital, human capital, and technological development affects economic growth

The physical capital stock increases from year to year as long as net investment (gross investment less the depreciation of the capital) is positive. Thus, countries with a higher rate of investment should have a growing physical capital stock and a higher rate of GDP growth. Note that the impact on growth of per capita GDP will be somewhat smaller if the population is growing because a proportion of net investment simply provides the capital needed to maintain the capital-to-labor ratio. Exhibit 8 shows the level of gross non-residential investment as a share of GDP. The exhibit shows significant variation across countries, with the investment share in the United States being low in comparison to other developed countries.

Exhibit 8: Business Investment as a Percentage of GDP

	Investment Percentage of GDP		
	2000	2008	2018
Developed Countries			
France	19.5	24.1	22.8
Germany	21.5	20.9	21.2
Ireland	23.9	24.4	24.5
Italy	20.3	21.8	18.0

	Investment Percentage of GDP		
	2000	2008	2018
Developed Countries			
Spain	26.2	29.6	21.9
United Kingdom	17.1	17.2	17.2
Australia	22.0	28.4	24.2
Japan	25.4	24.5	24.4
South Korea	30.6	33.0	30.2
Singapore	33.1	30.5	27.0
Canada	19.2	24.1	23.0
United States	19.9	21.1	21.1
Developing Countries			
Brazil	18.3	21.9	15.4
China	35.1	47.9	44.2
India	24.3	36.5	31.6
Mexico	25.5	22.8	23.0
South Africa	15.1	19.5	17.9

Source: IMF.

The correlation between economic growth and investment is high. Countries that devote a large share of GDP to investment, such as China, India, and South Korea, have high growth rates. Some of the fastest-growing countries in Europe in the 1990s and for long periods since the year 2000, including Ireland and Spain, have the some of the highest investment-to-GDP ratios. Countries that devote a smaller share of GDP to investment, such as Brazil and Mexico, have slower growth rates. The data show why the Chinese economy has expanded at such a rapid rate: annual GDP growth rate in excess of 10% over long periods. Investment spending in China on new factories, equipment, and infrastructure as a percentage of GDP is the highest in the world, at more than 40% of GDP.

As we discussed earlier, long-term sustainable growth cannot rely on pure capital deepening. How can we reconcile this notion with the strong correlation between investment spending and economic growth across countries? First, although diminishing marginal productivity will eventually limit the impact of capital deepening, investment-driven growth may last for a considerable period, especially in countries that start with relatively low levels of capital per worker.

A second, and closely related, explanation is that the impact of investment spending on available capital depends on the existing physical capital stock. As with the share of GDP devoted to investment, the stock of capital available per worker varies significantly across countries. In 2000, the average US worker had $148,091 worth of capital, compared with $42,991 in Mexico and $6,270 in India (Heston, Summers, and Aten 2009). The wide difference in physical capital per worker suggests that the positive impact of changes in the physical capital stock on growth is very significant in developing countries. Mexican workers have relatively little access to machinery or equipment, so adding even a little can make a big percentage difference. In developed countries, such as the United States, Japan, Germany, France, and the United Kingdom, the physical capital stock is so large that positive net investment in any given year has only a small percentage effect on the accumulated capital stock. For the developed countries, a sustained high level of investment over many years is required to have a meaningful relative impact on the physical capital stock even though the absolute size of the increase in any given year is still larger than in the developing countries.

Third, because physical capital is not really homogeneous, the composition of investment spending and the stock of physical capital matters for growth and productivity. Insights obtained from the endogenous theory of growth (discussed later) and from studies attempting to obtain a more accurate measure of TFP show that the composition of the physical capital stock is very important. These studies suggest that capital spending could be separated into two categories. The first is spending on information, computers, and telecommunications equipment (ICT investment). Capital spending on these goods is a measure of the impact of the information technology sector on economic growth. One of the key drivers of growth in the developed countries over the last decade has been the IT sector. Growth in the IT sector has been driven by technological innovation that has caused the price of key technologies, such as semiconductors, to fall dramatically. The steep decline in the price of high-technology capital goods has encouraged investment in IT at the expense of other assets.

The IT sector has grown very rapidly and has made a significant contribution to increasing the rate of economic and productivity growth. The greater use of IT equipment in various industries has resulted in **network externalities**. Computers allow people to interconnect through the internet and by email, enabling them to work more productively. *The more people in the network, the greater the potential productivity gains*. The effects of the network externalities are largely captured in TFP rather than observed as a distinct, direct effect. The share of ICT investment in GDP tends to be in the 3%–5% range for most developed economies. The IT sector is still relatively small in most countries, and IT spending actually declined as a share of GDP between 2000 and 2008 because the early 2000s recession disproportionately affected high-technology spending.

The other category of investment, non-ICT capital spending, includes non-residential construction, transport equipment, and machinery. High levels of capital spending for this category should eventually result in capital deepening and thus have less impact on potential GDP growth. In contrast, a growing share of ICT investments in the economy, through their externality impacts, may actually boost the growth rate of potential GDP.

It is worthwhile to note that there have been important "transformational technologies" at various stages of history. One need only consider the impact of the steam engine, the internal combustion engine, powered flight, atomic energy, vaccination, and so on, to realize that revolutionary advances are not unique to information, computers, and tele-communications. All of these are, to some extent, "general purpose technologies" (GPT) that affect production and/or innovation in many sectors of the economy. ICT capital clearly embodies this GPT characteristic. Nanotechnology could well become the next "super GPT," at which point investing in ICT may begin to look like mere capital deepening.

Technology

The most important factor affecting growth of per capita GDP is technology, especially in developed countries. Technology allows an economy to overcome some of the limits imposed by diminishing marginal returns and results in an upward shift in the production function, as we noted in Exhibit 4. Technological progress makes it possible to produce more and/or higher-quality goods and services with the same resources or inputs. It also results in the creation of new goods and services. Technological progress can also be one of the factors improving how efficiently businesses are organized and managed.

Technological change can be embodied in human capital (knowledge, organization, information, and experience base) and/or in new machinery, equipment, and software. Therefore, high rates of investment are important, especially investment in ICT goods. Countries can also innovate through expenditures, both public and private, on research and development (R&D). Expenditures on R&D and the number of patents issued, although not directly measuring innovation, provide some useful insight into innovative performance. Exhibit 9 shows R&D spending as a share of GDP for various countries. The developed countries spend the highest percentage of GDP on R&D because they must rely on innovation and the development of new products and production methods for growth. In contrast, developing countries spend less on R&D because these countries can acquire new technology through imitation or copying the technology developed elsewhere. The embodiment of technology in capital goods can enable relatively poor countries to narrow the gap relative to the technology leaders. It should also be noted that the relationship between economic growth and R&D spending is not clear-cut. Although technological innovation resulting from high R&D spending raises output and productivity in the long run, it may result in a cyclical slowing of growth as companies and workers are displaced by the new technologies. This is the Schumpeterian concept of creative destruction, which captures the double-edged nature of technological innovation.

Exhibit 9: Research and Development as a Percentage of GDP in Selected Countries

	1990	2009	2016
France	2.3	2.2	2.2
Germany	2.6	2.8	2.9
Ireland	0.8	1.8	1.2
Italy	1.2	1.3	1.3
Spain	0.8	1.4	1.2
United Kingdom	2.1	1.9	1.7
Australia	1.3	2.2	1.9
Japan	3.0	3.4	3.1
South Korea	1.7	3.1	4.2
Singapore	1.1	2.9	2.2
Canada	1.5	2.0	1.6
United States	2.6	2.9	2.7
China	NA	1.7	2.1
India	NA	0.8	0.8
Mexico	NA	0.4	0.5

Source: OECD.

The state of technology, as reflected by total factor productivity, embodies the cumulative effects of scientific advances, applied research and development, improvements in management methods, and ways of organizing production that raise the productive capacity of factories and offices. Because it is measured as a residual, TFP estimates are very sensitive to the measurements of the labor and capital inputs. Empirical work at the

Conference Board and the OECD accounts for changes in the composition and quality of both the labor and capital inputs. The resulting measure of TFP should capture the technological and organizational improvements that increase output for a given level of inputs. Exhibit 10 provides data for the periods 1995–2005 and 2005–2018 on the growth rate in labor productivity and total factor productivity. Labor productivity growth depends on both capital deepening and technological progress. The contribution of capital deepening can be measured as the difference between the growth rates of labor productivity and total factor productivity. For example, from 2005 to 2018, South Korea's labor productivity grew by 3.3% per year, of which 2.5% (3.3% − 0.8%) came from capital deepening, with the rest coming from changes in TFP (note that rounding causes minor discrepancies in the calculations in the exhibit). The larger the difference between the productivity growth measures, the more important capital deepening is as a source of economic growth. As we discussed previously, however, growth in per capita income cannot be sustained perpetually by capital deepening.

Exhibit 10: Labor and Total Factor Productivity

	Growth in Hours Worked (%)	Growth in Labor Prod. (%)	Growth in TFP (%)	Growth from Capital Deepening (%)	Growth in GDP (%)	Productivity Level 2018; GDP per Hour Worked ($)
Germany						70
1995–2005	−0.3	1.6	0.9	0.7	1.3	
2005–2018	0.8	0.8	0.2	0.7	1.6	
Ireland						84
1995–2005	3.2	4.1	1.7	2.4	7.3	
2005–2018	0.6	2.9	0.1	2.7	3.3	
United States						73
1995–2005	0.9	2.4	0.9	1.5	3.3	
2005–2018	0.9	1.2	0.0	1.3	1.9	
Japan						47
1995–2005	−1.0	2.1	0.4	1.7	1.1	
2005–2018	0.0	1.0	−0.1	1.1	1.0	
South Korea						39
1995–2005	0.0	4.3	2.4	1.9	4.3	
2005–2018	0.1	3.3	0.8	2.5	3.3	
China						15
1995–2005	1.1	6.7	1.5	5.2	7.8	
2005–2018	0.2	9.2	4.3	5.0	9.0	
India						9
1995–2005	2.1	4.2	1.9	2.3	6.3	
2005–2018	1.2	6.3	1.8	4.5	7.2	
Brazil						19
1995–2005	2.1	0.3	−0.3	0.6	2.4	
2005–2018	0.8	1.3	−0.7	1.9	2.0	
Mexico						21

	Growth in Hours Worked (%)	Growth in Labor Prod. (%)	Growth in TFP (%)	Growth from Capital Deepening (%)	Growth in GDP (%)	Productivity Level 2018; GDP per Hour Worked ($)
1995–2005	2.2	1.4	0.4	1.0	3.6	
2005–2018	2.1	0.1	−0.2	0.4	2.2	

Source: Conference Board Total Economy Database.

Exhibit 10 also provides data on the *level* of labor productivity or the amount of GDP produced per hour of work. The level of productivity depends on the accumulated stock of human and physical capital and is much higher among the developed countries. For example, China has a population of more than 1.3 billion people, compared with slightly more than 300 million people in the United States. Although the United States has significantly fewer workers than China because of its smaller population, its economy as measured by real GDP is much larger. This is because US workers have historically been more productive than Chinese workers as measured by GDP per hour worked, as shown in Exhibit 10. In contrast to the *level* of productivity, the *growth rate* of productivity will typically be higher in the developing countries, where human and physical capital are scarce but growing rapidly and the impact of diminishing marginal returns is relatively small.

An understanding of productivity trends is critical for global investors. A permanent increase in the rate of labor productivity growth will increase the sustainable rate of economic growth and raise the upper boundary for earnings growth and the potential return on equities. In contrast, a low growth rate of labor productivity, if it persists over a number of years, suggests poor prospects for equity prices. A slowdown in productivity growth lowers both the long-run potential growth rate of the economy and the upper limit for earnings growth. Such a development would be associated with slow growth in profits and correspondingly low equity returns.

EXAMPLE 7

Why the Sluggish Growth in the Japanese Economy?

Annual growth in real GDP in Japan averaged about 1% since 1990. This growth is in sharp contrast to the 4.2% annual growth rate experienced from 1971 to 1990. The sluggish growth in Japan should not be surprising. Japan's economy is growing at its potential rate of growth, which is limited by the following:

1. The labor input is not growing. Population growth has been essentially zero since 2000 (Exhibit 5), and average hours worked per year per person is declining (Exhibit 8).

2. There has been a lack of technological innovation. The lack of growth in the labor input could be offset through higher productivity derived from innovation and more efficient use of available inputs. However, this is not occurring in Japan. Total factor productivity (Exhibit 10) increased at a sluggish 0.4% annual rate from 1995 to 2005 and declined slightly between 2005 and 2018.

3. Diminishing returns to capital are very significant. Despite the negative growth in TFP, labor productivity growth remained relatively high. This means that all the growth in labor productivity in Japan resulted from capital deepening (Exhibit 10). The problem for Japan,

> as discussed in earlier, is that once the capital-to-labor ratio becomes high, further additions to capital have little impact on per capita output. Thus, the growth in labor productivity should slow.

1. Use the data for 2005–2018 and the labor productivity growth accounting equation to estimate the growth rate in potential GDP for Japan.

   Solution

   To estimate the growth rate in potential GDP, we use Equation 5, given by

   Growth rate of potential GDP = Long-term growth rate of labor force + Long-term growth rate in labor productivity

   To use this equation, we need to project the growth rate in the labor input and labor productivity.

   The hours worked data in Exhibit 10 are a potential source to use to estimate the growth rate of the labor input. Exhibit 10 shows the labor input for Japan unchanged between 2005 and 2018. This was partly caused by the negative impact of the global recession on hours worked. As an alternative, the labor input should grow at the same rate as the population plus the net change in immigration. The population data in Exhibit 5 show essentially zero population growth in Japan for the period 2000–2018. This trend is likely to continue. Thus, a reasonable estimate for potential GDP growth in Japan is around 1%. We get this estimate by assuming no growth in the labor input and a 1% annual increase in labor productivity (using data from Exhibit 10 for 2005–2018).

Public Infrastructure

The final expansion of the definition of the capital input is public infrastructure investment. Roads, bridges, municipal water, dams and, in some countries, electric grids are all examples of public capital. They have few substitutes and are largely complements to the production of private sector goods and services. Ashauer (1990) found that infrastructure investment is an important source of productivity growth and should be included as an input in the production function. As with R&D spending, the full impact of government infrastructure investment may extend well beyond the direct benefits of the projects because improvements in the economy's infrastructure generally boost the productivity of private investments.

9 SUMMARY OF ECONOMIC GROWTH DETERMINANTS

Long-term sustainable growth is determined by the rate of expansion of real potential GDP. Expansion of the supply of factors of production (inputs) and improvements in technology are the sources of growth. The factors of production include human capital, ICT and non-ICT capital, public capital, labor, and natural resources. Data for the sources of growth are available from the OECD and the Conference Board. Exhibit 11 provides data from the Conference Board on the sources of output growth for various countries. These estimates are based on the growth accounting formula.

Exhibit 11: Sources of Output Growth

	Contribution from:					
	Labor Quantity (%)	Labor Quality (%)	Non-ICT Capital (%)	ICT Capital (%)	TFP (%)	Growth in GDP (%)
Germany						
1995–2005	−0.2	0.1	0.3	0.2	0.9	1.3
2005–2018	0.4	0.1	0.6	0.3	0.2	1.6
Ireland						
1995–2005	2.0	0.3	2.6	0.7	1.7	7.3
2005–2018	0.0	0.3	2.5	0.3	0.1	3.3
United States						
1995–2005	0.6	0.3	0.7	0.8	0.9	3.3
2005–2018	0.4	0.3	0.7	0.5	0.0	1.9
Japan						
1995–2005	−0.6	0.4	0.6	0.3	0.4	1.1
2005–2018	0.0	0.3	0.5	0.3	−0.1	1.0
South Korea						
1995–2005	−0.5	0.8	1.1	0.5	2.4	4.3
2005–2018	0.0	0.1	1.9	0.5	0.8	3.3
China						
1995–2005	0.5	0.2	4.5	1.1	1.5	7.8
2005–2018	0.1	0.3	3.9	0.4	4.3	9.0
India						
1995–2005	1.0	0.2	2.7	0.5	1.9	6.3
2005–2018	0.7	0.6	3.4	0.8	1.8	7.2
Brazil						
1995–2005	0.8	0.1	1.1	0.7	−0.3	2.4
2005–2018	0.4	0.8	1.2	0.4	−0.7	2.0
Mexico						
1995–2005	1.2	0.2	1.4	0.4	0.4	3.6
2005–2018	1.0	0.1	1.1	0.2	−0.2	2.2

Notes: A standard growth accounting model (expanded version of Equation 4) is used to compute the contribution of each input to aggregate output (GDP) growth. The inputs include both the quantity and quality of labor and ICT and non-ICT capital. Each input is weighted by its share in national income, and TFP captures all sources of growth that are left unexplained by the labor and capital inputs. Rounding is used throughout.
Source: Conference Board Total Economy Database.

EXAMPLE 8

The Irish Economy

As shown in Exhibit 1, economic growth in Ireland since 1980 has been significantly higher than that experienced in the major European economies of Germany, France, and the United Kingdom. In 1970, the per capita GDP of Ireland, at $9,869, was 45.2% below the per capita GDP of the United Kingdom.

By 2010, per capita GDP in Ireland caught up with or exceeded most other developed European countries. Like most of the global economy, Ireland fell into a deep recession in 2009, with GDP contracting by more than 7%, before staging a recovery and reaching annual growth of more than 5% for several years in the 2010–2018 period. To understand the factors driving the Irish economy and the prospects for future equity returns, use the data in Exhibit 11 and the following population data to address these questions:

1. Using the growth accounting framework data, evaluate the sources of growth for the Irish economy starting from 1995.

   Solution

   The sources of growth for an economy include labor quantity, labor quality, non-ICT capital, ICT capital, and TFP. The growth accounting data in Exhibit 11 indicate that economic growth in Ireland from 1995 to 2018 is explained by the following factors:

Input	Contribution: 1995–2005		Contribution: 2005–2018	
Labor		**2.3%**		**0.3%**
Labor quantity	2.0%		0.0%	
Labor quality	0.3%		0.3%	
Capital/Investment		**3.3%**		**2.8%**
Non-ICT capital	2.6%		2.5%	
ICT capital	0.7%		0.3%	
TFP		**1.7%**		**0.1%**
Total: GDP growth		**7.3%**		**3.3%**

   In sum, the main driver of growth for the Irish economy since 1995 has been capital spending. It accounted for more than 45% of growth in 1995–2005 and has been the dominant factor contributing to growth in the Irish economy since 2005. Another way to look at growth in Ireland for the period 2005–2018 is that all the growth is through capital deepening. As shown in Exhibit 11, capital deepening added 2.7% to growth, which caused an increase in labor productivity of 2.9%.

2. What is likely to happen to the potential rate of growth for Ireland? What are the prospects for equity returns?

	2000	2010	2016	Avg. Annual Growth Rate
Population (millions)	3.8	4.5	4.9	1.6%
Net immigration total (2000–2010)		0.38m		
Net immigration total (2011–2016)		0.19m		
Population less immigrants (millions)	3.8	4.1	4.3	0.8%

Solution

If we look forward, prospects for the economy are not as favorable as in the past. To estimate the growth rate in potential GDP, we use Equation 5, given by

Growth rate of potential GDP = Long-term growth rate of labor force + Long-term growth rate in labor productivity

To use this equation, we need to project the growth rate in the labor input and labor productivity. The total hours worked data in Exhibit 11 are one potential source to use to estimate the growth rate of the labor input. Exhibit 11 shows the labor input increasing by 0.6% annually between 2005 and 2018. The problem here is that the decline in hours worked is overstated because of the negative impact of the 2008–2009 recession on hours worked. As an alternative, the labor input should grow at the same rate as the population plus the net change resulting from immigration. The population data for Ireland (given above) show that more than half of the population growth between 2000 and 2010 resulted from immigration. Since 2009, however, outward migration has replaced inward migration for a short period, and the rate of growth in labor input declined. Thus, a more reasonable, perhaps somewhat conservative, estimate for labor force growth is 0.3%. We also assume the following:

1. There is no increase in labor productivity coming from capital deepening as investment slows (resulting in essentially no growth in net investment and the physical capital stock).

2. TFP growth reverts to its average growth rate of 1.7% in the 1995–2005 period (see Exhibit 11).

3. Labor productivity grows at the same rate as TFP.

Thus, growth in potential GDP is 0.3% + 1.7% = 2.0%.

In summary, despite the projected rebound in TFP growth, overall potential growth in Ireland is likely to decline because labor input growth and capital deepening no longer contribute to overall growth. As discussed earlier, slower growth in potential GDP will limit potential earnings growth and equity price appreciation.

EXAMPLE 9

Investment Outlook for China and India

The Investment Policy Committee at Global Invest Inc. is interested in increasing the firm's exposure to either India or China because of their rapid rates of economic growth. Economic growth in China has been close to 9% over the last few years, and India has grown more than 7%. You are asked by the committee to do the following:

1. Determine the sources of growth for the two economies and review the data on productivity and investment using information from Exhibit 11. Which of the two countries looks more attractive based on the sources of growth?

   Solution

   The sources of economic growth include size of labor force, quality of labor force (human capital), ICT and non-ICT capital, natural resources, and technology. Looking at the sources of growth in Exhibit 11, we determine the following:

Input	Percent Contribution: 1995–2005	Percent Contribution: 2005–2018
India		
Labor quantity	1.0	0.7
Labor quality	0.2	0.6
Non-ICT capital	2.7	3.4
ICT capital	0.5	0.8
TFP	1.9	1.8
Total: GDP growth	6.3	7.2
China		
Labor quantity	0.5	0.1
Labor quality	0.2	0.3
Non-ICT capital	4.5	3.9
ICT capital	1.1	0.4
TFP	1.5	4.3
Total: GDP growth	7.8	9.0

   - The contribution of the labor quantity input is more important to growth in India than in China. Labor quantity contributed 1% to India's GDP growth over 1995–2005 and 0.7% over 2005–2018. The equivalent numbers for China are 0.5% and 0.1%, respectively. Looking ahead, we can project that labor is likely to be a major factor adding to India's growth. The population of India (Exhibit 5) is growing at a faster rate than that of China. The annual growth rate in population from 2005 to 2018 was 1.34% in India versus 0.50% in China. Also, hours worked in India (Exhibit 11) are growing at a faster rate than in China. Therefore, the workforce and labor quantity input should grow faster in India. The edge here goes to India.

   - The contribution to GDP made by the quality of the labor force is essentially identical in the two countries (0.2% in China versus 0.2% in India between 1995 and 2005 and 0.3% in China and 0.6% in India between 2005 and 2018). This factor is stronger in India.

   - The contribution of non-ICT capital investment is significantly higher in China (4.5% in China versus 2.7% in India between 1995 and 2005 and 3.9% in China and 3.4% in India between 2005 and 2018). The edge goes to China.

- The contribution of ICT capital investment was significantly higher in China (1.1% in China versus 0.5% in India between 1995 and 2005). Since 2005, it has contributed 0.4% to growth in China and 0.8% in India, which has an edge.

- Both countries spend a high percentage of GDP on capital investment (Exhibit 9). In 2018, investment spending as a percentage of GDP was 44% in China and 32% in India. The Chinese share is higher, and this provides China with an edge unless diminishing marginal returns to capital deepening become an issue. This scenario is not likely for a while, however, given the relatively low level of capital per worker in China. China and India still have a way to go to converge with the developed economies. The advantage goes to China.

- The contribution of technological progress is measured by TFP. Comparing the two countries, we find that TPF growth was higher in India over the period 1995–2005 (1.9% in India versus 1.5% in China). For the period 2005–2018, however, TFP growth was significantly higher in China (4.3% versus 1.8%). In addition, expenditures on R&D for 2016 (Exhibit 10) as a percentage of GDP were higher in China (2.1% in China and 0.8% in India). The edge here goes to China.

- Finally, growth in overall labor productivity (Exhibit 11) is considerably higher in China than India (9.2% in China versus 6.3% in India between 2005 and 2018). This dynamic resulted from both a greater increase in the capital-to-labor ratio in China (because of the high rate of investment, the physical capital stock is growing faster than the labor input) and faster technological progress in China. The edge here goes to China.

In sum, based on the sources of growth, China appears to be slightly better positioned for growth in the future.

2. Estimate the long-term sustainable earnings growth rate using data from 1995 to 2018.

Solution

Estimates of potential GDP using the inputs from Exhibit 11 for China and India are

Growth rate in potential GDP = Long-term growth rate of labor force (equals growth in hours worked in Exhibit 11) + Long-term growth rate in labor productivity.

China (using 1995–2018)

Growth in potential GDP = 0.6% + 7.9% = 8.5% (calculated as geometric mean growth rates using data for the 1995–2005 and 2005–2018 subperiods).

India (using 1995–2018)

Growth in potential GDP = 1.6% + 5.2% = 6.8%

3. Make an investment recommendation.

    Solution

    Growth prospects in both countries are very attractive. China's growth potential is higher, however, because of its greater level of capital spending and the greater contribution of technological progress toward growth. Long-term earnings growth is closely tied to the growth rate in potential GDP. Therefore, based on the previous calculations, earnings in China would be projected to grow at an annual rate of 8.5%, compared with 6.8% in India. Over the next decade, ignoring current valuation, the Chinese equity market would be projected to outperform the Indian market as its higher rate of sustainable growth translates into a higher rate of appreciation in equity values. Note that the global economy is evolving rapidly, and past trends may or may not be sustained. This is especially true of China and India. To provide concrete answers that do not require the reader to bring in additional information, our exercise solutions must assume that past patterns are indicative of the future.

10   THEORIES OF GROWTH

☐ | compare classical growth theory, neoclassical growth theory, and endogenous growth theory

The factors that drive long-term economic growth and determine the rate of sustainable growth in an economy are the subject of much debate among economists. The academic growth literature includes three main paradigms with respect to per capita growth in an economy—the classical, neoclassical, and endogenous growth models. Per capita economic growth under the classical model is only temporary because an exploding population with limited resources brings growth to an end. In the neoclassical model, long-run per capita growth depends solely on exogenous technological progress. The final model of growth attempts to explain technology within the model itself—thus the term endogenous growth.

Classical Model

Classical growth theory was developed by Thomas Malthus in his 1798 publication *Essay on the Principle of Population.* Commonly referred to as the Malthusian theory, it is focused on the impact of a growing population in a world with limited resources. The concerns of resource depletion and overpopulation are central themes within the Malthusian perspective on growth. The production function in the classical model is relatively simple and consists of a labor input with land as a fixed factor. The key assumption underlying the classical model is that population growth accelerates when the level of per capita income rises above the subsistence income, which is the minimum income needed to maintain life. This means that technological progress and land expansion, which increase labor productivity, translate into higher population growth. But because the labor input faces diminishing marginal returns, the additional output produced by the growing workforce eventually declines to zero. Ultimately, the population grows so much that labor productivity falls and per capita income returns back to the subsistence level.

The classical model predicts that in the long run, the adoption of new technology results in a larger but not richer population. Thus, the standard of living is constant over time even with technological progress, and there is no growth in per capita output. As a result of this gloomy forecast, economics was labeled the "dismal science."

The prediction from the Malthusian model failed for two reasons:

1. The link between per capita income and population broke down. In fact, as the growth of per capita income increased, population growth slowed rather than accelerating as predicted by the classical growth model.

2. Growth in per capita income has been possible because technological progress has been rapid enough to more than offset the impact of diminishing marginal returns.

Because the classical model's pessimistic prediction never materialized, economists changed the focus of the analysis away from labor to capital and to the neoclassical model.

Neoclassical Model

Robert Solow devised the mainstream neoclassical theory of growth in the 1950s (Solow 1957). The heart of this theory is the Cobb–Douglas production function discussed earlier. As before, the potential output of the economy is given by

$$Y = AF(K,L) = AK^\alpha L^{1-\alpha},$$

where K is the stock of capital, L is the labor input, and A is total factor productivity. In the neoclassical model, both capital and labor are variable inputs each subject to diminishing marginal productivity.

The objective of the neoclassical growth model is to determine the long-run growth rate of output per capita and relate it to (a) the savings/investment rate, (b) the rate of technological change, and (c) population growth.

Balanced or Steady-State Rate of Growth

As with most economic models, the neoclassical growth model attempts to find the equilibrium position toward which the economy will move. In the case of the Solow model, this equilibrium is the balanced or **steady-state rate of growth** that occurs when the output-to-capital ratio is constant. Growth is balanced in the sense that capital per worker and output per worker grow at the same rate.

We begin the analysis by using the per capita version of the Cobb–Douglas production function given earlier in Equation 3:

$$Y = Y/L = Ak^\alpha,$$

where $k = K/L$. Using their definitions, the rates of change of capital per worker and output per worker are given by

$$\Delta k/k = \Delta K/K - \Delta L/L$$

and

$$\Delta y/y = \Delta Y/Y - \Delta L/L.$$

From the production function, the growth rate of output per worker is also equal to

$$\Delta y/y = \Delta A/A + \alpha\Delta k/k. \tag{6}$$

Note that these and other rate of change equations are exact only for changes over arbitrarily short periods ("continuous time").

The physical capital stock in an economy will increase because of gross investment (*I*) and decline because of depreciation. In a closed economy, investment must be funded by domestic saving. Letting *s* be the fraction of income (*Y*) that is saved, gross investment is given by *I* = *sY*. Assuming the physical capital stock depreciates at a constant rate, δ, the change in the physical capital stock is given by

$$\Delta K = sY - \delta K.$$

Subtracting labor supply growth, $\Delta L/L \equiv n$, and rearranging gives

$$\Delta k/k = sY/K - \delta - n. \tag{7}$$

In the steady state, the growth rate of capital per worker is equal to the growth rate of output per worker. Thus,

$$\Delta k/k = \Delta y/y = \Delta A/A + \alpha \Delta k/k,$$

from which we get

$$\Delta y/y = \Delta k/k = (\Delta A/A)/(1 - \alpha).$$

Letting θ denote the growth rate of TFP (i.e., $\Delta A/A$), we see that the equilibrium sustainable growth rate of output per capita (= Growth rate of capital per worker) is a constant that depends only on the growth rate of TFP (θ) and the elasticity of output with respect to capital (α). Adding back the growth rate of labor (*n*) gives the sustainable growth rate of output.

$$\text{Growth rate of output per capita} = \frac{\theta}{1 - \alpha} \tag{8}$$

$$\text{Growth rate of output} = \frac{\theta}{1 - \alpha} + n$$

This is the key result of the neoclassical model. Note that θ/(1 − α) is the steady-state growth rate of labor productivity, so Equation 8 is consistent with the labor productivity growth accounting equation discussed earlier.

Substituting θ/(1 − α) into the left-hand side of Equation 7 and rearranging gives the equilibrium output-to-capital ratio, denoted by the constant Ψ.

$$\frac{Y}{K} = \left(\frac{1}{s}\right)\left[\left(\frac{\theta}{1-\alpha}\right) + \delta + n\right] \equiv \Psi \tag{9}$$

In the steady state, the output-to-capital ratio is constant and the capital-to-labor ratio (*k*) and output per worker (*y*) grow at the same rate, given by θ/(1 − α). On the steady-state growth path, the marginal product of capital is also constant and, given the Cobb–Douglas production function, is equal to α(*Y*/*K*). The marginal product of capital is also equal to the real interest rate in the economy. Note that even though the capital-to-labor ratio (*k*) is rising at rate θ/(1 − α) in the steady state, the increase in the capital-to-labor ratio (*k*) has no impact on the marginal product of capital, which is not changing. *Capital deepening is occurring, but it has no effect on the growth rate of the economy or on the marginal product of capital once the steady state is reached.*

EXAMPLE 10

Steady-State Rate of Growth for China, Japan, and Ireland

Earlier examples generated estimates of potential growth for China (8.5%), Japan (1.0%), and Ireland (2.0%). Given the following data, address these questions:

1. Calculate the steady-state growth rates from the neoclassical model for China, Japan, and Ireland.

   Solution

   Using Equation 8, the steady-state growth rate in the neoclassical model is given by

   $\Delta Y/Y = (\theta)/(1 - \alpha) + n$ = Growth rate of TFP scaled by labor factor share + Growth rate in the labor force

   Using the preceding equation and data, we can estimate steady-state growth rates for the three countries as follows:

   China: The labor share of output $(1 - \alpha)$ is given by the average of the labor cost as a percentage of total factor cost, which is equal to 0.561 for China. The growth rate in the labor force is 1.2%, and the growth rate of TFP is 2.9%.

   Steady-state growth rate = 2.9%/0.561 + 1.2% = 6.37%

   Japan: The labor share of output $(1 - \alpha)$ for Japan is 0.538. The growth rate in the labor force is 0.0%, and TFP growth is 0.2%.

   Steady-state growth rate = 0.2%/0.538 + 0.0% = 0.37%

   Ireland: The labor share of output $(1 - \alpha)$ is 0.574% for Ireland. The growth rate in the labor force is 0.3%, and TFP growth is 0.9%.

   Steady-state growth rate = 0.9%/0.574 + 0.3% = 1.87%

2. Compare the steady-state growth rates to the growth rates in potential GDP estimated in Examples 7–9 and explain the results.

	Labor Cost in Total Factor Cost (%)	TFP Growth (%)	Labor Force Growth (%)
China	56.1	2.9	1.2
Japan	53.8	0.2	0.0
Ireland	57.4	0.9	0.3

Sources: Conference Board Total Economy Database; labor cost based on 2008–2018, TFP growth based on 1995–2018. Labor force growth based on assumptions and estimates from earlier examples.

   Solution

   The growth rate in potential GDP for China (8.5%, estimated in Example 9) is significantly above the estimated 6.37% steady-state growth rate. The reason for this is that the economy of China is still in the process of converging to the higher income levels of the United States and the major economies in Europe. The physical capital stock is below the steady state, and capital deepening is a significant factor increasing productivity growth (see Exhibit 11) and the growth in potential GDP.

   This is not the case for Japan and Ireland. Both countries are operating at essentially the steady state. The estimated growth rate in potential GDP for Japan (1.0%, from Example 7) is only slightly above its 0.37% steady-state growth rate. Likewise, the estimated growth rate in potential GDP for Ireland (2.0%, from Example 8) is effectively equal to its estimated steady-state growth rate of 1.87%. Operating close to the steady state means

> that capital investment in these countries, which results in an increasing capital-to-labor ratio, has no significant effect on the growth rate of the economy. Only changes in the growth rates of TFP and labor and in the labor share of output have an impact on potential GDP growth.

An intuitive way to understand the steady-state equilibrium given in Equation 9 is to transform it into a savings/investment equation:

$$sy = \left[\left(\frac{\theta}{1-\alpha}\right) + \delta + n\right]k$$

Steady-state equilibrium occurs at the output-to-capital ratio where the savings and actual gross investment per worker generated in the economy (sy) are just sufficient to (1) provide capital for new workers entering the workforce at rate n, (2) replace plant and equipment wearing out at rate δ, and (3) deepen the physical capital stock at the rate $\theta/(1 - \alpha)$ required to keep the marginal product of capital equal to the rental price of capital.

Exhibit 12 shows the steady-state equilibrium graphically. The straight line in the exhibit indicates the amount of investment required to keep the physical capital stock growing at the required rate. Because the horizontal axis is capital per worker, the slope of the line is given by $[\delta + n + \theta/(1 - \alpha)]$. The curved line shows the amount of actual investment per worker and is determined by the product of the saving rate and the production function. It is curved because of diminishing marginal returns to the capital input in the production function. The intersection of the required investment and actual investment lines determines the steady state. Note that *this exhibit is a snapshot at a point in time*. Over time, the capital-to-labor ratio rises at rate $[\theta/(1 - \alpha)]$ as the actual saving/investment curve $[sf(k)]$ shifts upward because of TFP growth, and *the equilibrium moves upward and to the right along the straight line.*

Exhibit 12: Steady State in the Neoclassical Model

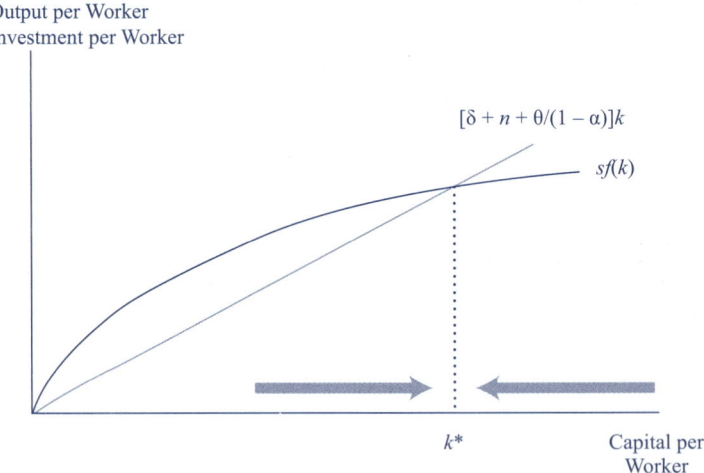

The impact of the various parameters in the model on the steady state can also be seen in the exhibit. At any point in time when the economy is on its steady-state growth path, the exogenous factors—labor supply and TFP—are fixed. We would like to know what effect each of the parameters in the model has on the steady-state capital-to-labor ratio and therefore on output per worker. For example, if there are two economies that differ only with respect to one parameter, what does that imply about their per capita incomes? All else the same, we can say the following regarding the impact of the parameters:

- *Saving rate (s)*: An increase in the saving rate implies a higher capital-to-labor ratio (k) and higher output per worker (y) because a higher saving rate generates more saving/investment at every level of output. In Exhibit 13, the saving/investment curve [$sf(k)$] shifts upward from an initial steady-state equilibrium at point A to a new equilibrium at point B. At the new equilibrium point, it intersects the required investment line [$\delta + n + \theta/(1 - \alpha)$] at higher capital-to-labor and output per worker ratios. Note that although the higher saving rate increases both k and y, it has no impact on the steady-state growth rates of output per capita or output (Equation 8).

Exhibit 13: Impact on the Steady State: Increase in the Saving Rate

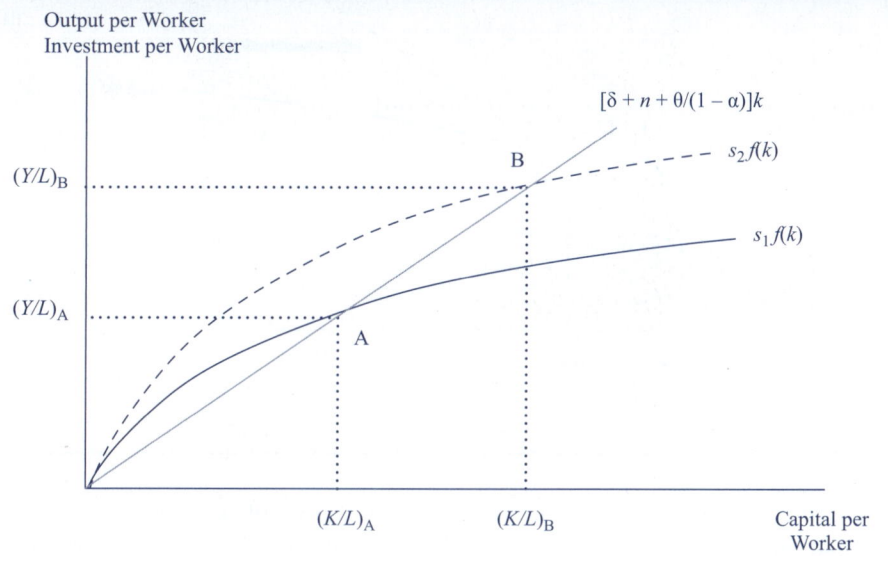

- *Labor force growth (n)*: An increase in the labor force growth rate reduces the equilibrium capital-to-labor ratio because a corresponding increase in the steady-state growth rate of capital is required. Given the gross saving/investment rate, this can be achieved only at a lower capital-to-labor ratio. Output per worker is correspondingly lower as well. In Exhibit 14, the higher population growth rate increases the slope of the required investment line. This shifts the steady-state equilibrium from point A to point B, where it intersects the supply of saving/investment curve at lower capital-to-labor and output per worker ratios.

- *Depreciation rate (δ)*: An increase in the depreciation rate reduces the equilibrium capital-to-labor and output per worker ratios because a given rate of gross saving generates less net capital accumulation. Graphically, it increases the slope of the required investment line and affects the steady-state equilibrium in the same way as labor force growth (Exhibit 14).

- *Growth in TFP (θ)*: An increase in the growth rate of TFP reduces the steady-state capital-to-labor ratio and output per worker for given levels of labor input and TFP. This result must be interpreted with care. Raising the growth rate of TFP means that output per worker will grow faster in the future (Equation 8), but at a given point in time, a given supply of labor, and a given *level* of TFP, output per worker is lower than it would be with a slower TFP growth rate. In effect, the economy is on a steeper trajectory off a lower base of output per worker. Graphically, it is identical to Exhibit 14 in that faster TFP growth steepens the required investment line (increases the slope), which intersects with the available saving/investment curve at lower capital-to-labor and investment per worker ratios.

Exhibit 14: Impact on the Steady State: Increase in Labor Force Growth

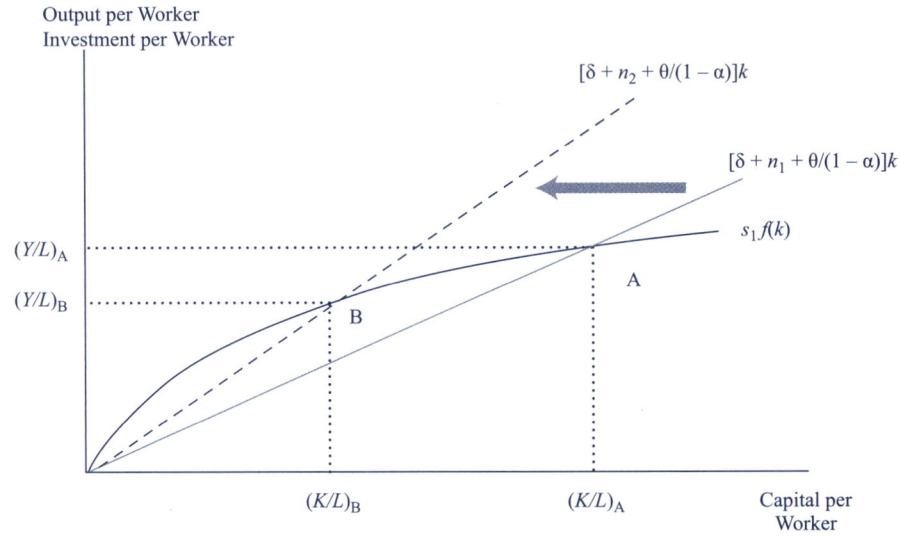

In sum, such factors as the saving rate, the growth rate of the labor force, and the depreciation rate change the *level* of output per worker but do not permanently change the *growth rate* of output per worker. A permanent increase in the growth rate in output per worker can occur only if there is a change in the growth rate of TFP.

So far we have focused on the steady-state growth path. What happens if the economy has not yet reached the steady state? During the transition to the steady-state growth path, the economy can experience either faster or slower growth relative to the steady state. Using Equations 6, 7, and 9, we can write the growth rates of output per capita and the capital-to-labor ratio as, respectively,

$$\frac{\Delta y}{y} = \left(\frac{\theta}{1-\alpha}\right) + \alpha s\left(\frac{Y}{K} - \Psi\right) = \left(\frac{\theta}{1-\alpha}\right) + \alpha s(y/k - \Psi) \tag{10}$$

and

$$\frac{\Delta k}{k} = \left(\frac{\theta}{1-\alpha}\right) + s\left(\frac{Y}{K} - \Psi\right) = \left(\frac{\theta}{1-\alpha}\right) + s(y/k - \Psi), \tag{11}$$

where the second equality in each line follows from the definitions of y and k, which imply $(Y/K) = y/k$. These relationships are shown in Exhibit 15.

Exhibit 15: Dynamics in the Neoclassical Model

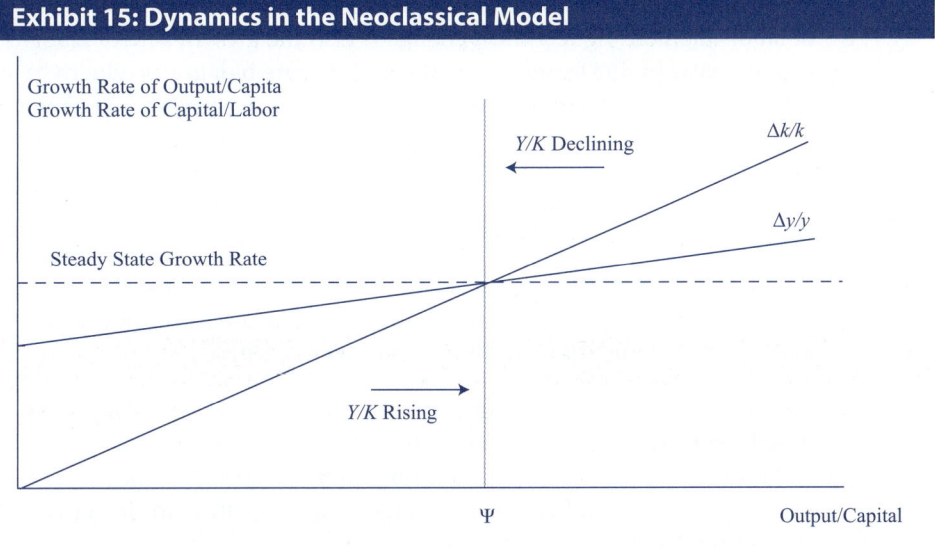

If the output-to-capital ratio is above its equilibrium level (ψ), the second term in Equations 10 and 11 is positive and the growth rates of output per capita and the capital-to-labor ratio are above the steady-state rate $\theta/(1 - \alpha)$. This corresponds to a situation in which actual saving/investment exceeds required investment and above-trend growth in per capita output is driven by an above-trend rate of capital deepening. This situation usually reflects a relatively low capital-to-labor ratio but could, at least in principle, arise from high TFP. Because $\alpha < 1$, capital is growing faster than output and the output-to-capital ratio is falling. Over time, the growth rates of both output per capita and the capital-to-labor ratio decline to the steady-state rate.

Of course, the converse is true if the output-to-capital ratio is below its steady-state level. Actual investment is insufficient to sustain the trend rate of growth in the capital-to-labor ratio, and both output per capita and the capital-to-labor ratio grow more slowly. This situation usually corresponds to a relatively high and unsustainable capital-to-labor ratio, but it could reflect relatively low TFP and hence relatively low output. Over time, output grows faster than capital, the output-to-capital ratio rises, and growth converges to the trend rate.

IMPLICATIONS OF NEOCLASSICAL MODEL

11

There are four major groups of conclusions from the neoclassical model:

1. Capital Accumulation

   a. Capital accumulation affects the level of output but not the growth rate in the long run.

   b. Regardless of its initial capital-to-labor ratio or initial level of productivity, a growing economy will move to a point of steady-state growth.

   c. In a steady state, the growth rate of output equals the rate of labor force growth plus the rate of growth in TFP scaled by labor's share of income $[n + \theta/(1 - \alpha)]$. The growth rate of output does not depend on the accumulation of capital or the rate of business investment. Those familiar with the "labor-augmenting" technical change formulation of the neoclassical model should note that in that formulation, the rate of labor-augmenting technical change is also the growth rate of labor productivity. In our formulation, the growth rate of labor productivity is $\theta/(1 - \alpha)$. So both formulations imply that long-run growth equals the growth rate of the labor supply (n) plus a constant growth rate of labor productivity.

2. Capital Deepening vs. Technology

   a. Rapid growth that is above the steady-state rate of growth occurs when countries first begin to accumulate capital; but growth will slow as the process of accumulation continues (see Exhibit 16).

   b. Long-term sustainable growth cannot rely solely on capital deepening investment—that is, on increasing the stock of capital relative to labor. If the capital-to-labor ratio grows too rapidly (i.e., faster than labor productivity), capital becomes less productive, resulting in slower rather than faster growth.

   c. More generally, increasing the supply of some input(s) too rapidly relative to other inputs will lead to diminishing marginal returns and cannot be the basis for sustainable growth.

   d. In the absence of improvements in TFP, the growth of labor productivity and per capita output would eventually slow.

   e. Because of diminishing marginal returns to capital, the only way to sustain growth in potential GDP per capita is through technological change or growth in total factor productivity. This results in an upward shift in the production function—the economy produces more goods and services for any given mix of labor and capital inputs.

3. Convergence

   a. Given the relative scarcity and hence high marginal productivity of capital and potentially higher saving rates in developing countries, the growth rates of developing countries should exceed those of developed countries.

   b. As a result, there should be a convergence of per capita incomes between developed and developing countries over time.

4. Effect of Savings on Growth

   a. The initial impact of a higher saving rate is to temporarily raise the rate of growth in the economy. Mathematically, this can be seen as follows: Equation 9 indicates that an increase in the saving rate (s) reduces the steady-state output-to-capital ratio (ψ). This makes the last term in Equations 10 and 11 positive, raising the growth rates of output per capita (y) and the capital-to-labor ratio (k) above the steady-state rate. In response to the higher saving rate, growth exceeds the steady-state growth rate during a transition period. However, the economy returns to the balanced growth path after the transition period.

   b. During the transition period, the economy moves to a higher level of per capita output and productivity.

c. Once an economy achieves steady-state growth, the growth rate does not depend on the percentage of income saved or invested. Higher savings cannot permanently raise the growth rate of output.

d. Countries with higher saving rates, however, will have a higher level of per capita output, a higher capital-to-labor ratio, and a higher level of labor productivity.

EXAMPLE 11

Comparative Statics and Transitional Growth in the Neoclassical Model

Beginning in steady-state equilibrium, an economy's saving rate suddenly increases from 20% of income to 30% of income. Other key parameters describing the economy are as follows:

Growth rate of TFP (θ)	= 0.02
Income share of capital (α)	= 0.35
Depreciation rate (δ)	= 0.10
Labor force growth rate (n)	= 0.01

The following table shows the output-to-capital ratio that will prevail in this economy at various points in time after the increase in the saving rate.

Years after Saving Rate Increase	Output-to-Capital Ratio
5	0.5947
10	0.5415
25	0.4857
50	0.4708
100	0.4693
New steady state	??

By rearranging the Cobb–Douglas production function (Equation 3), the proportional impact of the saving rate change on the capital-to-labor ratio can be expressed in terms of the proportional impact on the output-to-capital ratio. The proportional impact on per capita income can then be determined from the production function (Equation 3). Labeling the paths with and without the change in saving rate as "new" and "old" respectively, at each date we have:[a]

$$\frac{k_{new}}{k_{old}} = \left[\frac{(Y/K)_{new}}{(Y/K)_{old}}\right]^{\frac{1}{\alpha-1}}$$

and

$$\frac{y_{new}}{y_{old}} = \left(\frac{k_{new}}{k_{old}}\right)^{\alpha}.$$

1. Using Equations 8 and 9, calculate the steady-state growth rate of per capita income and the steady-state output-to-capital ratio both before and after

the change in the saving rate. What happens to the capital-to-labor ratio and output per capita?

Solution

From Equation 8, the steady-state growth rate of per capita income, both before and after the increase in the saving rate, is $\Delta y/y = \theta/(1 - \alpha) = 0.02/(1 - 0.35) = 0.0308$, or 3.08%. From Equation 9, the steady-state output-to-capital ratio is

$$\frac{Y}{K} = \left(\frac{1}{s}\right)\left[\left(\frac{\theta}{1-\alpha}\right) + \delta + n\right] \equiv \Psi.$$

Using the parameter values given, $\theta/(1 - \alpha) + \delta + n = 0.0308 + 0.10 + 0.01 = 0.1408$, so the steady-state output-to-capital ratio is $0.1408/0.2 = 0.7040$ with the initial 20% saving rate and $0.1408/0.30 = 0.4693$ with the new 30% saving rate. As shown in Exhibit 14, both the capital-to-labor ratio and output per worker are at higher *levels* in the new steady state. But once the new steady state is achieved, they do not grow any faster than they did in the steady state with the lower saving rate.

2. Use the output-to-capital ratios given in the preceding table along with Equation 10 and your answers to Question 1 to determine the growth rate of per capita income that will prevail immediately following the change in the saving rate and at each of the indicated times after the change. Explain the pattern of growth rates.

Solution

According to Equation 10, the growth rate of per capita income is given by

$$\frac{\Delta y}{y} = \left(\frac{\theta}{1-\alpha}\right) + \alpha s(y/k - \Psi).$$

Immediately following the increase in the saving rate, the relevant value of ψ becomes the new steady-state output-to-capital ratio (0.4693). The actual output-to-capital ratio does not change immediately, so y/k is initially still 0.7040. Plugging these values into the foregoing growth equation gives the growth rate of per capita income:

$\Delta y/y = 0.0308 + (0.35)(0.30)(0.7040 - 0.4693) = 0.0554$, or 5.54%

Similar calculations using the output-to-capital ratios in the preceding table give the following:

Years after Saving Rate Increase	Output-to-Capital Ratio	Growth Rate of Per Capita Income (%)
0	0.7040	5.54
5	0.5947	4.39
10	0.5415	3.84
25	0.4857	3.25
50	0.4708	3.09
100	0.4693	3.08
New steady state	0.4693	3.08

The growth rate "jumps" from the steady-state rate of 3.08% to 5.54% when the saving rate increases because the increase in saving/investment results in more rapid capital accumulation. Over time, the growth rate slows because the marginal productivity of capital declines as the capital-to-labor ratio increases. In addition, as the capital-to-labor ratio increases and the output-to-capital ratio declines, a greater portion of savings is required to maintain the capital-to-labor ratio, leaving a smaller portion for continued capital deepening. Roughly two-thirds of the growth acceleration has dissipated after 10 years.

3. Using the output-to-capital ratios given in the preceding table, calculate the proportional impact of the increased saving rate on the capital-to-labor ratio and on per capita income over time. With respect to these variables, how will the new steady state compare with the old steady state?

Solution

Using the output-to-capital ratio that will prevail five years after the saving rate increase, the proportional impact on the capital-to-labor ratio and on per capita income will be

$$\frac{k_{new}}{k_{old}} = \left[\frac{(Y/K)_{new}}{(Y/K)_{old}}\right]^{\frac{1}{\alpha-1}} = \left[\frac{0.5947}{0.7040}\right]^{\frac{-1}{0.65}} = 1.2964$$

and

$$\frac{y_{new}}{y_{old}} = \left(\frac{k_{new}}{k_{old}}\right)^{\alpha} = 1.2964^{0.35} = 1.0951$$

Thus, after five years, the capital-to-labor ratio will be 29.64% higher than it would have been without the increase in the saving rate, and per capita income will be 9.51% higher. Similar calculations for the other periods give the following:

Years after Saving Rate Increase	Proportionate Increase (%) in:	
	Capital-to-Labor Ratio	Per Capita Income
0	0.00	0.00
5	29.64	9.51
10	49.74	15.18
25	77.01	22.12
50	85.71	24.19
100	86.68	24.42
New steady state	86.68	24.42

In the new steady state, the capital-to-labor ratio will be 86.68% higher at every point in time than it would have been in the old steady state. Per capita income will be 24.42% higher at every point in time. Both variables will be growing at the same rate (3.08%) as they would have been in the old steady state.

[a] Note that the output-to-capital ratio would have been constant on the original steady state path. Because of the impact of total factor productivity, the capital-to-labor ratio and output per capita are not constant even in steady state. In comparing "paths" for these variables, we isolate the impact of the saving rate change by canceling out the effect of TFP growth. Mathematically, we cancel out A in Equation 3 to produce the equations shown here.

12 | EXTENSION OF NEOCLASSICAL MODEL

Solow (1957) used the growth accounting equation to determine the contributions of each factor to economic growth in the United States for the period 1909–1949. He reached the surprising conclusion that more than 80% of the per capita growth in the United States resulted from TFP. Denison (1985) authored another study examining US growth for the period 1929–1982 using the Solow framework. His findings were similar to Solow's, with TFP explaining nearly 70% of US growth. The problem with these findings is that the neoclassical model provides no explicit explanation of the economic determinants of technological progress or how TFP changes over time. Because technology is determined outside the model (i.e., exogenously), critics argue that the neoclassical model ignores the very factor driving growth in the economy. Technology is simply the residual or the part of growth that cannot be explained by other inputs, such as capital and labor. This lack of an explanation for technology led to growing dissatisfaction with the neoclassical model.

The other source of criticism of the neoclassical model is the prediction that the steady-state rate of economic growth is unrelated to the rate of saving and investment. Long-run growth of output in the Solow model depends only on the rates of growth of the labor force and technology. Higher rates of investment and savings have only a transitory impact on growth. Thus, an increase in investment as a share of GDP from 10% to 15% of GDP will have a positive impact on the near-term growth rate but will not have a permanent impact on the ultimately sustainable percentage growth rate. This conclusion makes many economists uncomfortable. Mankiw (1995) provided evidence rebutting this hypothesis and showed that saving rates and growth rates are positively correlated across countries. Finally, the neoclassical model predicts that in an economy where the stock of capital is rising faster than labor productivity, the return to investment should decline with time. For the advanced countries, the evidence does not support this argument because returns have not fallen over time.

Critiques of the neoclassical model led to two lines of subsequent research on economic growth. The first approach, originated by Jorgenson (1966, 2000), is termed the augmented Solow approach. It remains in the neoclassical tradition in that diminishing marginal returns are critical and there is no explanation for the determinants of technological progress. Instead, this approach attempts to reduce empirically the portion of growth attributed to the unexplained residual labeled technological progress (TFP). The idea is to develop better measures of the inputs used in the production function and broaden the definition of investment by including human capital, research and development, and public infrastructure. In addition, the composition of capital spending is important. Higher levels of capital spending on high-technology goods will boost productivity more than spending on machine tools or structures.

By adding inputs such as human capital to the production function, the augmented Solow model enables us to more accurately measure the contribution of technological progress to growth. The economy still moves toward a steady-state growth path, however, because even broadly defined capital is assumed to eventually encounter diminishing marginal returns. In essence, this line of research uses the growth accounting methodology and increases the number of inputs in the production function in order to provide a more accurate measure of technological progress. The second approach is the endogenous growth theory, which we examine in the next section.

ENDOGENOUS GROWTH MODEL

13

The alternative to the neoclassical model is a series of models known as endogenous growth theory. These models focus on explaining technological progress rather than treating it as exogenous. In these models, self-sustaining growth emerges as a natural consequence of the model and the economy does not necessarily converge to a steady-state rate of growth. Unlike the neoclassical model, there are *no diminishing marginal returns to capital for the economy as a whole* in the endogenous growth models. So increasing the saving rate permanently increases the rate of economic growth. These models also allow for the possibility of increasing returns to scale.

Romer (1986) provided a model of technological progress and a rationale for why capital does not experience diminishing marginal returns. He argued that capital accumulation is the main factor accounting for long-run growth, once the definition of capital is broadened to include such items as human or knowledge capital and research and development (R&D). R&D is defined as investment in new knowledge that improves the production process. In endogenous growth theory, knowledge or human capital and R&D spending are factors of production, like capital and labor, and have to be paid for through savings.

Companies spend on R&D for the same reason they invest in new equipment and build new factories: to make a profit. R&D spending is successful if it leads to the development of a new product or method of production that is successful in the marketplace. There is a fundamental difference, however, between spending on new equipment and factories and spending on R&D. The final product of R&D spending is ideas. These ideas can potentially be copied and used by other companies in the economy. Thus, R&D expenditures have potentially large positive externalities or spillover effects. This means that spending by one company has a positive impact on other companies and increases the overall pool of knowledge available to all companies. Spending by companies on R&D and knowledge capital generates benefits to the economy as a whole that exceed the private benefit to the individual company making the R&D investment. Individual companies cannot fully capture all the benefits associated with creating new ideas and methods of production. Some of the benefits are external to the company, and so are the social returns associated with the investment in R&D and human capital.

This distinction between the private and social returns or benefits to capital is important because it solves an important microeconomic issue. The elimination of the assumption of diminishing marginal returns to capital implies constant returns to capital and increasing returns to all factors taken together. If individual companies could capture these scale economies, then all industries would eventually be dominated by a single company—a monopoly. There is simply no empirical evidence to support this implication. Separating private returns from social returns solves the problem. If companies face constant returns to scale for all private factors, there is no longer an inherent advantage for a company being large. But the externality or social benefit results in increasing returns to scale across the entire economy as companies benefit from the private spending of the other companies.

The role of R&D spending and the positive externalities associated with this spending have important implications for economic growth. In the endogenous growth model, the economy does not reach a steady growth rate equal to the growth of labor plus an exogenous rate of labor productivity growth. Instead, saving and investment decisions can generate self-sustaining growth at a permanently higher rate. This situation is in sharp contrast to the neoclassical model, in which only a transitory increase in growth above the steady state is possible. The reason for this difference is that because of the externalities on R&D, diminishing marginal returns to capital do not set in. The production function in the endogenous growth model is a straight line given by

$$y_e = f(k_e) = ck_e, \tag{12}$$

where output per worker (y_e) is proportional to the stock of capital per worker (k_e), c is the (constant) marginal product of capital in the aggregate economy, and the subscript e denotes the endogenous growth model. In contrast, the neoclassical production function is a curved line that eventually flattens out (see Exhibit 4).

To understand the significance of introducing constant returns to aggregate capital accumulation, note that in this model the output-to-capital ratio is fixed (= c) and therefore output per worker (y_e) always grows at the same rate as capital per worker (k_e). Thus, faster or slower capital accumulation translates one for one into faster or slower growth in output per capita. Substituting Equation 12 into Equation 7 gives an equation for the growth rate of output per capita in the endogenous growth model:

$$\Delta y_e/y_e = \Delta k_e/k_e = sc - \delta - n$$

Because all the terms on the right-hand side of this equation are constant, this is both the long-run and the short-run growth rate in this model. Examination of the equation shows that *a higher saving rate (s) implies a permanently higher growth rate.* This is the key result of the endogenous growth model.

The positive externalities associated with spending on R&D and knowledge capital suggest that spending by private companies on these inputs may be too low from an overall societal point of view. This is an example of a market failure wherein private companies under-invest in the production of these goods. In this case, there may be a role for government intervention to correct for the market failure by direct government spending on R&D and/or providing tax breaks and subsidies for private production of knowledge capital. Higher levels of spending on knowledge capital could translate into faster economic growth even in the long run. Finally, according to the endogenous growth theory, there is *no reason why the incomes of developed and developing countries should converge.* Because of constant or even increasing returns associated with investment in knowledge capital, the developed countries can continue to grow as fast as, or faster than, the developing countries. As a result, there is no reason to expect convergence of income over time. We now turn to the convergence debate in more detail.

EXAMPLE 12

Neoclassical vs. Endogenous Growth Models

Consider again an economy with per capita income growing at a constant 3.08% rate and with a 20% saving rate, an output-to-capital ratio (c in the endogenous growth model, Equation 12) of 0.7040, a depreciation rate (δ) of 10%, and a 1% labor force growth (n).

1. Use the endogenous growth model to calculate the new steady-state growth rate of per capita income if the saving rate increases to 23.5%.

   Solution

   In the endogenous growth model, the new growth rate of per capita income is

   $$\Delta y_e/y_e = sc - \delta - n = (0.235)(0.7040) - 0.10 - 0.01 = 0.0554, \text{ or } 5.54\%.$$

   This is the same as the growth rate immediately following the increase in the saving rate (to 30% in that case) in the earlier example using the neoclassical model (Example 11). Unlike in the neoclassical model, in the endogenous growth model this higher growth rate will be sustained.

2. How much higher will per capita income be in 10 years because of the higher saving rate? How does this compare with the impact calculated in Example 11 using the neoclassical model? What accounts for the difference?

Solution

According to the endogenous growth model, per capita income will grow 2.46% (= 5.54% − 3.08%) faster with the higher saving rate. After 10 years, the cumulative impact of the faster growth rate will be

$$\exp(0.0246 \times 10) = \exp(0.246) = 1.2789.$$

So, per capita income will be almost 28% higher than it would have been at the lower saving rate. This increase is substantially larger than the 15.18% cumulative increase after 10 years found in Example 11 assuming a much larger increase in the saving rate (to 30% instead of 23.5%) in the neoclassical model. The difference arises because the endogenous growth model assumes that capital accumulation is not subject to diminishing returns. Therefore, the growth rate is permanently, rather than temporarily, higher.

3. In an effort to boost growth, the government is considering two proposals. One would subsidize all private companies that increase their investment spending. The second would subsidize only investments in R&D and/or implementation of new technologies with potential for network externalities. Interpret these proposals in terms of the neoclassical and endogenous growth models and assess their likely impact on growth. (Focus only on "supply-side" considerations here.)

Solution

Subsidizing all private investment would tend to have a significant, pure capital deepening component. That is, companies would be encouraged to buy more, but not necessarily better, plant and equipment. The neoclassical model indicates that this scenario is likely to result in a temporary surge in growth, but even if the higher rate of investment/saving is sustained, growth will again decline over time. On the positive side, this proposal is very likely to succeed, at least for a while, because it does not require investment in unproven technologies or ill-defined network effects. The impact of the other proposal is more uncertain but potentially much more powerful. If the investments in R&D and/or new technologies lead to new knowledge, greater efficiency, new products and methods, and/or network externalities, then the endogenous growth model suggests that growth is likely to be permanently enhanced.

CONVERGENCE HYPOTHESES

14

☐ | explain and evaluate convergence hypotheses

As is evident in Exhibit 1, a wide gap separates the living standards in developed and developing nations. The question is, will this difference persist forever or will the per capita income levels of the developing countries converge to those of the developed countries? Convergence means that countries with low per capita incomes should grow at a faster rate than countries with high per capita incomes. Thus, over time the per capita income of developing countries should converge toward that of the developed countries. Whether convergence occurs has major implications for the future growth prospects of developed versus developing countries. It also has important investment implications.

Neoclassical growth theory predicts two types of convergence: absolute convergence and conditional convergence. **Absolute convergence** means that developing countries, regardless of their particular characteristics, will eventually catch up with the developed countries and match them in per capita output. The neoclassical model assumes that all countries have access to the same technology. As a result, per capita income in all countries should eventually grow at the same rate. Thus, the model implies convergence of per capita *growth rates* among all countries. It does not, however, imply that the *level* of per capita income will be the same in all countries regardless of underlying characteristics; that is, it does not imply absolute convergence.

Conditional convergence means that convergence is conditional on the countries having the same saving rate, population growth rate, and production function. If these conditions hold, the neoclassical model implies convergence to the same *level* of per capita output as well as the same steady-state growth rate. In terms of Exhibit 13, these economies would have the same k^* and thus the same steady state. If they start with different capital-to-labor ratios, their growth rates will differ in the transition to the steady state. The economy with a lower capital-to-labor ratio will experience more rapid growth of productivity and per capita income, but the differential will diminish until they finally converge. Countries with different saving rates or population growth rates and thus different steady-state values for k^* will have different steady-state *levels* of per capita income, but their growth rates of per capita output will still converge.

The data (see Exhibit 17) indicate that some of the poorer countries are diverging rather than converging to the income levels of the developed countries. Thus, in addition to the first two convergence concepts, we have the notion of **club convergence**, where only rich and middle-income countries that are members of the club are converging to the income level of the world's richest countries. This means that the countries with the lowest per capita income in the club grow at the fastest rate. In contrast, countries outside the club continue to fall behind. Poor countries can join the club if they make appropriate institutional changes, such as those summarized earlier in our discussion of factors limiting growth in developing economies. Finally, countries may fall into a **non-convergence trap** if they do not implement necessary institutional reforms. For example, failure to reform labor markets has undermined growth in some European countries that have experienced weak growth in employment and high rates of unemployment over the last two decades. Certain institutional arrangements that initially enhance growth may later generate non-convergence traps if maintained too long. Import substitution policies enabled the Latin American countries to grow rapidly in the 1950s and 1960s but caused them to stagnate in the 1970s and 1980s.

If convergence, and especially club convergence, does occur, investing in countries with lower per capita incomes that are members of the club should, over long periods, provide a higher rate of return than investing in higher-income countries. Convergence means that the rate of growth of potential GDP should be higher in developing countries that have made the institutional changes that are a precondition for growth and that enable these countries to become members of the convergence club. With higher long-term growth in these economies, corporate profits should also grow at a faster rate. Given the faster rate of growth in earnings, stock prices may also rise at a faster rate. Of course, risk is also likely to be higher in these markets.

Nonetheless, it is reasonable to conclude that long-term investors should allocate a risk-tolerance-appropriate portion of their assets to those developing economies that have become members of the convergence club.

Convergence between the developed and developing countries can occur in two ways. First, convergence takes place through capital accumulation and capital deepening. Exhibit 16 illustrates the difference between developed and developing countries using the per capita neoclassical production function. The developed countries operate at point B, so increases in capital have almost no impact on productivity. In contrast, developing countries operate at point A, where increases in capital significantly boost labor productivity.

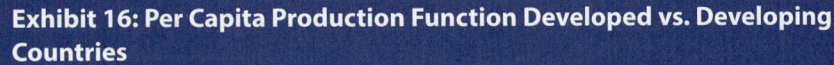

Exhibit 16: Per Capita Production Function Developed vs. Developing Countries

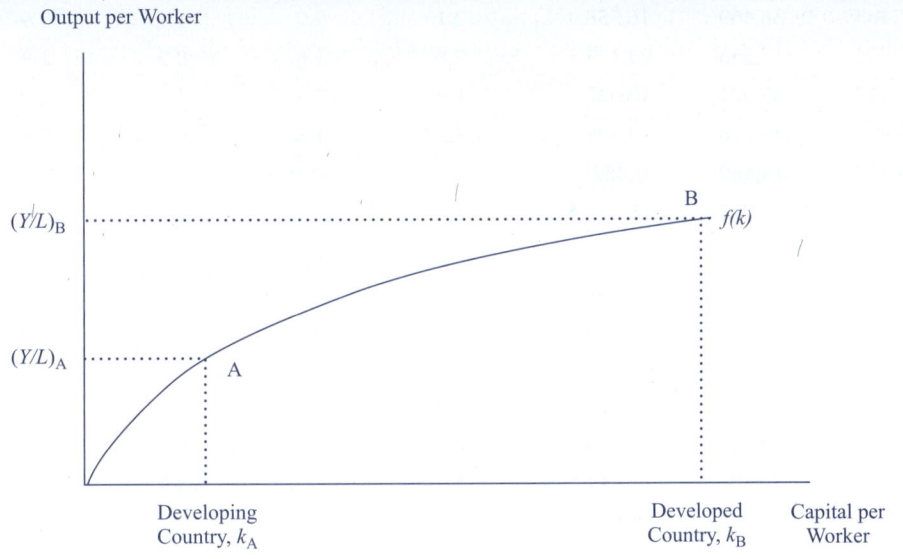

A second source of convergence is that developing countries can imitate or adopt technology already widely utilized in the advanced countries. Developing countries can learn from advanced countries as scientific and management practices spread with globalization. By importing technology from the advanced countries, the developing countries can achieve faster economic growth and converge to the income of the advanced countries. Technology transfers will narrow the income gap between developed and developing countries only if the poor countries invest the resources to master the technology and apply it to their economies. This spending is similar to R&D spending and allows the country to join the convergence club. The steady-state rate of growth for members of the convergence club will be determined by the global rate of technological progress. Without such spending, the country will be left out and will continue to fall behind the developed countries.

In contrast to the neoclassical model, the endogenous growth model makes no prediction that convergence should occur. This model allows for countries that start with high per capita income and more capital to grow faster and stay ahead of the developing countries. If the externalities associated with knowledge and human capital are large, the higher-income country can maintain its lead through high rates of investment in these capital inputs.

If the convergence hypothesis is correct, there should be an inverse relation between the initial level of per capita real GDP and the growth rate in per capita GDP. Exhibit 17 shows the countries in Exhibit 1 in descending order of per capita income in 1950. If incomes are converging across countries, the poor countries in 1950 should have a higher growth rate between 1950 and 2018 than the rich countries.

Exhibit 17: Real Per Capita GDP by Selected Economy

	Real GDP Per Capita (in US dollars)				Avg. Annual Growth in Per Capita GDP (%)			
	1950	1980	2000	2018	1950–80	1980–2000	2000–18	1950–2018
United States	14,559	29,136	45,640	55,650	2.3	2.3	1.1	2.0
New Zealand	13,795	20,526	27,514	35,676	1.3	1.5	1.5	1.4
Australia	13,219	24,403	36,469	46,555	2.1	2.0	1.4	1.9
Canada	12,053	27,356	37,555	44,135	2.8	1.6	0.9	1.9
United Kingdom	11,602	20,547	33,531	40,627	1.9	2.5	1.1	1.9
France	8,266	24,901	35,778	40,689	3.7	1.8	0.7	2.4
Venezuela	8,104	18,247	14,469	9,487	2.7	−1.2	−2.3	0.2
Argentina	6,164	14,710	15,011	18,255	2.9	0.1	1.1	1.6
Italy	5,954	24,937	36,085	35,233	4.9	1.9	−0.1	2.6
Ireland	5,496	16,707	39,345	70,032	3.8	4.4	3.3	3.8
South Africa	4,361	10,781	9,715	12,156	3.1	−0.5	1.3	1.5
Singapore	4,299	20,626	51,748	89,196	5.4	4.7	3.1	4.6
Mexico	4,180	13,546	15,811	18,313	4.0	0.8	0.8	2.2
Spain	3,964	18,353	30,347	35,679	5.2	2.5	0.9	3.3
Peru	3,464	7,314	6,498	12,644	2.5	−0.6	3.8	1.9
Japan	3,048	20,769	33,875	39,313	6.6	2.5	0.8	3.8
Brazil	2,365	11,372	11,470	14,360	5.4	0.0	1.3	2.7
Turkey	2,327	7,990	13,258	24,850	4.2	2.6	3.6	3.5
Philippines	1,296	4,390	4,277	7,943	4.2	−0.1	3.5	2.7
Korea	1,185	5,084	20,757	36,756	5.0	7.3	3.2	5.2
Egypt	1,132	5,228	8,452	11,881	5.2	2.4	1.9	3.5
Indonesia	804	2,911	5,863	11,760	4.4	3.6	3.9	4.0
Pakistan	666	2,080	3,406	5,049	3.9	2.5	2.2	3.0
India	658	1,297	2,546	6,999	2.3	3.4	5.8	3.5
China	402	722	3,682	16,098	2.0	8.5	8.5	5.6
Ethiopia	314	727	653	2,073	2.8	−0.5	6.6	2.8

Note: GDP per capita, constant prices at 2011 in US dollars, adjusted for PPP.
Source: IMF.

The results for the convergence hypothesis are mixed. The economies with the highest per capita income in 1950 were the United States, New Zealand, Australia, and Canada. The markets with the fastest growth rate over the period 1950–2018 were China and Korea, each growing at a rate above 5%. This result strongly supports convergence because the per capita incomes of these economies in 1950 were well below that of the United States. In addition, the results for Japan, Singapore, Spain, and Korea showed a convergence to the level of income in the advanced economies. In total, 17 of the 27 economies in our sample grew faster than the United States during the period.

However, South Africa, Argentina, Venezuela, and New Zealand were among those that fell further behind the United States. Interestingly, since 2000, convergence has been relatively strong overall, with 16 countries in our sample (60%) growing faster than the United States—including Ethiopia, the Philippines, Peru, Turkey, South Africa, Australia, and New Zealand—but has not continued among the most advanced economies: France, Japan, and Italy all lagged the United States, Canada, and Australia.

The evidence seems to suggest that poorer countries may converge if they develop the appropriate legal, political, and economic institutions. In addition, trade policy is an important factor, which we address in the next section.

GROWTH IN AN OPEN ECONOMY   15

☐   describe the economic rationale for governments to provide incentives to private investment in technology and knowledge

☐   describe the expected impact of removing trade barriers on capital investment and profits, employment and wages, and growth in the economies involved

The Solow model discussed earlier assumed a closed economy in which domestic investment equals domestic savings and there is no international trade or capital flows. Opening up the economy to trade and financial flows can significantly affect the rate of growth in an economy for the following reasons:

1. A country can borrow or lend funds in global markets, and domestic investment can be funded by global savings. Thus, investment is not constrained by domestic savings.

2. Countries can shift resources into industries in which they have a comparative advantage and away from industries in which they are relatively inefficient, thereby increasing overall productivity.

3. Companies have access to a larger, global market for their products, allowing them to better exploit any economies of scale and increasing the potential reward for successful innovation.

4. Countries can import technology, thus increasing the rate of technological progress.

5. Global trade increases competition in the domestic market, forcing companies to produce better products, improve productivity, and keep costs low.

According to the neoclassical model, convergence should occur more quickly if economies are open and there is free trade and international borrowing and lending. Opening up the economy should increase the rate at which countries' capital-to-labor ratios converge. The dynamic adjustment process can be described as follows:

1. Developing countries have less capital per worker, and as a result, the marginal product of capital is higher. Thus, the rate of return on investments should be higher in countries with low capital-to-labor ratios and lower in countries with high capital-to-labor ratios.

2. Global savers, seeking higher returns on investments, will invest in the capital-poor countries. In an open economy, capital should flow from countries with high capital-to-labor ratios to those that are capital poor.

3. Because of the capital inflows, the physical capital stock in the developing countries should grow more rapidly than in rich countries even if the saving rate is low in the poorer countries. Faster capital growth will result in higher productivity growth, causing per capita incomes to converge.

4. Because capital flows must be matched by offsetting trade flows, capital-poor countries will tend to run a trade deficit as they borrow globally to finance domestic investment. In contrast, the developed countries will tend to run trade surpluses as they export capital.

5. During the transition to the new steady state, the inflows of capital will temporarily raise the rate of growth in the capital-poor country above the steady-state rate of growth. At the same time, growth in the capital-exporting countries will be below the steady state.

6. Over time, the physical capital stock will rise in the capital-poor country, reducing the return on investments. As a result, the rate of investment and size of the country's trade deficit will decline. Growth will slow and approach the steady-state rate of growth. If investment falls below the level of domestic savings, the country will eventually shift from a trade deficit to a trade surplus and become an exporter of capital.

7. In the Solow model, after the reallocation of world savings, there is no permanent increase in the rate of growth in an economy. Both the developed and developing countries grow at the steady-state rate of growth.

In contrast to the neoclassical model, endogenous growth models predict that a more open trade policy will permanently raise the rate of economic growth. In these models, international trade increases global output through the following:

1. A selection effect, whereby increased competition from foreign companies forces less efficient domestic companies to exit and more efficient ones to innovate and raises the efficiency of the overall national economy.

2. A scale effect that allows producers to more fully exploit economies of scale by selling to a larger market.

3. A backwardness effect arising from less advanced countries or sectors of an economy catching up with the more advanced countries or sectors through knowledge spillovers.

Open trade also affects the innovation process by encouraging higher levels of spending on R&D and on human capital as companies invest to take advantage of access to larger markets and the greater flow of ideas and knowledge among countries. The rate of return to new investment increases, as does the rate of economic growth. In general, most countries gain from open trade, with the scale effect benefiting smaller countries and the backwardness effect benefiting the poorer, less developed countries. But trade can also retard growth in some cases, especially in small countries that lag behind the technology leaders. Opening these countries to trade may discourage domestic innovation because companies will recognize that, even if they innovate, they may lose out to more efficient foreign companies.

EXAMPLE 13

The Entry of China and India into the Global Economy

China and India effectively entered the global economy in the 1980s as they shifted toward more market-oriented policies and opened up to global trade. Their impact on global growth was significant. In 2018, according to the IMF, China and India accounted for 20% and 8% of world GDP (based on PPP), respectively, whereas the two countries combined for only 4.2% of global output in 1980. The entry of these two countries significantly increased the global supply of skilled and unskilled labor receiving relatively lower wages. As a result of the surge in available labor, global potential GDP increased sharply. Economic theory suggests that the supply-side increase in the global capacity to produce goods and services would increase global output and put downward pressure on prices.

The neoclassical model of growth can provide us with some further insights into the impact of China and India entering the global economy. At the time, China and India had relatively lower wages and capital compared with the United States and Europe. One would expect that the rate of return on capital would be higher in China and India and that capital would flow from the developed countries to China and India. Hence, both China and India would be expected to run trade deficits. This has been the case for India but, contrary to the model's prediction, China has run trade surpluses. These surpluses stem mainly from China's very high domestic saving rate.

Nonetheless, China has experienced large foreign direct investment (see Exhibit 18) inflows, which have reinforced its already high private investment rate. As China and India accumulate capital, their capital-to-labor ratios, real wage levels, and per capita income should converge toward those of the advanced economies. Depending on global aggregate demand conditions, wages might even have to fall in the developed countries in the process of shifting wealth and income to the developing economies. Because of the surge in the global supply of labor, the overall share of labor in global income should decline relative to capital. In addition, global productivity should rise as China and India account for a rising share of global output. In sum, over the long run, the growing share of global GDP going to China and India will benefit the global economy as more efficient utilization of resources allows global potential GDP to grow more rapidly for an extended period.

Although both the neoclassical and the endogenous models of growth show the benefits of open markets, over the last 50 years developing countries have pursued two contrasting strategies for economic development:

- *Inward-oriented policies* attempt to develop domestic industries by restricting imports. Instead of importing goods and services, these policies encourage the production of domestic substitutes, despite the fact that it may be more costly to do so. These policies are also called import substitution policies.

- *Outward-oriented policies* attempt to integrate domestic industries with those of the global economy through trade and make exports a key driver of growth.

Many African and Latin American countries pursued inward-oriented policies from the 1950s to the 1980s that resulted in poor GDP growth and inefficient industries producing low-quality goods. In contrast, many East Asian countries, such as Singapore and South Korea, pursued outward-oriented polices during this same period, which resulted in high rates of GDP growth and convergence with developed countries. These countries also benefited from the positive effects of foreign direct investment, which suggests that more open and trade-oriented economies will grow at a faster rate. The evidence strongly supports this case.

In Example 1, we compared the economic performance of Argentina and Venezuela with that of Japan, South Korea, and Singapore. In 1950, the per capita GDP of the two Latin American countries was well above that of the three East Asian countries. By 2010, however, the per capita GDPs of the three Asian countries were well above those of Argentina and Venezuela. The difference in the growth rates between Argentina and Venezuela and the three Asian countries is explained largely by the openness of their economies. Argentina and Venezuela were relatively closed economies, whereas the Asian countries relied on foreign investment and open markets to fuel growth.

Many African and Latin American countries have removed trade barriers and are pursuing more outward-oriented policies, and they experienced better growth. Brazil is a good example. Exports of goods and services increased from $64.6 billion in 2000 to $218 billion in 2018, an increase of more than 237%. As shown in Exhibit 18, exports as a share of GDP rose from 10.2% to 14.8% over this period.

Exhibit 18: Exports and Foreign Direct Investment of Selected Countries				
	1980	**1990**	**2000**	**2018**
Brazil				
Exports as a percentage of GDP	9.1%	8.2%	10.2%	14.8%
Inflows of foreign direct investment ($ billions)	NA	NA	$32.8	$61.2
China				
Exports as a percentage of GDP	5.9%	13.6%	20.9%	19.5%
Inflows of foreign direct investment ($ billions)	NA	NA	$38.4	$203.5
India				
Exports as a percentage of GDP	6.1%	7.1%	13.0%	19.7%
Inflows of foreign direct investment ($ billions)	NA	NA	$3.6	$42.1
Ireland				
Exports as a percentage of GDP	44.3%	54.6%	94.5%	122.3%
Inflows of foreign direct investment ($ billions)	NA	NA	$25.8	$28.1
Mexico				
Exports as a percentage of GDP	10.1%	18.7%	25.4%	39.2%
Inflows of foreign direct investment ($ billions)	NA	NA	$18.0	$32.7
South Africa				
Exports as a percentage of GDP	34.3%	23.5%	27.2%	30.1%
Inflows of foreign direct investment ($ billions)	NA	NA	$0.9	$5.3
South Korea				
Exports as a percentage of GDP	28.5%	25.3%	35.1%	44.0%
Inflows of foreign direct investment ($ billions)	NA	NA	$9.3	$14.5
United States				

	1980	1990	2000	2018
Exports as a percentage of GDP	9.8%	9.3%	10.7%	12.2%
Inflows of foreign direct investment ($ billions)	NA	NA	$159.2	$268.4

Source: OECD (2019).

EXAMPLE 14

Why Some Countries Converge and Others Do Not

As evident from the high rates of growth between 1950 and 2018 shown in Exhibit 18, China and South Korea are converging toward the income levels of the advanced economies. In contrast, the economies of Mexico and South Africa have not converged.

1. Using the data in Exhibit 18, give some reasons why this has occurred.

   Solution

   Two reasons largely account for the difference. First, growth in the Chinese and South Korean economies has been driven by high rates of business investment. As shown in Exhibit 9, investment as a share of GDP in 2018 was 44% in China, almost double the rate of 23.0% in Mexico and more than double the rate of 18% in South Africa. Although investment as a share of GDP in South Korea is lower than in China, it is well above that of Mexico and South Africa.

   Second, both China and South Korea have pursued an aggressive export-driven, outward-oriented policy focusing on manufactured goods. In 2018, exports were 44% of GDP for South Korea and 19.5% of GDP for China (Exhibit 18). In addition, foreign direct investment is a major factor underlying growth in China.

   On the other hand, South Africa's more inward-oriented economy attracted only $5.3 billion in foreign direct investment in 2018, significantly less than that of Ireland—a smaller but much wealthier and very open country—and the $203 billion inflow of foreign investment into China. These trends are changing, however, as many African and Latin American countries are increasingly relying on growing exports and foreign investment to increase GDP growth.

EXAMPLE 15

Investment Prospects in Spain: Estimating the Sustainable Growth Rate

You are a financial analyst at Global Invest Inc., an investment management firm that runs a number of global mutual funds with a significant exposure to Spain. The IBEX 35 Index, which reached a crisis-induced low of 6,065 in May 2012, remains far below its October 2007 peak of almost 16,000. The members of the investment policy committee at the firm believe the equity market in Spain is attractive and is currently being depressed by temporary problems in the banking and real estate markets of Spain, which they feel are overstated.

They believe that higher profits will ultimately drive the market higher but are concerned about the long-term prospects and the sustainable rate of growth for Spain. One of the research assistants at the firm gathers the data shown in Exhibit 19 from the OECD and the Conference Board.

Exhibit 19: Growth Data for Spain

	GDP in Billions of USD Adjusted for PPP	Gross Capital Spending as Percentage of GDP	Consumption of Fixed Capital (percent of GDP)	Labor Cost as Percentage of Total Factor Cost	Total Hours Worked (millions)	Output per Hour Worked in 2011 USD Adjusted for PPP	Growth in Total Factor Productivity (%)
2006	1,390	31.3	14.9	61.4	35,358	48	−0.5
2007	1,481	31.3	15.1	60.5	36,259	48	−0.4
2008	1,527	29.6	15.6	60.2	36,519	48	−1.6
2009	1,484	24.6	16.4	60.5	34,371	50	−1.7
2010	1,501	23.5	16.8	59.1	33,591	51	−0.1
2011	1,517	21.9	17.4	59.1	32,788	51	−0.8
2012	1,501	20.0	18.0	57.3	31,204	52	−1.2
2013	1,501	18.7	17.8	56.5	30,250	53	−1.0
2014	1,551	19.5	17.8	56.1	30,569	53	−0.3
2015	1,625	20.4	17.5	56.4	31,527	54	−0.9

Sources: OECD Stat Extracts and the Conference Board Total Economy Database.

According to the Conference Board website, the physical capital stock for Spain was estimated at $1,808 billion (adjusted for purchasing power parity) in 2005. The research analyst calculated the physical capital stock (K) for Spain for the years 2006–2015 using the following equation:

$$K_t = K_{t-1} + I - D,$$

where I is gross investment or gross capital spending and D is the depreciation or the consumption of fixed capital. So for 2006 and 2007, the physical capital stock is calculated as follows:

$$K_{2006} = \$1,808 + \$1,390\,(0.313 - 0.149) = \$2,036 \text{ billion}$$

$$K_{2007} = \$2,036 + \$1,481\,(0.313 - 0.151) = \$2,276 \text{ billion}$$

The physical capital stock for the remaining years is calculated in the same way and given by Exhibit 20.

Exhibit 20: Estimated Physical Capital Stock (USD billions)

2006	$2,036
2007	2,276
2008	2,490
2009	2,611
2010	2,713
2011	2,782
2012	2,812
2013	2,826

2014	2,851
2015	2,898

The investment policy committee asks you to use the preceding data to address the following:

1. Calculate the potential growth rate of the Spanish economy using the production function or growth accounting method (Equation 4), and determine the amount of growth attributed to each source.

   Solution

   The production function or growth accounting method estimates the growth in GDP using Equation 4:

   Growth in potential GDP = $\alpha \Delta K/K + (1 - \alpha)\Delta L/L + \Delta A/A$

   The annual growth rate in capital is calculated from Exhibit 20 as

   $(2{,}898/2{,}036)^{1/9} - 1 = 4.0\%$.

   The labor input is measured by the growth rate in total hours worked in the economy (Exhibit 19) and given by

   $(31{,}527/35{,}358)^{1/9} - 1 = -1.27\%$.

   The growth rate in total factor productivity (Exhibit 19) is calculated by using a geometric average of the growth rates for 2000–2009 and is equal to −0.68%. Finally, the labor share of output is given by the average of the labor cost as a percentage of total factor cost, which is 58.7% for 2006–2015 (Exhibit 19). Thus, the share of capital (α) is 1 − 0.587 = 41.3%. Using these numbers, the growth in potential GDP is

   Growth in potential GDP = $\alpha \Delta K/K + (1 - \alpha)\Delta L/L + \Delta A/A$

   $= (0.413)0.04 + (0.587)(-0.0127) + (-0.0068)$

   $= 0.23\%$

   Sources of growth for Spain over the period 2006–2015 were as follows:

Capital	$(0.413) \times (0.04) = 1.65\%$
Labor	$(0.587) \times (-0.0127) = -0.75\%$
TFP	$= -0.68\%$

2. Calculate the potential growth rate of the Spanish economy using the labor productivity method (Equation 5).

   Solution

   The labor productivity method estimates the growth in GDP using Equation 5:

   Growth rate in potential GDP = Long-term growth rate of labor force + Long-term growth rate in labor productivity

   As before, we use the growth in total hours worked to measure the growth in the labor force. The growth in labor productivity per hour worked is as follows:

   $(54/48)^{1/9} - 1 = 1.32\%$

Growth in potential GDP = -1.27% + 1.32% = 0.05%

Note that the estimate of potential GDP growth using the labor productivity approach is broadly similar to that obtained from the growth accounting method. In general, the two methods are likely to give somewhat different estimates because they rely on different data inputs. The growth accounting method requires measurements of the physical capital stock and TFP. As discussed earlier, TFP is estimated using various time-series or econometric models of the component of growth that is not accounted for by the explicit factors of production. As a result, the estimate of TFP reflects the average (or "smoothed") behavior of the growth accounting residual. The labor productivity approach is simpler, and it avoids the need to estimate the capital input and TFP. In contrast to the estimated value of TFP, labor productivity is measured as a pure residual; that is, it is the part of GDP growth that is not explained by the labor input (and only the labor input). The cost of the simplification is that the labor productivity approach does not allow a detailed analysis of the drivers of productivity growth.

3. How significant are capital deepening and technology in explaining growth for Spain?

Solution

Capital deepening occurs in an economy when there is an increase in the capital-to-labor ratio. The labor input for Spain is measured in terms of total hours worked in the economy. Thus, the capital-to-labor ratio for Spain is calculated by dividing the physical capital stock in Exhibit 20 by total hours worked in Exhibit 19. The results, shown in Exhibit 21, indicate that capital deepening was very significant in Spain: The amount of capital per hour worked increased from $57.6 in 2006 to $91.9 in 2015. In terms of the growth rate, the capital-to-labor ratio increased at an annual rate of 5.3%. The contribution of TFP is measured by the growth in total factor productivity. In contrast to capital deepening, TFP made a negative contribution to growth; the average rate of growth for TFP from 2006 to 2015 was −0.68%. However, TFP is estimated using various statistical techniques, and given the uncertainty around these estimates, it should be viewed with some caution.

Exhibit 21: Estimated Capital-to-Labor Ratio ($/hour worked)

2006	$57.6
2007	62.8
2008	68.2
2009	76.0
2010	80.8
2011	84.8
2012	90.1
2013	93.4
2014	93.3
2015	91.9

4. What is the steady-state growth rate for Spain according to the neoclassical model?

   Solution

   The steady-state growth rate in the neoclassical model is estimated by the following (see Equation 8):

   $$\Delta Y/Y = (\theta)/(1 - \alpha) + n$$

   = Growth rate of TFP scaled by labor factor share + Growth rate in the labor force

   Steady-state growth rate = $-0.68\%/(1 - 0.413) + (-1.27\%) = -2.4\%$

   As expected, the growth rate in potential GDP (calculated as in the solutions to 1 and 2) is above the steady-state growth rate. The reason for this is that Spain's economy is still in the process of converging to the higher income levels of the United States and the major economies in Europe. The physical capital stock is below the steady state, and capital deepening is a significant factor increasing productivity growth and the growth in potential GDP. Steady-state growth may be somewhat underestimated in our analysis given that TFP growth is likely to revert to the 1% annual rate of increase exhibited in other major developed economies. This shift is likely to be offset by a lower growth rate in the labor input (see Example 6). It should also be noted that the negative growth in the labor force used in the calculation is based on a period whose start coincides with high level of hours worked and ends in a year when the hours worked were particularly low. The hours worked actually rose subsequent to the 2006–2015 period.

5. Assess the implications of the growth analysis for future economic growth and equity prices in Spain.

   Solution

   The results suggest that potential GDP growth in Spain is close to 0%. As we saw in Exhibit 1, the growth rate of actual GDP since early 2000 has been 0.91% per year, close to the previous estimate of potential but well above the steady state. The problem is that all the growth in potential GDP results from the increase in the labor and capital inputs, with capital deepening being very significant as the capital-to-labor ratio is increasing at a 5.3% annual rate. The neoclassical model suggests that the impact of capital deepening will decline over time and the economy will move toward a steady-state rate of growth. Thus, growth based on capital deepening should not be sustainable over time.

   The other major question raised is whether the labor input can continue to decline at an annual rate of 1.3%. We examined this question in Example 6. In sum, potential GDP growth is likely to be negatively influenced over time by Spain's reliance on capital deepening. A positive impact may come from increasing labor input. The reversion of TFP growth to levels more typical of other European economies should also be a positive factor. Even if TFP does rebound, relatively slow growth in potential GDP in Spain will likely restrain future stock price increases.

SUMMARY

This reading focuses on the factors that determine the long-term growth trend in the economy. As part of the development of global portfolio equity and fixed-income strategies, investors must be able to determine both the near-term and the sustainable rates of growth within a country. Doing so requires identifying and forecasting the factors that determine the level of GDP and that determine long-term sustainable trends in economic growth.

- The sustainable rate of economic growth is measured by the rate of increase in the economy's productive capacity or potential GDP.

- Growth in real GDP measures how rapidly the total economy is expanding. Per capita GDP, defined as real GDP divided by population, measures the standard of living in each country.

- The growth rate of real GDP and the level of per capita real GDP vary widely among countries. As a result, investment opportunities differ by country.

- Equity markets respond to anticipated growth in earnings. Higher sustainable economic growth should lead to higher earnings growth and equity market valuation ratios, all other things being equal.

- In the long run, the growth rate of earnings cannot exceed the growth in potential GDP. Labor productivity is critical because it affects the level of the upper limit. A permanent increase in productivity growth will raise the upper limit on earnings growth and should translate into faster long-run earnings growth and a corresponding increase in stock price appreciation.

- For global fixed-income investors, a critical macroeconomic variable is the rate of inflation. One of the best indicators of short- to intermediate-term inflation trends is the difference between the growth rate of actual and potential GDP.

- Capital deepening, an increase in the capital-to-labor ratio, occurs when the growth rate of capital (net investment) exceeds the growth rate of labor. In a graph of output per capita versus the capital-to-labor ratio, it is reflected by a move along the curve (i.e., the production function).

- An increase in total factor productivity causes a proportional upward shift in the entire production function.

- One method of measuring sustainable growth uses the production function and the growth accounting framework developed by Solow. It arrives at the growth rate of potential GDP by estimating the growth rates of the economy's capital and labor inputs plus an estimate of total factor productivity.

- An alternative method measures potential growth as the long-term growth rate of the labor force plus the long-term growth rate of labor productivity.

- The forces driving economic growth include the quantity and quality of labor and the supply of non-ICT and ICT capital, public capital, raw materials, and technological knowledge.

- The labor supply is determined by population growth, the labor force participation rate, and net immigration. The physical capital stock in a country increases with net investment. The correlation between long-run economic growth and the rate of investment is high.

- Technological advances are discoveries that make it possible to produce more or higher-quality goods and services with the same resources or inputs. Technology is a major factor determining TFP. TFP is the main factor affecting long-term, sustainable economic growth rates in developed countries and also includes the cumulative effects of scientific advances, applied research and development, improvements in management methods, and ways of organizing production that raise the productive capacity of factories and offices.

- Total factor productivity, estimated using a growth accounting equation, is the residual component of growth after accounting for the weighted contributions of all explicit factors (e.g., labor and capital).

- Labor productivity is defined as output per worker or per hour worked. Growth in labor productivity depends on capital deepening and technological progress.

- The academic growth literature is divided into three theories —the classical view, the neoclassical model, and the new endogenous growth view.

- In the classical model, growth in per capita income is only temporary because an exploding population with limited resources brings per capita income growth to an end.

- In the neoclassical model, a sustained increase in investment increases the economy's growth rate only in the short run. Capital is subject to diminishing marginal returns, so long-run growth depends solely on population growth, progress in TFP, and labor's share of income.

- The neoclassical model assumes that the production function exhibits diminishing marginal productivity with respect to any individual input.

- The point at which capital per worker and output per worker are growing at equal, sustainable rates is called the steady state or balanced growth path for the economy. In the steady state, total output grows at the rate of labor force growth plus the rate of growth of TFP divided by the elasticity of output with respect to labor input.

- The following parameters affect the steady-state values for the capital-to-labor ratio and output per worker: saving rate, labor force growth, growth in TFP, depreciation rate, and elasticity of output with respect to capital.

- The main criticism of the neoclassical model is that it provides no quantifiable prediction of the rate or form of TFP change. TFP progress is regarded as exogenous to the model.

- Endogenous growth theory explains technological progress within the model rather than treating it as exogenous. As a result, self-sustaining growth emerges as a natural consequence of the model and the economy does not converge to a steady-state rate of growth that is independent of saving/investment decisions.

- Unlike the neoclassical model, where increasing capital will result in diminishing marginal returns, the endogenous growth model allows for the possibility of constant or even increasing returns to capital in the aggregate economy.

- In the endogenous growth model, expenditures made on R&D and for human capital may have large positive externalities or spillover effects. Private spending by companies on knowledge capital generates benefits to the economy as a whole that exceed the private benefit to the company.

- The convergence hypothesis predicts that the rates of growth of productivity and GDP should be higher in the developing countries. Those higher growth rates imply that the per capita GDP gap between developing and developed economies should narrow over time. The evidence on convergence is mixed.

- Countries fail to converge because of low rates of investment and savings, lack of property rights, political instability, poor education and health, restrictions on trade, and tax and regulatory policies that discourage work and investing.

- Opening an economy to financial and trade flows has a major impact on economic growth. The evidence suggests that more open and trade-oriented economies will grow at a faster rate.

REFERENCES

Ashauer, David. 1990. "Why Is Infrastructure Important?" In *Is There a Shortfall in Public Capital Investment?* Edited by Alicia Munnell. Federal Reserve Bank of Boston Conference Series No. 34.

Denison, Edward. 1985. *Trends in American Growth*. Washington, DC: Brookings Institution.

Grinold, Richard C., Kenneth F. Kroner. 2002. "The Equity Risk Premium: Analyzing the Long-Run Prospects for the Stock Market." Investment Insights5 (3): 7–33.

Heston, Alan, Robert Summers, Bettina Aten. 2009. Penn World Table Version 6.3. Center for International Comparisons of Production, Income and Prices at the University of Pennsylvania (August).

IMF2019. "Statistical Appendix." In *April 2019*. Washington, DC: International Monetary Fund.

Jorgenson, Dale. 1966. *Technology in Growth Theory*. Technology and Growth, Federal Reserve Bank of Boston Conference Series.

Jorgenson, Dale. 2000. *Raising the Speed Limit: US Economic Growth in the Information Age*. Brooking Papers on Economic Activity.

Levine, R. 2005. "Finance and Growth: Theory and Evidence." In *Handbook of Economic Growth*, ed. Philippe Aghion and Steven Durlauf. Amsterdam: Elsevier, B.V.

L'Her, J.-F., T. Masmoudi, and R. K. Krishnamoorthy. 2018. "Net Buybacks and the Seven Dwarfs." *Financial Analysts Journal* 74 (4): 57–85.

Mankiw, Gregory. 1995. "The Growth of Nations." Brookings Papers on Economic Activity. 10.2307/2534576

OECD2003. *The Sources of Economic Growth in the OECD Countries*. Paris: Organisation for Economic Co-Operation and Development.

Romer, Paul. 1986. "Increasing Returns and Long-Run Growth." Journal of Political Economy94 (5): 1002–37. 10.1086/261420

Solow, Robert. 1957. "Technical Change and the Aggregate Production Function." Review of Economics and Statistics39 (3): 312–20. 10.2307/1926047

Stewart, Scott, Christopher Piros, Jeffrey Heisler. 2011. *Running Money: Professional Portfolio Management*. McGraw-Hill/Irwin.

PRACTICE PROBLEMS

The following information relates to questions 1-9

Victor Klymchuk, the chief economist at ECONO Consulting (EC), is reviewing the long-term GDP growth of three countries. Klymchuk is interested in forecasting the long-term change in stock market value for each country. Exhibit 1 presents current country characteristics and historical information on select economic variables for the three countries.

Exhibit 1: Select Country Factors and Historical Economic Data

	Country Factors	2009–2019			
		Growth in Hours Worked (%)	Growth in Labor Productivity (%)	Growth in TFP (%)	Growth in GDP (%)
Country A	▪ High level of savings and investment ▪ Highly educated workforce ▪ Low tariffs on foreign imports ▪ Limited natural resources	0.9	2.4	0.6	3.3
Country B	▪ Developed financial markets ▪ Moderate levels of disposable income ▪ Significant foreign direct and indirect investments ▪ Significant natural resources	−0.3	1.6	0.8	1.3
Country C	▪ Politically unstable ▪ Limited property rights ▪ Poor public education and health ▪ Significant natural resources	1.8	0.8	−0.3	2.6

Klymchuk instructs an associate economist at EC to assist him in forecasting the change in stock market value for each country. Klymchuk reminds the associate of the following:

Statement 1:   "Over short time horizons, percentage changes in GDP, the ratio of earnings to GDP, and the price-to-earnings ratio are important factors for describing the relationship between economic growth and stock prices. However, I am interested in a long-term stock market forecast."

A client is considering investing in the sovereign debt of Country A and Country B and asks Klymchuk his opinion of each country's credit risk. Klymchuk tells the client the following:

Statement 2:   "Over the next 10 years, I forecast higher potential GDP growth for Country A and lower potential GDP growth for Country B. The capital per worker is similar and very high for both countries, but per capita output is greater for Country A."

The client tells Klymchuk that Country A will offer 50-year bonds and that he believes the bonds could be a good long-term investment given the higher potential GDP growth. Klymchuk responds to the client as follows:

Statement 3:   "After the next 10 years, I think the sustainable rate of economic growth for Country A will be affected by a growing share of its population over the age of 65, a declining percentage under age 16, and minimal immigration."

The client is surprised to learn that Country C, a wealthy, oil-rich country with significant reserves, is experiencing sluggish economic growth and asks Klymchuk for an explanation. Klymchuk responds by stating:

Statement 4:   "Although countries with greater access to natural resources are often wealthier, the relationship between resource abundance and economic growth is not clear. My analysis shows that the presence of a dominant natural resource (oil) in Country C is constraining growth. Interestingly, Country A has few natural resources but is experiencing a strong rate of increase in per capita GDP growth."

Klymchuk knows that growth in per capita income cannot be sustained by pure capital deepening. He asks the associate economist to determine how important capital deepening is as a source of economic growth for each country. Klymchuk instructs the associate to use the data provided in Exhibit 1.

Klymchuk and his associate debate the concept of convergence. The associate economist believes that developing countries, irrespective of their particular characteristics, will eventually equal developed countries in per capita output. Klymchuk responds as follows:

Statement 5:   "Poor countries will only converge to the income levels of the richest countries if they make appropriate institutional changes."

1. Based on the country factors provided in Exhibit 1, the country *most likely* to be considered a developing country is:

    A. Country A.

    B. Country B.

    C. Country C.

2. Based on Exhibit 1, capital deepening as a source of growth was *most* important for:

    A. Country A.

    B. Country B.

    C. Country C.

3. Based on Statement 1, over the requested forecast horizon, the factor that will *most likely* drive stock market performance is the percentage change in:

    A. GDP.

    B. the earnings to GDP ratio.

    C. the price-to-earnings ratio.

4. Based solely on the predictions in Statement 2, over the next decade Country B's sovereign credit risk will *most likely*:

    A. increase.

    B. decrease.

    C. not change.

5. Based on Statement 2, the difference in per capita output between Country A and Country B *most likely* results from differences in:

    A. capital deepening.

    B. capital per worker.

    C. total factor productivity.

6. Based on Statement 3, after the next 10 years, the growth rate of potential GDP for Country A will *most likely* be:

    A. lower.

    B. higher.

    C. unchanged.

7. Based on Statement 4 and Exhibit 1, the sluggish economic growth in Country C is *least likely* to be explained by:

    A. limited labor force growth.

    B. export driven currency appreciation.

    C. poorly developed economic institutions.

8. Based on Statement 4, the higher rate of per capita income growth in Country A is *least likely* explained by the:

    A. rate of investment.

    B. growth of its population.

    C. application of information technology.

9. The type of convergence described by Klymchuk in Statement 5 is *best* described as:

   A. club convergence.

   B. absolute convergence.

   C. conditional convergence.

The following information relates to questions 10-15

At an international finance and economics conference in Bamako, Mali, Jose Amaral of Brazil and Lucinda Mantri of India are discussing how to spur their countries' economic growth. Amaral believes that growth can be bolstered by removing institutional impediments and suggests several possibilities for Brazil: launching a rural literacy program, clarifying property rights laws, and implementing a new dividend tax on foreign investors.

Mantri responds that for India, capital deepening will be more effective, and she has proposed the following ideas: building a group of auto and textile factories in the southern states, developing a north–south and east–west highway network, and sponsoring a patent initiative.

In response, Amaral says to Mantri:

"Based on endogenous growth theory, one of those proposals is more likely to raise total factor productivity than result in pure capital deepening."

Although Mantri recognizes that India lacks the significant natural resources that Brazil has, she states that India can overcome this challenge by bolstering long-term growth through three channels:

Channel 1	Deepening the capital base
Channel 2	Making investments in technology
Channel 3	Maintaining a low rupee exchange rate

Each country's basic economic statistics were presented at the conference. Selected data for Brazil and India are presented in Exhibit 1. Adama Kanté, a fund manager based in Mali, is planning to increase the fund's allocation to international equities and, after some preliminary analysis, has determined the new allocation will be to Brazilian or Indian equities. After reviewing the data in Exhibit 1, Kanté decides that the allocation will be to Indian equities.

Exhibit 1: Economic Statistics for Brazil and India		
Economic Statistic	**Brazil**	**India**
GDP per capita, 2018	$14,360	$6,999
GDP per capita growth, 2000–2018	1.3%	5.8%
GDP growth, 2005–2018	2.0%	7.2%
- Growth resulting from labor productivity component	1.3%	6.3%

Economic Statistic	Brazil	India
- Growth resulting from capital deepening component	1.9%	4.5%

Kanté is concerned about the low standard of living in Mali and its large informal sector. To improve per capita GDP, Kanté is considering five specific strategies:

Strategy 1   Lower the country's tax rate.

Strategy 2   Introduce policies that encourage the return of highly educated Malian emigrants.

Strategy 3   Build daycare centers to increase women's participation in the workforce.

Strategy 4   Impose high tariffs on imports to protect the country's nascent industries.

Strategy 5   Use economic development bank loans to improve the country's transport and manufacturing infrastructure.

10. Which of Amaral's initiatives is *least likely* to achieve his stated growth objective?

   A. Dividend tax

   B. Rural literacy

   C. Property rights

11. Which proposal for India is Amaral *most likely* referring to in his response to Mantri?

   A. Patent initiative

   B. Highway network

   C. Auto and textile factories

12. The channel that is *least likely* to help India overcome its challenge of lacking significant natural resources is:

   A. Channel 1.

   B. Channel 2.

   C. Channel 3.

13. Based on Exhibit 1, which Indian economic statistic *least likely* supports Kanté's international equity allocation preference?

   A. GDP per capita

   B. Growth resulting from labor productivity

   C. Growth resulting from capital deepening

14. The strategy that is *least likely* to improve per capita GDP in Mali is:

   A. Strategy 1.

   B. Strategy 2.

   C. Strategy 3.

15. Which of the following strategies being considered by Kanté is *most likely* to undermine or delay convergence with developed economies?

A. Strategy 2

B. Strategy 4

C. Strategy 5

The following information relates to questions 16-21

Hans Schmidt, CFA, is a portfolio manager with a boutique investment firm that specializes in sovereign credit analysis. Schmidt's supervisor asks him to develop estimates for GDP growth for three countries. Information on the three countries is provided in Exhibit 1.

Exhibit 1: Select Economic Data for Countries A, B, and C

Country	Economy	Capital per Worker
A	Developed	High
B	Developed	High
C	Developing	Low

After gathering additional data on the three countries, Schmidt shares his findings with colleague, Sean O'Leary. After reviewing the data, O'Leary notes the following observations:

Observation 1: The stock market of Country A has appreciated considerably over the past several years. Also, the ratio of corporate profits to GDP for Country A has been trending upward over the past several years and is now well above its historical average.

Observation 2: The government of Country C is working hard to bridge the gap between its standard of living and that of developed countries. Currently, the rate of potential GDP growth in Country C is high.

Schmidt knows that a large part of the analysis of sovereign credit is to develop a thorough understanding of the potential GDP growth rate for a particular country and the region in which the country is located. Schmidt is also doing research on Country D for a client of the firm. Selected economic facts on Country D are provided in Exhibit 2.

Exhibit 2: Select Economic Facts for Country D

- Slow GDP Growth
- Abundant Natural Resources
- Developed Economic Institutions

Prior to wrapping up his research, Schmidt schedules a final meeting with O'Leary to see if he can provide any other pertinent information. O'Leary makes the following statements to Schmidt:

Statement 1: Many countries that have the same population growth rate, savings rate, and production function will have growth rates that converge over time.

Statement 2: Convergence between countries can occur more quickly if economies are open and there is free trade and international borrowing and lending; however, there is no permanent increase in the rate of growth in an economy from a more open trade policy.

16. Based on Exhibit 1, the factor that would *most likely* have the greatest positive impact on the per capita GDP growth of Country A is:

    A. free trade.

    B. technology.

    C. saving and investment.

17. Based on Observation 1, in the long run the ratio of profits to GDP in Country A is *most likely* to:

    A. remain near its current level.

    B. increase from its current level.

    C. decrease from its current level.

18. Based on Observation 2, Country C is *most likely* to have:

    A. relatively low real asset returns.

    B. a relatively low real interest rate.

    C. a relatively high real interest rate.

19. Based on Exhibit 2, the *least likely* reason for the current pace of GDP growth in Country D is:

    A. a persistently strong currency.

    B. strong manufacturing exports.

    C. strong natural resource exports.

20. The type of convergence described by O'Leary in Statement 1 is *best* described as:

    A. club convergence.

    B. absolute convergence.

    C. conditional convergence.

21. Which of the following growth models is *most* consistent with O'Leary's Statement 2?

    A. Classical

    B. Endogenous

    C. Neoclassical

SOLUTIONS

1. C is correct. Country C is the most likely to be a developing economy. Political instability, limited property rights, and poor public education and health are all factors that limit economic growth and thereby contribute to a relatively low standard of living.

2. A is correct. The associate economist can measure the effect of pure capital deepening by measuring the difference of the growth rates of labor productivity and total factor productivity. The larger the difference, the more important capital deepening is as a source of economic growth. From 2000–2010, Country A's labor productivity grew by 2.4% per year, of which 0.6% came from TFP growth and 1.8% from capital deepening (2.4% – 0.6% = 1.8%).

3. A is correct. In the long run, the GDP growth rate is the most important driver of stock market performance. Therefore, the associate economist should focus on the drivers of long-run potential GDP growth. The ratio of earnings to GDP cannot increase indefinitely because that would imply that profit would eventually absorb all of GDP. This ratio cannot shrink forever, either, because unprofitable companies will go out of business. Thus, the annualized growth rate of the earnings to GDP ratio must be approximately zero over long time horizons, and this ratio should not be a dominant factor in forecasting long-term stock market performance. Similarly, the price-to-earnings ratio cannot grow or contract at a finite rate forever because investors will not pay an excessive price for each dollar of earnings, nor will they give away earnings for free. Therefore the rate of change in the price-to-earnings ratio must be approximately zero over long time horizons and should not be a dominant factor in the forecast of long-term stock market performance.

4. A is correct. Credit rating agencies consider the growth rate of potential GDP when evaluating the credit risk of sovereign debt. The chief economist's expectation for lower potential GDP growth for Country B over the next decade increases the perceived credit risk of its sovereign bonds.

5. C is correct. The higher per capita output for Country A is most likely the result of differences in the cumulative impact of technological progress embodied in total factor productivity. Technological progress raises a country's productive capacity and causes an upward shift in the entire production function, resulting in higher output per worker for a given level of capital per worker.

6. A is correct. Demographic factors can positively or negatively contribute to a country's sustainable rate of economic growth. After the next 10 years, Country A is expected to experience a growing share of the population over the age of 65 and a declining percentage of the population under the age of 16. All else the same, this implies slower growth of the labor force and hence slower growth of potential GDP. Immigration could offset these demographic challenges. However, Statement 3 indicates that Country A is expected to experience minimal immigration.

7. A is correct. Country C is an example of a country endowed with an abundant natural resource yet experiencing slow economic growth. Although labor force growth is an important source of economic growth, it is the least likely explanation of the sluggish economic growth in Country C. As shown in Exhibit 1, growth in total hours worked has accounted for most of Country C's growth. Furthermore, export driven currency appreciation and poorly developed economic institutions are both likely causes of sluggish growth in countries with abundant

natural resources.

8. B is correct. Population growth can increase the growth rate of the overall economy but does not affect the rate of increase in *per capita* GDP. Therefore, population growth does not explain Country A's higher rate of per capita income growth. An increase in labor force participation could, however, raise the growth rate of per capita GDP.

9. A is correct. Klymchuk is referring to the concept of club convergence. The basic premise is that lower-income members of the club are converging to the income levels of the richest countries. This implies that the countries with the lowest per capita income in the club grow at the fastest rate. Countries outside the club, however, continue to fall behind.

10. A is correct. Amaral's initiative to implement a new dividend tax is likely to impede inflows of equity capital by making equity investment in Brazil less attractive for foreign investors. Capital flows, or lack thereof, have a major impact on economic growth because, in an open economy, world savings can finance domestic investment. As a potential source of funds, foreign investment breaks the vicious cycle of low income, low domestic savings, and low investment.

11. A is correct. Mantri's proposal to sponsor a patent initiative, which is likely to result in technology investment and improvement, is likely to cause a proportional upward shift in the entire production function, allowing the economy to produce higher output per worker for a given level of capital per worker. Technological progress also increases the marginal product of capital relative to its marginal cost.

12. C is correct. Maintaining a low currency exchange rate is a policy aimed at maintaining demand for the country's exports. It would have little direct impact on the potential growth rate of aggregate supply. It might boost long-term capacity growth indirectly, however, by encouraging adoption of leading edge technology. Nonetheless, it would not be expected to be as powerful as capital deepening and/or investment in technology.

13. A is correct. Kanté's decision to invest in equities in India is supported by the country's strong economic growth. For global investors, economic growth is important because equity composite valuations depend to a great extent on both the level of economic output (GDP per capita and GDP overall) and the rate of economic growth. Relative to Brazil, India's growth rate in per capita GDP has been much higher, and furthermore, the growth rate in GDP has also been much higher than that of Brazil. In contrast to the growth rate, the relatively low *level* of GDP per capita in India is less likely to indicate attractive equity investment opportunities. Low per capita GDP suggests that India may lack sufficient industrial and financial infrastructure to support some types of industries. It also indicates that domestic purchasing power is relatively limited, decreasing the potential for higher-margin, domestically oriented businesses.

14. A is correct. With Mali's low standard of living (i.e., GDP per capita and large informal workforce), the tax rate is unlikely to be an impediment to growth, so lowering the tax rate is not likely to be a major contributor to growth.

15. B is correct. The strategy for Mali to impose high tariffs (trade restrictions) on imports is likely to undermine rather than enhance growth and therefore is not supportive of convergence with developed economies. Freer trade (fewer trade restrictions) tends to enhance growth by, for example, inducing a shift of resources into industries in which the country has a comparative thereby increasing

overall productivity; forcing less efficient domestic companies to exit and more efficient ones to innovate; allowing domestic producers to more fully exploit economies of scale by selling to a larger market; and enabling less advanced sectors of an economy to catch up with more-advanced countries or sectors through knowledge spillovers.

16. B is correct. Country A is a developed country with a high level of capital per worker. Technological progress and/or more intensive use of existing technology can help developed countries increase productivity and thereby increase per capita GDP. Most developed countries have reasonably low trade barriers; thus, somewhat freer trade is likely to have only an incremental, and probably transitory, impact on per capita GDP growth. Also, because the country already has a high capital-to-labor ratio, increased saving/investment is unlikely to increase the growth rate substantially unless it embodies improved technology.

17. C is correct. The ratio of profits to GDP for Country A has been trending upward over the past several years and is now well above its historical average. The ratio of profits to GDP cannot rise forever. At some point, stagnant labor income would make workers unwilling to work without an increase in wages and would also undermine demand, making further expansion of profit margins unsustainable. Thus, the ratio of profits to GDP will likely decline in the long run toward its historical average.

18. C is correct. A high growth rate of potential GDP would cause real incomes to rise more rapidly and also translate into higher real interest rates and higher expected/required real asset returns. The real interest rate is essentially the real return that consumers/savers demand in exchange for postponing consumption. Faster growth in potential GDP means that consumers expect their real income to rise more rapidly. This implies that an extra unit of future income/consumption is less valuable than it would be if income were expected to grow more slowly. All else the same, the real interest rate will have to be relatively high in order to induce the savings required to fund required/desired capital accumulation.

19. B is correct. Country D is a country with abundant resources and has developed the economic institutions necessary for growth, yet the country is experiencing slow economic growth. It is likely that Country D is experiencing the Dutch Disease, whereby currency appreciation driven by strong export demand for natural resources makes other segments of the economy, in particular manufacturing, globally uncompetitive. Strong manufacturing exports indicate that Country D is globally competitive and likely to have adopted leading edge technology. Thus, it is unlikely that the slow growth reflects inability to maintain productivity growth. Similarly, strong exports suggest adequate demand for its products. Thus, strong exports are unlikely to be the cause of slow growth.

20. C is correct. Conditional convergence means that convergence is conditional on the countries having the same savings rate, population growth rate, and production function. If these conditions hold, the neoclassical model implies convergence to the same *level* of per capita output as well as the same steady-state growth rate.

21. C is correct. According to the neoclassical model, convergence should occur more quickly if economies are open and there is free trade and international borrowing and lending. Opening up the economy should increase the rate at which the capital-to-labor ratio converges among countries. In the neoclassical Solow model, however, after the reallocation of world savings, there is no permanent increase in the rate of growth in an economy. Both the developed and developing countries eventually grow at the same steady-state rate.

Economics of Regulation

by Chester S. Spatt, PhD.

Chester S. Spatt, PhD, is at Tepper School of Business at Carnegie Mellon University (USA).

LEARNING OUTCOMES

Mastery	The candidate should be able to:
☐	describe the economic rationale for regulatory intervention
☐	explain the purposes of regulating commerce and financial markets
☐	describe anticompetitive behaviors targeted by antitrust laws globally and evaluate the antitrust risk associated with a given business strategy
☐	describe classifications of regulations and regulators
☐	describe uses of self-regulation in financial markets
☐	describe regulatory interdependencies and their effects
☐	describe tools of regulatory intervention in markets
☐	describe benefits and costs of regulation
☐	describe the considerations when evaluating the effects of regulation on an industry

INTRODUCTION

1

Regulation can be described as a form of government intervention in markets that involves rules and their enforcement. It is an important topic because regulation has potential effects not only at the macro level on the economy but also at the micro level on companies and individuals. Regulation may develop either proactively in anticipation of consequences of changes in the market environment or reactively in response to some occurrence(s). For example, changes that resulted from technological advances in the markets because of new means of communication and applications of computers have led to a variety of regulation, both proactive and reactive. Regulation has also developed in response to financial crises and undesirable behaviors or actions that have occurred in the past. Regulations are necessary because in some situations market solutions are inadequate. In other words, regulations exist to protect end users from market failings.

A significant challenge for financial regulators is how to deal with systemic risk (the risk of failure of the financial system) and the consequences of risk taking by financial institutions. Issues such as labor regulation, environmental regulation, and electronic privacy are also receiving increased attention.

How regulations are developed and applied can have significant impacts on businesses. Changes in regulatory framework and regulatory uncertainty can also have substantial effects on business decisions. So, one of the significant challenges facing professionals in the finance industry is to anticipate and understand the consequences of potential changes in the regulatory environment and of specific regulations.

In the following sections, we describe the economic rationale of regulation, including how regulation improves fairness in markets and addresses the danger to society of financial system failure. We also provide an overview of regulators, the tools at their disposal, and how the work of regulators around the globe is interdependent. Lastly, we describe the assessment of costs and benefits of regulation and highlight practical issues that arise from the implementation of regulation.

2   ECONOMIC RATIONALE FOR REGULATION

☐ | describe the economic rationale for regulatory intervention

Regulations are necessary because market solutions are not adequate for all market situations. Conceptually, this need can be understood best using ideas from economic theory. One of the basic principles in economics is the "fundamental theorem of welfare economics." Assuming constant returns to scale, no frictions (such as costs for or restraints on trading and asymmetrical information), and no externalities, competitive market (equilibrium) allocations are efficient, or *Pareto optimal*. Note that market (equilibrium) allocations are ones in which i) agents maximize utility given relative prices and ii) markets clear. In such a scenario, there is no way to redistribute resources and make some agents better off without making others worse off. (Note that if resources can be redistributed such that any one agent can be made better off without making any other agent worse off, then the original allocation would not be *Pareto optimal*.) Furthermore, any efficient allocation of resources can be sustained as a market equilibrium for an appropriate set of prices. Hence, absent frictions and externalities, the market solution will be economically efficient and regulation would be needed only to ensure consumer protection and privacy rights.

The case for regulatory intervention rests on the presence of **informational frictions**, externalities, weak competition, and social objectives. Informational frictions are market inefficiencies that lead to sub-optimal outcomes. They include lack of access to information and inadequate information. Such frictions result in a variety of issues that regulators attempt to address. These issues include "adverse selection" (private information in the hands of some, but not all, market participants that allows the holder of that information to gain at the expense of others) and "moral hazard" (incentive conflicts that arise from the delegation of decision making to agents or from contracts that will affect the behavior of one party to the contract to the detriment of the other party). Asymmetrical information, in general, may give one entity an inherent advantage over another entity with which interaction occurs. The resulting regulation focuses on establishing rights and responsibilities of entities and on seeking to establish a level playing field in the dissemination of information in the market.

Externalities are spillover effects of production and consumption activities onto others who are not directly involved in a particular transaction, activity, or decision. A positive externality provides a spillover benefit, and a negative externality generates a spillover cost. Systemic risk posed by failures of financial institutions is an example of an externality, as is environmental pollution. Both can have far-reaching consequences for the public. One example of a positive externality would be home improvements, whereby neighbors may benefit from increases in their home values resulting from renovations to a nearby house, even though they have expended no resources to improve their own properties.

Weak competition can also give rise to regulatory intervention. Weak competition is considered to be detrimental to consumers owing to high prices, less choice, and lack of innovation. It is associated with scenarios in which a dominant firm has significant market power or in which firms collude and agree to keep prices high.

Social objectives are typically resolved by the provision of public goods that the market would not otherwise provide. An important feature of public goods is that consumption by one individual does not reduce the availability of the good for others. Usually funded by the government, public goods include defense, police protection, and education. Alternatively, social objectives may be achieved by placing regulatory obligations on firms—for example, by requiring energy companies to give discounts on energy bills to vulnerable customers or by requiring telecommunication companies to provide service to remote customers who would otherwise not be served because of the additional costs of providing such service.

It is difficult, if not impossible, to think of an area of life unaffected by regulation. Regulations address a broad range of issues and can be classified by their objectives. These include the following:

- Safety (for example, food and products)
- Privacy (for example, financial information)
- Protection (for example, intellectual property)
- Environmental (for example, pollution)
- Labor or employment (for example, workers' rights and employment practices)
- Commerce or trade (for example, consumers' rights and protection, investors' protection, and antitrust)
- Financial system (for example, prudential supervision of institutions, capital requirements, and insider trading)

Rationale for the Regulation of Financial Markets

The regulation of securities markets and financial institutions is essential because of the consequences to society of failures in the financial system. These consequences could be experienced at both micro and macro levels. Potential consequences include individual financial losses experienced by individuals, an overall loss of confidence, and disruption to commerce. These consequences were evident in the 2008 global financial crisis. Securities regulation focuses on such goals as protecting investors, creating confidence in markets, and encouraging capital formation. Although it is difficult to define precisely how regulation enhances confidence in the financial system, increasing confidence is cited as one of the motives for securities regulation. Many of the rules oriented toward transparency, equitable access to information (which, in turn, encourages capital formation), and protecting small investors implicitly serve to promote confidence in the markets.

Among the objectives of many financial regulators is the protection of consumers and investors, the safety and soundness of financial institutions, the smooth operation of payment systems, and access to credit. Other (macroeconomic) concerns of financial regulators, particularly central banks, include price stability, levels of employment/ unemployment, and economic growth.

A key focus of regulators is maintaining the integrity of markets, ensuring that they operate efficiently and that consumers and investors are informed and not exploited. This role is distinct from financial stability regulation, which is focused on specific outcomes. In addition to securities registration requirements, disclosure requirements are important to facilitate and support the marketplace and the confidence of investors. Disclosures allow investors to use available information to assess the consequences for investing in and valuing financial instruments and to allow markets to operate. Securities market disclosures occur at various levels, in various forms, and with varied and sometimes unexpected consequences. For example, in the European Union, the Markets in Financial Instruments Directive II (MiFID II), implemented in 2018, focuses on improving transparency in financial markets, including in fixed income, derivatives, and other over-the-counter markets in which prices and volumes were not previously publicly disclosed. The opacity of these markets meant that the buildup of risks prior to the 2008 financial crisis went largely undetected by regulators and market participants.

Disclosures are wide ranging and have high importance. They include financial reporting requirements and accounting standards, prospectus disclosure requirements in conjunction with both securities offerings and annual reports, disclosure requirements in the context of proxy proposals and contests, mutual fund disclosure rules, and financial market price transparency rules. Disclosure requirements tend to be oriented toward the protection of investors and the provision of information to investors (either to investors directly or to their service providers).

Many of the regulations governing securities markets are designed to mitigate agency problems that arise through delegation to intermediaries. For many financial transactions, parties need to act through others (agents), leading to the potential for agency conflicts. Among examples of regulations addressing potential agency conflicts are those related to mutual fund fees and governance, the governance of listed companies, rules for proxy voting in companies, best execution requirements for broker/ dealers, and treatment of inducements (commissions and other non-monetary benefits) that arise in the provision of investment advice and in portfolio management. For example, MiFID II requires advisers to disclose all costs and charges, including all one-off and ongoing charges, transaction costs associated with the financial instrument, all third-party payments received, and the total combined costs of these three categories. These disclosures must also be accompanied by an illustration that shows the cumulative effect of the overall costs and charges on the return to investors.

Historically, securities regulators have tended to focus primarily on protecting retail investors (individual investors with modest resources and less investment expertise than professional investors). This tendency has resulted in a lesser focus on financial regulation of hedge funds, private equity, and venture capital funds because of the type of investors (institutional and affluent individual investors) that invest in these funds. For these larger investors, regulators have taken more of a "buyer beware" stance. For larger investors, it is more difficult to define suitability standards. One approach is to require a more modest range of disclosure requirements related to offering memorandums for a variety of different types of transactions, alongside basic antifraud rules.

Regulations related to prudential supervision of financial institutions and financial stability are critical because of the cost that failure of a financial institution can impose on the economy, capital markets, and society. Prudential supervision is regulation and monitoring of the safety and soundness of financial institutions in order to promote financial stability, reduce system-wide risks, and protect customers of financial institutions. The failure of a bank can result in loss of savings and access to credit. The failure of an insurance company can result in unanticipated losses to those insured. If government-sponsored entities provide protection against these losses or the government chooses to cover all or a portion of these losses, the losses can be spread across a broader section of society than simply those directly affected. Additionally, the resulting loss of confidence in the financial system can have far-reaching consequences. Note that prudential supervision is part of prudential regulation, which includes setting capital adequacy and liquidity standards for such financial institutions as banks and insurers.

Types of prudential supervision include those that focus on diversifying assets, managing and monitoring risk taking, and ensuring adequate capitalization. In addition, regulators may set up funds to provide insurance against losses and mandate premiums or fees to be paid into these funds. Some regulators, such as those in the European Union, may also require that designated investment firms have in place appropriate recovery plans and resolution plans to be applied if they encounter financial distress.

The benefits of regulation, however, generally come with associated costs. For example, regulations that require certain entities or individuals to use insurance when undertaking certain activities may create moral hazard and result in greater risk-taking incentives. Similarly, regulations that increase capital-holding requirements can reduce the amount of capital available to be distributed in the market.

EXAMPLE 1

Rationale for Regulation

1. Which of the following is least likely to be a reason for the use of regulation?

   A. Systemic risk posed by the financial services industry

   B. Informational frictions in the form of private information

   C. Extensive disclosure of operating and financial information by companies seeking to attract investors' attention

Solution

C is correct. Extensive disclosures are not a reason for the use of regulation. They may be the result of regulation or a reflection of good business practices. Presence of systemic risk and informational frictions give rise to the need for regulation.

---

2. Prudential supervision is primarily concerned with:

   A. treatment of inducements in the provision of investment advice.

   B. provision of information about financial products to retail investors.

   C. safety and soundness of the financial system.

Solution

C is correct. The primary objective of prudential regulation is to ensure safety and soundness of the financial system.

3

REGULATION OF COMMERCE

☐ | explain the purposes of regulating commerce and financial markets

Government regulation in certain areas of commerce, such as consumer protection, commercial law, and antitrust, is critical to setting out an underlying framework for the operation of private markets and facilitating business decisions that involve a considerable degree of coordination.

Issues pertaining to externalities and public goods (for example, national defense and transportation infrastructure) are critical to the operation of national and global economies and are essential considerations for the work of investment analysts. The relevant decisions arise at a number of levels. Many of these decisions would be within the domain of national governments, but some of the relevant externalities are global.

Although common examples involve local environmental issues, such as pollution, global externalities—such as nuclear waste storage and global warming—occur across countries. So it is important to have international mechanisms to facilitate the coordination and acceptance of responsibilities among national governments (typically, national governments are best able to coordinate decisions within their respective countries). Some of these externalities have long-term consequences (costs) and implications. In most cases, these long-run consequences may be difficult to fully quantify and assess.

Government policy can be important for promoting commerce locally, nationally, regionally, and globally. Trade agreements are important to global commerce. At the national, regional, or local level, governments can facilitate basic features of the business environment, such as establishing the legal framework for contracting and setting standards. Regulation is also central to fundamental aspects of labor markets, such as workers' and employers' rights and responsibilities, as well as workplace safety. Immigration issues are also handled through regulation. Fundamental safety regulations with respect to drugs, food products, medical devices, and pollution are significant too.

Several issues have emerged as particularly relevant in the context of globalization and the internet. One issue is the recognition and protection of intellectual property. Government policies regulate intellectual property, prescribing standards and processes that define and govern patents, trademarks, and copyrights. The legal standards are country specific, and although most countries recognize the importance of protecting intellectual property, lack of enforcement and protection of intellectual property at a global level has emerged as an issue. Setting common technical standards is another global issue, given the focus on ensuring higher levels of interoperability between the technology and electronic tools used in commerce. Even something as basic as establishing domain names and the related standard setting requires some appropriate delegation of authority.

Technological change, including a shift toward digitization, is leading to an increasing amount of data being collected, processed, shared, and used in digital form at lower cost and on a larger scale than ever before. "Big Data" gives rise to potential market opportunities, such as the development of data-based business models that rely on the sharing of data and the extraction of commercial value from data. However, it is also giving rise to concerns about privacy and data protection. Privacy is particularly important with respect to medical, financial, academic, and employment records. New regulations, such as the General Data Protection Regulation (GDPR) and the proposed e-Privacy Regulation in the European Union, require entities, including businesses and governments, to apply certain protections and safeguards to personal data in their possession and maintain appropriate security procedures. The internet raises a broad set of issues involving privacy because of the breadth of information potentially available about a person's situation (financial and personal), activities, interactions, and purchases. How internet software navigates these privacy concerns will influence both the perceptions and actions of regulators, as well as the acceptance of software innovations and business models in the marketplace.

An effective legal environment is also crucial for the successful operation of commerce. Clearly defined rules governing contracts, their interpretation, and each party's legal rights under a contract are necessary. A framework for financial liability and dealing with bankruptcy is also necessary as an incentive to enter into economic contracts, particularly those that require long-term commitments. Such activities as construction projects, energy exploration, and extraction projects—and even mundane commercial activities, such as relocation decisions—involve significant long-term, dynamic commitments. Pre-commitment by society to a well-defined set of rules and standards is crucial to facilitating the willingness of market participants to engage in long-term commercial activities.

For example, consider the situation in which a company needs to incur significant costs to start a project. These costs are unrecoverable if the project does not progress; in other words, these are sunk costs. Without a strong legal framework to guarantee that the party will recover these initial costs, the party paying the sunk costs would be reluctant to incur them because of the potential of a "holdout" problem in which the other side exploits the fact that the sunk costs have been incurred to force a renegotiation of the deal. Such contractual difficulties would destabilize the operation of businesses and weaken the economy.

ANTITRUST REGULATION AND FRAMEWORK

4

☐ | describe anticompetitive behaviors targeted by antitrust laws globally and evaluate the antitrust risk associated with a given business strategy

In a global context, an implicit regulatory goal of government may be to restrict competition from other countries. In a domestic context, a regulatory goal often pursued is to promote competition in most economic sectors (this goal can alternatively be viewed as monitoring and preventing activities that restrict or distort competition). There are several dimensions to this goal. Regulatory approval or notification is typically required for mergers and acquisition of major companies in a specific market. When a merger or acquisition is expected to substantially reduce competition, regulators can block the merger or acquisition or suggest remedies to resolve a perceived issue (for example, divestiture of particular segments of the businesses to resolve an antitrust issue). When there are competing bids, the regulator can effectively decide the outcome based on its assessment of each bid's effects. Considering the potential response of competition or antitrust agencies is a central aspect to the evaluation of mergers and acquisitions.

Competition and antitrust laws also typically prohibit anticompetitive arrangements or practices, such as price collusion or exchanging certain information, and anticompetitive behavior by companies that dominate a market. Types of behavior that are problematic when undertaken by a dominant company (beyond mergers that substantially lessen competition) include exclusive dealings and refusals to deal, price discrimination, and engaging in predatory pricing. In response to antitrust issues, regulators not only may impose monetary sanctions but also may require companies to change their business (for example, divest portions or change operating/marketing practices). In some jurisdictions, such as the United States, the United Kingdom, Germany, Denmark, Ireland, France, and Australia, individuals can also face imprisonment for engaging in a cartel.

There has been an increasing focus on applying antitrust laws to the technology sector, which includes investigations of Google (owned by a holding company, Alphabet Inc.), Apple, Intel, and Microsoft. In Europe, for example, Google was found to have abused its dominant position in the internet search market by favoring its own comparison shopping service over those of its rivals. Similarly, Intel was found to have abused its dominant position by engaging in exclusive dealing with certain computer equipment manufacturers and retailers. Both companies challenged the claims on the basis that they have brought considerable benefits to consumers in terms of low prices and ever-improving quality. Using competition laws to challenge rivals can also represent a business strategy. An example of such a challenge is Microsoft's challenge in Europe that Google is unfairly impeding competition in the search engine market.

A significant issue that companies need to face in addressing antitrust (lack of competition) issues is that in many cases, they need to satisfy simultaneously a range of regulators across multiple jurisdictions. For example, a company may have to satisfy both the US Department of Justice and the European Union if it plans to use a common product and market strategy across jurisdictions. Despite language and cultural differences, it often is advantageous to adopt a unified strategy around the globe because of business imperatives and likely overlapping views among regulators of competition.

ANTITRUST REGULATION

1. Which of the following issues is least likely to be the subject of antitrust rules?

   A. Privacy and data protection

   B. Anticompetitive behavior by dominant companies in a market

   C. Mergers and acquisitions by major companies

Solution

A is correct. Privacy and data protection issues are regulated, but only as part of regulations besides antitrust rules.

---

5   CLASSIFICATION OF REGULATIONS AND REGULATORS

☐ | describe classifications of regulations and regulators
☐ | describe uses of self-regulation in financial markets

Regulations are sometimes enacted by legislative bodies (often these regulations are laws) but more typically arise from the determination of regulatory bodies.

Classification of Regulations and Regulators

Broadly speaking, regulators can be either sanctioned by the government or created by an industry on a voluntary basis.

Government-backed regulatory bodies can be either governmental departments and agencies or independent regulators, which derive their power and authority from the state. Government-backed regulatory bodies have legal authority to enact and enforce regulations within the parameters of the mandate given to them. In many instances, a legislative body enacts a statute at a broad level, leaving it to regulatory bodies to implement and apply the detail of the regulation.

ILLUSTRATION OF REGULATORY PROCESS

This description by the US Securities and Exchange Commission (SEC) is illustrative of how the process works: "Rulemaking is the process by which federal agencies implement legislation passed by Congress and signed into law by the President. Major pieces of legislation, such as the Securities Act of 1933, the Securities Exchange Act of 1934, and the Investment Company and Investment Adviser Acts of 1940, provide the framework for the SEC's oversight of the securities markets. These statutes are broadly drafted, establishing basic principles and objectives. To ensure that the intent of Congress is carried out in specific circumstances—and as the securities markets evolve technologically, expand in size, and offer new products and services—the SEC engages in rulemaking." (www. sec.gov/about/whatwedo.shtml)

Courts play an important role in regulation as well—helping interpret regulations and laws, defining permitted and proscribed regulatory practices, and, in some instances, imposing sanctions for regulatory violations. State-backed regulations can, therefore, be classified as comprising

- laws enacted by legislative bodies (**statutes**),
- rules issued by government agencies or other regulators (**administrative regulations or administrative law**), and
- interpretations of courts (**judicial law**).

Although government departments and agencies make many regulations, **independent regulators** can also make regulations in accordance with their powers and objectives. The authority of independent regulators, such as the Financial Conduct Authority in the United Kingdom, comes from their recognition, autonomy, and powers given to them by a statute, government department, or government agency, but they are not government agencies per se. One distinction between government agencies and independent regulators is that the latter typically do not rely on government funding and are often given a degree of autonomy in terms of decision making. Some argue that an advantage of independent regulators is that they are to some extent immune from political influence and pressure and can, therefore, take a more technical and long-term view of policies, which would achieve the objectives they have been created to pursue.

In contrast to state-backed government agencies or independent regulators, industry **self-regulatory bodies** are private organizations that both represent and regulate their members. Although these organizations are independent of the government and to an extent are isolated from political pressure, they may be subject to pressure from their members. Industry self-regulatory bodies derive authority from their members, who agree to comply with the organization's rules and standards and their enforcement. This authority does not have the force of law, but industry self-regulatory bodies do have the power to exclude or expel parties from being members. To ensure minimum standards are maintained, certain entry requirements (such as training or ethical standards) may be imposed.

Some industry self-regulatory bodies, particularly in the securities industry, are known as **self-regulating organizations (SROs)**. SROs differ from standard industry self-regulatory bodies in that they are given recognition and authority, including enforcement power, by a government body or agency. SROs are funded independently, rather than by the government. For example, the US SEC, the government agency that regulates the securities markets in the United States, allocates some regulatory responsibilities to the Financial Industry Regulatory Authority (FINRA), which is an SRO. It has the authority to enforce industry rules and federal securities laws.

> **FINRA**
>
> On its website, FINRA states:
> *FINRA is dedicated to protecting investors and safeguarding market integrity in a manner that facilitates vibrant capital markets.*
> *FINRA plays a critical role in ensuring the integrity of America's financial system—all at no cost to taxpayers. Working under the supervision of the Securities and Exchange Commission, we:*
>
> - *Write and enforce rules governing the ethical activities of all registered broker-dealer firms and registered brokers in the U.S.;*
> - *Examine firms for compliance with those rules;*
> - *Foster market transparency; and*
> - *Educate investors.*
>
> (http://www.finra.org/about)

The role of SROs varies among countries. In some countries, such as the United States, SROs have specific regulatory authority, and in other countries, self-regulating organizations are rarely or never recognized as independent regulators. For example, the Australian financial regulator, ASIC, has stated, "One of the many significant recent legislative amendments that was introduced in Australia with the Financial Services Reform Act 2001 was the removal of the official regulatory standing of SROs. SROs, whether they are exchanges, industry associations, or some other form of peer group, have traditionally set standards of behavior or codes of conduct for market participants" (https://asic.gov.au/media/1339352/integration-financial-regulatory-authorities.pdf). According to the World Bank, the role of self-regulation in Europe, with the exception of the United Kingdom, was limited because of civil law systems and the resulting reliance on government supervision. In the United Kingdom and other countries with common law systems, reliance on self-regulation has been more extensive. The roles of SROs in regulation in these countries range from non-existent to having some regulatory authority. Regulators are concerned with the corporate governance of SROs and the management of their conflicts of interest. The extent of the concern is a factor in deciding the regulatory role, if any, of the SRO in question.

The relatively simple classification of regulators (legislative bodies, government agencies, independent regulators, and courts) and regulations (statutes, administrative regulations, and judicial law) is useful but does not reflect the complexities and nuances that exist. In some cases, the classification of a regulator is clear, and in other cases, it is ambiguous. For example, the Public Company Accounting Oversight Board (PCAOB) is a non-profit corporation, established by the US Congress to oversee the audits of public companies. Previously, the audit profession was self-regulated. The PCAOB is funded primarily through annual fees paid by public companies, brokers, and dealers. The SEC oversees the PCAOB. The PCAOB is an independent regulator rather than a government agency, but it is not an SRO.

In Singapore, statutory boards are entities separate from the government, with specific legislation governing their operations. Most, if not all, statutory boards impose charges for some or all of their services. Those statutory boards that generate insufficient revenue to meet their expenses receive grants from the government to finance their operations. The grants are funded from the government's annual budget. The statutory boards are described as separate from the government, yet they are subject to specific legislation governing their operations and may receive government funding.

Whether Singapore's statutory boards are government agencies or independent regulators is ambiguous. The Singapore Economic Development Board (EDB), one such statutory board, describes itself as "a government agency under the Ministry of Trade and Industry...responsible for strategies that enhance Singapore's position as a global centre for business, innovation, and talent" (www.edb.gov.sg/en/about-edb/who-we-are.html). Another statutory board, the Accounting and Corporate Regulatory Authority (ACRA), describes itself as "the national regulator of business entities, public accountants and corporate service providers in Singapore" (www.acra.gov.sg/who-we-are/overview-of-acra). Although EDB clearly identifies itself as a government agency, it is less clear whether ACRA, given the description of a statutory board and the description of itself, should be classified as a government agency or an independent regulator.

Classifying regulatory bodies that exist in unions, such as the Union of South American Nations and the European Union, can also present challenges. For example, the European Commission, which has a mission to promote the general interest of the EU, can initiate legislation in the form of directives and regulations, which are subject to debate and approval by the European Parliament and the European Council (the co-legislators). The directives and regulations passed by the European Parliament and the European Council are jointly referred to as "EU law." Regulations have binding legal force in every EU member state on a par with national laws. Directives identify desired results and require national authorities to put laws in place to achieve them. Decisions are binding laws addressed to specific parties and are the result of specific cases (https://ec.europa.eu/info/law/law-making-process/types-eu-law_en). Regulations appear to have the characteristics of administrative regulations. Directives appear to have the characteristics of statutes; they are at a broad level, and another body needs to fill in the implementation details. Decisions appear similar to judicial law. Regardless of how a regulatory body is classified, it is important to identify the regulators and regulations that might affect the industry or company being analyzed.

EXAMPLE 3

Classification of Regulators

1. The media devotes considerable coverage to a regulatory body that has been given autonomy by the government and is empowered by statute. The regulatory body has recently raised the fees charged to the companies it regulates. The regulatory body in question is most likely to be a(n):

   A. self-regulatory organization.

   B. government agency.

   C. independent regulator.

Solution

C is correct. Independent regulators are given authority by the government and are empowered by statute. Unlike government agencies, they are funded by fees that they collect from the firms they regulate.

2. Which of the following is least likely to be a characteristic of a self-regulatory body?

   A. It represents and regulates its members.

   B. It carries out government policy.

   C. It can discipline members that violate its rules and principles.

Solution

B is correct. Self-regulating bodies do not carry out government policy. They are meant to be independent from government and immune to its influence.

Regulatory authorities may reference the work of outside bodies in their regulations. Examples of these outside bodies are accounting standard–setting bodies, such as the International Accounting Standards Board (IASB) and the Financial Accounting Standards Board (FASB), and credit-rating agencies. Regulatory authorities have the legal authority to enforce any regulation that references the work of these bodies. In the case of accounting standard–setting bodies—which are typically private sector, non-profit, self-regulated organizations—the requirement to prepare financial reports in accordance with specified accounting standards is the responsibility of regulatory authorities. The standard-setting bodies may set the standards, but the regulatory authorities recognize and enforce the standards. Ratings by credit-rating agencies—which are typically private sector, profit-oriented entities—were often referenced in regulations related to acceptable holdings by certain entities. Issues with conflicts of interest when the agencies were paid by the firms they rated, however, have resulted in efforts to reduce references to credit-rating agencies in regulations.

Although much of the focus of this reading is on the rules themselves and their development, impact, and implementation, regulatory enforcement and sanctions also play an important role. This division between development and enforcement of regulation also represents a possible way to classify laws or regulation. **Substantive law** focuses on the rights and responsibilities of entities and relationships among entities, and **procedural law** focuses on the protection and enforcement of the substantive laws. Regulators typically have responsibility for both substantive and procedural aspects of their regulations.

6   REGULATORY INTERDEPENDENCIES

☐   describe regulatory interdependencies and their effects

An interesting facet of regulation is how regulated entities view the regulation, which is often context specific. Although there are many examples in which regulated companies fight against new proposed regulations, an outright opposition is relatively rare. Regulated company efforts to fight particular regulations tend to attract more public attention than when the companies are sympathetic to the proposed regulations. Even more fundamentally, academics have argued that regulation can sometimes enhance and work to the benefit of the interests of the regulated. This argument is often called the "**regulatory capture**" theory (see Stigler 1971). For example, regulatory actions and determinations can restrict potential competition (for example, by limiting entry) or effectively coordinate the choices of rivals (by imposing certain quality standards or price controls). In the interactions between regulated entities and their regulators, the regulated entities may possess considerable expertise and knowledge, and some of the individual regulators may have worked in the industry or aspire to be in the industry in which the regulated entities operate. These interactions may reinforce regulatory capture.

Regulatory differences across jurisdictions can lead to shifts in location and behavior of entities because of **regulatory competition** and **regulatory arbitrage**. Regulators may compete to provide a regulatory environment designed to attract certain entities (regulatory competition). As a result, companies may engage in regulatory arbitrage; for example, they may identify and use some aspect of regulations that allows them to exploit differences in economic substance and regulatory interpretation in foreign and domestic regulatory regimes to the companies' benefit.

Interdependence in the actions of regulators dealing with the same issues and activities is important in the international arena. Many regulatory issues are relatively similar around the globe. This commonality reflects both similarities in the challenges confronting different countries and the diffusion of the underlying problems around the globe. Such issues as financial systemic risk, terrorism financing, money launder- ing, and climate change reflect global concerns and, therefore, are well suited to an approach based on regulatory cooperation and coordination. For other issues, however, domestic regulators in specific jurisdictions often adopt different perspectives or face different trade-offs when developing and applying regulations in their jurisdiction. These varying perspectives can lead to differences in regulatory treatments of the same issue across countries. For example, some jurisdictions have significantly greater disclosure requirements to protect investors than other jurisdictions have. Although such differences are often justified, "regulatory competition" can reduce the effective- ness of regulation in particular countries. Regulatory competition can lead to what is sometimes referred as a "race to the bottom," in which countries continually reduce their regulatory standards to attract as many companies as possible to their jurisdiction.

Consider issues related to global warming and pollution. How should governments manage and coordinate efforts around the globe? The relevant externality is not simply within countries but, rather, extends beyond country borders. One of the challenging aspects of this issue is that countries differ in how much they contribute to climate change and in terms of how they are affected by it. Put simply, the countries most affected by climate change may not be the ones that are contributing the most to it. What are the institutional and governance mechanisms that would be appropriate to address this issue on a global basis? Although an economist's solution to the problem of pollution externalities might be to tax pollution or to introduce an emission trading system (or a cap and trade system) in order to allocate the pollution to the parties that can absorb the cost, the practical application of the solution may be complicated. How should one allocate "permits" to pollute among countries? Should countries have the "right" to pollute related to their past pollution? If not, how would one accommodate differences in living standards? How should one address the equity issues associated with low wealth and developing countries' having a potential comparative advantage in absorbing pollution?

The point of this overall discussion of interdependencies among jurisdictions is not to suggest the existence of global governance or a global regulator but, rather, is to recognize the reality and implications of diverse trade-offs and preferences among regional, national, and local regulators. To a degree, the presence of diverse and com- peting jurisdictions influences the stances of national and regional regulators. Evidence that governments recognize the necessity for global regulatory cooperation and coordi- nation on some issues exists. For example, the Basel Accords established and promote internationally consistent capital requirements and risk management practices for large international banks. The Basel Committee on Banking Supervision has evolved into a standard setter for bank supervision, among other functions. Another example is the International Organization of Securities Commissions (IOSCO), a self-regulating organization but not a regulatory authority. Its members (national regulators) regulate a significant portion of the world's capital markets. This organization has established objectives and principles to guide securities and capital market regulation, to which its members agree to adhere.

> ### HOW IOSCO ENHANCES REGULATORY COOPERATION
>
> The member agencies of IOSCO have resolved, through its permanent structures,
>
> - "to cooperate in developing, implementing and promoting adherence to internationally recognized and consistent standards of regulation, oversight and enforcement in order to protect investors, maintain fair, efficient and transparent markets, and seek to address systemic risks;
>
> - to enhance investor protection and promote investor confidence in the integrity of securities markets, through strengthened information exchange and cooperation in enforcement against misconduct and in supervision of markets and market intermediaries; and
>
> - to exchange information at both global and regional levels on their respective experiences in order to assist the development of markets, strengthen market infrastructure and implement appropriate regulation" (www.iosco.org/about/?subsection=about_iosco).

IOSCO is a standard setter and an establisher of best practices for securities regulators, and it has developed a framework of matters to be addressed in the domestic laws of a jurisdiction to facilitate effective securities legislation (IOSCO, "Methodology for Assessing Implementation of the IOSCO Objectives and Principles of Securities Regulation," May 2017). This framework is shown in Exhibit 1.

The framework also serves as a useful, but by no means exhaustive, list of areas of regulation relevant to an analyst. Labor, consumer protection, and environmental, health, and safety laws, which are not included in the list, may also significantly affect a business or industry.

Awareness of the basic types of laws and regulations that affect economies, financial systems, industries, and businesses is useful to an analyst. This knowledge will help the analyst to identify areas of concern and to consider proactively potential effects of regulations, existing and anticipated.

Exhibit 1: IOSCO's Objectives and Principles of Securities Regulation

Effective securities regulation depends on an appropriate legal framework. The matters to be addressed in the domestic laws of a jurisdiction include the following:

1. **Company Law**
   1. company formation
   2. duties of directors and officers
   3. regulation of takeover bids and other transactions intended to effect a change in control
   4. laws governing the issue and offer for sale of securities
   5. disclosure of information to security holders to enable informed voting decisions
   6. disclosure of material shareholdings

2. **Commercial Code/Contract Law**
   1. private right of contract
   2. facilitation of securities lending and hypothecation

3. property rights, including rights attaching to securities, and the rules governing the transfer of those rights

3. **Taxation Laws**

    1. clarity and consistency, including, but not limited to, the treatment of investments and investment products

4. **Bankruptcy and Insolvency Laws**

    1. rights of security holders on winding up

    2. rights of clients on insolvency of intermediary

    3. netting

5. **Competition Law**

    1. prevention of anticompetitive practices

    2. prevention of unfair barriers to entry

    3. prevention of abuse of a market dominant position

6. **Banking Law**

7. **Dispute Resolution System**

    1. a fair and efficient judicial system (including the alternative of arbitration or other alternative dispute resolution mechanisms)

    2. enforceability of court orders and arbitration awards, including foreign orders and awards

Source: International Organization of Securities Commissions, "Methodology For Assessing Implementation of the IOSCO Objectives and Principles of Securities Regulation" (May 2017): Appendix 1, "The Legal Framework." www.iosco.org/library/pubdocs/pdf/IOSCOPD562.pdf

Even within countries, the objectives of diverse government regulators can differ and potentially lead to regulations that seem inconsistent. Bank supervisors (whether as a function of the central bank, another entity, or a combination of entities) generally focus on **prudential supervision**—regulation and monitoring of the safety and soundness of financial institutions in order to promote financial stability, reduce system-wide risks, and protect customers of financial institutions. The objectives of securities commissions or regulators are typically to protect investors; ensure that markets are fair, efficient, and transparent; and reduce systemic risk. In some situations, the goals of the bank supervisor and securities regulator can be in tension, resulting in conflicting objectives. For example, on the one hand, the bank supervisor may be reluctant or even unwilling to release the results of stress tests of financial institutions in order to promote financial stability and avoid systemic risk because of the potential loss of confidence. On the other hand, a securities regulator might advocate for the release of information that might be relevant to investor decision making and act to protect investors (see Spatt 2009).

A general conclusion is that regulation by different regulators, even with seemingly similar objectives, can lead to very different regulatory outcomes.

EXAMPLE 4

Regulatory Interdependencies

1. A country's securities regulator is looking to attract a higher number of smaller companies to its capital markets. It proposes to ease hurdles that companies face when preparing to list shares on the country's stock exchange. The proposals include the lowering of the frequency of financial

reporting, reducing the extent of disclosures required, and reducing the minimum size of company that can be accepted on the market.

This is an example of:

A. regulatory competition.

B. regulatory coordination.

C. regulatory capture.

Solution

A is correct. Regulatory competition occurs when regulators compete to provide a regulatory environment designed to attract certain entities.

2. Regulatory capture is most likely to be a concern where there is reliance on:

A. SROs.

B. government agencies.

C. government departments.

Solution

A is correct. Regulatory capture has been a concern when SROs are used.

---

7   REGULATORY TOOLS

☐ | describe tools of regulatory intervention in markets

Regulatory and government policies should be predictable as well as effective in achieving objectives. It is very difficult for any entity to function with confidence and success in an environment where the rules are unclear or in a state of flux (in other words, where there is considerable regulatory uncertainty). Regulatory choices or government policies that will be consistent over time are desirable. If these choices occur, the regulatory environment is likely to be stable despite the fact that, in many countries, governmental decision makers (with diverse political preferences) change on a regular basis. It is helpful to use regulatory tools that are consistent with maintaining a stable regulatory environment. Regulatory tools and government interventions in markets include the use of price mechanisms, such as taxes and subsidies; regulatory mandates and restrictions on behaviors, including establishing rights and responsibilities; provision of public goods; and public financing of private projects.

The issue of how to address pollution is a classic example in regulation. By taxing polluters (or subsidizing those who do not pollute, by using a suitable baseline), one can create a system in which marginal incentives are equated across economic agents. The advantage of such an arrangement is that, theoretically, the rights to pollute are redistributed in an "efficient" manner relative to a fixed allocation. In particular, the structure of the regulation allows market incentives to redistribute the pollution rights to those for whom they are the most valuable at the margin. There are important issues, however, about how to initially establish and distribute the amount of acceptable total pollution. In some situations, historical usage (amount of pollution produced) is used to allocate pollution rights One problem is that marginal incentives may be altered in anticipation of this allocation. In other situations, the allocation is the outcome of a political process, which can lead to considerable lobbying. At the heart of this example is the use of a price mechanism to create the appropriate marginal incentives and an efficient allocation of resources. The Coase theorem states that if an externality can be traded and there are no transaction costs, then the allocation of property rights will be efficient and the resource allocation will not depend on the initial assignment of property rights.

Governments can intervene in markets in ways other than through the price mechanism. These include restricting some activities (e.g., insider trading and short selling), mandating some activities (e.g., capital requirements for banks and registration with a securities commission for certain activities), providing public goods (e.g., national defense and transportation infrastructure), and financing private projects (e.g., loans to individuals or companies for specified activities that the government deems desirable to encourage). The extent of government provision of public goods and government financing of private projects depends on a number of factors, including the political philosophy of the country and/or government in power, the structure of the government, and the country's gross domestic product. The problem of **systemic risk** (the risk of failure of the financial system) as a result of the failure of a major financial institution has emerged as an issue in many countries around the world in the aftermath of the 2008 global financial crisis. Systemic risk and **financial contagion** (a situation in which financial shocks spread from their place of origin to other regions; in essence, a faltering economy infects other, healthier economies) are examples of negative externalities. In the EU, the European Systemic Risk Board, formed in December 2010, is an advisory EU body within the European Central Bank tasked with advising national macroprudential bodies to take steps to address risks.

Exhibit 2 focuses on how "bail-in" tools can mitigate systemic risk.

Exhibit 2: Bail-In Tools

Among the regulatory tools introduced following the 2008 financial crisis are so-called bail-in powers, which were endorsed by the Financial Stability Board and the G–20. A bail-in tool is seen as improving the toolkit for dealing with the failure of large, globally systemic banks. Bail-in involves shareholders of a failing institution being divested of their shares and creditors of the institution having their claims canceled or reduced to the extent necessary to restore the institution to financial viability. Bail-in policies are intended to ensure that shareholders and creditors of the failed institution, rather than taxpayers, pay the costs of the failure. This situation contrasts with how many governments dealt with the financial crisis of 2008, when banks and insurers were rescued by taxpayers in a number of countries. Such policies also allow the failed institution to continue to operate, so that it can introduce restructuring measures to address the cause of the failure. These policies can limit disruption to the customers of the institution and help maintain confidence in the banking system.

It is difficult to assess the extent to which the new approaches and tools, such as bail-in policies, will reduce systemic risk. There are a number of reasons for this difficulty. The types and sources of future crises are likely to be different from those of the past, so regulations designed with a prior crisis in mind may not prevent a future crisis. It can be difficult to assess the potential effectiveness of regulatory actions before an event and even after the fact. The mere fact that a crisis does not occur is not necessarily evidence that regulations prevented one. It is also plausible that some regulatory responses have the unintended consequence of mitigating one source of risk while increasing another source of risk. All these issues make effective regulation challenging to design.

Generally, more than one regulatory approach or policy is feasible and worthy of consideration in a specific situation. Two examples that illustrate a range of possible regulatory responses are (1) conflict-of-interest policies and (2) trading restrictions on insiders, which are explored in Exhibit 3 and Exhibit 4, respectively.

Exhibit 3: Regulating Conflicts of Interest

Consider the hypothetical scenario in which a potential employee of a regulator has some degree of financial exposure to a regulated company. Such exposure could come about in many ways (for example, spousal employment, a marketable position in an investment portfolio, or an illiquid position resulting from past employment) and at a variety of financial levels.

What types of regulatory policies might be appropriate to mitigate these risks? Among the potential regulatory responses are the following: The individual could be barred from employment at the regulatory agency or from working on specific (or all) projects involving the regulated company in question. The individual could sell the position; the sale could be voluntary or mandated. The individual could be required to disclose the nature of his potential conflict to higher-level decision makers to whom he will be providing recommendations. Other potential policies include a bar on involvement, resolution of the conflict, or disclosure of it.

Exhibit 4: Regulating Corporate Insiders

Turning to the case of corporate insiders, there are potential regulatory and corporate restrictions. Examples of regulatory responses are a ban from trading on non-public information and a requirement that when they do trade, the insiders disclose the trades. The company may impose a blackout period during which insiders are banned from trading on the company's stock (these periods often precede earnings announcements and continue for a short while afterward). The appropriate remedy depends on the underlying facts and circumstances, and arguably the appropriate standards would reflect the specific context.

An important aspect of effective regulation is the potential ability to impose sanctions on violators of the regulations; in other words, it is important to be able to enforce the regulations. IOSCO clearly identifies this aspect as one of the agreed-on principles of securities regulation: "The regulator should have comprehensive enforcement powers" (IOSCO, "Objectives and Principles of Securities Regulation," 2017). Enforcement of securities regulations and regulations on businesses may include sanctions for the violating corporation (business or company), the individual violator(s), or both. Corporate sanctions may be appropriate if the company caused harm to others. The sanctions often involve monetary fines/fees/settlement, and in the case of individuals, the sanctions may also involve prison terms. In some situations, such as in cases of accounting fraud, shareholders may actually be the victims. In such instances, if the stockholders were harmed by the wrongdoing, the case for sanctions, such as fines, against the company is often far from compelling. The sanctions may simply redistribute funds from current shareholders to the stockholders who were the specific victims, and the company incurs real resource costs.

For various reasons, it can be difficult to prosecute or achieve settlements with individual violators. First, it often is difficult to detect violations and to identify exactly which individuals were at fault. Second, the individuals possess strong incentives to fight in order to protect their reputation and livelihood. Indeed, individuals are often able to fight using corporate resources because of indemnification provisions in their employment contract. The intent of these provisions may be to protect risk-averse executives against inadvertent liability and to potentially align their interests with those of the stockholders, but the provisions instead may result in protecting executives to the detriment of the stockholders. The incentive to fight individual sanctions may be especially strong because of not only financial costs but also other costs, such as reputational costs.

EXAMPLE 5

Regulatory Tools

1. Globalization of capital markets is *most likely* to result in increased concerns about:

   A. financial contagion.

   B. regulatory competition.

   C. both contagion and regulatory competition.

Solution

C is correct. Globalization is likely to result in increased concerns about contagion and regulatory competition. It is easier for a financial shock to spread. Governments may use their regulatory environment to attract entities from around the world.

2. The regulatory tools *least likely* to be used by self-regulating organizations are:

   A. price mechanisms.

   B. restrictions on behaviors.

   C. provision of public goods.

Solution

A is correct. SROs are least likely to use price mechanisms. They typically regulate behaviors and often provide public goods in the form of standards.

COST–BENEFIT ANALYSIS

8

☐ describe benefits and costs of regulation

The effects of regulation can range from macro effects that impact large parts of the economy to micro effects on an individual business. Section 4.1 introduces the concept of cost–benefit analysis carried out by regulators. Section 4.2 illustrates how an analyst could approach the task of assessing the effect of regulation on a particular industry. Because regulations can evolve in response to market, technological, and societal changes, it is important to monitor issues of concern to regulators and ongoing developments to evaluate the implications of potential changes in regulation. Understanding the regulatory process will help an analyst recognize the types of challenges that regulators and policymakers face and formulate expectations of regulatory outcomes.

Basic Concepts of Cost–Benefit Analysis

In assessing regulation and regulatory outcomes, it is common practice for regulators to assess the overall benefits and costs of regulatory proposals to assess the trade-offs associated with a particular regulatory action and to assess alternative solutions. Regulators, guided by economic principles, strive to develop techniques to enhance the measurement of the costs and benefits of regulations. The general benefits of regulation as discussed in previous sections may be clear, but the measurement of the full impact of the regulation (both benefits and costs) can be challenging. In conducting cost–benefit analysis of regulation, it often is easier to assess the costs of regulation, although doing so can also be challenging.

Regulatory burden refers to the costs of regulation for the regulated entity; these costs are sometimes viewed as the private costs of regulation or government burden. **Net regulatory burden** is the private costs of regulation less the private benefits of regulation. Many regulators focus narrowly on the implementation costs of regulation (for example, how many compliance lawyers will need to be hired—and at what cost), but in many instances, the most significant costs are the indirect ones that relate to the ways in which economic decisions and behavior are altered and market allocations are changed.

Regulators view some of the costs associated with regulations as "unintended," but it is important to distinguish between two types of such costs. There may be implementation costs that were unanticipated (for example, if it turns out more compliance lawyers need to be hired than originally thought) and indirect costs because of unintended consequences. It is important for regulators to recognize that their evaluation of potential regulations should reflect indirect costs as well as the consequences that were the direct objective of the rule making. Furthermore, in some cases, regulatory filings and consultations in response to proposed regulations identify at least some of the "unintended consequences" prior to the implementation of the regulations. In these circumstances, it is difficult to argue that such consequences were unanticipated and unintended if they were identified prior to the implementation of the regulation. Unintended consequences are reflective of underlying policy risk and may result in high unanticipated costs.

Regulatory costs and benefits are especially difficult to assess on a prospective basis relative to a retrospective basis. An after-the-fact analysis allows a comparison of the item(s) of interest before and after the regulation occurs. This comparison allows for a more informed assessment of a regulation because the actual costs and benefits may be identifiable. In some instances, a trial or pilot analysis may be appropriate and helpful to more fully understand the potential impacts in advance of a proposed regulation. A potentially feasible and relevant approach in the context of an environment with frequent trading is to use natural experiments and trial phase-ins to generate data suitable for careful cost–benefit analysis. This approach facilitates the assessment of statistical evidence to evaluate the effects prior to the full implementation of the proposed regulation. Among the contexts in which US securities regulators have used such techniques are rules involving short sales, post-trade price reporting, and the tick size increment for trading. Such approaches are more feasible for a trading rule in a market with high trading frequency that will generate considerable data and run little risk of disrupting the real economy. Similar approaches, sometimes known as "regulatory sandboxes," are being introduced by regulators in such countries as the United Kingdom, Singapore, Australia, the United Arab Emirates, and Malaysia.

In the United States, administrative law requires that federal regulatory agencies conduct a cost–benefit analysis to assess the consequences of their actions. Court rulings have struck down regulatory actions because cost–benefit analyses performed were deemed inadequate. For example, the US Circuit Court of Appeals overturned the 2004 SEC rule requiring that mutual funds have independent chairs and at least

75% independent directors on such grounds (see *Chamber of Commerce v. SEC*, 412 F.3d 133 [D.C. Cir. 2005] and 443 F.3d 890 [D.C. Cir. 2006]). In 2011, as reported in the *Wall Street Journal*, "Striking a blow to the shareholder rights movement, a federal appeals court threw out a controversial new Securities and Exchange Commission regulation that would give investors more power to oust corporate directors.... The court issued a harsh rebuke to the SEC, saying it didn't adequately analyze the costs to U.S. companies of fighting in contested board elections" (*The Wall Street Journal*, 23 July 2011, "Court Deals Blow to SEC, Activists," Jessica Holzer). Requirements to undertake cost–benefit analyses (also known as "impact assessments") prior to the introduction of new regulations exist in a number of other jurisdictions, including in the EU and Australia.

Ideally, regulatory judgments should reflect economic principles and full consideration of the economic costs and benefits, rather than the preferences of current decision makers. Although the potential failure of the fundamental theorem of welfare economics suggests the potential relevance of regulation, it is important to use economic principles to identify and assess alternative remedies and specific actions.

ILLUSTRATION OF COST–BENEFIT ANALYSIS

To illustrate the issues that may be relevant to a regulator when considering a cost–benefit analysis, we focus here on a proposal for the introduction of new regulation in Europe to remove the red tape and compliance burdens faced by small and medium-sized enterprises (SMEs) when seeking an IPO of their shares or for issuing bonds on public markets. The proposed regulation is intended to address three problems. First, the "one-size-fits-all" approach to some areas of financial regulation has led to a perception that the costs of listing outweigh the benefits. Second, there has been a progressive decline in the number of smaller brokers and investment firms that specialize in trading shares of smaller companies. A small, local brokerage ecosystem is necessary to support smaller companies with the listing process. The third problem is the lack of investment in shares and bonds of small companies.

The objective of the proposed regulation would, therefore, be to revive IPOs and bond offerings of small companies. The cost–benefit assessment would examine two proposals: first, whether some of the existing regulations, such as MiFID II and the Market Abuse Regulation (MAR), could be adapted to accommodate smaller issuers. The costs and benefits of (1) targeted changes and clarifications to the existing regulations or (2) an overhaul of the provisions would be examined relative to a "baseline scenario" where the existing rules under MiFID II and MAR do not change. The second proposal would examine the cost and benefits of the introduction of new provisions. These could include simpler delisting rules, rules enabling easy transfer of a listing from less regulated "small company growth markets" to regulated markets, and less stringent free float requirements to make it more attractive for issuers, investors, and market operators.

A regulator carrying out cost–benefit analysis would need to assess the positive impact on the companies' investment and growth rates as a result of easier access to capital. The costs the regulator would have to consider include the additional regulatory oversight over the small companies in question and the consequences of any impact of corporate failures among the listed smaller firms on investor confidence and, consequently, the remaining firms' cost of capital.

COST–BENEFIT ANALYSIS

1. An investment adviser is discussing a client's portfolio exposure to the electric utilities sector. The sector's regulator has outlined series of proposals for new regulation, on which it is carrying out cost–benefit analysis. The

adviser makes two statements to the client about the regulator's cost–benefit analysis.

Statement 1　　"The regulator will assess and take into account as part of its cost–benefit analysis only the indirect costs of new regulation arising from changed economic decisions and behaviors."

Statement 2　　"Regulatory costs and benefits are easier to assess on a retrospective, after-the-fact basis."

Which statement is correct?

A. Only Statement 1 is correct.

B. Only Statement 2 is correct.

C. Both statements are correct.

Solution

B is correct. Statement 2 is correct because actual costs and benefits may be available during retrospective analysis, allowing a more informed assessment of regulation. Statement 1 is incorrect because both indirect and implementation costs will be taken into account.

9 ANALYSIS OF REGULATION

☐　｜describe the considerations when evaluating the effects of regulation on an industry

Christopher Decker (University of Oxford) contributed content for this discussion.

In the previous section, we considered cost–benefit analysis of new regulations from the point of view of the regulator that is in the process of developing new regulations or is analyzing the impact of regulatory intervention retrospectively, after the event. In this section, we focus on the considerations that an analyst or investor could take into account when evaluating the effects of a specific regulation on a particular industry or company for the purpose of making an investment recommendation. In-depth coverage of industry and company analysis is featured elsewhere in the CFA Program curriculum.

The fact that rules and regulations can take different forms and can affect industries and individual companies in different ways adds to the complexity of the task. Analysts need to understand not just how regulation affects companies and industries at present; they should also be able to understand and anticipate the impact of proposed new or changing regulations on the future prospects for companies and industries. Having assessed the impact of regulations on the company and its prospects, analysts can then use suitable valuation tools to establish fair values for the business and make investment recommendations. Although no framework or template is adequate for all the possible scenarios, there are certain steps an analyst can take that are common to most circumstances.

Assessment of the likelihood of regulatory change

The analyst will need to assess the likelihood of the proposed regulation actually being implemented. Understanding the regulator's intentions, the cost–benefit analysis framework used by the regulator, and the extent of engagement with the regulated companies will help the analyst draw conclusions about the likelihood that the proposed regulation will be implemented. Where relevant, public and political pressure may also play a role in determining the likelihood that regulatory intervention will materialize.

Assessment of the impact of regulatory change on a sector

Industry and company analysis performed by an analyst (explored in depth elsewhere) will incorporate the analyst's or investor's opinion on the impact of regulations. The following text describes some, but not all, of the effects that regulations may have.

Impact on revenues

Regulatory bodies sometimes introduce limits on prices, tariffs, rents, or fees that companies may charge, usually to protect consumers. Alternatively, certain products or services may be banned by the regulators, or companies may be required to provide product descriptions that discourage their consumption (food or tobacco product labeling). The analyst would need to estimate the impact of such regulatory interventions on the companies' turnover, noting that not all entities in the sector would be affected equally. For example, telecommunication and utilities companies in Europe have been subject to caps on prices and tariffs in the last few decades. Another example is the former biannual pricing revision process in Japan's pharmaceutical sector. The analyst would also need to be aware that if certain charges or fees are no longer allowed by the regulator, the companies may find alternative ways of generating revenues, helping to offset the negative impact of the regulation. For instance, the ban on commissions from financial product providers that financial advisory firms used to receive in parts of Europe led firms instead to charge their clients fees for giving financial advice. In this way, they could recoup some of the revenues they lost through the ban on commissions.

In some scenarios, pricing or charging may not be regulated or limited by the regulator in any way, but companies may be required to increase their pricing transparency and provide a detailed breakdown of their fees. For example, power utilities in the United Kingdom must provide transparent monthly bills and, if applicable, suggest that their customers switch to a different tariff if the customer could benefit from a lower monthly payment by switching.

Another form of regulation that relates to the revenue line is the arrangement in which utility companies, often natural monopolies, are allowed to earn only a certain return on their assets.

Cost impact

Compliance with some regulations results in additional costs for companies. These costs could take the form of higher operating expenses if, for example, manufactured products need to incorporate new safety features. Alternatively, these costs could take the form of higher capital expenditure if additional or new equipment is required. Analysts may also need to consider additional costs related to minimum wages, increased information disclosure, and data protection requirements. Companies may also incur additional costs resulting from the need to use (or not to use) certain raw materials, introduce product features, or subject themselves to regular inspections that make products or services safer for consumers. There may be costs related to expensive wastewater treatment for certain industries. The analyst will try to estimate such costs and incorporate their impact into forecasts of a company's future profitability. When quantification of specific additional costs is not possible or relevant, the analyst will need to take into account the potentially reduced flexibility of the company's operations. It may also be possible for some companies to pass on some additional costs to their customers. The analyst will need to understand the competitive position of the industry.

Examples of regulations that companies may be subjected to include labor laws that may impose limits on hours of work, such as the maximum working week in parts of Europe or, more globally, limits on the number of work hours for pilots and cabin crew in the aviation industry. Of course, some companies that adhere to high environmental, social, and governance standards would incur some of those costs regardless of government regulation. In the financial services industry, the increasing requirements in relation to record keeping, data protection, risk control, and prevention of money laundering often result in significant additional personnel, training, and information technology infrastructure expenses.

Business risk

Many industries have seen greater regulator involvement in the form of fines, requirements to pay compensation to customers, or bans on certain activities. Such events are difficult to forecast, and their impact may be hard to quantify and incorporate into future cash flow or growth forecasts. Analysts should take these types of events into account either by attempting to assign probabilities to them or by reflecting the risk in the discount rate used to value the company. For example, companies prone to a particular regulatory risk may deserve to trade on lower valuation multiples relative to peers or other industries. Or, when future earnings or cash flows are discounted to present values, the discount rate should reflect an additional risk premium.

EXAMPLE OF REGULATORY ANALYSIS

The scenario outlined earlier (in "Illustration of Cost–Benefit Analysis") considered proposed changes to the regulations concerning the IPO market for smaller companies. An analyst may wish to evaluate the impact of such changes to the rules in order to analyze prospects for a particular company (issuer) or to assess the portfolio fund flows into or out of the smaller companies segment. The analyst may also want to understand the impact on companies in the brokerage business involved in that segment of the market.

The analyst might consider a series of questions. One set of questions could concern the design of the proposal: Are there any exemptions from the new regulation, or will it apply to all small companies? What thresholds, if any, are used to determine whether a company is designated as small? Will the regulation be applied identically across all EU member states, or will each jurisdiction have an ability to tailor it to their own conditions? Will the regulation be subject to review or withdrawal later?

Another set of questions that an analyst might consider relates to the potential market and participant impacts: Who will benefit most from the regulation? Will it benefit high-growth companies in particular sectors or countries? What is the scale of the potential benefit associated with the regulation? What costs are associated with the regulation, and what is their scale? Will all participants face the same costs, or will they differ by market segment? Are the costs likely to be one-off in nature or recurring? Is the regulation likely to lead to market entry, expansion, or innovation by certain SMEs? Could the regulation lead to the potential exit of some existing providers of brokerage services or potentially crowd out other means of supplying capital and finance? How might the regulation change the behavior of SMEs? For example, will it reduce their reliance on bank loans?

Finally, the analyst might consider any wider impacts of the regulation on the market, industry, and society: Will the regulation affect financial stability or resilience? Could the regulation widen the opportunities for other investors, allowing them to better diversify their portfolios? Could there be potential spillover effects, allowing firms, for example, to shift between "junior markets" and more regulated markets? Could the impacts on financial markets be greater in some EU member states than in others? What are the possible macroeconomic impacts of the regulation? For example, could it improve capital inflows?

EXAMPLE 7

Analysis of Regulation

1. Jessica Wong, CFA, is an equity analyst responsible for the materials and industrial sectors in Europe. The regulatory authorities are preparing new rules on transportation, further limiting the age and exhaust emissions of the trucks used by industrial companies. What is likely to be of greatest concern to the analyst when evaluating the impact of the new rules on companies?

   A. Changes to costs related to the acquisition, operation, and maintenance of trucks

   B. Positive impact of reduced pollution on public health and subsequent health care cost savings in the wider society

   C. The methods and techniques used by the regulator during its cost–benefit analysis

Solution

A is correct. The analyst will want to understand and analyze the impact of the proposed regulations on the performance of companies she covers. Answers B and C relate to cost–benefit analysis carried out by the regulatory authority.

---

2. Which of the following questions would be the least relevant for the analyst to ask?

   A. Will the costs be one-off in nature, or will they be recurring?

   B. Will all companies in the sector be affected equally?

   C. What is the legal status of the regulator? Is it a government department, a government agency, or a self-regulating organization?

Solution

C is correct. The status of the regulator is the least important question. Answers A and B represent items that the analyst will find relevant when evaluating the impact of new regulations on the companies under coverage.

REGULATORS AND THE REGULATED

How may regulation affect the economics of businesses?

One example is the effect of the SEC's Regulation National Market System (NMS) on competition among equity trading platforms in the United States. Regulation NMS, adopted in 2005, was intended to reflect technological advances and achieve the objectives of efficient, competitive, fair, and orderly markets. Since the 2005 adoption of Regulation NMS, the market share of the trading floor of the NYSE has fallen substantially to account for a fraction of the overall NYSE volumes. Prior to Regulation NMS, NYSE "specialists" or market makers could take up to 30 seconds to react to orders sent by other platforms. The other platforms were checking whether the NYSE would execute at a more favorable price than the original platform had quoted. This process provided considerable opportunity for an NYSE specialist to observe subsequent pricing and to exploit the implicit optionality in the process. This process also made it hard for the rival platform to compete. Consequently, the NYSE could position itself to attract and concentrate much of the market liquidity, and so it came to resemble a natural monopoly. After Regulation NMS, which the NYSE had endorsed, the advantage to the NYSE diminished (see the discussion of the impact of Regulation NMS in Angel, Harris, and Spatt 2011)). Because of the change in regulation, many new trading platforms developed and trading execution fragmented. Clearly, the structure of regulation plays a crucial role with respect to the viability of different order tactics and even the viability of the business models underlying different trading platforms.

The history of the money market mutual fund industry is another example of how regulation can affect business models. Money market mutual funds in the United States first arose in the early 1970s in response to Regulation Q, which imposed a ceiling on the interest rates paid by banks for various types of bank deposits. When market interest rates rose above the ceiling, there was considerable migration from bank deposits toward marketed fixed-income instruments, such as Treasury bills and notes. Money market mutual funds developed in response to the binding Regulation Q rate ceilings. During the 2008 global financial crisis, the collapse of a major US money market mutual fund (the Reserve Fund) led to a run until the government launched a short-term insurance program to protect money market mutual fund balances. Government policy (motivated by an attempt to stabilize the financial system) helped protect this product. In response to resulting pressures from banks and the new advantage that the money market fund industry obtained, however, the Federal Deposit Insurance Corporation subsequently raised its insurance limit from $100,000 to $250,000. As this example illustrates, regulatory constraints have played a major role in the organization of short-term deposits in the United States. Changes in the effective regulatory structure have led to dramatic changes in the competitive landscape.

Government regulation can affect the structure of the industry. The issues can be seen in the pricing of joint products in the utility industries. For example, it can be difficult to separate fully the underlying economics associated with the production, transmission, and distribution of such services as electricity, telecommunications, and water. Suppose, for example, that there is a natural monopoly with respect to transportation (transmission and distribution) of a utility service but that there is competition in complementary activities (such as gas or electricity production or retail competition in telecommunications). How much should the provider of the natural monopoly services be able to obtain from the consumer or other companies providing upstream services, such as an energy product or access to a communication network? Although for some products there is increased and vigorous competition, these issues are still important with respect to the returns available from building various types of infrastructure. Although the market can sort out the allocation of profits and pricing across stages when there is vigorous competition at each stage, these issues are challenging in the case of a natural monopoly. Monopoly power is at the root of one of the most important traditional uses of regulation—to set pricing and returns at utility providers. In many jurisdictions, a government regulator sets or approves public utility prices because a utility provider has a monopolistic position.

SUMMARY

Knowledge of regulation is important because regulation has potentially far-reaching and significant effects. These effects can range from macro-level effects on the economy to micro-level effects on individual entities and securities.

Regulation originates from a variety of sources and in a variety of areas. A framework that includes types of regulators and regulation as well as areas of regulation that may affect the entity of interest (including the economy as an entity) is useful. The framework will help in assessing possible effects of new regulation. It can also help in assessing the effects of regulation on various entities.

More than one regulator may develop regulations in response to a particular issue. Each of the relevant regulators may have different objectives and choose to address the issue using different regulatory tools.

In developing regulations, the regulator should consider costs and benefits. In the analysis, the net regulatory burden (private costs less private benefits of regulation) may also be relevant. Potential costs and benefits, regardless of the perspective, may be difficult to assess. A critical aspect of regulatory analysis, however, is assessing the costs and benefits of regulation.

The following are some key points of the reading.

- The existence of informational frictions and externalities creates a need for regulation. Regulation is expected to have societal benefits and should be assessed using cost–benefit analysis.

- The regulation of securities markets and financial institutions is extensive and complex because of the consequences of failures in the financial system. These consequences include financial losses, loss of confidence, and disruption of commerce.

- The focus of regulators in financial markets includes prudential supervision, financial stability, market integrity, and economic growth.

- Regulatory competition is competition among different regulatory bodies to use regulation in order to attract certain entities.

- The breadth of regulation of commerce necessitates the use of a framework that identifies potential areas of regulation. This framework can be referenced to identify specific areas of regulation, both existing and anticipated, that may affect the entity of interest.

- Legislative bodies, regulatory bodies, and courts typically enact regulation.

- Regulatory bodies include government agencies and independent regulators granted authority by a government or governmental agency. Some independent regulators are self-regulating organizations.

- Typically, legislative bodies enact broad laws or statutes. Regulatory bodies issue administrative regulations, often implementing statutes. Courts interpret statutes and administrative regulations; these interpretations may result in judicial law.

- Interdependence in the actions and potentially conflicting objectives of regulators is an important consideration for regulators, regulated entities, and those assessing the effects of regulation.

- Regulation that arises to enhance the interests of regulated entities reflects regulatory capture.

- Regulators have responsibility for both substantive and procedural laws. The former focuses on rights and responsibilities of entities and relationships among entities. The latter focuses on the protection and enforcement of the former.

- Regulatory arbitrage is the use of regulation by an entity to exploit differences in economic substance and regulatory interpretation or in regulatory regimes to the entity's benefit.

- There are many regulatory tools available to regulators, including regulatory mandates and restrictions on behaviors, provision of public goods, and public financing of private projects.

- The choice of regulatory tool should be consistent with maintaining a stable regulatory environment. "Stable" does not mean unchanging but, rather, refers to desirable attributes of regulation, including predictability, effectiveness in achieving objectives, time consistency, and enforceability.

- In assessing regulation and regulatory outcomes, regulators should conduct ongoing cost–benefit analyses, develop techniques to enhance the measurement of these outcomes, and use economic principles to guide them.

- Net regulatory burden to the entity of interest is an important consideration for analysts.

REFERENCES

Angel, James, Lawrence Harris, Chester Spatt. 2011. "Equity Trading in the 21st Century." Quarterly Journal of Finance1 (1): 1–53.

International Organization of Securities Commissions (IOSCO)"Objectives and Principles of Securities Regulation," May 2017

IOSCO"Methodology for Assessing Implementation of the IOSCO Objectives and Principles of Securities Regulation," May 2017

Spatt, Chester. 2009. "Regulatory Conflict: Market Integrity vs. Financial Stability." University of Pittsburgh Law Review. University of Pittsburgh. School of Law71 (3): 625–39.

Stigler, George J. 1971. "The Economic Theory of Regulation." Bell Journal of Economics2 (1): 3–21.

PRACTICE PROBLEMS

The following information relates to questions 1–7

Cate Stephenson is an analyst in the economics research division of an international securities firm. She is conducting research on the regulatory environment in certain European countries. Stephenson begins with an analysis of a hypothetical country, Genovia.

Genovia has recently introduced a new accounting statute. In Genovia, there is an independent regulator—"Le régulateur." Le régulateur is not a self-regulating organization (SRO). There is also an SRO—"L'organisation." L'organisation is not an independent regulator.

In her research report, Stephenson makes the following statements:

Statement 1	Le régulateur has been given legal authority by the government to enforce the new statute.
Statement 2	L'organisation issues administrative regulations related to the new statute using government funding.
Statement 3	L'organisation has member companies that accept the authorization of L'organisation to set and enforce rules and standards.

Stephenson and her supervisor discuss the intended and unintended effects of implementing the new statute, and Stephenson makes two comments.

Comment 1	It is likely that some unintended consequences will be identified in regulatory filings prior to implementation of the new legislation.
Comment 2	Indirect costs arise because of unintended consequences and may result in high unanticipated costs.

Stephenson reads a report titled "International Trade," which has three sections about Genovia's policies and regulations.

- The first section of the report discusses policies that legislators may implement to accomplish Genovia's objective of promoting free trade on industrial goods.
- The second section of the report covers corporate domicile. Stephenson learns that regulators in Genovia recently amended regulations to encourage foreign businesses to move their corporate domicile to Genovia.
- The third section of the report reviews the regulation of commerce. Genovia's goal is to establish an environment that encourages foreign businesses to increase trade with domestic businesses. Stephenson considers two features of Genovia's regulation of commerce.

Feature 1	Recent court decisions have upheld financial liability and bankruptcy laws.
Feature 2	A legal structure that governs contracts and each party's rights is in place.

Stephenson then reviews two initiatives by Genovia to improve domestic policies and regulations.

- The first initiative by Genovia is its passage of conflict-of-interest regulations. Regulators implement regulatory restrictions and regulatory mandates that apply to employees of securities firms. One of Stephenson's research colleagues writes reports on a company in which he owns shares.

- The second initiative by Genovia is to reduce pollution and promote renewable electricity generation. Two years ago, the government implemented taxes on fossil fuels and subsidies on hydropower and other renewables. Stephenson reviews the changes in sources of electricity production since the policies were introduced, shown in Exhibit 1.

Exhibit 1: Genovia's Domestic Electricity Generation Production

Sector	Year 0	Year 1	Year 2
Fossil fuels	462	446	426
Hydropower	186	231	273
Other renewables	97	120	154
Total	745	797	853

Note: Amounts are in terawatt hours (TWh).

1. Which of Stephenson's statements regarding Le régulateur and L'organisation is correct?

   A. Only Statement 1 is correct.

   B. Only Statement 2 is correct.

   C. Both Statement 1 and Statement 2 are correct.

2. Is Stephenson's Statement 3 correct?

   A. Yes

   B. No, because L'organisation is given the authority to enforce regulations by a government agency

   C. No, because pressure from its member companies prevents L'organisation from enforcing its rules and standards

3. Which of Stephenson's comments to her supervisor is most likely correct?

   A. Only Comment 1 is correct.

   B. Only Comment 2 is correct.

   C. Both Comment 1 and Comment 2 are correct.

4. Which of the following policies would *best* address Genovia's objective of promoting free trade on industrial goods?

   A. Imposing tariffs on foreign-produced goods

    B. Allowing a floating currency

    C. Providing subsidies to domestic companies

5. By amending regulations to encourage foreign businesses to change their corporate domicile, regulators are engaging in regulatory:

    A. capture.

    B. arbitrage.

    C. competition.

6. Which feature discussed in the third section of "International Trade" will *most likely* help Genovia achieve its goal of encouraging foreign businesses to increase trade with domestic businesses?

    A. Only Feature 1

    B. Only Feature 2

    C. Both Feature 1 and Feature 2

7. Based on Exhibit 1, which government policy has been *most effective* in helping Genovia achieve its second initiative?

    A. Tax on fossil fuels

    B. Subsidy on hydropower

    C. Subsidy on other renewables

The following information relates to questions 8-11

Tiu Asset Management (TAM), a hypothetical financial services firm, recently hired Jonna Yun. A member of TAM's global equity portfolio team, Yun is assigned the task of analyzing the effects of regulation on the financial services sector of a particular country. In her first report to the team, Yun makes the following statements:

Statement 1   The country's regulator, a government agency, concerned about systemic risk, is calling for an accelerated adoption of centralized derivatives settlement (as opposed to bilateral settlement between two counterparties)—a more stringent rule—ahead of other major countries that are considering a similar move.

Statement 2   Regulators use various tools to intervene in the financial services sector.

Statement 3   Regulations may bring benefits to the economy, but they may also have unanticipated costs.

Statement 4   The country's regulatory authorities are considering a regulation that is similar to Regulation Q in the United States, which imposed a ceiling on interest rates paid by banks for certain bank deposits.

8. What is the *most likely* basis for the concerns noted in Statement 1?

    A. Externalities

    B. Regulatory arbitrage

    C. Informational friction

9. The tools *least likely* to be used by regulators to intervene in financial markets owing to informational frictions are:

    A. blackout periods.

    B. capital requirements.

    C. insider-trading restrictions.

10. Which of the following is *most likely* an unanticipated effect of regulation?

    A. Hiring compliance lawyers

    B. Setting legal standards for contracts

    C. Establishing employers' rights and responsibilities

11. After Regulation Q was imposed, the demand for money market funds *most likely*:

    A. increased.

    B. decreased.

    C. remained unchanged.

SOLUTIONS

1. A is correct. Le régulateur, as an independent regulator but not an SRO, has legal authority from the Genovia government to regulate. Therefore, Le régulateur both enacts and enforces regulations related to the new accounting statute in Genovia.

2. A is correct. L'organisation is an SRO but not an independent regulator, so it is a private entity that is not affiliated with Genovia's government. SROs that are not independent regulators receive authority from their members, who agree to comply with the organization's rules and standards and its enforcement thereof.

3. C is correct. Comment 1 is correct because regulatory filings, in response to proposed regulations, often identify at least some of the unintended consequences prior to the implementation of the regulation. Comment 2 is correct because the cost of unintended consequences, including both indirect costs and unanticipated implementation costs, can be high.

4. B is correct. A floating currency allows international trade in Genovia to be market based. International disputes about whether a country is manipulating or fixing its currency price often center on issues related to competitiveness.

5. C is correct. Regulatory competition describes actions by regulators to encourage behaviors. Regulators may compete to provide a regulatory environment designed to attract certain entities (regulatory competition). By amending regulations, Genovia's regulators seek to encourage foreign companies to change their corporate domicile.

6. C is correct. Genovia needs unambiguous laws concerning financial liability and bankruptcy to encourage foreign businesses to enter into contracts, particularly those that are long term and may involve sunk costs. The court decisions help Genovia achieve its goal. Also, clearly defined rules governing contracts, their interpretation, and each party's legal rights under a contract are necessary. Thus, both features help Genovia achieve its goal.

7. C is correct. At the end of Year 2, the compound annual growth rate (CAGR) for each sector is calculated as follows: $(\text{Year 2}/\text{Year 0})^{0.5} - 1$.

    Fossil fuels: $(426/462)^{0.5} - 1 = -4\%$

    Hydropower: $(273/186)^{0.5} - 1 = 21\%$

    Other renewables: $(154/97)^{0.5} - 1 = 26\%$

    The CAGR indicates that the 26% increase in production from the subsidy on other renewables has been more effective than the 4% decrease in production from the tax on fossil fuels or the 21% increase in production from the subsidy on hydropower. Thus, the subsidy on other renewables of 26% is the highest, indicating that this policy has been the most effective in helping Genovia achieve its second initiative.

8. B is correct. Firms based in the country are likely to be concerned because of the earlier timing of the application of new (more stringent) regulations in the country than in other large countries. With more stringent regulations, some business may flow to less stringent regulatory environments or jurisdictions.

9. A is correct. Blackout periods are established by *companies* in response to

concerns about insider trading. Thus, blackout periods are not a tool used by regulators to intervene in the financial services sector. Capital requirements are used by government regulators to reduce systemic risk and financial contagion. Insider-trading restrictions are used by regulators concerned about insiders using their greater knowledge to the disadvantage of others; insider-trading restrictions respond to informational frictions.

10. A is correct. The hiring of more lawyers to deal with compliance is an example of an "unintended" implementation cost. Establishing legal standards for contracts and employers' rights and responsibilities are objectives (intended consequences) of some regulation.

11. A is correct. Regulation Q set a ceiling on the interest rates paid by banks for various types of deposits, which resulted in investors' shifting funds to money market funds.

Glossary

Abnormal earnings See *residual income*.

Abnormal return The amount by which a security's actual return differs from its expected return, given the security's risk and the market's return.

Absolute convergence The idea that developing countries, regardless of their particular characteristics, will eventually catch up with the developed countries and match them in per capita output.

Absolute valuation model A model that specifies an asset's intrinsic value.

Absolute version of PPP An extension of the law of one price whereby the prices of goods and services will not differ internationally once exchange rates are considered.

Accounting estimates Estimates used in calculating the value of assets or liabilities and in the amount of revenue and expense to allocate to a period. Examples of accounting estimates include, among others, the useful lives of depreciable assets, the salvage value of depreciable assets, product returns, warranty costs, and the amount of uncollectible receivables.

Accumulated benefit obligation The actuarial present value of benefits (whether vested or non-vested) attributed, generally by the pension benefit formula, to employee service rendered before a specified date and based on employee service and compensation (if applicable) before that date. The accumulated benefit obligation differs from the projected benefit obligation in that it includes no assumption about future compensation levels.

Accuracy The percentage of correctly predicted classes out of total predictions. It is an overall performance metric in classification problems.

Acquisition When one company, the acquirer, purchases from the seller most or all of another company's (the target) shares to gain control of either an entire company, a segment of another company, or a specific group of assets in exchange for cash, stock, or the assumption of liabilities, alone or in combination. Once an acquisition is complete, the acquirer and target merge into a single entity and consolidate management, operations, and resources.

Activation function A functional part of a neural network's node that transforms the total net input received into the final output of the node. The activation function operates like a light dimmer switch that decreases or increases the strength of the input.

Active factor risk The contribution to active risk squared resulting from the portfolio's different-than-benchmark exposures relative to factors specified in the risk model.

Active return The return on a portfolio minus the return on the portfolio's benchmark.

Active risk The standard deviation of active returns.

Active risk squared The variance of active returns; active risk raised to the second power.

Active share A measure of how similar a portfolio is to its benchmark. A manager who precisely replicates the benchmark will have an active share of zero; a manager with no holdings in common with the benchmark will have an active share of one.

Active specific risk The contribution to active risk squared resulting from the portfolio's active weights on individual assets as those weights interact with assets' residual risk.

Adjusted funds from operations (AFFO) Funds from operations adjusted to remove any non-cash rent reported under straight-line rent accounting and to subtract maintenance-type capital expenditures and leasing costs, including leasing agents' commissions and tenants' improvement allowances.

Adjusted present value As an approach to valuing a company, the sum of the value of the company, assuming no use of debt, and the net present value of any effects of debt on company value.

Adjusted R^2 Goodness-of-fit measure that adjusts the coefficient of determination, R^2, for the number of independent variables in the model.

Administrative regulations or administrative law Rules issued by government agencies or other regulators.

Advanced set An arrangement in which the reference interest rate is set at the time the money is deposited.

Advanced settled An arrangement in which a forward rate agreement (FRA) expires and settles at the same time, at the FRA expiration date.

Agency issues Conflicts of interest that arise when the agent in an agency relationship has goals and incentives that differ from the principal to whom the agent owes a fiduciary duty. Also called *agency problems* or *principal–agent problems*.

Agglomerative clustering A bottom-up hierarchical clustering method that begins with each observation being treated as its own cluster. The algorithm finds the two closest clusters, based on some measure of distance (similarity), and combines them into one new larger cluster. This process is repeated iteratively until all observations are clumped into a single large cluster.

Akaike's information criterion (AIC) A statistic used to compare sets of independent variables for explaining a dependent variable. It is preferred for finding the model that is best suited for prediction.

Allowance for loan losses A balance sheet account; it is a contra asset account to loans.

Alpha The return on an asset in excess of the asset's required rate of return; the risk-adjusted return.

American Depositary Receipt A negotiable certificate issued by a depositary bank that represents ownership in a non-US company's deposited equity (i.e., equity held in custody by the depositary bank in the company's home market).

Analysis of variance (ANOVA) The analysis that breaks the total variability of a dataset (such as observations on the dependent variable in a regression) into components representing different sources of variation.

Application programming interface (API) A set of well-defined methods of communication between various software components and typically used for accessing external data.

Arbitrage 1) The simultaneous purchase of an undervalued asset or portfolio and sale of an overvalued but equivalent asset or portfolio, in order to obtain a riskless profit on the price differential. Taking advantage of a market inefficiency in a risk-free manner. 2) The condition in a financial market in which equivalent assets or combinations of assets sell for two different prices, creating an opportunity to profit at no risk with no commitment of money. In a well-functioning financial market, few arbitrage opportunities are possible. 3) A risk-free operation that earns an expected positive net profit but requires no net investment of money.

Arbitrage-free models Term structure models that project future interest rate paths that emanate from the existing term structure. Resulting prices are based on a no-arbitrage condition.

Arbitrage-free valuation An approach to valuation that determines security values consistent with the absence of any opportunity to earn riskless profits without any net investment of money.

Arbitrage opportunity An opportunity to conduct an arbitrage; an opportunity to earn an expected positive net profit without risk and with no net investment of money.

Arbitrage portfolio The portfolio that exploits an arbitrage opportunity.

Ask price The price at which a trader will sell a specified quantity of a security. Also called *ask, offer price,* or *offer.*

Asset-based approach Approach that values a private company based on the values of the underlying assets of the entity less the value of any related liabilities.

Asset-based valuation An approach to valuing natural resource companies that estimates company value on the basis of the market value of the natural resources the company controls.

At market contract When a forward contract is established, the forward price is negotiated so that the market value of the forward contract on the initiation date is zero.

Authorized participants (APs) A special group of institutional investors who are authorized by the ETF issuer to participate in the creation/redemption process. APs are large broker/dealers, often market makers.

Autocorrelations The correlations of a time series with its own past values.

Autoregressive model (AR) A time series regressed on its own past values in which the independent variable is a lagged value of the dependent variable.

Backtesting The process that approximates the real-life investment process, using historical data, to assess whether an investment strategy would have produced desirable results.

Backward propagation The process of adjusting weights in a neural network, to reduce total error of the network, by moving backward through the network's layers.

Backwardation A condition in the futures markets in which the spot price exceeds the futures price, the forward curve is downward sloping, and the convenience yield is high.

Bag-of-words (BOW) A collection of a distinct set of tokens from all the texts in a sample dataset. BOW does not capture the position or sequence of words present in the text.

Balance sheet restructuring Altering the composition of the balance sheet by either shifting the asset composition, changing the capital structure, or both.

Bankruptcy A declaration provided for by a country's laws that typically involves the establishment of a legal procedure that forces creditors to defer their claims.

Barbell portfolio Fixed-income portfolio that combines short and long maturities.

Base error Model error due to randomness in the data.

Basic earnings per share (EPS) Net earnings available to common shareholders (i.e., net income minus preferred dividends) divided by the weighted average number of common shares outstanding during the period.

Basis The difference between the spot price and the futures price. As the maturity date of the futures contract nears, the basis converges toward zero.

Basis trade A trade based on the pricing of credit in the bond market versus the price of the same credit in the CDS market. To execute a basis trade, go long the "underpriced" credit and short the "overpriced" credit. A profit is realized as the implied credit prices converge.

Bearish flattening Term structure shift in which short-term bond yields rise more than long-term bond yields, resulting in a flatter yield curve.

Benchmark value of the multiple In using the method of comparables, the value of a price multiple for the comparison asset; when we have comparison assets (a group), the mean or median value of the multiple for the group of assets.

Best ask The offer to sell with the lowest ask price. Also called *best offer* or *inside ask.*

Best bid The highest bid in the market.

Best offer The lowest offer (ask price) in the market.

Bias error Describes the degree to which a model fits the training data. Algorithms with erroneous assumptions produce high bias error with poor approximation, causing underfitting and high in-sample error.

Bid price In a price quotation, the price at which the party making the quotation is willing to buy a specified quantity of an asset or security.

Bid–ask spread The ask price minus the bid price.

Bill-and-hold basis Sales on a bill-and-hold basis involve selling products but not delivering those products until a later date.

Blockage factor An illiquidity discount that occurs when an investor sells a large amount of stock relative to its trading volume (assuming it is not large enough to constitute a controlling ownership).

Bond indenture A legal contract specifying the terms of a bond issue.

Bond risk premium The expected excess return of a default-free long-term bond less that of an equivalent short-term bond.

Bond yield plus risk premium (BYPRP) approach An estimate of the cost of common equity that is produced by summing the before-tax cost of debt and a risk premium that captures the additional yield on a company's stock relative to its bonds.

Bonus issue of shares A type of dividend in which a company distributes additional shares of its common stock to shareholders instead of cash.

Book value The net amount shown for an asset or liability on the balance sheet; book value may also refer to the company's excess of total assets over total liabilities. Also called *carrying value.*

Book value of equity Shareholders' equity (total assets minus total liabilities) minus the value of preferred stock; common shareholders' equity.

Book value per share The amount of book value (also called carrying value) of common equity per share of common stock, calculated by dividing the book value of shareholders' equity by the number of shares of common stock outstanding.

Bootstrap aggregating (or bagging) A technique whereby the original training dataset is used to generate n new training datasets or bags of data. Each new bag of data is generated by random sampling with replacement from the initial training set.

Bootstrapping The use of a forward substitution process to determine zero-coupon rates by using the par yields and solving for the zero-coupon rates one by one, from the shortest to longest maturities.

Bottom-up approach With respect to forecasting, an approach that usually begins at the level of the individual company or a unit within the company.

Breakup value The value derived using a sum-of-the-parts valuation.

Breusch–Godfrey (BG) test A test used to detect autocorrelated residuals up to a predesignated order of the lagged residuals.

Breusch–Pagan (BP) test A test for the presence of heteroskedasticity in a regression.

Bullet portfolio A fixed-income portfolio concentrated in a single maturity.

Bullish flattening Term structure change in which the yield curve flattens in response to a greater decline in long-term rates than short-term rates.

Bullish steepening Term structure change in which short-term rates fall by more than long-term yields, resulting in a steeper term structure.

Buy-side analysts Analysts who work for investment management firms, trusts, bank trust departments, and similar institutions.

Buyback A transaction in which a company buys back its own shares. Unlike stock dividends and stock splits, share repurchases use corporate cash.

CDS spread A periodic premium paid by the buyer to the seller that serves as a return over a market reference rate required to protect against credit risk.

Callable bond A bond containing an embedded call option that gives the issuer the right to buy the bond back from the investor at specified prices on pre-determined dates.

Canceled shares Shares that were issued, subsequently repurchased by the company, and then retired (cannot be reissued).

Capital asset pricing model (CAPM) A single factor model such that excess returns on a stock are a function of the returns on a market index.

Capital charge The company's total cost of capital in money terms.

Capital deepening An increase in the capital-to-labor ratio.

Capitalization of earnings method In the context of private company valuation, a valuation model based on an assumption of a constant growth rate of free cash flow to the firm or a constant growth rate of free cash flow to equity.

Capitalization rate The divisor in the expression for the value of perpetuity. In the context of real estate, it is the divisor in the direct capitalization method of estimating value. The cap rate equals net operating income divided by value.

Capitalized cash flow method In the context of private company valuation, a valuation model based on an assumption of a constant growth rate of free cash flow to the firm or a constant growth rate of free cash flow to equity. Also called *capitalized cash flow model*.

Capitalized income method In the context of private company valuation, a valuation model based on an assumption of a constant growth rate of free cash flow to the firm or a constant growth rate of free cash flow to equity.

Capped floater Floating-rate bond with a cap provision that prevents the coupon rate from increasing above a specified maximum rate. It protects the issuer against rising interest rates.

Carry arbitrage model A no-arbitrage approach in which the underlying instrument is either bought or sold along with an opposite position in a forward contract.

Carry benefits Benefits that arise from owning certain underlyings; for example, dividends, foreign interest, and bond coupon payments.

Carry costs Costs that arise from owning certain underlyings. They are generally a function of the physical characteristics of the underlying asset and also the interest forgone on the funds tied up in the asset.

Cash available for distribution See *adjusted funds from operations*.

Cash-generating unit The smallest identifiable group of assets that generates cash inflows that are largely independent of the cash inflows of other assets or groups of assets.

Cash settlement A procedure used in certain derivative transactions that specifies that the long and short parties settle the derivative's difference in value between them by making a cash payment.

Catalyst An event or piece of information that causes the marketplace to re-evaluate the prospects of a company.

Ceiling analysis A systematic process of evaluating different components in the pipeline of model building. It helps to understand what part of the pipeline can potentially improve in performance by further tuning.

Centroid The center of a cluster formed using the k-means clustering algorithm.

Chain rule of forecasting A forecasting process in which the next period's value as predicted by the forecasting equation is substituted into the right-hand side of the equation to give a predicted value two periods ahead.

Cheapest-to-deliver The debt instrument that can be purchased and delivered at the lowest cost yet has the same seniority as the reference obligation.

Classification and regression tree A supervised machine learning technique that can be applied to predict either a categorical target variable, producing a classification tree, or a continuous target variable, producing a regression tree. CART is commonly applied to binary classification or regression.

Clean surplus relation The relationship between earnings, dividends, and book value in which ending book value is equal to the beginning book value plus earnings less dividends, apart from ownership transactions.

Club convergence The idea that only rich and middle-income countries sharing a set of favorable attributes (i.e., are members of the "club") will converge to the income level of the richest countries.

Cluster A subset of observations from a dataset such that all the observations within the same cluster are deemed "similar."

Clustering The sorting of observations into groups (clusters) such that observations in the same cluster are more similar to each other than they are to observations in other clusters.

Cobb–Douglas production function A function of the form $Y = K^{\alpha} L^{1-\alpha}$ relating output (Y) to labor (L) and capital (K) inputs.

Coefficient of determination   The percentage of the variation of the dependent variable that is explained by the independent variables. Also referred to as the R-squared or R^2.

Cointegrated   Describes two time series that have a long-term financial or economic relationship such that they do not diverge from each other without bound in the long run.

Collateral return   The component of the total return on a commodity futures position attributable to the yield for the bonds or cash used to maintain the futures position. Also called *collateral yield*.

Collection frequency (CF)   The number of times a given word appears in the whole corpus (i.e., collection of sentences) divided by the total number of words in the corpus.

Commercial real estate properties   Income-producing real estate properties; properties purchased with the intent to let, lease, or rent (in other words, produce income).

Commodity swap   A type of swap involving the exchange of payments over multiple dates as determined by specified reference prices or indexes relating to commodities.

Company fundamental factors   Factors related to the company's internal performance, such as factors relating to earnings growth, earnings variability, earnings momentum, and financial leverage.

Company share-related factors   Valuation measures and other factors related to share price or the trading characteristics of the shares, such as earnings yield, dividend yield, and book-to-market value.

Comparables   Assets used as benchmarks when applying the method of comparables to value an asset. Also called *comps*, *guideline assets*, or *guideline companies*.

Compiled financial statements   Financial statements that are not accompanied by an auditor's opinion letter.

Complexity   A term referring to the number of features, parameters, or branches in a model and to whether the model is linear or non-linear (non-linear is more complex).

Composite variable   A variable that combines two or more variables that are statistically strongly related to each other.

Comprehensive income   All changes in equity other than contributions by, and distributions to, owners; income under clean surplus accounting; includes all changes in equity during a period except those resulting from investments by owners and distributions to owners. Comprehensive income equals net income plus other comprehensive income.

Comps   Assets used as benchmarks when applying the method of comparables to value an asset.

Concentrated ownership   Ownership structure consisting of an individual shareholder or a group (controlling shareholders) with the ability to exercise control over the corporation.

Conditional convergence   The idea that convergence of per capita income is conditional on the countries having the same savings rate, population growth rate, and production function.

Conditional heteroskedasticity   A condition in which the variance of residuals of a regression are correlated with the value of the independent variables.

Conditional VaR (CVaR)   The weighted average of all loss outcomes in the statistical (i.e., return) distribution that exceed the VaR loss. Thus, CVaR is a more comprehensive measure of tail loss than VaR is. Sometimes referred to as the *expected tail loss* or *expected shortfall*.

Confirmation bias   A belief perseverance bias in which people tend to look for and notice what confirms their beliefs, to ignore or undervalue what contradicts their beliefs, and to misinterpret information as support for their beliefs.

Confusion matrix   A grid used for error analysis in classification problems, it presents values for four evaluation metrics including true positive (TP), false positive (FP), true negative (TN), and false negative (FN).

Conglomerate discount   When an issuer is trading at a valuation lower than the sum of its parts, which is generally the result of diseconomies of scale or scope or the result of the capital markets having overlooked the business and its prospects.

Constant dividend payout ratio policy   A policy in which a constant percentage of net income is paid out in dividends.

Constant returns to scale   The condition that if all inputs into the production process are increased by a given percentage, then output rises by that same percentage.

Contango   A condition in the futures markets in which the spot price is lower than the futures price, the forward curve is upward sloping, and there is little or no convenience yield.

Contingent consideration   Potential future payments to the seller that are contingent on the achievement of certain agreed-on occurrences.

Continuing earnings   Earnings excluding nonrecurring components. Also referred to as *core earnings*, *persistent earnings*, or *underlying earnings*.

Continuing residual income   Residual income after the forecast horizon.

Continuing value   The analyst's estimate of a stock's value at a particular point in the future.

Control premium   An increment or premium to value associated with a controlling ownership interest in a company.

Convergence   The tendency for differences in output per capita across countries to diminish over time. In technical analysis, the term describes the case when an indicator moves in the same manner as the security being analyzed.

Conversion period   For a convertible bond, the period during which bondholders have the right to convert their bonds into shares.

Conversion price   For a convertible bond, the price per share at which the bond can be converted into shares.

Conversion rate (or ratio)   For a convertible bond, the number of shares of common stock that a bondholder receives from converting the bond into shares.

Conversion value   For a convertible bond, the value of the bond if it is converted at the market price of the shares. Also called *parity value*.

Convertible bond   Bond that gives the bondholder the right to exchange the bond for a specified number of common shares in the issuing company.

Convexity   A measure of how interest rate sensitivity changes with a change in interest rates.

Cook's distance   A metric for identifying influential data points. Also known as Cook's D (D_i).

Core earnings   Earnings excluding nonrecurring components. Also referred to as *continuing earnings*, *persistent earnings*, or *underlying earnings*.

Core real estate investment style   Investing in high-quality, well-leased, core property types with low leverage (no more than 30% of asset value) in the largest markets with strong, diversified economies. It is a conservative strategy designed to avoid real estate–specific risks, including leasing, development, and speculation in favor of steady returns. Hotel properties are excluded from the core categories because of the higher cash flow volatility resulting from single-night leases and the greater importance of property operations, brand, and marketing.

Corpus A collection of text data in any form, including list, matrix, or data table forms.

Cost approach An approach that values a private company based on the values of the underlying assets of the entity less the value of any related liabilities. In the context of real estate, this approach estimates the value of a property based on what it would cost to buy the land and construct a new property on the site that has the same utility or functionality as the property being appraised.

Cost of carry model A model that relates the forward price of an asset to the spot price by considering the cost of carry (also referred to as future-spot parity model).

Cost of debt The required return on debt financing to a company, such as when it issues a bond, takes out a bank loan, or leases an asset through a finance lease.

Cost of equity The return required by equity investors to compensate for both the time value of money and the risk. Also referred to as the required rate of return on common stock or the required return on equity.

Cost restructuring Actions to reduce costs by improving operational efficiency and profitability, often to raise margins to a historical level or to those of comparable industry peers.

Country risk premium (CRP) The additional return required by investors to compensate for the risk associated with investing in a foreign country relative to the investor's domestic market.

Country risk rating (CRR) The rating of a country based on many risk factors, including economic prosperity, political risk, and ESG risk.

Covariance stationary Describes a time series when its expected value and variance are constant and finite in all periods and when its covariance with itself for a fixed number of periods in the past or future is constant and finite in all periods.

Covered bonds A senior debt obligation of a financial institution that gives recourse to the originator/issuer and a predetermined underlying collateral pool.

Covered interest rate parity The relationship among the spot exchange rate, the forward exchange rate, and the interest rates in two currencies that ensures that the return on a hedged (i.e., covered) foreign risk-free investment is the same as the return on a domestic risk-free investment. Also called *interest rate parity*.

Cox-Ingersoll-Ross model A general equilibrium term structure model that assumes interest rates are mean reverting and interest rate volatility is directly related to the level of interest rates.

Creation basket The list of securities (and share amounts) the authorized participant (AP) must deliver to the ETF manager in exchange for ETF shares. The creation basket is published each business day.

Creation units Large blocks of ETF shares transacted between the authorized participant (AP) and the ETF manager that are usually but not always equal to 50,000 shares of the ETF.

Creation/redemption The process in which ETF shares are created or redeemed by authorized participants transacting with the ETF issuer.

Credit correlation The correlation of credit (or default) risks of the underlying single-name CDS contained in an index CDS.

Credit curve The credit spreads for a range of maturities of a company's debt.

Credit default swap A derivative contract between two parties in which the buyer makes a series of cash payments to the seller and receives a promise of compensation for credit losses resulting from the default.

Credit derivative A derivative instrument in which the underlying is a measure of the credit quality of a borrower.

Credit event An event that defines a payout in a credit derivative. Events are usually defined as bankruptcy, failure to pay an obligation, or an involuntary debt restructuring.

Credit protection buyer One party to a credit default swap; the buyer makes a series of cash payments to the seller and receives a promise of compensation for credit losses resulting from the default.

Credit protection seller One party to a credit default swap; the seller makes a promise to pay compensation for credit losses resulting from the default.

Credit risk The risk of loss caused by a counterparty's or debtor's failure to make a promised payment. Also called *default risk*.

Credit spread The compensation for the risk inherent in a company's debt security.

Credit valuation adjustment The value of the credit risk of a bond in present value terms.

Cross-validation A technique for estimating out-of-sample error directly by determining the error in validation samples.

Cumulative preferred stock Preferred stock that requires that the dividends be paid in full to preferred stock owners for any missed dividends prior to any payment of dividends to common stock owners.

Current exchange rate For accounting purposes, the spot exchange rate on the balance sheet date.

Current rate method Approach to translating foreign currency financial statements for consolidation in which all assets and liabilities are translated at the current exchange rate. The current rate method is the prevalent method of translation.

Curvature One of the three factors (the other two are level and steepness) that empirically explain most of the changes in the shape of the yield curve. A shock to the curvature factor affects mid-maturity interest rates, resulting in the term structure becoming either more or less hump-shaped.

Curve trade Buying a CDS of one maturity and selling a CDS on the same reference entity with a different maturity.

Customer concentration risk The risk associated with sales dependent on a few customers.

Cyclical businesses Businesses with high sensitivity to business- or industry-cycle influences.

Data preparation (cleansing) The process of examining, identifying, and mitigating (i.e., cleansing) errors in raw data.

Data snooping The practice of determining a model by extensive searching through a dataset for statistically significant patterns.

Data wrangling (preprocessing) This task performs transformations and critical processing steps on cleansed data to make the data ready for ML model training (i.e., preprocessing), and includes dealing with outliers, extracting useful variables from existing data points, and scaling the data.

Deep learning Machine learning using neural networks with many hidden layers.

Deep neural networks   Neural networks with many hidden layers—at least 2 but potentially more than 20—that have proven successful across a wide range of artificial intelligence applications.

Default risk   See *credit risk*.

Defined benefit pension plans   Plans in which the company promises to pay a certain annual amount (defined benefit) to the employee after retirement. The company bears the investment risk of the plan assets.

Defined contribution pension plans   Individual accounts to which an employee and typically the employer makes contributions during their working years and expect to draw on the accumulated funds at retirement. The employee bears the investment and inflation risk of the plan assets.

Delay costs   Implicit trading costs that arise from the inability to complete desired trades immediately. Also called *slippage*.

Delta   The relationship between the option price and the underlying price, which reflects the sensitivity of the price of the option to changes in the price of the underlying. Delta is a good approximation of how an option price will change for a small change in the stock.

Dendrogram   A type of tree diagram used for visualizing a hierarchical cluster analysis; it highlights the hierarchical relationships among the clusters.

Depository Trust and Clearinghouse Corporation   A US-headquartered entity providing post-trade clearing, settlement, and information services.

Diluted earnings per share   (Diluted EPS)Net income, minus preferred dividends, divided by the weighted average number of common shares outstanding considering all dilutive securities (e.g., convertible debt and options); the EPS that would result if all dilutive securities were converted into common shares.

Dilution   A reduction in proportional ownership interest as a result of the issuance of new shares.

Dimension reduction   A set of techniques for reducing the number of features in a dataset while retaining variation across observations to preserve the information contained in that variation.

Diminishing marginal productivity   When each additional unit of an input, keeping the other inputs unchanged, increases output by a smaller increment.

Direct capitalization method   In the context of real estate, this method estimates the value of an income-producing property based on the level and quality of its net operating income.

Discount   To reduce the value of a future payment in allowance for how far away it is in time; to calculate the present value of some future amount. Also, the amount by which an instrument is priced below its face value.

Discount factor   The price equivalent of a zero rate. Also may be stated as the present value of a currency unit on a future date.

Discount for lack of control   An amount or percentage deducted from the pro rata share of 100% of the value of an equity interest in a business to reflect the absence of some or all of the powers of control.

Discount for lack of marketability   An amount of percentage deducted from the value of an ownership interest to reflect the relative absence of marketability.

Discount function   Discount factors for the range of all possible maturities. The spot curve can be derived from the discount function and vice versa.

Discounted abnormal earnings model   A model of stock valuation that views intrinsic value of stock as the sum of book value per share plus the present value of the stock's expected future residual income per share.

Discounted cash flow (DCF) method   Income approach that values an asset based on estimates of future cash flows discounted to present value by using a discount rate reflective of the risks associated with the cash flows. In the context of real estate, this method estimates the value of an income-producing property based on discounting future projected cash flows.

Discounted cash flow method   Income approach that values an asset based on estimates of future cash flows discounted to present value by using a discount rate reflective of the risks associated with the cash flows. In the context of real estate, this method estimates the value of an income-producing property based on discounting future projected cash flows.

Discounted cash flow model   A model of intrinsic value that views the value of an asset as the present value of the asset's expected future cash flows.

Dispersed ownership   Ownership structure consisting of many shareholders, none of which has the ability to individually exercise control over the corporation.

Divestiture   When a seller sells a company, segment of a company, or group of assets to an acquirer. Once complete, control of the target is transferred to the acquirer.

Dividend   A distribution paid to shareholders based on the number of shares owned.

Dividend coverage ratio   The ratio of net income to dividends.

Dividend discount model   (DDM) A present value model of stock value that views the intrinsic value of a stock as present value of the stock's expected future dividends.

Dividend discount model (DDM)   The model of the value of stock that is the present value of all future dividends, discounted at the required return on equity.

Dividend displacement of earnings   The concept that dividends paid now displace earnings in all future periods.

Dividend imputation tax system   A taxation system that effectively assures corporate profits distributed as dividends are taxed just once and at the shareholder's tax rate.

Dividend index point   A measure of the quantity of dividends attributable to a particular index.

Dividend payout ratio   The ratio of cash dividends paid to earnings for a period.

Dividend policy   The strategy a company follows with regard to the amount and timing of dividend payments.

Dividend rate   The annualized amount of the most recent dividend.

Dividend recapitalization   Restructuring the mix of debt and equity, typically shifting the capital structure from equity to debt through debt-financed share repurchases. The objective is to reduce the issuer's weighted average cost of capital by replacing expensive equity with cheaper debt by purchasing equity from shareholders using newly issued debt.

Dividend yield   Annual dividends per share divided by share price.

Divisive clustering   A top-down hierarchical clustering method that starts with all observations belonging to a single large cluster. The observations are then divided into two clusters based on some measure of distance (similarity). The algorithm then progressively partitions the intermediate clusters into smaller ones until each cluster contains only one observation.

Document frequency (DF) The number of documents (texts) that contain a particular token divided by the total number of documents. It is the simplest feature selection method and often performs well when many thousands of tokens are present.

Document term matrix (DTM) A matrix where each row belongs to a document (or text file), and each column represents a token (or term). The number of rows is equal to the number of documents (or text files) in a sample text dataset. The number of columns is equal to the number of tokens from the BOW built using all the documents in the sample dataset. The cells typically contain the counts of the number of times a token is present in each document.

Dominance An arbitrage opportunity when a financial asset with a risk-free payoff in the future must have a positive price today.

Double taxation system Corporate earnings are taxed twice when paid out as dividends. First, corporate pretax earnings are taxed regardless of whether they will be distributed as dividends or retained at the corporate level. Second, dividends are taxed again at the individual shareholder level.

Downstream A transaction between two related companies, an investor company (or a parent company) and an associate company (or a subsidiary) such that the investor company records a profit on its income statement. An example is a sale of inventory by the investor company to the associate or by a parent to a subsidiary company.

Dual-class shares Shares that grant one share class superior or even sole voting rights, whereas the other share class has inferior or no voting rights.

Due diligence Investigation and analysis in support of an investment action, decision, or recommendation.

Dummy variable An independent variable that takes on a value of either 1 or 0, depending on a specified condition. Also known as an *indicator variable*.

Duration A measure of the approximate sensitivity of a security to a change in interest rates (i.e., a measure of interest rate risk).

Durbin–Watson (DW) test A test for the presence of first-order serial correlation.

Dutch disease A situation in which currency appreciation driven by strong export demand for resources makes other segments of the economy (particularly manufacturing) globally uncompetitive.

ESG integration An ESG investment approach that focuses on systematic consideration of material ESG factors in asset allocation, security selection, and portfolio construction decisions for the purpose of achieving the product's stated investment objectives. Used interchangeably with **ESG investing**.

Earnings surprise The portion of a company's earnings that is unanticipated by investors and, according to the efficient market hypothesis, merits a price adjustment.

Earnings yield EPS divided by price; the reciprocal of the P/E.

Economic profit Equal to accounting profit less the implicit opportunity costs not included in total accounting costs; the difference between total revenue (TR) and total cost (TC). Also called *abnormal profit* or *supernormal profit*.

Economic sectors Large industry groupings.

Economic value added (EVA®) A commercial implementation of the residual income concept; the computation of EVA® is the net operating profit after taxes minus the cost of capital, where these inputs are adjusted for a number of items.

Economies of scale A situation in which average costs per unit of good or service produced fall as volume rises. In reference to mergers, the savings achieved through the consolidation of operations and elimination of duplicate resources.

Edwards–Bell–Ohlson model A model of stock valuation that views intrinsic value of stock as the sum of book value per share plus the present value of the stock's expected future residual income per share.

Effective convexity A *curve convexity* statistic that measures the secondary effect of a change in a benchmark yield curve on a bond's price.

Effective duration Sensitivity of the bond's price to a 100 bps parallel shift of the benchmark yield curve, assuming no change in the bond's credit spread.

Effective spread Two times the difference between the execution price and the midpoint of the market quote at the time an order is entered.

Eigenvalue A measure that gives the proportion of total variance in the initial dataset that is explained by each eigenvector.

Eigenvector A vector that defines new mutually uncorrelated composite variables that are linear combinations of the original features.

Embedded options Contingency provisions found in a bond's indenture or offering circular representing rights that enable their holders to take advantage of interest rate movements. They can be exercised by the issuer, by the bondholder, or automatically depending on the course of interest rates.

Ensemble learning A technique of combining the predictions from a collection of models to achieve a more accurate prediction.

Ensemble method The method of combining multiple learning algorithms, as in ensemble learning.

Enterprise value Total company value (the market value of debt, common equity, and preferred equity) minus the value of cash and investments.

Enterprise value multiple A valuation multiple that relates the total market value of all sources of a company's capital (net of cash) to a measure of fundamental value for the entire company (such as a pre-interest earnings measure).

Equity charge The estimated cost of equity capital in money terms.

Equity investment A company purchasing another company's equity but less than 50% of its shares. The two companies maintain their independence, but the investor company has investment exposure to the investee and, in some cases depending on the size of the investment, can have representation on the investee's board of directors to influence operations.

Equity REITs REITs that own, operate, and/or selectively develop income-producing real estate.

Equity risk premium (ERP) Compensation for bearing market risk.

Equity swap A swap transaction in which at least one cash flow is tied to the return on an equity portfolio position, often an equity index.

Error autocorrelations The autocorrelations of the error term.

Ex ante **tracking error** A measure of the degree to which the performance of a given investment portfolio might be expected to deviate from its benchmark; also known as *relative VaR*.

Ex ante version of PPP The hypothesis that expected changes in the spot exchange rate are equal to expected differences in national inflation rates. An extension of relative purchasing power parity to expected future changes in the exchange rate.

Ex-dividend Trading ex-dividend refers to shares that no longer carry the right to the next dividend payment.

Ex-dividend date The first date that a share trades without (i.e., "ex") the right to receive the declared dividend for the period.

Excess earnings method Income approach that estimates the value of all intangible assets of the business by capitalizing future earnings in excess of the estimated return requirements associated with working capital and fixed assets.

Exercise date The date when employees actually exercise stock options and convert them to stock.

Exercise value The value of an option if it were exercised. Also sometimes called *intrinsic value.*

Expanded CAPM An adaptation of the CAPM that adds to the CAPM a premium for small size and company-specific risk.

Expectations approach A procedure for obtaining the value of an option derived from discounting at the risk-free rate its expected future payoff based on risk neutral probabilities.

Expected exposure The projected amount of money an investor could lose if an event of default occurs, before factoring in possible recovery.

Expected shortfall The average loss conditional on exceeding the VaR cutoff; sometimes referred to as *conditional VaR* or *expected tail loss.*

Expected tail loss See *expected shortfall.*

Exploratory data analysis (EDA) The preliminary step in data exploration, where graphs, charts, and other visualizations (heat maps and word clouds) as well as quantitative methods (descriptive statistics and central tendency measures) are used to observe and summarize data.

Exposure to foreign exchange risk The risk of a change in value of an asset or liability denominated in a foreign currency due to a change in exchange rates.

Extendible bond Bond with an embedded option that gives the bondholder the right to keep the bond for a number of years after maturity, possibly with a different coupon.

Extra dividend A dividend paid by a company that does not pay dividends on a regular schedule, or a dividend that supplements regular cash dividends with an extra payment.

F1 score The harmonic mean of precision and recall. F1 score is a more appropriate overall performance metric (than accuracy) when there is unequal class distribution in the dataset and it is necessary to measure the equilibrium of precision and recall.

FX carry trade An investment strategy that involves taking long positions in high-yield currencies and short positions in low-yield currencies.

Factor A common or underlying element with which several variables are correlated.

Factor betas An asset's sensitivity to a particular factor; a measure of the response of return to each unit of increase in a factor, holding all other factors constant.

Factor portfolio See *pure factor portfolio.*

Factor price The expected return in excess of the risk-free rate for a portfolio with a sensitivity of 1 to one factor and a sensitivity of 0 to all other factors.

Factor risk premium The expected return in excess of the risk-free rate for a portfolio with a sensitivity of 1 to one factor and a sensitivity of 0 to all other factors. Also called *factor price.*

Factor risk premiums The expected return in excess of the risk-free rate for a portfolio with a sensitivity of 1 to one factor and a sensitivity of 0 to all other factors. Also called factor price.

Failure to pay When a borrower does not make a scheduled payment of principal or interest on any outstanding obligations after a grace period.

Fair market value The price, expressed in terms of cash equivalents, at which a property (asset) would change hands between a hypothetical willing and able buyer and a hypothetical willing and able seller, acting at "arm's length" in an open and unrestricted market, when neither is under compulsion to buy or sell and when both have reasonable knowledge of the relevant facts. Fair market value is most often used in a tax reporting context in the United States.

Fair value The amount at which an asset could be exchanged, or a liability settled, between knowledgeable, willing parties in an arm's-length transaction; the price that would be received to sell an asset or paid to transfer a liability in an orderly transaction between market participants.

Fama–French models Factor models that explain the drivers of returns related to three, four, or five factors.

Feature engineering A process of creating new features by changing or transforming existing features.

Feature selection A process whereby only pertinent features from the dataset are selected for model training. Selecting fewer features decreases model complexity and training time.

Features The independent variables (X's) in a labeled dataset.

Finance (or capital) lease A lease that is viewed as a financing arrangement.

Financial contagion A situation in which financial shocks spread from their place of origin to other locales. In essence, a faltering economy infects other, healthier economies.

Financial leverage The use of fixed sources of capital, such as debt, relative to sources without fixed costs, such as equity.

Financial transaction A purchase involving a buyer having essentially no material synergies with the target (e.g., the purchase of a private company by a company in an unrelated industry or by a private equity firm would typically be a financial transaction).

First-differencing A transformation that subtracts the value of the time series in period $t - 1$ from its value in period t.

First-order serial correlation The correlation of residuals with residuals adjacent in time.

Fitting curve A curve which shows in- and out-of-sample error rates (E_{in} and E_{out}) on the y-axis plotted against model complexity on the x-axis.

Fixed price tender offer Offer made by a company to repurchase a specific number of shares at a fixed price that is typically at a premium to the current market price.

Fixed-rate perpetual preferred stock Nonconvertible, noncallable preferred stock that has a fixed dividend rate and no maturity date.

Flight to quality During times of market stress, investors sell higher-risk asset classes such as stocks and commodities in favor of default-risk-free government bonds.

Float Amounts collected as premium and not yet paid out as benefits.

Floored floater Floating-rate bond with a floor provision that prevents the coupon rate from decreasing below a specified minimum rate. It protects the investor against declining interest rates.

Flotation cost Fees charged to companies by investment bankers and other costs associated with raising new capital.

Forced conversion For a convertible bond, when the issuer calls the bond and forces bondholders to convert their bonds into shares, which typically happens when the underlying share price increases above the conversion price.

Foreign currency transactions Transactions that are denominated in a currency other than a company's functional currency.

Forward curve A series of forward rates, each having the same time frame.

Forward dividend yield A dividend yield based on the anticipated dividend during the next 12 months.

Forward-looking estimates Estimates based on current and expectations. Also referred to as ex ante estimates.

Forward P/E A P/E calculated on the basis of a forecast of EPS; a stock's current price divided by next year's expected earnings.

Forward price Represents the price agreed upon in a forward contract to be exchanged at the contract's maturity date, T. This price is shown in equations as $F_0(T)$.

Forward pricing model The model that describes the valuation of forward contracts.

Forward propagation The process of adjusting weights in a neural network, to reduce total error of the network, by moving forward through the network's layers.

Forward rate An interest rate determined today for a loan that will be initiated in a future period.

Forward rate agreement An over-the-counter forward contract in which the underlying is an interest rate on a deposit. A forward rate agreement (FRA) calls for one party to make a fixed interest payment and the other to make an interest payment at a rate to be determined at contract expiration.

Forward rate model The forward pricing model expressed in terms of spot and forward interest rates.

Forward rate parity The proposition that the forward exchange rate is an unbiased predictor of the future spot exchange rate.

Forward value The monetary value of an existing forward contract.

Franchising An owner of an asset and associated intellectual property divests the asset and licenses intellectual property to a third-party operator (franchisee) in exchange for royalties. Franchisees operate under the constraints of a franchise agreement.

Franking credit A tax credit received by shareholders for the taxes that a corporation paid on its distributed earnings.

Free cash flow method Income approach that values an asset based on estimates of future cash flows discounted to present value by using a discount rate reflective of the risks associated with the cash flows.

Free cash flow to equity The cash flow available to a company's common shareholders after all operating expenses, interest, and principal payments have been made and necessary investments in working and fixed capital have been made.

Free cash flow to equity model A model of stock valuation that views a stock's intrinsic value as the present value of expected future free cash flows to equity.

Free cash flow to the firm The cash flow available to the company's suppliers of capital after all operating expenses (including taxes) have been paid and necessary investments in working and fixed capital have been made.

Free cash flow to the firm model A model of stock valuation that views the value of a firm as the present value of expected future free cash flows to the firm.

Frequency analysis The process of quantifying how important tokens are in a sentence and in the corpus as a whole. It helps in filtering unnecessary tokens (or features).

Functional currency The currency of the primary economic environment in which an entity operates.

Fundamental factor models A multifactor model in which the factors are attributes of stocks or companies that are important in explaining cross-sectional differences in stock prices.

Fundamentals Economic characteristics of a business, such as profitability, financial strength, and risk.

Funds available for distribution (FAD) See *adjusted funds from operations.*

Funds from operations (FFO) Net income (computed in accordance with generally accepted accounting principles) *plus* (1) gains and losses from sales of properties and (2) depreciation and amortization.

Futures price The pre-agreed price at which a futures contract buyer (seller) agrees to pay (receive) for the underlying at the maturity date of the futures contract.

Futures value The monetary value of an existing futures contract.

Gamma A numerical measure of how sensitive an option's delta (the sensitivity of the derivative's price) is to a change in the value of the underlying.

General linear *F*-test A test statistic used to assess the goodness of fit for an entire regression model, so it tests all independent variables in the model.

Generalize When a model retains its explanatory power when predicting out-of-sample (i.e., using new data).

Global CAPM (GCAPM) A single-factor model with a global index representing the single factor.

Going-concern assumption The assumption that the business will maintain its business activities into the foreseeable future.

Going-concern value A business's value under a going-concern assumption.

Goodwill An intangible asset that represents the excess of the purchase price of an acquired company over the value of the net identifiable assets acquired.

Gordon growth model A DDM that assumes dividends grow at a constant rate into the future.

Grant date The day that stock options are granted to employees.

Green bond Bonds in which the proceeds are designated by issuers to fund a specific project or portfolio of projects that have environmental or climate benefits.

Greenmail The purchase of the accumulated shares of a hostile investor by a company that is targeted for takeover by that investor, usually at a substantial premium over market price.

Greenwashing The risk that a green bond's proceeds are not actually used for a beneficial environmental or climate-related project.

Grid search   A method of systematically training a model by using various combinations of hyperparameter values, cross validating each model, and determining which combination of hyperparameter values ensures the best model performance.

Gross domestic product   The market value of all final goods and services produced within the economy during a given period (output definition) or, equivalently, the aggregate income earned by all households, all companies, and the government within the economy during a given period (income definition).

Gross lease   A lease under which the tenant pays a gross rent to the landlord, who is responsible for all operating costs, utilities, maintenance expenses, and real estate taxes relating to the property.

Ground truth   The known outcome (i.e., target variable) of each observation in a labelled dataset.

Growth accounting equation   The production function written in the form of growth rates. For the basic Cobb–Douglas production function, it states that the growth rate of output equals the rate of technological change plus α multiplied by the growth rate of capital plus $(1 - \alpha)$ multiplied by the growth rate of labor.

Growth capital expenditures   Capital expenditures needed for expansion.

Guideline assets   Assets used as benchmarks when applying the method of comparables to value an asset.

Guideline companies   Assets used as benchmarks when applying the method of comparables to value an asset.

Guideline public companies   Public-company comparables for the company being valued.

Guideline public company method   A variation of the market approach; establishes a value estimate based on the observed multiples from trading activity in the shares of public companies viewed as reasonably comparable to the subject private company.

Guideline transactions method   A variation of the market approach; establishes a value estimate based on pricing multiples derived from the acquisition of control of entire public or private companies that were acquired.

Harmonic mean   A type of weighted mean computed as the reciprocal of the arithmetic average of the reciprocals.

Hazard rate   The probability that an event will occur, given that it has not already occurred.

Hedonic index   Unlike a repeat-sales index, a hedonic index does not require repeat sales of the same property. It requires only one sale. The way it controls for the fact that different properties are selling each quarter is to include variables in the regression that control for differences in the characteristics of the property, such as size, age, quality of construction, and location.

Heteroskedastic   When the variance of the residuals differs across observations in a regression.

Heteroskedasticity   The property of having a nonconstant variance; refers to an error term with the property that its variance differs across observations.

Hierarchical clustering   An iterative unsupervised learning procedure used for building a hierarchy of clusters.

High-leverage point   An observation of an independent variable that has an extreme value and is potentially influential.

Highest and best use   The concept that the best use of a vacant site is the use that would result in the highest value for the land. Presumably, the developer that could earn the highest risk-adjusted profit based on time, effort, construction and development cost, leasing, and exit value would be the one to pay the highest price for the land.

Historical exchange rates   For accounting purposes, the exchange rates that existed when the assets and liabilities were initially recorded.

Historical scenario analysis   A technique for exploring the performance and risk of investment strategies in different structural regimes.

Historical simulation   A simulation method that uses past return data and a random number generator that picks observations from the historical series to simulate an asset's future returns.

Historical simulation method   The application of historical price changes to the current portfolio.

Historical stress testing   The process that tests how investment strategies would perform under some of the most negative (i.e., adverse) combinations of events and scenarios.

Ho–Lee model   The first arbitrage-free term structure model. The model is calibrated to market data and uses a binomial lattice approach to generate a distribution of possible future interest rates.

Holdout samples   Data samples that are not used to train a model.

Homoskedasticity   The property of having a constant variance; refers to an error term that is constant across observations.

Horizontal ownership   Companies with mutual business interests (e.g., key customers or suppliers) that have cross-holding share arrangements with each other.

Human capital   An implied asset; the net present value of an investor's future expected labor income weighted by the probability of surviving to each future age. Also called *net employment capital*.

Hybrid approach   With respect to forecasting, an approach that combines elements of both top-down and bottom-up analyses.

Hyperparameter   A parameter whose value must be set by the researcher before learning begins.

iNAVs   "Indicated" net asset values are intraday "fair value" estimates of an ETF share based on its creation basket.

ISDA Master Agreement   A standard or "master" agreement published by the International Swaps and Derivatives Association. The master agreement establishes the terms for each party involved in the transaction.

I-spreads   Shortened form of "interpolated spreads" and a reference to a linearly interpolated yield.

Idiosyncratic risk premium (IRP)   The additional return required for bearing company-specific risks.

Illiquidity discount   A reduction or discount to value that reflects the lack of depth of trading or liquidity in that asset's market.

Impairment   Diminishment in value as a result of carrying (book) value exceeding fair value and/or recoverable value.

Impairment of capital rule   A legal restriction that dividends cannot exceed retained earnings.

Implementation shortfall   (IS) The difference between the return for a notional or paper portfolio, where all transactions are assumed to take place at the manager's decision price, and the portfolio's actual return, which reflects realized transactions, including all fees and costs.

Implied volatility   The standard deviation that causes an option pricing model to give the current option price.

In-sample forecast errors The residuals from a fitted time-series model within the sample period used to fit the model.

Income approach A valuation approach that values an asset as the present discounted value of the income expected from it. In the context of real estate, this approach estimates the value of a property based on an expected rate of return. The estimated value is the present value of the expected future income from the property, including proceeds from resale at the end of a typical investment holding period.

Incremental borrowing rate (IBR) The rate of interest that the lessee would have to pay to borrow using a collateralized loan over the same term as a lease.

Incremental VaR (IVaR) A measure of the incremental effect of an asset on the VaR of a portfolio by measuring the difference between the portfolio's VaR while including a specified asset and the portfolio's VaR with that asset eliminated.

Indenture A written contract between a lender and borrower that specifies the terms of the loan, such as interest rate, interest payment schedule, or maturity.

Independent board directors Directors with no material relationship with the company with regard to employment, ownership, or remuneration.

Independent regulators Regulators recognized and granted authority by a government body or agency. They are not government agencies per se and typically do not rely on government funding.

Index CDS A type of credit default swap that involves a combination of borrowers.

Industry risk premium (IP) The additional return that is required to bear industry-specific risk.

Industry shocks Unexpected changes to an industry from regulations or the legal environment, technology, or changes in the growth rate of the industry.

Industry structure An industry's underlying economic and technical characteristics.

Influence plot A visual that shows, for all observations, studentized residuals on the y-axis, leverage on the x-axis, and Cook's D as circles whose size is proportional to the degree of influence of the given observation.

Influential observation An observation in a statistical analysis whose inclusion may significantly alter regression results.

Information gain A metric which quantifies the amount of information that the feature holds about the response. Information gain can be regarded as a form of non-linear correlation between Y and X.

Information ratio (IR) Mean active return divided by active risk; or alpha divided by the standard deviation of diversifiable risk.

Informational frictions Forces that restrict availability, quality, and/or flow of information and its use.

Inside ask See *best ask*.

Inside bid See *best bid*.

Inside spread The spread between the best bid price and the best ask price. Also called the *market bid-ask spread*, *inside bid-ask spread*, or *market spread*.

Insiders Corporate managers and board directors who are also shareholders of a company.

Intangible assets Assets without a physical form, such as patents and trademarks.

Inter-temporal rate of substitution The ratio of the marginal utility of consumption s periods in the future (the numerator) to the marginal utility of consumption today (the denominator).

Interaction term A term that combines two or more variables and represents their joint influence on the dependent variable.

Intercept dummy An indicator variable that allows a single regression model to estimate two lines of best fit, each with differing intercepts, depending on whether the dummy takes a value of 1 or 0.

Interest rate risk The risk that interest rates will rise and therefore the market value of current portfolio holdings will fall so that their current yields to maturity then match comparable instruments in the marketplace.

Interlocking directorates Corporate structure in which individuals serve on the board of directors of multiple corporations.

International CAPM (ICAPM) A two-factor model with a global index and a wealth-weighted currency index.

International Fisher effect The proposition that nominal interest rate differentials across currencies are determined by expected inflation differentials.

Intrinsic value The amount gained (per unit) by an option buyer if an option is exercised at any given point in time. May be referred to as the exercise value of the option.

Inverse price ratio The reciprocal of a price multiple—for example, in the case of a P/E, the "earnings yield" E/P (where P is share price and E is earnings per share).

Investment value The value to a specific buyer, taking account of potential synergies based on the investor's requirements and expectations.

Joint test of hypotheses The test of hypotheses that specify values for two or more independent variables in the hypotheses.

Joint venture Two or more companies form and control a new, separate company to achieve a business objective. Each participant contributes assets, employees, know-how, or other resources to the joint venture company. The participants maintain their independence otherwise and continue to do business apart from the joint venture, but they share in the joint venture's profits or losses.

Judicial law Interpretations of courts.

Justified price multiple The estimated fair value of the price multiple, usually based on forecasted fundamentals or comparables.

Justified (fundamental) P/E The price-to-earnings ratio that is fair, warranted, or justified on the basis of forecasted fundamentals.

K-fold cross-validation A technique in which data (excluding test sample and fresh data) are shuffled randomly and then are divided into k equal sub-samples, with $k-1$ samples used as training samples and one sample, the kth, used as a validation sample.

K-means A clustering algorithm that repeatedly partitions observations into a fixed number, k, of non-overlapping clusters.

K-nearest neighbor A supervised learning technique that classifies a new observation by finding similarities ("nearness") between this new observation and the existing data.

Kalotay–Williams–Fabozzi (KWF) model An arbitrage-free term structure model that describes the dynamics of the log of the short rate and assumes constant drift, no mean reversion, and constant volatility.

Key rate durations Sensitivity of a bond's price to changes in specific maturities on the benchmark yield curve. Also called *partial durations*.

kth-order autocorrelation The correlation between observations in a time series separated by k periods.

LASSO Least absolute shrinkage and selection operator is a type of penalized regression which involves minimizing the sum of the absolute values of the regression coefficients. LASSO can also be used for regularization in neural networks.

Labeled dataset A dataset that contains matched sets of observed inputs or features (X's) and the associated output or target (Y).

Labor force Everyone of working age (ages 16 to 64) who either is employed or is available for work but not working.

Labor force participation rate The percentage of the working age population that is in the labor force.

Labor productivity The quantity of goods and services (real GDP) that a worker can produce in one hour of work.

Labor productivity growth accounting equation States that potential GDP growth equals the growth rate of the labor input plus the growth rate of labor productivity.

Lack of marketability discount An extra return to investors to compensate for lack of a public market or lack of marketability.

Latency The elapsed time between the occurrence of an event and a subsequent action that depends on that event.

Law of one price A principle that states that if two investments have the same or equivalent future cash flows regardless of what will happen in the future, then these two investments should have the same current price.

Leading dividend yield Forecasted dividends per share over the next year divided by current stock price.

Leading P/E A P/E calculated on the basis of a forecast of EPS; a stock's current price divided by next year's expected earnings.

Learning curve A curve that plots the accuracy rate (= 1 − error rate) in the validation or test samples (i.e., out-of-sample) against the amount of data in the training sample, which is thus useful for describing under- and overfitting as a function of bias and variance errors.

Learning rate A parameter that affects the magnitude of adjustments in the weights in a neural network.

Level One of the three factors (the other two are steepness and curvature) that empirically explain most yield curve shape changes. A shock to the level factor changes the yield for all maturities by an almost identical amount.

Leverage A measure for identifying a potentially influential high-leverage point.

Leveraged buyout (LBO) An acquirer (typically an investment fund specializing in LBOs) uses a significant amount of debt to finance the acquisition of a target and then pursues restructuring actions, with the goal of exiting the target with a sale or public listing.

Libor–OIS spread The difference between Libor and the overnight indexed swap rate.

Likelihood ratio (LR) test A method to assess the fit of logistic regression models and is based on the log-likelihood metric that describes the model's fit to the data.

Limit order book The book or list of limit orders to buy and sell that pertains to a security.

Linear classifier A binary classifier that makes its classification decision based on a linear combination of the features of each data point.

Linear trend A trend in which the dependent variable changes at a constant rate with time.

Liquidating dividend A dividend that is a return of capital rather than a distribution from earnings or retained earnings.

Liquidation value The value of a company if the company were dissolved and its assets sold individually.

Liquidity preference theory A term structure theory that asserts liquidity premiums exist to compensate investors for the added interest rate risk they face when lending long term.

Liquidity premium An extra return that compensates investors for the risk of loss relative to an investment's fair value if the investment needs to be converted to cash quickly.

Local currency The currency of the country where a company is located.

Local expectations theory A term structure theory that contends the return for all bonds over short periods is the risk-free rate.

Log-linear model With reference to time-series models, a model in which the growth rate of the time series as a function of time is constant.

Log odds The natural log of the odds of an event or characteristic happening. Also known as the *logit function*.

Logistic regression (logit) A regression in which the dependent variable uses a logistic transformation of the event probability.

Logistic transformation The log of the probability of an occurrence of an event or characteristic divided by the probability of the event or characteristic not occurring.

Long/short credit trade A credit protection seller with respect to one entity combined with a credit protection buyer with respect to another entity.

Look-ahead bias A bias caused by using information that was unavailable on the test date.

Lookback period The time period used to gather a historical data set.

Loss given default The amount that will be lost if a default occurs.

Macroeconomic factor model A multifactor model in which the factors are surprises in macroeconomic variables that significantly explain equity returns.

Macroeconomic factors Factors related to the economy, such as the inflation rate, industrial production, or economic sector membership.

Maintenance capital expenditures Capital expenditures needed to maintain operations at the current level.

Majority shareholders Shareholders that own more than 50% of a corporation's shares.

Majority-vote classifier A classifier that assigns to a new data point the predicted label with the most votes (i.e., occurrences).

Marginal VaR (MVaR) A measure of the effect of a small change in a position size on portfolio VaR.

Market approach Valuation approach that values an asset based on pricing multiples from sales of assets viewed as similar to the subject asset.

Market conditions Interest rates, inflation rates, and other economic characteristics that comprise the macroeconomic environment.

Market conversion premium per share For a convertible bond, the difference between the market conversion price and the underlying share price, which allows investors to identify the premium or discount payable when buying a convertible bond rather than the underlying common stock.

Market conversion premium ratio For a convertible bond, the market conversion premium per share expressed as a percentage of the current market price of the shares.

Market efficiency A finance perspective on capital markets that deals with the relationship of price to intrinsic value. The traditional efficient markets formulation asserts that an asset's price is the best available estimate of its intrinsic value. The rational efficient markets formulation asserts that investors should expect to be rewarded for the costs of information gathering and analysis by higher gross returns.

Market fragmentation Trading the same instrument in multiple venues.

Market impact The effect of the trade on transaction prices. Also called *price impact*.

Market model A regression model with the return on a stock as the dependent variable and the returns on a market index as the independent variable.

Market value of invested capital The market value of debt and equity.

Mature growth rate The earnings growth rate in a company's mature phase; an earnings growth rate that can be sustained long term.

Maximum drawdown The worst cumulative loss ever sustained by an asset or portfolio. More specifically, maximum drawdown is the difference between an asset's or a portfolio's maximum cumulative return and its subsequent lowest cumulative return.

Maximum likelihood estimation (MLE) A method that estimates values for the intercept and slope coefficients in a logistic regression that make the data in the regression sample most likely.

Mean reversion The tendency of a time series to fall when its level is above its mean and rise when its level is below its mean; a mean-reverting time series tends to return to its long-term mean.

Metadata Data that describes and gives information about other data.

Method based on forecasted fundamentals An approach to using price multiples that relates a price multiple to forecasts of fundamentals through a discounted cash flow model.

Method of comparables An approach to valuation that involves using a price multiple to evaluate whether an asset is relatively fairly valued, relatively undervalued, or relatively overvalued when compared to a benchmark value of the multiple.

Midquote price The average, or midpoint, of the prevailing bid and ask prices.

Minority interest The proportion of the ownership of a subsidiary not held by the parent (controlling) company.

Minority shareholders Particular shareholders or a block of shareholders holding a small proportion of a company's outstanding shares, resulting in a limited ability to exercise control in voting activities.

Mispricing Any departure of the market price of an asset from the asset's estimated intrinsic value.

Model specification The set of independent variables included in a model and the model's functional form.

Molodovsky effect The observation that P/Es tend to be high on depressed EPS at the bottom of a business cycle and tend to be low on unusually high EPS at the top of a business cycle.

Momentum indicators Valuation indicators that relate either price or a fundamental (such as earnings) to the time series of their own past values (or in some cases to their expected value).

Monetary assets and liabilities Assets and liabilities with value equal to the amount of currency contracted for, a fixed amount of currency. Examples are cash, accounts receivable, accounts payable, bonds payable, and mortgages payable. Inventory is not a monetary asset. Most liabilities are monetary.

Monetary/non-monetary method Approach to translating foreign currency financial statements for consolidation in which monetary assets and liabilities are translated at the current exchange rate. Non-monetary assets and liabilities are translated at historical exchange rates (the exchange rates that existed when the assets and liabilities were acquired).

Monetizing Unwinding a position to either capture a gain or realize a loss.

Monte Carlo simulation A technique that uses the inverse transformation method for converting a randomly generated uniformly distributed number into a simulated value of a random variable of a desired distribution. Each key decision variable in a Monte Carlo simulation requires an assumed statistical distribution; this assumption facilitates incorporating non-normality, fat tails, and tail dependence as well as solving high-dimensionality problems.

Mortgage A loan with real estate serving as collateral for the loan.

Multicollinearity When two or more independent variables are highly correlated with one another or are approximately linearly related.

Multiple linear regression Modeling and estimation method that uses two or more independent variables to describe the variation of the dependent variable. Also referred to as *multiple regression*.

Mutual information Measures how much information is contributed by a token to a class of texts. MI will be 0 if the token's distribution in all text classes is the same. MI approaches 1 as the token in any one class tends to occur more often in only that particular class of text.

N-grams A representation of word sequences. The length of a sequence varies from 1 to *n*. When one word is used, it is a unigram; a two-word sequence is a bigram; and a 3-word sequence is a trigram; and so on.

n-Period moving average The average of the current and immediately prior $n - 1$ values of a time series.

NTM P/E Next 12-month P/E: current market price divided by an estimated next 12-month EPS.

Naked credit default swap A position where the owner of the CDS does not have a position in the underlying credit.

Name entity recognition An algorithm that analyzes individual tokens and their surrounding semantics while referring to its dictionary to tag an object class to the token.

Negative serial correlation A situation in which residuals are negatively related to other residuals.

Nested models Models in which one regression model has a subset of the independent variables of another regression model.

Net asset balance sheet exposure When assets translated at the current exchange rate are greater in amount than liabilities translated at the current exchange rate. Assets exposed to translation gains or losses exceed the exposed liabilities.

Net asset value per share (NAVPS) Net asset value divided by the number of shares outstanding.

Net lease A lease under which the tenant pays a net rent to the landlord and an additional amount based on the tenant's pro rata share of the operating costs, utilities, maintenance expenses, and real estate taxes relating to the property.

Net liability balance sheet exposure When liabilities translated at the current exchange rate are greater assets translated at the current exchange rate. Liabilities exposed to translation gains or losses exceed the exposed assets.

Net operating income (NOI) Gross rental revenue minus operating costs but before deducting depreciation, corporate overhead, and interest expense. In the context of real estate, a measure of the income from the property after deducting operating expenses for such items as property taxes, insurance, maintenance, utilities, repairs, and insurance but before deducting any costs associated with financing and before deducting federal income taxes. It is similar to EBITDA in a financial reporting context.

Net regulatory burden The private costs of regulation less the private benefits of regulation.

Network externalities The impact that users of a good, a service, or a technology have on other users of that product; it can be positive (e.g., a critical mass of users makes a product more useful) or negative (e.g., congestion makes the product less useful).

Neural networks Computer programs based on how our own brains learn and process information.

No-arbitrage approach A procedure for obtaining the value of an option based on the creation of a portfolio that replicates the payoffs of the option and deriving the option value from the value of the replicating portfolio.

No-growth company A company without positive expected net present value projects.

No-growth value per share The value per share of a no-growth company, equal to the expected level amount of earnings divided by the stock's required rate of return.

Non-cash rent An amount equal to the difference between the average contractual rent over a lease term (the straight-line rent) and the cash rent actually paid during a period. This figure is one of the deductions made from FFO to calculate AFFO.

Non-convergence trap A situation in which a country remains relatively poor, or even falls further behind, because it fails to implement necessary institutional reforms and/or adopt leading technologies.

Non-monetary assets and liabilities Assets and liabilities that are not monetary assets and liabilities. Non-monetary assets include inventory, fixed assets, and intangibles, and non-monetary liabilities include deferred revenue.

Non-renewable resources Finite resources that are depleted once they are consumed; oil and coal are examples.

Non-residential properties Commercial real estate properties other than multi-family properties, farmland, and timberland.

Nonearning assets Cash and investments (specifically cash, cash equivalents, and short-term investments).

Normal EPS The EPS that a business could achieve currently under mid-cyclical conditions. Also called *normalized EPS*.

Normal Q-Q plot A visual used to compare the distribution of the residuals from a regression to a theoretical normal distribution.

Normalized EPS The EPS that a business could achieve currently under mid-cyclical conditions. Also called *normal EPS*.

Normalized earnings The expected level of mid-cycle earnings for a company in the absence of any unusual or temporary factors that affect profitability (either positively or negatively).

Normalized P/E P/E based on normalized EPS data.

Notional amount The amount of protection being purchased in a CDS.

Off-the-run A series of securities or indexes that were issued/created prior to the most recently issued/created series.

Offshoring Refers to relocating operations from one country to another, mainly to reduce costs through lower labor costs or to achieve economies of scale through centralization, but still maintaining operations within the corporation.

Omitted variable bias Bias resulting from the omission of an important independent variable from a regression model.

On-the-run The most recently issued and most actively traded sovereign securities.

One hot encoding The process by which categorical variables are converted into binary form (0 or 1) for machine reading. It is one of the most common methods for handling categorical features in text data.

One-sided durations Effective durations when interest rates go up or down, which are better at capturing the interest rate sensitivity of bonds with embedded options that do not react symmetrically to positive and negative changes in interest rates of the same magnitude.

One-tier board Board structure consisting of a single board of directors, composed of executive (internal) and non-executive (external) directors.

Opportunity cost Reflects the foregone opportunity of investing in a different asset. It is typically denoted by the risk-free rate of interest, r.

Option-adjusted spread (OAS) Constant spread that, when added to all the one-period forward rates on the interest rate tree, makes the arbitrage-free value of the bond equal to its market price.

Orderly liquidation value The estimated gross amount of money that could be realized from the liquidation sale of an asset or assets, given a reasonable amount of time to find a purchaser or purchasers.

Other comprehensive income Items of comprehensive income that are not reported on the income statement; comprehensive income minus net income.

Other post-employment benefits Promises by the company to pay benefits in the future, such as life insurance premiums and all or part of health care insurance for its retirees.

Out-of-sample forecast errors The differences between actual and predicted values of time series outside the sample period used to fit the model.

Outlier An observation that has an extreme value of the dependent variable and is potentially influential.

Outsourcing Shifting internal business services to a subcontractor that can offer services at lower costs by scaling to serve many clients.

Overfitting Situation in which the model has too many independent variables relative to the number of observations in the sample, such that the coefficients on the independent variables represent noise rather than relationships with the dependent variable.

Overnight indexed swap (OIS) rate An interest rate swap in which the periodic floating rate of the swap equals the geometric average of a daily unsecured overnight rate (or overnight index rate).

PEG ratio The P/E-to-growth ratio, calculated as the stock's P/E divided by the expected earnings growth rate.

Pairs trading An approach to trading that uses pairs of closely related stocks, buying the relatively undervalued stock and selling short the relatively overvalued stock.

Par curve A sequence of yields-to-maturity such that each bond is priced at par value. The bonds are assumed to have the same currency, credit risk, liquidity, tax status, and annual yields stated for the same periodicity.

Par swap A swap in which the fixed rate is set so that no money is exchanged at contract initiation.

Parametric method A method of estimating VaR that uses the historical mean, standard deviation, and correlation of security price movements to estimate the portfolio VaR. Generally assumes a normal distribution but can be adapted to non-normal distributions with the addition of skewness and kurtosis. Sometimes called the *variance–covariance method* or the *analytical method*.

Partial regression coefficient Coefficient that describes the effect of a one-unit change in the independent variable on the dependent variable, holding all other independent variables constant. Also known as *partial slope coefficient*.

Parts of speech An algorithm that uses language structure and dictionaries to tag every token in the text with a corresponding part of speech (i.e., noun, verb, adjective, proper noun, etc.).

Payout amount The loss given default times the notional.

Payout policy The principles by which a company distributes cash to common shareholders by means of cash dividends and/or share repurchases.

Payouts Cash dividends and the value of shares repurchased in any given year.

Penalized regression A regression that includes a constraint such that the regression coefficients are chosen to minimize the sum of squared residuals *plus* a penalty term that increases in size with the number of included features.

Pension obligation The present value of future benefits earned by employees for service provided to date.

Perfect capital markets Markets in which, by assumption, there are no taxes, transaction costs, or bankruptcy costs and in which all investors have equal ("symmetric") information.

Perpetuity A perpetual annuity, or a set of never-ending level sequential cash flows, with the first cash flow occurring one period from now.

Persistent earnings Earnings excluding nonrecurring components. Also referred to as *core earnings, continuing earnings,* or *underlying earnings*.

Physical settlement Involves actual delivery of the debt instrument in exchange for a payment by the credit protection seller of the notional amount of the contract.

Point-in-time data Data consisting of the exact information available to market participants as of a given point in time. Point-in-time data is used to address look-ahead bias.

Portfolio balance approach A theory of exchange rate determination that emphasizes the portfolio investment decisions of global investors and the requirement that global investors willingly hold all outstanding securities denominated in each currency at prevailing prices and exchange rates.

Positive serial correlation A situation in which residuals are positively related to other residuals.

Potential GDP The maximum amount of output an economy can sustainably produce without inducing an increase in the inflation rate. The output level that corresponds to full employment with consistent wage and price expectations.

Precision In error analysis for classification problems it is ratio of correctly predicted positive classes to all predicted positive classes. Precision is useful in situations where the cost of false positives (FP), or Type I error, is high.

Preferred habitat theory A term structure theory that contends that investors have maturity preferences and require yield incentives before they will buy bonds outside of their preferred maturities.

Premise of value The status of a company in the sense of whether it is assumed to be a going concern or not.

Premium leg The series of payments the credit protection buyer promises to make to the credit protection seller.

Premiums Amounts paid by the purchaser of insurance products.

Present value model A model of intrinsic value that views the value of an asset as the present value of the asset's expected future cash flows.

Present value of growth opportunities The difference between the actual value per share and the no-growth value per share. Also called *value of growth*.

Presentation currency The currency in which financial statement amounts are presented.

Price improvement When trade execution prices are better than quoted prices.

Price momentum A valuation indicator based on past price movement.

Price multiples The ratio of a stock's market price to some measure of value per share.

Price-to-earnings ratio (P/E) The ratio of share price to earnings per share.

Priced risk Risk for which investors demand compensation for bearing (e.g., equity risk, company-specific factors, macroeconomic factors).

Principal components analysis (PCA) An unsupervised ML technique used to transform highly correlated features of data into a few main, uncorrelated composite variables.

Principle of no arbitrage In well-functioning markets, prices will adjust until there are no arbitrage opportunities.

Prior transaction method A variation of the market approach; considers actual transactions in the stock of the subject private company.

Private market value The value derived using a sum-of-the-parts valuation.

Pro forma financial statements Financial statements that include the effect of a corporate restructuring.

Probability of default The likelihood that a borrower defaults or fails to meet its obligation to make full and timely payments of principal and interest.

Probability of survival The probability that a bond issuer will meet its contractual obligations on schedule.

Procedural law The body of law that focuses on the protection and enforcement of the substantive laws.

Projection error The vertical (perpendicular) distance between a data point and a given principal component.

Prospective P/E A P/E calculated on the basis of a forecast of EPS; a stock's current price divided by next year's expected earnings.

Protection leg   The contingent payment that the credit protection seller may have to make to the credit protection buyer.

Protection period   Period during which a bond's issuer cannot call the bond.

Provision for loan losses   An income statement expense account that increases the amount of the allowance for loan losses.

Prudential supervision   Regulation and monitoring of the safety and soundness of financial institutions to promote financial stability, reduce system-wide risks, and protect customers of financial institutions.

Pruning   A regularization technique used in CART to reduce the size of the classification or regression tree—by pruning, or removing, sections of the tree that provide little classifying power.

Purchasing power gain   A gain in value caused by changes in price levels. Monetary liabilities experience purchasing power gains during periods of inflation.

Purchasing power loss   A loss in value caused by changes in price levels. Monetary assets experience purchasing power loss during periods of inflation.

Purchasing power parity (PPP)   The idea that exchange rates move to equalize the purchasing power of different currencies.

Pure expectations theory   A term structure theory that contends the forward rate is an unbiased predictor of the future spot rate. Also called the *unbiased expectations theory*.

Pure factor portfolio   A portfolio with sensitivity of 1 to the factor in question and a sensitivity of 0 to all other factors.

Putable bond   Bond that includes an embedded put option, which gives the bondholder the right to put back the bonds to the issuer prior to maturity, typically when interest rates have risen and higher-yielding bonds are available.

Qualitative dependent variable   A dependent variable that is discrete (binary). Also known as a *categorical dependent variable*.

Quality of earnings analysis   The investigation of issues relating to the accuracy of reported accounting results as reflections of economic performance. Quality of earnings analysis is broadly understood to include not only earnings management but also balance sheet management.

Random forest classifier   A collection of a large number of decision trees trained via a bagging method.

Random walk   A time series in which the value of the series in one period is the value of the series in the previous period plus an unpredictable random error.

Rate implicit in the lease (RIIL)   The discount rate that equates the present value of the lease payment with the fair value of the leased asset, considering also the lessor's direct costs and the present value of the leased asset's residual value.

Rational efficient markets formulation   See *market efficiency*.

Readme files   Text files provided with raw data that contain information related to a data file. They are useful for understanding the data and how they can be interpreted correctly.

Real estate investment trusts (REITs)   Tax-advantaged entities (companies or trusts) that own, operate, and—to a limited extent—develop income-producing real estate property.

Real estate operating companies (REOCs)   Regular taxable real estate ownership companies that operate in the real estate industry in countries that do not have a tax-advantaged REIT regime in place or that are engage in real estate activities of a kind and to an extent that do not fit in their country's REIT framework.

Real interest rate parity   The proposition that real interest rates will converge to the same level across different markets.

Real options   Options that relate to investment decisions such as the option to time the start of a project, the option to adjust its scale, or the option to abandon a project that has begun.

Rebalance return   A return from rebalancing the component weights of an index.

Recall   Also known as *sensitivity*, in error analysis for classification problems it is the ratio of correctly predicted positive classes to all actual positive classes. Recall is useful in situations where the cost of false negatives (FN), or Type II error, is high.

Recency bias   The behavioral tendency to place more relevance on recent events.

Reconstitution   When dealers recombine appropriate individual zero-coupon securities and reproduce an underlying coupon Treasury.

Recovery rate   The percentage of the loss recovered.

Redemption basket   The list of securities (and share amounts) the authorized participant (AP) receives when it redeems ETF shares back to the ETF manager. The redemption basket is published each business day.

Reference entity   The borrower (debt issuer) covered by a single-name CDS.

Reference obligation   A particular debt instrument issued by the borrower that is the designated instrument being covered.

Regime   With reference to a time series, the underlying model generating the times series.

Regular expression (regex)   A series of texts that contains characters in a particular order. Regex is used to search for patterns of interest in a given text.

Regularization   A term that describes methods for reducing statistical variability in high-dimensional data estimation problems.

Regulatory arbitrage   Entities identify and use some aspect of regulations that allows them to exploit differences in economic substance and regulatory interpretation or in foreign and domestic regulatory regimes to their (the entities') advantage.

Regulatory burden   The costs of regulation for the regulated entity.

Regulatory capture   Theory that regulation often arises to enhance the interests of the regulated.

Regulatory competition   Regulators may compete to provide a regulatory environment designed to attract certain entities.

Reinforcement learning   Machine learning in which a computer learns from interacting with itself or data generated by the same algorithm.

Relative-strength indicators   Valuation indicators that compare a stock's performance during a period either to its own past performance or to the performance of some group of stocks.

Relative VaR   See *ex ante tracking error*.

Relative valuation models   A model that specifies an asset's value relative to the value of another asset.

Relative version of PPP   The hypothesis that changes in (nominal) exchange rates over time are equal to national inflation rate differentials.

Renewable resources   Resources that can be replenished, such as a forest.

Rental price of capital   The cost per unit of time to rent a unit of capital.

Reorganization   A court-supervised restructuring process available in some jurisdictions for companies facing insolvency from burdensome debt levels. A bankruptcy court assumes control of the company and oversees an orderly negotiation process between the company and its creditors for asset sales, conversion of debt to equity, refinancing, and so on.

Repeat sales index   As the name implies, this type of index relies on repeat sales of the same property. In general, the idea supporting this type of index is that because it is the same property that sold twice, the change in value between the two sale dates indicates how market conditions have changed over time.

Replacement cost   In the context of real estate, the value of a building assuming it was built today using current construction costs and standards.

Reporting unit   For financial reporting under US GAAP, an operating segment or one level below an operating segment (referred to as a component).

Required rate of return on equity   The minimum rate of return required by an investor to invest in an asset, given the asset's riskiness. Also known as the required return on equity.

Residential properties   Properties that provide housing for individuals or families. Single-family properties may be owner-occupied or rental properties, whereas multi-family properties are rental properties even if the owner or manager occupies one of the units.

Residual autocorrelations   The sample autocorrelations of the residuals.

Residual income   Earnings for a given period, minus a deduction for common shareholders' opportunity cost in generating the earnings. Also called *economic profit* or *abnormal earnings*.

Residual income method   Income approach that estimates the value of all intangible assets of the business by capitalizing future earnings in excess of the estimated return requirements associated with working capital and fixed assets.

Residual income model   (RIM) A model of stock valuation that views intrinsic value of stock as the sum of book value per share plus the present value of the stock's expected future residual income per share. Also called *discounted abnormal earnings model* or *Edwards–Bell–Ohlson model*.

Restricted model   A regression model with a subset of the complete set of independent variables.

Restructuring   Reorganizing the capital structure of a firm.

Return on invested capital   A measure of the profitability of a company relative to the amount of capital invested by the equity- and debtholders.

Reverse carry arbitrage   A strategy involving the short sale of the underlying and an offsetting opposite position in the derivative.

Reverse stock split   A reduction in the number of shares outstanding with a corresponding increase in share price, but no change to the company's underlying fundamentals.

Reverse stress testing   A risk management approach in which the user identifies key risk exposures in the portfolio and subjects those exposures to extreme market movements.

Reviewed financial statements   A type of non-audited financial statements; typically provide an opinion letter with representations and assurances by the reviewing accountant that are less than those in audited financial statements.

Rho   The change in a given derivative instrument for a given small change in the risk-free interest rate, holding everything else constant. Rho measures the sensitivity of the option to the risk-free interest rate.

Risk-based models   Models of the return on equity that identify risk factors or drivers and sensitivities of the return to these factors.

Risk budgeting   The establishment of objectives for individuals, groups, or divisions of an organization that takes into account the allocation of an acceptable level of risk.

Risk decomposition   The process of converting a set of holdings in a portfolio into a set of exposures to risk factors.

Risk factors   Variables or characteristics with which individual asset returns are correlated. Sometimes referred to simply as *factors.*

Risk-free rate   The minimum rate of return expected on a security that has no default risk.

Risk parity   A portfolio allocation scheme that weights stocks or factors based on an equal risk contribution.

Robust standard errors   Method for correcting residuals for conditional heteroskedasticity. Also known as *heteroskedasticity-consistent standard errors* or *White-corrected standard errors.*

Roll   When an investor moves its investment position from an older series to the most current series.

Roll return   The component of the return on a commodity futures contract attributable to rolling long futures positions forward through time. Also called *roll yield.*

Rolling down the yield curve   A maturity trading strategy that involves buying bonds with a maturity longer than the intended investment horizon. Also called *riding the yield curve.*

Rolling windows   A backtesting method that uses a rolling-window (or walk-forward) framework, rebalances the portfolio after each period, and then tracks performance over time. As new information arrives each period, the investment manager optimizes (revises and tunes) the model and readjusts stock positions.

Root mean squared error (RMSE)   The square root of the average squared forecast error; used to compare the out-of-sample forecasting performance of forecasting models.

Sale-leaseback   A situation in which a company sells the building it owns and occupies to a real estate investor and the company then signs a long-term lease with the buyer to continue to occupy the building. At the end of the lease, use of the property reverts to the landlord.

Sales comparison approach   In the context of real estate, this approach estimates value based on what similar or comparable properties (comparables) transacted for in the current market.

Sales risk   The uncertainty regarding the price and number of units sold of a company's products.

Scaled earnings surprise   Unexpected earnings divided by the standard deviation of analysts' earnings forecasts.

Scaling   The process of adjusting the range of a feature by shifting and changing the scale of the data. Two of the most common ways of scaling are normalization and standardization.

Scatterplot matrix   A visualization technique that shows the scatterplots between different sets of variables, often with the histogram for each variable on the diagonal. Also referred to as a *pairs plot.*

Scenario analysis   A technique for exploring the performance and risk of investment strategies in different structural regimes.

Schwarz's Bayesian information criterion (BIC or SBC)   A statistic used to compare sets of independent variables for explaining a dependent variable. It is preferred for finding the model with the best goodness of fit.

Scree plots   A plot that shows the proportion of total variance in the data explained by each principal component.

Screening   The application of a set of criteria to reduce a set of potential investments to a smaller set having certain desired characteristics.

Seasonality   A characteristic of a time series in which the data experience regular and predictable periodic changes; for example, fan sales are highest during the summer months.

Secured overnight financing rate (SOFR)   A daily volume-weighted index of rates on qualified cash borrowings collateralized by US Treasuries that is expected to replace Libor as a floating reference rate for swaps.

Security selection risk   See *active specific risk*.

Segmented markets theory   A term structure theory that contends yields are solely a function of the supply and demand for funds of a particular maturity.

Self-regulating organizations (SROs)   Self-regulating bodies that are given recognition and authority, including enforcement power, by a government body or agency.

Self-regulatory bodies   Private, non-governmental organizations that both represent and regulate their members. Some self-regulating organizations are also independent regulators.

Sell-side analysts   Analysts who work at brokerages.

Sensitivity analysis   Analysis that shows the range of possible outcomes as specific assumptions are changed.

Sentence length   The number of characters, including spaces, in a sentence.

Serial correlation   A condition found most often in time series in which residuals are correlated across observations. Also known as *autocorrelation*.

Serial-correlation consistent standard errors   Method for correcting serial correlation. Also known as *serial correlation and heteroskedasticity adjusted standard errors*, *Newey–West standard errors*, and *robust standard errors*.

Service period   For employee stock options, usually the period between the grant date and the vesting date.

Settled in arrears   An arrangement in which the interest payment is made (i.e., settlement occurs) at the maturity of the underlying instrument.

Settlement   The closing date at which the counterparties of a derivative contract exchange payment for the underlying as required by the contract.

Shadow banking   Lending by financial institutions that are not regulated as banks.

Shaping risk   The sensitivity of a bond's price to the changing shape of the yield curve.

Share repurchase   A transaction in which a company buys back its own shares. Unlike stock dividends and stock splits, share repurchases use corporate cash.

Shareholder activism   Strategies used by shareholders to attempt to compel a company to act in a desired manner.

Shareholders' equity   Total assets minus total liabilities.

Simulation   A technique for exploring how a target variable (e.g. portfolio returns) would perform in a hypothetical environment specified by the user, rather than a historical setting.

Single-name CDS   Credit default swap on one specific borrower.

Sinking fund bond   A bond that requires the issuer to set aside funds over time to retire the bond issue, thus reducing credit risk.

Size premium (SP)   Additional return compensation for bearing the additional risk associated with smaller companies.

Slope dummy   An indicator variable that allows a single regression model to estimate two lines of best fit, each with differing slopes, depending on whether the dummy takes a value of 1 or 0.

Soft margin classification   An adaptation in the support vector machine algorithm which adds a penalty to the objective function for observations in the training set that are misclassified.

Sovereign yield spread   The spread between the yield on a foreign country's sovereign bond and a similar-maturity domestic sovereign bond.

Special dividend   A dividend paid by a company that does not pay dividends on a regular schedule, or a dividend that supplements regular cash dividends with an extra payment.

Specific-company risk premium (SCRP)   Additional return required by investors for bearing non-diversifiable company-specific risk.

Spin off   When a company separates a distinct part of its business into a new, independent company. The term is used to describe both the transaction and the separated component, while the company that conducts the transaction and formerly owned the spin off is known as the parent.

Split-rate tax system   In reference to corporate taxes, a split-rate system taxes earnings to be distributed as dividends at a different rate than earnings to be retained. Corporate profits distributed as dividends are taxed at a lower rate than those retained in the business.

Spot curve   A sequence of yields-to-maturity on zero-coupon bonds. Sometimes called *zero* or *strip curve* (because coupon payments are "stripped" off the bonds).

Spot price   The current price of an asset or security. For commodities, the current price to deliver a physical commodity to a specific location or purchase and transport it away from a designated location.

Spot rate   The interest rate that is determined today for a risk-free, single-unit payment at a specified future date.

Spot yield curve   The term structure of spot rates for loans made today.

Stabilized NOI   In the context of real estate, the expected NOI when a renovation is complete.

Stable dividend policy   A policy in which regular dividends are paid that reflect long-run expected earnings. In contrast to a constant dividend payout ratio policy, a stable dividend policy does not reflect short-term volatility in earnings.

Standardized beta   With reference to fundamental factor models, the value of the attribute for an asset minus the average value of the attribute across all stocks, divided by the standard deviation of the attribute across all stocks.

Standardized unexpected earnings   Unexpected earnings per share divided by the standard deviation of unexpected earnings per share over a specified prior time period.

Statistical factor model   A multifactor model in which statistical methods are applied to a set of historical returns to determine portfolios that best explain either historical return covariances or variances.

Statutes   Laws enacted by legislative bodies.

Steady-state rate of growth   The constant growth rate of output (or output per capita) that can or will be sustained indefinitely once it is reached. Key ratios, such as the capital–output ratio, are constant on the steady-state growth path.

Steepness   The difference between long-term and short-term yields that constitutes one of the three factors (the other two are level and curvature) that empirically explain most of the changes in the shape of the yield curve.

Stock dividend   A type of dividend in which a company distributes additional shares of its common stock to shareholders instead of cash.

Stop-loss limit   Constraint used in risk management that requires a reduction in the size of a portfolio, or its complete liquidation, when a loss of a particular size occurs in a specified period.

Straight bond   An underlying option-free bond with a specified issuer, issue date, maturity date, principal amount and repayment structure, coupon rate and payment structure, and currency denomination.

Straight debt   Debt with no embedded options.

Straight-line rent   The average annual rent under a multi-year lease agreement that contains contractual increases in rent during the life of the lease.

Straight-line rent adjustment   See *non-cash rent*.

Straight voting   A shareholder voting process in which shareholders receive one vote for each share owned.

Stranded assets   Assets that are obsolete or not economically viable.

Strategic transaction   A purchase involving a buyer that would benefit from certain synergies associated with owning the target firm.

Stress tests   A risk management technique that assesses the portfolio's response to extreme market movements.

Stripping   A dealer's ability to separate a bond's individual cash flows and trade them as zero-coupon securities.

Studentized residual   A *t*-distributed statistic that is used to detect outliers.

Substantive law   The body of law that focuses on the rights and responsibilities of entities and relationships among entities.

Succession event   A change of corporate structure of the reference entity, such as through a merger, a divestiture, a spinoff, or any similar action, in which ultimate responsibility for the debt in question is unclear.

Sum-of-the-parts valuation   A valuation that sums the estimated values of each of a company's businesses as if each business were an independent going concern.

Summation operator   A functional part of a neural network's node that multiplies each input value received by a weight and sums the weighted values to form the total net input, which is then passed to the activation function.

Supernormal growth   Above-average or abnormally high growth rate in earnings per share.

Supervised learning   A machine learning approach that makes use of labeled training data.

Support vector machine   A linear classifier that determines the hyperplane that optimally separates the observations into two sets of data points.

Survivorship bias   The exclusion of poorly performing or defunct companies from an index or database, biasing the index or database toward financially healthy companies.

Sustainable growth rate   The rate of dividend (and earnings) growth that can be sustained over time for a given level of return on equity, keeping the capital structure constant and without issuing additional common stock.

Swap curve   The term structure of swap rates.

Swap rate   The fixed rate to be paid by the fixed-rate payer specified in a swap contract.

Swap rate curve   The term structure of swap rates.

Swap spread   The difference between the fixed rate on an interest rate swap and the rate on a Treasury note with equivalent maturity; it reflects the general level of credit risk in the market.

Synergies   The combination of two companies being more valuable than the sum of the parts. Generally, synergies take the form of lower costs ("cost synergies") or increased revenues ("revenue synergies") through combinations that generate lower costs or higher revenues, respectively.

Systematic risk   Risk that affects the entire market or economy; it cannot be avoided and is inherent in the overall market. Systematic risk is also known as non-diversifiable or market risk.

Systemic risk   Refers to risks supervisory authorities believe are likely to have broad impact across the financial market infrastructure and affect a wide swath of market participants.

TED spread   A measure of perceived credit risk determined as the difference between Libor and the T-bill yield of matching maturity.

Tail risk   The risk that losses in extreme events could be greater than would be expected for a portfolio of assets with a normal distribution.

Takeover premium   The amount by which the per-share take-over price exceeds the unaffected price expressed as a percentage of the unaffected price. It reflects the amount shareholders require to relinquish their control of the company to the acquirer.

Tangible assets   Identifiable, physical assets such as property, plant, and equipment.

Tangible book value per share   Common shareholders' equity minus intangible assets reported on the balance sheet, divided by the number of shares outstanding.

Target   In machine learning, the dependent variable (Y) in a labeled dataset; the company in a merger or acquisition that is being acquired.

Target capital structure   A company's chosen proportions of debt and equity.

Target payout ratio   A strategic corporate goal representing the long-term proportion of earnings that the company intends to distribute to shareholders as dividends.

Taxable REIT subsidiaries   Subsidiaries that pay income taxes on earnings from non-REIT-qualifying activities like merchant development or third-party property management.

Technical indicators   Momentum indicators based on price.

Temporal method   A variation of the monetary/non-monetary translation method that requires not only monetary assets and liabilities, but also non-monetary assets and liabilities that are measured at their current value on the balance sheet date to be translated at the current exchange rate. Assets and liabilities are translated at rates consistent with the timing of their measurement value. This method is typically used when the functional currency is other than the local currency.

Term frequency (TF)   Ratio of the number of times a given token occurs in all the texts in the dataset to the total number of tokens in the dataset.

Term premium   The additional return required by lenders to invest in a bond to maturity net of the expected return from continually reinvesting at the short-term rate over that same time horizon.

Terminal price multiples   The price multiple for a stock assumed to hold at a stated future time.

Terminal share price   The share price at a particular point in the future.

Terminal value of the stock   The analyst's estimate of a stock's value at a particular point in the future. Also called *continuing value of the stock*.

Test sample   A data sample that is used to test a model's ability to predict well on new data.

Theta   The change in a derivative instrument for a given small change in calendar time, holding everything else constant. Specifically, the theta calculation assumes nothing changes except calendar time. Theta also reflects the rate at which an option's time value decays.

Time series   A set of observations on a variable's outcomes in different time periods.

Tobin's *q*   The ratio of the market value of debt and equity to the replacement cost of total assets.

Token   The equivalent of a word (or sometimes a character).

Tokenization   The process of representing ownership rights to physical assets on a blockchain or distributed ledger.

Top-down approach   With respect to forecasting, an approach that usually begins at the level of the overall economy. Forecasts are then made at more narrowly defined levels, such as sector, industry, and market for a specific product.

Total factor productivity (TFP)   A multiplicative scale factor that reflects the general level of productivity or technology in the economy. Changes in total factor productivity generate proportional changes in output for any input combination.

Total invested capital   The sum of market value of common equity, book value of preferred equity, and face value of debt.

Tracking error   The standard deviation of the differences between a portfolio's returns and its benchmark's returns; a synonym of *active risk*. Also called *tracking risk*.

Tracking risk   The standard deviation of the differences between a portfolio's returns and its benchmarks returns. Also called *tracking error*.

Trailing dividend yield   The reciprocal of current market price divided by the most recent annualized dividend.

Trailing P/E   A stock's current market price divided by the most recent four quarters of EPS (or the most recent two semi-annual periods for companies that report interim data semi-annually). Also called *current P/E*.

Training sample   A data sample that is used to train a model.

Tranche CDS   A type of credit default swap that covers a combination of borrowers but only up to pre-specified levels of losses.

Transaction exposure   The risk of a change in value between the transaction date and the settlement date of an asset of liability denominated in a foreign currency.

Treasury shares/stock   Shares that were issued and subsequently repurchased by the company.

Trend   A long-term pattern of movement in a particular direction.

Triangular arbitrage   An arbitrage transaction involving three currencies that attempts to exploit inconsistencies among pairwise exchange rates.

Trimming   Also called truncation, it is the process of removing extreme values and outliers from a dataset.

Triple-net leases   Leases that require each tenant to pay its share of the following three operating expenses: common area maintenance and repair expenses; property taxes; and building insurance costs. Also known as *NNN leases*.

Two-tier board   Board structure consisting of a supervisory board that oversees a management board.

Unbiased expectations theory   A term structure theory that contends the forward rate is an unbiased predictor of the future spot rate. Also called the *pure expectations theory*.

Unconditional heteroskedasticity   When heteroskedasticity of the error variance is not correlated with the regression's independent variables.

Uncovered interest rate parity   The proposition that the expected return on an uncovered (i.e., unhedged) foreign currency (risk-free) investment should equal the return on a comparable domestic currency investment.

Underlying earnings   Earnings excluding nonrecurring components. Also referred to as *continuing earnings*, *core earnings*, or *persistent earnings*.

Unexpected earnings   The difference between reported EPS and expected EPS. Also referred to as an *earnings surprise*.

Unit root   A time series that is not covariance stationary is said to have a unit root.

Unrestricted model   A regression model with the complete set of independent variables.

Unsupervised learning   A machine learning approach that does not make use of labeled training data.

Upfront payment   The difference between the credit spread and the standard rate paid by the protection buyer if the standard rate is insufficient to compensate the protection seller. Also called *upfront premium*.

Upfront premium   See *upfront payment*.

Upstream   A transaction between two related companies, an investor company (or a parent company) and an associate company (or a subsidiary company) such that the associate company records a profit on its income statement. An example is a sale of inventory by the associate to the investor company or by a subsidiary to a parent company.

Validation sample   A data sample that is used to validate and tune a model.

Valuation   The process of determining the value of an asset or service either on the basis of variables perceived to be related to future investment returns or on the basis of comparisons with closely similar assets.

Value additivity   An arbitrage opportunity when the value of the whole equals the sum of the values of the parts.

Value at risk (VaR)   The minimum loss that would be expected a certain percentage of the time over a certain period of time given the assumed market conditions.

Value of growth   The difference between the actual value per share and the no-growth value per share.

Variance error   Describes how much a model's results change in response to new data from validation and test samples. Unstable models pick up noise and produce high variance error, causing overfitting and high out-of-sample error.

Variance inflation factor (VIF)   A statistic that quantifies the degree of multicollinearity in a model.

Vasicek model A partial equilibrium term structure model that assumes interest rates are mean reverting and interest rate volatility is constant.

Vega The change in a given derivative instrument for a given small change in volatility, holding everything else constant. A sensitivity measure for options that reflects the effect of volatility.

Venture capital investors Private equity investors in development-stage companies.

Vertical ownership Ownership structure in which a company or group that has a controlling interest in two or more holding companies, which in turn have controlling interests in various operating companies.

Vested benefit obligation The actuarial present value of vested benefits.

Vesting date The date that employees can first exercise stock options.

Visibility The extent to which a company's operations are predictable with substantial confidence.

Voting caps Legal restrictions on the voting rights of large share positions.

Web spidering (scraping or crawling) programs Programs that extract raw content from a source, typically web pages.

Weighted average cost of capital (WACC) A weighted average of the after-tax required rates of return on a company's common stock, preferred stock, and long-term debt, where the weights are the fraction of each source of financing in the company's target capital structure.

Weighted harmonic mean See *harmonic mean*.

Winsorization The process of replacing extreme values and outliers in a dataset with the maximum (for large value outliers) and minimum (for small value outliers) values of data points that are not outliers.

Write-down A reduction in the value of an asset as stated in the balance sheet.

Yield curve factor model A model or a description of yield curve movements that can be considered realistic when compared with historical data.

Zero A bond that does not pay a coupon but is priced at a discount and pays its full face value at maturity.

Zero-coupon bond A bond that does not pay interest during its life. It is issued at a discount to par value and redeemed at par. Also called *pure discount bond*.